Jury Selection

Jury Selection

An Attorney's Guide to Jury Law and Methods

V. Hale Starr
Ph.D. in Communication

Mark McCormick
Justice, Supreme Court of Iowa

with contributions from

Danny E. Cupit
Member, Mississippi Bar

Browne Greene
Member, California Bar

Dwight W. James
Member, Iowa Bar

Stanley J. Levy
Member, New York Bar

Roger Pardieck
Member, Indiana Bar

Little, Brown and Company
Boston Toronto

Library of Congress Catalog Card No. 84-82019

ISBN 0-316-81100-9

Fourth Printing

MV NY

Published simultaneously in Canada
by Little, Brown & Company (Canada) Limited

Printed in the United States of America

VHS

To the memory of C. Jay

MM

To Marcia, Michael, and Paul

Summary of Contents

Contents

List of Figures, Forms, Photographs, and Tables

Foreword

For me this book is the culmination of a dream. The dream began years ago when as a fledgling trial lawyer I was astounded and disappointed at the dearth of literature on the subject of jury selection. The dream was that someday someone would write a book for trial lawyers that would combine a comprehensive statement of the law with the methodology of jury selection. The breakthrough that led to the publication of the present book was the sudden emergence of the new courtroom professional called the jury selection specialist. Now, in this one magnificent book, the trial lawyer can find an encyclopedic summary of substantive and procedural law governing jury selection combined with a full and definitive explanation of all of the current scientific methodology being employed in that process.

V. Hale Starr ranks with Hans Zeisel and a handful of other persons as a pioneer jury selection specialist. As one who uses her services and has been associated with her professionally for many years, I feel qualified to say that I can think of no other person in her field so brilliantly able to express in writing the relevant principles and practices. Her extensive background in teaching and business coupled with impressive academic credientials and years of extensive experience in the field have uniquely prepared her for this monumental undertaking. She has continued her own research and her study of the research of others; she continues to learn and to teach what she has learned. Having counseled with Dr. Starr in the planning of this book, I have the honor of suggesting that I was "present at the creation." I have the greater honor of announcing that the finished product has exceeded my high expectations.

The legal framework for Dr. Starr's exegesis has been provided by Justice Mark McCormick of the Supreme Court of Iowa. Justice McCormick brought to this task a rich background as trial lawyer, trial judge, and appellate jurist. In the first three chapters of the book he sets the stage for what follows by succinctly and clearly summarizing substantive and procedural law as well as issues at the cutting edge of the law affecting jury selection.

Against this background, Dr. Starr takes us through issues and methods: background investigations, community attitude surveying, voir dire techniques and strategy, the science of nonverbal communication, and courtroom application of all of the relevant scientific methodology. The book is enriched by many helpful examples and a plentitude of sage advice; forms and checklists are furnished as useful tools. The heart of the book is the discussion of nonverbal communication. This is the first time, to my knowledge, that this fascinating and critical subject has been so fully and plainly explained.

This book is written for the practitioner as well as the theorist. It will be useful to a lawyer who merely wishes to know what to look for in employing a jury selection specialist as well as to a lawyer who wishes to use the methodology without employing a professional. The book represents the state of the art in the field.

Here then is an outstanding book that covers the most important procedure in every jury trial. It belongs within arms' reach of every trial lawyer and every other person who is interested in the law and science of jury selection.

Stanley Preiser
Preiser & Wilson
Charleston, West Virginia

Preface

Trial lawyers have become increasingly interested in recent years in the use of scientific methodology in jury selection. This methodology couples the lawyer's skill with the social scientist's understanding of human behavior. More lawyers are seeking the assistance of psychologists, sociologists, market researchers, and communication specialists in selecting juries and in analyzing the courtroom behavior of juries and witnesses.

Techniques that were initially used only in complex and celebrated cases arising out of the anti-war and civil rights movements are now being used much more widely and as a result more specialists are offering jury selection services to lawyers. Although still used in only a small percentage of trials, their use has far-reaching implications:

> Jury selection is a fast-growing application of the psycho-social sciences. Its practitioners — a few dozen sociologists, psychologists, market researchers and others — use public opinion surveys, in-depth interviews, computer analysis correlating jurors' backgrounds and attitudes and laboratory simulations of impending trials to help lawyers select jurors likely to favor their side, exclude those likely to be hostile to it and present their cases in ways psychologically designed to benefit from the unconscious needs and motives of the jurors. The implications of this new use of behavioral research are significant: Jurors are not viewed as free moral agents, able to assess impartially where the

> truth lies, but as organisms whose emotional and mental processes are determined by "predictor variables." . . . [W]hen subtle questions fail to smoke out the truth, jury research can provide it in the form of statistical probabilities.[1]

Although these applications are fairly recent, techniques for measuring community attitudes have existed since 1920. In the 1950s, standardized attitude and personality scales were developed, and investigations into demographic variables (such as sex, race, age, occupation, and marital status) provided significant correlations with behavior. More recently, widespread use of computers has simplified statistical analysis and as a result "the potential for selecting juries scientifically [has gone] from feasible to easy."[2]

There are those who warn that scientific jury selection threatens the integrity of the legal system and increases the advantage of the rich and celebrated over the poor and obscure.[3] Even though evidence exists that scientific jury selection has been helpful in a number of significant cases, it is unlikely that the methodology is as powerful as either its proponents or critics sometimes contend. Social or behavioral science cannot guarantee a favorable verdict. Careful application of these techniques, however, can enable the attorney to make certain predictions about jury response to evidence or witnesses.

This book describes and explains scientific jury selection for the trial attorney. Since all jury selection takes place in the context of the law governing the right to trial by jury, *Jury Selection* begins with a thorough grounding in the legal framework of this right. Justice Mark McCormick of the Iowa Supreme Court authored part 1 of the book (chapters 1 to 3) in which he reviews the history of the right to trial by jury; the role of statutes, rules, and caselaw in jury selection; and developments in the law of the jury trial.

[1]Morton Hunt, Putting Juries on the Couch, N.Y. Times Nov. 28, 1982 (Magazine) at 70-88.

[2]Saks, Social Scientists Can't Rig Juries, 9 Psychology Today 48, 57 (Jan. 1976).

[3]See Etzioni, Creating an Imbalance, 10 Trial 28 (1974).

A comprehensive exposition of pretrial investigation, jury selection methodologies, voir dire, and nonverbal communication follows the law of juries in parts 2 through 4 (chapters 4-14) of the book. Dr. V. Hale Starr, a communication specialist who has worked as a forensic consultant with trial attorneys for eight years, wrote the chapters in parts 2 and 4. Both Dr. Starr and Justice McCormick, with the assistance of Roger Pardeick, a prominent trial lawyer from Indiana, authored part 3 on voir dire. Part 5 ties together the principles and methods described in the preceding parts in a comprehensive sample jury selection.

In addition to the above, four prominent trial attorneys have contributed their views on selected topics in jury selection and nonverbal communication.

The following chapter-by-chapter breakdown further explains the structure of *Jury Selection*:

Chapter 1 traces the history of the right to trial by jury under the federal and state constitutions and the rulings of the Supreme Court.

Chapter 2 discusses the role of statutes, rules, and caselaw in jury selection, under both federal and state law.

Chapter 3 is an expansive treatment of current developments in the law of juries, including areas of continuing controversy and model approaches to the jury system.

Chapter 4 reviews pretrial investigation, an old concept with numerous new applications.

Chapter 5 explains the use of community attitude assessments in support of change of venue motions as well as in developing profiles of best and worst jurors.

Chapter 6 covers staging a trial simulation to explore jurors' reactions to specific case issues.

Chapter 7 is a concise overview of demographic analysis of the jury list.

Chapter 8 introduces voir dire with a review of its purposes and the potential pitfalls for the trial attorney.

Chapter 9 offers a detailed look at the mechanics of both judge-conducted and attorney-conducted voir dire.

Chapter 10 contains advice on preparing for and conducting a strategic voir dire. The chapter includes detailed questioning techniques.

Chapter 11 introduces nonverbal communication as an analytical tool for the attorney to use in jury selection and at trial;

Chapter 12 covers the first of the three major aspects of nonverbal communication: the *appearance* of the jury.

Chapter 13 discusses the second of these aspects: the *voices* of jurors.

Chapter 14 covers analysis of the *movements* of jurors as the third major aspect of nonverbal communication. All three chapters on nonverbal communication provide the attorney with suggestions for gaining added insight into the attitudes, biases, and personalities of both prospective and seated jurors.

Chapter 15 examines a jury selection process in detail to demonstrate the use of scientific methodologies, voir dire techniques, and jury psychology.

Jury Selection is designed to maximize the attorney's understanding of the problems and opportunities inherent in the selection of a jury. Every trial lawyer should be able to use information provided in the book. The lawyer who comes to the book with a good understanding of his or her case can select those topics that best apply. It is not necessary to employ professionals to take advantage of scientific jury selection. Nor is it necessary to use all of the voir dire and communication techniques in every case. Each section of *Jury Selection* is self-contained with the intention that the book serve as a reference tool and practical handbook.

The outcome of any trial depends largely on the quality of the evidence and the commitment and experience of the attorney. It is hoped that this book will eliminate much, if not all, of the guesswork that now confronts the trial lawyer in jury selection.

V.H.S.
M.M.

January 1985

About the Authors

V. Hale Starr (Ph.D., Communication Research, University of Iowa) is the president of Starr & Associates, a legal consulting firm. She is on the Board of Directors of the Association of Trial Behavior Consultants and is a member of the Speech Communication Association, the American Sociological Association, and the International Communication Association.

Mark McCormick (LL.B., Georgetown University; LL.M., University of Virginia) is a justice of the Supreme Court of Iowa, who has previously served as both a district court judge and an assistant county attorney. He lectures frequently, has written several law review articles, and has been on the National Judicial College faculty.

About the Contributors

Danny E. Cupit (J.D., University of Mississippi) practices primarily in the areas of personal injury litigation and workers' compensation. He is a member of the American Bar Association, the American Trial Lawyers Association, the Mississippi Trial Lawyers Association, and the Mississippi State Bar Association.

Browne Greene (LL.B., George Washington University) specializes in product liability and negligence cases. He is a diplomate on the American Board of Trial Advocates, vice president of the California Trial Lawyers Association, and a recipient of a Trial Lawyer of the Year Award from the Los Angeles Trial Lawyers Association.

Dwight W. James (LL.B., Drake University) is the current governor of the Association of Trial Lawyers of Iowa, and is a fellow of both the Iowa Academy of Trial Lawyers and the American College of Trial Lawyers. He has been certified as a civil trial advocate by the National Board of Trial Advocacy.

Stanley J. Levy (LL.B., Columbia University) is currently a trustee of the Asbestos Litigation Group as well as chairman of the Official Committee of Asbestos Claimants. He is a member of the Environmental Law Committees of the Association of Trial Lawyers of America and of the ABA's Tort and Insurance Practice Section.

Roger Pardieck (J.D., Indiana University) is on the NITA faculty at the Notre Dame Law School. He is a member of the Association of Trial Lawyers of American, the American College of Trial Lawyers, the American Board of Trial Advocates, and the American Bar Association. He is a frequent lecturer and an author of numerous articles.

Acknowledgments

Finding the time and place to write was often challenging. For answering this challenge plus providing encouragement to work, warm thanks go to Anne Norris and the Black Hills, and to Terry Newman and the Great Plains.

A knowing and caring critic adds quality to a manuscript. For her unique touch, deep thanks go to my associate and friend, Lin S. Lilley.

Special thanks are due to Dr. Mark L. Knapp, nonverbal communication researcher, for reviewing the chapters on nonverbal communication and offering excellent advice. Thanks also to Dana Downie, whose fine photographs appear in chapters 14 and 15.

The final stages of preparing a manuscript require the skills of someone patient, persistent, and pleasant, who is willing and capable of spending hours either on the phone with the editor, at the office tracking some obscure reference, or in the library verifying footnotes and quotations. For his excellence and hard work, sincere thanks are offered to Dan Johnson.

Many thanks are offered to my associates and co-workers at Starr & Associates for their understanding, encouragement, and interest.

Of course, this book would not have been possible without the experience, support, and education provided to the personnel at Starr & Associates by the many lawyers across America who have shown us friendship as well as a working relationship: John Fitzgerald, Jr., Rapid City, South Dakota; Stanley Preiser, Charleston, West Virginia; Robert F. Hill, Denver, Colorado; Theodore N. Miller, Chicago, Illinois; Browne Greene and Charlie O'Reilly, Los Angeles, California; Charles R. McRae, Pascagoula, Mississippi; Thomas T. Anderson, Indio, California; Kermit A. Brashear III, Omaha, Nebraska; Charles Brega, Denver, Colorado; Lee Kreindler and Stanley Levy, New York, New York; Roxanne Conlin, Michael Galligan, and Dwight James, Des Moines, Iowa; Thomas W. Conklin, Chicago, Illinois; John Mozola, Amarillo, Texas; Danny Cupit, Jackson, Mississippi; John P. Edmonds, Chillicothe, Illinois; Lex Hawkins, Des Moines, Iowa; Bernard Kelly and L. Ames Luce, Anchorage, Alaska; George LaMarca, Des Moines, Iowa; Verne Lawyer, Des Moines, Iowa; Ted Lockyear, Evansville, Indiana; Peter Chase Neumann, Reno, Nevada; Roger Pardieck, Seymour, Indiana; Tom Riley, Cedar Rapids, Iowa; Thomas L. Ryan, Fort Wayne, Indiana; Robert R. Smiley, Washington, D.C.; Gerry L. Spence, Jackson, Wyoming; Jo Stone, Denver, Colorado; Ted Warshafsky, Milwaukee, Wisconsin; George Shadoan, Rockville, Maryland; William E. Johnson, Frankfort, Kentucky; David Hamilton, Reno, Nevada; Russell Hart and Steve Yeager, Lafayette, Indiana; and Joseph P. Shein, Philadelphia, Pennsylvania.

V. Hale Starr

Jury Selection

PART I

The Law of Juries

CHAPTER

1

History of the Right to Trial by Jury

§1.0 Constitutional Foundations

The right to trial by jury is firmly established in the United States Constitution. As adopted in 1789, the Constitution provided that the trial of all crimes except impeachment shall be by jury.[1] Two additional provisions were added in 1791 as part of the Bill of Rights. The sixth amendment assures a person accused of crime "a speedy and public trial, by an impartial jury of the State and district wherein the crime shall have been committed, which district shall have previously been ascertained by law. . . ."[2] This provision merely amplified the right protected in the original Constitution.[3] The seventh amendment guarantees the right in federal civil cases: "In all suits at common law, where the value in controversy shall exceed twenty dollars, the right of trial by jury shall be preserved. . . ."[4]

Constitutions adopted by the original states also guaranteed

§1.0 [1]U.S. Const. art. III, §2.

[2]Id. amend. VI.

[3]Callan v. Wilson, 127 U.S. 540, 549, 85 S. Ct. 1301, 1303, 32 L. Ed. 223, 226 (1888).

[4]U.S. Const. amend. VII.

the right to jury trial.[5] A similar assurance was provided in the constitution of every state that subsequently joined the union.[6] Today the right to trial by jury is protected in some form by both federal and state law.[7] Moreover, the United States Supreme Court has held that the right to jury trial in serious criminal cases must be recognized by the states as part of their obligation to provide due process of law to all persons within their jurisdiction.[8]

The American commitment to jury trial is explained in part by the fact that it was among the rights of Englishmen for which the revolution was fought. The Declaration of Independence accused the King of depriving colonists "in many cases of the benefits of Trial by Jury" and of transporting colonists to England for trial "for pretended offenses." English vice-admiralty courts sat in the colonies without juries, and this was perceived by colonists as a step toward slavery.[9]

Alexander Hamilton strongly defended the constitutional guarantee of the right in criminal trials:

> The friends and adversaries of the plan of the convention, if they agree on nothing else, concur at least in the value they set upon trial by jury; or if there is any difference between them it consists in this: the former regard it as a valuable safeguard to liberty; the latter represent it as the very palladium of free government. For my own part, the more the operation of the institution has fallen under my observation, the more reason I have for holding it in high estimation; and it would be superfluous to examine to what extent it deserves to be esteemed useful or essential in a representative republic, or how much more merit it may be entitled to as a defense against the oppressions of a hereditary monarch, than as a barrier to the tyranny of popular magistrates in a popular government.[10]

[5] Duncan v. Louisiana, 391 U.S. 149, 153, 88 S. Ct. 1444, 1450, 20 L. Ed. 2d 491, 498 (1968).

[6] F. Busch, 1 Law and Tactics in Jury Trials 17-42 (1959).

[7] Ibid.

[8] Duncan v. Louisiana, 391 U.S. 149, 88 S. Ct. 1444, 20 L. Ed. 2d 491 (1968).

[9] J. Pole, The Pursuit of Equality in American History 24 (1978).

[10] The Federalist No. 83, at 499 (A. Hamilton) (The New American Library 1961).

These sentiments can best be understood in their historical context. Those who emigrated from England " 'brought with them this great privilege as their birthright and inheritance, as a part of that admirable common law which had fenced around and interposed barriers on every side against the approaches of arbitrary power.' "[11]

The concept of jury trial as it existed at the time of the American Revolution was not the product of a preconceived theory of jurisprudence. Rather, it was the outgrowth of forms previously in use and contained elements of several systems of varying origin.[12] Historians have traced these elements to Anglo-Saxon and Norman institutions bearing the influence of systems in ancient Greece, Rome and Germany.[13] The concept resulted from several centuries of experience, rather than from a specific plan.

§1.1 Jury Law under Decisions of the Supreme Court

The United States Supreme Court originally assumed that the jury assured in the Constitution had the characteristics of the common law jury as it existed in 1789. Thus, for example, the Court said in 1898 that the jury referred to in the sixth amendment was a jury "constituted as it was at common law, of twelve persons, neither more nor less."[1] In 1930 the Court stated that a sixth amendment jury was characterized by three essential features: "(1) that the jury should consist of twelve men, neither more nor less; (2) that the trial should be in the presence and under the superintendence of a judge having a

[11] Thompson v. Utah, 170 U.S. 343, 349-350, 18 S. Ct. 620, 622, 42 L. Ed. 1061, 1066 (1898) (quoting 2 Story, Comm. on Const. §1772 (1833)).

[12] W. Forsyth, History of Trial by Jury 6 (1852).

[13] M. Lesser, History of the Jury System (1894).

§1.1 [1] Thompson v. Utah, 170 U.S. 343, 349, 18 S. Ct. 620, 622, 42 L. Ed. 1061, 1066 (1898).

power to instruct them in respect of the facts; and (3) that the verdict should be unanimous."[2]

The Court subsequently held, however, that two of these characteristics are not essential. A jury need not have 12 members, and decisions of 12-person juries, at least in state courts, need not be unanimous.

§1.1.1 *Jury Size*

In 1970, the Court held in *Williams v. Florida*[3] that the Constitution did not necessarily require a jury of 12 persons. It upheld a Florida statute that provided for a 6-person jury in serious criminal cases despite a claim that the sixth amendment as applied to the states through the fourteenth amendment was thereby violated.[4] The Court said the following:

> We do not pretend to be able to divine precisely what the word "jury" imported to the Framers, the First Congress, or the States in 1789. It may well be that the usual expectation was that the jury would consist of 12, and that hence, the most likely conclusion to be drawn is simply that little thought was actually given to the specific question we face today. But there is absolutely no indication in "the intent of the framers" of an explicit decision to equate the constitutional and common-law characteristics of the jury. Nothing in this history suggests, then, that we do violence to the letter of the Constitution by turning to other than purely historical considerations to determine which features of the jury system, as it existed at common law, were presented in the Constitution. The relevant inquiry, as we see it, must be the function that the particular feature performs and its relation to the purposes of the jury trial. Measured by this standard, the 12-man requirement cannot be regarded as an indispensable component of the Sixth Amendment.[5]

[2] Patton v. United States, 281 U.S. 276, 288, 50 S. Ct. 253, 254, 74 L. Ed. 854, 858 (1930).

[3] 399 U.S. 78, 90 S. Ct. 1893, 26 L. Ed. 2d 446 (1970).

[4] Ibid.

[5] Id. at 98-101, 90 S. Ct. at 1904-1905, 26 L. Ed 2d at 459-460.

The Court asserted the purpose of a jury trial is "to prevent oppression by the Government."[6] This purpose, according to the Court, "is not a function of the particular numbers of the body that makes up the jury."[7] After acknowledging that the jury should be large enough to promote group deliberation and to provide an opportunity for a representative cross-section of the community, the Court said it had little reason to think those goals could not be achieved by a jury of six members, particularly if unanimity were required.[8] The Court did not believe the reliability of the jury as factfinder is a function of its size.[9] It said that a few experiments with different sized juries had shown no discernible difference in results reached.[10]

The same conclusion was reached under the seventh amendment in *Colgrove v. Battin*[11] in which the Court held that a jury of six members in federal court did not violate the Constitutional right to trial by jury in a civil case.

The *Williams* and *Colgrove* decisions sparked criticism of the empirical studies cited by the Court, and substantial additional research on jury size. Many of the resulting writings were cited in the opinion of Justice Blackmun, joined by Justice Stevens, in *Ballew v. Georgia.*[12] Although the Court unanimously agreed in *Ballew* that a Georgia criminal trial to a jury of five persons deprived the defendant of his right to trial by jury under the sixth and fourteenth amendments, the Court did not agree on a reason for a constitutional distinction between a six-person and a five-person jury. Commentators have suggested that the line was drawn at six in *Ballew* because the empirical studies did not support the Court's assertion in *Williams* of the absence of a correlation between jury size and function.[13] Most of the stud-

[6] Id. at 101, 90 S. Ct. at 1905, 26 L. Ed. 2d at 460.

[7] Id. at 101, 90 S. Ct. at 1906, 26 L. Ed. 2d at 460.

[8] Ibid.

[9] Id. at 101-102, 90 S. Ct. at 1906-1907, 26 L. Ed. 2d at 460-461.

[10] Id. at 102, 90 S. Ct. at 1906, 26 L. Ed. 2d at 460-461.

[11] 413 U.S. 149, 93 S. Ct. 2448, 37 L. Ed. 2d 522 (1973).

[12] 435 U.S. 223 n.10, 230-233, 98 S. Ct. 1029, 1034-1035, 55 L. Ed. 2d 234, 241–242 (1978).

[13] See, e.g., Note, The Impact of Jury Size on the Court System, 12 Loy. L.A.L. Rev. 1103 (1979); Note, Constitutional Law — Five Jurors are Not Enough, 46 Tenn. L. Rev. 847 (1979).

ies cited by Justice Blackmun purported to show that juries of six are significantly inferior to juries of twelve.[14] Thus, they tended to undermine the foundation of *Williams* rather than constitute a foundation for the distinction in *Ballew*.

§1.1.2 Unanimity Requirements

In *Johnson v. Louisiana*,[15] the Supreme Court held that neither due process nor equal protection was denied by a Louisiana law permitting conviction on the vote of nine of twelve jurors in criminal cases in which punishment was at hard labor. Because the case was tried before the decision in *Duncan v. Louisiana*,[16] the sixth amendment issue was not involved.[17]

The sixth amendment issue was confronted in *Apodaca v. Oregon*,[18] decided on the same date. The Court held that an Oregon constitutional provision allowing conviction in non-capital criminal prosecutions by vote of ten of twelve jurors did not violate the sixth amendment right to trial by jury as made applicable to the states by the fourteenth amendment. A plurality of the Court employed the same method of analysis as in *Duncan*. Stating that the purpose of the jury is to prevent government oppression, the plurality repeated that the jury's essential feature "lies in the interposition between the accused and his accuser of the commonsense judgment of a group of laymen. . . ."[19] The justices asserted that a requirement of unanimity "does not materially contribute to the exercise of this commonsense judgment."[20] In terms of the jury function the plurality perceived no difference between juries required to

[14] Ibid.

[15] 406 U.S. 356, 92 S. Ct. 1620, 32 L. Ed. 2d 152 (1972).

[16] 391 U.S. 145, 88 S. Ct. 1444, 20 L. Ed. 2d 491 (1968).

[17] See De Stefano v. Woods, 392 U.S. 631, 88 S. Ct. 2093, 20 L. Ed. 2d 1308 (1968).

[18] 406 U.S. 404, 92 S. Ct. 1628, 32 L. Ed. 2d 184 (1972).

[19] Id. at 411, 92 S. Ct. at 1633, 32 L. Ed. 2d at 191, quoting Williams v. Florida, 399 U.S. 78, 100, 90 S. Ct. 1893, 1906, 26 L. Ed. 2d 446, 460 (1970).

[20] Id. at 411, 92 S. Ct. at 1633, 32 L. Ed. 2d at 191.

act unanimously and those permitted to decide cases by votes of ten to two or eleven to one.[21] The plurality said that unanimity is not essential to give effect to the requirement that jury panels reflect a cross-section of the community.[22] In casting the fifth vote for the Court's holding, Justice Powell agreed that the sixth amendment as applied to the states through the fourteenth amendment does not require unanimous verdicts in state prosecutions. He contended, however, that the sixth amendment did require unanimous verdicts in federal trials.[23] Consequently the question whether the sixth amendment permits nonunanimous verdicts in federal criminal trials is unresolved.[24]

In *Burch v. Louisiana,*[25] the Court confronted a question that it said lay at the "intersection" of its decisions concerning jury size and unanimity. That question was whether a conviction by a nonunanimous six-person jury in a state criminal trial for a nonpetty offense violated the right of an accused to trial by jury guaranteed by the sixth and fourteenth amendments. Acknowledging, as did the Blackmun opinion in *Ballew,* that a bright line could not be drawn, the Court again concluded that it must nevertheless draw the line "somewhere if the substance of the jury trial right is to be preseved."[26] Persuaded in part by the practice in most other states requiring verdicts by six-person juries to be unanimous, the Court held that the Constitution requires such verdicts to be unanimous.[27]

[21] Id. at 412, 92 S. Ct. at 1633, 32 L. Ed. 2d at 191.

[22] Id. at 414-415, 92 S. Ct. at 1634, 32 L. Ed. 2d at 192-193.

[23] Johnson v. Louisiana, 406 U.S. 356, 371, 92 S. Ct. 1635, 1637, 32 L. Ed. 2d 152, 165 (1972).

[24] The issue is likely to remain unresolved so long as Federal Rule of Criminal Procedure 31(a), which requires unanimous verdicts, is interpreted as precluding waiver. See, e.g., United States v. Pachay, 711 F.2d 488, 490-91 (2d Cir. 1983).

[25] 441 U.S. 130, 99 S. Ct. 1623, 60 L. Ed. 2d 96 (1979).

[26] Id. at 138, 99 S. Ct. at 1627, 60 L. Ed. 2d at 103.

[27] Id. at 139, 99 S. Ct. at 1627-1628, 60 L. Ed. 2d at 104. The Court observed that 25 states apparently allow six-person juries in at least some nonpetty cases. Of those states, only Louisiana and Oklahoma appeared to allow nonunanimous verdicts. Ibid., n.12.

From the Supreme Court's decisions commencing with *Duncan v. Louisiana* it is now apparent, however, that at the state level the 12-person jury and unanimous verdict are not essential elements of trial by jury under the United States Constitution. At the federal level, it is clear that 12-person juries are not required in civil cases. At both levels, it is now established that juries of at least six persons are required and, when they are used, their verdicts must be unanimous.

Constitutional adjudication has also resulted in rules defining the class of cases to which the right to trial by jury applies, when and how the right may be waived, and how juries are to be selected.

§1.1.3 Applicability of a Right to Jury Trial in Civil Cases

The Supreme Court has thus far declined to hold that the seventh amendment right to jury trial in civil cases is binding on the states.[28] Therefore the seventh amendment applies only in federal courts.

The Court has long held that the right to jury trial in civil cases is not limited to actions at common law as they existed in 1791:

> The phrase "common law," found in this clause, is used in contradistinction to equity, and admiralty, and maritime jurisdiction. . . . By *Common law,* [the Framers] meant . . . not merely suits, which the *common law* recognized among its old and settled proceedings, but suits in which *legal* rights were to be ascertained and determined, in contradistinction to those where equitable rights alone were recognized, and equitable remedies were administered. . . . In a just sense, the amendment then may well be construed to embrace all suits which are not of equity and admiralty jurisdiction, whatever might be the pecu-

[28] See, e.g., Alexander v. Virginia, 413 U.S. 836, 93 S. Ct. 803, 37 L. Ed. 2d 993 (1973).

liar form from which they may assume to settle legal rights. (emphasis in original)[29]

In *Curtis v. Loether,*[30] the Court confirmed that the seventh amendment applies to actions enforcing statutory rights, "and requires a jury trial upon demand, if the statute creates legal rights and remedies, enforceable in an action for damages in the ordinary courts at law."[31] The court held that an action for damages under the fair housing provisions of the Civil Rights Act of 1968 was an action to enforce legal rights within the meaning of the seventh amendment.[32] The action was plainly distinguishable from administrative law actions and bankruptcy actions to which the right to jury trial does not attach.[33]

The procedural combination of actions at law and equity does not affect the jury trial right. Its application does not depend "upon the form of the action or procedural devices by which the parties happen to come before the court."[34] When legal claims are involved, they are triable by jury.[35]

An unanswered question exists, however, concerning the extent to which "the practical abilities and limitations of juries" will affect the right to jury trial in civil cases. By a footnote in *Ross v. Bernard,*[36] the Court suggested this was a factor to be considered in determining the legal nature of an issue. Whether a "complexity" exception now exists has been considered in two significant subsequent Court of Appeals decisions.

[29] Parsons v. Bedford, 28 U.S. (3 Pet.) 432, 445-446, 7 L. Ed. 732, 736-737 (1830).

[30] 415 U.S. 189, 94 S. Ct. 1005, 39 L. Ed. 2d 260 (1974).

[31] Id. at 195, 94 S. Ct. at 1008, 39 L. Ed. 2d at 266.

[32] Id. at 196, 94 S. Ct. at 1009, 39 L. Ed. 2d at 267.

[33] Id. at 195-196, 94 S. Ct. at 1008-1009, 39 L. Ed. 2d at 266-267, citing NLRB v. Jones & Laughlin Steel Corp., 301 U.S. 1, 57 S. Ct. 615, 81 L. Ed. 893 (1937) (administrative proceedings), and Katchen v. Lanly, 382 U.S. 323, 86 S. Ct. 467, 15 L. Ed. 2d 391 (1966) (bankruptcy action).

[34] Ross v. Bernard, 396 U.S. 531, 541, 90 S. Ct. 733, 739, 24 L. Ed. 2d 729, 737 (1970).

[35] Id. at 542, 90 S. Ct. at 739, 24 L. Ed. 2d at 737.

[36] 396 U.S. 531, 539, 90 S. Ct. at 738, 24 L. Ed. 2d at 736, n.10 (1970).

In one, *In re United States Financial Securities Litigation,*[37] the court refused to read a complexity exception into the seventh amendment. In the other, *In re Japanese Electronic Products Antitrust Litigation,*[38] the court held that such an exception exists. The court reasoned that "due process precludes trial by jury when a jury is unable to perform [its] tasks with a reasonable understanding of the evidence and legal rules."[39] This question is not likely to go away until it is resolved by the Supreme Court. Modern litigation is becoming more complex, and, under the leadership of Chief Justice Burger, the Judicial Conference of the United States is studying the possibility of curtailing or eliminating by court rule jury trials in complex federal cases.[40]

§1.1.4 Applicability of a Right to Jury Trial in Criminal Cases

In *Duncan v. Louisiana,*[41] the Court held that the fourteenth amendment guarantees a right to jury trial in all cases where the sixth amendment would require jury trial if the case were tried in federal court.

Under the sixth amendment, the right to jury trial does not apply to petty offenses.[42] Cases carrying possible penalties of up to six months' incarceration do not require a jury trial if they otherwise qualify as petty.[43] Although the possible penalty is not always conclusive in determining the nature of the offense, it is "of major relevance" and, if severe enough, may be conclu-

[37] 609 F.2d 411 (9th Cir. 1979).

[38] 631 F.2d 1069 (3d Cir. 1980).

[39] Id. at 1084.

[40] See Kuhlman, Pontikes, and Stevens, Jury Trial, Progress, and Democracy, 14 J. Mar. L. Rev. 679, 682 (1981).

[41] 391 U.S. 145, 88 S. Ct. 1444, 20 L. Ed. 2d 491 (1968).

[42] Cheff v. Schnackenberg, 384 U.S. 373, 86 S. Ct. 1523, 16 L. Ed. 2d 629 (1966).

[43] Ibid.

sive.[44] Historically most cases involving possible penalties of more than six months in prison have been triable by jury.[45] In the federal system, a statute defines petty offenses as those punishable by no more than six months in prison and a $500 fine.[46]

Guided by these objective criteria, the *Duncan* Court held that the Louisiana offense punishable by two years in prison was a serious crime to which the jury trial right was applicable.[47] In a separate decision filed the same day, *Dyke v. Taylor Implement Mfg. Co.,*[48] the Court held that a six-month sentence is short enough to be "petty." Because the contempt punishment was imposed under a Tennessee statute authorizing a maximum penalty of ten days in jail and a fine of $50, the Court characterized it as petty and held the right to jury trial did not apply.[49] In *Bloom v. Illinois,*[50] also filed the day of the *Duncan* decision, the Court refused to exempt serious state criminal contempt cases from the jury trial requirements. When no maximum penalty for contempt is fixed by statute, the sentence actually imposed becomes the most important criterion of seriousness.[51] For example, a term of probation for five years that if breached would result in incarceration for no more than six months was held to be a petty offense in *Frank v. United States.*[52]

A state characterization of an offense called jostling that carried a maximum sentence of one year was held to be a serious offense under the federal standard in *Baldwin v. New York.*[53]

[44] Duncan v. Louisiana, 391 U.S. 145, 159, 88 S. Ct. 1444, 1453, 20 L. Ed. 2d 491, 502 (1968).

[45] Id. at 161, 88 S. Ct. at 1453-1454, 20 L. Ed. 2d at 503.

[46] 18 U.S.C. §1 (1982).

[47] 391 U.S. at 161-162, 88 S. Ct. at 1454, 20 L. Ed. 2d at 503.

[48] 391 U.S. 216, 88 S. Ct. 1472, 20 L. Ed. 2d 538 (1968).

[49] Id. at 220, 88 S. Ct. at 1475, 20 L. Ed. 2d at 543.

[50] 391 U.S. 194, 88 S. Ct. 1444, 20 L. Ed. 2d 522 (1968).

[51] Frank v. United States, 395 U.S. 147, 149, 89 S. Ct. 1503, 1505-1506, 23 L. Ed. 2d 162, 166 (1969).

[52] 395 U.S. 147, 89 S. Ct. 1503, 23 L. Ed. 2d 162 (1969).

[53] 399 U.S. 66, 90 S. Ct. 1886, 26 L. Ed. 2d 437 (1970).

The Court observed that no state, including New York, denied a jury trial to an accused who was subject to a possible prison term of more than six months: "In the entire nation, only New York City alone denies an accused the right to interpose between himself and a possible prison term of over six months, the commonsense judgment of a jury of his peers."[54]

Post-verdict adjudications of contempt based on multiple incidents of direct contempt during trial that resulted in consecutive sentences of six months each, when no statutory maximum sentence existed, were held to be a single offense subject to the right of jury trial for sixth amendment purposes in *Codispoti v. Pennsylvania*.[55] Where concurrent sentences of six months each are imposed in the same situation, the right does not apply.[56] It is possible that a corporation that is merely fined for contempt will not have the right to jury trial.[57]

In *Callan v. Wilson*,[58] the Supreme Court held that a federal two-tier trial system, permitting trial by jury only in a de novo trial on appeal to the second tier, violated the sixth amendment by unduly burdening the defendant's right to jury trial. Eighty-eight years later, however, the Court upheld a state two-tier trial system in *Ludwig v. Massachusetts*.[59] Apart from the fact the latter case involved a state court, the only factual difference was that the Massachusetts system allowed the defendant to submit to conviction at the first tier and then appeal to the second tier without a full trial.[60]

The Supreme Court has held that a juvenile proceeding is not a criminal prosecution for sixth amendment jury trial purposes.[61]

[54] Id. at 72-73, 90 S. Ct. at 1889-1890, 26 L. Ed. 2d at 442 (plurality opinion).
[55] 418 U.S. 506, 94 S. Ct. 2687, 41 L. Ed. 2d 912 (1974).
[56] Taylor v. Hayes, 418 U.S. 488, 94 S. Ct. 2697, 41 L. Ed. 2d 897 (1974).
[57] Muniz v. Hoffman, 422 U.S. 454, 95 S. Ct. 2158, 45 L. Ed. 2d 319 (1975).
[58] 127 U.S. 540, 8 S. Ct. 1301, 32 L. Ed. 223 (1888).
[59] 427 U.S. 618, 96 S. Ct. 2781, 49 L. Ed. 2d 732 (1976).
[60] Id. at 630-631, 96 S. Ct. at 2787-2788, 49 L. Ed. 2d at 741-742.
[61] McKeiver v. Pennsylvania, 403 U.S. 528, 91 S. Ct. 1976, 29 L. Ed. 2d 647 (1971).

§1.1.5 *Waiver of the Right to Jury Trial in Civil Cases*

In civil cases, of course, the right to jury trial may be waived by unilateral act of the litigant.[62] Waiver may occur through stipulation, agreement, or consent in writing.[63] It may also be implied.[64] Under the Federal Rules of Civil Procedure, failure to serve and file a timely demand for jury trial waives the right.[65] The court, however, has discretion on subsequent motion to order a jury trial on some or all issues.[66]

§1.1.6 *Waiver of the Right to Jury Trial in Criminal Cases*

One writer has asserted that the Supreme Court cases from *Duncan* to *Ballew* that purport to reaffirm identical constitutional jury policies are "profoundly deceptive."[67] This is because in 1791 when the sixth amendment was adopted, almost all criminal prosecutions were tried to juries:

> Well into the nineteenth century, jury trial was the routine dispositive procedure for cases of serious crime. Bench trial — that is, trial by a professional judge sitting without lay participation of any sort — developed in the United States in the second half of the nineteenth century and was not made generally available until well into the twentieth century. Contemporary legal thought resisted bench trial for cases of serious crime, precisely because it so impaired the purposes of the jury guarantee.[68]

[62] Baylis v. Travelers' Ins. Co., 113 U.S. 316, 5 S. Ct. 494, 28 L. Ed. 989 (1885).

[63] Ibid.

[64] Kearney v. Case, 79 U.S. (12 Wall.) 275, 20 L. Ed. 395 (1871).

[65] Fed. R. Civ. P. 38(c).

[66] Fed. R. Civ. P. 39(b).

[67] See Langbein, Mixed Court and Jury Court: Could the Continental Alternative Fill the American Need? 1981 A.B. Found. Research J. 195, 216.

[68] Ibid.

Part of this phenomenon is attributable to the brevity of eighteenth century trials. Short trials resulted from the fact that neither prosecution nor defense was represented by counsel in ordinary trials, there was no counsel-conducted voir dire, the defendant usually testified, evidence was presented less formally, rules of evidence were subject to trial court control, and appeal was rare.[69]

By 1945 only 15 percent of criminal prosecutions in the United States were tried by jury.[70] Ten percent of the cases were tried to the court alone, and 75 percent were disposed of on guilty pleas.[71]

Even though the Supreme Court held in 1892 that state law permitting waiver of jury trial in criminal cases did not violate fourteenth amendment due process,[72] the Court stated in 1898 in *Thompson v. Utah*[73] that the sixth amendment did not permit waiver of the right to trial by jury in a federal prosecution. It was not until *Patton v. United States*[74] was decided in 1930 that the Court first recognized the right of a defendant to waive jury trial and be tried by the court. The *Patton* Court reasoned that the provision for jury trial was a personal right of the accused rather than part of the structure of government. The Court held, however, that the maintenance of the jury as a factfinding body in criminal cases is of such importance in our traditions that no waiver can be effective without the consent of the prosecutor and the judge as well as the "express and intelligent consent of the defendant."[75]

In 1965, in *Singer v. United States*,[76] the Court upheld a federal rule of criminal procedure conditioning bench trial on consent of the government and approval of the court. The Court said: "We can find no Constitutional impediment to conditioning a

[69] Id. at 217-18.
[70] H. Kalven & H. Zeisel, The American Jury 18 (1966).
[71] Ibid.
[72] Hallinger v. Davis, 146 U.S. 314, 13 S. Ct. 105, 36 L. Ed. 986 (1892).
[73] 170 U.S. 343, 18 S. Ct. 620, 42 L. Ed. 1061 (1898).
[74] 281 U.S. 276, 50 S. Ct. 253, 74 L. Ed. 854 (1930).
[75] Id. at 312, 50 S. Ct. at 263, 74 S. Ct. at 870.
[76] 380 U.S. 24, 85 S. Ct. 783, 13 L. Ed. 2d 630 (1965).

waiver of this right on the consent of the prosecuting attorney and the trial judge when, if either refuses to consent, the result is simply that the defendant is subject to an impartial trial by jury — the very thing that the Constitution guarantees him."[77] The Court reserved the question "whether there might be some circumstances where a defendant's reasons for wanting to be tried by a judge alone are so compelling that the Government's insistance on trial by jury would result in the denial to a defendant of an impartial trial."[78] Courts subsequently have found such circumstances.[79]

Waiver, of course, must be voluntary and intelligent; it will not be presumed from a silent record.[80] Threats or promises made to induce a plea bargain will not necessarily vitiate the validity of a guilty plea and attendant jury waiver.[81] To demonstrate a due process violation, it is necessary to show that the prosecutor imposed a penalty on the defendant in retaliation for the defendant's exercise of a lawful right.[82] Because the defendant is free to reject a plea bargain, the prosecutor does not impose a penalty by merely pursuing a course of action that could have been taken in the absence of plea negotiations.[83] Moreover, a guilty plea will not be upset merely because it is induced by a desire to avoid conviction of a higher offense.[84] Similarly, a plea is not valid when induced by erroneous advice of counsel, when the advice is within the range of normal competency.[85]

[77] Id. at 36, 85 S. Ct. at 790, 13 L. Ed. 2d at 638.

[78] Id. at 37-38, 85 S. Ct. at 791, 13 L. Ed. at 639.

[79] See, e.g., United States v. Panteleakis, 422 F. Supp. 247 (D.R.I. 1976) (complexity of trial).

[80] Boykin v. Alabama, 395 U.S. 238, 89 S. Ct. 1709, 23 L. Ed. 2d 274 (1969).

[81] Bordenkircher v. Hayes, 434 U.S. 357, 98 S. Ct. 663, 54 L. Ed. 2d 604 (1978).

[82] See United States v. Goodwin, 457 U.S. 368, 102 S. Ct. 2485, 73 L. Ed. 2d 74 (1982).

[83] Bordenkircher v. Hayes, 434 U.S. 357, 363, 98 S. Ct. 663, 667, 54 L. Ed. 2d 604, 610-611 (1978).

[84] Brady v. United States, 397 U.S. 742, 90 S. Ct. 1463, 25 L. Ed. 2d 747 (1970).

[85] Parker v. North Carolina, 397 U.S. 790, 90 S. Ct. 1458, 25 L. Ed. 2d 785 (1970); McMann v. Richardson, 397 U.S. 759, 90 S. Ct. 1441, 25 L. Ed. 2d 763 (1970).

§1.1.7 *Jury Selection: The Fair Cross-Section Principle*

At common law there was no list of persons declared by law to be eligible for jury service.[86] The sheriff was charged with summoning the proper number of "good and lawful men."[87] Most of the original states adopted statutes providing for the preparation of jury lists by officials other than the sheriff.[88] In the absence of statute, it was recognized that a court had inherent authority to summon jurors through open venire in aid of its jurisdiction.[89] Until adoption of the Federal Rules of Civil Procedure in 1946, federal courts were required to conform selection practices to those in the states in which the courts were located.[90]

In *Thiel v. Southern Pacific Co.*,[91] the Supreme Court said the following:

> The American tradition of trial by jury, considered in connection with either criminal or civil proceedings, necessarily contemplates an impartial jury drawn from a cross-section of the community. . . . This does not mean, of course, that every jury must contain representatives of all the economic, social, religious, racial, political and geographical groups of the community; frequently such complete representation would be impossible. But it does mean that prospective jurors shall be selected by court officials without systematic and intentional exclusion of any of these groups. Recognition must be given to the fact that those eligible for jury service are to be found in every stratum of society. Jury competence is an individual rather than a group or class matter. That fact lies at the very heart of the jury system. To disregard it is to open the door to class distinctions and discriminations which are abhorrent to the American ideals of trial by jury.[92]

[86] 1 F. Busch, Law and Tactics in Jury Trials §54 at 417 (1959).
[87] Ibid.
[88] Id. at 418.
[89] Clawson v. United States, 114 U.S. 477, 5 S. Ct. 949, 29 L. Ed. 179 (1885).
[90] 1 F. Busch, Law and Tactics in Jury Trials §56 at 417 (1959).
[91] 328 U.S. 217, 66 S. Ct. 984, 90 L. Ed. 1181 (1946).
[92] Id. at 220, 66 S. Ct. at 985-986, 90 L. Ed. at 1184-1185.

Even before the sixth amendment was held applicable to the states, the Court used the fourteenth amendment to invalidate a state system that systematically excluded blacks from jury service.[93] The Court said it was "part of the established tradition in the use of juries as instruments of public justice that the jury be a body truly representative of the community."[94] In *Brown v. Allen,*[95] the Court disclaimed any intention to impose on states its conception of the proper source of jury lists, "so long as the source reasonably reflects a cross-section of the population suitable in character and intelligence for that civic duty."[96] Finally, after holding in *Duncan v. Louisiana*[97] that the sixth amendment's provision for jury trial is binding on the states through the fourteenth amendment, the Court confirmed in *Taylor v. Louisiana*[98] that "the selection of a petit jury from a representative cross section of the community is an essential component of the Sixth Amendment right to jury trial."[99]

In departing from the common law rule that women were unqualified to be jurors, the Court observed it was the current judgment of the country, reflected in legislative or constitutional provisions in every state and at the federal level, that women are qualified.[100] Moreover, the Court concluded that a venire from which women were systematically excluded could not satisfy the fair cross-section rule.[101]

At the root of the Court's holding in *Taylor* is the principle that representativeness is essential to the capacity of the jury to fulfill its purpose of making "the commonsense judgment of the community" that guards against government oppression: "This prophylactic vehicle is not provided if the jury pool is

[93] Smith v. Texas, 311 U.S. 128, 61 S. Ct. 164, 85 L. Ed. 84 (1940).
[94] Id. at 130, 61 S. Ct. at 165, 85 L. Ed. at 86.
[95] 344 U.S. 443, 73 S. Ct. 397, 97 L. Ed. 469 (1953).
[96] Id. at 474, 73 S. Ct. at 416, 97 L. Ed. at 498.
[97] 391 U.S. 145, 88 S. Ct. 1444, 20 L. Ed. 2d 491 (1968).
[98] 419 U.S. 522, 95 S. Ct. 692, 42 L. Ed. 2d 690 (1975).
[99] Id. at 529, 95 S. Ct. at 697, 42 L. Ed. 2d at 697.
[100] Id. at 534, 95 S. Ct. at 699, 42 L. Ed. 2d at 699-700.
[101] Id. at 537, 95 S. Ct. at 701, 42 L. Ed. 2d at 702.

made up of only special segments of the populace or if large, distinctive groups are excluded from the pool."[102] Impartiality in a particular case cannot be assured in the constitutional sense unless the jury is drawn from a pool broadly representative of the community.

Total exclusion of an identifiable group is not necessary to constitute a violation. Substantial underrepresentation will also violate the Constitution if it results from purposeful discrimination.[103] Furthermore, although it is not sufficient merely to show underrepresentation, that factor combined with deficiencies in the selection system may be enough to establish a prima facie case of intentional discrimination.[104]

§1.1.8 Proof of Discrimination

To establish a constitutional violation, the complaining party must show (1) "a recognizable distinct class, singled out for different treatment under the laws, as written or as applied,"[105] and (2) substantial underrepresentation, usually proved by comparing the percentage of the group in the whole population to the proportion in the jury pool over a significant period of time.[106] The complaining person need not be a member of the excluded group.[107] When the party has shown substantial underrepresentation of the group, a prima facie case has been made, and the government has the burden of producing evidence to rebut it.[108]

[102] Id. at 531, 95 S. Ct. at 698, 42 L. Ed. 2d at 698.

[103] See Turner v. Fouche, 396 U.S. 346, 90 S. Ct. 532, 24 L. Ed. 2d 567 (1970).

[104] See Washington v. Davis, 426 U.S. 229, 96 S. Ct. 2040, 48 L. Ed. 2d 597 (1976).

[105] Castaneda v. Partida, 430 U.S. 482, 495, 97 S. Ct. 1272, 1280, 51 L. Ed. 2d 498, 510 (1977). Although the case related to representativeness of a grand jury, the principles are equally applicable to petit jury cases.

[106] Ibid.

[107] Taylor v. Louisiana, 419 U.S. 522, 527, 95 S. Ct. 692, 695, 42 L. Ed. 2d 690, 695 (1975).

[108] Castaneda v. Partida, 430 U.S. 482, 496, 97 S. Ct. 1272, 1280, 51 L. Ed. 2d 498, 511 (1977).

What constitutes a cognizable group subject to this standard depends on contemporary community conditions.[109] It must be a commonly recognized fairly large group of people who share distinctive perspectives.[110] Among cognizable groups that have been recognized by various courts are blacks, Hispanic-Americans, native Americans, women, persons who work for a daily wage, common laborers, nontheists, students and professors, young people, and persons who object in principle to the death penalty.[111]

In *Swain v. Alabama,*[112] the Supreme Court held that a prima facie case of purposeful discrimination in the exercise of peremptory challenges is not made out merely by showing underrepresentation of blacks on the petit jury. The prosecutor's participation must be shown, and, to "pose the issue," the defendant must "show the prosecutor's systematic use of peremptory challenges against Negroes over a period of time."[113] Underlying this holding is the conviction that it is inconsistent with the role of the peremptory challenge to allow inquiry into the reason for its use:

> To subject the prosecutor's challenge in any particular case to the demands and traditional standards of the Equal Protection Clause would entail a radical change in the nature and operation of the challenge. The challenge, pro tanto, would no longer be peremptory, each and every challenge being open to examination, either at the time of the challenge or at a hearing afterwards. The prosecutor's judgment underlying each challenge would be subject to scrutiny for reasonableness and sincerity. And a great many uses of the challenge would be barred.[114]

[109] See Hernandez v. Texas, 347 U.S. 475, 478, 74 S. Ct. 667, 670, 98 L. Ed. 866, 870 (1954).

[110] Ibid.

[111] ABA Standards, Juror Use and Management 16 (approved draft 1983).

[112] 380 U.S. 202, 85 S. Ct. 824, 13 L. Ed. 2d 759 (1965).

[113] Id. at 227, 85 S. Ct. at 839, 13 L. Ed. 2d at 776.

[114] Id. at 221-222, 85 S. Ct. at 836-837, 13 L. Ed. 2d at 773.

Two state courts have taken a contrary position under their state jury trial guarantees.[115] Under those holdings, a defendant may establish a prima facie case by (1) making as complete a record as possible, (2) showing the excused jurors belong to a cognizable group, and (3) establishing group bias as the basis for the challenges from all the circumstances.[116] The prosecution can rebut the prima facie case by producing evidence that the challenges were not motivated by group bias alone.[117]

One division of a state intermediate court reached the same conclusion under the sixth amendment of the United States Constitution.[118] The court reasoned that the Supreme Court decisions in *Duncan*[119] and *Taylor*[120] had undermined *Swain* and had created a sixth amendment basis for precluding use of peremptory challenges to exclude blacks from juries just because they are blacks.[121] When it reasonably appears to a trial court that the prosecuting attorney is using peremptory challenges for that purpose, the court was said to have a duty to demonstrate that blacks were not being systematically excluded.[122] Another division of the same state's intermediate court reached a contrary result.[123] The controversy was apparently put to rest when the state's highest court followed *Swain*.[124] The majority of state courts continue to treat *Swain* as

[115] People v. Wheeler, 22 Cal. 3d 258, 583 P.2d 748, 148 Cal. Rptr. 890 (1978); Commonwealth v. Soares, 377 Mass. 461, 387 N.E.2d 499, *cert. denied,* 444 U.S. 881, 100 S. Ct. 170, 62 L. Ed. 2d 110 (1979); cf. State v. Crespin, 94 N.M. 486, 612 P.2d 716 (Ct. App. 1980) (apparently also relying on state constitution).

[116] See Comment, 25 Vill. L. Rev. 339, 359 (1979-1980).

[117] Ibid.

[118] See People v. Gosberry, 65 Ill. Dec. 99, 109 Ill. App. 3d 674, 440 N.E.2d 954 (1982); People v. Payne, 62 Ill. Dec. 744, 106 Ill. App. 3d 1034, 436 N.E.2d 1046 (1982).

[119] Duncan v. Louisiana, 391 U.S. 145, 88 S. Ct. 1444, 20 L. Ed. 2d 491 (1968).

[120] Taylor v. Louisiana, 419 U.S. 522, 95 S. Ct. 692, 42 L. Ed. 2d 690 (1975).

[121] 62 Ill. Dec. at 749-750, 106 Ill. App. 3d at 1041-1042, 436 N.E.2d at 1052.

[122] Id. at 748, 106 Ill. App. 3d at 1040, 436 N.E.2d at 1050.

[123] See People v. Teague, 64 Ill. Dec. 401, 108 Ill. App. 3d 891, 439 N.E.2d 1066 (1982).

[124] See People v. Williams, 97 Ill. 2d 252, 73 Ill. Dec. 360, 454 N.E.2d 220 (1983).

controlling.[125] So far, the United States Supreme Court has not expressly retreated from that holding.[126]

Moreover, despite the fair cross-section requirement, the Court has refused to dictate selection procedures. So long as the system is facially neutral, it will not be invalidated merely because it is capable of discriminatory application.[127] Thus, even the use of "key man"[128] and "blue ribbon"[129] systems have not been found to violate the Constitution.[130] The Court has noted, however, that such systems are susceptible to abuse as applied.[131]

§1.1.9 *Jury Selection: Impartiality*

Even before the sixth amendment right to trial by jury was applied to the states, the Supreme Court held that the right to trial by an impartial jury is essential to due process.[132] The Court said, however, that a person is not disqualified by having formed "some impression or opinion as to the merits of the case. . . . It is sufficient if the juror can lay aside his impressions

[125] See, e.g., State v. Grady, 93 Wis. 2d 1, 286 N.W.2d 607 (1979).

[126] Three members of the present Court believe the states should continue for the present to serve as laboratories for a period of further study. Two members of the Court would overrule *Swain* now. See McCray v. New York, 103 S. Ct. 2438, 77 L. Ed. 2d 1322 (1983) (denying certiorari).

[127] Carter v. Jury Commn., 396 U.S. 320, 336-337, 90 S. Ct. 518, 526-527, 24 L. Ed. 2d 549, 560-561 (1970).

[128] Under a "key man" system, jury commissioners select potential jurors from the community at large, in contrast to random selection procedures. See Castaneda v. Partida, 430 U.S. 482, 485, 97 S. Ct. 1272, 1275, 51 L. Ed. 2d 498, 504 (1977).

[129] Under a "blue ribbon" system, special jurors are selected from the general panel based on perceived special qualifications to hear important and intricate cases. See Fay v. New York, 332 U.S. 261, 67 S. Ct. 1613, 91 L. Ed. 2043 (1947).

[130] See Castaneda v. Partida, 430 U.S. 482, 97 S. Ct. 1272, 51 L. Ed. 2d 498 (1977); Moore v. New York, 333 U.S. 565, 68 S. Ct. 705, 92 L. Ed. 881 (1948); Fay v. New York, 332 U.S. 261, 67 S. Ct. 1613, 91 L. Ed. 2d 2043 (1947).

[131] Castaneda v. Partida, 430 U.S. 482, 498, 97 S. Ct. 1272, 1282, 51 L. Ed. 2d 498, 512 (1977).

[132] In re Murchison, 349 U.S. 133, 136, 75 S. Ct. 623, 625, 99 L. Ed. 942, 946 (1955) ("A fair trial in a fair tribunal is a basic requirement of due process.").

or opinion and render a verdict based on the evidence presented in court."[133]

External influences may be strong enough to destroy the possibility of jury impartiality. One example is "mob domination" that produces a wave of public passion making acquittal almost an impossibility.[134] The same effect may be produced by pervasive and prejudicial publicity.[135] Moreover, when a change of venue would otherwise be warranted because of local prejudice, state law may not categorically deny it merely because the charge is a misdemeanor.[136]

The risk of juror prejudice from television coverage of a trial is not alone sufficient to require preclusion of such coverage in all cases.[137] If television coverage produces a circus atmosphere, however, it may result in a denial of due process.[138]

The Supreme Court has distinguished between a juror's knowledge of a case and a juror's predisposition concerning it. The latter may be disqualifying, but the former is not.[139] Voir dire examination of potential jurors may reveal such extensive admitted bias that it draws into question the actual impartiality of jurors who deny bias. It may also demonstrate that, despite knowledge of the case, a sufficient number of jurors can put their impressions aside and an impartial jury can be selected.[140] The defendant has the burden to demonstrate the existence of actual partiality that cannot be laid aside.[141]

The Supreme Court has imposed different standards governing inquiry into racial prejudice on voir dire in federal and state

[133] Irvin v. Dowd, 366 U.S. 717, 722-723, 81 S. Ct. 1639, 1642-1643, 6 L. Ed. 2d 751, 756 (1961).

[134] Frank v. Mangum, 237 U.S. 309, 35 S. Ct. 382, 59 L. Ed. 969 (1915).

[135] See Sheppard v. Maxwell, 384 U.S. 333, 95 S. Ct. 2031, 16 L. Ed. 2d 600 (1966); Rideau v. Louisiana, 373 U.S. 723, 83 S. Ct. 1417, 10 L. Ed. 2d 663 (1963); Irvin v. Dowd, 366 U.S. 717, 81 S. Ct. 1639, 6 L. Ed. 2d 751 (1961).

[136] Groppi v. Wisconsin, 400 U.S. 505, 91 S. Ct. 490, 27 L. Ed. 2d 571 (1971).

[137] Chandler v. Florida, 449 U.S. 560, 101 S. Ct. 802, 66 L. Ed. 2d 740 (1981).

[138] Estes v. Texas, 381 U.S. 532, 85 S. Ct. 1628, 14 L. Ed. 2d 543 (1964).

[139] Murphy v. Florida, 421 U.S. 794, 801, 95 S. Ct. 2031, 2036, 44 L. Ed. 2d 589, 595 (1975).

[140] Id. at 804, 95 S. Ct. at 2037-2038, 44 L. Ed. 2d at 596.

[141] Ibid.

courts. Under its supervisory authority, it requires federal trial courts to make specific inquiry on request when the circumstances show a "reasonable possibility" that racial prejudice will influence the jury.[142] A reasonable possibility exists when the defendant is accused of a violent crime against a person of a different race or ethnic group.[143] When the defendant is merely a member of a minority group, an inquiry into prejudice against that group is not required.[144] Similarly, the Constitution does not require special inquiry into prejudice in a state case even when a member of a minority race or ethnic group is accused of a violent crime against a member of another racial or ethnic group.[145] Special inquiry is mandated by due process only when racial issues are "inextricably bound up with the conduct of the trial."[146] Consequently, it was a constitutional violation for the state trial court in *Ham v. South Carolina*[147] to refuse voir dire inquiry into racial prejudice when the black defendant asserted he was framed on a drug charge by law enforcement authorities in retaliation for his civil rights activities. But it was not a constitutional violation to refuse inquiry in *Ristaino v. Ross*[148] merely because the black defendant was accused of a violent crime against a white victim.[149]

The Court is reluctant to relieve the defendant of the burden to prove actual bias. In *Smith v. Phillips*[150] the defendant learned after trial that a juror had submitted an application during the trial for a position as an investigator in the district attorney's

[142] Rosales-Lopez v. United States, 451 U.S. 182, 101 S. Ct. 1629, 68 L. Ed. 2d 22 (1981) (plurality opinion).

[143] Ibid.

[144] Ibid.

[145] Ristaino v. Ross, 424 U.S. 589, 96 S. Ct. 1017, 47 L. Ed. 2d 258 (1976).

[146] Id. at 598, 96 S. Ct. at 1021, 47 L. Ed. 2d at 264.

[147] 409 U.S. 524, 93 S. Ct. 848, 35 L. Ed. 2d 46 (1973).

[148] 424 U.S. 589, 96 S. Ct. 1017, 47 L. Ed. 2d 258 (1976).

[149] One federal court has held that a trial court did not abuse its discretion in conducting voir dire en masse as one means of countering effects of massive publicity. See United States v. Blanton, 719 F.2d 815 (6th Cir. 1983). Another court found a constitutional violation in the failure of a court to question jurors individually in a capital case. See McCorquodale v. Balkcom, 705 F.2d 1553 (11th Cir. 1983).

[150] 455 U.S. 209, 102 S. Ct. 940, 71 L. Ed. 2d 78 (1982).

office. A posttrial hearing was held in which the juror testified. The trial judge found insufficient evidence of actual bias and refused to upset the verdict. The Supreme Court held that bias could not be imputed in these circumstances.[151] The Court said due process does not require a new trial every time a juror has been placed in a compromising situation.[152] Rather, "[d]ue process means a jury capable and willing to decide the case solely on the evidence before it, and a trial judge ever watchful to prevent prejudicial occurrences and to determine the effect of such occurrences when they happen."[153] In so holding, the Court relied on *Remmer v. United States*[154] in which the Court ruled that any third-party communication with a juror during trial concerning the case at trial is not automatically a ground for upsetting a verdict but is instead "presumptively prejudicial" with the burden on the government to prove the contact was harmless.[155] The lesson from these cases appears to be that even in an extreme case the issue of actual bias must be resolved by the trial court after giving the defendant an opportunity for hearing.

Moreover, a juror's mistaken answer to a question on voir dire will not alone entitle the affected party to a new trial. The party must first demonstrate that the juror failed to answer honestly a question on voir dire and that a correct response would have provided a valid basis for a challenge for cause.[156]

§1.1.10 Jury Selection: Openness

The guarantee of openness in criminal trial proceedings embraces the voir dire of potential jurors.[157] A presumption of

[151] Id. at 215, 102 S. Ct. at 945, 71 L. Ed. 2d at 85.

[152] Ibid.

[153] Ibid.

[154] 347 U.S. 227, 74 S. Ct. 450, 98 L. Ed. at 654 (1954).

[155] Id. at 229, 74 S. Ct. at 451, 98 L. Ed. at 656.

[156] McDonough Power Equipment, Inc. v. Greenwood, 104 S. Ct. 845, 78 L. Ed. 2d 663 (1984).

[157] Press Enterprise Co. v. Superior Court of California, 104 S. Ct. 819, 78 L. Ed. 2d 629 (1984).

openness exists that can be overcome only by proof of an overriding interest based on findings that closure is necessary to preserve higher values and is narrowly tailored to serve that interest.[158] When limited closure is ordered, upon sufficient showing, the constitutional values may be satisfied later by making a transcript of the closed proceedings available within a reasonable time, so long as the protected interest is not harmed.[159]

[158] Ibid.
[159] Ibid.

CHAPTER

2

The Role of Statutes, Rules, and Caselaw in Jury Selection

§2.0 Introduction

Supreme Court adjudication of the right to trial by jury assured under the federal Constitution is only part of the picture. Through its supervisory authority over the federal courts, the Supreme Court may impose higher standards than the Constitution requires. Congress, of course, may do the same through legislation affecting the federal court system.

Each has exercised its prerogative in the area of jury selection. For example, in *Ristaino v. Ross,*[1] the Court imposed a duty on federal trial courts to inquire into racial bias even though such inquiry was not mandated by the Constitution. With the encouragement of the Judicial Conference of the United States,[2] Congress has eliminated in the federal system the "key man" and "blue ribbon" methods of selecting juries that have been upheld by the Court when attacked on Constitutional grounds.[3] Congress declared, "It is the policy of the

§2.0 [1]424 U.S. 539, 96 S. Ct. 1017, 47 L. Ed. 2d 258 (1976).

[2]National College of the State Judiciary, Jury 25-26 (1975).

[3]See Castaneda v. Partida, 430 U.S. 482, 97 S. Ct. 1272, 51 L. Ed. 2d 498 (1977); Moore v. New York, 333 U.S. 565, 68 S. Ct. 705, 92 L. Ed. 881 (1948), and Fay v. New York, 332 U.S. 261, 67 S. Ct. 1613, 91 L. Ed. 2043 (1947). For a definition of these terms, see §1.1.9, nn. 128 & 129 supra.

United States that all litigants in federal courts entitled to trial by jury shall have the right to grand and petit juries selected at random from a fair cross section of the community in the district or division wherein the court convenes."[4] Furthermore, despite the constitutionality of exemption statutes,[5] the statute adds, "It is further the policy of the United States that all citizens shall have the opportunity to be considered for service on grand and petit juries in the district courts of the United States, and shall have an obligation to serve as jurors when summoned for that purpose."[6]

Similarly, the states are free to extend greater protections to their citizens than are provided by the federal Constitution.[7] Thus a state constitution may guarantee the right to a 12-person jury despite the Supreme Court holding that a 6-person jury is authorized by the federal Constitution.[8] Moreover, a state court may establish rules governing voir dire that include rights not federally mandated.[9] Furthermore, so long as federal rights are not infringed, states may determine for themselves how juries are to be selected.[10]

§2.1 Analyzing the Law of Jury Selection: Relevant Factors

It is obvious that constitutions, statutes, rules, and caselaw must be examined before one may have a complete picture of the law of jury selection in any jurisdiction. Relevant subjects

[4] 28 U.S.C. §1861 (1982).

[5] See Rawlins v. Georgia, 201 U.S. 638, 26 S. Ct. 560, 50 L. Ed. 899 (1906).

[6] 28 U.S.C. §1861 (1982).

[7] See generally, Brennan, State Constitutions and the Protection of Individual Rights, 90 Harv. L. Rev. 489 (1977).

[8] See 1 F. Busch, Law and Tactics in Jury Trials §24 (1959).

[9] See, e.g., People v. Williams, 29 Cal. 2d 392, 628 P.2d 869, 174 Cal. Rptr. 317 (1981).

[10] Carter v. Jury Commn., 396 U.S. 320, 90 S. Ct. 518, 24 L. Ed. 2d 549 (1970).

include jury size, unanimity requirements, jury waiver, source lists, juror qualifications, exemption, selection methods, questionnaires, orientation, voir dire, and challenges.

§2.1.1 Jury Size

In the federal system, defendants in criminal cases are entitled by rule of criminal procedure to a jury of 12 persons unless they stipulate in writing to a lesser number.[1] The federal district courts are authorized by local rule to provide for 6-person juries in civil cases.[2] At least 81 of the 94 district courts have done so.[3]

Thirty-four states allow juries of less than twelve in some courts in criminal actions.[4] Thirty-eight states authorize trial by juries of less than twelve in some courts in some civil actions.[5]

§2.1.2 Unanimity Requirements

The rule of unanimity still applies in criminal and civil cases in federal courts.[6] The rule cannot be waived in criminal cases.[7]

§2.1 [1]Fed. R. Crim. P. 23(a).

[2]Colgrove v. Battin, 413 U.S. 419, 93 S. Ct. 2448, 37 L. Ed. 2d 522 (1973).

[3]National Center for State Courts, Facets of the Jury System: A Survey 5 (1976).

[4]Ibid. They are Alaska, Arizona, Colorado, Connecticut, Florida, Georgia, Idaho, Indiana, Iowa, Kansas, Kentucky, Louisiana, Massachusetts, Michigan, Minnesota, Mississippi, Missouri, Montana, Nebraska, New Hampshire, New Mexico, New York, North Dakota, Ohio, Oklahoma, Oregon, South Carolina, South Dakota, Tennessee, Texas, Utah, Virginia, Washington, and Wyoming. Id. at 41-43. The provision lacks statutory implementation in North Dakota. Id. at 44.

[5]Id. at 5. They are Alaska, Arizona, Colorado, Connecticut, Delaware, Florida, Georgia, Idaho, Illinois, Indiana, Iowa, Kansas, Kentucky, Louisiana, Maine, Massachusetts, Michigan, Minnesota, Mississippi, Missouri, Montana, Nebraska, Nevada, New Jersey, New Mexico, New York, North Dakota, Ohio, Oklahoma, Oregon, South Carolina, South Dakota, Texas, Utah, Virginia, Washington, West Virginia, Wyoming. Id. at 41-43.

[6]Fed. R. Crim. P. 31(a); Fed. R. Civ. P. 48.

[7]See, e.g., United States v. Pachay, 711 F.2d 488 (2d Cir. 1983)

Unanimity is also required in criminal cases in states that have adopted the Uniform Rules of Criminal Procedure.[8]

Four states permit nonunanimous verdicts in criminal cases.[9] Over half the states allow nonunanimous verdicts in civil cases.[10]

§2.1.3 *Waiver of Jury*

In the federal system and 19 states, waiver of jury trial in criminal cases requires government consent and court approval.[11] Ten states permit unilateral waiver by the defendant.[12] Except for North Carolina, the remainder require either consent of the government or approval of the court. North Carolina does not allow waiver.[13]

No jurisdiction bars or imposes conditions on the right of a party to agree to waiver of jury trial in a civil case.

§2.1.4 *Source Lists*

In the federal system, the names of jurors are to be selected from voter registration lists or actual voting lists supplemented

[8] National Conference of Commissioners on Uniform State Laws, Uniform Rules of Criminal Procedure, Rule 535(b) (1974).

[9] Louisiana, Oklahoma, Oregon and Texas. National Center for State Courts, Facets of the Jury System: A Survey 9 (1976).

[10] Ibid. They are Alaska, Arizona, Arkansas, California, Hawaii, Iowa (jury must first deliberate six hours), Idaho, Kentucky, Louisiana, Maine, Massachusetts, Michigan, Minnesota (jury must deliberate six hours), Mississippi, Missouri, Montana, Nebraska (jury must deliberate six hours), Nevada, New Jersey, New Mexico, New York, Ohio, Oklahoma, Oregon, Pennsylvania, South Dakota, Texas, Utah, Virginia, Washington, and Wisconsin. Id. at 41-43.

[11] The states are Alabama, Alaska, Arizona, Delaware, Indiana, Iowa, Kansas, Kentucky, Nevada, New Mexico, North Dakota, South Dakota, Tennessee, Texas, Utah, Vermont, Virginia, Wisconsin, and Wyoming. Note, Criminal Jury Trials in Iowa: A Time for Revision, 31 Drake L. Rev. 187, 213-214 (1981).

[12] They are Colorado, Connecticut, Illinois, Louisiana, Maryland, Minnesota, New Hampshire, Ohio, Oklahoma, and West Virginia. Ibid.

[13] Ibid.

by "some other source or sources of names in addition to voter lists where necessary to foster the policy and protect the rights secured by [the federal statute]."[14] Each district court is required to devise its own plan, which must be approved by a reviewing panel.[15] The adequacy of a voter registration list as a source of persons to serve on juries has generally been sustained when attacked on constitutional grounds.[16]

The states are given considerable leeway in application of the fair cross-section principle.[17] The Supreme Court will not impose on states its conception of the proper source of jury lists "so long as the source reasonably reflects a cross-section of the population suitable in character and intelligence for that civic duty."[18] Thus, states are not obliged to use source lists and random selection methods as in the federal system. As a result, states have retained systems that give authority to jury commissioners to exercise a wide range of choice in selecting jurors.[19] Even "key man" systems may be utilized.[20] The point is that these systems are facially neutral. They have a potential for abuse but are not inherently defective. The burden remains on an objector to prove that underrepresentation of a protected group is due to "systematic exclusion" of the group in the jury selection process.[21]

Some states, nevertheless, have modified their systems to follow the federal example. The National Commissioners on Uniform State Laws lent impetus to this movement by promulgating a Uniform Jury Selection and Service Act in 1970.[22] The

[14] 28 U.S.C. §1863(b)(2) (1982).

[15] 28 U.S.C. §1863(a) (1982).

[16] See, e.g., United States v. Clifford, 640 F.2d 150 (8th Cir. 1981).

[17] Taylor v. Louisiana, 419 U.S. 522, 538, 95 S. Ct. 692, 701, 42 L. Ed. 2d 690, 702 (1975).

[18] Carter v. Jury Commn., 396 U.S. 320, 333-334, 90 S. Ct. 518, 525, 24 L. Ed. 2d 549, 559 (1970).

[19] Ibid.

[20] See Castaneda v. Partida, 430 U.S. 482, 97 S. Ct. 1272, 51 L. Ed. 2d 498 (1977).

[21] Duren v. Missouri, 439 U.S. 357, 365, 99 S. Ct. 664, 668, 58 L. Ed. 2d 579, 586-587 (1979).

[22] 13 Uniform Jury Selection and Service Act, 13 U.L.A. 509 (1980).

commissioners noted three principal reasons for developing the act. First was the desire to avoid problems, pinpointed in the Supreme Court cases, that might lead to a judicial declaration that certain states' jury panels were unlawful.[23] Second was the objective of providing the states with a unified selection method calculated to give all citizens an opportunity to serve and to create an obligation for them to serve when summoned.[24] Third was the goal of preventing forum shopping by achieving uniformity in jury selection between the federal and state systems and among the states.[25]

The uniform act provides for a jury commission in each county or district.[26] The commission administers a random selection system with implementing features designed to maximize the opportunity for service and to make it difficult to avoid the obligation.[27] The act bears a strong resemblance to the federal statute.[28]

The uniform act has been adopted in at least eight states.[29] Other states have adopted the source list and other features of the uniform act.[30] Therefore, it is not uncommon for states to use voter registration lists, drivers' license lists, utility customer and other lists to form the pool from which jurors are selected.

§2.1.5 *Juror Qualifications*

In approving juror qualification requirements the Supreme Court noted the following in *Carter v. Jury Commission*:[31]

[23] Ibid.
[24] Ibid.
[25] Ibid.
[26] Id. at 510.
[27] Ibid.
[28] Id. at 512.
[29] They are Colorado, Idaho, Indiana, Maine, Michigan, Minnesota, Mississippi, and North Dakota. See Am. Jur. 2d Desk Book, 1982 Supp. at 185.
[30] See, e.g., Iowa Code ch. 609 (1983).
[31] 396 U.S. 320, 90 S. Ct. 518, 24 L. Ed. 2d 549 (1970).

> Nearly every State requires that its jurors be citizens of the United States, residents of the locality, of a specified minimum age, and able to understand English. Many of the States require that jurors be of "good character" or the like; some, that they be "intelligent" or "well-informed." (Footnotes omitted).[32]

Under the federal statute, any person is qualified unless he (or she)

> (1) is not a citizen of the United States eighteen years old who has resided for a period of one year within the judicial district;
> (2) is unable to read, write, and understand the English language with a degree of proficiency sufficient to fill out satisfactorily the juror qualification forms;
> (3) is unable to speak the English language;
> (4) is incapable, by reason of mental or physical infirmity, to render satisfactory jury service; or
> (5) has a charge pending against him for the commission of, or has been convicted in a State or Federal court of record of, a crime punishable by imprisonment for more than one year and his civil rights have not been restored.[33]

The Uniform Jury Selection and Service Act contains an analogous provision. It requires, however, that a person claiming a physical or mental disability "may be required to submit a physician's certificate as to the disability, and the certifying physician is subject to inquiry by the court at its discretion. . . ."[34]

It is obvious that the federal and uniform acts seek to limit disqualification to a few objective factors that most persons would agree are disabling. The effect should be to eliminate subjectivity in the selection process and increase the representativeness of the panel.

[32]Id. at 334, 90 S. Ct. at 525, 24 L. Ed. 2d at 559-560. Citations to state statutes are provided id. at 334-335, n.31-33, 90 S. Ct. at 525-526, 24 L. Ed. 2d at 559-560.

[33]28 U.S.C. §1865(b) (1982).

[34]Uniform Jury Selection and Service Act §8, 13 U.L.A. 525-526 (1980).

§2.1.6 Exemptions

The same spirit is reflected in exemption provisions. Exemptions traditionally have been granted to every occupational group with sufficient legislative influence to obtain passage of an exemption statute. The practice has withstood constitutional attack.[35]

Now, however, exemptions have been significantly cut back under both the federal and uniform acts. Under the federal statute, the jury selection plan must provide for exemption for armed forces members, members of fire and police departments, and public officials.[36] The uniform act simply provides that "[n]o qualified prospective juror is exempt from jury service."[37] The reasoning of the commissioners is that the public policy favoring representativeness is better achieved through a system of individual excuses based on a showing in an individual case of "undue hardship, extreme inconvenience, or public necessity."[38] The commissioners' assertion is that "[t]he individual should not be given an automatic exemption merely because he comes within a particular class, but rather should be required to make out a case of hardship to the court."[39]

§2.1.7 Selection Methods

Even though the key man system of jury selection has not been precluded on federal constitutional grounds,[40] modern authority generally endorses the principle of random selection.[41]

The federal statute makes it the policy of the United States in

[35] See Rawlins v. Georgia, 201 U.S. 638, 26 S. Ct. 560, 50 L. Ed. 899 (1906).
[36] 28 U.S.C. §1863(b)(6) (1982).
[37] Uniform Jury Selection and Service Act §10, 13 U.L.A. 528 (1980).
[38] Id. at 529 (commissioners' comment).
[39] Ibid.
[40] See Castaneda v. Partida, 430 U.S. 482, 97 S. Ct. 1272, 51 L. Ed. 2d 498 (1977).
[41] See, e.g., ABA Standards, Trial Courts §2.61 (approved draft 1976); ABA Standards, Trial by Jury §2.1(a) (approved draft 1968).

federal courts to select grand and petit juries at random "from a fair cross-section of the community."[42] The names are to be placed in a master jury wheel, or a device similar in purpose and function, in accordance with the selection plan.[43] After screening for disqualifications and exceptions, the names of qualified jurors are placed in a qualified jury wheel.[44] The jury commission or clerk is required to draw names at random from the qualified jury wheel for service on grand and petit jury panels.[45]

Similar requirements are imposed in the Uniform Jury Selection and Service Act. The policy is one of random selection.[46] Names of prospective jurors are taken from the master list at random and placed in the master jury wheel.[47] After screening for disqualifications, the names of qualified jurors[48] are placed in the qualified jury wheel. The jury wheel may be a mechanical or electronic device suitable for storing names.[49] Panels are drawn at random from the qualified jury wheel when required.[50]

§2.1.8 Use of Jury Questionnaires

The use of jury questionnaires has become common. In the federal system, the questionnaire is called a "juror qualification form."[51] The form is approved by the Judicial Conference of the United States. It elicits the "name, address, age, race, occupation, education, length of residence within the judicial district, distance from residence to place of holding court, prior jury

[42] 28 U.S.C. §1861 (1982).
[43] 28 U.S.C. §1863(b)(3) (1982).
[44] 28 U.S.C. §1866(a) (1982).
[45] Ibid.
[46] Uniform Jury Selection and Service Act §1, 13 U.L.A. 512 (1980).
[47] Id. §6 at 520-521.
[48] Id. §9 at 526-527.
[49] Id. §3(5) at 515.
[50] Id. §7(a) at 523-524.
[51] 28 U.S.C. §1864 (1982).

service, and citizenship of a potential juror. . . ."[52] The form also obtains the data necessary to determine if the person meets the statutory qualifications or exemption standards.[53] It is mailed to the persons whose names are drawn from the master jury wheel.[54] On the basis of information provided on the form, the court determines whether the person is disqualified or exempt.[55] The remaining names are put in a qualified jury wheel from which grand and petit jury panels are made up.[56]

The Uniform Act provides for similar use of a jury qualification form.[57] It also expressly permits public access to the completed forms of qualified jurors:

> The names of qualified jurors drawn from the qualified jury wheel and the contents of jury qualification forms completed by those jurors shall be made available to the public unless the court determines in any instance that this information in the interest of justice should be kept confidential or its use limited in whole or in part.[58]

Thus a qualification form may serve as an aid to voir dire examination as well as a means of screening out disqualified or exempt jurors.

Even when not used for preliminary screening, jury questionnaires are frequently employed to obtain basic information about jurors to assist the parties in jury selection. For example, a questionnaire may be sent to jurors at the time they are summoned to duty. It may be accompanied by a return envelope with prepaid postage and instructions to complete and return it by a certain date. This procedure is intended to facilitate and shorten voir dire examination.[59]

[52] 28 U.S.C. §1869(b) (1982).
[53] Ibid.
[54] 28 U.S.C. §1864 (1982).
[55] 28 U.S.C. §1865 (1982).
[56] 28 U.S.C. §1866 (1982).
[57] Uniform Jury Selection and Service Act §§7-9, 13 U.L.A. 523-527 (1980).
[58] Id. §9 at 526-527.
[59] National College of the State Judiciary, Jury 49 (1975).

§2.1.9 Jury Orientation

Jury orientation may consist of providing jurors with a handbook or an oral presentation or both. A modern variation of the oral presentation is the use of audiovisual materials to record a standard introduction to jury service that can be shown to the panel when it is summoned.[60]

The purpose of orientation is to inform the prospective jurors concerning the nature of the judicial process and their role in it.[61] In the past, orientation was sometimes challenged as objectionable in principle or on the basis of content. It does not appear that any jurisdiction today disapproves of orientation in principle.[62]

§2.1.10 Voir Dire

The voir dire stage of the trial is intended to permit questioning of prospective jurors as a predicate for the exercise of challenges.[63] The purpose is to select a fair and impartial jury.

In the federal system the court may permit the parties or their attorneys to conduct the examination or may do the questioning itself. When the court does the questioning, it must permit the parties or their attorneys to supplement the inquiry by such additional questions "as it deems proper or shall itself submit to the prospective jurors such additional questions of the parties or their attorneys as it deems proper."[64] A 1977 survey of federal judges showed that in practice 75 percent of the judges excluded oral participation of counsel in voir dire.[65]

[60] See discussion in §3.9 infra.

[61] See Center for Jury Studies; Methodology Manual for Jury Systems, §§5.1-5.9 (1979).

[62] National College of the State Judiciary, Jury 48-49 (1975).

[63] See, e.g., Swain v. Alabama, 380 U.S. 202, 218-219, 85 S. Ct. 824, 834, 13 L. Ed. 2d 759, 771 (1965).

[64] Fed. R. Crim. P. 24(a); Fed. R. Civ. P. 47(a).

[65] See G. Bermant, Conduct of the Voir Dire Examination: Practices and Opinions of Federal District Judges 5 (Federal Judicial Center 1977).

State practices vary. In approximately thirteen states the examination is conducted by the judge only. In approximately eighteen states the examination is primarily done by the attorneys. In the remainder, the judge and attorneys share the examination.[66]

In both the federal and state systems, trial judges are vested with considerable discretion in determining the scope of voir dire interrogation.[67]

Courts have approved the propriety of a wide range of questions:

> A juror may be asked any question directed to ascertaining whether he possesses the necessary statutory qualifications for jury service. Where fairly related to the parties or issues involved, a juror may, according to the weight of authority, be asked questions relating to his nativity and ancestry; necessary property qualifications; moral deficiencies; his education (schools and colleges he has attended), and his knowledge of the English language; his state of health and the condition of his ordinary faculties; his previous jury service; membership on grand jury which returned the indictment he is called upon to try as a petit juror; membership on a previous jury which heard the same evidence as would be offered in the case in which he is called; interest in another case pending for trial at the same term of court; his relationship to the parties or their attorneys; his direct or indirect financial interest in the outcome of these; his relationship (as partner, employer, employee, landlord, tenant, debtor, creditor, bail or surety) to one of the parties; membership in an organization to which one of the parties belongs; his marital status, and if he has children; his social, religious, fraternal, labor union, and political affiliations; his present and former places of residence; his present and former places of employment and, if married, the gainful employment, if any, of a spouse; if the case is a criminal one, whether he has been con-

[66] National Center for State Courts, State Court Organization: 1980, Table 42 (1981).

[67] See 6 C. Wright & A. Miller, Federal Practice and Procedure, §2482 at 469 (1971) (federal); 1 F. Busch, Law and Tactics in Jury Trials, §84 at 564 (1959) (state).

> nected with any organization whose object is to suppress and punish crime, and whether he or any member of his family or a close friend has ever been [the] prosecuting witness or defendant in a criminal case; if the case is a civil one, whether he or any member of his family or a close friend has been in a position similar to that of the plaintiff or defendant (e.g., in an action for damages for personal injuries, whether he or any member of his family or a close friend has suffered accidental injury or made claim for damages for such an injury, or has ever been charged with negligence or had a claim made against him); whether he has ever been engaged in litigation and its nature; knowledge of the facts in the instant case, or acquaintance with any of the parties, attorneys or witnesses; his friendship, animosity, prejudice or bias against or for one of the parties; his prejudice against the race or nationality or political affiliations or religion of a party or his attorney or witnesses; or against the occupation of a party or against particular types of actions of defenses; whether he has any preconceived opinion as to the merit or demerit of the case, and in a criminal case, of the defendant's guilt or innocence; and his opinions respecting capital punishment and circumstantial evidence. (Footnotes omitted.)[68]

Courts have also disapproved certain types of questions:

> A juror may not, in the absence of statutory authority, be required to answer any question calculated to humiliate him or bring him into disrepute. It is also generally held that he may not be asked the meaning of various legal terms which will be used during the trial, but the court in its discretion may allow such questions, particularly where ability to understand the English language is a statutory qualification, and the object of the examination is to determine if the juror possesses that qualification. A juror may not be cross-examined, and it is held that the court, in its discretion, may curtail an unduly protracted examination. The asking of hypothetical questions, that is, questions containing a recital of assumed facts and concluding with an inquiry as to what verdict a juror would give if such facts

[68] 1 F. Busch, Law and Tactics in Jury Trials, §84 at 564-577 (1959). (Copyright © 1959 by Michie Company. Reprinted by permission.)

> were proved, is not favored; but here again, it has been held that the court, in its discretion, may permit such questions under certain circumstances. Similarly, it is generally held that a juror may not be asked how he would vote in certain contingencies. The courts are divided on whether a juror may be asked what his verdict would be if the evidence should be equally balanced. It is generally held that a juror may not be asked what he would do if the court gave certain instructions, or if a certain state of the evidence should develop, or what his attitude would be toward a certain witness who is expected to testify. It has been held that a juror may be asked if he would be prejudiced against a defendant if he failed to take the witness stand in his own defense, but refusal to permit this question has been held not to constitute reversible error. It has been held that the trial court properly refused to permit defendant's attorney to ask juror if the fact a prior jury had disagreed would influence his verdict. Questions are not favored where their tendency is to encourage a disagreement, such as whether a juror would change his opinion formed after mature deliberation because a majority of his fellow jurors were of a contrary opinion. It has been held proper to state to a juror in a criminal case that the defendant is presumed to be innocent until proved guilty beyond a reasonable doubt and to ask him if he will give the defendant the benefit of that presumption until it is overcome by proof beyond a reasonable doubt; but the propriety of the question has been doubted in other cases. (Footnotes omitted.)[69]

In most jurisdictions the interrogation occurs in the presence of the entire panel, but the trial court has discretion to order otherwise. The voir dire may be collective or individual. A fixed number of prospective jurors are generally called forward for interrogation. When they have been examined, the parties have an opportunity to exercise challenges for cause and peremptory challenges. Replacement jurors are called forward as necessary and questioned. If a striking procedure exists, the parties also exercise strikes to reduce the group to the 12 jurors who will try the case.[70]

[69] Id. at 577-589.
[70] Id. at 548-551.

§2.1.11 Challenges for Cause

Two main kinds of challenges to prospective jurors exist in all jurisdictions. They are challenges for cause and peremptory challenges.

Challenges for cause are sometimes categorized as challenges to the array, challenges for favor, and principal challenges. A *challenge to the array* is simply a challenge to the entire panel based on some alleged irregularity in the process of summoning or selecting the prospective jurors.[71] A *challenge for favor* is a challenge to an individual prospective juror where the facts raise a suspicion of bias.[72] A *principal challenge* is a challenge to an individual prospective juror based on alleged incompetency as a matter of law.[73] A challenge for cause in general is a challenge to an individual prospective juror in which a reason is advanced for the person's alleged disqualification.[74] All challenges for cause must be predicated on an express reason as to why the court should not permit the person to sit on the jury. The object, of course, is to arrive at a fair and impartial jury.[75]

Challenges for cause are the responsibility of the parties and must be urged in timely manner.[76] Generally, the rule is that all challenges must be exercised before the jury is sworn.[77] Nevertheless it has been suggested that when the court handles voir dire it should excuse prospective jurors on its own motion if grounds for challenge appear.[78] Ordinarily all challenges for cause must be exercised before peremptory challenges are employed.[79] There is also a prevailing rule that any error in failing

[71] Id. §70 at 481 (1959).
[72] Ibid.
[73] Id. at 482.
[74] Id. §72 at 485-487.
[75] Ibid.
[76] See ABA Standards, Trial by Jury §2.5, Commentary at 68 (approved draft 1968).
[77] Ibid.
[78] Id. at 67.
[79] 1 F. Busch, Law and Tactics in Jury Trials, §75 at 498 (1959).

to sustain a challenge for cause is waived if a party proceeds to trial without using all peremptory challenges.[80] The ruling on a challenge for cause involves an exercise of trial court discretion.[81]

§2.1.12 *Peremptory Challenges*

A peremptory challenge gives a party the right to have an individual prospective juror excused without explanation.[82] The history of the peremptory challenge was reviewed by the Supreme Court in *Swain v. Alabama.*[83] In English trials for felonies at common law, the defendant was allowed to challenge 35 jurors peremptorily, and the prosecutor had an unlimited number of such challenges.[84] In this country, both sides were given a substantial number of statutory peremptory challenges in both the federal and state systems.[85] Although usually fewer in number, peremptory challenges were also allowed in civil cases.[86]

A procedure that has the same effect as peremptory challenges is the struck jury system. It is used either in combination with peremptory challenges or as an alternative method. Historically, 48 persons would be summoned from the jury list and each side would alternately strike 12 names, the remaining 24 jurors being summoned for the case.[87] In a modern adaptation of this method, Alabama uses the struck jury system in both civil and criminal cases.[88] The theory of the peremptory challenge and struck jury system is that the parties should have the

[80] Id. at §79.

[81] See 2 C. Wright & A. Miller, Federal Practice and Procedure, §383 at 361-362 (1982).

[82] Id. §384 at 372.

[83] 380 U.S. 202, 211-220, 85 S. Ct. 824, 831-835, 13 L. Ed. 2d 759, 767-772 (1965).

[84] Ibid.

[85] Ibid.

[86] Ibid.

[87] Id. at 217, n.21, 85 S. Ct. at 834, 13 L. Ed. 2d at 771.

[88] Ala. Code §§12-16-100-01 and 12-16-140 (1977).

opportunity to eliminate a certain number of prospective jurors without fear of incurring a person's hostility through a challenge for cause:[89]

> The function of the challenge is not only to eliminate extremes of partiality on both sides, but to assure the parties that the jurors before whom they try the case will decide on the basis of the evidence placed before them and not otherwise. In this way the peremptory satisfies the rule that "to perform its high function in the best way 'justice must satisfy the appearance of justice.' "[90]

In *Swain* the Court also said the following:

> The essential nature of the peremptory challenge is that it is one exercised without a reason stated, without inquiry and without being subject to the court's control. . . . While challenges for cause permit rejection of jurors on a narrowly specified, provable and legally cognizable basis of partiality, the peremptory permits rejection for a real or imagined partiality that is less easily designated or demonstrable. . . . It is often exercised upon the "sudden impressions and unaccountable prejudices we are apt to conceive upon the bare looks and gestures of another," . . . upon a juror's "habits and associations," . . . or upon the feeling that "the bare questioning [of a juror's] indifference may sometimes provoke a resentment." . . . It is no less frequently exercised on grounds normally thought irrelevant to legal proceedings or official action, namely, the race, religion, nationality, occupation or affiliations of people summoned for jury duty. (Citations and footnotes omitted.)[91]

In the federal system, a party in a civil case ordinarily has three peremptory challenges.[92] The number of peremptories in

[89]Swain v. Alabama, 380 U.S. 202, 219-220, 85 S. Ct. 824, 834-835, 13 L. Ed. 2d 759, 772 (1965).

[90]Id. at 219, 85 S. Ct. at 835, 13 L. Ed. 2d at 772, quoting In re Murchison, 349 U.S. 133, 136, 75 S. Ct. 623, 625, 99 L. Ed. 942, 946 (1955).

[91]Id. at 220, 85 S. Ct. at 836, 13 L. Ed. 2d at 772.

[92]28 U.S.C. §1870 (1982).

a criminal case depends on the possible punishment.[93] Each side has twenty peremptory challenges in a capital case.[94] In other felony cases the government has six peremptories and the defendant has ten.[95] In misdemeanor cases each side has three.[96]

State statutes and rules vary, but all states allow peremptory challenges or provide a struck jury sytem in both civil and criminal cases.[97] In most states the number of challenges and procedures are analogous to those in the federal system.[98] In criminal cases, when multiple parties are involved, statutes and rules deal with the problem in various ways. Some provide that all codefendants must join in every peremptory challenge made by a single defendant. Other statutes and rules variously include (1) that the trial court has discretion to increase the number of challenges, (2) that each defendant has additional challenges, (3) that each has a certain number of challenges but fewer than if the defendant were tried alone, (4) that challenges be divided among defendants with trial court discretion to permit additional challenges, and (5) that each defendant shall have the same number of challenges as if tried separately.[99] The Uniform Rules of Criminal Procedure provide that the court allow each defendant additional challenges, to be exercised separately, and, if a motion for severance has been denied, to give each defendant the same number as the state.[100]

[93] Fed. R. Crim. P. 24(b).
[94] Ibid.
[95] Ibid.
[96] Ibid.
[97] See Swain v. Alabama, 380 U.S. 202, 217, 85 S. Ct. 824, 834, 13 L. Ed. 2d 759, 770-771 (1965).
[98] See ABA Standards, Trial by Jury §2.6, Commentary at 72 (approved draft 1968).
[99] Id. at 73-74.
[100] Uniform Rules of Criminal Procedure, Rule 512(d), 10 U.L.A. 263 (1974).

CHAPTER

3

Current Issues and Developments in Jury Law

§3.0 Introduction

The United States is unique in its adherence to the system of trial by jury in civil and criminal cases. Approximately ninety-eight percent of the world's civil jury trials and ninety percent of the criminal jury trials are conducted in this country.[1] The use of juries in civil cases has virtually gone into eclipse in the rest of the world. They are used in some Canadian provinces and Australian states.[2] In England they are used only in the trial of personal torts like libel and slander.[3] Although juries were used for trying major crimes in many European countries in the nineteenth century, today they are used in only a handful of countries outside of the English-speaking world.[4]

Even in this country the percentage of case dispositions by jury trial is surprisingly small. Only one or two percent of civil cases are ultimately decided by juries.[5] Less than ten percent of

§3.0 [1]H. Zeisel, The American Jury, Chief Justice Earl Warren Conference on Advocacy in the United States 65 (1977).

[2]Id. at 93, n.1.

[3]Ibid.

[4]Ibid.

[5]Id. at 66.

felony charges are tried to juries, and the percentage is less for misdemeanors.[6] Most civil cases, of course, are settled before trial, and most criminal convictions occur through guilty pleas that often are based on plea bargains.

Despite this limited use of the jury, it remains the centerpiece of our system. Its impact extends far beyond the small percentage of cases tried by jury: "The importance of the jury . . . transcends these percentages; it is partly the expectation of what a jury is likely to do in a particular case that informs the decisions as to whether or not to settle or plead guilty, or whether or not to waive a jury."[7]

§3.1 General Sources of Controversy about the Jury System

Considerable controversy has traditionally surrounded the jury system. This phenomenon is a natural concomitant of the jury's central role in resolving disputes under the rule of law:

> The Anglo-American jury is a remarkable political institution. We have had it with us for so long that any sense of surprise over its main characteristics has perhaps somewhat dulled. It recruits a group of twelve laymen, chosen at random from the widest population; it convenes them for the purpose of the particular trial; it entrusts them with great official powers of decision; it permits them to carry on deliberations in secret and to report out their final judgment without giving reasons for it; and, after their momentary service to the state has been completed, it orders them to disband and return to private life.
>
> The jury represents a deep commitment to the use of laymen in the administration of justice — a commitment that finds its

[6] Ibid. (The trend appears to be toward an increase in the use of juries in criminal cases. See Flango & Roper, Rise or Fall of the American Jury, 7 St. Ct. J. 27 (No. 4 1983)).

[7] Ibid.

> analogue in the widespread use of lay judges in the criminal courts of other countries. The jury is, thus, by definition, an exciting experiment in the conduct of serious human affairs. It is not surprising that, virtually from its inception, it has been subject to deep controversy, attracting at once the most extravagant praise and the harshest criticism.[1]

The controversy over the merits of the jury system intensifies when a jury in a highly publicized case returns a verdict that runs counter to public opinion. This presents a paradox. Opponents of the system charge that the system has failed because the jury has gone against popular judgment. Defenders of the system point out that this illustrates its strength and value. According to the latter view, the jury stands as a bulwark between the force of public opinion and the rights of the individual under the rule of law.

Developments and current issues relating to jury trial include (1) differences in result between trial by jury and bench trials, (2) effect on the right of trial by jury of plea bargains and pretrial conferences, (3) factors of inefficiency and delay attendant to jury trial, (4) considerations of jury size, (5) consequences of unanimity requirements, (6) methods of selecting prospective jurors, (7) procedures relating to choosing a jury, and (8) techniques of jury orientation and instruction. Each of these will be discussed below.

§3.2 Disparities in Results between Jury and Bench Trials

Studies conducted during the University of Chicago jury project showed a rate of disagreement between judge and jury in

§3.1 [1]H. Zeisel, The American Jury, Chief Justice Earl Warren Conference on Advocacy in the United States, 65, 66 (1977).

jury cases of approximately twenty percent.[1] Most of the study involved criminal cases, but some data was gathered in civil cases.

§3.2.1. *Disparities in Civil Cases*

In civil cases the judges and juries agreed on verdicts for the plaintiff in 47 percent of the cases and for the defendant in 31 percent of them.[2] The judge would rule for the plaintiff in an additional 12 percent where the jury would not, and the jury would rule for the defendant in an additional 10 percent where the judge would not.[3] The disagreement is thus quite balanced.

On the average, the civil jury awarded more in damages than the judge.[4] In the 47 percent of civil cases in which the judge and jury agreed on a verdict for the plaintiff, the jury awarded more than the judge would in 22 percent and the same amount in 8 percent. The judge awarded more than the jury would in 17 percent of the cases.[5]

The project directors concluded that jurors as a group can understand cases as well as judges.[6] They also concluded that the major reason for jury disagreement with judges is a jury propensity to inject a community sense of justice into the controversy: "The upshot is that, when the jury reaches a different conclusion from the judge on the same facts, it does so, not because it is a sloppy or inaccurate finder of facts, but because it gives recognition to values which fall outside the official rules."[7]

New Jersey's experiment with mandatory pretrial conferences included an analysis of judge-jury agreement on liability

§3.2 [1]H. Zeisel, The American Jury, Chief Justice Earl Warren Conference on Advocacy in the United States 65, 68 (1977).

[2]Id. at 69.

[3]Ibid.

[4]Ibid.

[5]Ibid.

[6]Ibid.

[7]Id. at 70.

decisions in civil personal injury cases. The New Jersey results were reasonably similar to those in the Chicago Jury Project.[8] They also tended to confirm the Chicago results relating to differences in damage awards.[9]

§3.2.2. *Disparities in Criminal Cases*

The Chicago study showed that judges and juries agreed on conviction in 64 percent of the criminal cases and on acquittal in 14 percent of them.[10] However, the judge would convict in an additional 19 percent of the cases where the jury would acquit, and the jury would convict in 3 percent of the cases in which the judge would acquit.[11] It thus appears that in criminal cases the disagreement of juries with judges favors defendants.

Judge and jury differences in criminal cases are fully analyzed in Kalven and Zeisel's definitive work, *The American Jury*,[12] based on their University of Chicago studies of criminal cases. In the majority of cases, disagreement occurred because of differing views of the evidence.[13] Apart from this factor, differences were attributable principally to jury sentiments about the law or the defendant.[14] The jury's view of the facts, however, was the sole cause of disagreement in only one-third of the cases.[15] In the remaining two-thirds of the cases the disagreement was based in part or solely on jury values and sentiments.[16]

Several conclusions from the study should be useful to lawyers who try criminal cases. The findings should provide a more informed basis for deciding whether to waive jury trial.

[8] M. Rosenberg, The Pretrial Conference and Effective Justice 65 (1964).
[9] Id. at 66.
[10] H. Zeisel, The American Jury, Chief Justice Earl Warren Conference on Advocacy in the United States 65, 66 (1977).
[11] Ibid.
[12] H. Kalven & H. Zeisel, The American Jury (1966).
[13] Id. at 111.
[14] Id. at 115.
[15] Id. at 116.
[16] Ibid.

One conclusion is that a jury is more likely than a judge to acquit in a close case involving a serious charge when a defendant with no record testifies in his or her own behalf and denies guilt.[17] Moreover, a jury generally imposes a more stringent notion of what constitutes proof beyond a reasonable doubt than a judge does.[18]

A sympathetic defendant will be more influential with a jury than with a judge.[19] This element exists in approximately one out of five trials and is decisive in about twenty percent of the judge-juror agreements.[20] Consequently it accounts for disagreement in four percent of all cases. When the defendant is unattractive, the jury is more likely to convict than the judge.[21]

A jury is inclined to be impressed with defendants charged with crimes in situations involving aggression or provocation by the victim.[22] Frequently the jury response is to return a verdict on a lesser charge rather than to acquit.[23] A jury is also more likely than a judge to react adversely to the use of excessive force by the police.[24]

In criminal cases as well as civil cases, juries have a tendency to weigh the conduct of the complainant in deciding the merits of the case. They tend to identify the government's case with the victim in assessing the guilt of the defendant.[25] This phenomenon is particularly marked in rape cases. Juries tend to examine the woman's conduct closely and sometimes harshly. The result is a tendency of juries toward conviction on lesser charges or acquittals in cases where suggestion exists of "assumption of risk" or "contributory behavior" by the victim.[26]

[17] Id. at 179.
[18] Id. at 189.
[19] Id. at 217.
[20] Ibid.
[21] Ibid.
[22] Id. at 221-241.
[23] Id. at 240.
[24] Id. at 236-239.
[25] Id. at 242-243.
[26] Id. at 249-254.

Another interesting point of disagreement is the jury's tendency toward leniency in cases where a victim and the defendant were drinking together before some act of violence on which the charge is based. This leniency does not arise from sympathy for an intoxication defense, but from the jury's use of the victim's drinking as a basis for taking the victim's complaint less seriously.[27]

Another area in which the jury has a tendency to interpose its notion of equity is in situations of only slight or technical harm to the victim. This includes cases where the injury or loss is perceived as trivial, where an attempted crime does not succeed, where restitution has been made, where the complainant is reluctant, or where the societal cost is small.[28] This tendency explains in part traditional jury leniency in drunk driving cases in which no accident has occurred.[29]

A defendant will also fare better with a jury than with a judge in cases where the jury is likely to perceive the law as too severe or unpopular. Examples are game laws, liquor laws, gambling laws, and drunk driving laws.[30] It will be interesting to see whether juries will change their reaction to drunk driving charges in light of widespread recent efforts to educate the public about the harm threatened and caused by drunk driving, coupled with legislation easing the prosecutor's evidentiary burden and increasing penalties.

Minor sentiments that account for jury leniency are notions that a defendant has been "punished enough,"[31] that a threatened punishment is "too severe,"[32] that the defendant is being treated unequally,[33] that police methods have been improper,[34] and that the conduct involved was inadvertent.[35]

[27] Id. at 254-257.
[28] Id. at 258-285.
[29] Id. at 266.
[30] Id. at 286-297.
[31] Id. at 301-305.
[32] Id. at 306-312.
[33] Id. at 313-317.
[34] Id. at 318-323.
[35] Id. at 324-328.

In view of present controversy concerning the insanity defense, it is interesting that judges and juries tend to agree on the outcome of cases in which that defense is raised as well as those in which the intoxication defense is urged.[36] The insanity defense is involved in only 2 percent of all criminal cases — most involving homicide charges; psychiatrists testify in the same percentage of cases.[37]

Several explanations have been advanced for the judge-jury disagreement in the 3 percent of criminal cases in which the judge would acquit whereas the jury would convict. One is that judges are more likely than juries to give the benefit of the doubt in close cases to defendants whose behavior is particularly offensive.[38] Another is that when a defendant's credibility is involved, the judge appears to have a more discriminatory insight.[39] In addition, the judgment of the jury is harsher than that of the judge when a defendant has a prior record or does not testify.[40] Finally, the differing knowledge concerning factors favorable to the defendant accounts for some of the disagreements.[41]

Study of the source of judge-jury disagreement on the outcome of criminal cases should reassure those who believe in the value of jury equity. Juries bring to bear a sense of justice that lies outside the rules, but in doing so they apply community values. Their disagreements with judges are not based on incompetence or difficulty in understanding issues or evidence. Moreover, any substantial departure from the practice of choosing juries from a cross-section of the community will skew the system. An elite or insular group will impose its own values, and no guarantee exists that they will conform with community values.

[36] Id. at 329-338.
[37] Id. at 330.
[38] Id. at 382.
[39] Id. at 385-387.
[40] Id. at 389.
[41] Id. at 391-394.

§3.3 Bargains and Pretrial Conferences

Plea bargaining, like bench trial of serious crimes, is an American invention of the nineteenth century.[1] Resort to guilty pleas and waiver of jury trial account for the small percentage of criminal cases that are actually tried with juries.[2] In the controversy over plea bargaining, the popular perception seems to be that the system inures to the benefit of criminal defendants. It appears, however, that many defendants either make bad bargains or suffer because of their refusal to make any bargain.

The prosecution does not always have a strong case. When it does not, the plea bargain serves as means of obtaining convictions without having to go through a jury trial with a high risk of acquittal. In some federal district courts these marginal cases constitute approximately one-half of the guilty-plea cases.[3] A statistical analysis of those cases shows that at least one-third of all persons pleading guilty in those districts would have been acquitted if their cases had gone to trial.[4] Perhaps as many as two-thirds of the defendants in the marginal cases would have been acquitted if they had insisted on their trial rights.[5]

The irrationality of the plea bargaining system is further demonstrated by the effect upon defendants who exercise their constitutional right to jury trial and suffer conviction. Because they have gambled and lost, they ordinarily end up with a more severe sentence:

> By imposing a penalty upon the exercise of procedural rights in those cases in which there is a reasonable likelihood that the rights will be vindicated, the plea negotiation system creates a

§3.3 [1]Langbein, Mixed Court and Jury Court: Could the Continental Alternative Fill the American Need?, A.B. Found. Research J. 195, 216 (1981).

[2]Ibid.

[3]Finkelstein, A Statistical Analysis of Guilty Plea Practices in the Federal Courts, 89 Harv. L. Rev. 293, 309 (1975).

[4]Id. at 309-310.

[5]Ibid.

> significant danger to the innocent. Many of the rights it discourages are rights designed to prevent the conviction of innocent defendants. To the extent these rights are rendered nonoperative by the plea negotiation system, innocent defendants are endangered.[6]

This is one reason many thoughtful persons advocate abolition of plea bargaining.[7]

On the civil case side, the pretrial conference has been touted as a means for promoting efficiency in the handling of litigation. For those who look to it as a means of discouraging jury trials, the results must be disappointing. The New Jersey pretrial study demonstrated that pretrial conferences do not encourage parties to waive jury trial. In fact a pretrial conference tends to confirm their desire for a jury.[8] This result should comfort those who oppose the use of pretrial conferences on the ground that they are calculated to undermine the right to jury trial.

§3.4 Improving Jury Management

Amidst skyrocketing litigation costs, the jury system has been targeted as an alleged source of inefficiency and a waste of time and money.[1] One may well question at the outset whether the jury can be a significant part of the economic problem when such a small percentage of cases is actually tried by jury. Moreover, actual jury fees and expenses constitute less than five percent of the budget for the federal court system and little more than that in state systems.[2] Comparatively, the cost of

[6] National Advisory Commission on Criminal Justice Standards and Goals, Courts, 48 (1973).

[7] Id. at 46-49.

[8] M. Rosenberg, The Pretrial Conference and Effective Justice 54 (1964).

§3.4 [1] See, e.g., Weihl, A State Looks at the Six-Member Jury, The Judges J. 11 (1972).

[2] A. Padawer-Singer, Justice or Judgments?, Annual Chief Justice Earl Warren Conference on Advocacy in the United States 46-48 (1977).

space, facilities, and personnel account for a far greater proportion of court expenditures.[3]

Nevertheless, reduction of costs is a worthy objective of improved jury management. Other legitimate objectives include increased efficiency in jury operations and a concomitant improvement in the attitude of citizens toward jury duty.

An impressive group of administrative and judicial organizations joined in an effort to devise standards for jury use and management in state courts.[4] They included the Conference of State Court Administrators, the National Association for Trial Court Administrators, the National Conference of State Trial Judges, the National Conference of Special Court Judges, the National Conference of Metropolitan Courts, the National Bar Association, the National Conference of Federal Trial Judges, the Lawyers' Conference, and the Appellate Judges' Conference.[5] The study was staffed by the National Center for State Courts. A special committee of the Judicial Administration Division of the American Bar Association also participated in the endeavor with the idea that the standards would ultimately be submitted to the association for adoption.[6]

The standards went through a preliminary draft and a tentative draft. After approval of the tentative draft by the participating organizations, the standards were adopted by the ABA in January 1983.[7]

In an introductory guiding statement, the drafters stated the following:

> Efficient court administration and management will best guarantee preservation of the jury system and enhance the quality of the decision-making process. Specifically, courts must seek to define those qualities and characteristics which constitute effective jury use and management. Courts must ensure

[3] Id. at 49.

[4] ABA Standards, Jury Use and Management iii (approved draft 1983).

[5] Ibid.

[6] Ibid.

[7] The 1982 tentative draft was approved as written by the House of Delegates of the ABA at its January 1983 meeting.

> that jury resources are utilized to the maximum degree of efficiency, while minimizing inconvenience to individual citizens. Courts must identify those procedures and processes that have proven successful in increasing the economies of jury service and must present such findings in a manner that will be suitable for application in courts throughout the United States.[8]

They also defined the scope of the standards:

> Management of a jury system includes every aspect of selecting jurors and using their services from identifying prospective jurors and accurately predicting the court's need for jurors, to providing adequate and comfortable facilities during their service as jurors.[9]

The resulting Standards Relating to Juror Use and Management represent a consensus viewpoint of the study participants. They incorporate and build upon standards previously developed and adopted by the leading organizations in the field.[10] It is likely they will serve as a model for statutory and procedural reform in jury management.

§3.4.1 *Administration of the Jury System*

The standards include a general provision relating to administration of the jury system:

> The responsibility for administration of the jury system should be vested exclusively in the judicial branch of government.
>
> (a) All procedures concerning jury selection and service should be governed by court rules and regulations promulgated by the state's highest court or judicial council.

[8] ABA Standards, Jury Use and Management 1 (approved draft 1983). (Reprinted by permission.)

[9] Ibid.

[10] Id. at 2.

(b) A single unified jury system should be established in any area in which two or more courts conduct jury trials. This applies whether they are of the same or differing subject matter or geographic jurisdiction.

(c) Responsibility for administering the jury system should be vested in a single administrator acting under the supervision of a presiding judge of the court.[11]

It is reasonable that procedures by which citizens are called for service in the court system should be subject to judicial control, and rule-making flexibility enables courts to keep pace with management advancements.[12]

Efficiency can also be achieved by combining the administration of all local courts in one location under a single authority. Source lists, summoning procedures, and orientation can be handled at that place. As jurors are needed, they can be assigned to courts from the central pool.[13]

In urban areas, administrative control of the jury system can be implemented by a manager working on the administrative staff. Among the duties that should be assigned to such a person are the following:

— Supervising all aspects of jury selection;
— Setting up liaison between jury management system and other court personnel to ensure two-way information flow:
  anticipated trial activities;
  the number of jurors available;
  and other matters affecting the supply of jurors needed . . . ;
— Integrating management of juror selection and use so that the operation of each complements the other;
— Maintaining statistical records:
  response and qualification rates on persons sent questionnaires or summoned;
  number of jurors used (and not used) daily; and

[11] ABA Standards, Jury Use and Management, §10 at 96 (approved draft 1983).
[12] Id. at 96-97.
[13] Id. at 97.

other statistics necessary to determine how many questionnaires to send out, how many jurors to summon, etc., in the future;
— Predicting both on a long-range and day-to-day basis the number of jurors needed at court;
— Managing the activities of jurors while at work;
— Maintaining attendance records;
— Notifying jurors to come to court;
— Preparing panels for jurors to be sent for voir dire;
— Providing training for all court personnel involved with jurors;
— Providing appropriate identification (such as a badge) for jurors;
— Planning for better management and recommending improvements when needed;
— Arranging for payment of jurors.[14]

3.4.2 Notification

The ABA also believes that efficiencies and cost savings will result from its standard on notification and summoning procedures:

(a) The notice summoning a person to jury service and the questionnaire eliciting essential information regarding that person should be
  (i) combined in a single document;
  (ii) phrased so as to be readily understood by an individual unfamiliar with the legal and jury systems; and,
  (iii) delivered by first class mail.
(b) A summons should clearly explain how and when the recipient must respond and the consequences of a failure to respond.
(c) The questionnaire should be phrased and organized so as to facilitate quick and accurate screening, and should request only that information essential for

[14] Id. at 98-99.

(i) determining whether a person meets the criteria for eligibility;
(ii) providing basic background information ordinarily sought during voir dire examination; and
(iii) efficiently managing the jury system.

(d) Policies and procedures should be established for enforcing a summons to report for jury service and for monitoring failures to respond to a summons.[15]

The use of a combined questionnaire and summons is considered to have several advantages:

> Filling out and screening a well-designed questionnaire not only takes less time than an interview but is less subject to bias and distortion. . . . Sending out one form instead of two eliminates duplication of work, thus reducing material and postage expenses. In addition, the combined method eliminates the need for a qualified list or wheel, which may become outdated between the time prospective jurors are qualified and the time they are summoned. It also relieves some of the uncertainty and confusion felt by prospective jurors as a result of this interval between qualification and summoning. Finally, the combined qualification and summoning method has been shown to increase the percentage of eligible persons who respond to the initial notice.[16]

First class mail is recommended as more effective and less expensive than other methods of notice.[17] The forms should be designed so they are easy to fill out and screen. They should elicit sufficient background information to obviate the necessity of standard voir dire questions on that subject.[18] Information showing how the juror can be reached and requests for excuse or deferment, with supporting data, should also be obtained through use of the questionnaire.[19]

[15] Id. §11 at 103.
[16] Id. at 104.
[17] Id. at 105.
[18] Id. at 106.
[19] Id. at 107.

§3.4.3 *Monitoring*

Another standard provides for monitoring of the jury system:

> Courts should collect and analyze information regarding the performance of the jury system on a regular basis in order to ensure
>
> (a) the representativeness and inclusiveness of the jury source list;
> (b) the effectiveness of qualification and summoning procedures;
> (c) the responsiveness of individual citizens to jury duty summonses;
> (d) the efficient use of jurors; and
> (e) the cost effectiveness of the jury system.[20]

Monitoring enables the administrator to determine how the system is working, whether changes should be made, and how best to allocate resources to meet the system's objectives.[21]

§3.4.4 *Maximizing Use of Jurors*

Efficiency and cost savings can also result from improved use of jurors. The ABA has a standard on that subject:

> (a) Courts should employ the services of prospective jurors so as to achieve optimum use with a minimum of inconvenience to jurors.
> (b) Courts should determine the minimally sufficient number of jurors needed to accommodate trial activity. This information and appropriate management techniques should be used to adjust both the number of individuals

[20] Id. §12 at 111.
[21] Ibid.

summoned for jury duty and the number assigned to jury panels.

(c) Courts should ensure that each prospective juror who has reported to the courthouse is assigned to a courtroom for voir dire before any prospective juror is assigned a second time.

(d) Courts should coordinate jury management and calendar management to make effective use of jurors.[22]

Implementation of this standard should reduce waste and improve the attitude of citizens toward jury duty. It is well established that inefficient juror use fosters dissatisfaction with jury service.[23]

Panels should have only the number of persons necessary to ensure selection of a jury in a particular case. The panels are frequently too large, and experience demonstrates that the fear that they will be depleted is usually unfounded.[24] Effective management and monitoring can establish a suitable panel size for the ordinary case, a basis for predicting actual need for prospective jurors, and efficient scheduling practices.

§3.4.5 *Improving Facilities*

Another standard has at least a tangential effect on the system's efficiency:

> Courts should provide an adequate and suitable environment for jurors.
>
> (a) The entrance and registration area should be clearly identified and appropriately designed to accommodate the daily flow of prospective jurors to the courthouse.
>
> (b) Jurors should be accommodated in pleasant waiting facilities furnished with suitable amenities.

[22] Id. §13 at 116.
[23] Id. at 116-117.
[24] Id. at 117-118.

(c) Jury deliberation rooms should include space, furnishings and facilities conducive to reaching a fair verdict. The safety and security of the deliberation rooms should be ensured.

(d) To the extent feasible, juror facilities should be arranged to minimize contact between jurors, parties, counsel and the public.[25]

The drafters assert that "[a]dequate facilities play an integral part in the realization of a well-managed, efficient jury operation:"[26]

> It is difficult, for example, to maintain an efficient jury operation when people must gather in overcrowded rooms and when jury management personnel are not located adjacent to the jury assembly room. Poor spacial arrangement and unsatisfactory environmental conditions in addition to inadequate facilities can reduce the efficiency of operations. Inadequate attention to the accessibility of court facilities can reduce the representativeness of the jury pool by, in effect, excluding many otherwise eligible persons whose mobility is impaired. The standard recognizes the need for an adequate and suitable environment for jurors, not only to allow them to wait in comfort and dignity but also to orient them to the trial process, to carry out administrative details, and to properly accommodate the movements, voir dire, and selection process in trial proceedings.[27]

§3.4.6 Juror Compensation

Even juror compensation can affect a system's efficiency. When compensation is inadequate, it imposes a hardship on some citizens and makes it difficult for them to serve. In some

[25] Id. §14 at 126.
[26] Ibid.
[27] Ibid.

situations, jury service causes problems with employment.[28] An ABA standard also addresses this problem:

> (a) Persons called for jury service should receive:
> (i) a nominal amount in recognition of out-of-pocket expenses for the first day they report to the courthouse;
> (ii) a reasonable fee for each succeeding day they report.
> (b) Such amounts and fees should be paid promptly.
> (c) State law should prohibit employees from discharging, laying-off, denying advancement opportunities to, or otherwise penalizing employees who miss work because of jury service.[29]

In 1980 the average juror fee was an estimated $10 per day, ranging from $2 per day in parts of South Carolina to $40 per day after the third day of service in one Massachusetts county.[30] As much as 68 percent of jury system costs are being borne by private business through such subsidies as paid leave provisions in labor agreements.[31]

No doubt exists that jury trials take longer than nonjury trials. This was thoroughly documented in the New Jersey pretrial study.[32] Another study showed that the average jury trial is 67 percent longer than the average bench trial.[33] Voir dire, instructions, and prolonged final arguments can be avoided in a bench trial. One factor usually left out of the calculation, however, is the time it takes a judge to decide a case. Whereas juries deliberate on their own time and usually reach a verdict within a few hours after submission of the case, judges have been known to take weeks, months, and, unfortunately, even

[28] Id. at 131.
[29] Ibid. §15 at 131.
[30] Id. at 133, n.1.
[31] Id. at 133, n.4.
[32] M. Rosenberg, The Pretrial Conference and Effective Justice 158-159, n.57 (1964).
[33] H. Zeisel, H. Kalven & B. Buchholz, Delay in the Court 79 (1959).

years to decide cases. Moreover, the time taken by the judge to deliberate and write a decision may constitute an extensive incursion into the judge's availability to preside over other trials.[34] It has been suggested that no time would be saved by abolishing trial by jury when all factors are considered.[35] Accordingly, some question exists concerning whether abolishing trial by jury would actually reduce the time consumed by litigation.

Jury trial is of course a matter of constitutional right in all jurisdictions in serious criminal cases and at least some civil cases. Accepting that reality, the movement for reform to promote efficiency and cost savings has generally focused on paring the system to its minimum constituents, instead of merely improving management techniques. In fact, improved management has probably received less emphasis in most quarters than such measures as cutting back voir dire, reducing jury size, and allowing nonunanimous verdicts.[36]

Studies suggest that measures to shorten voir dire, reduce jury size, and permit nonunanimous verdicts do not appreciably reduce costs, save time, or promote efficiency.[37] Questions concerning the effect of such measures on the right to jury trial are another matter.

Reducing jury size does not bring about a proportionate reduction in jury cost or voir dire time because proportionately more jurors have been required on the panels from which the smaller juries are chosen.[38] In addition, voir dire tends to be prolonged because of greater care exercised by counsel in selecting the smaller jury.[39] One study showed no saving in voir dire on trial time.[40]

[34] L. Moore, The Jury 166 (1973).

[35] Ibid.

[36] See A. Padawer-Singer, Justice or Judgments?, Annual Chief Justice Earl Warren Conference on Advocacy in the United States 49 (1977).

[37] Id. at 50-51.

[38] Id. at 50.

[39] Ibid.

[40] Ibid.

§3.5 Jury Size

Independent of issues relating to cost, time, and general efficiency is the question of the effect of jury size on the values thought to be essential to the right to jury trial. Those values include maintaining the reliability of the jury as a factfinder, promoting deliberations, and providing a reasonable possibility of obtaining a fair cross-section of the community.[1]

Assuming the community is stratified in keeping with the human tendency to see and evaluate things differently, it is obvious that the larger the jury the greater the representation of community viewpoints. If representation of these viewpoints is critical to the jury's reliability, a larger jury is more likely to be reliable than a small one.[2] Moreover, the larger the jury the more likely it is that minority viewpoints will be represented.[3] Furthermore, the larger the jury, the more probable it is that deliberations will be thorough.[4]

As a consequence, a six-person jury produces a wider range and variation of verdicts in civil cases than a twelve-person jury.[5] Thus a litigant takes a greater gamble on the outcome with a smaller jury.[6] Where six-person juries are provided for, this may result in increased jury waiver.[7] In criminal cases, a larger jury presents a greater opportunity for a hung jury, not because of the greater likelihood of one or two holdouts but because of the greater opportunity for more substantial alignments of viewpoint.[8]

The Columbia University Jury Project tested the Supreme Court's view that six-person juries do not significantly affect

§3.5 [1]Williams v. Florida, 399 U.S. 78, 101-102, 90 S. Ct. 1893, 1905-1906, 26 L. Ed. 2d 446, 460-461 (1970).

[2]See Zeisel, . . . And Then There Were None: The Diminution of the Federal Jury, 38 U. Chi. L. Rev. 710, 715-720 (1971).

[3]Ibid.

[4]Ibid.

[5]Id. at 717.

[6]Id. at 719.

[7]Ibid.

[8]Id. at 719-720.

the goals of the jury system by conducting 92 experiments with actual jurors.[9] The study showed essential differences in jury composition, deliberations, and decision-making processes.[10]

Less heterogeneity was found in the six-person jury. Fewer six-member juries had women and blacks on them, and the panels had less representation of educational levels and age categories.[11] This had consequences on verdicts. In criminal cases, for example, fewer blacks than whites voted for guilty, and college graduates voted to acquit more often than persons with only an elementary education.[12]

Discussion during deliberations was more spirited in the larger juries.[13] Jurors with a minority view at the commencement of deliberations persuaded the majority to their viewpoint in 13 percent of the 12-person juries but only in about 2 percent of the six-person juries.[14]

Chance factors determined the verdicts in 24 percent of the six-person verdicts because the jurors arrived at the jury room with the same viewpoint in that many cases.[15] Only a little over four percent of the twelve-person juries entered the jury room with as many as ten jurors in agreement.[16]

Jury size thus does seem to make a substantial difference in the outcome of cases. It does, however, appear to have significant impact on verdict reliability, group deliberations, and jury representativeness.

The ABA jury standards provide that juries in criminal cases should have 12 members "if a penalty of confinement may be imposed upon conviction" and at least 6 persons for offenses punishable by a lesser penalty.[17] The ABA recommends that

[9] A. Padawer-Singer, Justice or Judgments?, Annual Chief Justice Earl Warren Conference on Advocacy in the United States 51-53 (1977).

[10] Id. at 53.

[11] Ibid.

[12] Ibid.

[13] Ibid.

[14] Id. at 54.

[15] Id. at 57.

[16] Ibid.

[17] ABA Standards, Juror Use and Management, §17 at 150 (approved draft 1983).

civil juries have at least 6 but not more than 12 members.[18] These recommendations are based on the data suggesting that important values of the jury system may be lost as jury size decreases.[19]

§3.6 Consequences of Unanimity Requirements

In the Columbia study, nonunanimous juries displayed less willingness to negotiate or listen to minority viewpoints.[1] The chance of a predeliberation verdict increases as the percentage of jurors who must agree on a verdict decreases.[2] Therefore, the study suggests that the unanimity rule requires jurors to deliberate more thoroughly and carefully, and makes them less susceptible to predeliberation alignments.

A unanimity rule for criminal cases is endorsed in the Uniform Rules of Criminal Procedure.[3] The drafting committee asserts that the rule is desirable for uniformity, reliability of verdicts, effectuation of the burden of proof requirements, and implementation of the representativeness function of the jury.[4] The committee also argues that a change will tilt the conviction-acquittal ratio in favor of the government.[5]

The ABA jury standards also provide for a unanimity rule in criminal cases.[6] That committee endorses the option of nonunanimous verdicts in civil cases provided that at least three-quarters of the jury members be required to concur in the

[18] Ibid.

[19] Id. at 150-153.

§3.6 [1] A. Padawer-Singer, Justice or Judgments?, Annual Chief Justice Earl Warren Conference on Advocacy in the United States 54 (1977).

[2] Id. at 57.

[3] Rules of Criminal Procedure, Rule 535(b), 10 U.L.A. 189 (1974).

[4] Id. at 280-285.

[5] Id. at 283-284.

[6] ABA Standards, Juror Use and Management, §17 at 150 (approved draft 1983).

verdict.[7] Differing rules of the states in civil cases are perceived as a basis for thorough study of the actual differences in verdicts under the rules.[8]

§3.7 The ABA Proposals: Methods of Selecting Prospective Jurors

Several of the ABA juror use and management standards address substantive issues rather than merely issues of cost and efficiency. In so doing they seek to implement the spirit as well as the letter of the constitutional right to trial by jury. The standards constitute a pragmatic basis for avoiding the pitfalls associated with some of the existing state systems.

The ABA has proposed six standards relating to selection of prospective jurors.[1] These standards seek to implement the United States Supreme Court decisions requiring panels to be drawn from a cross-section of the community and proscribing systematic exclusion of cognizable groups.

§3.7.1 Opportunity for Jury Service

Citizens in all cognizable groups should be given the opportunity to serve.

> The opportunity for jury service should not be decided or limited on the basis of race, national origin, gender, age, religious belief, income, occupation, or any other factor that discriminates against a cognizable group in the jurisdiction.[2]

[7] Ibid.

[8] Id. at 153.

§3.7 [1] ABA Standards, Juror Use and Management 16-66 (approved draft 1983).

[2] Id. §1 at 16.

This standard seeks to impose on the administrator of the selection system a duty to avoid discriminatory practices at all stages of the selection process.[3]

§3.7.2 *Source Lists*

Source lists should be comprehensive and representative:

(a) The names of potential jurors should be drawn from a source list compiled from one or more regularly maintained lists of persons residing in the court jurisdiction.
(b) The jury list should be representative and should be as inclusive of the adult population in the jurisdiction as is feasible.
(c) The court should periodically review the jury source list for its representativeness and inclusiveness of the adult population in the jurisdiction.
(d) Should the court determine that improvement is needed in the representativeness or inclusiveness of the source lists corrective action should be taken.[4]

This standard distinguishes between inclusiveness and representativeness. Inclusiveness refers to the proportion of the adult population on the source list, whereas representativeness refers to the proportionate presence of cognizable groups on the list.[5]

A reasonable goal is 85 percent inclusiveness.[6] The nature of the list will affect its representativeness. Generally, voter lists supplemented by lists of licensed drivers will provide for inclusiveness and representativeness.[7]

[3] Id. at 16-17.
[4] Id. §2 at 23.
[5] Id. at 24.
[6] Id. at 25.
[7] Id. at 26.

§3.7.3 *Random Selection*

Another standard incorporates the principle of random selection:

(a) Random selection procedures should be used throughout the juror selection process. Any method may be used, manual or automated, that provides each eligible and available person with an equal probability of selection.
(b) Random selection procedures should be employed in
  (i) selecting persons to be summoned for jury service;
  (ii) assigning prospective jurors to panels; and
  (iii) calling prospective jurors for voir dire.
(c) Departures from the principle of random selection are appropriate
  (i) to exclude persons ineligible for service in accordance with standard 4;
  (ii) to excuse or defer prospective jurors in accordance with standard 6;
  (iii) to remove prospective jurors for cause or if challenged peremptorily in accordance with standards 8 and 9; and
  (iv) to provide all prospective jurors with an opportunity to be called for jury service and to be assigned to a panel in accordance with standard 13.[8]

Randomness is thus prescribed at each stage of the selection process, the only exceptions being limited to situations carefully circumscribed in other standards.

§3.7.4 *Eligibility*

A broad standard of eligibility is established:

All persons should be eligible for jury service except those who
(a) are less than eighteen years of age, or

[8]Id. §3 at 36.

(b) are not citizens of the United States, or
(c) are not residents of the jurisdiction in which they have been summoned to serve, or
(d) are not able to communicate in the English language, or
(e) have been convicted of a felony and have not had their civil rights restored.[9]

This standard departs from the subjective criteria provided in many state statutes.[10] It requires citizenship and residency but not a period of residency. It conforms, however, to the Federal Jury Selection and Service Act[11] and Uniform Jury Selection and Service Act.[12]

§3.7.5 *Availability for Service*

Another standard addresses the term of and availability for service:

> The time that persons are called upon to perform jury service and to be available therefor, should be the shortest period consistent with the needs of justice.
> (a) A term of service of one day or the completion of one trial, whichever is longer, is recommended. However, a term of one week or the completion of one trial, whichever is longer, is acceptable.
> (b) Persons should not be required to maintain a status of availability for jury service for longer than two weeks except in areas with few jury trials when it may be appropriate for persons to be available for service over a longer period of time.[13]

[9] Id. §14 at 47.

[10] See Carter v. Jury Commn., 396 U.S. 320, 334, 90 S. Ct. 518, 525, 24 L. Ed. 2d 549, 559-560 (1970).

[11] 28 U.S.C. §1865(b) (1982).

[12] Uniform Jury Selection and Services Act §8(b)1, 13 U.L.A. 525 (1980).

[13] ABA Standards, Juror Use and Management, §5 at 55 (approved draft 1983).

At least 39 jurisdictions have adopted a "one-day or one-trial term" of service for jurors.[14] Under this concept, an individual's term is completed by serving for one day, if not selected to serve as a juror, or for one trial if selected.[15] It is intended to eliminate juror inconvenience and hardship with a resulting increase in the inclusiveness and representativeness of panels.[16]

§3.7.6 Avoiding Service

The standards carefully limit exemption, excuse, and deferral:

> (a) All automatic excuses or exemptions from jury service should be eliminated.
> (b) Eligible persons who are summoned may be excused from jury service only if:
>   (i) their ability to receive and evaluate information is so impaired that they are unable to perform their duties as jurors and they are excused for this reason by a judge; or
>   (ii) they request to be excused because their service would be a continuing hardship to them or to members of the public, or they have been called for jury service during the two years preceding their summons, and they are excused by a judge or duly authorized court official.
> (c) Deferrals of jury service for reasonably short periods of time may be permitted by a judge or duly authorized court official.
> (d) Requests for excuses and deferrals and their disposition should be written or otherwise made of record. Specific uniform guidelines for determining such requests should be adopted by the court.[17]

[14] Ibid.
[15] Ibid.
[16] Id. at 56.
[17] Id. §6 at 60.

This standard conforms with the modern idea that no automatic exemptions should exist and that excuses should be granted only on the basis of serious disability and severe hardship.[18]

§3.8 Voir Dire and Resulting Verdicts

It is not uncommon for a lawyer to assert an ability to win a verdict with the first 12 jurors called to the jury box. An experiment in the United States District Court for the Northern District of Illinois suggests that a criminal defense attorney who fails to exercise voir dire challenges increases the risk of conviction of his client to such an extent that the lawyer's services could not be deemed effective.[1]

The study purported to show a causal connection between the voir dire performance of counsel and a reduction in the likelihood of a guilty verdict.[2] The director of the study said the following:

> The first conclusion, perhaps a surprising one, emerging from this study is that there are cases in which the jury verdict is seriously affected, if not determined, occasionally by one lawyer doing a significantly superior job of challenging hostile jurors than his opponent. Lawyers apparently do win, as they occasionally boast, some of their cases during, or at least with the help of voir dire.[3]

This phenomenon may be seen as good and bad. It is good in its confirmation of the value of advocacy in the judicial system. It is bad in its suggestion that unequal performance of counsel

[18] Id. at 61-62.

§3.8 [1] See H. Zeisel, The American Jury, Annual Chief Justice Earl Warren Conference on Advocacy in the United States 81-84 (1977).

[2] Id. at 84.

[3] Ibid.

at voir dire may determine the outcome of the case without the jury having even heard the evidence. If the goal of the system is justice, the goal is not served by a system that permits the outcome to turn on the performance of counsel. In any event, however, the phenomenon highlights the importance of voir dire.

Considerable controversy surrounds this stage of the trial process. On one side are proponents of expanded voir dire procedures to give advocates more latitude to explore juror prejudice and bias.[4] The other side argues that controls on voir dire are necessary to keep it within its intended purpose.[5] Restraints have been imposed by courts as a means of saving time and protecting juror privacy.[6]

§3.8.1 *The ABA Proposals: In General*

In an effort to accommodate the competing concerns about voir dire, the ABA has adopted a median position:

> Voir dire should be limited to matters relevant to determining whether to remove a juror for cause and to exercising peremptory challenges.
>
> (a) To reduce the time required for voir dire, basic background information should be made available in writing to counsel for each party on the day on which jury selection is to begin.
>
> (b) The trial judge should conduct a preliminary voir dire examination. Counsel should then be permitted to question panel members for a reasonable period of time.
>
> (c) The judge should ensure that the privacy of prospective jurors is reasonably protected, and that questioning is consistent with the purpose of the voir dire process.

[4]See, e.g., Ryan & Neeson, Voir Dire: A Trial Technique in Transition, 4 Am. J. of Trial Advoc. 523 (1981).

[5]See, e.g., Braswell, Voir Dire: Use and Abuses, 7 Wake Forest L. Rev. 49 (1970).

[6]See, e.g., Levit, Nelson, Ball & Chernick, Expediting Voir Dire: An Empirical Study, 44 S. Cal. L. Rev. 916 (1971).

(d) In criminal cases, the voir dire process should always be held on the record. In civil cases, the voir dire process should be held on the record unless waived by the parties.[7]

The providing of background information is intended to shorten voir dire.[8] Not making the information available until the day of trial is intended to prevent out-of-court contact with panel members.[9] In exceptional cases, the standard contemplates a recess to permit counsel to evaluate the information before proceeding with voir dire.[10]

In permitting counsel to ask questions of panel members, the standard departs from federal procedure and conforms with the practice common to many states. The standard also opts, however, for relatively tight judicial control of the voir dire process.

The provision for reporting voir dire reflects the critical role of the process. Ordinarily a verbatim record would be necessary to support a claim of error on appeal. An objection without a record is of little avail on appeal, just as a record without an objection is generally inadequate. The very fact that the record is being made may encourage the court and counsel to stay within the rules.

§3.8.2 The ABA Proposals: Challenges for Cause

The ABA provides a standard governing challenges for cause incorporating the principle that if the judge determines during voir dire that any individual is unable or unwilling to hear the case "fairly and impartially," the individual should be removed from the panel on motion of counsel or the judge's own mo-

[7] ABA Standards, Juror Use and Management, §7 at 68 (approved draft 1983).

[8] Id. at 69.

[9] Ibid.

[10] Ibid.

tion.[11] Because the integrity of the trial process is at stake, the ABA believes the decision to question a panel member's impartiality should not be left solely to the tactical decisions of counsel.[12]

§3.8.3 *The ABA Proposals: Peremptory Challenges*

Regarding peremptory challenges, the ABA standards provide the following:

> (a) The number of and procedure for exercising peremptory challenges should be uniform throughout the state.
> (b) Peremptory challenges should be limited to a number no larger than necessary to provide reasonable assurance of obtaining an unbiased jury.
> (c) In civil cases, the number of peremptory challenges should not exceed three for each side.
> (d) In criminal cases, the number of peremptory challenges should not exceed
>   (i) ten for each side when a death sentence may be imposed upon conviction;
>   (ii) five for each side when a sentence of imprisonment for more than six months may be imposed upon conviction; or
>   (iii) three for each side when a sentence of incarceration of six months or fewer, or when only a penalty not involving incarceration may be imposed.
>
> One additional peremptory challenge should be allowed for each defendant in a multi-defendant proceeding.
> (e) Where juries of fewer than twelve persons are used in civil or petty offense cases, the number of peremptory challenges should not exceed two for each side.
> (f) One peremptory challenge should be allowed to each side in a civil or criminal proceeding for every two alternate jurors to be seated.

[11] Id. §8 at 80.
[12] Id. at 81.

(g) The trial judge should have the authority to allow additional peremptory challenges when justified.

(h) Following completion of the voir dire examination, counsel should exercise their peremptory challenges by alternately striking from the list of panel members until each side has exhausted or waived the permitted number of challenges.[13]

Independent of the issue of saving time, cutting back the number of peremptory challenges has been urged as a means of preventing their use to upset the representativeness of the trial jury. This prompted the limitations in the ABA standard.[14]

The standard also recommends the struck jury system. It is designed to permit all panelists to be questioned before peremptory challenges are exercised.[15] It contemplates a procedure in which the size of the panel equals the sum of the number of jurors and alternates to be seated plus the total number of peremptory challenges available to the parties plus the statistically projected number of those likely to be removed for cause. Voir dire inquiry is made, and any removals for cause occur. Then peremptory challenges are exercised alternately by the parties. If more than the requisite number of jurors remain, the unstruck jurors are called in the order in which they appear on the list, and they constitute the trial jury.[16]

Voir dire procedures are the focus of considerable debate. Because lawyers have come to believe, with apparent justification, that trials are often won or lost at this stage of the trial process, tension will continue to exist between advocates of an expansive right of inquiry and advocates favoring restrictions. As long as this stage of the process is perceived as critical, parties will continue to attempt to learn as much about prospective jurors as they can. If they cannot do it in court,

[13] Id. at 83.
[14] Id. at 84.
[15] Id. at 86.
[16] Ibid.

they will probably do it out of court.[17] One court has observed, "For it is when the door of inquiry is closed in busy courtrooms that the pressure of need breaks open in private investigations conducted outside the courtroom."[18]

§3.8.4 *The Rise of Social Science Techniques as an Aid in Jury Selection*

Restrictions on voir dire have been imposed simultaneously with the development of sophisticated social science techniques to assist in jury selection. This development has been encouraged by the difficulty of obtaining information about prospective jurors through other sources. Prosecutors in criminal cases for years have had access to pretrial information about prospective jurors. The majority of courts hold that the defense does not have access to this information as a matter of right.[19] In the federal system even a jury list may be kept confidential until the day of trial except in treason and capital cases.[20] Other records and materials on jurors need not be released except in accordance with the district plan.[21] A contrary position is taken in the Uniform Rules of Criminal Procedure.[22] An interesting issue of due process and equal protection is presented concerning whether a defendant without resources to make an independent investigation should have a right either to the prosecutor's information or public funds to make an investigation.[23]

[17] See Orfield, Trial Jurors in Federal Criminal Cases, 29 F.R.D. 43, 115 (1962).

[18] Kiernan v. Van Schaik, 347 F.2d 775, 780 (3d Cir. 1965).

[19] See, e.g., Lemon v. Supreme Court of New York, 245 N.Y. 24, 156 N.E. 84 (1927).

[20] 18 U.S.C. §3432 (1982).

[21] 28 U.S.C. §1867(b) (1982).

[22] Uniform Rules of Criminal Procedure, Rule 421(a), 10 U.L.A. 114 (1974).

[23] Cf. English v. Missildine, 311 N.W.2d 292 (Iowa 1981) (holding that an indigent defendant has a federal due process right to reasonably necessary investigative services).

In at least one case, which has sparked controversy, an appellate court has upheld a trial court's holding that jurors' rights of privacy outweighed a criminal defendant's desire for information concerning potential jurors.[24] The case illustrates the tension between jurors' rights and the party's desire for information on which to base peremptory challenges. It also illustrates the lengths to which appellate courts go in deferring to trial court discretion in voir dire rulings.[25]

Social science techniques include background investigations of potential jurors,[26] community surveys,[27] and courtroom observations.[28] These techniques, of course, are calculated to give the voir dire process more focus and may assist in shortening rather than extending it.

The opportunity for pretrial investigation of potential jurors has been recognized as "an inherent part of the jury system as it has developed."[29] Yet it has always been subject to reasonable limitation to protect against abuses and to safeguard the jurors' right to privacy.[30] One court has carefully circumscribed the right of litigants to make background investigations. After saying, "[W]e are aware of no rule prohibiting the interviewing of persons other than prospective jurors and members of their families as part of such an investigation," the court added the following:

> However, it is essential that in interviewing third parties investigators do not, by design or effect, influence, solicit, intimidate or propagandize either the persons interviewed or, indirectly, the prospective juror. The risk of this improper influence occurring may be minimized by certain precautions. First, the investigators should be persons who are not closely related or

[24] United States v. Barnes, 604 F.2d 121 (2d Cir. 1979), *cert. denied,* 446 U.S. 907, 100 S. Ct. 1833, 64 L. Ed. 2d 260 (1980).

[25] See, generally, Note, The Defendant's Right to an Impartial Jury and the Rights of Prospective Jurors, 48 U. Cinn. L. Rev. 985, 991-994 (1979).

[26] See chapter 4 for discussion of this technique.

[27] See chapter 5 for discussion of this technique.

[28] See chapter 10 for discussion of this technique.

[29] Commonwealth v. Allen, 379 Mass. 564, 577, 400 N.E.2d 229, 237 (1980).

[30] Ibid.

> associated with a litigant or his family. Second, the investigators should, where possible, avail themselves of sources of information other than third-party interviews, if such sources are likely to provide the desired data. Third, ideally investigators would be employed on a mutual or cooperative basis between parties, with the resulting information available to both sides. If the investigation is not being made on behalf of all parties to a particular case, the investigators should not disclose the identity of the particular party or parties for whom it is being conducted. In any event, counsel are expected to retain effective control over the activities of their investigators.[31]

This subject is also covered in ABA standards governing the prosecution and defense functions. As to the prosecutor, the standard provides the following:

> In those cases where it appears necessary to conduct a pretrial investigation of the background of jurors the prosecutor should restrict himself to investigatory methods which will not harass or unduly embarrass potential jurors or invade their privacy and, whenever possible, he should restrict his investigation to records and sources of information already in existence.[32]

A comparable provision is applicable to defense counsel.[33]

These constraints respond to concerns expressed by courts that have otherwise recognized the right of litigants to employ background investigations.[34] If adequately supervised by the court or counsel, such investigations should be no more intrusive than those conducted routinely by government bodies, insurance companies, and others.

Community attitude surveys have been frequently employed in criminal cases in connection with a motion for change of venue based on alleged community prejudice. The right to use

[31] Id., 379 Mass. at 579, 400 N.E.2d at 238-239.

[32] ABA Standards, Prosecution Function §5.3(b) (approved draft 1971).

[33] ABA Standards, Defense Function §7.2(b) (approved draft 1971).

[34] See Sinclair v. United States, 279 U.S. 749, 49 S. Ct. 471, 73 L. Ed. 938 (1929); Kiernan v. Van Schaik, 347 F.2d 775 (3d Cir. 1965).

such evidence is now well established. An ABA standard on the subject provides the following:

> In addition to the testimony or affidavits of individuals in the community, which shall not be required as a condition of the granting of a motion for change of venue or continuance, qualified public opinion surveys shall be admissible as well as other materials having probative value.[35]

At least one court has held it error to refuse to admit such evidence.[36] Nevertheless, other courts have not found it to be indispensable. Appellate courts have generally upheld trial court refusals in criminal cases to order public opinion surveys for indigents at public expense.[37] Of course, even when survey results are admitted, they are not conclusive.[38]

Observations of jurors during voir dire are not intrusive and are similar to the kinds of observations lawyers have made for years on a less sophisticated level. Thus the place of background investigations, community attitude surveys, and courtroom observations is well established in the law. These techniques are legitimate and may be utilized by a litigant with means.

A remaining serious question is whether a party with resources sufficient to employ social science techniques in jury selection has an unfair advantage over an adversary who does not.[39] In criminal cases, of course, this would present a special problem if the prosecution was able to use the techniques and the defendant was not. The issue arises even in civil cases. There, however, it is in the context of possible subversion of

[35] ABA Standards, Fair Trial and Free Press §3.2(b) (approved draft 1968).

[36] See Sollitt v. District Court, 180 Colo. 114, 502 P.2d 1108 (1972).

[37] See, e.g., State v. Tison, 129 Ariz. 526, 633 P.2d 335 (1981); State v. Powers, 96 Idaho 833, 537 P.2d 1369 (1975); State v. Armstrong, 616 P.2d 341 (Mont. 1980).

[38] See State v. Williams, 205 Neb. 56, 287 N.W.2d 18 (1979); State v. Mayberry, 52 N.J. 413, 245 A.2d 481 (1968), *cert. denied,* 393 U.S. 1093, 89 S. Ct. 673, 21 L. Ed. 2d 593 (1969).

[39] See Note, Computers and Scientific Jury Selection: A Calculated Risk, 55 J. Urb. L. 345, 366 (1978).

the purpose of obtaining a jury impartial to both sides in the case.

Although the subject is still open for debate, two justifications have been advanced for the seeming inequity allowed by the courts regarding the use of social science techniques in jury selection. One is that this is nothing other than a fundamental inequity that has always existed in our courts.[40] The other is that the techniques are not such a powerful tool that they prevent cases from being decided on the evidence. They may make a difference but that difference occurs in close cases.[41] There is science in magic but no magic in science. As with any new development, the debate about scientific jury selection will surely continue.

§3.9 Techniques of Jury Orientation and Pretrial Instruction

Approximately eighty percent of the persons summoned for jury duty have not served before.[1] Therefore it is important that they be provided meaningful information concerning what is expected of them at each stage of the proceeding. The ABA committee on jury standards has addressed this subject in a proposed standard that provides in relevant part as follows:

> (a) Courts should provide some form of orientation or instructions to persons called for jury service
> (i) upon initial contact prior to service;
> (ii) upon first appearance at the courthouse;
> (iii) upon reporting to the courtroom for voir dire;

[40] See Saks, The Limits of Scientific Jury Selection: Ethical and Empirical, Jurimetrics J. 509, 518 (Fall 1976).

[41] Id. at 519-528.

§3.9 [1] ABA Standards, Juror Use and Management 140 (approved draft 1983).

(iv) directly following empanelment;
(v) during the trial;
(vi) prior to deliberations; and
(vii) after the verdict has been rendered or when a proceeding is terminated without a verdict.

(b) Orientation programs should be
(i) designed to increase prospective jurors' understanding of the judicial system and prepare them to serve competently as jurors;
(ii) presented in a uniform and efficient manner using a combination of written, oral and audiovisual materials.

(c) The trial judge should
(i) give preliminary instructions directly following empanelment of the jury that explain the jury's role, the trial procedures including note-taking and questioning by jurors, the nature of the evidence and its evaluation, the issues to be addressed, and the basic relevant legal principles; . . . .

(e) All communications between the judge and members of the jury panel from the time of reporting to the courtroom for voir dire until dismissal should be in writing or on the record in open court. Counsel for each party should be informed of such communication and given the opportunity to be heard.[2]

Information that should be provided before the prospective jurors report for duty should cover when and where to report, directions to the court, parking and transportation facilities, court hours, first-day activities, length of service, procedures and grounds for requesting deferral or excuse, penalties for not responding, procedures for reporting, compensation, appropriate dress, eating places near the court, what to bring, standby procedures, and where to call for additional information.[3] This information would normally be provided in writing.

Upon their initial appearance the jurors should be told how

[2]Id. §16 at 138-139.
[3]Id. at 140.

the names of prospective jurors are chosen, the function of voir dire, why more persons are summoned than may be needed, why a certain amount of waiting and delays may be necessary, the functions of jury and judge, the difference between criminal and civil trials, the responsibilities of various court employees, proper juror conduct, what the deliberation process is like, what certain legal terms mean, what the trial process involves, and the meaning and possibility of sequestration, if pertinent. Audiovisual materials are useful in presenting this information.[4] Much of it can also be presented in jury handbooks. It should be fair, accurate, and impartial. Extemporaneous remarks should be avoided because of the risk of misstatements.

Additional information relating to voir dire should be conveyed when the panelists are called to a courtroom for that process. They should be informed of its purpose, the difference between removals for cause and peremptory challenges, the nature of the case to be tried and its estimated length.[5]

The ABA believes that after the jury is empaneled, the judge should give preliminary instructions on the jury's role and responsibilities, the basic principles of law to be applied in this case, and the order and nature of the presentations.[6] These instructions should also be written and subject to objection by counsel. The jury should also be admonished at this time concerning its duty not to discuss the case with anyone until it is submitted for decision, to report any attempts at any improper influence, and not to form or express an opinion concerning the case until it is submitted.[7] The purpose of these preliminary instructions is to tell the jurors the general principles that govern their task so they will undertake it more intelligently.[8] They should know the rules of the game before it starts.

[4]Id. at 140-141.
[5]Id. at 141.
[6]Id. at 143.
[7]Id. at 141.
[8]National College of the State Judiciary, Jury 58 (1975).

PART II

Pretrial Preparation

CHAPTER

4

Pretrial Investigation

§4.0 Introduction

There are times when the voir dire process provides insufficient information about jurors to allow wise and advantageous use of peremptory challenges or challenges for cause. Attorneys should consider pretrial investigation of jurors for such cases.

Cases that could benefit from pretrial investigation are those that have received extensive pretrial publicity, will be afforded a limited voir dire, or present a major concern about community bias and prejudice. This last consideration is especially important if the case involves a racial minority, a prominent citizen, political considerations, or if some aspect of the case will have a direct effect on the lives of the jurors or local citizens generally.

The problem of limited voir dire most frequently arises in federal court, since Rule 24 of the Federal Rules of Criminal Procedure gives the judge the right to conduct voir dire alone — a right that is frequently exercised. In state courts, voir dire is dependent upon local custom. In some of them, voir dire is limited to 20 minutes or less; in other courts, judges follow federal precedent and conduct the inquiry without assistance.

In such instances, minimal verbal information is produced by the jurors in the courtroom with the result that the trial attorney will have limited data on which to base peremptory challenges. Therefore, additional methods of checking jurors' attitudes, biases, and prejudices must be pursued. Among these methods is the pretrial investigation.

§4.1 Right to Conduct a Pretrial Investigation

There is no doubt that pretrial investigations are both legal and common. Nevertheless, the trial attorney considering their use must be thoroughly familiar with the case law concerning them. Every conceivable precaution must be exercised to avoid even the hint of jury tampering or any other impropriety.

In 1929, the Supreme Court of the United States established some criteria that limit contact with jurors in pretrial investigation. In *Sinclair v. United States,*[1] the defense had used private detectives to follow jurors during the trial. The Court found that this interfered with the jury process and that the conduct of the private investigator was intimidating and "tended to obstruct the honest and fair administration of justice."[2] Since *Sinclair,* the courts have held that, while pretrial investigations aimed at discovering information about the jury are legal, any direct contact with the potential juror or the juror's family is prohibited.

In *Dow v. Carnegie-Illinois Steel Corp.,*[3] the court approved an investigator's questioning of neighbors and friends of a potential juror about the employment, education, and political views of the persons on the jury list.

> Litigants are given the right to challenge jurors. In order to exercise that right intelligently in densely populated areas where the realm of one's own acquaintances is necessarily limited, a reasonable investigation of jurors is helpful and, conse-

§4.1 [1]279 U.S. 749, 49 S. Ct. 471, 73 L. Ed. 938 (1929).
[2]Id. at 764, 49 S. Ct. at 476, 73 L. Ed. at 946.
[3]224 F.2d 414 (3d Cir. 1955).

> quently, such investigatory procedures are widely used. It has not been demonstrated that such investigations (whereby a prospective juror may know that someone working for lawyers has asked questions about him) would normally have a tendency to intimidate the juror, even if it could be assumed that the knowledge by a juror of such an investigation would work for the benefit of one party rather than another in a case such as this.[4]

The courts have been especially supportive of investigations conducted by federal prosecutors. In *United States v. Falange,*[5] the prosecutor gave jury lists to the FBI to check for any information in its files that would be of any interest to the government. He further requested information from local and state police and from credit agencies. This procedure was upheld by the court.[6]

§4.2 Conducting the Pretrial Investigation

The attorney, in considering the advisability of conducting a pretrial investigation, must weigh the risks involved against the benefits. While the information may be extremely helpful, the costs, both financial and social, must be considered.

There are three major risks involved in conducting a pretrial investigation: (1) a charge of jury tampering, (2) discovery of the investigation by prospective jurors resulting in a negative reaction on their part, and (3) a negative reaction from the judge on disclosure of the pretrial investigation.

No danger of a charge of jury tampering should exist if proper precautions are followed at every step of the investigation. However, the trial attorney should thoroughly research

[4]Id. at 431.

[5]426 F.2d 930 (2d Cir. 1970).

[6]See Martin v. United States, 266 F.2d 97 (5th Cir. 1959); Commonwealth v. Smith, 350 Mass. 600, 215 N.E.2d 897 (1966); and People v. Ruef, 14 Cal. App. 576, 114 P. 48 (1911).

the judge's past reactions to pretrial investigations. Additionally, the attorney should find out the specific local laws governing pretrial investigations and provide *every* person involved in the process with the information so that the investigation is carried out within the law.

It is distinctly possible the jurors will learn of the investigation, especially if it is extensive. If friends, neighbors, or coworkers are contacted, it is likely that the prospective juror will hear of it. This will not be a problem when individual voir dire is conducted — as in many political cases or in cases that have received extensive pretrial publicity. At that time, the juror can be told about the investigation; the reaction of the prospective juror can provide insight into the overall bias and prejudgment that the juror would bring to the case.

If the jurors who have participated in voir dire, however, converse with other members of the jury pool, some prospective jurors may know of the investigation before they are called up for questioning. In such instances, jurors often react with righteous indignation at having had their private lives invaded. Mary Timothy, jury foreperson in the Angela Davis trial, addressed the issue as follows:

> Jurors have a right to be free from investigation of their private lives. In the Angela Davis trial, the panel of veniremen was investigated very thoroughly — both through the extensive public voir dire questioning in the open court with the representatives of the press in attendance — and also through the use of volunteer defense investigators who checked the neighborhoods in which we lived and the attitudes of our neighbors and fellow employees toward us. Psychologists advised the attorneys, and even a handwriting expert was used to analyze our suitability to serve.
>
> Similar investigations have been made in other recent trials.
>
> In all these cases the defendant has been successful — either by gaining an acquittal or . . . a hung jury.
>
> The government, losing so many of these politically important cases, is bound to blame the juries rather than the inadequacy of its own cases and so will be forced to expand the already formidable investigations of prospective jurors. . . .
>
> Thus, in an effort towards more sophisticated jury selecting,

> dossiers would need to be compiled on all citizens and kept up-to-date.
>
> And the jury system, devised as a fortification of democracy, would lead us to a police state![1]

While these concerns might seem exaggerated, it is clear that this type of reaction from jurors is likely to produce an unhealthy atmosphere for jury selection.

When jurors become aware of the pretrial investigation and have strenuous objections, the court's reassurance that the investigation is the prerogative of the trial attorney representing a client is usually sufficient to offset the surface resentment. Sometimes, however, the resentment and anger is so deep-seated that the juror must be removed by either a challenge for cause or a peremptory challenge. This option may be a high price to pay for the pretrial investigation since the people who are struck are generally those who are most zealous in protecting the rights of the individual.

In most cases, jurors seem to understand the need for investigation. Jay Schulman, a doctor of sociology who has done extensive work with pretrial investigations and community attitude studies, explored juror reaction to pretrial investigations and found that jurors tend to accept the need for such procedures:

> Although it is morally regressive to emulate the enemy, a people's lawyer has no political alternative, given the state's enormous advantages, to seeking and using third-party information. Indeed, almost no venire people interviewed after the Harrisburg, Camden and Gainesville trials objected to the defense making direct inquiries about them among their friends, neighbors and co-workers. One venireman put it this way: "When I want to hire someone, I certainly check out his references! I would think that you would want to check out the pedigree of jurors who are going to decide on prison terms or not."[2]

§4.2 [1]M. Timothy, Jury Woman, 306-307 (1974).

[2]Schulman, A Systematic Approach to Successful Jury Selection, Guild Notes, Nov. 1973, at 17.

The best way to minimize the danger of a juror becoming aware of the pretrial investigation is for investigators to take necessary precautions and for the attorney to disclose the pretrial investigation at the beginning of voir dire. Questions should then be asked that will determine whether any of the prospective jurors are offended by the investigation having been conducted. At this time, an explanation of the necessity of the investigation should be given. The investigation must not appear merely inquisitive, for it is important that the trial attorney demonstrate that a pretrial investigation is never frivolously conducted nor the results frivolously used.

The trial attorney must also anticipate a negative reaction from the trial judge when the investigation is disclosed. The attorney should have a brief ready for the judge explaining the procedure, the rationale, and the legal justification for the investigation. In this way, the pretrial investigation does not become a potential trap for the harried trial attorney. Rather, it provides the advocate another opportunity to demonstrate seriousness, earnestness, and preparedness in facing the issues of the trial.

The pretrial investigation can feasibly be conducted by five different types of investigators: (1) a commercial jury investigation service, (2) a private investigator, (3) members of the trial team (paralegal or legal secretary or junior attorney), (4) volunteers who are interested in serving the interest of the client, or (5) a local attorney who is selected for the special work of analyzing the jury pool.

Using a *commercial jury investigation service* is a quick method of obtaining information about prospective jurors. In many areas, where jurors serve for more than two weeks and the names of prospective jurors are made public, a private investigation service or a law firm can conduct a pretrial investigation of all persons on the jury list. Usually the investigator does not attempt to contact the prospective juror. Instead, the information is pulled from juror questionnaires that prospective jurors fill out for the court, public sources of information (telephone books, city directories), and from other readily available sources (automobile license registrations, credit services). Frequently, the resulting "jury books" are later updated to include information concerning verdicts and juror behavior in any cases the juror may have sat for during the two week jury duty, with a short description of the issues that the juror considered. Melvin Belli discusses jury books as follows:

> In most "big cities" there are "jury services." These are like the "Winter Book" at Hialeah. They putatively tell how a juror will "run." At least some information is given as to his religion, his political party, how he voted in other cases. But I've found, unless a particular juror out-and-out aligns himself with one side or the other, repeatedly that these "winter books" aren't as valuable as some lawyers believe. In the first place, if one relies too heavily on them he loses his individual intuitive skill in picking juries. Secondly, and obviously, a juror may not react to one type of a case like another, but most importantly, he may react to one lawyer completely differently than he did to another.[3]

While the ready availability of information from a commercial jury investigation service may be an advantage, the information is often extremely expensive and, due to the large number of jurors involved, frequently inaccurate or out-of-date.

These criticisms also apply to the information that can be provided by a *private investigator,* often used in a community that does not offer the professional jury investigation service.

However, since much of the information in a jury book is public, it is possible that *volunteers* can be used to conduct the pretrial investigation, especially if the trial is of major interest to some sector of the community. Each volunteer must be carefully chosen as someone who will accurately record the data as it is obtained and be judicious in selecting and organizing information. Since the volunteers will be uneducated in procedures used to obtain information, it is important that a single individual be designated as the coordinator of the project. This coordinator must have direct access to the trial attorney or someone

[3]M. Belli, foreword to The Chosen Ones by W. Bryan, Jr., pp. x-xi (1971).

on the trial team who can answer questions at any moment. This is especially important if friends, neighbors or co-workers are to be contacted, since any hint of jury tampering must be constantly guarded against.

The exact information to be researched must be specified for the volunteers and the probable sources of information must be identified. Volunteers can be a problem since often they tend to be advocates for the client. Careful training of the volunteers will decrease the possibility that in their contacts with the community they will expose information or opinions damaging to the overall trial process. But the trial attorney should be fully aware that this possibility exists. Using volunteers has as its greatest disadvantage the lack of direct control over actions and procedures. The great advantage, however, is that the workers are inexpensive, and usually eager and willing.

Perhaps the best person to conduct the pretrial investigation is a member of the trial team. This could be a paralegal, legal secretary, or junior attorney — any professional not urgently needed in the preparing of evidence or issues that will be presented in the trial. When a member of the trial team is utilized in this process, the chances of bringing on jury tampering charges are minimized. Again, almost all of the information that is available to a commercial jury investigation service will be available to a member of the trial team. Since it is inconceivable that one person could perform the tremendous task of investigating an extensive list of potential jurors, a trial team member could be used to coordinate work done by volunteers. If the trial team waits to investigate only those jurors who will actually be assigned to its case, time becomes a major consideration, necessitating that more than one person conduct the investigation. Under such circumstances, not only must the information be obtained quickly, it must be processed quickly so that is is readily available to the attorney for voir dire and the intelligent exercise of peremptory challenges or challenges for cause.

When the trial attorney is from outside the area, an *attorney from the local community* can be added to the trial team as the person in charge of investigating the venire. In *The Chosen*

Ones,[4] Dr. William Bryan discussed the difficult task of investigating the 243 persons on the petit jury panel and the 200 persons on the reserve panel in Monmouth County, New Jersey, while preparing for the 1966 Coppolino trial:

> Every one of these prospective jurors had to be investigated prior to the trial of Dr. Carl Coppolino in Freehold, New Jersey. To begin this process, Attorney Joseph F. Mattice of Asbury Park, New Jersey, was retained by F. Lee Bailey as local counsel to accomplish this herculean task in a minimum amount of time and with a minimum amount of effort. Mr. Mattice proved to be an excellent choice; for he not only accomplished one of the best pre-trial jury investigations I have ever seen, but was an invaluble aid at the time of the trial in answering questions put to him by Mr. Bailey and myself about particular idiosyncrasies of the jurors, many of whom he had personally known for years. For this reason, I heartily recommend that any attorney trying a case out of his jurisdiction should associate himself with local counsel who has lived in the jurisdiction for a long time and who has an intimate personal knowledge of a great many of the townspeople. This is especially important in a small town or rural type area.[5]

Use of a reliable local attorney assures the trial attorney that the investigation is being conducted in a professional and ethical manner with a proper awareness of the resources in the community. The trial attorney should be aware, however, that prejudices resulting from the relationships beween members of the community and the local attorney will affect the information gathered. If the local attorney's responsibilities are kept strictly to the gathering of data, without involving his or her attitudes and opinions, the arrangement can be highly rewarding.

The cost of bringing a local attorney onto the case is normally higher than employing a commercial jury service or private investigator. If cost is a primary consideration, the use of a local attorney is frequently not the first choice.

[4] W. Bryan, Jr., The Chosen Ones (1971).
[5] Id. at 38.

§4.2.1 *Venire Lists and Juror Questionnaires*

The first and obvious step in a pretrial investigation is to obtain the venire list. Second, the project coordinator should check to see if there is a juror questionnaire available at the courthouse. Since the potential juror will have personally completed the questionnaire, it is a reliable source. In some cases, if there is a qualified handwriting analyst in the area, it is helpful to have the handwriting on questionnaires analyzed. The third step is to circulate the venire list among a carefully selected group of concerned individuals including the trial attorney, other members of the trial team, the client, and friends or supporters of the client. Each should be asked to give information about any familiar name on the list and to evaluate the person's desirability for service on the jury. Each one of these evaluations should be supported with reasons. After the list has been processed by these individuals, it should be passed on to whoever has been chosen to process and secure the additional information.

At this time, a detailed plan for gathering and processing the information should be developed. The specific information about each desirable juror should be itemized. Often the best way to do this is to design a questionnaire to be used by all those working in the process of gathering information.

Next, precise details on how and where to obtain the information should be provided to the workers. Explicit instruction must also be given on the method for reporting information back to the trial team. This should include directions on how, when, and to whom the information should be sent. Usually, the information is collected by the individual assigned the coordination of the project. When each worker is provided with an exact list of instructions concerning how to avoid any prospect of a jury tampering charge, the worker should be told to be honest and open about the purpose for gathering the information. Any devious action could provide a backlash of charges if it is exposed to the judge.

As an important last step, there must be some method for evaluating the information. Some data will be totally or partially wrong, some will be contradictory, and some will be the product of guesswork. In all cases, there must be a process of verification and a method by which the relative importance of information is weighed for use during voir dire.

§4.2.2 *Training the Investigator*

To be of maximum usefulness, the investigator should go through a training session. First, each investigator should know what information is needed, why it is needed, and how it is going to be used. An understanding of the information's relevance will prevent the investigator from overlooking any vital information. The coordinator of the pretrial investigation should also inform each investigator about the exact type of report to file, the format to use, and the due date. At the training session, a list of sources should be identified along with instruction on how to use them. Some time also should be spent advising the investigators on jury tampering and how to avoid even its appearance. The investigators should have a clear understanding of how to answer questions about the pretrial investigation, especially if friends or neighbors of the prospective jurors are to be approached. They should not be sent out to investigate until they understand every aspect of the investigative process.

§4.2.3 *Sources of Information*

City directories, Polk's Directories, and Crisscross Directories can provide information concerning the prospective juror's occupation, employer, marital status, a spouse's or other family member's occupation, the number of family members who make up the household, the number of children, and, if of working age, the occupation of the children. These directories are usually available in the public library or at the local Chamber of Commerce.

Another accessible source of information is the voter registration list, which often includes the juror's age as well as the juror's political party.

Records of past jury service, which are maintained in some federal and state courts, will identify the cases a juror has sat on previously along with the final verdicts. While these records are sometimes difficult to obtain, if it can be demonstrated that one side has access to the information, the other side can generally obtain court permission to question the jurors during voir dire about their jury service.[6]

In many areas, the court sends questionnaires to potential jurors (see samples of states' juror questionnaires in appendix 1). Such questionnaires are public documents and the parties should be allowed access to them under provisions like the California Public Records Act. The act provides for public inspection and copying[7] of "any writing containing information relating to the conduct of the public's business prepared, owned, used, or retained by any state or local agency,"[8] unless the writing is subject to one of the listed exemptions.[9] To date, none of the exemptions has been held to apply to the questionnaires or the jury lists.

The American Bar Association supports this right of access in its Standards Relating to Trial by Jury: "Before voir dire examination begins, the court and counsel should be provided with data pertinent to the qualifications of the prospective jurors and to matters ordinarily raised in voir dire examination. . . ."[10] The standard is amplified in an accompanying commentary:

> It has been suggested that if certain basic information about prospective jurors were made available in advance of voir dire, considerable time would be saved. . . . Presumably, such information could be obtained by jury officials at the time they determine the juror's qualifications. The committee which drafted the Illinois rule on voir dire examination suggested

[6] See State v. Holmes, 347 So. 2d 221 (La. 1977).
[7] Cal. Govt. Code §§6253 & 6256 (West 1980).
[8] Id. at §6252(d).
[9] Id. at §6252(e).
[10] ABA Standards, Trial by Jury §2.2 (1978).

> that the attorneys, in advance of the voir dire examination, be given a list of prospective jurors showing their names, addresses, number of years employed, ownership of real estate, marital status, and number of children. Experience has shown that such information will shorten materially the voir dire examination.[11]

In the Angela Davis trial, the defense requested the court to make available the jury questionnaires on all 5,040 prospective jurors, and the court so ordered.

Additional information can be obtained from researching litigation records at the courthouse. Particular attention should be paid to small claims actions, deed transfers, bankruptcy actions, and traffic court records since prior experience as a plaintiff or defendant is significant.

Credit checks can sometimes be obtained; however, before the expense and trouble of checking a potential juror's credit is undertaken, the lawyer should decide exactly how such information would be used.

If union membership is a potential item of significance, a list of active members can usually be obtained from unions. Also, union members might be willing to discuss the opinions of fellow members about various union activities and principles.

If time, money, and workers are available, other procedures for obtaining information can be pursued. The local newspaper files can be checked to see whether any prospective jurors have written letters to the editor or have been involved in community campaigns that might indicate a bias. Such research, of course, is more reasonable in a small community.

The pretrial investigation must be aimed at seeking accurate, valuable, and pertinent information. There is no need to invade the juror's privacy. Gathering information just for the pleasure of having additional data will only waste the trial team's time and money, and will be of no benefit in the overall trial process. If the information does not have some *direct* bearing on the issues involved in the trial, then it is of no value, no matter how easy to obtain or how interesting.

[11] Ibid. (quoting Tone, Voir Dire, New Supreme Court Rule 24-1: How It Works, 47 Ill. B.J. 140, 145-146 (1958)).

All of the information must be accumulated at least two or three days prior to the beginning of the voir dire so that it can be tabulated, summarized, and evaluated by the trial team.

§4.2.4 *Specifying Information Desired*

The basic rule in guiding pretrial investigation is simple: Only seek information that will have meaning for the jury selection process. Relevant information that provides a basis for determining the bias or prejudgment of the prospective juror is all that is of interest. Information should either provide guidelines for exercising challenges or a basis for voir dire questions. Always the information should be relevant to assessing the juror's suitability. This paramount consideration is often overlooked, resulting in wasted time, money and effort.

§4.2.5 *Use of the Pretrial Investigation Questionnaire*

"I want some information about these jurors," is too often the only direction that is provided to investigators. This simply will not produce a systematic flow of the type of information needed to evaluate prospective jurors. Therefore, the trial attorney should produce either a list of desired information or design a questionnaire that will define areas of interest. The following sample questionnaire identifies areas of interest for which it is feasible to secure information.

A great deal of information can be gained with this type of questionnaire, some of which is not essential. Therefore, the attorney should tailor the questionnaire to the needs of the specific case. To do this, the attorney should weigh the cost and difficulty of obtaining the information against its value in selecting jurors. If the attorney cannot identify in advance how particular information would be of assistance, then the information should not be sought during the investigation. However, the attorney should not decide to eliminate a category of information because it is available for some jurors and not others. That certain information about a particular juror is not available, but is readily available for others, is significant since it denotes an individual's visibility in the community.

Form 4-1
Pretrial Investigation Questionnaire (Civil)

JUROR NAME____________________Venire Number______

EVALUATION: Leader____ Follower____ Loner____

	1. Trial Attorney	*2. Trial Attorney*	*Jury Worker*	*Client*	*Average*
Pretrial	____	____	____	____	____
Voir Dire	____	____	____	____	____
Strike or Keep	____	____	____	____	____

COMMENTS OF INTEREST:

STRIKE? ____Yes ____No
Order of Strike________
Liability: ____ Good
____ Neutral
____ Poor
Award: ____ High
____ Moderate
____ Low
Overall Evaluation:

PERSONAL INFORMATION:

Sex____ Age____ Current Marital Status______ Number of Children____

Height___ Estimated____ Weight___ Est.______ Body Type___

Known ____ Known____________

Physical appearance: (attractiveness, dress, physical defects, facial hair, etc.)

____

____

____

Habits: (especially drinking, drugs, smoking) How methodical or erratic?

____

____

____

Hobbies, recreational activities:

____

____

____

Personality descriptions from friends, neighbors, co-workers:

____

____

____

____

Friends: (occupations, interviewer's impression of personality, education level, activities, length of friendships, etc.)

____

____

____

____

____

EDUCATION: Highest level achieved____ Major area of study:____

Where attended High School?________ College?________

Year graduated High School ________ College ________

GPA______ Est.______ Known____ Absenteeism______ Conduct______

____

____

____

OCCUPATION:____________

Check one:

Laborer _____

Blue-collar _____

White-collar _____

Executive _____

Foreman _____

Place of Employment____________

How long?____________

Date of last promotion____________

Probable salary____________

Other jobs for additional income?_____Yes _____No

Kind?____________

Description of employer: (purpose of company, how long in business, how sound economically, number of employees, union status and/or problems, reputation in community, pension plan, profit sharing, etc.)

____

____

____

____

____

____

____

Security clearances?____________________

Typical duties include:____________________

____

Decision making areas:____________________

____

Prior employment record:____________________

____

History of activity in union or professional organization:

____

Business reputation:____________________

SPOUSE'S OCCUPATION AND EMPLOYMENT HISTORY:
(include all information asked for above in regard to potential juror, if available.)

____

____

____

____

____

____

____

RESIDENCE: _____Apartment

_____Duplex

_____Condominium

_____Single Family Dwelling

_____Other (describe) ____________________

Own?_____ Rent?_____ Mortgage held by____________________

Type and description of neighborhood____________________

____

Neighbors: (occupations, income level, political interests, etc.)

____

____

____

(See also Residential Observation Check Sheet)

ETHNIC DATA: Race__________ Racial bias if known__________

Description of interactions with other racial groups:__________

____

____

Other languages read or spoken:____________________

VEHICLES: Number______ Drivers______

Description, make, year, condition of each:

____

____

Other: ____Boats ____Cycles ____Campers ____Bikes ____Other Specify:

Bumper stickers:________________________ ________

____

Driving record: (tickets, accidents, arrests, etc.)

____

LITIGATION RECORD:

Small claims court?______ Divorce court?______

Civil cases?______ Witness?______ Crime victim?______

Law enforcement connections:________________________

Armed forces history: Date________ Branch________

Rank________

Honors/problems____________________________

Discharge: Type________________________ Date________

Gun registration____________________________

Past trouble with law____________________________

MEDICAL HISTORY: Present health________________________

Deformities or disabilities:____________________________

Explain nature and effect:____________________________

____

Known major illnesses____________________________

Visual limitations__________ Auditory limitations__________

Suicide attempts__________ Mental health history__________

____

PAST JUROR HISTORY: (list court, type of case, lawyers involved, verdict, etc.)

____

____

____

SPOUSE or PREVIOUS SPOUSE INFORMATION: (Give information for each spouse, use back of form for more than one.)

Prior or current marriages________ Children by prior marriage____

Age______ Race________

Physical description____________________________

Source of income______________ Occupation______________ (see spouse's occupation section)

Personality____________________

Solidity of relationship____________________________

FAMILY HISTORY: (Identify parents, children, siblings. Where do they live? Reputations? Occupations? Items of interest.)

____

____

____

____

____

MEDIA EXPOSURE: Newspaper(s)________________________

TV in home?____Periodical subscriptions:________________

____

Letters to the editor:____________________________

POLITICAL AFFILIATION: Party of registration______________

Voted in elections on____________________________

History of candidate support________________________

History of party activity__________________________

RUMORS, MISCELLANEOUS INFORMATION:

____

____

____

____

____

____

____

____

§4.2.6 Use of the Residential Observation Checklist

In addition to the information provided in this general pretrial investigation, a residential observation — having someone drive past the home (or business) of the prospective juror and get a detailed description of the area — is often useful. If it can be done unobtrusively, a photograph of the residence and its surrounding area should be taken. The photograph should include both the juror's home (or business) and neighboring properties to allow for comparisons. Among other factors, the tidiness and upkeep of the homes are of interest.

In observing the area, note should be made of the probable property value, the types of people who reside in the area, the types of cars driven by the residents, and any recreational items in the yards (boats, motorcycles, basketball hoops on the garage). Decals, symbols, flags, religious statues, or bumper stickers are of special interest since they reveal attitudes or opinions held by the occupants of a particular residence. However, if the prospective juror is a young adult who still lives at home, some information gained from a residential observation might be more applicable to the parents.

A residential observation should include information such as that requested in the following sample questionnaire.

Form 4-2
Residential Observation Checklist

JUROR NAME______________________Venire Number______

Address____

Type of housing: ____ Single family housing ____ Duplex

____ Apartment complex ____ Condominium

____ Other (specify)______________________________

Ownership: ____ own ____ rent ____ lives with parent

____ other (specify)______________________________

Type of neighborhood: ____ low income ____ middle income

____ high income ____ all white ____ all black

____ mixed ____ other ____________________________

Describe neighborhood:___________________________

____

Color of house____________ Ornamentation__________

Yard______________ Condition (repair)______________

Security measures: (dog, locks, warnings, fences, etc.)________

____

Signs of children? ____ yes ____ no If yes, their ages_______

Signs/symbols on house: (flags, stickers, placards, etc.)

____

Garage:____ yes ____ no Cars/vehicles/boats, etc. ________

____

Bumper stickers___________________________________

What impression does this residence make upon you? What type of person lives there?

____

____

Attach photographs: Front____ Rear____ Garage____

Neighbor's house____

Special items of interest________________

§4.2.7 Organizing the Information into a Usable Form

All of the information gathered must be processed so that it is usable by the trial attorney and readily accessible during voir dire. The project coordinator is responsible for providing the finished product to the attorney on time. While cross-referenced note cards can be used, a looseleaf notebook that allows pages to be easily rearranged and removed is generally preferred. A second notebook may also be used so that as prospective jurors are drawn their data sheets can be transferred to create a file of seated jurors.

In the notebook there should be a separate page or series of pages for each juror marked with the jury list identification number. New numbers must be given as jurors are drawn and assigned to the jury box. The notebook section on each juror should provide the following: (1) all data and a summary of that data, (2) a pretrial assessment of juror desirability by all members of the trial team (see chapter 7, Demographic Analysis), (3) a space to record voir dire observations, (4) a space for a final recommendation for disposition of the prospective juror, and (5) blank pages for general notes.

While the coordinator may find all of the background data useful in evaluating the verbal and nonverbal information gained during the voir dire process, the trial attorney might find using notebooks too cumbersome. An alternative is for the coordinator to provide the attorney with a summary of information on a note card. The summary should include (1) an indication of the assessment of juror desirability, (2) suggested voir dire questions for the particular person, and (3) room for the attorney to make notations.

§4.3 Evaluating Information from Pretrial Investigations

In *United States v. Quarles,*[1] the Supreme Court stated the following: "Juries fairly chosen from different walks of life bring into the jury box a variety of different experiences, feelings, intuitions and habits."[2] Professor Hans Zeisel, coauthor of *The American Jury,*[3] takes this fact about juries further. He points out that although every juror in the box sees the same trial and hears the same witnesses, attorneys, and judge, each, according to his or her predispositions and life experiences, will evaluate the process in vastly different ways. This is especially so when the evidence is not completely clear or is contradictory, according to Zeisel: "But since, as a rule, it is not possible to say in advance how clear or how close the trial evidence will be, it is the better part of wisdom to be prepared for the close case and to select the jury accordingly with care, so that jurors with extreme predispositions can be discovered."[4]

It is imperative that as many juror biases and prejudgments as possible be determined during the pretrial investigation or during the voir dire. Therefore, evaluating the information that has been collected about the jurors becomes a vitally important task. The thoroughness of the evaluation, however, is controlled by the available time. If the jury pool list is not going to be available prior to trial, then the entire venire must be evaluated. It will take considerably more time to evaluate information on every possible juror than it would to wait until the final jury pool of 50 or 60 jurors has been pulled.

The most effective procedure for evaluating pretrial data on each juror involves all members of the trial team. The process

§4.3 [1]350 U.S. 11, 76 S. Ct. 1, 100 L. Ed. 8 (1955).

[2]Id. at 18, S. Ct. at 6, 100 L. Ed. at 15.

[3]H. Kalven, Jr. & H. Zeisel, The American Jury (1966).

[4]Excerpt from Affidavit of H. Zeisel, dated July 3, 1944, and offered in case D. Minn. No. 4-71 Civ. 435, pending. "In re coordinated pre-trial proceedings and antitrust action."

takes from four to ten minutes per juror, depending upon the available information and the ease with which each item of information can be evaluated. One person reads aloud the coordinator's summary and then each team member assigns the juror a rank on a scale of one to ten. These scores are then recorded by the coordinator on the juror's trial notebook sheet. If there is disagreement on the assigned value, each person should explain why a particular score was assigned. Sometimes it becomes apparent that additional information is desired; this becomes the coordinator's task to be accomplished before that juror is questioned.

During the process of evaluating juror information additional questions for voir dire can be identified. For instance, "Mrs. Smith", a prospective juror, was a teacher until three years ago. Did she teach primary or secondary students? What subject matter? Why is she no longer teaching? There may be a considerable difference in the desirability of an elementary teacher who quit teaching to be at home with her children and a high school biology teacher who lost her job when budget cuts went into effect.

The entire process of evaluation, when completed, should provide the following: (1) a pretrial rating of desirability for every person on the prospective jury panel; (2) a list of prospective jurors who have been identified as candidates for a challenge for cause and the appropriate strategy outlined; (3) a compilation of voir dire questions to be asked each prospective juror; and (4) an evaluation of the panel as to the probability that a "good" jury can be drawn.

This last step is especially important in civil cases where there is a settlement offer on the table or a possibility that one will be forthcoming. There are times when even though the jury panel has been carefully selected it is heavily stacked with undesirable jurors. For example, during a pretrial rating of jurors in a malpractice case in Richmond, Virginia, it was found that 62 percent of the potential jurors had direct contact with the medical profession, while 12 percent had a history of severe illness with extensive hospitalization. The trial team agreed that this was one of the worst possible jury pools for selecting a panel that might award a sizable verdict to their client. Settlement was an attractive option.

Finally, two notes of warning must be given regarding the pretrial investigation. The first is especially well phrased by the National Jury Project in its book, *Jurywork: Systematic Techniques*[5]:

> Don't fall into the trap of relying too heavily on network information because it is more tangible than other pieces of information such as survey scores or interpretation of nonverbal behavior.
>
> Network information is not always reliable. Sometimes it comes from someone who does not know the juror well, or who has had a bad experience with the juror, or who might not want to say anything negative about the person because of their relationship. For this reason it is advisable to get as many reports as possible about each juror.
>
> Be suspicious of network reports, especially if they are extremely glowing or damning. Evaluate reports carefully in terms of the biases and associations of the people who gave the information. When network reports contradict impressions that members of the defense team have formed during the voir dire, the in-court evaluations should be carefully reviewed and the network information weighed with extreme caution.[6]

The second warning is one that underscores every consideration in doing a pretrial investigation: What effect will the investigation have on the jury and judge if it becomes known? It is often an avoidable waste of resources to have done all the work of a pretrial investigation for a jury that is dismissed due to the judge's decision that the pretrial investigation prejudiced the jury or invaded the jurors' privacy.

[5]Lawrence, MacPherson & Wiley, The Community Network Model for Collecting Juror Background Information, in Jurywork: Systematic Techniques (1979).

[6]Id. at 150.

CHAPTER

5

Community Attitude Assessment

§5.0 Introduction

Community attitude assessments can be used in any major civil or criminal case as the basis for constructing a profile of the most or least desirable juror. A determination of the least desirable juror is often particularly valuable, since potential jurors are eliminated at the impaneling rather than actually selected. A profile of both best and worst jurors, however, will allow the trial attorney to exercise peremptory challenges more logically and effectively.

In addition, community attitude assessments are invaluable for use in the following areas: (1) securing a change of venue in both civil and criminal cases (however, their use has had greater visibility and success in criminal cases), (2) supporting a motion for more extensive voir dire, (3) supporting a motion for individual voir dire where potential jurors are questioned one at a time apart from other potential jurors,[1] (4) supporting a motion seeking lawyer-conducted voir dire, (5) supporting a challenge to the composition of the jury panel, (6) testing a trial

§5.0 [1]Small group voir dire is sometimes just as acceptable. It saves time while still allowing for more extensive examination about sensitive topics without fear of contamination of an entire panel. Small groups are usually composed of three or four persons at a time.

strategy, and (7), when there is a choice of areas in which to file the lawsuit, determining the area with the greatest number of desirable potential jurors.

This chapter will be most helpful in assisting the attorney to (1) become familiar with a valuable aid in jury selection, (2) learn what questions to ask when selecting someone to direct and conduct the community attitude assessment, and (3) expose the areas that should be covered in either direct or cross-examination of an expert on community attitude assessments.

One note of caution: If the community attitude assessment is to be used in support of a change of venue motion, and especially if that venue change is opposed by the adversary, then it is not advisable for the attorney handling the case to personally conduct the study. Most community attitude assessments conducted in support of a change of venue are discredited at the methodology level. Therefore the principal investigator[2] must be qualified, unbiased and objective.

§5.1 Determining the Purpose of the Study

The first step is frequently the most ignored step: determination of the study's purpose. This should not be a general statement (i.e., to determine the community attitude about helicopter crashes, or to determine the level of the community's familiarity with the "Sunday Morning Murders"); instead, the purpose should be stated in such a way that the scope of the study will be defined. Such a statement of purpose for a change of venue study might be as follows:

[2]"Principal investigator" is a term borrowed from government grant research. It describes the duties and responsibilities of the person accountable for constructing the questionnaire, determining the pool from which subjects will be drawn, devising sampling method(s), instructing the interviewers, constructing the coding device by which material is changed from alphabetic to numeric, and conducting the analysis and making conclusions.

> The purposes of this community attitude study are the following: (1) determine the extent of information retention concerning this case within the community, (2) assess the name recognition level of this client within the area from which potential jurors will be called, (3) verify whether the community opinion is that this client is held to be guilty or not guilty of the crime charged, (4) determine the accuracy of the information held by the public, (5) determine the spread and belief-value attached to that information available from the public media that will not be admissible in court during the course of the trial, and (6) determine the level, by respondent's self-report,[1] of his or her ability to give the client a fair trial.

Once the purpose has been clearly stated, the study will have direction and goals. The statement of purpose should serve as the guideline for constructing the questionnaire and assessing the final results.

§5.2 Types of Community Attitude Assessments

The purpose, time, money and available expertise will determine how extensive a study to conduct. There are four basic ways to gather information for a community attitude assessment: (1) the poll, (2) the survey, (3) the community attitude study, and (4) the psychological interview.

§5.1 [1]"Self-report" refers to the verbal self-assessment made by an individual of his or her level of prejudice. In other words, say a potential juror is asked, "Will the fact that you are an insurance claims investigator have any effect on your ability to be a fair and impartial juror and to bring back a substantial award if you see that we have proven liability?" and he replies, "No, it would have no effect." That is the self-report of prejudice. This may well be contradicted by an assessment of behavior or a psychological interpretation of a full range of opinions and attitudes.

§5.2.1 Polls

A poll is the easiest to conduct and analyze but also the most limited for generating information. A poll should consist of no more than ten questions: two questions determining the respondent's qualifications to participate in the poll (i.e., residency and voter registration), four questions dealing with the topic at issue, and four questions for soliciting demographic information (i.e., age, marital status, occupation, education, and religion). All of the questions should be in a forced-choice format.[1] A poll should take a respondent only two or three minutes to complete, and most people will be willing to answer these types of questions. Also, dropouts[2] are likely to occur only 1 percent of the time, since the questions invite only superficial responses and do not probe for further explanations.

Designing a poll questionnaire — drawing up the questions and pretesting them (see §5.8 *infra*) — generally requires only two or three hours. A coding system for results (see §5.11 *infra*) is also simple to design, requiring little training and time, since analysis of responses will be limited by their superficial nature.

In summary, the poll is mechanically the easiest type of questionnaire format to use; however, it is also the least satisfactory for measuring depth of attitude or opinion, or for determining

§5.2 [1] A "forced-choice" format simply means that the respondent is asked to choose from selected responses. For instance, in the question "Would you say that you are _____very satisfied, _____somewhat satisfied, or _____not at all satisfied with your local police force?," the responses are limited to the four answers contained in the question, plus "I don't know" or "I refuse to answer that question." Questions that would logically be answered "yes," "no," "sometimes," or "maybe" are also forced-choice questions even though those answers are not identified as the responses within the wording of the question.

[2] A "dropout" is a person who initially agrees to answer the questions, but then refuses to complete the process. The two most common reasons for refusing to continue are that (1) the time required to finish and (2) the questions are increasingly personal or sensitive. Some people will refuse to discuss questions relating to sex, rape, murder, or finance, whether face-to-face or over the telephone.

the extent to which information is dispersed through the community.

§5.2.2 *Surveys*

A survey is very much like a poll except that it covers more than one topic area and, therefore, involves more questions. Questions should again be in a forced-choice format. A survey should include up to six questions about each of three, possibly four, subject areas. One survey questionnaire might cover the following topic areas: (1) attitudes concerning the responsibility of merchants for the quality of their merchandise,[3] (2) market research information concerning use and purchase of tires,[4] (3) awareness of a particular company and its reputation,[5] (4) opinion of a particular company's product,[6] and questions of a demographic nature (i.e., age, marital status, occupation, spouse's occupation, education, religion, and income).[7]

[3]Questions might include the following: (1) Who is most responsible for the quality of merchandise that you might purchase at a national department store: _____the local store manager, _____the purchasing agents, _____the manufacturer of the product, _____the government, which set the standards for manufacturing? (2) If you purchase an item for $50 that has a one year warranty, do you feel that you should be able to return it for repair to the local store where you purchased within the first year? _____yes, _____no, _____I don't know.

[4]Questions might include the following: (1) Which is more important to you when you purchase new tires: _____price or _____tire quality? (2) When was the last time you purchased new tires? _______________ (3) How may did you purchase? _____one, _____two, _____three, _____four, _____five.

[5]Questions might include the following: (1) What manufacturing companies do you associate with the making of good tires? _______________ _______________. (2) Which of the following companies do you think makes the most expensive tires?_____ brand *A*, _____ brand *B*, or _____ brand *C*. (3) Which of the following companies do you think makes the best tire for endurance on the road? _____ brand *A*, _____ brand *B*, or _____ brand *C*.

[6]Questions in this section might include the following: (1) Have you heard of the brand *A* tire? _____yes _____no. (2) Would you use a set of brand *A*'s tires on your car? _____yes _____no _____I don't know.

[7]Note that sex of the respondent is not one of the questions. The interviewer can generally tell the sex of the respondent from the sound of his or her voice.

A survey should not exceed 35 questions, and should allow for approximately six minutes of the respondent's time to fully respond to each. Dropout rates will increase to about three and one half percent due to the additional amount of time required to complete the interview.

Designing the survey questionnaire will normally require about six hours; again, this would include the time necessary for drawing up the questions and then pretesting them. A coding system for responses will be no more complicated to design and teach than for a poll; however, it will require more time to complete since there are many more questions.

Analysis of survey results will give much more information than analysis of poll results, since cross-tabulations (see §5.14 *infra*) of various questionnaire topics can be made to determine the relationship between behavior and opinion.[8] Analysis of a survey does not require any more skill than is necessary for analysis of a poll; however, it requires more time since, again, there are more questions to compare.

In summary, a survey is only slightly more mechanically difficult to conduct than the poll. The information available from a survey is more extensive, but it is still limited by the superficial nature of the responses. While the analysis of survey results does give a better measure of the spread of information within a community, it does not measure the depth of attitudes or opinions.

§5.2.3 Community Attitude Study

A community attitude study differs from a poll or a survey in that it adds the use of open-ended questions to the question-

[8] Analysis by cross-tabulation of the survey on tires might show, for instance, whether a person who thought the local manager of national department store was most responsible for merchandise quality also believed that Goodyear produced the most reliable tire. Or it might show whether the person who only purchased one tire as needed had different expectations about quality control than the person who purchased four new tires whenever he or she deemed that the tires currently on the car had excessive mileage.

naire. An open-ended question[9] allows the respondent to reveal attitudes and opinions more fully since the person is given the opportunity to speak openly and freely. When the respondent is allowed to volunteer information, which is recorded verbatim, there is a better chance to assess the person's opinion correctly.

The open-ended question is especially useful when it is used as a follow-up to a forced-choice question. When attempting to identify the kind of person most likely to make a high award in an aviation case, for instance, a sequence of questions like the following should be asked. The sequence begins with a forced-choice question:

> In 1977, two Boeing 747s collided at Tenerife in the Canary Islands and some claimants were awarded $650,000 by a jury. Do you think that amount was probably ____ pretty fair, ____ too much, or ____ too little?

It is followed by an open-ended question:

> On what do you base your opinion?

Analysis of the open-ended question response in conjunction with the forced-choice question response will often reveal certain basic differences about whether a person feels that an award was fair. For example, some persons might express a belief in the jury system that explains why they support the award. Others might believe that $650,000 is a fair award for the type of damages that can occur in a crash involving two 747s.

[9] An "open-ended question" generally begins with the words "what," "why," or "how." Open-ended questions that might be used in a community attitude study that is to support a motion for a change of venue might include the following: (1) What do you most remember about the shooting? (2) What specifically have you read or heard about this case or this defendant? (3) What is the reputation of this defendant in this community? Open-ended questions that might be used for a civil case include the following: (1) In your opinion, what kind of a case would be worthy of a million dollar verdict? (2) What criteria or method would you use in determining the amount of an award for pain and suffering?

A community attitude study should range in length from 20 to 60 questions. It should take the interviewer about ten minutes to conduct the interview. It is generally not too difficult to keep people on the phone for such a short time; however, for each additional minute, there is an increasing likelihood of dropouts. If 60 questions are included in the questionnaire, it will probably require 20 to 25 minutes to complete. A questionnaire this long should only be used when well-trained, highly skilled, and experienced interviewers are involved.

The likelihood of persons refusing to participate in the study is a function of the length of the questionnaire (the time required to complete it should be hinted at during an introductory statement) and the sensitivity of the subject matter. In rural or small communities participation can also be affected by people discussing the fact that they have been contacted and speculating about the reasons for the study.[10] Dropout rates increase to an average of 6.8 percent for a community attitude study in a change of venue case when the media coverage has been extensive, where the community is rural, when the victim or defendant is well known, and when people are reluctant to get involved in discussing the case.

Designing the questionnaire will require eight to ten hours, and sometimes more, depending on the pretesting time necessary. Open-ended questions require more pretesting time than forced-choice questions. A coding system for results is more complicated to design for open-ended questions, since it cannot be done until the interview process has been completed. The person responsible for devising the coding key for the open-ended questions must read all of the responses before subjecting them to content analysis (see §5.14 *infra*).

Coders will require more training and supervision when they are asked to code open-ended questions. Also, coding time will be significantly longer. Whereas it normally requires less than 3 hours to code 100 polls and 9 hours to code as many 30-

[10] When a study is done in a rural or small community it is wise to plan to complete the study in one or two days so that the results are not contaminated by rumor or speculation.

question surveys, it will likely require more than 20 hours to code 100 community attitude studies that include 45 questions, 4 of which are open-ended.

Analysis of the community attitude study includes measuring the number of responses to each question, cross-tabulation of responses, and interpretation of the response patterns. The last reveals the depth of opinion, bias, and prejudice existing in the community. For instance, compare the patterns in the following responses from two participants in a community attitude study used to support a motion for a change of venue. Note that they appear at the beginning, middle and end of the questionnaire.

Question 5: Do you normally read ____ only headlines, ____ mainly local news, ____ only special sections, ____ just scan for items of interest, ____ or do you read the whole paper?
Respondent One: Read the whole paper.
Respondent Two: Scan for items of interest.

Question 17: What have you read or heard about the shooting?
Respondent One: This man is supposed to have shot this woman in her bedroom.
Respondent Two: Carney broke into this young widow's home, tied her up, raped her and then shot her in cold blood four or five times with her poor little kid watching in shock.

Question 28: Do you think David Carney is probably ____ guilty or ____ not guilty as charged?
Respondent One: I don't know.
Respondent Two: Guilty.

Question 29: Would you want to serve on Carney's jury?
Respondent One: No.
Respondent Two: Yes.

Question 30: Could you sit on his jury and give him a fair trial?
Respondent One: I don't know.
Respondent Two: Yes.

Question 36: Do you think it is possible that Carney is not guilty?
Respondent One: Yes.
Respondent Two: Anything's possible, but I doubt it.

From examining the patterns in these responses, one could conclude that respondent 2 is very knowledgeable about the case, has concluded that defendant Carney is guilty, and, despite a response to the contrary, could not give Carney a fair trial.[11] On the other hand, respondent 1 is fairly open (note the use of the words "supposed to have shot" in response to question 17) and probably has not prejudged the defendant. In the hearing for the change of venue, all of this information should be shared with the judge. It can be seen from the above examples that analysis of a community attitude study requires more time and skill than is necessary for a poll or survey. The required skill is possessed by most social psychologists, psychologists, or sociologists, especially those who are familiar with linguistic or content analysis.

In summary, the community attitude study is the most effective and accurate medium for assessing community prejudgment or bias. However, it is also more complex to conduct and analyze. Greater skill is required of all personnel.

§5.2.4 *Psychological Interview*

A psychological interview is a lengthy, in-depth discussion of a situation or case between a highly skilled interviewer (preferably a psychologist or a person well trained in interviewing techniques) and a member of the target community. The psychological interview is relatively unstructured. While the areas of interest are well defined and clearly delineated, the inter-

[11]This is a common response pattern discovered in community attitude studies and reveals the difficulty in relying on voir dire to be effective in removing biased individuals.

viewer has discretion in phrasing questions so as to elicit the desired information.

The most difficult aspect of the psychological interview is recording the responses. Since the interview is conversational in nature, it is difficult to write down everything said. To do so would inhibit the responses. The best way to deal with this problem is to tape-record the conversation and then transcribe the tapes.[12] Coding of this material is very difficult. Subjective analysis can be difficult to defend in court. The interpretation of information is open to challenge by opposing experts. Due to the length and complexity of this type of interview, it is generally reserved for use in determining the nature of a community, the life experiences of persons residing in the community, and the effect those experiences will have on the issues in the particular case. The persons interviewed should be from the following two groups: (1) community leaders who will describe both their experiences working with the community and its demographic make-up, and (2) a cross-section of citizens who are likely to serve as jurors.

Questions for the community leaders should generally be directed toward determining the following: (1) What are the most powerful organizations in town? Why are they powerful? (2) Describe the various neighborhoods located in town. What are the basic concerns of each neighborhood? Who are the leaders of that neighborhood? What is the racial, ethnic, economic, and educational composition of each neighborhood? What is felt to be the major crime problem for each area? (3) Who are the major employers? How are they connected with each other? Do they cooperate or are they rivals? Are they unionized? Have they had any union problems? Is any violence related to those problems? (4) What is the employee situation in

[12] Tape-recording any conversation without the consent of the person being interviewed can offer some special problems if the information is later going to be introduced in court. Even if this is not a consideration, careful deliberation should be made before it is decided to record interviews without the interviewee's consent. Surprisingly, many people are quite willing to speak openly and completely about almost any topic, even with full knowledge that the conversation is being recorded.

the community? Is there much unemployment or job dissatisfaction? Have there been strikes in the last year? Where? What has been the most disruptive labor issue? (5) What is the attitude toward local government? What was the most controversial issue or race in the last election? Why was it so controversial? What were the positions of the various sides? Has there been any post-election change in these positions or controversies? (6) What are the major media influences? Who are the opinion leaders? Who writes letters to the editor of the newspaper or calls the local talk shows (not necessarily the names of persons, but the groups or organizations that these people represent)? (7) What are the issues that these leaders see as important in this particular trial? How do they think the community will react to these issues and why? What would they do in order to win the case? Do they think the case could be won? How do they react to each of the parties or witnesses? What is their reaction to presentation of evidence? Whom do they consider to be an expert in the area? (8) What group or groups in the community would be the least prejudiced and the most accepting of jurors for this particular case? Why? What groups would be the most prejudiced and least accepting jurors? Why?

Questions for the cross-section of community members likely to serve as jurors should cover the same topics, but the respondent should answer as an individual rather than as a spokesperson for the community. The nature of these interviews should be much more personal and should probe into the nature of the respondent's stereotypes and basic prejudices.

In summary, a psychological interview elicits a personal, introspective, and descriptive view of a community. It represents the most subjective view of the community. It is useful in determining the type of prejudice in the community concerning a specific case, but is less useful in measuring the extent of prejudice. The trial attorney who is forced to work in an unfamiliar community will frequently find it desirable to conduct this type of interview, either personally or with the assistance of a team of trained interviewers. It is an expensive process, in terms of both the time involved and the cost of conducting the interviews. The psychological interview is generally used by large law firms where the information can be pooled and the cost spread over many cases. It might be used by a smaller firm in a case where the stakes are high enough to justify the cost. It is especially useful to public prosecutors or defenders.

Basic considerations in deciding on which type of community assessment to conduct will include time, finances, personnel, and purpose. Frequently, attorneys are deterred by the cost of the project. To guard against this tendency the lawyer should select the best method for the purpose; then the financial considerations should be surveyed to see how costs can be kept within reason. The use of volunteers — both expert and lay volunteers — should be considered if it is determined that they would not be a detriment to the project. Educational institutions should not be overlooked as a source of both expert advice and volunteer labor — or at least inexpensive labor. Frequently, professors will be willing to take on a special project, especially if they can see some social or educational value to the project. Anthropology, sociology, social psychology, and psychology departments are often the best sources of assistance. However, one should not overlook journalism or speech departments that have a communication research division.

§5.3 Personnel Selection

The personnel involved in conducting a community attitude assessment generally include the principal investigator, project director, interviewers, coders, computer operators, statistician, and typists. Experience and previous training requirements are dependent on the needs of the particular project. If rigorous examination and cross-examination of the final conclusions can be expected, then a higher value should be placed on prior training and experience. It should be noted that courtroom standards for qualifying a person as an expert should be considered if the study is to be formally presented in court. This is particularly true for studies conducted in support of a contested change of venue.

The selection of the *principal investigator* is probably the most crucial decision in determining the value and effectiveness of the final product. This person is responsible for constructing the questionnaire, hiring and supervising the project director, determining the sample selection and contact method, determining the pool from which subjects will be drawn, instructing the interviewers, constructing the coding key by which material is given a numeric value, analyzing the results, and determining the final conclusions for the project based on the results of the data. (Each of these elements shall be explained fully in the following sections). In addition, this person will set the standards for the project, especially for data collection and preservation methods. He or she needs to recognize and be guided by the ethical rules and procedures for social scientific research. The principal investigator is the person who will present, possibly in court, the results and conclusions of the study and to support the methodology used. Therefore, the person must be unquestionably both expert and ethical.

The *project director's* qualifications and effectiveness are also important. This person is responsible for hiring the interviewing and coding staff, training and supervising them, selecting the sample, and preserving records necessary to support the authenticity of the data and the methodology used. The project director will be required to present, in court if necessary, the details of the sampling, training, interviewing, and coding. Many studies are discounted for lack of a rigid adherence to a methodology. For this reason, the project director must be meticulous.

It is important, when feasible, to divide the roles of principal investigator and project director. To do so assures the maximum protection for the authenticity and accuracy of the study. One major criticism of the community attitude assessment is that the principal investigator will force the data to justify a certain conclusion. The intrusion of the project director into the midst of this process provides a cushion against this objection.

Also, this division of labor reduces the stress and tension of the project for all involved.

The *interviewers* need to be friendly, objective, articulate, and competent persons, who can maintain accurate records and follow directions. Interviewing skills are relatively easy to teach[1] provided the individual has a pleasant, confident manner and projects a sincere interest in people. It is important that the interviewer be disinterested in the outcome of the study and be convinced of its impartiality. The interviewer's basic job is to establish a pleasant but businesslike contact with the respondent, to read the questions exactly as written and follow up with the appropriate probes,[2] to obtain clear and complete answers from the respondent and record them precisely and legibly on the answer sheets. Some people, while clearly qualified to work as interviewers, will not perform well or enjoy the task. Some people find it difficult to call strangers on the phone and ask them to respond to questions. Interviewers should always work under close supervision of the project director,[3] so that those unsuited to the task can be reassigned so they will not have direct contact with the public.

Volunteers can be used as interviewers; however, special control must then be used to verify the objectivity of their work product and the accuracy with which they record responses. The availability of volunteers may make a project feasible. Their use is acceptable when supervision and evaluation of their performance is rigidly controlled.

§5.3 [1]This does not apply to psychological/sociological interviewing, which requires extensive special training.

[2]A probe is a question is used to encourage a respondent to answer more fully or more completely. The probe is never evaluative. It must be neutral. The probe does not offer additional information. It only seeks additional information. Typical probe questions might include the following: (1) Could you clarify that for me? (2) Would you like to add any other information? (3) Is that all that you have read or heard? (4) Would you explain what you mean by that?

[3]There are occasions when interviewers should not work under direct supervision. Circumstances related to space and time considerations will be determinative. Other supervisory techniques should then be used to ascertain whether the interviewers are working effectively and efficiently.

The voice of the interviewer is the most important single consideration in hiring. The person must be able to project a friendly, pleasant attitude while maintaining an absolutely neutral position regarding questions. Tone of voice, inflection, or delivery style must not invite a particular response or approve a particular expression of opinion. Interviewers must not let their own opinion be reflected in the results of the survey.

Women, especially those with mature and gentle voices, make the best interviewers. Male voices are generally perceived as more authoritative and demanding,[4] which is why males are frequently used in bill collection. Both male and female respondents tend not to feel threatened by a female voice. Nor are respondents likely to feel that a female interviewer is evaluating their responses or finding them wanting. Both male and female respondents tend to be greater self-disclosers[5] to female interviewers. Since females are generally more available for this type of work, it is fortunate that they are highly valued. Males may be used as interviewers if they have exceptional skill or experience.

The *coders* task is relatively simple. They must follow a coding key that has been constructed by the principal researcher for transferring a written information into a numeric form (see §5.11 *infra*). The coders have absolutely no discretion. They must follow the coding key exactly. Accuracy is their principal responsibility. If time and money allow, each interview should be coded twice. Both codings should be identical; if they are not, the project director should check the areas of disagreement to determine the proper numeric value of the response. Generally discrepancies occur in the coding of open-ended or forced-choice responses where the respondent has offered a qualified response.

A *statistician* is required only when the principal investigator

[4]This information is based on linguistic analysis that has been conducted by various collection agencies and is not part of any formal research done on interviewing.

[5]Jourard & Lasakow, Some Factors in Self-Disclosure, 56 J. of Abnormal and Social Psychology 91, 91-98 (1958); Benney, Riesman and Star, Age and Sex in the Interview, 62 Am. J. of Soc. 143, 143-152 (No. 2, Sept. 1956).

needs assistance determining the appropriate sample size, setting up the computer program, or performing a complicated analysis. Generally, statistical tasks are carried out by the principal investigator.

Computer operators are generally available from a professional computer service or an educational institution. They are used in the process of moving coded information into the statistical data base (see §5.14 *infra*). Computer operators should be selected on the basis of dependability and accuracy.

A skilled *typist* will be required for preparing the final report. Accuracy and speed are the primary qualifications.

§5.4 Personnel Training and Supervision

Personnel training and supervision are the immediate responsibilities of the project director, although the techniques and materials are agreed on generally by both the principal investigator and the project director. Training manuals for interviewers and coders are prepared in advance.

The training manual for the interviewers should contain both general instructions on interviewing and specific instructions for conducting the particular questionnaire or interview. (See the training manual example in appendix 2.)

The training manual for coders should be much more brief. It should cover general rules and procedures plus the coding key.

Training of the interviewers should be done in one general session.[1] A typical general training session agenda for a telephone study should cover the following:

1. Introduction of the project personnel.
2. General introduction to the project, with special em-

§5.4 [1]If experienced interviewers are used, especially those who have worked under the project director before, a general training session may be unnecessary. Brief instructions concerning the particular project, either individually or collectively, will be sufficient.

phasis on the time limitations and scope of the project. (It is important that there be no discussion of the purpose of the study or the facts of the case involved. If at all feasible, the interviewers should not be informed about which side of the case contracted for the study. This is not always possible, as, for instance, with a change of venue study when the press has revealed to the public that such a study will be undertaken.)

3. Go over the interviewers' manual in detail. Cover every item. Encourage the interviewers to make notes on their own copy of the manual.
4. Cover the questionnaire in detail. Read *every* question. Emphasize the necessity of reading each question exactly as written in a clear, pleasant tone with neutral inflection.
5. Practice reading the questionnaire. Include every interviewer, even the experienced ones.
6. Discuss the probe questions, and particularly when and how they are to be used.
7. Go over the telephone-dialing record sheets. Explain the marking system and practice using it.
8. Emphasize the need for maintaining clear and accurate records.
9. Emphasize the need for accurate, legible recording of responses, especially with open-ended questions or remarks of interest that explain or modify an answer to a forced-choice question.
10. Explain the daily check-in system.
11. Establish work periods.
12. Assign work space.
13. Discuss how to handle the problem respondent. Clarify the procedures to be used. Identify whom respondent can contact for more information.

Training for the response coders is much simpler and may be done either in a group or individually, depending upon the preference of the project director. After covering the background information about the project, the trainer should take a questionnaire, a coding sheet, and a coding key and code the questionnaire with the assistance of a trainee. Then the trainee should complete two or three more under the supervision of the trainer.

Careful training and supervision of the interviewers and coders is essential in producing a reliable and valid study.

§5.5 Time Requirements

Time is usually at a premium in conducting a community attitude assessment since there is almost always a court deadline that governs the scheduling of the study. The assessment can be conducted efficiently in three or four weeks, depending on availability of personnel and facilities. The following considerations dictate the deadlines for the assessment.

Design and pretesting of the questionnaire (see §5.7 *infra*) will require two or three days.

Printing and collating the questionnaires, telephone dialing call sheets (see §5.9 *infra*), interviewer manuals, coders' manuals, and coding sheets should require one day.

The amount of time required for the randomization of the telephone numbers (see §5.7 *infra*) will depend on the source of the numbers. This tedious job requires a major proportion of the project director's time. At least one full day should be set aside *before* the start of the project so that enough numbers can be generated to keep the interviewers busy for the first calling period.

Interviewer training will require four or five hours, especially if first-time interviewers are being used. Generally the morning or afternoon prior to the first calling period is set aside for training time.

Interviewing should be completed in three or four days. Otherwise, there is a danger that responses will be tainted by prior knowledge of the interview. In cases that receive extensive media coverage, there is always the risk that the study will be made public. It is best, therefore, to complete the study as quickly as possible.

Weekends are ideal for telephoning. The best time periods are on Friday evening from 7:00 to 9:30; Saturday from 10:00 A.M. to noon, 1:00 to 5:00 P.M., and 7:00 to 9:00 P.M.; and Sunday from 1:30 to 5:30 P.M. and from 7:00 to 9:00 P.M. This gives a total of 16½ hours during the weekend.

In order to estimate the number of interviewers needed to complete the project within that time period, follow this procedure:

1. Multiply the average amount of time required to complete the questionnaire by 2.2 (ten minutes times 2.2 equals 22 minutes or $10 \times 2.2 = 22$).
2. Multiply this amount by the total number of interviews in the project (22 minutes times 300 interviews equals 6,600 minutes).
3. Divide that number by 60 to estimate the number of hours (6,600 minutes divided by 60 minutes equals 110 hours).
4. Divide that number by the number of hours in the targeted calling periods in order to arrive at the number of interviewers needed (110 hours divided by 17 hours equals 6.47, indicating that 7 full-time interviewers should be used.

To estimate the number of coders needed, determine the average amount of time required to code one questionnaire and multiply that number by the total number to be coded (5.6 average coding time multiplied by 300 interviews equals 1,680 minutes, divided by 60 minutes equals 28 hours). Two coders who begin work on Saturday morning with completed questionnaires, and then keeping up with the interview crew, would be finished by Monday evening.

Most professional computer service companies will require seven days from the time they receive the coded data until they generate the computer programmed results.

Analysis of the data and preparation of the final report will require three to five days. This does not change much regardless of how many interviews are conducted; in other words, the analysis of 150 interviews requires just about as much time as the analysis of 600 interviews.

A bank of phones in one location is ideal for supervision of the project. Each interviewer should have a desk or table where she or he can work out of the hearing of other interviewers, or at least out of noisy areas. She will need a telephone, dialing record sheets, plenty of questionnaires, and extra pens for recording answers. Do *not* use pencils or other erasable markers; the interviewer should record all responses in ink so that if the questionnaires are examined later, it will be easier to determine if responses have been altered.

The project director will also need a desk and supplies appropriate to preparing the telephone dialing record sheets and checking the completed questionnaires. She or he should have ready access to all of the interview stations.

The coders should have a nearby work area and be supplied with coding sheets and pencils.

§5.6 Selection of the Sample

Sampling is the process by which a portion of the total population is selected for examination, that examination in this case being participation as a respondent to a survey. Fortunately, statistical research has proven there is no need to contact every member of a targeted group for an accurate survey of opinion. Otherwise it would be too costly in terms of time and money. Contact with a selected part of that population will reveal adequately representative information. Dr. Raymond Barker, professor of marketing at Bowling Green State University, illustrates the adequacy of a survey sample by drawing an analogy to a physician who tests the blood of a patient by removing a representative sample. There is no need to remove all of the patient's blood to determine its nature and composition.[1]

If the results of the sample are going to be generalized as reflective of the whole, then a probability sample is used. In a probability sample, every person in the population has an equal chance of being selected for contact. This is not true in a nonprobability sample, such as the reference system that is used to identify community leaders for the psychological/sociological interview. The nonprobability sample is not acceptable for analyzing the attitudes of prospective jurors, since there is no statistical basis for claiming that the attitudes of the sample could be generalized as representative of the whole population.

Probability sampling methods include (1) quota sampling, (2) area sampling, (3) stratified sampling, and (4) random sampling. *Quota* sampling involves identifying certain factors in the target population (i.e., sex, age, voting status, political affiliation) and attempting to represent them in the sample in proportion to their number in the population as a whole. *Area* sampling involves identifying certain geographic locations as being representative of the whole and then interviewing every nth[2] person (this method is frequently preferred in face-to-face interviewing). *Stratified* sampling permits the tailoring of the sample by selecting persons from all significant major groups in the population in proportion to the numerical size of those groups. For instance, if 80 percent of the population is white and 20 percent is nonwhite, a stratified sample would need approximately 80 percent of its respondents to be white. *Random* sampling is the selection by chance of persons from within the whole population, all persons having an equal opportunity to be selected.

Random selection is generally used in surveying or polling. It is statistically the most reliable and pragmatically the easiest

§5.6 [1] A. B. Blankenship, Professional Telephone Surveys 61 (1977).

[2] "Nth" is a statistical reference that implies the selection of a particular number that then becomes consistent in use; in this case, every 10th or 7th or 35th person might be contacted.

method to use for a study involving contact by telephone. Random samples may be generated by either the straight, systematic, or stratified approach. The *straight* method is analogous to drawing numbers from a fishbowl containing all possible choices. In actuality, the numbers are either computer generated or pulled from existing random number tables. The latter is the most time consuming method. The *systematic* method involves picking every nth name from a master list. As long as there is no bias in the way the master list is put together, there is no bias in the sampling list. The *stratified* method involves working from a list that is somehow classified prior to selecting the names, resulting in a sampling of various levels of the total population. Since social strata are not represented in actual potential jury panels, the stratified random selection has no real value to this type of community attitude assessment. That is, there is no requirement that every jury panel must be 50 percent male or female or that every panel must be composed of 25 percent of each different age group, for example, people 18 to 25, 26 to 40, 41 to 60, and over 60.

The systematic random selection is the method most feasible for use in the community survey conducted for jury analysis.[3]

The size of the sample depends on the level of confidence desired for the results. Generally, a standard error rate of 5 percent is allowable for studies that are to be presented at a court hearing in support of a change of venue motion or a motion for additional peremptory challenges.[4] This means that since such a study will have a 95 percent confidence level, the results should be accurate to within ± 5 percent. Therefore, if the study found 45 percent of the community to be prejudiced, the range of predictability for prejudice in the community would be from a low of 40 percent to a high of 50 percent. For

[3]For further reading in the area of conducting surveys or measuring community attitude, read these basic texts: H. Cantril, Gauging Public Opinion (1947); H. H. Remmers, Introduction to Opinion and Attitude Measurement (1954).

[4]In profiling the most and least desirable jurors, a standard error of 5 percent might be acceptable.

the sample to be predictive of the universe (target population), the sample must be (1) representative of the population and (2) sufficiently large to minimize the standard error. However, sample size does not have to be huge — a sampling of 300 will be large enough to keep from exceeding a 5 percent error for an entire state. Both Gallup and Roper expect a 1 to 3 percent error rate with their national polls, which are based on 3,500 to 5,000 people — approximately 1⁄100th of one percent of the population of interest. In 1948, Roper predicted how Chicago would vote in the national election and was accurate to within 1.5 percent of the actual vote, based on polling only 75 voters. A statistician can be of help in determining the appropriate size of the sample for a study.

Once the size of the sample and the sampling method have been decided, the actual work of picking the telephone numbers and assigning them to the interviewers must be done. Professor Blankenship points out two mechanical aspects of sampling that must be observed:

> The professional telephone survey firm always provides the list of selected telephone numbers to its interviewers. The professional telephone survey firm never, even when working from directories or other lists, has its interviewers look up telephone numbers. These are always supplied for two important reasons. One reason is that selection of the lists calls for professional, meticulous, clerical talent, and the work should be done under supervision. Otherwise, there is too much risk of dilution of purity of the sample chosen. The other reason . . . is the research firm finds it essential to keep these telephone lines in use as much of the time as possible. It cannot afford to take the interviewer away from his or her key job: using one of those lines.
>
> The list provided for dialing must be many times the total interviews required. Market Opinion Research, for instance, in consumer surveys, provides a list size which is anywhere from four to ten times the number of required interviews. This sounds as though the completion rate is too low. This is not the case, as many lines have been disconnected, many are business telephones, and for many there is repeatedly no answer.[5]

[5] A. B. Blankenship, Professional Telephone Surveys 43 (1977).

An interview telephone dialing record should be used. It contains the telephone numbers that have been randomly selected for the community. These numbers, and only these numbers, are the ones called by the interviewers. The dialing record includes columns for indicating the six possible results of an attempted contact: (1) busy number, (2) no answer, (3) refusal — the respondent declines to participate from the beginning or breaks off the interview, (4) noneligible — no qualified respondent is available (i.e., nonregistered voters, persons of an age that is not acceptable for jury duty, or nonresidents of the community), (5) business number, or (6) completed interview. Occasionally, a person will indicate that he or she is busy but would have time later. The interviewer should then make an appointment for a call-back at another time. This should be noted on the dialing record sheet, and the call-back made at the appointed time. (See sample interview telephone dialing record with complete instructions for its use in appendix 2.)

§5.7 Constructing the Questionnaire

Designing a questionnaire requires special knowledge and expertise and should not be attempted by the novice, especially if the results of the study will be defended in court. However, such expertise is much more available than one may think, since almost every university has someone in the sociology, psychology, or communication department who has training in constructing a questionnaire.

The poll is the simplest questionnaire to construct since it is limited to ten or fewer questions, all in a forced-choice format. Yet, even in designing a questionnaire for a poll, care must be taken to follow basic interviewing techniques. The survey, community attitude study, and psychological/sociological interview are each progressively more difficult to construct. Each type of community attitude assessment requires different techniques and questionnaire considerations. However, to cover each of these would require more time and detail than is necessary in achieving a basic understanding of the process. Therefore, this section will emphasize the process by which a community attitude study is constructed by telephone. The community attitude study serves as a good example because it (1) combines aspects of all four assessment types and (2) is the type most commonly used for jury analysis.

Background source materials should be examined before beginning to construct the questionnaire. If the study is to be used to support a change of venue motion, the background materials should be limited to those available to the general public. The limitation is in keeping with the purpose of the change of venue study, which is to determine what information and attitudes currently exist within the community. It is essential that no new information about the case be released to the community. Therefore, the only case materials that should be examined before constructing the questionnaire for a change of venue study are media reports identifying rumors circulating in the community, or other materials that are easy to obtain and analyze. Newspaper coverage, however, tends to be the most factual and least sensational. Due to the limited broadcast time allotted per story, radio and television reporters tend to sensationalize their coverage. It is important to consider this factor when reviewing news coverage. Also, always keep source materials for courtroom identification.

If the study is not limited to a change of venue but will be used for analysis of the case's issues, testing of a trial strategy, or profiling a jury, then the source materials should include everything that might shed light on the issues that will be important to the particular case. Once the background material has been reviewed and the purpose of the study clearly defined, then actual questionnaire construction can begin.

The questionnaire format most common to the community attitude study consists of seven different sections: (1) the introduction, (2) screening questions, (3) questions for ascertaining the source of information, (4) questions concerning the amount of information prevalent in the community, (5) questions determining the general attitude toward the case's major issues and other case-specific questions, and (6) demographic information. Both forced-choice and open-ended questions should be included in the questionnaire design.

§5.7.1 *The Introduction*

The introduction needs to be brief, informative, and inviting to overcome any normal reluctance on the part of the respondent to participate in an interview over the phone. An effective introduction for use in either criminal or civil cases might be the following:

> Hello. My name is ________________. I'm working as a research assistant for ________________, who is doing a survey concerning the public's view of issues in this community. We would appreciate it if you would share your opinions with us about several issues. All of your responses will be treated anonymously. Okay?

The introduction should be just long enough to briefly explain the purpose of the study. Also, the introduction should not make any false claims nor employ any deliberately misleading statements. The respondents may be curious about the purpose of the study and have questions they want satisfied before agreeing to participate in the study. Supplemental statements should be prepared ahead of time for such occasions (see appendix 3).

§5.7.2 *Screening and Source of Information Questions*

Screening questions are included in the questionnaire to make certain that only eligible respondents are included in the sample. These normally reflect the requirements for jury service in the area. Typical screening questions include the following:

1. Are you a resident of ________ County?
2. Are you a registered voter of this county? or How many registered voters live in this household?
3. Are you between the ages of 18 and 70? (Or whatever ages reflect those required for jury service in the area.)

If the person does not answer the screening questions affirmatively, then he or she must be marked as "not eligible" for participation as a respondent in the survey. The person should be thanked for his or her time and the conversation discontinued.

Include six to eight questions in the questionnaire concerning major sources of information for the respondent. These questions should look for sources of private information, as well as check for reliance on mass media. Typical questions in this section would include the following:

1. What daily newspaper do you read?
2. Do you watch TV news regularly?
3. Do you listen to radio news regularly?
4. What is your *major* source of news information: Discussion with friends or neighbors? Conversation at work? Listening to the radio, watching television? Or reading the newspaper?
5. Do you tend to believe the information provided to you by these news sources?
6. Which do you think is most accurate: newspaper, radio or television?

No question should be asked without a reason. The information obtained from asking the question should have some meaning for the study and should allow for interpretation. For instance, in a change of venue study, one issue might be the extent of media coverage devoted to the case. Questions should determine the respondent's dependence on the media for information and the degree of trust and reliance on the media information as an accurate source. However, extensive questioning about a source of information should only be used if that source can be identified as being particularly prejudicial or biased in its coverage.

§5.7.3 *Questions about the Amount of Information in the Community*

Once the source of the information has been determined, the respondent should be questioned about the amount of information concerning the case that is prevalent in the community. The first step is to see if the case is voluntarily mentioned in response to a general question: "What crime that has occurred within the last six months do you remember reading or hearing about?" Then, the respondent's memory of the incident should be specifically addressed: "Do you remember reading or hearing about the 'Sunday Morning Murders'?" Next, open-ended questions would be used to examine the nature of the information remembered: "What do you remember about that incident?" or "Do you remember who the victims were?" or "Has someone been arrested in connection with that murder?"

§5.7.4 *Attitudes toward the Case's Major Issues and Other Case-Specific Questions*

General attitude and case-specific questions usually require the assistance of an expert in the area of questionnaire design. It is important that each question be worded clearly, neutrally, and unemotionally. Avoid questions that are not limited to one idea (i.e., "Would you expect the owner of the airplane to have insurance to cover his liability or do you think he should personally have to pay for the damages?"). Ambiguous words or phrases should not be used (i.e., "Does it *bother* you *a lot* to *be on* the streets after dark?"). Word use plays a very important part in determining the effectiveness of a question. Therefore, it is important to consider the various interpretations the respondents might give a particular word or group of words. For instance, what does it mean to say "driving after drinking"?

Does it imply that the driver had consumed a small amount of alcohol or does it mean the driver was drunk? In change of venue cases, it is important to ask as directly as possible, what kind of verdict the respondent favors: "Do you think he is probably guilty as charged?" or "Do you think the plaintiff should be compensated for this injury?"

A full knowledge and understanding of the law and issues concerning a case is required before a questionnaire can be constructed that will identify attitudes predictive of juror behavior. Therefore, it is essential that the trial lawyer have extensive input in defining the issues from which the questions will be drawn up. Useful information will be obtained only if the proper questions are included in the questionnaire. All too frequently, those involved in the study realize during response analysis that a crucial question has been omitted. For instance, in one complex civil case it was essential to determine how potential jurors felt about awarding damages to a plaintiff — a smoker — who had been exposed to asbestos, when no medical expert would isolate either factor as the direct cause of the plaintiff's lung cancer. Six hundred respondents were asked about their attitudes toward smoking; exposure to asbestos in work-related and non-work-related activities; the responsibility of the manufacturer, employer, or government in providing accurate warnings of danger. In all, respondents were asked over 60 questions in an interview that required 25 minutes to complete. Yet three basic questions were omitted: "Do you smoke?", "Have you ever smoked?", and "Why did you quit?" or "Why did you never smoke?" Since these questions were important in determining the profile of a desirable or undesirable juror, the same respondents had to be contacted a second time, again by long distance, so that this information could be considered for the final profile. Once included in the final analysis, the additional information turned out to be the single most predictive element. So, the basic rule of questionnaire construction must not be overlooked: *Never* ask for information you don't need and *always* ask every question needed to understand and interpret accurately the data collected.

§5.7.5 *Demographic Questions*

The final section of the questionnaire contains the demographic questions. When the study is to be used for building the profile of a desirable or undesirable juror, it is necessary to include a greater number of demographic questions that will correspond to juror questionnaires or voir dire. Age, sex, race, occupation, marital status, spouse's occupation, education level, spouse's education level, ethnicity, religion, union membership, group memberships, and income all can be included in the questionnaire *if* that information will be available later about each potential juror. For instance, religion is often an unknown factor in evaluating prospective jurors; seldom is a question concerning religious preference allowed in voir dire. If the study is to be used as evidence in court to support a motion for change of venue, the only information necessary is that which will demonstrate that the population surveyed has the same characteristics as the people eligible for jury service. This probably would include only sex, age, marital status, occupation and race.

§5.7.6 *Pretesting Questions*

Pretesting the questions as they are drawn up verifies the validity and clarity of each question, as well as each section of the questionnaire and the overall design. Pretesting can be performed by at least two different methods. The principal investigator, who is responsible for the ultimate questionnaire design, should contact people in a test population at random to ask whether they understand a certain question, whether the wording of the question is unclear or misleading, what information they think the question is trying to elicit, whether they feel the wording of the question limits their responses, whether they are led to answer the question in a certain pattern, and whether they believe there would be a better way to ask the same question. Test questions should be worded variously to test respondent reactions to different words and phrases. If a question is found to be unclear, misleading, limiting, leading, or capable of producing a predictable response, it should be eliminated from the questionnaire.

The test population should be somewhat like the project population but should *not* be the population in which the survey actually will be conducted. Use of a test population avoids contaminating of the survey population with discussion in the community about the pretesting of the questionnaire. It also provides a control group[1] for comparison with the survey population. When contacting persons in the test population, the principal investigator could use this type of introductory statement:

> My name is ________________. I am putting together a questionnaire for a different community from the one in which you live, and I need some advice on whether my questions are good or bad. Would you be willing to listen to my questions and tell me how you react to them?

People are generally quite responsive to this approach.

As soon as a question or section of the questionnaire meets with complete approval by three or more persons, the principal investigator may move into the second phase of the pretesting.

The ordering of the questionnaire sections and questions within the sections should be pretested next, by either the principal investigator or one or two assistants, to determine what effect, if any, it has on response patterns. While some response patterns can be expected,[2] any pattern that leads the respon-

§5.7 [1] A "control group" is a statistical term used to identify a group that is like a second group except that it has not been exposed to the test variable. It is frequently used to demonstrate the reliability or validity of a study.

[2] It is well known that questions that are moderately to highly personal should be placed near the end of the questionnaire. Otherwise, people are likely to refuse to answer any questions or to discontinue the interview. Once respondents have answered several questions, they gain confidence in the interviewer and in the interview process, plus they have an investment in the process and are more likely to respond and continue the interview. It is for

dents to reply in a systematic or predictable way should be avoided. Time and finances will control how many tests of question sequence are desirable, but 15 to 30 are generally recommended.

Pretesting the questions will also suggest the range of possible and probable responses likely for each question, allowing the questionnaire's design to anticipate more response choices. This will simplify the process of designing the response coding key.

§5.8 Method of Contacting Respondents

There are three methods of contacting a respondent: (1) personal contact, (2) telephone contact, or (3) contact by mail. The personal contact is also known as the face-to-face contact or door-to-door contact.

The personal contact method was the preferred choice of professional surveyors until recently. It reached all of the population; it allowed for more direct contact and feedback. However, times are changing. In 1975, *Time* quoted Mervin Field, a West Coast pollster, as saying, "Twenty years ago we could count on getting 85% [of the sample contacted personally] with reasonable effort. Now we're hard-pressed to get 60%."[1] Dr. A. B. Blankenship, professor of marketing research at Bowling Green State University, points out further problems with personal contact interviewing:

> The rise in resistance [to answering the door to personal interviewers] seems to be greatest in ghettos and in affluent areas. The problem is compounded because most personal interview-

---

this reason that the demographic questions, which are considered to be highly personal, are placed at the end of the interview, while other sensitive questions are placed immediately before the demographic questions.

§5.8 [1]Time, Nov. 10, 1975, at 6.

> ing must be done during the late afternoon and evening to be sure to get working people into the sample. . . . [It is difficult to get] interviewers to go out at night. . . . [Also] many people no longer are willing to open their doors after dark to a stranger, whether man or woman. The increasing crime rate presents very serious problems to personal interviewing.[2]

Professor Blankenship also points out the difficulty of assuring the quality of the personal interview due to lack of supervision, inadequacy of pay per interview, and lack of control over the interviewing process. For these reasons, falsification of information can be a genuine problem with the personal interview.[3] The personal contact interview is now the most costly to conduct successfully in terms of time, energy, and money.

Contact by mail is the least preferred method because it is difficult to obtain sufficient return for a reliable study. Professor Paul L. Erdos suggests that 80 percent is the desired response to a mail survey and suggests, "No mail survey can be considered reliable unless it has a minimum of 50 percent response. . . .[4] Blankenship reports, "The completion rate of mail surveys often is low. Most research textbooks report that about 15 percent completion is all that can be expected in a general population survey, but this figure is woefully underestimated."[5] Also, the availability of a mailing list for the total population of a community is nonexistent, even in small communities. Most available lists are incomplete, inaccurate, and selective. Frequently, the best mailing list is the telephone book.[6]

Another major problem with contact by mail is that there is no way to determine specificity of respondent; that is, the person to whom the questionnaire is sent might not be the one who fills in the responses. Because of this problem of ensuring the accuracy of the sample, contact by mail offers no advantage

[2] A. B. Blankenship, Professional Telephone Surveys 20 (1977).
[3] Id. at 40.
[4] P. L. Erdos, Professional Mail Surveys (1970).
[5] A. B. Blankenship, Professional Telephone Surveys 40 (1977).
[6] Id. at 39.

over telephone contact. Such defects make mail contact unreliable for jury studies.

This leaves the telephone contact. Blankenship reports that telephone contact is now the least costly and most efficient survey method due to increased telephone ownership,[7] availability of phone banks that allow for better supervision, and the likelihood of a high completion rate.[8] Unless there is some overriding reason that makes personal contact desirable or necessary, the telephone contact is the method generally used in a community attitude survey.

Once the method of respondent contact has been determined, the next question is what "frame" should be used. The frame is the list that is used to identify the universe of potential respondents. Possible frames for consideration include voter registration lists (especially in areas where voter registration is the primary source for drawing up the jury pool), the jury wheel from which the jury panel will be selected, and the names and phone numbers of community citizens listed in the telephone book.

Voter registration lists would be a desirable frame except (1) they usually cost a significant amount of money to obtain; (2) they are frequently two to four years out of date, depending on the date of the last national election; and (3) they require a tremendous amount of time to put into working order, since the lists generally do not include current telephone numbers. Using voter registration lists will usually add several hundred dollars and many days to conducting a study.

The list of names on the current jury wheel would be the ideal frame; however, there are the following problems: (1) The lists are almost impossible to obtain (in almost every jurisdiction, these lists are well protected and are inaccessible. Even with a court order, the list has not been "available" in some

[7] About ninety-seven percent of families in the United States had telephone service as of 1981. (Statistical Abstract of the United States 1984, U.S. Bureau of the Census (104 ed. 1983)).

[8] See A. B. Blankenship, Professional Telephone Surveys 18-19, 41-46 (1977).

jurisdictions.) (2) There is a risk of contacting a person currently on a jury panel which might be interpreted as jury tampering. (3) Often the lists do not have telephone numbers, again requiring additional time to put the list in working order. (This last problem is magnified by the current practice of listing telephone numbers under the name of the male head of household, and not identifying the names of spouse and children who also are members of a particular household.) Thus while a considerable amount of time, energy, and money could be spent in attempting to obtain the current jury wheel list, these attempts seldom meet with success, and, even if obtainable, they do not always produce a workable frame.

The last logical source of a frame that identifies the universe of potential respondents is the telephone book. This is a readily accessible source that is highly accurate. Critics may question whether it is a representative listing of the population from which the jury panel will be drawn. To respond to this criticism, the following steps should be followed: (1) Find out from the local phone company the percentage of local homes that have, or do not have, phone service. (These statistics are readily available, if not by asking for them, then by subpoena.) The proportion will likely be close to the national average of over 95 percent. (2) Determine the percentage of potential jurors on the last several jury panels who do not have a listed phone number. (3) Use screening questions to identify potential jurors when calling from the phone book listings (i.e., "Are you a registered voter in ____________ County?" or "How many registered voters of ____________ County reside at this number?") and eliminate nonregistered voters as possible respondents.[9] (4) Check for challenges to selecting the array exclusively from voter registration lists. Most state supreme court decisions regarding jurors make no distinction between the qualifications of nonregistered voters and registered voters in terms of the way they view the court system. The lawyer who would object to using phone contacts in which there has

[9]Be careful to frame screening questions that match the criteria for voter eligibility.

been no attempt to verify that the respondent is also a registered voter may well be faced with a dilemma — either registered voters are different from nonregistered voters (hence, a challenge to the composition of the jury panel) or they are not different (hence, any resident of the area, whether a registered voter or not, is a viable respondent as long as he or she meets the other federal or state requirements for jury service).

There are two potential biases that should be eliminated before using telephone directories as the source of respondent contacts. First, find out who the nonowners of telephones are within the area and whether they represent a distinct demographic group eligible for jury service. Do this by checking the last few jury panels to determine if consistently there are people who do not list a telephone number. If such a group exists, then there is strong support for a bias in using the telephone directory as a frame. Second, determine the extent of the use of unlisted phone numbers in the area, and try to find out the identity of the class or type of person who is apt to have an unlisted number. Using the last four or five jury panel lists, determine the percentage of persons from that class who have served on a jury. Again, if a statistically significant number of persons with unlisted phone numbers have been called to jury service recently, then it is likely the telephone directory would be a biased frame.

If the local telephone directory passes these two tests for bias, then it will serve as a reliable, valid, and feasible frame.

The use of a computer generated phone number list is also a reliable, valid, and feasible frame. However, such a method produces many numbers that have not been assigned to customers by the phone company. This increases the difficulty of obtaining a qualified respondent and also significantly adds to the amount of interviewer time required to complete the study. Therefore, unless there is a valid reason for opting for computer generated numbers, it is an unnecessary expenditure of time, energy, and finances. The actual telephone book listing with proper use of qualifying questions in the questionnaire is the preferred method.

§5.9 Conducting the Interview

In order to produce the greatest number of completed questionnaires and to have reliable information recorded on them, the interviewers must be well trained and confident in their abilities. They must be very familiar with the questionnaire, the proper way to record responses, and the telephone dialing record sheets.

There are certain basic rules and procedures that must be followed. The interviewers should know them thoroughly, since the ability to follow the rules and procedures is basic to the performance of a good interviewer.

§5.9.1 Following the Interview Schedule

The interviewer must adhere exactly to the interview schedule, the introduction and questions, reading the questions to the respondent exactly as they appear on the questionnaire. Questions may be repeated but they cannot be explained. The interviewer must not offer any interpretation of the question nor give any example of what the question may mean. If the respondent indicates that he or she does not understand the question after it is repeated twice, the interviewer should say the following: "I cannot explain the question. I can only repeat it. Could you answer the question based on what you think it means?" If the person responds in the negative, the interviewer can then say, "Should I record your response to this question as "I don't understand it" or would you rather I record one of these responses. . . ." She or he would then read the available responses to that question and continue.

The interviewer must read the questions slowly, clearly, without emotion, and with neutral intonation and inflection. She or he should not rush the respondent to a response.

The interviewer must never argue or disagree with a respondent, nor express approval or disapproval of any comment volunteered by a respondent. The interviewer must be friendly and pleasant at all times to all respondents, even to those who become aggressive and abusive. It is important that a neutral and objective attitude be displayed at all times.

§5.9.2 Recording Responses

The interviewer should record responses to open-ended questions verbatim, in a legible hand. When the respondent volunteers information of interest to forced-choice questions, that information should also be recorded verbatim. Use of the third person should be avoided in recording responses, in favor of the first person. When the respondent speaks too rapidly for accurate transcription, the interviewer should interject: "Could you repeat that? I want to be sure that I'm getting all this down right."

The interviewer must record all the responses accurately, even the forced-choice answers. The coder can only decode what is on the interview schedule. Every question must be marked with a response, even if it is "IDK" for "I don't know," "NA" for "No Answer," or "NR" for "No Response," indicating that the respondent has a response but doesn't think it is appropriate. Also, the interviewer should not mark more than one response. If a respondent indicates two or more responses, the interviewer should have the respondent choose one: "This question asks which one is *the most* important. Choosing between the two responses you just indicated, which one do you think is *the most* important?" However, the interviewer should *never* force the respondent to make a choice he or she is not comfortable making. After one or two attempts to encourage a single response (the appropriate number of probes should be decided on by the principal investigator during the construction stage), the interviewer should record the response so as to alert the coder to its qualified nature.

The interviewer should never make a decision about what she or he *thinks* the respondent said. For instance, if the respondent answers a question with, "Well, I don't know, yes, I suppose it could be viewed that way," the interviewer must not decide what the respondent intends. Instead, the interviewer should ask a follow-up question. "The responses that I could check for your answer are as follows: yes, no, or I don't know. Which would you like me to check as your response to that question?"

The interviewer must be careful not to supply information beyond what is contained in the question. She or he should never lead the respondent to a particular answer. While this is acceptable in the courtroom during voir dire, the interview process is not an attempt to rehabilitate the potential juror nor an attempt to support a challenge for cause. The interview process is merely an attempt to accurately and systematically record the attitudes and opinions currently prevalent in the community. This is why a neutral tone must be maintained at all times.

The interviewer must be conservative in recording responses. Even if the interviewer thinks that a question has been answered in a prior response, the interviewer should ask the question and not guess at the response.

§5.9.3 Wrapping Up the Interview

The interviewer should try to keep the interview as short as possible without losing response accuracy. She or he will, however, want to complete as many interviews as possible in the allocated time. Also, the interviewers should not take up too much time and risk losing the respondent. At the end of the interview, the interviewer should thank the respondent for his or her cooperation. At this point, the interviewer can expect additional questions about the purpose of the interview. She or he should give a full and accurate disclosure of all the information she or he is allowed to give. If even more information is sought, the respondent can be told to call — collect if necessary — the appropriate person involved in directing the study.

§5.9.4 *Maintaining Confidentiality*

Generally, people will be concerned about how public their responses will be or whether their names will be used in the report. This is why they are assured in the opening statement of the interview that all of their responses will be treated anonymously. If they ask for reassurance on this matter, the interviewer should provide them with the following information: first, the interviewer does not know the respondent's name, only his or her telephone number. (Interviewers should not be given names or addresses with their telephone list). No name is attached to the questionnaire. Last, all results are compiled as totals of all responses, and then broken down into averages. In the end, the report will only indicate, for instance, that 40 percent answered "yes," 45 percent answered "no," and 15 percent said "maybe."

Respondents can also be assured that their phone numbers were picked by a random sampling method; it was by chance that their telephone numbers were included on the list for the project.

§5.10 Coding the Questionnaire

Coding is the process by which the written information (the alphabetic) is converted to numerical equivalents (the numeric) so that it can be processed by a computer. Coding may not be required if the various question responses can be tabulated and totaled.

The value of the number assigned to a response has no real meaning. That is, if the response to a question is either "yes" or "no," it does not matter whether the "yes" is assigned a value of 1 or 2 or 7. The coding number is merely a method of separating the two responses. The computer will print out a tabulation of the number of times (the frequency) a particular number appears as a response to a particular question. Therefore, if the value "1" is assigned to "yes" and "2" is assigned to "no," the computer printout would indicate that out of 300 questionnaires there were 175 responses for "1" and 125 for "2", which would then be interpreted as 175 "yeses" and 125 "nos."

There must be a coding designation for every question on every questionnaire. If a blank appears, the computer will handle that blank as missing data which will skew the results.

Setting up the coding key should be handled by a person familiar with the computer program to be used in processing the study data. That person should also help establish the training procedures for the coders.

§5.11 Verification Calls

The project director or the principal investigator should contact six to ten percent of the respondents for verification. These calls are to check on the following areas: (1) that the interviewer made the contact as recorded, (2) that the interviewer was friendly and neutral in her dealing with the respondent, and (3) that the responses were accurately recorded on the interview sheets.

The interviewers should be forewarned that the verification calls will be made. They should be told that any problem in verifying the contact and the recording of responses will result in discontinuation of the interviewer and may necessitate throwing out all of that interviewer's work to avoid jeopardizing the validity of the study.

Verification calls should be made as the interview calls are being made, so that a poor interviewer can be identified immediately. Furthermore, all verification calls should be completed prior to analysis of the data. When telephone contacts are by long distance, the phone bill provides additional check on when calls were made and how long they lasted.

Verification calls will sometimes cause the respondent concern about the confidentiality of the interview. Again, the respondent should be assured that only the telephone number is recorded on the interview, and that he or she is one of a small number of the total respondents who has been selected at random for this check on the work performed by the interviewers.

§5.12 Determining the Completion Rate

The completion rate reflects the reliability of the sample. It is based on the total number of dialings made to get the desired number of completed interviews. Roughly, the completion rate is computed as follows: Count the number of telephone calls made; subtract from that number all out-of-order numbers, ineligible households called, plus the estimated proportion of the non-reached households which would belong in the above categories (this last is based on experience and performance by the community). This number is referred to as the base number. It is divided by the number of completed interviews for the rough completion rate. Different formulas take into account busy numbers, no answers, and re-contact numbers.

In a poll or marketing research project where the topic is not particularly sensitive and the questions are all forced-choice, a completion rate of seventy percent or better is usually expected. However, in a survey that deals with a sensitive topic or one that has excited community concern, the rate of refusals or drop-outs might be especially high. Accurate records of refusals and drop-outs, and the stated reason for such behavior, should be used to determine the completion rate. Community attitude studies for support of a motion for change of venue may have a completion rate of roughly less than sixty percent with a drop-out percentage of seven to ten percent (higher drop-out percentages can be expected in communities affected by either fear or outrage) and a refusal rate in excess of twelve percent.

The completion rate should be estimated at the end of each

contact day. One of the best methods for affecting the completion rate is careful supervision of the interviewers. If call-backs are not made for busy or unanswered numbers, the phone number list will be exhausted quickly, lowering the completion rate significantly. No number should be considered an exhausted number until a contact has been attempted at least three times during different call periods.

§5.13 Analysis of the Results

The basic statistic used in analysis of the data is the *frequency*, or marginal, which gives the number and percent of the respondents who fall into each category of response for a question. A basic frequency table for fair trial response for the question "Could you serve on his jury and give him a fair trial?" would look like the following:

	Frequencies	
	Number	*Percent*
Yes	153	51.0
No	119	39.7
IDK[1]	28	9.3
Totals	300	100.0

Reading this table, you would know that 119 respondents, or 39.7 percent of the 300 respondents, did not feel that they could serve on a jury and give the defendant a fair trial. One hundred fifty-three respondents, or 51 percent of the total, believed they could, and 28 respondents, or 9.3 percent of the total, were not sure if they could be fair.[2]

§5.13 [1] "IDK" indicates the respondent answered "I Don't Know."

[2] All of the frequencies and cross-tabulation results used in this section are taken from an actual community attitude study performed in support of a successful motion for a change of venue.

While frequencies are interesting, they do not begin to reveal the whole story about information collected in the questionnaire. Say, for instance, that the frequencies show that 168 respondents (56 percent of the total) were female while 132 (44 percent) were male; also, that 144 respondents (48 percent) believed the defendant was guilty as charged, 52 respondents (17.3 percent) refused to answer the question, and 73 respondents (24.3 percent) responded that they didn't know. Only 31 respondents (10.3 percent) indicated that the defendant was not guilty. This information would be interesting but not as interesting as the answers to the following questions: How many of the respondents who thought the defendant was guilty also thought they could give the defendant a fair trial? Are males or females more likely to believe in the guilt of the defendant?

To find the answers to these questions, a *cross-tabulation* can be run. Cross-tabulations show how the set of responses from one question relates to the set of responses to another question or questions. To answer the first question above, the frequencies for the questions concerning guilt are compared with those concerning the ability to give a fair trial. A cross-tabulation of those questions would look like Table 5-1.

Results of this cross-tabulation include the following: (1) of the 153 respondents who indicated they could give the defendant a

Table 5-1
Cross-Tabulation: Belief in Guilt *Times* Able to Give Fair Trial

	Is the defendant:									
Could give a fair trial?	*Guilty*		*Not guilty*		*No answer*		*I don't know*		*Total*	
	#	%	#	%	#	%	#	%	#	%
Yes	94	31.3	28	9.3	4	1.3	27	9.0	153	50.9
No	48	16.0			34	11.3	37	12.3	119	39.6
IDK	2	.7	3	1.0	14	4.8	9	3.0	28	9.5
Totals	144	48.0	31	10.3	52	17.4	73	24.3	300	100.0

fair trial, 94 respondents, or 61.4 percent, indicated that they felt the defendant is guilty as charged, and (2) of the 52 respondents who refused to answer the question about the defendant's guilt, 34 respondents, or 65.4 percent, indicated that they could not give the defendant a fair trial. The results of this cross-tabulation are a better indication of the level of prejudice against the defendant shown by the community than the frequencies obtained separately from these two questions. The first result should also indicate to the trial attorney that rehabilitation by the prosecutor could be fairly successful and that challenges for cause could be difficult to secure.

A second cross-tabulation of these results can be made according to respondents' sexes. Such a cross-tabulation shows that of the 94 respondents who indicated that although they believed the defendant was guilty they could give him a fair trial, 68 respondents were male and 26 were female. If these breakdowns were in keeping with the proportion by sex of the population sampled, only 41 of the 94 respondents would have been male while 53 would have been female. Weighing these figures, it can be seen that males are far more likely to believe they can set aside their prejudice and be fair in reaching a verdict. This information would be very useful to the trial attorney during the voir dire process when deciding whether to challenge a particular juror for cause.

If the profiles of the desirable and undesirable jurors are desired, more complex and sophisticated techniques are used. Regression analysis, interaction analysis, or discriminant analysis are the statistical programs most frequently used to develop these profiles. Use of a computer makes the process fairly quick and easy. A research-oriented social or behavioral scientist can help in deciding which approach or statistical analysis best suits the available data. That person should also have the skills necessary to interpret results and explain them clearly, so that every person on the trial team can use them.

Regression, interaction, or discriminant analysis assesses the relative importance of the information collected in the demographic section of the questionnaire for classifying respondents as desirable or undesirable. Ratings based on demographic information provide a more logical way to evaluate potential jurors and their *probable* performance on a certain case. Demographic ratings indicate how a certain type of person is likely to feel about certain issues and what his or her probable behavior will be in the jury room. (For instance, a 44-year-old married businessman, who has two children, is active in the community, and has two years of college might be one type.) The demographic information, however, is compared to the case-specific questionnaire responses as a basis for *prediction* of verdict outcome.

§5.14 Records that Should Be Introduced in Court

If the study is to be used in support of a motion in court, the following materials should be available for introduction as court exhibits:

1. The source materials used by the principal investigator to become familiar with the issues of the case;
2. The instructions for randomizing the sample;
3. The list from which the phone numbers were pulled during the process of randomization (If telephone books were used, the ones actually marked should be introduced);
4. The interview telephone dialing records with all markings or comments made by the interviewers;
5. The incomplete questionnaires;
6. The completed questionnaires (These should be photocopied if the originals would be of value at a later time. Remember that once they are introduced into court, the information is available to the opposing side of the case);

7. All training materials (especially the interviewers' and coders' training manuals);
8. The coding key;
9. A sample questionnaire;
10. The final report.

The records should be so well marked and maintained that if the project director or the principal investigator were to be given a telephone number of a respondent, or even the number of someone who discontinued an interview, the completed or partial interview could be pulled and placed into the questioner's hand within minutes.

Coding sheets and computer analysis records should not always be placed into evidence during a hearing. If the data contained on these sheets would allow the opposition to identify the probable characteristics of the most desirable or least desirable juror, these sheets should be kept as work product and should not be introduced in court. On the other hand, if it appears that coding sheets and computer analysis printouts could be demanded as proof of a reliable, valid study, then the juror information should be omitted from the printouts except as required to demonstrate that the sample reflected the demographic characteristics of the whole. It is uncommon to have data that both supports a change of venue motion and provides juror profiles. Generally, only one kind of analysis can be supported by the data.

The project director is usually charged with maintaining the records until they are presented in court. Presentation in court of the actual results of the community attitude study must be carefully handled. If the results of the study are discounted, it is usually because the methodology has flaws. Assuming the methodology is sound, the results must be given substantial weight, if not by the trial judge, then by the appellate court. The project director and the principal investigator must prepare thoroughly for their testimony. It is important that the court understand why each step was followed and why each bolsters the credibility of the results.

§5.15 A Lawyer's Perspective on Use of the Community Attitude Assessment — Stan Levy, New York City

No one seriously suggests that a community attitude study can or should replace the expertise, skill, experience, and instinct of the experienced trial lawyer. It cannot and never will. Indeed, that is why trial lawyers almost unanimously condemn efforts to eliminate or restrict the scope of attorney-conducted voir dire. Increasingly, however, lawyers are recognizing that a carefully devised and conducted community attitude study can be — in the right case — a significant supplement to the attorney's skill and instinct.

The following are essential factors to consider in determining whether to embark on a community attitude study: (1) Are you psychologically and emotionally prepared to accept the survey as possibly providing a tool that can help you select the jury? (2) Are you willing to invest the time needed to assure that the survey is done — and done right — and that you get the most out of the information it uncovers? and (3) Is the case large enough or important enough to justify the cost?

Once a decision has been made to go forward with your survey — and you should want the best and most accurate survey possible for the money — the first step on this perilous journal is to obtain professional help.

It is critical to select the principal investigator with some care. Some articles have suggested that all you need to do is turn to the Yellow Pages of the telephone book and look under marketing research or market consultants and pick anyone listed, since one is as good as another. This is just not the case and that advice should be rejected out-of-hand. This is a specialized area where communication, psychology, public relations, polling statistics, computer analysis, and an understanding of the legal system all are significant elements and frequently are difficult to find in one person or firm.

The ideal principal investigator is someone who already has been involved in conducting community attitude studies for litigation because he or she already will have gone through the process and have an understanding of how the information will be used in litigation. The investigator must understand the legal issues in the case, how the jury system works, and how the survey can affect the jury selection, and, therefore, the entire litigation.

The investigator should have a background in psychology and communications. It is essential that questions are worded carefully to avoid being ambiguous, biased, or misleading. Moreover, the overall questionnaire must be properly organized with a full awareness that the order or placement of questions can influence, if not totally distort, the survey results. Finally, the investigator must be able to analyze and interpret the results and communicate them to the lawyer.

A knowledge of statistics and computers is also necessary. A community attitude study involves a probability sample. The investigator must assure that the sample is adequate to assure that the results provide accurate attitudinal and personal data reflective of the community as a whole. Moreover, the data obtained must be calculated, cross-checked, and analyzed to assure that it is usable for the intended purposes.

By no means least important, the investigator must be able to work with the attorney. The lawyer and the investigator must collaborate in developing the questions to be used in the survey. They must work together in evaluating the responses to the questions. In addition, the investigator must be able to assist the attorney in developing the best juror and worst juror profiles, in developing the questions to ask on voir dire, and in deciding which issues to communicate during voir dire and how to communicate them best. In short, they will be working closely together, and it is important that they are able to work together smoothly and effectively.

After some discussion with the investigator, the attorney should define the purpose of the study and assemble the relevant facts for the investigator as a prerequisite to formulating the questionnaire.

The investigator must understand the essential elements of the case as well as know the purpose of the study. Here the attorney bears the responsibility for communicating the relevant facts to the investigator and for defining the issues in the litigation. It may be possible to accomplish this during a conference. However, it may be necessary for the lawyer to prepare a written factual statement and possibly provide the investigator with significant exhibits and depositions. Whatever method is used, it is essential that the investigator be provided with the full facts of the case, including both its strengths and its weaknesses. The investigator must be fully familiar with the facts of the case and understand the issues before he or she begins to develop the questions for the questionnaire.

The heart of the survey is the questionnaire. The questions and their order are critical. No matter how scientifically correct or how artfully conducted, the survey will be a failure if the end product is not helpful and does not fulfill the specified purpose. While the investigator will develop the questions and structure the questionnaire, the attorney cannot avoid the task of reviewing the questionnaire and understanding why each question was included. Careful attention to this element of the survey preparation cannot be overemphasized.

Every trial attorney carefully analyzes his case before trial. In part, this analysis includes an effort to determine what type of person he wants on the jury and what type he wants to be sure to eliminate. Obviously, each attorney brings to this process his individual analysis of the particular case as well as personal prejudices and instincts.

Regardless of the type of personal injury case, most defense lawyers would be ecstatic with a jury of 60-year-old bank officers, insurance company officials, corporate executives, and accountants. Conversely, the plaintiff's lawyer in a child's injury case would love to see a jury of middle-class parents in their mid-30s who have young children and come from a racial or religious minority background. While you might not consciously put a numerical value on the different types of potential jurors, nonetheless, we all mentally grade these different types of jurors based on personal experience with demographic factors.

Of course, the factors of a particular case may alter the subjective evaluation of demographic factors. If the attorney is trying an admitted liability case involving the death of a corporate official earning in the six figure range, a jury of accountants and bank presidents might not be as unpleasant a prospect as it might be in a different liability case. In the admitted liability case, the jury will be asked to award damages based on the decedent's very high income and the spouse's high standard of living. In such a case, one might well want jurors who are willing to accept that high income level, the estate and country club level of living, and not be appalled at doing the arithmetic that demands a seven-figure verdict. The facts of the case can alter the instinctive evaluation.

How does the lawyer weave the community attitude survey data and evaluation into his selection process? In a sense the survey provides data and tends to impose a preselection consideration and discipline to the process.

It would be nice to develop an exact profile of the ideal juror and then have 12 ideal jurors appear and be seated without challenge. However, it is rare that even one ideal juror appears. A best and worst juror scale allows the attorney to predetermine the relative merit and weight to be given to various demographic factors that will likely exist for every juror. When the juror list is obtained, the juror scale can be used to make a preliminary evaluation of the panel for potentially good jurors. Maybe more important, the list can be used to highlight jurors who pose potential problems and must be examined with greater detail. Indeed, identifying potential problem jurors can be critical for conducting the actual voir dire, since you will know ahead which potential jurors must be questioned. You will also know the areas that must be explored either to establish a basis for challenge for cause or to satisfy yourself about the priorities for use of peremptory challenges.

A paralegal or associate counsel can do the numerical quantification using the predetermined scale. He or she can determine that one juror totals out as a "+4" and another as a "−3." But the ultimate decision to keep a juror or use a challenge remains with the trial lawyer.

The jury profile can point out areas of concern. It can alert counsel to hidden predictive factors. It can provide a basis for selection. But no survey and no simple scorecard will ever replace the instinct and gut reaction of an experienced and sensitive trial lawyer who is fully familiar with the intricacies of his case.

In the end, some lawyers use such homegrown bottom-line factors as "Would I like to have a beer with the juror after the trial?" or "Would I like to spend an evening with the juror?" or, maybe more tellingly, "Do I feel comfortable with the juror?"

In one study the indicators all called for a particular juror, a middle-aged Italian man, to be challenged. However, trial counsel felt that the man would be a good juror and that there was something appealing about him. The attorney decided to leave the juror on the panel. When polled, that juror wanted to award almost twice the average award. The lawyer's instinct had rebelled against the scientific study indicators, and his instinct was right. The lesson is that despite all the studies and all the "science," the trial lawyer should go with his own instinct and assessment.

The scientific survey and the scorecard are aids and guides. But they don't tell us all we need to know and they don't speak with exactitude or certainty. No one can understand all the factors that affect a juror. No study has yet been devised that can accurately predict how a juror will react to certain facts or the trial's development, or how he or she will ultimately vote. The community attitude survey helps by providing more information, more pointers, and more guidance. But the bottom line is, and must always remain, the instinct and experience of the trial lawyer.

§5.16 A Lawyer's Perspective on Use of the Community Attitude Assessment in Civil Cases to Support a Change of Venue Motion — Danny Cupit, Jackson, Mississippi

The use of community attitude surveys to support changes of venue in criminal trials because of adverse pretrial publicity or prejudicial community bias against the defendant is not new.

However, the growing acceptability of community attitude surveys as reliable evidence of a community's attitude has also brought an expansion of their use to support motions to change venue in civil trials.

The rule has been succinctly stated as follows:

> It has long been recognized as a general rule that a defendant, in order to establish a deprivation of due process, must show that potential jurors were actually prejudiced by the publicity. [Citations omitted.] This burden of proof requires a showing that community prejudice actually invaded the jury box infecting the opinions of the prospective jurors. [Citations omitted.] However, when the defendant proffers evidence of pervasive community prejudice in the form of highly inflammatory publicity or intensive media coverage, prejudice is presumed and there is no further duty to establish actual bias. [Citations omitted.][1]

It is against this backdrop that a motion to change venue in a civil action because of prejudicial pretrial publicity or community bias should be considered. The movant will be asking the court to discard the traditional use of voir dire to determine jury bias and to *presume* based upon the evidence presented that actual jury bias exists as a matter of law and voir dire would be useless.

In this context, the community attitude survey assumes a critical role. If it shows pervasive community bias, then, under the applicable law referred to above, actual juror bias may be presumed. If it does not or if its validity can be questioned, then such actual bias should not be presumed and the motion should be denied. The critical issue, therefore, in determining juror impartiality is not whether the juror was exposed to pretrial publicity, but whether such publicity has made such a deep impression as to close the juror's mind against evidence offered at trial or whether the juror exposed to such publicity can lay aside his or her opinion and render a verdict based on the evidence presented in court.

§5.16 [1]United States v. Capo, 595 F.2d 1086, 1090 (5th Cir. 1979).

For the trial attorney in a civil action to effectively resist a change of venue motion based in whole or in part upon evidence of a community attitude survey, it is absolutely essential that he or she (a) have a good working knowledge of the generally accepted standards used in conducting a valid study; (b) have a clear understanding of the purpose or objective of the study; (c) obtain a detailed and thorough analysis of the methods used in the particular study in issue; (d) thoroughly analyze the data obtained and the conclusions reached in the study in issue.

Presumably, if the defendant has gone to the trouble and expense of conducting a community attitude survey to support a motion to change venue,. the case is significant enough to justify the plaintiff's expenditure of resources to oppose it. It would be a fatal error to assume that spontaneous courtroom tactics will be effective enough to successfully resist a well prepared motion to change venue supported by a convincing community attitude survey. Preparation in opposition to the motion is essential.

Chapter 5 of this book provides a good source of information for the trial attorney to begin obtaining a working knowledge of the acceptable standards used in conducting community attitude surveys. However, it is also recommended that at an early stage of the preparation process in opposing a community attitude survey the attorney secure the services of an expert in the field of community attitude surveys to act not only as an advisor and consultant in preparation, but also as a potential expert witness to give opinion testimony at the hearing of the motion to change venue. Such an expert can provide valuable guidance to the trial attorney in the evaluation of the community attitude survey conducted to support the change of venue and point out weaknesses in the study. In all probability, it will be necessary for the attorney opposing the change of venue to offer opinion testimony at the hearing on the proper methods of conducting such a survey and on the weaknesses or invalidity of the survey offered to support the motion to change venue. The earlier the services of the expert can be secured, the more complete the preparation to oppose the motion to change venue and the analysis of the supporting survey can be.

Once a fundamental working knowledge of the principles involved in conducting a community attitude survey has been gained, the attorney opposing the motion should undertake broad discovery on all aspects of the community attitude survey that will be offered to support the motion. This is done to evaluate fully the adequacy of the procedures used in conducting the community attitude survey. Initially, counsel should seek to secure the production of various documents used in developing and conducting the community attitude survey. These documents include the training manuals prepared and used to train the interviewers, the actual questionnaires and responses given in the interviews, all working papers used by those actually conducting the survey, correspondence between those conducting the survey and the parties securing the services of the company conducting the survey, any contracts or memorandums of understanding concerning the employment of those conducting the community attitude survey, the actual survey itself when completed, and any other documents that might be probative of the methods used or the techniques followed in conducting the survey.

Secondly, efforts should be made to take the depositions of all persons who played a significant role in the conduct of the community attitude survey used to support the motion. It is important to note here that just because a particular individual's name appears on the finished product, it does not necessarily mean the survey is more accurate. Many times in this field, organizations holding themselves out as having expertise in this rapidly growing field are built around a well-known personality or a person with known expertise in polling, surveying techniques, or statistics. Such a person, however, may or may not have day-to-day involvement in the organization and may simply be lending his or her name to the organization in order to secure business. If that individual's name appears on the community attitude survey as a participant, it is important to establish what role he or she actually played in the preparation of the survey. Likewise, it is important to take depositions of everyone who was significantly involved in the process. Those who participated in the planning and development of the survey and prepared the overall objectives may not necessarily be the persons who coordinated or supervised the actual project to see that it was conducted in accordance with the goals and objectives of the survey. Additionally, there might be an overall project director, a person who conducts a general review of the finished product and participates in writing the final report but may or may not have been directly involved in conducting the survey. It is important to establish just who had responsibility for specific aspects of the survey and to ascertain their experience, background, and qualifications. Obviously, depositions of these individuals will be helpful not only to probe their knowledge of the project and quality of their work, but also to evaluate their experience as potential witnesses in court.

There also must be thorough discovery concerning the methodology used in conducting the survey and the procedures followed to insure the integrity of the finished product. A good working knowledge of the standards used in conducting a valid community survey is required in order to properly examine the deponent relative to matters concerning methodology.

An essential ingredient in the validity of any community attitude survey is accuracy in gathering and recording the data obtained in the surveys. Therefore, the procedures used in conducting the survey are of vital importance to insure that bias in the responses is minimized and that the responses are accurately recorded. For instance, were the questions asked in the survey pretested to determine if they suggested certain responses? Were the interviewers trained prior to conducting the interviews to insure that the questions were asked properly and the responses recorded properly? What were the skills and educational levels of the interviewers? Were they men or women? Were the responses written in ink or in pencil, which could be altered? Were the responses actually kept so they could be verified later, or have they been thrown away? Do the numerical calculations check out? Was the design of the questionnaire suggestive of responses?

If the accuracy of the survey cannot be established, then the reliability of its conclusions can be seriously questioned. If the methodology used and procedures followed do not insure valid and accurate results, then the validity of the entire survey can be put into serious doubt.

The nature and form of the questions themselves must be technically reliable before the answers given can be a reliable reflection of true opinion.[2] If the questions themselves are leading or otherwise suggest a response, then the reliability of the answer to the question can be put in doubt. Additionally, the order or sequence of the questions in the survey can frequently suggest an answer. As other chapters in this book more fully explain, proper methodology requires that such leading questions be eliminated to the maximum extent possible in order to insure the integrity of the survey technique.

Another critical area to be explored in the discovery process relates to the sample used in developing the survey. A community attitude survey by definition is a representative sampling of the attitudes of a larger group. A fundamental rule in the concept of sampling is that a sample is reflective only of the group surveyed, and the conclusions reached from the sample cannot be scientifically extended to other groups. Thus, it is important to understand specifically what group is being surveyed. For instance, a survey of women's attitudes toward the death penalty would not be accurately reflected in a sampling that included men. For the survey of women to be valid, the sample would have to exclude men from the group from which the sample was taken.

Since the community attitude survey used in the context of this chapter would normally be an attempt to survey the attitudes of potential jurors, then it is important for the sample to be drawn only from potential jurors in the jurisdiction in which the motion is filed. If the sample is drawn from groups that

[2] A. N. Oppenheim, Questionnaire Design and Attitude Measurement, chs. 2,3,5,6 (1966); R. L. Kahn & C. F. Cannell, The Dynamics of Interviewing, chs. 5,6 (1957); C. Backstrom & G. Hursh, Survey Research, ch. 3 (1963).

cannot be potential jurors, then there is a risk that the sample will not be random, nor will it be a pure sample of the group sought to be surveyed. Each federal court district is required by the Jury System Improvement Act of 1978, 28 U.S.C. §1861, et seq., to develop a jury plan that provides a method for selecting jurors to serve in the district. The plan excludes from the system all individuals who are disqualified from jury service by statute and that the court itself feels should be excluded from jury duty. A typical plan also designates certain groups of people who are excludable — that is, who may be excluded upon request, but are not automatically excluded. If the survey is to be of potential jurors, then it is important that the sample be drawn only from those who would qualify under the court's jury selection plan to serve as jurors in the case in which the motion is being filed. By way of example, convicted felons are normally excluded from jury service, as are individuals over 65 years of age, persons who cannot read or write, and nonresidents. If the sample is drawn from groups which include these individuals, then its validity can be questioned.

Similarly, if individuals who are eligible for jury duty are excluded from the sample pool for one reason or another, then the sample drawn is also subject to question. For example, individuals are normally eligible to serve on juries if they are 18 years of age or older. If the survey is of potential jurors but the sample is drawn only from persons 21 years of age or older, then a significant group has been excluded from the pool from which the sample has been drawn. Thus, extreme care should be given in determining what group is to be surveyed and what group the sample is drawn from. An otherwise valid community attitude survey which draws a sample from an improper group can be nullified.

Another fundamental requirement of the validity of the survey is the randomness in the sampling process. Most organizations conducting community attitude surveys have persons on their staff who are experienced in statistics and sampling and are sensitive to the need for the sampling process to be of a random nature. If the expert employed by the attorney resisting the change of venue motion does not possess expertise in the field of statistics and sampling, then it is important that the services of such an individual be secured to assist in evaluation of this aspect of the community attitude survey. Such expertise is critical to the survey since no valid statistical conclusions can be drawn from an improper sample or from a sample that does not insure randomness in its process.

After completion of discovery, it will be necessary to conduct a thorough analysis of the data obtained in the community attitude survey. It is essential that the data reflected in the finished report be accurately supported in the raw data obtained through discovery. The survey is simply the basis for the conclusions reached, and if the supporting data is not accurately compiled, then the validity of the conclusions can be undermined. Care should be taken to see that the mathematical computations in the tables reflected in the finished product are accurate. Also, the raw data developed in discovery should be reflected accurately in the tables in the finished product. If there are inaccuracies in the actual numbers, then in all probability the percentages relied upon in the conclusions will be erroneous. This tedious work can pay huge dividends if inaccuracies can be found, and it should not be presumed that a community attitude survey compiled in an attractive and heavily documented report carries with it the accuracy that is essential to the validity of the survey.

Finally, a thorough analysis of the conclusions reached in the survey must be undertaken. For the conclusions to be valid, they must be supported by the data in the survey. The experts secured to assist in opposing the community attitude survey can be of vital importance in assessing the conclusions reached. However, logic is probably the key element in comparing the conclusions reached with the supporting data.

CHAPTER

6

Trial Simulation

§6.0 In General

A trial simulation is an attempt to stage an upcoming trial in miniature. The major issues of a trial are capsulized to discover the reactions of prospective jurors to evidence and arguments that could be offered during the course of the trial. The issues included in the simulation can be modified to suit the needs of the attorneys. The trial simulation is primarily beneficial in civil cases where questions of liability are often debatable or confusing, or hinge on jurors' acceptance of expert opinions. Presenting the issues to *jurors* will best answer the question, "Is this case worthy of taking into court?" Although most commonly used in civil cases, trial simulations can also help in criminal cases when the issues are complex or if there is a choice of defense strategies.

Trial simulation can also be beneficial in the following ways: (1) determining the most desirable trial strategy, (2) measuring the effectiveness of opening and closing statements, (3) measuring the effectiveness of expert witnesses, (4) determining the value of various kinds of demonstrative evidence, (5) assessing the effectiveness of an attorney in the courtroom, (6) providing valuable data for evaluating the desirability of an out-of-court settlement, and (7) determining a profile of desirable and undesirable jurors.

§6.1 Preparing a Trial Simulation

The trial simulation might include voir dire, opening statements, presentation of witnesses and demonstrative evidence, closing arguments, instructions from the judge to the jury, and recorded juror deliberations. More often, a limited number of these elements is included since emphasis is given only to items of particular concern to the attorneys involved. For instance, if the effectiveness of the opening statement and closing argument are of major concern, the simulation could include opening statements presented by both sides, a synopsis of the testimony expected from witnesses, and the closing arguments. Jurors would then be asked to use this information to deliberate and reach a verdict.

While there is value in practicing an opening statement, closing argument, or trial strategy a month or two before the case is presented in court, having recordings and transcriptions of jury deliberations available for trial can be of particular value.

In the simulation, the trial attorney should present the case to four or five times as many jurors as would be seated for the actual trial. For instance, in a civil case where normally eight jurors would serve, the attorney should present the case to thirty-two individuals. These jurors should be divided into four panels, either by a voir dire process or by an evaluation of the demographic information that has been collected on each individual. One panel should comprise the most desirable of the thirty-two people serving as jurors, while another panel should be made up of the least desirable jurors. The other two panels probably will comprise those most like the real jury panel after peremptory challenges have been exercised. At the end of the presentation, each panel will go into a closed room and deliberate until a verdict is reached. The transcribed deliberations are then made available to the trial attorney. Combined with the measurements that have been taken by the principal investigator throughout the presentation of the trial simulation, the transcripts provide valuable information on how frequently and at what points a juror changed his or her mind during the course of the trial, what information or witnesses prompted that change, what the individual's evaluations were at the end of the simulation, and how this individual opinion or attitude altered during the course of jury deliberations.

Whenever possible, the simulation should be held in a courtroom in order to reproduce the awe and solemnity that most jurors feel in a courthouse. Use of an official courtroom also promotes a sense of seriousness about the trial simulation, thereby reducing any tendency toward levity caused by an awareness that the proceeding is not a *real* trial.

Often an educational facility such as the local law school will have a courtroom that can be rented or even used free of charge. Also, a courtroom at the local courthouse might be available for rent, especially if the judge in charge understands that general information gained could have an application beyond the particular case. In fact, judges are often concerned about the effectiveness of their instructions to juries. If instructions for the upcoming trial are to be tested during the simulation, most judges will be eager to cooperate by providing the setting for the trial simulation, or even to act as the presiding judge. It is a simple matter to include testing of the judge's instructions in the trial simulation.

§6.1.1 Personnel: Nonjurors

The essential personnel are as follows: prospective jurors, a judge, the plaintiff's attorney, the defense attorney, prospective witnesses (or tape recordings or deposition-like statements of such witnesses), the principal investigator, four group facilitators, and a transcriber.

The duties of the judge, plaintiff's attorney, defense attorney, and prospective witnesses are the same as in an actual trial. They will conduct the business of the trial in a professional manner and in keeping with the law of the jurisdiction, using a reduced (frequently a greatly reduced) amount of time to perform their functions.

The principal investigator will be primarily responsible for the following: (1) instructing the jurors as to their duties, (2) training the group facilitators, (3) providing transcriptions of the jury deliberations, (4) analyzing those jury deliberations, and (5) drawing the juror profile of the most and least desirable jurors. The principal investigator also will work with the lawyers in determining the time table of the simulation so that all the desired activities will proceed with maximum efficiency. The measurements and questionnaires to be filled out by the jurors during the trial simulation are constructed by the principal investigator.

A group facilitator will work with each of the four panels of prospective jurors. His or her responsibilities will include (1) collecting the jurors' background information, (2) collecting the measurements during the trial presentation, (3) acting as bailiff during jury deliberation, and (4) being responsible for the accurate recording of the jury deliberations. Generally, group facilitators need no special training but do need to have a sense of responsibility, a friendly appearance and demeanor, and the ability to listen and remain quiet during deliberations. This last quality is of particular importance since it is imperative that the facilitator remain apart from the circle of jurors, listen to the discussion without interruption or correction. This requirement may be difficult to adhere to when jurors are misunderstanding the law or are confused about testimony, but it must be respected.

The group facilitator also records the speaking order of the jurors to assist the transcriber in correctly assigning particular statements, since when a tape recorder is used for a 12-person jury, it can be difficult when listening to the tape to determine exactly which person made which statement. Court reporters may be used for maximum accuracy. The presence of a court reporter, however, openly recording everything said is much more inhibiting than a tape recorder. While a tape recording may make transcription more difficult, research shows that most people tend to forget its presence after a few minutes. It has the added advantage of providing paralanguage information (vocal cues such as pitch, tone, and intensity) that is lost in a court transcription.

The transcribers will be responsible for producing a script of the jurors' deliberations from the tape recordings or the court reporter's notes. The transcriber needs typing accuracy, speed, and (when a tape recording is used) a good ear for hearing the differences between voices.

§6.1.2 Personnel: Jurors

The jurors are the most important ingredient in determining the success and accuracy of a trial simulation. For this reason, they must reflect the profile of typical persons in the community who serve on trial juries. While it is easy to put together a panel of law and college students or professors, social workers, and ministers because they are interested in the educational aspects of participating in such a communication experiment, such jurors would not be representative of the attitudes of persons in a community most likely to serve on a trial jury.

The first requirement for persons who will serve on a trial simulation panel is that they be qualified to serve on a jury in the particular community; they should meet the citizenship, age, and occupational requirements for the district or community. Second, they should be unfamiliar with the lawyers, the case, the witnesses, and the plaintiff or defendant. Third, they should be willing participants who fully understand the process and accept it as a method of pretrial preparation. It is best to have the jurors sign a statement of consent that indicates that they have been given the appropriate amount of background information and that they understand the purpose of the trial simulation. Fourth, the jurors should be paid for their participation in the study, according to the amount paid for actual jury service in the area. This is an important consideration since payment for the simulation jurors' time will increase their sense of involvement and responsibility. It is advisable that the compensation be below minimum wage since overpayment could affect the jurors' objectivity and cause them to identify with the person who is the source of payment. Overidentification with one side or the other will build a bias into

Form 6-1
Juror's Trial Simulation Consent Form

Decision Making Studies

By ______________________________
(*Name of researcher*)

____
(*Address*)

____
(*City, State, Zip*)

____
(*Telephone*)

I agree to participate in a communication research study conducted by ________________, Communication Specialist.

The purpose of this study is to determine what kind of information or evidence is most helpful in helping people to reach a decision.

The format utilized in the study is a simulation of a trial since the verdict reached by a jury is a real life situation in which strangers come together to reach consensus on a question.

The information used in this trial simulation is derived from an actual case which has not yet been tried in a court.

The results of this evening's study (1) will be used in a long-range study over cases and time concerning the decision-making process and (2) will be made available to the people involved in providing the information.

(*Signed*)______________________________

(*Date*)______________________________

the study that will undermine the accuracy of the trial simulation as a tool for making predictions about the actual jury.

If the use of volunteers is necessary to make the trial simulation financially feasible, they should be carefully screened so that a rating can be assigned to the depth and strength of each volunteer's biases. Volunteers are assumed to be biased by whatever compels them to offer their services. Their use is not recommended, however, since it is difficult to effectively insure against biases and since using volunteers makes it impossible to generalize information to form accurate profiles of the most and least desirable jurors.

The jurors will be asked to perform the following acts: (1) listen to the proceedings, (2) respond to the questionnaire and record their thinking process on measurement instruments provided to them by the principal investigator, and (3) deliberate as a panel until they reach a unanimous decision or until the end of a prespecified time period.

The number of jurors needed depends on both the size of the panel that will actually try the case in court and the number of jury panels to be used in the simulation. Four jury panels are usually recommended with three recording and one listening jury. Since the listening jury listens but does not record measurements, it is the most like the jury that will be used during the actual trial. The simulation judge will instruct the panels to listen to the evidence with an open mind and to avoid reaching a decision until they have heard all the evidence presented. The use of a listening jury simulates more accurately an actual trial jury and helps assess the effect that recording responses at each stage of the simulation has on the final verdict.

Persons on the three recording juries will respond to a questionnaire or other measurement instrument at the end of each presentation made during the trial simulation. This provides a full record of when the jurors begin to reach or alter their decisions.

§6.1.3 Basic Sources of Jurors

Frequently, the most difficult part of planning a trial simulation is obtaining appropriate jurors. It is best to assign one person to this task. The best source of jurors is, of course, the current jury wheel. However, access to this source requires cooperation from court officers, which, unfortunately, can be difficult to obtain. There are reasons the judge might cooperate: (1) a desire to see the case settled out-of-court, (2) a willingness to view the simulation an educational experience, (3) a desire to test the effectiveness of jury instructions, or (4) an interest in comparing his or her evaluation of the desired verdict with those of the simulation jury. Seldom is the court willing to risk contaminating the current jury pool by asking members to participate in a trial simulation. However, the judge might be willing to ask for volunteers from a jury panel that is concluding service, or may make lists of past jury panels available. These individuals can be contacted by mail or telephone to be given an explanation of the trial simulation process and be asked to participate as jurors.

In cases where the lawyer does not want to approach the court to seek cooperation in securing jurors, there are three other approaches to obtaining jurors: (1) advertising, (2) contacting persons on prior jury lists without the knowledge of the court, and (3) seeking the cooperation of civic, religious, or special interest groups within the community.

§6.1.4 Advertising for Jurors

Advertising for jurors can be productive. An advertisement seeking participation in a study could be placed in the local newspaper or shopper paper. If the ad is placed in the classified advertising section of the newspaper, it should be placed under both help wanted and personals. If only the help wanted section is used, it is likely that too many of the applicants will be unemployed and the panel will be skewed. Similarly, if only the personals section is used, single and divorced people may dominate the panel, which would also skew the results.

A typical advertisement would read as follows:

> PARTICIPANTS WANTED: We need participants for a communication study in decisionmaking on Saturday, July 20, starting at 9:00 A.M. No special skills required. Your reward will be

> an interesting experience and $20 in compensation. Phone 555-5555 betweeen 3:00 P.M. and 9:00 P.M. Sunday or after 6:00 P.M. Monday-Wednesday. Phone 555-1555 during business hours.

The best time to run the ad is on the Sunday morning and either two days before or two days after. This should be sufficient to secure enough applicants from which to make the final choice.

When applicants answer the ad, they are given an information sheet like form 6-2.

Form 6-2
Basic Participant Information Form

My name is ____________________ and I am a research assistant for ____________________ who is working on a human projects research problem. *(Name)* is in charge of the research project. This project will be examining how people work together in processing information to arrive at a decision. The purpose of the study is to determine what kind of information or evidence is the most useful in helping people actually reach a decision. The format used in the study is a simulation of a trial since the verdict reached by a jury is a real-life situation in which strangers come together to reach consensus on a question. The information used in this trial simulation is derived from an actual case that has not been tried yet in court.

You will not, of course, be exposed to all of the information to that case. The case is expected to take *(length of time)* when it is presented in court and you will be listening to only three hours of information and evidence. As you listen to the information and evidence presented, you will be asked to make certain evaluations of how useful or how important the information is in helping you reach a decision. Then, after the three-hour courtroom presentation, you will be placed in a jury-like group and you will deliberate as a group to reach a decision. We will tape-record these deliberations. The results of Saturday morning's study will be used in two ways: first, it will be used by *(name)* in a long-range study over cases and time concerning the jury decision-making process, and, second, some of the information will be made available to the individuals involved in providing the case information. If you are selected as a participant, you may also have the information made available to you in summary form at the cost of the printing and mailing charges.

Now that you have heard a little more about the project, are you interested in working with us as a participant in the study?

Good! There is some information that I must have from you.

PARTICIPANT INFORMATION SHEET

Name			
Address			
Age			
Marital Status			
Occupation			
Spouse's Occupation			
Highest Level of Education			
Prior Court Experience			
Association with Legal or Medical Profession			
Telephone No.			

Thank you. ___*(Name)*___ will be arriving on Thursday at which time the final participants will be selected and notified. ___*(Name)*___ will be looking for a cross-section of the population — in other words, people of all ages, backgrounds, and experiences, much as you would find in a true jury situation. I do hope that you will be one of those who will be working with us on Saturday morning. Where can I reach you Thursday evening?

Participants will be selected from the list of persons who have answered the ad in such a way that the range of age, marital status, and occupation will be varied. These participants are called back and told where and when to go for the simulation.

§6.1.5 Other Sources of Jurors

Prior jury lists are a good secondary source of jurors. People on such lists can be contacted by phone or mail to explain to them the trial simulation process. While the explanation should be general enough to avoid creating a bias, it should be specific enough to identify the project, build interest in it, and obtain willing and knowing cooperation. Again, both pay and interesting experience should be stressed as the reward for participation. Care should be taken to avoid including persons who have been repeatedly excluded from jury service. If a person has been struck from a jury panel several times, that person is not representative of persons who serve on actual juries and therefore should not be considered for the simulation.

The attorney might decide that neither advertisements or jury lists are workable methods for a specific case in a particular locality. It might then be feasible and logical to work with civic, religious, or special interest group leaders to secure possible jurors. If this method is chosen, past jury lists should be analyzed to identify persons most likely to be represented on a jury drawn from the locality. Such an examination might suggest that housewives, retired people, farmers, union members, and employees of a large local industry constitute three-fourths of jurors actually seated for recent trials. The principal investigator or representative of the lawyer (whoever is most likely to be able to secure cooperation) should then contact the leaders of the groups that represent these people. The local unions, Parent Teacher Association, Association of Retired People, senior citizens' center, and personnel section of the local large industry might be good places to start. The leaders of such groups would be asked to suggest the names of people who might be willing to help out on a special project. The project should be explained in a way that avoids creating a bias toward one side of a case or the other. The people so identified would then be contacted, informed of the project, and asked to participate. They might also be asked to identify a friend or acquaintance who would like to participate. That friend can then be contacted and interviewed to see if he or she would be a suitable participant. Friends, however, should not be placed on the same jury panel in the trial simulation. While this method is the least desirable way of putting together a list of jurors, it can be used if particular care is taken.

§6.2 Conducting the Simulation

Once jurors have been selected, arrangements have been made for the use of a courtroom, and personnel have been trained, the simulation is ready to start. At this point, the attorneys become responsible for the major part of the work. While the communication researcher can structure the simulation, all of the information that is included must come from the attorneys. One of the attorneys will represent the plaintiff and the other the defendant. Since the simulation forces all of the trial information to be presented to the mock jury in a limited amount of time, the attorneys must turn their attention to determining what evidence to present. They must also determine the minimum amount of time in which it will be feasible to present opening statements and closing arguments. Time must be allowed for the work of the communication researcher who will be taking measurements at intervals throughout the trial. Each measurement takes from one to two minutes, depending on the questions.

§6.2.1 Structuring Simulation Time

The attorneys really have two or three highly viable simulation structures within which they can work. The most common approach is to conduct the trial simulation in one evening or afternoon, which means that the total presentation from the time the participants arrive until the end of jury deliberations must be limited to four or five hours. A second approach, one preferred for especially complex trials that are expected to last a long time, is the two-day simulation. With this approach the trial is simulated on one evening and jurors return the next evening for the deliberation process. The closing arguments and the judge's instructions could be part of the second evening's presentation.

A typical schedule for a single evening trial simulation follows.

6:30 P.M.	Participants arrive at the courthouse and are greeted by the principal investigator and group facilitators. They are escorted to the courtroom and assigned positions on the four panels, based on the information contained on the initial questionnaire concerning attitudes toward case-related issues. The participants then sign informed consent forms and are instructed on procedures for the evening's presentation.
7:00 P.M.	Judge presents basic case information and gives instructions on juror behavior.
7:10 P.M.	Opening statement by plaintiff's attorney.
7:40 P.M.	Opening statement by defense attorney.
8:00 P.M.	Witness statement: plaintiff; cross-examination.
8:05 P.M.	Witness statement: police officer who was at the scene; cross-examination.
8:10 P.M.	Witness statement: eyewitness; cross-examination.
8:15 P.M.	Witness statement: accident reconstruction expert; cross-examination. Introduction of demonstrative evidence: scene models.

8:20 P.M.	Witness statement: plaintiff's doctor; cross-examination.
8:25 P.M.	Witness statement: physical therapist; cross-examination. Introduction of demonstrative evidence: film on a day in the life of the plaintiff (7 minutes).
8:35 P.M.	Witness statement: defendant; cross-examination.
8:40 P.M.	Witness statement: defense expert on accident reconstruction; cross-examination.
8:45 P.M.	Closing argument: plaintiff's attorney.
9:10 P.M.	Closing argument: defense attorney.
9:25 P.M.	Judge's instructions.
9:30 P.M.	Posttrial questionnaire filled out by all jurors.
9:35 P.M.	Break.
9:50 P.M.	Juror deliberations begin and are tape recorded.
10:55 P.M.	(Earlier if jurors have reached a unanimous verdict.) After-verdict questionnaire completed; jurors are paid; tapes of the deliberations are collected.

§6.2.2 Presenting Witnesses

Witnesses can be presented to the jury in several different ways. A videotaped statement or tape recording accompanied by a picture can be played for the jurors. The simplest method, which is in many ways just as effective as taped testimony, is the use of a deposition. Because most jurors have reached a decision by the end of the opening statements — if not before — many simulations only include voir dire, the introduction of the parties, and the opening statements. If the attorneys have no desire to test the effectiveness of closing arguments, this approach adequately presents the issues in the case and obtains jurors' reactions to the hinge issues[1] involved in the case.

Again, all of the information that is included in the trial simulation must come from the attorneys involved. This gives them an opportunity to do a shortened dry run of the case before they have to place the case before an actual jury. As with any rehearsal, there are untold benefits to be had from the additional general preparation as well as from the opportunity to smooth rough edges from the presentation of the opening statement and the closing argument.

§6.3 Simulation Measures

The measures used to evaluate witnesses, opening statements, closing arguments, and physical evidence in the trial simulation are of three types: (1) multiple choice questions, (2) open-ended questions, and (3) semantic differentials. Multiple choice questions are used as often as possible for easier recording and analysis of the mock jurors' responses. However, open-ended questions provide the greatest amount of insight into the working of the jurors' minds by allowing the jurors to give their personal reactions to various elements of the simulation.

The semantic differential is a communication research device used for measuring meaning as it is perceived. It is measured on a graduated scale that falls between two adjectives of opposite meaning. The scale is divided into nine grades (sometimes seven) that are given artificial values from 1 to 9 with 9 representing the highest value. Due to the averaging process, the extremes of 1 and 9 will seldom occur. Therefore, when 9 is the highest value on a scale, a value of 7.5 or higher should be perceived as high, while a value of 2.5 or lower would be perceived as low. Each measure should have two scales for report-

§6.2 [1]"Hinge issue" is a term for an issue that will cause the case to swing one way or the other.

ing results. The first will chart the individual responses of all jurors who participated in the trial simulation. The second will chart the average responses for jurors who found liability, as opposed to the average response for those who did not, plus an average for all respondents. The individual response scale is intended to provide a check for consistency. The scales will need to be compared to see if the individual responses are averaging out because extremes responses or if the responses are fairly varied. For instance, a response of several 9s and several 1s will average out to 5, whereas several 4s and 6s will also average out to 5. If the pattern were of the extremes of 9s and 1s, it would be valuable to know why such extreme responses were given. Such a pattern may indicate that bias or prejudice is at work.

Measures are taken at all four stages of the trial simulation process: (1) presimulation, (2) trial simulation, (3) predeliberation, and (4) postdeliberation.

§6.3.1 *Presimulation Measures*

The presimulation measures include signing the consent form, if that has not already been done; answering questions that would indicate attitude or life experience relevant to the hinge issues of the trial; and giving demographic information (age, sex, marital status, occupation, spouse's occupation, level of education, religious affiliation, and other information of interest as well as information that is reported on the local juror information sheet). Usually the questions concerning attitudes, life experiences, and demographic information are included in one questionnaire referred to as the General Information Sheet. A sample of a General Information Sheet is shown in form 6-3.

§6.3.2 *Trial Simulation Measures*

At the end of each event in the mock trial, including voir dire, the opening statement, presentation by a witness or pre-

Form 6-3
General Information Sheet

PARTICIPANT NO._____

NAME____________________________________ Age_______ Sex_____
Address_________________________________ Phone No.__________
Marital Status________________Occupation________________
Spouse's Occupation____________________________________
Number of children, their sex and ages______________________
What is highest education level you achieved?________________
What church are you affiliated with?______________________
How long have you resided in your community?________________
Do you own or rent your home?___________________________
Would you say that you are usually (a) a happy person, (b) an unhappy person, or (c) somewhere in between?_______
When you ride an escalator, do you usually let it (a) carry you along or (b) walk with it?________________________________
When people break a rule or law, should they be punished?_______
In your opinion, do people "get off" too easily today when they are charged with a crime?________________________________
Do you think the courts are usually too liberal in their sentencing?____
Do you think violence is increasing in America today?__________
Have you ever been in court?_______ If yes, in what way?_______

____

Have you ever been involved in a lawsuit?_______ If yes, in what way? Witness, plaintiff, juror, defendant, or other?___________

____

Are you active in politics?_______ Are you registered to vote?_______
Are you associated in any way with an insurance company?_______
What is the largest amount of money you spent (or committed yourself to spend) at one time?________________________

____

What crime do you believe is most serious in your community today?____
In your opinion, which crime is worst? _____child abuse
_____murder _____robbery

sentation of physical evidence, a measure of reaction should be taken from members of the recording juries. Each one of the following measures can be adapted to fit the specific needs of the attorneys conducting the simulation. The measures used to evaluate the attorney's opening statement and closing argument should be similar so that direct comparisons can be made concerning the effectiveness of these two elements in regard to the verdict. A sample of the measure that would be used to evaluate an opening statement or a closing argument is shown in form 6-4.

Form 6-4
Measure for Opening Statement

At this point, I think the lawyer is

	9	8	7	6	5	4	3	2	1	
fair	___	___	___	___	___	___	___	___	___	unfair
emotional	___	___	___	___	___	___	___	___	___	unemotional
logical	___	___	___	___	___	___	___	___	___	illogical
honest	___	___	___	___	___	___	___	___	___	dishonest
warm	___	___	___	___	___	___	___	___	___	cold
calm	___	___	___	___	___	___	___	___	___	excited
impressive	___	___	___	___	___	___	___	___	___	unimpressive
sincere	___	___	___	___	___	___	___	___	___	insincere
believable	___	___	___	___	___	___	___	___	___	unbelievable
effective	___	___	___	___	___	___	___	___	___	ineffective
intelligent	___	___	___	___	___	___	___	___	___	dumb

At this point, I _____ understand the issues, _____ am confused about the issues, _____ have no opinion.

At this point, I favor the plaintiffs _____very strongly, _____strongly, _____somewhat, _____weakly, _____not at all.

At this point, I believe the defendant is liable: _____yes _____no

The advice I would most like to give this attorney is

____

Measures used to evaluate the effectiveness of each witness can differ for lay and expert witnesses. At the end of each standard form specific questions can be asked that will help to assess the witness's information and presentation style. A standard measure for the evaluation of witnesses, either lay or expert, is shown in form 6-5.

Form 6-5
Witness Measure

I found this witness to be

very helpful in reaching decision	__	__	__	__	__	__	__	__	__	not at all helpful in reaching decision
	9	8	7	6	5	4	3	2	1	
sincere	__	__	__	__	__	__	__	__	__	insincere
logical	__	__	__	__	__	__	__	__	__	illogical
believable	__	__	__	__	__	__	__	__	__	unbelievable
biased	__	__	__	__	__	__	__	__	__	unbiased
effective	__	__	__	__	__	__	__	__	__	ineffective
honest	__	__	__	__	__	__	__	__	__	dishonest
intelligent	__	__	__	__	__	__	__	__	__	dumb
very impressive	__	__	__	__	__	__	__	__	__	not at all impressive

At this point, I favor the plaintiff _____very strongly, _____strongly, _____somewhat, _____weakly, _____not at all.

At this point, I believe the defendants are liable _____yes _____no.

I would like the following questions answered:_________________________

____

This witness would be better if_________________________________

____

Additional comments:_____________________________________

____

It is important to evaluate exactly how jurors react to different types of physical evidence — a film, a mock-up of the accident scene, a series of drawings or models, the vehicle itself or its parts. All of these can be evaluated for their impact on the jury. While the measure of physical evidence is the one that many attorneys often elect to exclude from the trial simulation, it is advisable to have some type of evaluation of physical evidence. Inclusion of this measure could be an extremely important part of the trial simulation even though it generally does not add much time to the presentation. A standard measure for the evaluation of physical evidence is illustrated in form 6-6.

Form 6-6
Physical Evidence Measure

I found that seeing this physical evidence

	9	8	7	6	5	4	3	2	1	
helped me to understand	___	___	___	___	___	___	___	___	___	only confused me
impressed me	___	___	___	___	___	___	___	___	___	did not impress me
made it more believable	___	___	___	___	___	___	___	___	___	did not aid in making it more believable
was effective support for the witness's testimony	___	___	___	___	___	___	___	___	___	was not effective support for the witness's testimony
was very helpful to me in reaching a decision	___	___	___	___	___	___	___	___	___	was not at all helpful to me in reaching a decision

was necessary to the case	— — — — — — — — — —	was not necessary to the case

This evidence would have been more effective if

____

____

____

The trial simulation ends with the judge giving the standard instructions expected to be used in the actual trial. It is essential to measure the mock jurors' reactions to the judge's instructions, for it is well known that certain authoritarian or rigid personality types are very responsive to judicial instructions and are inclined to follow the law to the letter. A standard measure that is used to do this is shown in form 6-7.

Form 6-7
Measure of Reaction to Judge's Instructions

My understanding of the law of the case as it has been given by the judge:

_____ has not changed my feeling about the case.
_____ has totally changed my feeling about the case.
_____ has modified my feeling about the case.
_____ other (specify) ______________________________

State below what effect on your decision-making process the instructions from the judge have had on you.

____

____

____

Do you understand the instructions? _____yes _____no
_____most of them _____all except the one about: ____________

§6.3.3 Predeliberation Measure

Before the jury begins its deliberations, every juror, including members of the listening jury, should fill out a measure. This will provide a basis for the evaluation of how the deliberation process affects the individual's final decision. A standard measure for these reactions is shown in form 6-8.

The first two end-of-presentation questions have proven particularly useful in civil cases. These two questions allow an analysis of how the jurors have changed their minds during presentation of arguments and evidence. Frequently, there are dramatic shifts of opinion when new evidence is introduced.

One of the greatest values of this measure is that it indicates the impact of bias on each juror in reaching the final verdict. It has been found that jurors who favor the plaintiff strongly or very strongly at the end of opening statements will often return a verdict that favors the plaintiff. Likewise, jurors who favor the plaintiff barely or not at all at the end of opening statements will often return a verdict in favor of the defendant.

Jurors without a particular opinion are the ones most likely to be affected by attorneys' arguments or information presented

Form 6-8
End-of-Presentation Measure

At this point, I favor the plaintiff:

____ very strongly
____ strongly
____ somewhat
____ weakly
____ not at all

At this point, I believe that the defendant is liable:

____ yes ____ no

Since I found the defendant liable, the dollar amount that I would award to the plaintiff is $________

Even though I do not find the defendant liable, if I were to award a dollar amount for this injury/suffering, I would award $________

through witnesses. At the end of the trial, these three groups (those who favor the plaintiff, those who favor the defendant, and those who initially do not have a strong opinion) can be divided by demographics and analyzed to develop profiles of the most and least desirable jurors.

§6.3.4 *Postdeliberation Measure*

After the verdict measure has been taken, the four different juries are taken to individual rooms to deliberate and decide on verdicts. These deliberations are tape-recorded and monitored by the group facilitator.

After the juries have completed their deliberations, the jurors are asked to fill out a final form that evaluates the overall simulation process. Once that is done they will receive payment for the participation. The types of questions that may be included in this measure are shown in form 6-9.

Form 6-9
Postverdict Measure

1. I am satisfied with the decision reached by my group:
   _____yes _____somewhat _____no
2. In my group, I was given opportunity to express myself fully:
   _____yes _____somewhat _____no
3. I changed my opinion a lot since I marked my decision concerning liability and award after the testimony of the plaintiff:
   _____yes _____no
4. Listening to the comments and arguments of the other jurors was important to me in reaching the final verdict:
   _____very important _____important _____somewhat important _____not at all important
5. Rank the items below from 1, the most important in helping you reach your decision, to 5, the least important:

   _____ opening statement by plaintiff's attorney
   _____ opening statement by defendant's attorney

_____ information provided by witnesses
_____ physical evidence
_____ information provided by plaintiff

6. The single most important fact to me was ________________
7. What information would you have liked to know that was not presented to you?
8. What information was presented that you now feel was unimportant or not essential?
9. Was information presented during the trial simulation that you now think was dishonest, biased, unfair, or incomplete?
   _____yes _____no
   If yes, please specify:
10. Which lawyer was the most effective?
11. On what do you base your last answer?

§6.4 Sample Results from Simulation Measurements

Suppose that a trial simulation has been conducted for the plaintiff's attorney in a liability lawsuit concerning a defective door latch on a truck. The plaintiff is now a paraplegic. The accident occurred after a Christmas party where plaintiff Mr. Denny Mindon, a 29-year-old auto mechanic, had partaken of several drinks.

§6.4.1 Opening Statements Measure

The first measure considered is a comparison of the effectiveness of opposing attorneys at the completion of their opening statements. Examination of table 6-1 indicates that there was very little difference in the overall averages for all respondents in the way they evaluated the two attorneys. The attor-

Table 6-1
Comparison of Attorneys at Completion of Opening Statements

	Average for those who find liability		*Average for those who do not find liability*		*Average for all respondents*	
	Plaintiff attorney	*Defense attorney*	*Plaintiff attorney*	*Defense attorney*	*Plaintiff attorney*	*Defense attorney*
Fair	8.2	7.3	6.3	7.7*	7.3	7.6
Emotional	7.0	5.0*	8.3	5.4*	7.7	5.3*
Logical	7.8	7.3	5.8	8.0*	6.8	7.8*
Honest	8.5	7.3*	7.8	7.8	8.2	7.7
Warm	8.5	7.0*	7.3	7.4	7.8	7.3
Calm	7.8	7.7	7.6	8.2	7.8	8.1
Impressive	8.2	7.0*	7.0	8.1*	7.6	7.9
Sincere	8.8	7.3*	6.8	8.0*	7.6	7.8
Believable	8.8	7.7*	7.2	8.0	8.0	7.9
Effective	8.3	7.3*	6.8	8.0*	7.6	7.8

1 = lowest possible score
9 = highest possible score
* = significant differences

ney for the plaintiff received above average scores in every area, except that the logic of his argument was only found to be average. The defense attorney received above average scores in every area, except that he was only average in displaying emotion. However, when the groups are broken down into those who found liability at the end of the simulation and those who did not, there are several significant differences that stand out.[1] The group that found liability believed that the attorney for the plaintiff was significantly more emotional, honest, warm, impressive, sincere, believable, and effective than the defense

§6.4 [1] A "significant difference" statistically indicates that conclusions could be drawn that would allow a final outcome to be predicted.

attorney. Those who found the defendant not liable, believed that the defense attorney was significantly more fair, logical, impressive, sincere, effective, and significantly less emotional than the plaintiff's attorney. These measures imply that each juror brought into the jury box prejudices that acted as a filter through which opening statements were processed. Such findings should reinforce the importance of voir dire and of determining the level of prejudice within each juror at the beginning of the trial.

In addition to being requested to compare the two opening statements, the participants were asked the following question: "Now that you have heard opening statements by both sides, what issues in the case are uppermost in your mind?"

Juror 1: After listening to the defense, I have found out that Mr. Mindon had been drinking before the accident and that he had been in a more complicated accident than his attorney had stated.

Juror 2: Why didn't he have his seat belt fastened? Didn't he check to see if the door was closed? Why didn't they call an ambulance after the accident? Why was he moved after he was thrown from his car before the ambulance could get there? Was there danger of fire? It seems to me that there was a lot about this accident, both before and after, that hasn't been explained to us.

Juror 3: Why weren't we told earlier that Mr. Mindon was drinking?

Juror 4: Had Mindon been drinking enough to cloud his judgment and his action? Does he really remember whether or not he closed the door?

Juror 5: Did Mindon really close the door or did he close it only partially? I also have a real question: Can a truck "fishtail" and go into a ditch, etc., at 20 miles an hour?

Juror 6: Amount of alcohol drunk? The speed of truck on the road? Did friend injure Denny by moving him? Did the injury occur inside the car before he was thrown out or after he was thrown out or when he was being moved?

Juror 7: Whose responsibility is it to prove that the door latch was defective? Was this the only time the door failed? Isn't it strange that it would fail only after a Christmas party when he had been drinking?

Juror 8: Who designs a door latch? Who's responsible for the design? What was Mindon's condition at the time of the accident?

Juror 9: Did Denny ultimately cause all of his own problems?

Juror 10: Denny stopped his truck to talk to a friend. He most likely left hurriedly and neglectfully in getting back into his truck.

Juror 11: Even if the company made a defective door latch, should they have to support an injured person the rest of their life? Maybe [they] should just pay the medical bills. He gambled and lost by not wearing a seat belt. Why wasn't there an ambulance called? How was he driving? How much did he have to drink? What time was the accident? How many miles was he from his work place at the time of the accident? What was his blood alcohol content at the time of the accident?

Juror 12: If the lock was defective and the fact Denny might have had serious injuries anyway because of him not wearing a seat belt and if the door was properly latched [sic]. No person should be awarded money only because a big corporation has a lot of money. Every person is responsible for his own safety to a great degree. If we don't care for our own safety and take all necessary precautions, why should a big corporation?

From the preceding comments it is obvious that the attorney for the plaintiff broke one of the primary rules concerning opening statements: If there is a fact that can hurt you, be certain that you are the one to reveal it to the jury. The jurors' comments reveal that the attorney for the plaintiff should have gone into greater detail about the facts surrounding the accident. He should have revealed that his client had been drinking at a Christmas party prior to the accident. The speed of Mindon's car and any fishtailing that occurred also should have been explored and explained.

§6.4.2 *Evaluating Witnesses*

The effectiveness of witnesses can be evaluated by examining jurors' reactions as indicated on the measure for each witness. Table 6-2 allows for comparisons of overall reactions. Comments offered by the jurors are also recorded.

Randall Kedwich, the plaintiff's expert who testified that the latch was defective, was not well received by the majority of the jurors. The jurors' comments reveal that he was dull, boring, and not believable. His examination of a latch similar to the one on Mindon's car was not impressive. The jurors wanted to know why he had not examined the car latch on Mindon's car. No explanation was offered on this point.

The ratings offered by each juror are added and then averaged. These averages, especially when compared to the final verdict, are highly revealing. As shown in table 6-3, jurors who found liability had a positive overall reaction to the expert, unlike those jurors who rejected liability. Since the majority of the jurors (ten jurors out of twelve) did not find liability and were negative in their evaluation of this key witness, it is important to note their ratings and opinions.

Both the pro-liability and the no-liability groups viewed the expert as logical and unemotional. However, the no-liability group found him unimpressive, unhelpful in reaching a decision, biased, relatively ineffective, and barely believable.

Witnesses are also compared according to their ratings on the postdeliberation measure. Each juror was asked to rate the witnesses for importance to the case and their credibility. The evaluation of the importance of witnesses as illustrated in table 6-4 shows one major problem facing the plaintiffs. Six witnesses were evaluated in the trial simulation, three of which (Denny Mindon, Mrs. Mindon, and Dr. Dalton) supported the compensation aspect of the case. The passenger, Steven Roberts, and the plaintiff's expert, Kedwich, were the liability witnesses. The defense presented one witness, Dee Wojowski. From studying the table, it is obvious that the jurors who found liability were most influenced by the compensation witnesses. Not only were those witnesses ranked high for their impor-

Table 6-2
Witness Evaluation
Expert Witness, Randall Kedwich

	Participant[1] number	*Very impressive*	*Very helpful in reaching decision*	*Emotional*	*Logical*	*Believable*	*Biased*	*Effective*	*Technical aspects understandable*	*More clarification*	*Favor plaintiff[2]*	*Find liability*
Recording Jury 1	1	3	5	5	7	4	7	3	Yes	No	W	No
	2	6	5	4	9	5	7	5	Yes	No	NAA	No
	3	9	9	3	8	9	3	9	Yes	No	S	Yes
	4	5	5	1	8	7	9	6	Yes	No	W	No
	5	8	5	2	8	8	8	8	Yes	Yes	SW	No
	6	4	3	3	6	4	8	5	Yes	No	W	No
Recording Jury 2	7	5	2	1	9	9	9	1	No	Yes	SW	No
	8	8	5	1	8	8	8	8	Yes	Yes	SW	No
	9	6	9	3	8	7	2	6	Yes	No	W	Yes
	10	1	1	1	7	4	9	2	No	No	NAA	No
	11	5	4	5	9	9	9	7	No	No	W	No
	12	3	4	3	6	7	7	5	Yes	Yes	W	No

[1]*Comments:*

Juror 1. Mr. Kedwich should have had contact with Mr. Mindon and his latch system.

Juror 2. How many doors and mechanisms were tested?

Juror 6. Kedwich was boring. Part of his information was useful.

Juror 7. Photo was of more help than explanation — there should have been more examination of Mindon vehicle.

Juror 9. The latch could have been open due to a mechanical problem — it is hard to determine.

Juror 10. This witness is not at all convincing and checking a purchased door-lock system has nothing to do with one in accident (a waste of time). I think Kedwich is not speaking the truth.

Juror 11. Isn't it strange that the only time Mindon's latch didn't work was after he'd been drinking at a Christmas party? Why didn't Kedwich check the Mindon latch?

[2]*Key:* Favor Plaintiff:
VS = very strongly
S = strongly
SW = somewhat
W = weakly
NAA = not at all

Table 6-3
Group Comparison of Witness Evaluations

Attribute	*Averages for those who found liability*	*Averages for those who did not find liability*	*Averages for all respondents*
Impressive	7.5	4.8	5.3
Helpful in reaching decision	9.0	3.9	4.8
Emotional	3.0	2.6	2.7
Logical	8.0	7.9	7.9
Believable	8.0	6.5	6.8
Biased	2.5	8.1	7.2
Effective	7.5	5.0	5.4

Table 6-4
Importance of Witnesses in Determining Final Decision

	*Importance ranking**		*Credibility rating***	
	Jurors who found liability	*Jurors who did not find liability*	*Jurors who found liability*	*Jurors who did not find liability*
Denny Mindon	2	2	7.3	5.1
Mrs. Mindon	4	4	6.9	5.8
Passenger	4	4	6.8	5.1
Plaintiff expert, Mr. Kedwich	3	4	6.5	5.0
B. D. Dalton, M.D.	1	4	8.6	8.2
Defense Expert, Dee Wojowski	4	1	7.1	8.7

*Importance ranking: 1 = very important
2 = important
3 = somewhat important
4 = unimportant
5 = not at all important

**Credibility rating: 1 = lowest value
9 = highest value

tance in helping jurors reach a final decision but also for their credibility. The pro-liability jurors gave only average ranking to the two experts, while giving the defense expert a higher credibility rating than the plaintiff's expert, even though the plaintiff's expert was ranked higher in importance than the defense's expert. From this analysis, it is apparent that the jurors who found liability did so primarily because of the traumatic nature of the injury, based on their feelings of sympathy or empathy. Jurors finding liability only used the "facts" presented by the experts to support the action they favored.

The group that did not find liability gave high credibility ratings to only two witnesses, Dr. Dalton and Ms. Wojowski, the defense's expert witness. However, Dr. Dalton was found to be unimportant in determining the final decision for this group, while the expert for the defense was found to be very important. Those not finding liability were influenced by the plaintiff in their final decision. Examining his credibility score of 5.1, just barely above average, however, reveals that it was the plaintiff's lack of credibility that impressed this group. Dr. Dalton's high credibility rating was significant because those not finding liability never considered compensation.

This table clearly indicates that before actually going to trial the plaintiff's team must improve the testifying skills of their primary expert or obtain a more credible expert. Furthermore, the testimony of the plaintiff and his wife should be examined closely to make certain their statements are not exaggerated and they do not proffer claims that cannot be totally supported. Also, the plaintiff's drinking problems must be brought out in direct examination, rather than allowing them to be exposed in cross-examination.

§6.4.3 *Track Analysis*

At the end of each measure the jurors were asked to respond to this question: "At this point, I favor the plaintiff very strongly, strongly, somewhat, weakly, or not at all." When the responses to this question are tracked on a chart (see figure

6-1), it is easy to identify the events that influenced the jurors' decisions.

The track analysis for Juror 3 is typical of those who found for the plaintiff — the minority of the jurors. This analysis reveals that the opening statement by the plaintiff's attorney was received very positively, while the defense attorney's statement caused a dramatic decrease in support. This confirms the harm that the omission of information causes and reaffirms the conclusions drawn from the analysis of the opening statements. The testimony of the plaintiff and his passenger did not move the juror (table 6-4 shows that these witnesses received minimal credibility ratings). Dr. Dalton, who was highly credible, moved the juror back to a positive evaluation of the plaintiff's case. That position was held until the closing argument of the plaintiff's attorney, which again moved the juror to the strongest possible position in favor of the plaintiff. While the defense was somewhat effective in reducing this support, the juror ultimately supported the plaintiff's case.

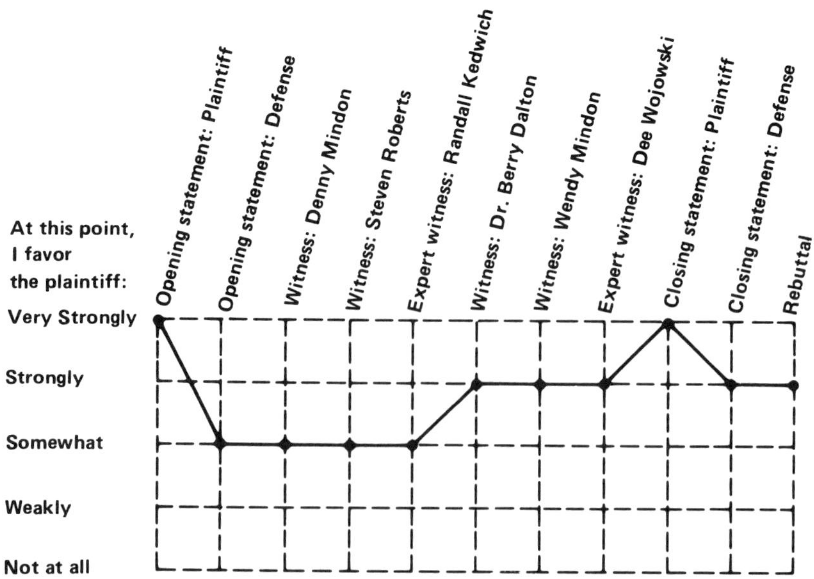

Figure 6-1. Track Analysis

Notice that the beginning and end positions are both supportive of the plaintiff. This pattern is found in approximately eighty percent of jurors, supporting the contention that people view facts through the funnel of their biases and attitudes. It also demonstrates the importance of identifying the personality type and attitudinal profile of a prospective juror prior to placing that person on a jury.

§6.4.4 *Measure after Rebuttal*

After rebuttal, each juror is asked to record the verdict he or she would give at that moment. This records the state of mind of each juror as he or she leaves the trial simulation and enters the deliberation stage. Table 6-5 records the initial verdict of each juror in this trial simulation.

Of the 24 jurors, 9 or 37.5 percent favored awarding compensation. However, the majority of the people on Juries 1, 2 and 3 did not find liability, and the final verdict of each of these juries was for the defense. But, in Jury 4, four of the six jurors initially favored the plaintiff and this jury returned a final verdict in favor of the plaintiff, awarding $1.2 million.

Note that in each case the majority controlled the final verdict. This supports the research reported in *The American Jury* that indicates that the initial majority view will be supported in over ninety percent of final verdicts.[2]

If the plaintiff's attorney were interested in the amount of compensation that might be awarded if liability were found, these results would be encouraging since compensation averages over $2 million and the one verdict for the plaintiff was $1.2 million. It is clear that if the plaintiff can improve the liability case so as to increase the number of jurors likely to find in the plaintiff's favor, the compensation will be substantial. However, if there is no way to improve the liability case, settlement might be attractive.

[2]See H. Kalven, Jr. & H. Zeisel, The American Jury 487-489 (1966).

Table 6-5
Individual Verdicts after Rebuttal

	Favor plaintiff	*Defendants liable*	*Compensation*
Jury 1 (verdict after deliberation = no liability)			
Juror 1	NAA	No	—
2	NAA	No	—
3	S	Yes	$750,000
4	NAA	No	—
5	W	No	—
6	NAA	No	—
Jury 2 (verdict = no liability)			
Juror 7	SW	No	—
8	S	No	$200,000
9	SW	Yes	$1,500,000
10	NAA	No	—
11	NAA	No	—
12	W	No	—
Jury 3 (verdict = no liability)			
Juror 13	S	Yes	$750,000
14	SW	No	—
15	S	Yes	$3 million
16	NAA	No	—
17	W	No	—
18	NAA	No	—
Jury 4 (verdict = $1.2 million)			
Juror 19	NAA	No	—
20	S	Yes	$5 million
21	VS	Yes	$5 million
22	VS	Yes	$1 million
23	VS	Yes	$1 million
24	NAA	No	—

Key: Favor Plaintiff: VS = very strongly
S = strongly
SW = somewhat
W = weakly
NAA = not at all

§6.4.5 *Demographic Analysis*

One of the items that should be of great interest to the trial attorney is the demographic analysis of jurors 3, 8, 9, 13, 15, 20, 21, 22 and 23. These nine awarded substantial compensation. The analysis of their commonalities as compared to those of the remaining jurors could be used to determine if there are demographic characteristics that would be predictive of desirable or undesirable jurors. In this case the following profile emerged: The desirable juror was a white male between the ages of 42 and 55 who had experience with auto mechanics and who acknowledged that, on occasion, he had driven after taking 2 or 3 drinks. He was married, had a high school or technical education, and was employed in a blue-collar job. (For an explanation of demographic analysis see chapter 7.)

§6.5 Deliberation Analysis

Each jury deliberation is tape recorded and transcribed. A content analysis of this information reveals in greater detail the thinking process involved in each deliberation. It also identifies questions the jurors would have liked answered during the presentation and which arguments were effective in persuading the jury. It reveals the thinking process used to justify the verdict finally agreed on and demonstrates the role the group's opinion leaders played with the other jurors.

All of this information is compacted into a list of problems and recommendations for use in further trial preparation. This helps the trial team improve its strategy so that it can be thoroughly prepared to meet the demands of the courtroom.

CHAPTER

7

Demographic Analysis of the Jury Panel

§7.0 In General

Demographic analysis of a jury panel is a system of pretrial analysis for evaluating whether a potential juror's attitudes are likely to favor or disfavor the view of the issues that will be presented in court by the trial team. This method of jury analysis can be used only in jurisdictions where a jury list is available prior to the date of trial.

The effectiveness of the demographic analysis depends on two basic considerations: (1) the amount of demographic information available about each prospective juror prior to jury selection, and (2) the accuracy of the criteria used in evaluating this demographic information.

§7.1 Evaluating Demographic Information

Demographic information about potential jurors is available from several likely sources, the most promising being the jury list itself. Background information may be available from studies made by private investigators or trial staff investigators.

Volunteers might also generate demographic information by checking voter registration lists, credit reports, union membership lists, Polk's Directories, Criss-Cross Directories, and other general sources. Sometimes valuable demographic information can be gathered simply from talking to people who are knowledgeable about the community.[1]

Before a demographic analysis is of any value in the jury selection process, the trial attorney should know at least the age, sex, and occupation of every person on the jury list. Marital status, spouse's occupation, and number of children should also be known.

§7.1.1 Statistical Analysis

The concept behind a demographic analysis is that a value can be placed on each category of demographic characteristic. This can be useful in jury selection since it is hypothesized that there is a consistent relationship between demographic variables and attitudes toward the issues of a case. For instance, assume it can be shown that divorced people tend to be strongly supportive of a particular case issue, while married people tend to be somewhat negative, and single people tend to be mildly supportive. Generally, widowed people have no tendency to demonstrate a consistent, predictable attitudinal pattern. We could then assign a value to each demographic characteristic of marital status like the following: divorced equals a value of +3, single equals +1, widowed equals 0 and married equals −2. This same process would then be followed in determining values for other demographic categories: sex (male-female), age (18-25, 26-39, 40-65, over 65 might be used as categories), and occupation (executive, white-collar, professional, clerical, blue-collar, gray-collar, retired, and unemployed might be used as categories).

§7.1 [1]This kind of information, however, is frequently unreliable. Before relying too heavily on it, several sources should verify the information. It is too easy for a person to get confused about the identity or reputation of another.

Only demographic categories that reflect the actual information available about the jury panel will be scored. For example, if the religious preference of prospective jurors will not be known, there is no sense in determining a value for different religions.

When each demographic variable has been given a value, then these are summed so that each juror can be assigned an a priori[2] value. This value indicates how acceptable or unacceptable the potential juror is likely to be for this particular case.

The effectiveness of a priori assignments depends on the reliability of the method for determining and assigning demographic values. By far the most reliable method is statistical analysis, like that performed in analysis of the data derived from a community attitude study. This kind of analysis, usually performed by computer program, results in the assignment of weights[3] to each classification of demographic variables. Application of these weights to the analysis of the demographic information will again provide a final score of acceptability or unacceptability for each prospective juror.

§7.1.2 *Nonstatistical Analysis*

If there are no data available for a statistical analysis, then a less precise approach to demographic analysis can be taken. The lawyer should assemble a team of psychologists, sociologists, communication researchers, and experienced trial lawyers and explain the hinge issues of the case. Taking each of the demographic variables separately, this team should discuss the following question: "All other things being equal, would I rather have ____________________ or ____________________ or

[2]"A priori" is a statistical term used to designate the value that is assigned before actual examination. In this usage, it would be the value assigned a potential juror prior to the voir dire examination.

[3]"Weights" are numerical assessments, either positive or negative, that reflect how important or valuable a demographic variable is in predicting or determining a corresponding attitude.

__________?" The blanks would be filled with the categories of each demographic variable. For instance, "All other things being equal, would I rather have a male or a female?" or "All other things being equal, would I rather have a person who is between the ages of 18 and 25, 26 and 39, 40 and 65, or over 65?" Each category should be examined logically and objectively, drawing on any information about probable attitudinal predispositions that team members can provide from their particular discipline. Once this question is answered (for the purposes of this example assume the team decides it would rather have a male than a female juror), the next question would be, "How much more would I prefer a person in this category than I would prefer a person in another demographic category of this variable?" In short, a numerical value must now be assigned to each category. After considerable discussion, the team might decide that a male should be given a value of +2, but that a female has neither a negative nor a positive value for this particular case and therefore should be assigned the value 0.

Once a value has been assigned for each category of each demographic variable, then the team should reexamine the categories to determine which demographic variables will most influence the final verdict. Will the possible juror's sex be more important than his or her race? Will age be more important than occupation? In other words, a ranking of demographic characteristics should be made. The trial team might decide that race and occupation are of equal importance in determining negative or positive attitudes toward the case, and that these two variables are three times as important as the person's sex, twice as important as marital status, and one-and-one-half times more important than age. This would give the demographic variables the following weights:

Variable	*Weight*
Sex	1.0
Marital status	1.5
Age	2.0
Occupation	3.0
Race	3.0

Each weight would be multiplied by the previous numerical value assigned to a category of demographic variable so that the final score given that category would reflect both the value within the demographic variable categories and across the demographic variables. To demonstrate how this weighting system works, examine the demographic variables of race, age, and sex in the following table.

Suppose that the trial team went through the process of determining the value placed on each category for each demographic variable and reached the following conclusions:

Variable	*Category*	*Value*
Race	White	0
	Black	+1
Age	18-25	−.5
	26-35	0
	36-50	+2
	51-65	+1
	Over 65	−1
Sex	Female	+1
	Male	−1

The next step would be to multiply the demographic variable's weights by the demographic category's values, as was done for table 7-1.

Table 7-1
Determining the Final Score

Variable	*Category*	*Value*	*Times the weight*	*Final score*
Race	White	0	3.0	0
	Black	+1	3.0	+3
Age	18-25	−.5	2.0	−1
	26-35	0	2.0	0
	36-50	+2	2.0	+4
	51-65	+1	2.0	+2
	Over 65	−1	2.0	−2
Sex	Female	+1	1.0	+1
	Male	−1	1.0	−1

The process of assigning weights is performed by the computer when it is programmed with the values for each demographic variable and the categories within each variable.

When determining the values and scores assigned to the variables used in the demographic analysis, past experience and current research should be the guidelines. The trial team should put aside any personal bias and operate on a level of objectivity and logic. While this is difficult to accomplish, it is not impossible.

§7.2 Sample Demographic Analysis

To better understand how demographic analysis works in analyzing a jury list, consider the following example. Suppose that the case is a Mississippi civil suit for substantial damages brought against a white landlord by a young black woman who suffered permanent injury in a fall from her third floor low-rent apartment. She claims the fall occurred due to negligence of the landlord in both his construction and his upkeep of the stairs and railings. Further, suppose that the trial team for the plaintiff had authorized a community attitude study to determine the profile of favorable and unfavorable jurors. The values in table 7-2 for the demographic variables of sex, race, marital status, age, and occupation (those variables provided to the attorney on the jury list) were determined with the specifics of the case in mind.

The trial team received the following jury list of eighteen prospective jurors. Twelve of these jurors will be drawn and directed to the jury box and then a struck jury system will be used with the plaintiff and defense attorneys striking alternately until six jurors remain for the trial panel. A list of potential jurors and their demographic characteristics follows.

1. Anne Kuhn — white female, 24, single, records clerk.
2. Calvin E. Peterson — black male, 56, married, porter.

3. Josephine N. Cook — white female, 51, married, self-employed as owner of a tavern.
4. Jimmie Golder — black male, 28, married, computer attendant for a telephone company.
5. Lawrence T. Colachero — white male, 31, married, foreman electrician for an electric company.
6. Joan Hillberg — white female, 27, single, graduate student working on a master's in business administration.
7. Anita Neelam — white female, 57, married, product analyst for a tool manufacturing company.
8. Alvina Marshall — white female, 59, married, housewife.
9. Wilmer T. Mitchell — white male, 56, divorced, retired carpenter.
10. Karla L. Clevland — white female, 31, married, homemaker.
11. Lelia Sue Torman — black female, 27, single, clerk-typist for state government agency.
12. David L. Sundstrom — white male, 36, married, programmer-analyst for medical insurance company.
13. Carmen Brocharo — white female, 24, single, a registered nurse at a nursing home.
14. Donald E. Oldham — white male, 35, divorced, student and alcoholism counselor.
15. John K. Danson — white male, 49, married, manager for a wrecker service.
16. Dolores S. Koremacher — black female, 55, medical nurse practitioner at a regional hospital.
17. Ted Black — white male, 33, married, research analyst personnel specialist for a construction company.
18. Noah Abrahams — black male, 47, married, housekeeping supervisor for a Jewish home care company.

The pretrial rating for each prospective juror based on the value assigned by the demographic analysis can now be computed. For instance, juror 1 would have a score of 0 for being a female, −1 for her race, −3 for her marital status, −3 for her age, and

Table 7-2
Listing of Variables and Values

Variable	*Category*	*Value*
Sex	Male	+3
	Female	0
Race	Black	+2
	White	−1
Marital status	Single	−3
	Married	+2
	Divorced	+1
	Widowed	−1
Age	18-25	−3
	26-39	+1
	40-65	+2
	Over 65	−1
Occupation	Student	−5
	Retired	−2
	Medical	−1
	Housewife	0
	Self-employed	−6
	White-collar	+2
	Blue-collar	+4
	Gray-collar	+1
	Clerical	−1
	Supervisor	+4
	Social worker	−3

−1 for her occupation, for a total of −8. An analysis of all 18 jurors is in table 7-3.

According to table 7-3 there would be eleven jurors (jurors 2, 18, 4, 15, 5, 17, 12, 7, 8, 9, 10 in descending order of desirability) who would likely be pro-plaintiff, one juror (juror 16) who would likely be neutral, and six jurors (jurors 11, 14, 3, 1, 6, 13 in ascending order of undesirability) who would likely be anti-plaintiff if their life experiences, as reflected in the demographic analysis, are consistent with prospective jurors of the same demographic description. From examining table 7-3, one can see that the four most desirable jurors would be 2, 18, 4,

Table 7-3
Demographic Analysis

Juror number	*Sex*	*Race*	*Marital status*	*Age*	*Occupation*	*Total*
1	0	−1	−3	−3	−1	−8
2	+3	+2	+2	+2	+4	+13
3	0	−1	+2	+2	−6	−3
4	+3	+2	+2	+1	+2	+10
5	+3	−1	+2	+1	+4	+9
6	0	−1	−3	+1	−5	−8
7	0	−1	+2	+2	+2	+5
8	0	−1	+2	+2	0	+3
9	+3	−1	+1	+2	−2	+3
10	0	−1	+2	+1	0	+2
11	0	+2	−3	+1	−1	−1
12	+3	−1	+2	+1	+2	+7
13	0	−1	−3	−3	−1	−8
14	+3	−1	+1	+1	−5	−1
15	+3	−1	+2	+2	+4	+10
16	0	+2	−3	+2	−1	0
17	+3	−1	+2	+1	+2	+8
18	+3	+2	+2	+2	+4	+13

and 15 while the four least desirable jurors would be 1, 6, 13, and 3.

§7.2.1 *Reliability of Demographic Analysis*

It is important to remember that the reliability of the demographic analysis is dependent on the criteria employed in determining the values for categories of demographic variables and assigning weight to demographic variables. If this process is performed with logic and rationality, especially if it is accomplished by statistical analysis of community data, the final assessment should have value in the actual jury selection.

Indeed, psychologist Michael Saks, a skeptic of demographic

analysis in jury selection, admits that "intuitive, instinctive judgments, when put to the test, have proved notoriously unreliable."[1] He states further, "When the same information is available to a human decisionmaker and a mathematical model, almost without exception the mathematical model makes more reliable and accurate predictions. After 60 studies comparing clinical versus statistical prediction, the humans beat the computer only once."[2]

Furthermore, in actual courtroom use almost all of the lawyers who have used demographic analysis as a pretrial technique in preparation for jury selection have found it preferable to their own instinctive judgments. This does not mean that verbal and nonverbal information gained during voir dire should be ignored. Instead, the demographic analysis should be used as a baseline for determining expected attitudinal propensities.

Another comment from Saks highlights the value of a statistical pretrial demographic analysis:

> These findings [that in only one out of 60 tests was human judgment found to be superior to scientific methodology] were as much of a shock (and offense to the human ego) to the people who discovered them as to you who read about them. The original intention was to aid human decisionmakers by providing a floor of statistical accuracy below which they could not fall. But the floor turned out to be a ceiling. We are indeed fallible creatures. In the Harrisburg trial, one of the two jurors who held out for conviction had been vetoed by the computer. That advice, however, was overruled by Ramsey Clark, who felt certain the juror was a good choice.[3]

§7.2 [1]Saks, Social Scientists Can't Rig Juries, 9 Psychology Today 48, 49 (Jan. 1976).

[2]Id. at 49-50.

[3]Id. at 50.

PART III

Voir Dire

CHAPTER

8

Introduction to Voir Dire

§8.0 In General

Comprehensive voir dire examination of the jury panel is a necessary concomitant of the constitutional right to trial by a fair and impartial jury. Voir dire provides the attorneys' only opportunity to obtain information directly from members of the jury panel concerning their qualifications. The purpose of the examination is to permit the litigants to make intelligent determinations concerning the exercise of challenges for cause and peremptory challenges.

Some attorneys boast that they can try a case to the first 12 persons seated in the jury box with as much success as an attorney who employs comprehensive voir dire. They insist that their advocacy skills, rather than careful voir dire, will determine the outcome. This boasting denies the complex sociological and psychological makeup of people. Each potential juror brings to the jury box a lifetime of opinions, biases, and prejudices.

Furthermore, the critical importance of voir dire is illustrated by research demonstrating that approximately eighty percent of jurors make up their minds by the conclusion of opening statements.[1] Other research,[2] conducted in trial simulations

§8.0 [1]H. Kalven, Jr. & H. Zeisel, The American Jury 352-372 (1966).
[2]Unpublished research by V. Hale Starr, Ph.D.

and community attitude surveys, suggests that jurors' decisions are made even earlier. Seventy to seventy-five percent of jurors have a definite opinion about the case by the end of voir dire. The effectiveness of voir dire or opening statements is generally not what determines jurors' early opinions. Rather, they are based on previously held opinions, biases, and prejudices.

Voir dire should not be left to last minute preparation. Because it can be the single most important factor determining the outcome of a case, it should be one of the most carefully prepared parts of the trial strategy.

§8.1 Purposes of Voir Dire

It is obvious that voir dire provides a unique opportunity to probe for jurors' prejudices and to obtain information that bears on their qualifications. These purposes are a useful predicate for the exercise of challenges. Voir dire serves other important functions as well, such as relaxing the jurors, establishing credibility, conditioning jurors to accept the law, educating them about the particular case, avoiding situations that might result in mistrial, nominating the foreperson, and laying a foundation for the opening statement and closing argument.

§8.1.1 Discovering Juror Attitudes and Background

The Supreme Court has not prescribed how the goal of a fair and impartial jury is to be achieved. Impartiality, of course, is a state of mind. Despite the absence of a specific formula, the courts have recognized the rights of litigants to probe for the hidden prejudices of jurors.

When an attorney has discovered through voir dire inquiry that a prospective juror is prejudiced against the case, a determination can be made whether to challenge the juror for cause or to exercise a peremptory challenge. Not every juror with a prejudice needs to be struck from the panel. It may be sufficient that voir dire forces certain jurors to confront their inherent prejudices. For example, questioning may make white jurors aware of a subconscious prejudice against nonwhites. Since most people are aware that prejudice must not be permitted to affect the outcome of a trial, the jurors are likely to monitor their prejudices during deliberations.

If the attorney has obtained information before trial about panel members, the information is likely to be principally of a demographic nature. Age, marital status, occupation, spouse's occupation, union membership, political affiliation, religion, education, and memberships are considered demographic factors. Other information is also necessary before the attorney can feel comfortable predicting how the juror will react in a particular case. Such information concerns the emotional response system of the individual juror. For example, in a civil case where damages for the probability of developing arthritis is at issue, it might make a difference if a prospective juror has a relative or acquaintance who suffers from the condition. If so, the juror would probably be aware of the pain and suffering caused by arthritis and have some sympathy for a person similarly afflicted. It might be different, however, if the juror were the person afflicted. A juror who has not been compensated for pain and suffering resulting from arthritis might feel that a plaintiff should not be compensated either.

§8.1.2 Relaxing the Jurors

The majority of jurors come to the courtroom without prior jury experience. Voir dire provides an opportunity to put them at ease with their task. If jurors are tense or anxious, they may not be capable of giving the necessary attention to the evidence.

Relaxing the jurors does not mean letting them forget their high duty. Instead, it means removing the occasion for anxiety by giving the jurors a clear understanding of procedures to be followed. In addition, the attorney should be at ease:

> Develop a spirit that will reflect warmth, concern and humanity. Remember that you are in the court of law and that you are an officer of the court — but also remember that you are a human being. The two identities need not create conflict. You can be both "careful and casual" (as the ad for men's sportswear says) and exude a feeling of both friendliness and formality (witness Henry Kissinger). The achievement of such demeanor demands attention to your relationship with the humans around you — the bailiff, the clerk, the client — everyone.[1]

Every effort should be made to relax the jurors at the outset of voir dire and to keep them at ease throughout the process.

§8.1.3 Establishing Lawyer Credibility

Every attorney strives to make a good impression on jurors. The purpose should be not so much to put the jurors in awe of the lawyer's skill as to enhance the lawyer's credibility. Voir dire provides the attorney with an opportunity to communicate personally with members of the jury panel. Theodore Koskoff, in a speech before the American Trial Lawyers Association in 1974, commented on the technique for making a good first impression:

> Motivational techniques in moving a group as a group are different from moving 12 individuals. To move a group, one must appeal to common denominator motivations like decency, honor, humanity, justice, the juror's oath, etc. This must be done from the voir dire through to the summation. As the voir dire is our first contact with the jury, that first impression of both the client and lawyer on the jury is most important. It must immediately, through sincerity, honesty and no obvious trick questions, be a good impression.[2]

§8.1 [1]Address by Attorney Charles R. Garry, founder of Association of Trial Lawyers of America, Association of Trial Lawyers of America Convention on Jury Selection (1976).

[2]Address by Attorney Theodore Koskoff, past president Association of Trial Lawyers of America, Association of Trial Lawyers of America Convention on Jury Selection (1974).

Some attorneys attempt to impress jurors by memorizing their names, occupations, and other personal information obtained from jury questionnaires. After the jury panel in a recent civil case listened to the defense attorney call panel members by name and ask specific questions about their occupations without referring to notes, 84 percent of the panel members said they were impressed with the attorney's intelligence and concern for them as individuals.

Whatever technique is used, the objective is to have the jurors look at the attorney and client as people like themselves. In 1936 Clarence Darrow asserted, "Every knowing lawyer seeks for a jury of the same sort of men as his client; men who will be able to imagine themselves in the same situation and realize what verdict the client wants."[3] Sociologists and psychologists today would rephrase this by saying that the lawyer seeks jurors who are "similar others" as opposed to "dissimilar others." If this is not accomplished during voir dire, it will not be accomplished.

§8.1.4 Educating the Juror on Points of Law

Although the term conditioning may have ominous implications, the concept of conditioning jurors means nothing other than making them aware of their responsibility to follow specific controlling principles of law in a case that might otherwise be inconsistent with their predilections.

For example, in a criminal case the question of the burden of proof is one that particularly requires the jury's understanding. The following series of questions and answers is illustrative of a possible voir dire colloquy on this subject.

Q: *[by defense attorney]* Do you understand that you are required as a juror to be convinced beyond a reasonable doubt about the guilt of the defendant, Mr. ________, before you can bring in a guilty verdict?

A: Yes I do.

[3] P. M. Stern, Lawyers on Trial 173 (1980).

Q: If after having heard all the evidence you suspected that the defendant might be guilty of the acts charged, what verdict would you bring in?
A: I guess I would have to bring in a verdict of not guilty.
Q: You wouldn't convict someone just because you suspect that he was guilty, is that right?
A: Yes, I couldn't convict just on suspicion.
Q: If you thought it was possible that the defendant had committed the acts charged by the state, what would be your verdict then?
A: I guess I'd still have to say that the defendant was not guilty.
Q: You couldn't bring in a verdict of guilty just on the possibility that the defendant was guilty, is that right?
A: Yes, that's right.
Q: If after hearing all the evidence you thought the defendant probably committed the acts charged by the state, what would be your verdict?
A: I would still have to say that the defendant was not guilty.
Q: Do I understand you then to say that you could not bring in a verdict of guilty if you thought that it was only possible or probable that the defendant was guilty?
A: Yes, I would have to be convinced beyond a reasonable doubt.

Conditioning jurors on the law may be just as important in a civil case. Many persons are exposed to advertising by insurance companies that implies that any increases in insurance premiums are caused by large jury verdicts. This may make potential jurors reluctant to consider returning substantial verdicts in meritorious cases. The following questions and answers illustrate possible voir dire questions on this subject:

Q: *[by plaintiff's attorney]* Are you aware that money is the only form of compensation that a person can seek in our present system of justice?
A: Yes, I guess so.

Q: In our system people like you are required to determine what amount constitutes a fair, just, adequate, and reasonable award for a given injury. Do you have any quarrel with that system?
A: No, no quarrel.
Q: Naturally you will want to hear all of the evidence first. But after you have heard the evidence, if in your opinion it would take a very substantial sum of money to make fair compensation to the plaintiff, would you hesitate to award it in this case?
A: No, I wouldn't hesitate.
Q: By adequate, I mean that it is sufficient to compensate for all of the elements of damage, whatever they may be, small or large. Do you understand my meaning?
A: Yes, I think so.
Q: I want to be sure that you do not have some artificial financial limit that you carry around in your head beyond which you would not award any more money. I say this because some people, no matter how badly they think the plaintiff has been treated or how much money he has have lost or how much damage he has suffered or how much pain or suffering he has endured, will in their minds, without telling anyone else, just simply say "I would not award any more than *X* dollars," whatever that figure may be. Do you feel that way?
A: I have no ceiling in my head.
Q: Let me ask all this from another perspective. Does $1 million in actual damages sound like a high verdict to you?
A: No, I guess that's okay.
Q: Does $1 million sould like a lot of money to you?
A: Well, yes, it's a lot of money.
Q: Can you imagine, as you sit here prior to trial, any set of circumstances that could be presented to you as a juror that would allow you to award $1 million to any plaintiff in any lawsuit?
A: Well, yes, I guess I could.
Q: In other words, does the word reasonable when it is used

in relation to the concept of damages in a court case imply to you a certain amount of money or an amount of money that has a certain dollar ceiling on it?

A: No, I would have no ceiling.

If jurors do not give appropriate responses to these inquiries, the attorney must consider whether there is justification for a challenge.

§8.1.5 Educating Jurors about the Particular Case

When attorneys advise the jury panel about the nature of a case, they sometimes hesitate to reveal certain facts for fear they might prove damaging. Research in trial simulation and community studies indicates there are two unforgivable sins that can be committed by a trial attorney during voir dire and the opening statement. The first is to make a claim that will not be substantiated; the second is to omit possibly damaging facts.

The omission of facts that are seemingly unfavorable to the case can lead jurors to the conclusion that the lawyer has lied to them. This, of course, is likely to have a disastrous effect on the verdict. It is a far better practice to diminish the effects of potentially damaging facts by bringing them up before they are revealed accidentally or by the opposition. Whenever this candid approach has been tested in credibility studies and trial simulations, it has proved to have positive results.

Consider a 1979 case in which a young man accused of murder arising from a fight over a debt claimed self defense. There was no question that at some point during the trial, evidence would show that the debt was the result of a drug purchase. Community attitude studies previously showed that local residents were especially harsh in their attitude toward drug use and drug dealing. For this reason, the defense attorneys were reluctant to mention in voir dire that their client was a drug user. Pretrial testing of the effect of disclosure, however, persuaded the attorneys to reveal it during voir dire. The trial resulted in an acquittal. After trial three jurors revealed that they were impressed with the honesty and credibility of the attorneys who took the initiative in revealing the potentially damaging evidence.

§8.1.6 Avoiding Mistrials

Trials are expensive both in time and money. No one profits from a mistrial. It is therefore desirable to use voir dire to the extent possible to avoid the necessity for aborting the trial.

The occasion for mistrial can arise from the asking of as well as the failure to ask certain questions. The method of conducting voir dire may create problems that would not otherwise exist. Consider a medical malpractice case tried in a small rural county in which one of the members of the jury panel was an insurance agent. The plaintiff's attorney had asked for individual voir dire, but his request had been denied. When the attorney reached the insurance agent during voir dire, he asked him what kind of insurance he sold. The agent responded, "I sell just about everything including life, auto, home fire protection, and malpractice insurance." The attorney then asked, "Did you sell malpractice insurance to the defendant?" The defense attorney moved for mistrial, and it was granted. If the panel members had been interrogated out of the hearing of the other jurors, this inflammatory exchange would not have affected the entire panel.

Consider also a contract case involving the performance of computers in which a young man was seated in the jury without having been asked his attitude concerning computers. In fact, the man had a negative impression of computers because of an unfortunate experience in attempting to get an bank account adjusted. In the middle of a computer expert's testimony on the fourth day of trial, the man stood up and shouted emotionally, "I've had enough of this nonsense! We all know that computers can't do what they are supposed to do and that humans aren't smart enough to tell them what to do!" After calling the trial to order, the judge ordered a mistrial. A more thorough voir dire inquiry could have avoided this incident.

§8.1.7 Nominating the Foreperson

When the attorney is able to identify a member of the jury panel who has leadership ability and an open mind about the major issues of the case, voir dire should be used to point out this potential foreperson to other members of the panel. This, of course, must be done with sincerity and subtlety. The attorney can do this by pointing out the desired characteristics of a foreperson, such as an ability to make sound decisions. While the lawyer should not actually nominate a person to lead the jury, by making frequent eye contact with the candidate and by repeating key phrases used by the juror during voir dire the attorney can plant the suggestion.

§8.1.8 Preparing for the Opening Statement and Summation

Voir dire can be used in four ways to set the stage for a trial strategy. First, the lawyer should ask questions during voir dire concerning crucial issues in the case — no more than four such issues should be included — in order to identify attitudes or prejudgments. The attorney should take careful notes on each juror's responses since the responses may necessitate alterations to the strategy for presenting witnesses, evidence, or arguments. For example, if the attorney discovers that the majority of jurors view issues rationally and not emotionally, the attorney should avoid emotional appeals in the final argument.

Second, the lawyer should obtain commitments from jurors that will be referred to during final argument. These commitments do not involve anything sinister. Rather, they include pledges to be open-minded and to apply the proper standard of proof to the evidence. It is important to remember, however, that these pledges are of little value unless the jury is reminded of them during the final argument.

Third, lawyers should psychologically condition the jury by using catch phrases that reflect favorably on important issues in the case. Discreet repetition of these catch phrases during voir dire will make it inevitable that whenever the subject of the phrase is referred to during trial, the jurors will automatically think of the corresponding catch phrase.

Finally, voir dire should be used to emphasize the qualifications of persons selected to serve on the jury. The jurors who are finally seated are the *chosen ones*. They should be made to feel that they are considered the most open-minded, most intelligent, and least prejudiced members of the panel. They should not feel that they are mere survivors of a negative process. This is of practical importance because jurors who have a positive attitude about themselves and their role are jurors who will respond to reminders in the opening statement and summation about their responsibility to deliver a fair and impartial verdict.

§8.2 Types of Juror Prejudice

To be able to identify and expose prejudice the attorney should be aware of the different types of prejudice, the difficulty in exposing it, and techniques for attempting to discover it.

Prejudice can be placed in four categories: (1) beliefs, (2) predispositions, (3) emotional response systems, and (4) prejudgments.

§8.2.1 Beliefs

Beliefs are values and judgments shared within a cultural environment. When a culture defines the world as flat, persons within that culture conduct their daily lives based on that belief. If a society adopts a class structure and defines it as worthy, even persons adversely affected will operate to some degree within the rules and regulations of that structure. A person's belief system defines his or her reality.

Even though most lawyers will not be concerned about

whether a particular juror believes the world is flat, lawyers must be concerned about other rather fundamental belief systems. For instance, if a person does not accept the legitimacy of psychology, that person would not be a suitable juror for a plaintiff in a civil case in which damages were being sought for emotional or psychological trauma.

The attorney must also be aware of whether jurors share beliefs, since consensus, which is the sharing of a belief within a group, is the chief means by which a belief system is reenforced and made to appear to be "the truth."

§8.2.2 Predispositions

Predispositions are acquired response patterns that affect a person's inclination to accept or reject some thing, situation, person, or event. Predispositions may take the form of preferences, attitudes or values.

Preferences are tendencies to accept or reject things, persons, or events. One's culture frequently emphasizes and reenforces them. For example, many Americans prefer hot dogs, hamburgers, and apple pie. Similarly, jurors will prefer things that find acceptance in society. They generally can be counted on to behave in a manner that reflects society's preferences.

Attitudes are more complex and comprehensive than preferences. Attitudes concern a person's reactions to minority groups, economics, politics, religion, and similar factors. An attitude establishes a basis for a ready-made response; when it is negative, it is considered a prejudice. The prejudiced person is one who has an emotionally charged negative attitude toward some social category such as blacks or Jews or democrats. The prejudiced person does not stop to determine how to respond to individuals within a societal group, but will reject a group categorically. Because prejudice makes it easier to deal with complexity, it causes people to be resistant to change.

Value systems comprise the broad and rather abstract predispositions that identify the goals of society. A value system is frequently so deeply ingrained that the individual is not aware of the extent to which it dictates behavior and reaction. Value systems have great impact on motivations, emotions, orientation, and other personality traits of which persons are not often consciously aware.

§8.2.3 Emotional Response System

The third category of prejudice is the individual's emotional response system. An individual's previous experiences may cause certain words or images to recall a whole sequence of events that is highly charged with emotion. Use of these images or words in the courtroom can trigger a potential juror's emotional response system.

For example, a person who has been assaulted or has witnessed assault of another will have more emotionally charged reaction to an assault case than a person who has never had such an experience. Through effective questioning, the attorney must discover the individuals with emotional response systems that will have an impact on the case. It must be determined next whether the probable reaction will be helpful or not.

§8.2.4 Prejudgments

The fourth category of prejudice is prejudgment. It is probably the most serious kind of prejudice the attorney will confront because prejudgment involves the juror's conscious decision about the case. This type of prejudice is most prominent in cases that have had widespread media coverage. In such situations the prospective juror may reject the idea that additional information is necessary to help decide the case.

Prejudgment occurs more frequently in cases where a highly emotional issue is involved. This happens more often in criminal than in civil trials.

A juror who reveals a prejudgment can be excused for cause. Unfortunately, however, many persons who have formed prejudgments about the case believe they have a stake in its outcome and are reluctant to reveal the depth of their feeling.

§8.2.5 Combined Prejudices

Prejudice is most serious when a juror is affected by more than one type. For example, an individual may believe that a person is not likely to be arrested unless there is good cause. Furthermore, gruesome pictures on television of a mutilated corpse may have triggered the individual's revulsion against the perpetrator of a crime. Having followed the story through the police search and the arrest of the suspect, this person may firmly believe that he or she has sufficient evidence to determine the guilt of the defendant.

Despite the fact that mere knowledge about an event does not establish prejudice, knowledge combined with prejudice will create a serious impediment to impartiality. Community attitude studies[1] conducted in more than 11 states in support of change of venue motions have revealed the following widespread beliefs that make it difficult for a defendant in a criminal case to have the advantage of the presumption of innocence: (1) Approximately eighty-five percent of potential jurors believe that media coverage tends to be fair and impartial. (2) Approximately ninety-two percent of prospective jurors do not believe that the police arrest innocent people. (3) Approximately eighty-five percent of respondents are satisfied with their local police force. The percentage is higher in rural areas than in urban areas. (4) Seventy-eight percent of potential jurors believe that people who are arrested are probably guilty of the crime charged. (5) Ninety-two percent of potential jurors believe that if the defendant does not take the stand, it is because of his or her vulnerability to cross-examination. (6) Sixty-two percent of potential jurors believe a person who has committed one crime is likely to have committed a second crime as

§8.2 [1]Unpublished research, V. Hale Starr, Ph.D.

charged, even if there is no similarity between the crimes. (7) Seventy percent of males and fifty-eight percent of females who express an opinion that the defendant is guilty will still claim they can be fair and impartial jurors. (8) Forty-nine percent of potential jurors who state that the defendant is probably guilty and claim they could be fair and impartial jurors will still say that it is not possible that the defendant could be innocent.

Comparable research has not been done for civil cases, but it is unrealistic to think that potential jurors do not bring prejudices to those cases as well. Research has established that witnesses for the defense in civil cases generally start with a higher level of expected credibility than witnesses for the plaintiff. Also, it has been shown that doctors possess extremely high levels of credibility when they testify for the defense, but not when they testify for a plaintiff.

§8.3 Why Jurors Retain Prejudices during Voir Dire

Four major reasons exist for jurors not revealing prejudice during voir dire. They are the following: (1) peer pressure and self-esteem, (2) genuine inability to gauge the level of their own prejudice, (3) willingness to lie about the level of prejudice, and (4) lack of opportunity to reveal prejudice because the right questions were not directed to them.

Something strange happens to people as they walk through the courtroom door to take their place in the pool of prospective jurors. No matter how hard they may have tried to be relieved from jury duty, once they are part of the panel they seem to believe that their character and community status require that they be seated on the jury. The community values the stamp of fairness and impartiality that is implicit in jury service. Potential jurors will rarely risk the contempt of fellow jurors by admitting bias; therefore, when jurors are asked about their ability to be fair and impartial, they predictably answer in the affirmative.

Many people are not aware that a certain thought pattern or belief system is prejudicial. Similarly, many individuals are unaware of the words or images that trigger their emotional response systems. They will respond that they have no prejudice, with total unawareness that their prejudice exists. This kind of prejudice is difficult to discern and expose during voir dire.

Other potential jurors are sometimes willing to lie, in an effort either to be selected for or excused from jury service. Their reasons for doing so are diverse. People who lie in order to be excused from service often believe that their other obligations are more important than their duty to serve on a jury. For example, a farmer during planting season, a warehouse foreman during inventory time, or an accountant during tax season may feel that his or her duties are more pressing than jury duty.

Of greater danger to the jury system are those persons who will lie to secure a seat on the jury. Some members of this group are people who are so excited about the idea of serving on a jury that they are willing to go to almost any length to be selected. This occurs most frequently when considerable media attention has been focused on the case and when one of the trial lawyers has a reputation for flamboyance.

An even greater threat is the person who has prejudged the case and feels a civic duty to remain on the jury so that justice can be done. Such prospective jurors quickly learn the "right" responses to voir dire questions and are careful to fit into the acceptable pattern. Questioning that only requires the juror to raise a hand to affirm a prejudice, or questioning that is not probing, makes it especially easy for such an individual to conceal prejudgment. It is easier to lie by omission than by commission, and it is easier for the lie of omission to go undetected.

Sometimes, however, jurors are simply not given the opportunity to reveal potential prejudice. Consider, for example, a criminal trial in which the alleged victim of an assault had been in three prior barroom fights during the evening of the alleged assault. The defendant was a member of a family believed in the small rural community to be among the criminal element.

The prosecutor felt that an extensive voir dire was unnecessary and did not ask many questions. The brother of one of the jurors, however, had been hit between the eyes with a pool cue in a barroom brawl with the victim. That juror was predisposed to believe that the alleged victim was not an innocent party in the assault. The result was a hung jury.

In a fairly simple civil case, the lawyers had neglected to ask during voir dire whether any of the jurors knew each other. It happened that two members of the panel were stepbrothers with different last names who had hated each other since they were children. They were both seated on the jury. During the deliberations, the jury eventually sent a note to the judge saying that because all of them were fighting so hard among themselves it was impossible to reach a verdict. It is not difficult to guess the probable cause of the disagreement.

Because it is difficult to anticipate every area of possible prejudice, it is wise to end voir dire questioning with a simple invitation to the jurors. "Is there any reason, whether we have mentioned it previously or not, why you do not feel that you could be a fair and impartial juror in this case?"

§8.4 Exposing Prejudice

No attorney can reasonably expect to discover all the underlying attitudes, opinions, and beliefs that may affect a potential juror. Yet, two general methods are useful for bringing a juror's prejudices to light. One is out-of-court investigation and the other is adequate voir dire. If time and money permit, the lawyer can conduct extensive pretrial investigation of the beliefs, lifestyle, and experience of potential jurors. More commonly, however, the lawyer must depend on the opportunity to conduct an adequate voir dire.

Ideally voir dire should be extensive enough to inquire about the possible prejudices of each potential juror without making the panel bored with the proceeding or impatient with the attorney. The more complex the trial, the more likely it is that a complete and extensive voir dire will be necessary, if only to provide more time to explain the case to the jury. Furthermore, judges are more amenable to extensive voir dire in complex cases expected to run long because they want to avoid having to declare a mistrial due to misconduct of a prejudiced juror.

An adequate voir dire must be extensive in scope, individual in contact, and preferably conducted by the attorney. The mechanics and techniques of voir dire are more thoroughly explored in subsequent chapters.

CHAPTER

9

Mechanics of Voir Dire

§9.0 Basic Voir Dire Procedure

Voir dire is generally conducted in one of the following three ways: (1) The judge exercises complete control over the questioning of jurors but permits counsel to submit written questions. The judge has discretion about whether or not to ask the questions or to allow the attorney to ask certain questions directly. (2) The attorney controls the questioning of jurors with the judge monitoring the proceeding for possible abuse. (3) The judge conducts initial questioning of the panel and then turns the questioning over to the attorney.

While each of the three basic methods of conducting voir dire has its particular merits, the overriding purpose is always to impanel an impartial jury. No juror is completely neutral and voir dire does not seek total impartiality in any juror. Rather, the object is to choose jurors who have only random biases that are a result of the person's traits and views. These traits and views are distinct from specific grudges against any one party or cause.[1]

§9.0 [1]See generally Levit, Nelson, Ball & Chernik, Expediting Voir Dire: An Empirical Study, 448 Cal. L. Rev. 916 (1971).

§9.0.1 *Judge-Conducted Voir Dire*

Judge-conducted voir dire is the prevalent method of voir dire in federal cases.[2] For this reason it has been called the *federal method.* Advocates of this method list several reasons in support of it. The most generally agreed on are expediency and the elimination of abuses by attorneys.

Attorneys often use voir dire to (1) establish rapport with the jury, (2) condition the jury, (3) orient the panel, and (4) introduce the merits of the case. Advocates of judge-conducted voir dire argue that establishing rapport with the jury is not an appropriate use of voir dire.[3] They contend that lawyers use voir dire to woo jurors and to begin arguing their case, and that such uses are not consonant with the inquiry's intended purpose of a fair and impartial jury. Attorneys have also been criticized for their use of leading questions during voir dire. One federal judge noted that he originally permitted lawyers to conduct voir dire after he had asked preliminary questions. However, he found that almost every time the lawyer conducted voir dire, he argued his case, sought advantages, or became repetitious.[4] The judge would admonish the attorney, but after a short time the attorney would almost invariably revert to former tactics.

The remedy for these abuses has been for the judge to conduct the voir dire. There are some who argue that since the

[2] A 1977 Survey by the Federal Judicial Center produced the following results:

- 49% of federal judges conducted voir dire using only their own questions.
- 19% of federal judges conducted the voir dire but asked some questions submitted by counsel.
- 16% of federal judges conducted the preliminary examination and then allowed the attorneys to examine the panel.
- 5% of federal judges allowed the attorneys to conduct the entire examination.

See 61 Judicature 73 (1977).

[3] See Atkins, Jury Voir Dire: The Judge's Perspective, 2 Litigation 19, 20 (1976).

[4] Id. at 20.

judge is a neutral party, he or she is better suited than the attorney to conduct the examination.

The other major criticism of attorney-conducted voir dire is that it is time consuming. One study indicates that the average judge-conducted voir dire takes less than an hour.[5] Allowing lawyers to conduct voir dire without good cause wastes time and money. Since judge-conducted voir dire permits attorneys to submit questions to the judge, advocates can still obtain all the information necessary for the intelligent exercise of challenges.

§9.0.2 Attorney-Conducted Voir Dire

The arguments in support of attorney-conducted voir dire are numerous. One of the aims of voir dire is to elicit candid remarks from jurors so that their biases can be discovered and as impartial a jury as possible can be selected.

The voir dire is basically an interview with prospective jurors. Frankness in interview situations is induced in a number of ways. These include (1) a warm and friendly demeanor on the part of the interviewer, (2) a socially acceptable yet comfortable distance between the interviewer and interviewee, (3) eye contact, and (4) positive feedback.[6]

While it is argued that judges can elicit truthful responses from prospective jurors, research indicates otherwise. Consider the different roles attorneys and judges have in the trial process. According to the American Bar Association Standards, the trial judge has the responsibility not only to conduct the trial in an orderly fashion, but also to maintain the dignity of the office and "enhance public confidence in the administration of justice by his personal appearance and demeanor."[7] In keep-

[5]See Costantino, Abolish Lawyer's Voir Dire of Juries, 8 Litigation 5 (1982). (The study surveyed 420 district courts and found that 82 percent of the civil voir dires were less than an hour with the average time at 43.9 minutes. In criminal cases, 65 percent of the voir dires lasted less than one hour.)

[6]See Suggs & Sales, Jury Self-Disclosure in the Voir Dire: A Social Science Analysis, 56 Ind. L.J. 245 (1981).

[7]ABA Standards, Function of the Trial Judge §1.3 (approved draft 1972).

ing with this goal, many trial judges wear the official black robe, the effect of which is to place the judge in an impersonal role as the "supreme being" of the courtroom. In addition, the judge sits elevated above the rest of the courtroom behind a bench that physically sets him off from the rest of the courtroom. These factors do not necessarily indicate that a judge would be less effective than an attorney in eliciting honest answers from the jurors, but studies have indicated that the more formal the conditions for an interview, the less honest persons are in their responses. The judge may actually elicit false responses, since people generally feel a need to respond in an acceptable manner when talking to authority figures, especially in novel situations. Also, people tend to pick up on nonverbal clues. If the judge conducts the voir dire and has negative feelings toward one party or its counsel, these feelings may be communicated to the jurors during questioning. Negative feelings "will almost surely" be conveyed to jurors in such instances through nonverbal communication.[8] If this does occur, there would be little the attorney could do to counteract the judge's inadvertent but nevertheless biased communication.

The same danger does not exist when the attorney conducts voir dire. To begin with, jurors are aware that the attorney is an adversary, and as such is out to do the best job for his or her client. Thus the attorney would not be jeopardizing his or her role in the jury trial system by becoming friendly with the jurors, establishing eye contact, or giving positive feedback through body cues or other expressions.

In addition, the attorney is better physically situated than the judge to elicit open and honest responses, being at eye level with jurors and able to move around the courtroom. Thus the attorney's role and location in the courtroom are best suited to the purpose of voir dire.

Another factor to consider is the judge's commitment to expediency compared to the attorney's commitment to the client. Judges are generally under a great deal of pressure to expedite court proceedings. Even the ABA standards list effective use of

[8]Suggs & Sales, 56 Ind. L.J. at 258.

time as one of the judge's concerns.[9] Crowded dockets also add pressure to speed up the legal process. Cutting the voir dire short is generally viewed as an appropriate method of expediting the trial.[10] Conversely, the attorney is not pressured to expedite the trial; the attorney's interests are in securing a fair panel. Not that judges do not have this goal in mind, but the attorney is more willing to spend the time needed to conduct a thorough and productive voir dire. Expediency at the cost of justice is not practical. As one author put it:

> [L]imited voir dire examination undercuts the ability of the litigant to exercise his peremptory challenges, which are essential to the jury trial right. Also implicated is the equal protection clause, because of the relative disadvantage of the poor litigant, deprived of a full voir dire as compared with the wealthy litigant, who has other resources for gathering information about the jury.[11]

The attorney is also better suited to question the jurors because he or she generally has a deeper knowledge of the case. Courts have recognized this fact:

> [A] judge cannot have the same grasp of the facts, the complexities and nuances as the trial attorneys entrusted with the preparation of the case. The court does not know the strength and

[9] ABA Standards, Function of the Trial Judge §1.4 (approved draft 1972). (The standard referred to here states that the judge has an "[o]bligation to use judicial time effectively." This of course would include cutting voir dire short if the judge felt it was not a good use of judicial time. It should also be noted that ABA standards are merely suggested guides for conduct. They are not binding unless a court has officially adopted the standard through its disposition of case law.)

[10] One judge earned a reputation as the "fastest gavel in the West" by managing to select a jury for a very complicated civil case in 20 minutes. Roscoe Pound — American Trial Lawyers Foundation, The American Jury System: Final Report 24 (1977).

[11] Babcock, Voir Dire: Preserving "Its Wonderful Power," 27 Stan. L. Rev. 545 (1975). (This idea has also been expounded by the courts. In United States v. Ledee, 549 F.2d 990, 993 (5th Cir. 1977), the court stated, "Peremptory challenges are worthless if trial counsel is not offered an opportunity to gain the necessary information upon which to base such strikes.")

> weaknesses of each litigant's case. Justice requires that each lawyer be given an opportunity to ferret out possible bias and prejudice of which the juror himself may be unaware until certain facts are revealed.[12]

Finally, there is the argument that the constitutional right to counsel carries with it the right to have one's counsel personally question prospective jurors. This argument is given added weight by the historical background of the sixth and ninth amendments to the Constitution. Prior to the American Revolution colonists were often confronted with juries stacked against them by the government, especially in political trials. The debates concerning the drafting of the amendments indicate a concern for protecting individuals from government controlled courts and juries. The drafters intended that the language used in the Constitution and in the amendments would sufficiently protect not only the right to trial by jury but also the right to examine and challenge jurors.[13] At least one court has concluded that "the right to be represented by counsel carries with it the right of counsel to interrogate the members of the jury panel."[14]

§9.0.3 *Voir Dire Conducted by Both Judge and Attorney*

A voir dire conducted by both the judge and the attorney is probably the best method. The judge conducts the preliminary examination by asking jurors general questions, and then turns the voir dire over to the attorney. The judge often remains in

[12] United States v. Ledee, 549 F.2d 990, 993 (quoting Frates and Greer, Jury Voir Dire: The Lawyer's Perspective, 2 A.B.A. Litigation 2 (1976)).

[13] For an in-depth analysis see Gutman, The Attorney-Conducted Voir Dire of Jurors: A Constitutional Right, 39 Brooklyn L. Rev. 290 (1972).

[14] LaRosa v. State, 414 S.W.2d 668, 671 (Tex. Crim. App. 1967). (The court was actually discussing the right to a fair and impartial jury and made the specific statement in reference to the Texas Constitution, Article I, §10, which provides the criminal defendant with the right to present his or her case personally or with the assistance of counsel. The court construed this as the right of counsel to personally examine the prospective jurors.)

the courtroom to guard against attorney abuses of the voir dire. While advocates of expediency may assert that this system is too time consuming, it offers several important advantages. First, since jurors are often unaware of their prejudices, the ability to select an impartial jury relies on the ferreting out these hidden biases. The voir dire must give an adequate opportunity to probe the social and psychological makeup of the jurors. The attorney's familiarity with the subtleties of the case make him or her better equipped to bring out the information that will lead to the detection of these hidden biases. Second, even if the voir dire could be conducted within a set time, as some have suggested, the limit could give the appearance of injustice and might cause a loss of faith in the system on the part of jurors and litigants.

A full and complete voir dire allows the attorney to exercise challenges intelligently and provides the best opportunity to eliminate biases against the parties. This approach tends to foster the idea that because the system is primarily concerned with resolution of disputes, priority is given to fairness over expediency. Finally, a thorough and proper voir dire may actually save judicial time by avoiding the necessity of retrial. One court has ruled that [t]he right of fair trial by an impartial jury is destroyed when the right to make an intelligent judgment as to whether a juror should be challenged is lost or unduly impaired. When this occurs, the verdict should be set aside and a new trial granted.[15]

§9.1 Seeking a Change in the Voir Dire Method

Whatever approach to voir dire is expected to be used in a case, the attorney is ordinarily not precluded from seeking to have it changed. If the attorney feels that the court's standard approach will not result in a full and adequate voir dire, an alter-

[15] Minnis v. Jackson, 330 So. 2d 847, 848 (Fla. Dist. Ct. App. 1976).

native should be requested. Judges usually have a great deal of discretion in determining the type of voir dire to allow and are more receptive to suggestions for changes when they are made as pretrial motions. While the pretrial request cannot guarantee the attorney an active part in the voir dire, it can result in a more thorough questioning of jurors by the judge.

When a change in voir dire method is requested by motion, certain types of information should be included. The attorney should outline "the areas of inquiry, the reasons requiring the questioning, and the authorities . . . compelling it."[1] In addition, the attorney should request permission to do the questioning. If the attorney is in a jurisdiction where judges do not usually allow attorneys to conduct voir dire, the attorney should suggest self-imposed constraints. For instance, the attorney might agree not to argue his or her case or try to indoctrinate jurors during the voir dire. By making these concessions the attorney may stand a better chance of being permitted to actively participate in the voir dire. It should be remembered that agreeing to a few constraints is better than being forced to accept a judge-conducted voir dire.

The attorney will also want to support the motion with a memorandum that backs up the argument for allowing the attorney to conduct the voir dire. The argument for attorney-conducted voir dire supported by relevant citations, might read as follows:

1) The law in this state sets up qualifications that trial jurors must meet;
2) If no opportunity is given to examine these jurors to see whether they meet these qualifications, the law is meaningless;
3) A right with no remedy is no right at all, and no remedy for the unqualified juror exists without a method of testing the juror's qualifications and;
4) Voir dire is the only tool provided by law for testing for juror qualifications.[2]

§9.1 [1]Turley, Voir Dire: Preparation and Execution, 8 Litigation 19, 20 (1982).

[2]Selecting the Jury—Plaintiff's View, 5 Am. Jury Trials 143-246.

Following the argument for attorney-conducted voir dire, the attorney should list the subjects that have been held by courts to be appropriate for inquiry by counsel, accompanied by appropriate citations. If the subject is controversial or confusing, the attorney should include a legal comment or discussion section on that topic, again supporting all propositions with authority. For example, the right to question jurors concerning the racial aspects of a case will require more of an explanation than merely a statement that courts previously have allowed such questioning. Each of the listed subjects should be individually numbered to enable the court to find them without having to read entire paragraphs.

In addition to a thorough memorandum, the pretrial motion can be supported by affidavits from experts. The affidavits might cover topics such as the effect pretrial publicity may have had on the prospective jurors.[3] Furthermore, the attorney may want to request a hearing on the motion. Some judges are willing to grant such motions if it can be shown that prominent and respected attorneys will serve as expert witnesses.[4]

Regardless of the type of trial, the motion should show the need for extensive and thorough voir dire in the particular case. Finally, the motion should be submitted at least several days before trial to permit the judge to read it and make a decision without having to rush. Even if the judge denies the motion, it will serve as proof of the lawyer's efforts to acquire an adequate voir dire if the case is appealed on the basis of a partial jury.

The following is an example of part of a memorandum in support of adequate voir dire:

I. VOIR DIRE EXAMINATION OF JURORS MUST BE CONDUCTED ORALLY AND DIRECTLY BY COUNSEL

Before *People v. Crowe,* 8 Cal. 3d 815 (1973), the law and practice was for voir dire to be conducted orally and directly by counsel. *People v. Adams,* 21 Cal. App. 3d 972 (1971), Cal. Penal Code sec. 1078 (before amendment in 1974).

[3]See A. Ginger, Jury Selection in Criminal Trials 290, 297 (1977).
[4]Id. at 290-91.

In *Crowe* the court interpreted the then-language of sec. 1078 as not requiring oral and direct voir dire by counsel. *People v. Barger*, 40 Cal. App. 3d 662 (1974), *People v. Dorsey*, 43 Cal. App. 3d 953 (1974).

In 1974, After *Crowe, Barger* and *Dorsey*, the Legislature amended sec. 1078. The effect of the 1974 amendment was to nullify *Crowe's* decision. See Brosnaham: *Trial Handbook for California Lawyers* (Bancroft-Whitney, April 1976 Pocket Part). Thus, the statute now explicitly provides:

> It shall be the duty of trial courts to examine prospective jurors to select a fair and impartial jury. He shall permit reasonable examination of prospective jurors by counsel for the People and for the Defendant, *such examination to be conducted orally and directly by counsel*. Penal Code sec. 1078, as amended (words underlined added by 1974 amendment.)

II. THE FOLLOWING SUBJECT MATTERS HAVE BEEN HELD TO BE APPROPRIATE FOR INQUIRY BY COUNSEL:

1. Personal background and information about jurors. *Walker v. Greenberger*, 63 Cal. App. 2d 457 (1944, occupation).
2. Prior jury experience. *People v. Wismer*, 58 Cal. App. 679 (1922).
3. Juror's acceptance of difference between proof by a preponderance and guilt beyond a reasonable doubt. *People v. Deriso*, 222 Cal. App. 2d 478 (1963), *People v. Tuthill*, 31 Cal. 2d 92 (1947).[5]

§9.2 Submitting Questions

Generally the attorney has the opportunity to submit questions for a judge-conducted voir dire. The judge has sole discretion about whether to ask all or any of the questions submitted by the attorney. In order to increase the likelihood of their being asked, the attorney should limit the questions to 20 or 30 that

[5]Extract from memorandum in support of adequate voir dire provided by the National Jury Project, Berkeley, Cal.

are "clearly relevant to issues in the case" along with an additional group of demographic questions.[1] The attorney should be prepared to explain why each question is necessary. If too many questions are submitted, it may be difficult to demonstrate that all of them are relevant. It is better to submit a limited number of thoughtful questions, each one designed to elicit the specific information. Also, if the judge is prepared to ask a set number of questions from the attorney, then the smaller list will increase the chances that the more important ones will be asked since there will be fewer questions to choose from.

The attorney should also prepare follow-up questions. Some of these are likely to be asked by the judge on his or her own initiative, but it is best to be prepared in the event the judge allows more questions to be submitted. To do this the attorney must anticipate answers to the initial questions in order to avoid antagonizing the judge by taking too much time in drawing up additional questions. It is important for the attorney to pay close attention to the juror's responses in order to determine whether a question was understood. This will help in designing follow-up questions not otherwise anticipated. When the attorney notices that a juror is confused, he or she should ask the judge to clarify the question. Often such occasions give rise to follow-up questions that elicit further information from the juror. The attorney should also be ready to ask for a complete answer when a judge cuts off a juror's response. Not only will full responses yield more information, but such close attention to the proceeding will also show the juror that the attorney is listening closely to the juror's responses.

§9.3 Introductory Remarks by Judge

The majority of people called for jury duty have never been inside a courtroom or seen a trial. If they have, it is likely they

§9.2 [1]National Jury Project, Jury Work, Systematic Techniques 38 (1979).

were in court as spectators only. Thus, to most prospective jurors the trial process is mysterious and they approach it with expectations shaped by television. As a result, many prospective jurors are anxious, uncomfortable, and even frightened. They can usually be put at ease simply by informing them about the trial process and their role in it. Instead of feeling like intruders in a strange world made up of lawyers and judges, the jurors can be made to feel like a part of the system. They should be made to realize that their participation in the system can be a pleasant, rather than frightening, experience.

The judge plays an important role in relaxing prospective jurors and making them feel like participants. While every judge has a unique style in addressing prospective jurors, there are certain topics every judge should cover.

First, the judge should welcome the jurors to the courtroom and introduce himself or herself, the court personnel, the lawyers, and the parties if they are present.[1] This gives jurors a feeling of familiarity with the other participants in the lawsuit and prevents them from having to wonder about various persons' roles. In addition, the judge should briefly state the nature of the action without going into the facts in depth, explaining that the lawyers will explain more during the voir dire.

Following introductions, the judge should explain to panel members how they came to be selected as prospective jurors.[2] At this point, the voir dire process can also be explained,[3] emphasizing that, while attorneys will not intentionally embarrass jurors, some personal questions will be necessary to insure that an impartial jury is selected. The judge should encourage the jurors to be frank and honest in their answers, possibly even explaining that voir dire literally means *to speak the truth.* Both types of challenges, peremptory challenges and challenges for cause, should be discussed. The judge should stress that being

§9.3 [1]See W. Jordan, Jury Selection 12 (1980).

[2]See Musser, Instructing the Jury — Pattern Instruction, 6 Am. Jury Trials 923, 939 (1967).

[3]See W. Jordan, Jury Selection 14 (1980).

challenged in no way reflects on a juror's personal integrity. The jurors should be made to understand that since the lawyers are ultimately looking out for their clients' best interests, a challenge does not constitute a personal attack. Also, jurors should be cautioned not to let the challenging of another juror affect their attitudes toward either party involved in the trial.

The jurors should be impressed with the importance of their role in the trial system during the explanation of voir dire. The judge needs to impress on jurors the need for them to be honest and to take their duties seriously. Judge Rubey M. Hulen once made the following remark:

> When jurors are treated as officers of the court, when they are told that they are not advocates of either side, have no personal interest in the case, but sit in the jury box as judges to judge facts, just as the judge is there as the judge of law, and when jurors are accorded the respect due them, it is the exceptional man or woman who will not respond by giving his best efforts to perform his or her duties fairly, honestly and impartially.[4]

Thus, it is extremely important for the judge to impress on jurors what their duties are, the impact of their duties, and the importance of jury service. They should then be told the reasons that will permit them to be excused from jury duty. It has been found that by explaining the importance of citizen participation in the system before allowing requests for exemption, the number of people asking to be excused is decreased.[5]

In the same fashion that a judge elaborates on a juror's duties, the roles of the judge and attorneys in the trial should be explained. The judge may also want to tell the jury panel not to discuss the case among themselves or anyone else, including members of their families. They should also be cautioned not to converse with the parties to the action, or the attorneys and witnesses involved. A warning should be given against accept-

[4] Hulen, Twelve Good Men and True: The Forgotten Men of the Courtroom, 38 A.B.A.J. 813, 815 (1952).

[5] See Musser, Instructing the Jury — Pattern Instruction, 6 Am. Jury Trials 923, 939 (1967).

ing favors from anyone who may be concerned with the trial, no matter how slight the favor may seem.

At this point the judge should explain the rest of the trial procedure to the jury panel. This should include who will be doing what and when, and why the trial will proceed in a particular manner. In addition, jurors should be told how long the trial is expected to last and what types of delays may occur, such as objections, recesses, and bench conferences. This gives the jury an overview of the trial process and can prevent feelings of confusion and alienation.

Finally, the jurors should be told about the deliberation process, emphasizing that throughout the trial they will be free to accept or reject any and all testimony. Some judges also prefer to give other instructions at this time regarding such niceties of law as the burden of proof and presumption of innocence. The current trend seems to be to give instructions as their need arises during the trial. This approach avoids confusing jurors by giving them too much to absorb at once.[6]

Two examples of judge's introductory remarks follow.

§9.3.1 *Sample Introductory Remarks by Judge*

New York Civil Impanelment[7]

. . . Seat No. 1 is in the lower lefthand as I face it with Seat No. 7 directly above it in the upper lefthand corner. Don't be thrown off by the two seats that we have over there on the far right. So as your names are called if you would please exchange seats with whoever is sitting in the seat you have been called

[6]See Strawn & Munsterman, Helping Juries Handle Complex Cases, 65 Judicature 444 (1982); Schwarzer, Jury Instructions: We Can Do Better, 8 Litigation 5 (1982).

[7]Partial transcript of New York civil impanelment conducted by Commissioner Nye in the Los Angeles Superior Court, July 31, 1970. See Levit, Nelson, Ball & Chernick, Expediting Voir Dire, An Empirical Study, 44 S. Cal. L. Rev. 916, 979-982 (1971).

for, then we'll have you properly lined up and we'll tell you what the lawsuit is all about.

Fill the box, please. . . .

At the moment, as you can see, neither of those parties is present here in this courtroom. You should, of course, attach no significance whatever one way or the other to the fact that neither party is presently with us. I'm sure you will hear and see all that you need to hear and see to bring this case to a proper conclusion at the appropriate time.

(Statement of Appearance of Counsel)

Do any of you know or recognize either of these gentlemen, or do you recognize the names of plaintiff or defendant? All right.

By his complaint, plaintiff is seeking damages for personal injuries that he alleges he sustained in an accident on September 8, 1965, at the intersection of 17th and Central Avenue in Los Angeles. In his complaint he alleges that his accident and the injuries of which he complains were caused by the negligence of the defendant. In her answer, the defendant denies that she was negligent; she denies that she was the cause of any accident; she denies the nature and extent of the injuries as alleged by plaintiff and she further asserts that if there were any negligence at all in connection with this accident, it was plaintiff's negligence.

Now, the law that will govern the situation will be given to you at the conclusion of the case by the trial court. If you are selected as a trial juror in this case, will you follow the law just as the court gives it to you, regardless of any personal thoughts that you might have about the law. I see you are all nodding your heads and I hear some of you answering in the affirmative and I take it what you're saying then, is that: If you are selected as a juror in this case and if, when you hear the law that the court tells you applies to this case, you find yourself disagreeing with it or perhaps being surprised that that's the law, for the purpose of disposing of this case, at least, you'll put aside all previous thoughts that you had about what the law is or should be and you'll follow the law that the court tells you should be applied to the facts of this case as you, the jury, determine those facts to be. Is that the frame of mind that you're all in? Very good. That's the frame of mind you are supposed to be in, so far we're all ahead of the game.

I will be leaving the room shortly and your further questioning will be taken over by the attorneys. Please, of course, give them your undivided attention so that you can hear and understand their questions and you can answer them fully and candidly.

Counsel, of course, can question only the twelve of you whose names have just been called. The others of you, of course, should listen just as carefully because you might be called upon to join the prospective panel. You should answer the questions as they are being asked, but, of course, silently to yourself. In that way much time can be saved if later you join the prospective panel of jurors.

In view of your answer here a minute ago, that regardless of your personal thoughts you'll follow the law as the court gives it to you, counsel will now not ask you any questions at all about the law or your understanding or attitude about any of the particular laws that might apply to this case. They won't burden you with lengthy and complicated hypothetical questions that are designed to test you or find out in advance how you might vote, and since nothing you hear in this room is evidence, they will, of course, not ask you any questions at all based on the facts that give rise to this lawsuit. What they will ask you, and perhaps at some length, will deal with your background, education, occupation; your driving experience; whether or not you have ever been involved in an accident; were you injured; if so, to what extent and what recovery have you had from those injuries. These are the types of things they will explore with you and these are the things that they owe their clients the duty of exploring with you to find out as much as they can about your frame of mind in connection with those subjects.

During the course of your selection, if I should return to the room, perhaps just sit over there and watch and listen for a while, please attach no significance whatever to that. Also, I'm sure that I can predict that as your selection progresses, counsel — probably both of them — will exercise what many of you have heard before called peremptory challenges; that is, they can excuse one or more of you from service on this jury and not have to say anything to anybody about why they are excusing you. When that happens, please don't worry or wonder about it. Don't attach any significance in so far as it affects this lawsuit to the exercise of such challenge and above all, don't take any personal offense at it. No personal offense is ever intended; none should ever be inferred. In exercising a peremptory challenge, counsel are not in any way attempting to comment either directly or indirectly on your integrity or your intelligence or your ability or competence as a juror. It simply means that they have listened to all the answers you gave to the many questions that were asked of you and they have come to the conclusion that it's possible that you might be uncomfortable for any one of many reasons sitting in judgment on this particular case and perhaps not even realize it yourself. And then, of course, too, it's possible if that's true, that this discomfort might find its way somehow or other into your deliberations and verdict, and again, without you even realizing it. So, if counsel does have that feeling, even if it's completely wrong, he owes his client the duty of exercising a right that the law gives him to cover that very situation so that he doesn't have to submit his client's rights to someone that he's afraid may be uncomfortable in passing on those rights. That's the only significance and none other should ever be attached to it.

Please remember, also, that the trial of this case has now begun. As you can tell from looking around you, you're not in a regular courtroom, but for the purpose of selecting a jury for a trial of this case, this room, with all of its shortcomings, is a courtroom and what's taking place here is part of the trial of this case and is, therefore, a regular session of the Superior Court. It's being conducted by counsel in their capacities as officers of the court and outside the presence of the trial judge, for the obvious purpose of saving everybody lots of time.

With respect to counsel, of course, I'm sure you all know this but I don't think it ever hurts to repeat it in each case, and that is that from now until the conclusion of this case, for those of you who are selected as jurors and until the selection is completed for all the rest of you, there cannot be any further contact or communication of any kind except that which takes place during a regular session of this trial between any of you and either of counsel or any of the parties at any later time, and that's for the obvious reason that our system of justice requires a complete impartiality from its trier of law and triers of fact, and that requisite impartiality demands that at all times throughout the course of every trial, clear through to the end of it, there be a very definite aloofness between counsel and their clients on the one side and the trier of the law, the judge, and the triers of the fact, the jury, on the other side. So, if during the course of this trial at any time or at any place you should happen to run across counsel, you'll probably find that they'll simply nod or smile, perhaps wave, but keep right on going and they'll do that, not because they think they're better than you are, or they're tired of looking at you, or any other reason such as that. They'll do it because, as officers of the court, they know they cannot stop and chat with you during the course of this case on anything, no matter how much they might want to or you might want them to.

After the case is over, no holds barred, then. You can talk to your heart's content, but during the course of the case, simply a good morning and keep on going. So, now if it happens you'll understand why it's happening and you won't be upset because you think plaintiff's attorney highhatted you or defendant thinks he's better than you are. You'll know why it's being done, and if you think about it, I'm sure you'll realize that is just the way you want it to be.

Gentlemen, you may begin the selection of your jury.

(Commissioner retires.)

§9.3.2 *Sample Introductory Remarks by Judge*

Jury Orientation

(Introduction of the parties and their attorneys by the Court. The Court should inform the members of the jury panel that the attorneys may be referred to, during the trial, as attorneys, lawyers, or counsel.)

The case which we are about to try is a civil case as distinguished from a criminal case. It is a suit filed by John Doe, who is called the Plaintiff, against Jane Doe, who is called the Defendant, for damages claimed to be due for (insert a very brief statement as to the type or kind of suit that is to be tried, e.g., "Injuries alleged to have been suffered as a proximate result of the defendant").

(Number) members will constitute the jury in this case, and they will consider all of the evidence produced during the trial, and reach a decision with the help of certain instructions from the Court as to the law applicable to this case.

It will be the sole responsibility of the jurors chosen to try the case to determine the facts from all the evidence produced during the trial.

It has been estimated that the trial will last (number) days. (The judge should then inquire if there are any members of the jury panel who would be unable to serve during the trial if selected as jurors.)

In this case, it will not be necessary to keep the jurors together at noon or at night until the case is finally presented to you for your deliberation and decision.

Explanation to the Jury Panel on Voir Dire

(Insert Number) members of the jury panel will be called to the jury box. Upon being called into the jury box, you will take an oath that you will truthfully answer all questions as to whether or not you can serve as a juror in this case. Your answer should be direct and complete as to all questions that may be asked by the court or by the counsel.

Each side may excuse, not exceeding (number) of the members without cause, leaving a jury of (number). Therefore, do not be embarrassed or consider it any reflection upon you if you are one of those excused. By using this method of selecting a jury, both sides are able to participate more frankly in the selection of the jury and the chances are greater this way to obtain a jury consisting of members who are absolutely fair and impartial. This procedure is part of our American System of Justice and is fair to both sides.

Instruction Regarding Juror's Conduct during Trial Admonition

Members of the jury: The court will be in recess until (insert time), but before we separate I must instruct you of your duty during the trial and all recesses not to discuss with, or otherwise, communicate among yourselves or anyone else, nor permit anyone to communicate with you upon any subject concerning the case now being tried, and not to form or express any opinion on the case until after it has been finally submitted to you for your verdict. Should anyone attempt to communicate with you about this case, immediately notify me personally.

Do not talk to any counsel, any party, or any witness upon any matter what-so-ever, whether it has anything to do with the case or not. Do not view the premises (place of occurrence) involved or make any effort to obtain any information as to the facts or law of the case other than what is presented to you during this trial.

Do not read any newspaper articles, listen to any broadcasts nor view any telecasts pertaining to this case or any facts or law concerning it.

Oath on Voir Dire

Do you, each of you, solemnly swear (or affirm) to answer truthfully the questions asked by the court or counsel concerning your service as a juror in this case, (So Help you God)?[8]

[8]Not every state requires the prospective jurors to take an oath; however, the oath is traditional in many courts. At the request of the juror, the word "affirm" should be substituted for the word "swear" and the words "So help me God" should be omitted.

§9.4 Remarks by Attorney

Although attorneys will choose their own approaches to the jury, all of them should include the following in their introductory statements:

1. Explain exactly what voir dire is and why it is used.
2. Address the likelihood that some jurors will feel their private lives are being invaded.
3. Explain the need for detailed and extensive questioning.
4. Introduce the party involved.
5. Introduce the nature of the case.
6. Expose the jurors to the hinge issues of the case.
7. Attempt to dispel any negative feelings toward the client, lawyer, or case caused by voir dire questioning.
8. Prepare the jurors for objections by the opposing counsel.

When preparing jurors for objections, the attorney has two areas of concern: objections during voir dire and objections during trial. Because some jurors may feel that objections are attempts to block the truth, the attorney may wish to prepare the jurors by making the following statements:

> As jurors you are probably going to feel that attorneys who make objections to testimony are trying to block the truth or trying to keep something from coming into evidence that would help you make up your minds about the case. We hope you realize that it is our duty to object when we feel some bit of information is inappropriate. We have here issues of fact that must be decided by you, the jurors. Certain information might be interesting to you, but it also might cloud the issues if, according to the law, it has no bearing on the facts. Therefore when irrelevant information is offered, one of the attorneys might object. The judge must then determine whether the evidence is proper. If he (or she) sustains the objection, he agrees that the evidence is not proper. If he overrules the objection, he believes that the evidence is proper.

Five sample introductory statements to be made to the jury at the start of voir dire follow.

§9.4.1 *Sample Introductory Remarks by Attorney (Criminal Case)*

My name is Bill H. of Newark, New Jersey. My client, Sherry Jo D., is seated here at my right side. We represent the defendants in this case, which means that Sherry Jo has been charged with the crime of third degree assault. We are here this morning to select a jury. That is why you are here also. In order to do that, we must conduct a process that is called voir dire, which simply means to speak. This is my chance, as Sherry Jo's lawyer, to speak to you, one on one, so that we can decide whether or not Sherry Jo can find 12 people who can listen to her case with open and unprejudiced minds and without having made any predeterminations from what they have read in the newspaper or may have heard from their friends and neighbors. In order to find out what your judgments are, what your attitudes are, how you feel about Sherry Jo and about what the prosecution is saying about Sherry Jo, I have to ask you some questions.

I have no intention of prying into your personal lives or of embarrassing you in any way. However, as an attorney, I have a duty to my client to ask you certain questions which you may find embarrassing, certain questions which you may not even want to answer. I hope that you will bear with me and that you will understand that the need for your answers justifies the need for asking these questions.

I know that I do not have to remind you that you all took an oath to tell the truth and to answer these questions openly and honestly. If we both do our jobs — that is, if I ask you the right questions and you give me truthful answers — then Sherry Jo and I should be able, at the end of this time of sharing questions and answers, to select the 12 fairest and most impartial jurors from among the panel.

And now, I would like each of you to stand and to briefly tell me your name and address, your occupation, your spouse's occupation if you have a spouse, the number of children you have, and, if they are old enough to work, their jobs. Because I know that that's a lot of information for you to remember, I have a flip chart on which I have listed in order these questions so you can simply follow that list and supply us with the answers. Now, we'll just take you in order, beginning with you, sir, Mr. Jack M., in seat number one. If you just stand and give us the answers to these questions. Thank you very much, sir.

§9.4.2 *Sample Introductory Remarks by Attorney (Civil Case)*

I am Dwight E. of the firm of E., S., H., F. and B. located in downtown Cleveland. We have some 27 lawyers in our firm and we have been located in this area since 1923.

Therefore, some of you might know either me or my partners or other members of our firm and later on I will be asking you some questions about that. I would also like to introduce to you Mr. James C. M., the president of A & G Manufacturing, who is the defendant in this civil matter. His wife, Mrs. M., is seated beside him and his three children are in the front row behind the barrier. Will they please stand. Thank you.

We are about to begin that part of the trial which is called voir dire. It means a chance for the lawyers to talk directly to the prospective jurors. Voir dire means to speak, and since I heard all of you take the oath to speak the truth, I am confident that you will do so. What I am about to do, I am doing not only for myself and my client, but also on behalf of Attorney J. and his client. Together we would like the jury panel to know that while the questions may tend to be rather personal, they are not being asked with the intention of prying into the juror's affairs.

These questions are being asked for good reason. First, it is important that both sides agree before the case begins that the jury was chosen as fairly as possible. Second, they must also be able to agree that the members of the jury are open-minded — that is, that they will have no tendency to lean in favor of either side and that they have no prejudgments or expectations of what the final verdict will be. In other words, these questions must be asked to assure both sides of the lawsuit that the jury is a fair one.

My first questions will be addressed to all of you as a group and then I will have some questions for each of you individually.

§9.4.3 Sample Introductory Remarks by Attorney

I know the judge a few minutes ago introduced all of us seated here at these tables, but I would like to go over that again for you. From looking at your trial experience sheets, I realize that most of you are here for the first time. My name is Craig M. and I am an attorney who practices law just across the street with my partner, David N. Our clients are seated here at the table with us and they are Professor and Mrs. Frank I. The gentleman seated behind me at the other table is Attorney Jerry R. of the law firm of M., B., W. and C. The gentleman to his left is the doctor in this malpractice case, Dr. Jerry W.

I am aware that this is an experience unlike many experiences you have had. You have entered this courtroom, a room that is in itself dramatic. The judge maintains order in the courtroom and tells us what the law is. Seated next to that black-robed judge is a court reporter who is busily recording every word that is spoken in this courtroom; and yes, he will be recording the answers that you give us.

I know that some of you feel that you haven't been treated very well this morning. First of all, you were asked to be here at an exceedingly early hour. Then you were asked to wait until you were all sent into a large room where you viewed a film about what jury duty was going to be like. Then you sat in that large room and waited for someone to call you to a courtroom where you might have the opportunity to be selected as a juror. Some of you were unfortunate enough to be selected to come to this courtroom where we were still busy in the judge's chambers going through certain motions and making certain decisions as to how this trial was going to proceed. So you were faced with further periods of waiting without really understanding what was happening or why it was happening. And then you were marched into this courtroom and asked to swear that you would answer truthfully the questions which are about to be asked. And now, I must tell you that some of those questions that you will have to answer are going to be of a highly personal nature.

I am certain that at this time the majority of you are wondering how justice can ever work and how it was that you ever got yourself into this spot. I can only say, Mr. J., that what has occurred so far this morning is a necessary part of our system of justice and that I hope that you will not hold anything that you have experienced thus far this morning against me or my client. How do you feel about that, Mr. J.? (After Mr. J. has responded, continue with the following.) I am sure, Mr. J., that you will understand that these questions are not being asked to satisfy my own personal curiosity or to embarrass you in any way in front of your fellow jurors. They are being asked so that we can determine if there is anything in your background or in your life experiences that would make it difficult for you to serve as a juror on this particular case. Do you understand that, Mr. J.?

§9.4.4 Sample Introductory Remarks by Attorney

The judge has already introduced all of us but I would just like to remind you who I am. My name is Karen F. and I represent Joe K. in this case.

I know that is is natural for jurors to resent prying questions. I am, therefore, going to attempt to explain to you the purpose that I have in asking these questions and to prepare you for the questions that are going to come. I must make certain that the jury we select will give Mr. K., the defendant, the same fair and impartial consideration that each of you would expect to have given to one of your own or to yourself if you were, by some act of fate, placed in my defendant's place. That is the purpose of these questions that I am about to ask.

Forgive me if you feel that any of these questions are of a highly personal nature. Believe me, I am going to confine my questioning to those areas which have direct relevance to my client's case and which we feel will assist us in determining that he will receive in this courtroom a trial by his peers that will be fair and impartial.

§9.4.5 Sample Introductory Remarks by Attorney

Members of the panel, we are now about to start that stage of the trial which is called voir dire. Attorneys have as many ways of pronouncing that phrase as they have ways of conducting the voir dire. I say *voĭr diré.* My opponent, the attorney from the prestigious Boston firm, will, no doubt, say *voir dire.* The process is the same. It simply means that this is the chance for us, the attorneys, to ask you, the prospective jurors, questions.

Let me give you a little more background about what all of this is really about. You see, everybody in this courtroom has already been assigned a job. Judge H., the lady that you see seated behind the bench who is wearing the black robe and who has been giving us the law this morning, has that as her duty and her obligation. As the judge, she is the one who determines the law. At various times during the course of this trial, either I or my opponent will be making objections. These objections will be as to whether or not the trial is being conducted according to the law. The judge's job is to make the decision as to whether or not these objections are valid; if they are valid, she will say that they are sustained; if she feels the objections are not valid, she will say, "overruled." That's her job and that job is filled.

Seated in front of the judge is Ms. Jane C., a court reporter. She is charged with recording exactly and precisely every word that is spoken in this courtroom while the court is in session so that those words can later be transcribed and be made a court record. That is her job and those are her duties and responsibilities.

Seated just to her left and at the end of the jury box is the man wearing the yellow coat that has "Deputy Sheriff" on it. That man is the bailiff and his name is Tom B. It is his job to make certain that all of the jurors' needs are taken care of. He will see that you have a place to go when you are excused from the courtroom, he will see that order is maintained among the jurors, and he will provide assistance to the judge. That is Tom's job and he has been performing it very well for 11 years.

As I said, my name is Ronald H., attorney for the plaintiff. Over the last several months it has been my duty to examine witnesses, to read depositions, to examine the evidence and to prepare this case to bring it into court to present my client's side. Seated next to me is my client, Frank L., the man who has brought this lawsuit.

Seated behind me is the attorney for the defendant, Alex B. His client is the manufacturing company of H & K Incorporated. In the same ways that I have been investigating on behalf of my client, he has been investigating on behalf of his client. It is his duty to come into this courtroom today and represent his client, H & K Incorporated. That's his job.

Everybody in this room has a job and everyone in this room has been preparing for his or her job with 12 exceptions. Those 12 exceptions are the members of the jury who will be the decisionmakers in this case. It is they who will listen to the evidence, weigh that evidence, and determine the credibility of the witnesses. They will sit here from eight o'clock until five o'clock, day in and day out, until all of the evidence is in and all of the witnesses have been heard and all of the arguments have been made. And then those 12 decisionmakers who have listened carefully will retire alone to the jury room, where not even the bailiff is allowed to accompany them. And those 12 decisionmakers must be fair; they must be unbiased; they must be unprejudiced.

Now, my opponent, Mr. B., and I both realize that people are the products of their backgrounds and their life experiences. Don't you agree with that, Mrs. J.? (Pause for her answer.)

There are a lot of jobs in the world. There are some jobs that I don't want and there are some jobs for which I am not qualified. If I were called by the government to perform a job for the government, that wouldn't necessarily mean that it is a job for which I am suited or that it is a job that I want.

What I'd like each of you to consider is that this is simply another job interview. I am going to be asking you some questions, a lot of questions in some cases. Some of you will think that these questions are of a highly personal nature; some of you will wonder what these questions have to do with the case that is before us. I can only assure you, I can only promise you, that I will not ask you a question which is meaningless and which has no value to me. Each one of these questions will provide me and my opponent with some indication as to how well this job suits you. There are many cases that are going to be going on trial in this courtroom. There might very well be another case which is more suited to your life experiences, your talents, your attitudes and your abilities. So we are going to ask you questions and we are going to look at your answers; and from those questions and answers we are going to make determinations as to which of the 12 of you are best suited to be the fairest and most impartial jurors in this case.

I'd like to tell you, to advise you of your rights, that if for some reason you feel that this is a case that you don't want to sit on — if there is something in your background, something in your political or religious or educational experiences or beliefs that will make it difficult, if not impossible, for you to sit on this case — please feel free to let us know that. As thorough as we are going to try to be, Mr. B. and I cannot possibly think of every question that should perhaps be asked in this case, so we are going to have to rely upon you and your honesty and your reasonableness to let us know if you can think of a reason why you could not be fair and impartial in sitting as a juror on this case.

Now, I know that we have been talking for a long time, but the only reason that I have taken this rather long way of introducing the concept of voir dire to you is that this is a very serious, a very important, and a very necessary part of the trial.

Everything that is going to happen here over the course of the next few days is going to happen for the benefit of the 12 people and 2 alternates who will occupy these seats; so it is important to me and to my client that these seats are filled with people who will give us a fair trial and who will listen to all of the evidence that we present to them with an open mind. Thank you.

And now, let's start with you, Mrs. J.

§9.5 Preserving the Record

An appeal based on inadequate or inappropriate voir dire arises from several types of circumstances. For example, new trials have been granted based on a juror's false responses during voir dire.[1] However, false responses will not always warrant a new trial. The court should consider "the temporal remoteness of the matter inquired about, the ambiguity of the question, the prospective juror's inadvertence or willfulness in falsifying or failing to answer, the failure of the juror to recollect, and the materiality of the matter inquired about."[2] Similar factors are considered when determining whether a trial judge's failure to grant a challenge for cause resulted in prejudice by forcing counsel to accept an undesirable juror. Also, the voir dire is sometimes challenged on appeal if an attorney has asked inappropriate questions or made prejudicial remarks to the jury. In such cases, however, the attorney who has raised the issue will have to show what transpired and how it worked to the client's detriment. It is extremely important to have the voir dire on record so that the attorney can back up his or her argument.

§9.5 [1]See, e.g., United States v. Varges, 606 F.2d 341 (1st Cir. 1979); Cavalier Insurance v. Faulk, 368 So. 2d 6 (Ala. 1979).

[2]Id. at 7 (quoting Martin v. Mansell, 357 So. 2d 964, 967 (Ala. 1978)).

The only way to show on appeal that a juror replied falsely or failed to divulge certain information when asked is through the record.[3] If there is no record of the voir dire, then the appeal probably will not be successful. This does not mean, however, that every voir dire needs to be recorded. Many cases with little merit that go to a jury trial will not likely be appealed. For such cases it would not be worthwhile to record the voir dire. Criminal cases, however, that involve a person's life or freedom and civil cases that involve thousands of dollars will usually merit an appeal if there are sufficient grounds.

[3]See W. Jordan, Jury Selection 44 (1980).

CHAPTER

10

Voir Dire Techniques

§10.0 Preparing for Voir Dire

Considerations in determining the approach to examination of the panel involve choosing which attorney will handle voir dire, attempting to influence the time and circumstances under which the inquiry will be conducted, and participating in the decision about whether panel members will be questioned as a group or individually.

§10.0.1 Choosing the Attorney to Conduct Voir Dire

Often more than one lawyer is involved in the preparation and trial of a case. Only one lawyer, however, should have primary responsibility for examination of the jury. The voir dire process introduces the personalities of the lawyers to the jury. Like all first impressions, it will have long-lasting effects. Because voir dire is of such critical significance to the outcome of the case, the choice of the lawyer who will conduct it should be carefully made.

Trial lawyers often have large egos. When two or more lawyers participate in a trial, however, they must put their egos to one side in the best interests of their client. Thus, voir dire should not simply be used to give an attorney a chance to feel important. It provides the best opportunity to establish personal rapport with prospective jurors. It requires expert interviewing skills.

Ordinarily the lawyer who conducts voir dire should also be responsible for the opening statement and closing argument. Clearly, for trial strategy to reach a persuasive peak, the controlling theme must be consistently and repeatedly emphasized throughout. Consistency will be enhanced if the same person handles each of these responsibilities.

If the trial strategy requires that a second lawyer will handle one or two of these tasks, the lawyer who has the most skillful questioning technique should conduct voir dire. If this is someone other than the lawyer or lawyers who are going to give the opening statement and closing argument, all of them should agree on the questions to be used during voir dire. They should carefully select words and phrases that will be given special emphasis during the trial.

§10.0.2 Observing the Time and Place for Voir Dire

The attorney must give careful consideration to the time of day that voir dire will be conducted. The standard practice varies with the jurisdiction and the court, where it is affected by juror orientation processes and the court's calendar.

Depending on the procedures of the court, a prospective juror may have been in the courtroom for two or two and a half hours before the start of voir dire. Sometimes an hour of that time has been spent waiting for something to happen. Therefore, some panel members are likely to be irritated.

Even after jurors have occupied the jury box for the beginning of trial, there is no assurance that their waiting is over. The judge and attorneys may still be occupied with motions and other pretrial issues in the judge's chambers. Eventually, the trial judge will move to the bench and make whatever preliminary remarks are customary in the jurisdiction. Depending on how information is presented at this time, the delay can prove to have been either helpful or harmful to a litigant. Some judges will also ask some general background questions of the jury panel. These questions ordinarily concern the panel members' names, marital status, occupations, spouses' occupation, number of children, places of residence, length of time at that residence, and whether the panel members know any of the parties in the case.

This practice varies among jurisdictions. In some counties in Mississippi, for example, a general orientation is conducted by a jury clerk using a film and instruction booklet. When the panel enters the courtroom, the plaintiff's attorney makes the first statement to the entire panel, which may consist of 60 to 100 people. The attorney then conducts the voir dire. At the end of voir dire, the attorney will either exercise challenges for cause or accept the entire jury. Next the defense attorney makes opening remarks and then conducts the defense voir dire. After each attorney has concluded his or her examination and has either exercised challenges for cause or accepted the panel, the peremptory challenges are exercised.

Regardless of the sequence of events, attorneys should be aware that a delay ordinarily has an adverse effect on the jury panel. As the day wears on, people may become bored, irritable, and in some instances even hostile. When conducting voir dire, the attorney must act and speak in a way that does not worsen the situation.

Usually voir dire is conducted in the courtroom with prospective jurors either in the jury box or in the spectators' gallery. Because a courtroom is a formal, dignified setting that may be intimidating, many jurors are subdued and cautious in their voir dire responses. Little can be done by the attorney, however, to counteract this atmosphere of formality. Any effort to introduce levity into the situation may backfire since jurors may view it as inappropriate and undignified. Testing during trial simulations has shown that jurors find joking out of place in the courtroom when it is artificially inserted in the proceeding by the attorney.

§10.0.3 *Questioning Jurors in Groups or Individually*

Jurors may be examined individually, in pairs, in small groups, or all at once. In jurisdictions using the struck jury method, the panel will consist of 12 persons plus enough additional panel members to anticipate the removal of jurors by challenge. In other jurisdictions the panel members may number 60 to 100 persons. In still others, only the number of persons who will serve on the jury will initially be called.

The strategy for determining which questions to ask and what questioning method to use will depend on communication techniques tailored to the number of panel members present. In large groups, each person has a smaller share of communication time. Consequently, the person tends to give more structured and formal responses that reveal little information of a personal nature. Single-word responses are likely. As the size of the group gets smaller, each person will feel freer to take a larger share of time. Thus, the smaller the number of persons interviewed, the greater the information that will be derived.

Some judges insist on the large group approach on the grounds that it saves time. In many cases, however, it does not. One situation in which it does not is when one juror's inappropriate statement before the group contaminates the entire panel, and a mistrial must be declared. Another such situation arises when an attorney addresses many questions to panel members individually. It will take more time to get meaningful responses from jurors in this inhibiting setting than when the jurors are questioned individually or in small groups.

When the jurors must be examined in large groups, the attorney should attempt to require jurors to respond as individuals. For example, a physical response should be requested, such as raising a hand or giving a shake of the head, and the attorney should take particular note of jurors who are reluctant to respond with the rest of the group. Such persons are just as likely to be unwilling to follow the attorney's suggestions in closing argument.

§10.1 Developing Rapport with the Panel

The attorney should be aware that the courtroom is a strange environment for the jurors. As the jurors file into the courtroom, they will carefully examine every aspect of the setting and every action that occurs. They will try to fit their observations into their own experience in an effort to make sense out of them. Lawyers should realize that most jurors' perceptions about court comes from television. Most of what occurs in the courtroom, especially in the opening moments, cannot begin to compare with the drama of *Perry Mason*. Yet the attorney needs to create a favorable impression on the jurors.

The attorney should look prepared and confident. He or she should enter the courtroom well in advance of the anticipated arrival of the prospective jurors so that the proper table is claimed, the necessary trial materials are neatly arranged, and the attorney is sitting in a watchful and anticipatory posture observing the jurors as the jurors observe him or her.

It is at this time that some of the keenest observations can be made about the probable attitudes and prejudices of the jurors. Jurors will not be offended by the direct and observing nature of the attorney; they will be offended if they feel they are being scrutinized and categorized.

One way for an attorney to communicate his or her concern for the jurors is to establish eye contact with them. This contact should be brief but sincere; it should never be so prolonged that it is interpreted as challenging or flirtatious. It is simply a mechanism by which the attorney says to the prospective juror, "I am interested in you and the kind of person you are so that I know whether you can be fair to my client."

§10.1.1 Making a Good First Impression

The lawyer should be aware that jurors begin to judge a lawyer's competency and credibility from their very first look at him or her. Therefore, the lawyer's deliberate attention to creating a positive first impression is wise and necessary.

Some experienced trial lawyers advise that it is best to treat the prospective jurors like royalty; others advise that they should be treated like a best friend; still others suggest that the best way to handle jurors is as if the lawyer were courting them. Whatever style is adopted, it should be consistent and natural to the lawyer. It is important to remember that the majority of jurors are strangers and may resent being singled out for more favorable treatment. A respectful attitude toward jurors is essential.

An excellent tactic for making jurors feel important is to address them by name during voir dire. If the lawyer has not had an opportunity to examine the jury list and memorize the names, he or she can at least carefully record their names as the jurors are called into the jury box. The lawyer should refer to that list when addressing jurors so that they know the lawyer is making a deliberate attempt to identify them as individuals.

The lawyer can make a good impression on the jury "by good humor, by special acts of kindness, by creating an impression of fairness, by tact, by simplicity and by courtesy."[1] The humor should be natural and appropriate, not sarcastic or in the form of stories. Forced humor, for instance, is not appropriate and may make a bad impression. The kindness should also be appropriate, such as picking up on a juror's physical discomfort and requesting, for example, that blinds be shut, or water provided. Such acts of kindness should be "subtle and related to the conduct of the case."[2] The impression of fairness can be created both by choosing words that indicate the attorney is seeking justice and by certain conduct, such as acknowledging a familiar juror as an acquaintance at the outset of the voir dire. Tact includes using good phraseology to avoid embarrassing jurors during the questioning or when challenges are being exercised. Simplicity includes choosing direct and

§10.1 [1]Richard Haynes, Humanizing the Defendant in Criminal Cases, American Trial Lawyers Association Counseling Cassettes (Vol. 9B, 1978).
[2]Ibid.

plain words to communicate with the jurors. Finally, courtesy to the jurors, the opposing counsel, and the judge is vital. With proper attention to this combination of factors, the lawyer will make a good initial impression.

§10.1.2 Maintaining Proximity

Because proximity is an important element in creating the illusion of friendship, the lawyer should get as physically close to the jurors as possible and then maintain that closeness. The lawyer should stand so that eye contact can be maintained with everyone on the panel being questioned, even if this is difficult.

In fact, the lawyer should establish eye contact with everyone involved in the proceeding and be certain that each person can hear and understand what is being said. Even when talking to an individual, the attorney should make everyone else in the courtroom feel part of the proceeding.

The attorney should also stand close to the client at times, touching the client in a friendly manner to demonstrate the rapport they share.

§10.1.3 Talking to Witnesses

The attorney must always be aware that he or she is being closely watched, indeed scrutinized, while in the presence of the jury. Whether the attorney is in the hallway, the elevator, or the courtroom, the attorney must act in a manner that conveys his or her sincerity. If an attorney is talking to a witness outside the courtroom or even talking informally in the courtroom, the interaction will be carefully watched and may well be misinterpreted. If the attorney seems to be smiling frequently at the witness and nodding his or her head, the juror will have a tendency to interpret this type of behavior as coaching the witness. Conversely, if the attorney is shaking his or her head at the witness or is frowning, the juror may interpret this as an indication that the attorney is dissatisfied with the testimony that the witness intends to give. It is never too early to be on guard. It is sometimes too late.

§10.2 Conducting Voir Dire

The technique of questioning panel members during voir dire calls into consideration the extent of questioning, types of questions, handling of sensitive topics, and dealing with unanticipated responses.

Many attorneys are fearful of open-ended questions and avoid them whenever possible during voir dire. There are good reasons for such reluctance. For example, the juror might reveal something harmful to the client or the case that may not be sufficient grounds for a mistrial. An ill-prepared lawyer might lose control of the voir dire procedure to an aggressive or verbose person. The well-prepared attorney, however, can use the open-ended question to let jurors reveal much about themselves and their attitudes. Asking jurors about the work they perform, for instance, provides an excellent opportunity to evaluate their self-esteem and decision-making skills with minimal risk of exposing damaging information. Most jurors feel comfortable and knowledgeable about their occupations. Thus, their responses can provide a window to their personalities. An individual who is interested in his or her job and describes it in an open and interesting manner is likely to be optimistic and positive. A prospective juror who is critical and negative by nature will most likely reveal this attitude in comments about his or her occupation.

To obtain an accurate picture of the potential jurors, the jurors must be permitted to talk. As much can be learned from how the juror responds as from the response itself.

Many lawyers fear the loss of control that comes with allowing a juror to speak openly in the courtroom; however, it is better to lose control of the proceedings during voir dire than it is to lose control of the jury after it has adjourned to the jury room for deliberations.

While it is possible to observe behavior, dress, demeanor, and use of space to tell a great deal about an individual, this information is particularly useful when it is coupled with verbal information. Both channels of communication are necessary to have a full and complete analysis of the attitude and personality of the prospective juror.

There is another reason for encouraging the juror to talk. It doesn't take very long for jurors to become conditioned to the hackneyed phrases used in the courtroom. They quickly learn how best to conduct themselves and how to answer the pat and repetitious questions asked by the advocates. Once they have observed how the first few prospective jurors have answered questions, they will know the *right* responses and will know how to make them. But if the lawyer lets the jurors talk freely, they will stray from the beaten path of redundant phrases and reveal their true thoughts and attitudes.

§10.2.1 Determining the Extent of Questioning

Obviously, certain questions can be asked of the whole panel; those who respond affirmatively would then be examined individually. For example, most persons own and drive automobiles; however, a small percentage of people do not. A jury panel might be asked generally, "Would anyone on the panel who does not have a valid driver's license or who does not know how to drive a car, please raise a hand." This should secure responses from those persons who do not know how to drive. Only those persons would then be questioned individually.

Ordinarily, any question that is not designed to obtain a commitment from the jurors can be directed to the whole panel. This includes most questions designed merely to obtain information. The attorney should design a set of general questions to be asked at the outset. Once those questions have been asked, individual questioning can begin.

Individual questions are asked for several reasons: (1) to secure specific information from a particular juror that will be different from the information other jurors will volunteer; (2) to obtain promises and commitments of future behavior, especially behavior during deliberation, from that juror; and (3) to encourage that juror to share a particular attitude or view of a hinge issue in the case that would be desirable for all jurors to share.

With this last concern, it is sometimes better for the juror to volunteer an attitude about the case than for the trial attorney to state it. Consider a case in which a person on trial for murder pleads self-defense in protecting his life and property. The attorney might select a particular juror and go through the following sequence of questions:

Q: Mr. Smith, how do you feel about violence?
A: I don't like it, of course.
Q: I share that opinion with you. I happen to think that violence is abhorrent. But is there any time when you feel that acts of violence are justified?
A: Well, yes, I do.
Q: And when would you consider it justified for you to commit an act of violence?
A: If my life were threatened.
Q: And would that be the only time?
A: Well, if my family were threatened or my property were threatened, or maybe even if my country were threatened, I guess I would have to condone an act of violence, but I guess that's it.
Q: In other words, if you were called upon to defend your family, your property, or your life, you would feel that an act of violence was justified?
A: Yes. Yes, I would.

Once this series of responses has been obtained from a particular juror, it might be detrimental to try to obtain a like series of responses from all members of the panel. A general interrogation — "Is there anyone here who wouldn't share Mr. Smith's opinion? Would you please raise your hand?" — might be sufficient to delve into differing attitudes that might exist in other panel members. If one of the panel members were to say that under no circumstances would an act of violence be justified, the lawyer could ask that person how he or she would respond to instructions from the court that self-defense is a full and complete defense to murder. This short procedure, which elicits attitudes from prospective jurors rather than dictating or lecturing them, generally wins a favorable response.

The lawyer's attempt to elicit desirable responses by using open-ended questions is risky. The lawyer must feel fairly confident about selecting a juror who will give the appropriate line of responses. If the attorney is working from a fairly solid understanding of human nature or has access to expert advice about which prospective jurors should be addressed, he or she will be in a better position. This does not mean, however, that an open-ended question should be used only when sociological or psychological advice is available. Most trial attorneys have a very good *feel* for the personalities and attitudes of the prospective jurors, especially after beginning eye-to-eye exchanges with them during a well-prepared voir dire.

Research shows that neither sequential or random questioning offers any particular advantage. The important thing is that jurors feel that they are being treated as individuals with full and complete consideration for their dignity.

§10.2.2 *Determining the Depth of Questioning*

Just as every defendant or plaintiff desires his or her day in court, so does every person who has ever been called for jury duty expect to be fully examined in voir dire. Yet many attorneys believe that if the first few jurors are questioned in depth the jurors at the end of the panel will become impatient with the process. For that reason, they may question the members at the end of the panel only briefly. In fact, jurors have a negative reaction to such attempts to hold their interest. If the first few jurors are questioned thoroughly, jurors who are questioned summarily will feel slighted. Attorneys must remember that ordinary people do not often have an opportunity to reveal in a public forum what they think about important issues. The jurors at the end of the panel are likely to be as eager to express their views as those questioned at the beginning of the process. It is flattering to those first few jurors to have the opportunity to explore their opinions in depth. Prospective jurors farther down the list feel anticipation as they contemplate their responses to the same questions — how they will improve upon them or how they will impress the court with their understanding or how they will challenge the lawyer with a thought that is new and innovative. The attorney begins to apologize for taking too much time and, in fact, even apologizes for taking time to rush through a few more questions for the rest of the jury. All too often the questioning of those final jurors goes something like the following sequence:

Q: Your name is Mrs. Sarah Marshall?
A: Yes.
Q: And you live at 1016 West Main?
A: Yes, I do.
Q: And you are married?
A: Yes.
Q: Do you work outside the home?
A: No, I am a homemaker.
Q: Do you know anything about this case, ma'am, other than what you have heard here today?
A: Oh, I vaguely remember reading something about it. (Long pause)
Q: Could you assure us that if sworn as a juror, you would decide the case on the basis of the evidence here?
A: Yes, sir.
Q: And not on anything you have read? Can you think of any reason why you could not be a fair and impartial juror?
A: No.
Q: Have you heard the questions asked of other prospective jurors?
A: Yes, I have.
Q: If they were asked of you, would your answers have been any different?
A: No, sir, I don't think so.

Q: They would be substantially the same?
A: Yes.
Q: Can you think of any reason now why you could not be a fair and impartial juror?
A: No, sir.
Q: Good. Pass the juror for cause.

This juror, who has sat through two, three, or even four hours of questioning, has now had all of three minutes to express herself. She feels cheated, and with every right. If a question is worth asking individually to the first five or six jurors, that question is worth asking individually to all of the jurors. The lawyer will antagonize far more jurors by neglecting them and ignoring their feelings and their biases than by boring them.

Lawyers, therefore, should attempt to give prospective jurors an equal opportunity to participate. The same admonition applies to questioning potential alternate jurors. Alternates are not often called to serve; however, if they do serve, they may resent the fact they were treated as second-class citizens during voir dire.

§10.2.3 Explaining Questions

Lawyers should allow the jurors, as much as possible, to understand the purpose of the questions. When jurors feel that they understand what is occurring, they will be more relaxed, more comfortable, and more revealing in their answers.

Unfortunately, research indicates that the credibility of lawyers is only slightly more than the credibility of used car salesmen and politicians. Pretrial questioning shows that prospective jurors expect to be tricked by lawyers in the courtroom. People who anticipate being tricked will be wary and will withhold information. Therefore the attorney must be as open, sincere, and reasonable as possible with the panel of prospective jurors.

§10.2.4 Avoiding Unnecessary Questions

All too often attorneys ask questions not because they expect the answers to be meaningful but simply because they are the kinds of questions normally included by experienced trial attorneys in voir dire. But it soon becomes clear that having enough time for relevant inquiry is a much greater problem than having enough conventional questions.

Of what value is the current marital status of a prospective juror unless the lawyer plans to use that information in exercising challenges or in preparing case strategy? If there is no reason for preferring one status over another, there is no reason to use the question.

§10.2.5 Avoiding Embarrassing Questions

A lawyer should never, under any circumstances or for any reason, ask a question that would humiliate a juror in front of other members of the jury. There are times when it can be anticipated that jurors will be embarrassed by certain questions (for example, attitudes toward sex, prior criminal convictions, whether they have had abortions). If it is essential to the case that this type of information be solicited from the jurors, then the judge should be petitioned for individual voir dire.

Sometimes a question that appears innocent on the surface can cause embarrassment to a prospective juror. For instance, a woman who was pregnant before marrying may feel embarrassed if a question about how long she has been married is followed by a request for the ages of her children. It is better to avoid this type of question unless for some reason it is imperative to know whether there are women on the panel who have borne illegitimate children or who married because they were pregnant.

There might also be prospective jurors who are sensitive about their lack of education, their occupations (especially if it is inconsistent with their level of education), or because they do not understand certain terminology. The attorney should give careful thought in the preparation and phrasing of voir dire questions to avoid situations in which the prospective juror will be made to feel ill at ease for any reason. Should it occur that a prospective juror is embarrassed or humiliated, the attorney should smooth out the situation as quickly as possible. Sometimes it is best to apologize; other times, it is better to avoid emphasizing the situation by simply ignoring it. Seldom is sarcasm or punning a suitable response to the situation.

§10.2.6 Avoiding Boring Questions

Every attorney worries about boring the jury. If the attorney knows the case well enough and has carefully planned the questions that will be included in the voir dire, boredom is unlikely. The attorney should carefully design the questions so that they fall in three categories: (1) those that will be asked of the entire panel, to which they will respond by raising a hand; (2) routine questions (such as name, age, marital status, occupation, spouse's occupation, residence, prior jury service), some of which will have been answered at the beginning of the voir dire; and (3) special questions intended to elicit information that will be valuable in exercising peremptory challenges or that are asked in order to educate the jurors, condition them, or get commitments from them.

Instructions to jurors on such difficult matters of law as reasonable doubt, burden of proof, preconceived notions of guilt or presumption of innocence, should always be presented in questions and never in the form of lectures. No question or introduction to a question should exceed five or six sentences. When questions are asked, the panel feels involved. If a lecture method is used, jurors' sense of involvement will be diminished and they will likely become bored. Research has shown that the length of time spent in voir dire does not alone bore jurors. There is, however, a high correlation between boredom and the juror's sense of being lectured to. During postjury-service interviews, many jurors indicate a feeling that could perhaps best be termed sympathetic boredom. They experience this while waiting for the lawyer to ask them the questions being addressed to other members on the panel.

§10.2.7 Avoiding the Words "Bias" and "Prejudice"

If you ask people if they are biased or if they are prejudiced or if they have prejudged a situation, you can expect their answer to be negative. The words "bias" and "prejudice" and "prejudgment" have negative connotations, especially to a person being considered for a "fair and unbiased" panel. People will, however, admit to having experiences, feelings, and thoughts.

Never ask prospective jurors, then, if they have a "prejudice." Instead, ask them what their "thoughts" are about a certain subject or how they "feel" about it or what "experiences" they have had in that area. Their responses will reveal the level of their bias or prejudice or prejudgment about a certain concept or a certain person.

§10.2.8 Handling Sensitive Topics

When voir dire concerns sensitive or potentially embarrassing information, the lawyer should seek to have jurors questioned in small panels, or individually in the judge's chambers or conference room. When voir dire is conducted outside the formal courtroom and in the presence of only two or three other prospective jurors, it will ordinarily result in far more revealing and honest responses. Jurors are more open in this kind of setting.

An experience in a Connecticut medical malpractice suit is illustrative. The defendant obstetrician was known to perform abortions. Although abortion was not involved in the suit, it was necessary to determine if prospective jurors' attitudes about abortion might influence their ability to make a fair decision in the case. Because abortion is such a volatile issue, the judge permitted individual voir dire in the courtroom out of the presence of other jurors.

Well over 100 jurors were examined individually before 12 could be seated. In the individual sessions with the judge and the attorneys, over 40 of the prospective jurors admitted that they themselves had had an abortion, a member of their family had had an abortion, or that they had been active participants in petition drives or group activities designed to drive the defendant doctor out of town. Each of these jurors was excused for cause. In the privacy of the quiet courtroom, individuals did not feel threatened about revealing their personal attitudes toward abortions or the doctor who performed them, even though they were fully aware that all of their comments were being recorded by the court reporter and heard by all of the officers of the court. With the removal of peer pressure, they were more willing to be open about their experiences and prejudices.

Attorneys are aware that there are some questions that cannot be asked because of the social pressure or because of a high level of prejudice. It is impractical in any court today to ask the question: "Are you prejudiced against blacks?" Some attorneys will try to elicit this information in what they feel is a more subtle way. While this is admirable, the attorney should avoid the appearance of being clever. In a recent case, a lawyer asked the following series of questions: "Have you ever had an experience where a black or a Mexican pulled a knife on you? Was that knife a pocket knife or was it one that is more commonly known as a sticker? Have you ever seen brass knuckles worn by a black man or by a Mexican?" All the lawyer accomplished was allowing each member of the prospective jury panel to understand that the lawyer was prejudiced against Mexicans and blacks.

An even more common failing among attorneys is the use of a particular tone of voice to encourage a seemingly acceptable response, only to use that response to attack the juror as a person she or he has exposed as being neither fair, nor unbiased, nor unprejudiced. The attorney is the loser in this kind of exchange.

§10.2.9 *Avoiding Provocation from Responses*

Every lawyer would rather have more friends seated in the jury box than strangers or enemies, and it is generally accepted that voir dire can create both. No matter what the provocation, the lawyer must endeavor at all times to remain calm. This will win the respect of jurors who remain in the jury box, while preventing the antagonism of one juror to contaminate those who will eventually be impaneled. A lawyer is well aware that the antagonistic juror can be excused from service either through a challenge for cause or through a peremptory challenge. The manner in which this is done is an important consideration.

Recently, while conducting a jury selection in Nebraska, a lawyer addressed the panel and asked, "Is there anything that I have not referred to, that I have not directly addressed that makes you believe that it might be difficult for you to be a fair and impartial juror in this case?" A young, tall, heavily bearded male, who had previously identified himself as a self-employed artist, jumped up from his seat in anger and shouted, "I am so angry that I am shaking. I can't stand what's going on in this courtroom. I don't like you and I don't like your client and I don't like what's going on here. How can they call this justice?"

The lawyer would have been perfectly justified in turning to the judge and immediately requesting that the prospective juror be removed for cause. Instead, he remained calm, collected his thoughts, and addressed the juror: "If you will be seated, sir, we can discuss this." And he paused while the juror resumed his seat. The lawyer then asked, "Am I to understand that what has occurred this afternoon in this courthouse is at variance with what you expected to occur?" The angry young man was somewhat surprised at this approach and he very calmly answered, "Yes, that's so. I didn't expect this kind of prying into my private life and it really upsets me."

The lawyer's next question was, "I also take it that this is not in keeping with your concept of justice?" Again, the prospective juror answered in the affirmative. Next the lawyer commented, "You indicated that you were so upset by what you were hearing and observing that you were shaking. Isn't that true?" The juror affirmed this. The lawyer then said, "Do you understand that what is occurring here during the voir dire, during this time when we have to talk to you, we are carrying out the course of law that has been prescribed to us as lawyers by our state laws?"

The lawyer continued, "Do you understand that it is not my job to make you like me or to make you like what is going on in this courtroom but that my job is to represent my client according to the law?" The juror responded, "I understand that. I just don't think it's right." The lawyer thought for a moment and then he asked, "You indicated previously that you did not know my client. Isn't that so?" The prospective juror nodded his head in the affirmative. The lawyer continued, "And you also indicated that you had never met me before today, isn't that true?" Again, the juror nodded his head in the affirmative.

The lawyer then continued, "And yet now you tell me that you don't like my client, you don't like me, and that you are so angry that you are shaking and that you are unhappy with what is occurring here today. Isn't that true?" The juror once more stood up with clenched fists at his side and exclaimed, "I am so angry. I can't remember when I have been this angry. I just want to tear things up. I know I can't go on with this."

At this time, the lawyer turned to the judge and said, "Judge, I ask that this juror be excused for cause. He obviously does not agree with our system of justice and finds it so upsetting that it would be an undue hardship to ask him to serve as a juror in this trial." The challenge for cause was honored.

Questioning of the impaneled jurors after the trial ended brought forth comments that they had a great deal of respect for the attorney who did not turn on the angry young man with an equal degree of anger, but had treated him as an adult. Yet the lawyer had shown all of the jurors that this young man was simply not suited to be a fair and impartial juror, not only in this case for this lawyer and this client, but for any case under any circumstances.

§10.2.10 Obtaining and Using Commitments

Lawyers frequently advise other lawyers to obtain commitments from jurors to follow the law as given in the judge's instructions and to perform their duty even if the duty is an unpopular one that will not win favor with friends and neighbors. Such commitments are not easy to obtain during voir dire since they require a lot of time and often cause the juror to experience considerable stress. Research has shown, however, that when such commitments are obtained, they are honored. When such commitments are made, they should be mentioned during closing argument. In posttrial interviews, jurors have indicated that they had had sleepless nights and had spent countless hours searching their consciences about such commitments that were not even invoked during the closing argument. This was the unfortunate result of over-training that has been found to yield inadequate results.

§10.2.11 Handling the Sympathy Issue

One of the points often stressed during voir dire is the need for fair and impartial jurors. When the ability of jurors to be fair is being discussed, the topic of sympathy usually emerges. Sympathy for an injured person is a normal reaction and is usually dealt with by defense attorneys in the voir dire. Thus, jurors who feel this natural sympathy will feel comforted by the defense attorney who makes statements like the following: "Human beings are sympathetic and no one is more sympathetic than I am. If you aren't sympathetic, then you probably aren't human. But if you decide this case based on sympathy, then . . ."[1] Jurors will probably hear similar remarks from the judge. The problem is that jurors, in an attempt to be fair, will lean over backwards to be fair to the opposing party because of

§10.2 [1]This example is based on an example given in Jamail, The Anatomy of a Personal Injury Suit as Viewed by a Trial Lawyer for the Plaintiff, 18 S. Tex. L.J. 167, 168 (1977).

their feelings of sympathy and because of the court's instructions to be fair and decide the case on the merits, not on feelings.[2] The plaintiff's lawyer must be prepared for this over-reaction.

One method of dealing with the possibility of jurors leaning too far in their fairness is to condition and educate the jurors. The original sympathy will have arisen because the jurors will have been encouraged by the plaintiff's lawyer to see the injured party as a human being. The defense attorney is justified in admonishing the jury against these feelings of sympathy. Once such emotions become an issue, the plaintiff's lawyer should address it by carefully explaining that the client does not want sympathy. By doing so, the attorney can counteract the effects the defendant lawyer's speech may have on the jurors. One commentator suggests that the following approach be taken by the plaintiff's attorney in addressing the jury on such feelings of sympathy:

> You may not find a verdict on the basis of sympathy. The responsibility of this defendant may not be determined because of your sympathetic attitude toward my client. This is the law and this is the proper law. I say to you now that sympathy is a form of charity: Charity is demeaning to a person of pride. My client was and is and has a right to be a person of pride. I want you to promise that throughout this case whenever you hear about sympathy, and you will not hear about it from me again, you will resist it and you will not permit your verdict to be tainted by sympathy. Because like charity, it is not only demeaning, it is usually inadequate.[3]

The commentator notes that this approach usually will prevent the defense attorney from talking about sympathy again, and if he does, "the jurors usually give each other knowing looks."[4]

[2] See Sorenson, Juror Selection and the Behavioral Sciences, 2 Litigation 30, 31 (1976).

[3] Jamail, The Anatomy of a Personal Injury Suit as Viewed by a Trial Lawyer for the Plaintiff, 18 S. Tex. L.J. 167, 168 (1977).

[4] Ibid.

Thus, the attorney can minimize the possible adverse effects of warnings about sympathy.

§10.3 Communicating with the Jury

Vocabulary and phrasing play an important role in the voir dire. The object of the voir dire is to obtain a jury that is fair and impartial. This goal cannot be attained without carefully considering the wording and phrasing of the questions addressed to the jurors. Before jurors will speak honestly and openly, they need to feel comfortable. The lawyer's attitude and demeanor play a large role in putting the jurors at ease, but so does the choice of words. The attorney must be sure to speak on an appropriate level.

§10.3.1 Avoiding Complex Language

In recent years, educators increasingly have complained about the low level language skills of the average high school graduate. Jury analysis has been performed in 11 different states to determine the average level of eduction of persons who actually serve on panels. It was discovered that the average juror has either a high school education or less. This is significant for two reasons: (1) People who have college degrees or advanced degrees are more frequently excused from jury service. (2) Attorneys on both sides of a case tend not to want persons with advanced degrees on their panels, so educated persons are often excused through peremptory challenges. The reason most commonly given for the exercise of those peremptory challenges is that the attorneys do not want a "one-person jury." The attorneys fear that a person with a higher level of education will exercise undue influence over the other jurors during deliberations.

Since recent tests have indicated that high school graduates tend to have eighth grade level vocabularies, it is imperative that lawyers be particularly careful not to use any language that will confuse jurors. One commentator made the following statements:

> In our talk and in our writing, we unnecessarily mystify our work, baffle our clients, and alienate the public. We could change this, and we should.
>
> Most lawyers must plead guilty to killing the English language. . . .
>
> Lawyers commit unnatural acts on language. . . .
>
> Judged by standards of esthetics, efficiency, or accuracy, legal language is deplorable. . . .
>
> Lawyer language is pompous. . . .
>
> Lawyers are so careful they become clumsy and repetitive. They alone find the need to "cease" as well as "desist," to "give" as well as "bequeath and devise." An Arkansas judge once told of a contempt order that was reported to have been "reversed, vacated and held null and void"; he suggested that the judge add "and stomped on."[1]

When conducting voir dire, speak simply. If legal terminology must be used, always define it with everyday language, using illustrations and charts if necessary.

There are attorneys who use complex language to impress jurors with their superior knowledge. To do so only "impresses" the jurors with their pomposity.

Trial lawyers F. Lee Bailey and Henry Rothblatt also advise avoidance of complex language. They have made the following comments:

> Many attorneys use complex legal language in an effort to impress the jury with their brilliance. Aside from tending to confuse the issues, this often antagonizes the jury. Nobody likes an egotist. Impress them with your humility, not with your brilliance — and the key to humility is simplicity.
>
> Let's take an example. Suppose you are defending a person

§10.3 [1]Goldfarb, Lawyer Language, 3 Litigation 3, 3-4 (1977).

charged with assault and your defense is that the accused acted in self-defense. Some lawyers might phrase the question in this manner: "Do you believe that a person is justified in injuring his attacker if, by the exercise of ordinary discretion and care, he has reasonable ground to believe that he is in imminent danger of losing his life or of incurring great bodily harm?" The accuracy of the law involved in that question is not to be doubted, but its value as a question is. The lay mind would have difficulty grasping it. The response, therefore, would be worthless.

I would suggest a more simplified question, such as follows: "Do you believe that a person is justified in injuring another if he honestly believes that he is in actual danger of being harmed by his attacker?"

This question employs simple, everyday language. It also explains to the jury the law of self-defense.[2]

§10.3.2 Tailoring Vocabulary to the Audience

Studies have indicated that people relate on three basic levels: adult-adult, parent-child, and child-child.[3] Since the ideal level for communication between a juror and a lawyer is adult-adult, the attorney needs to be careful not to speak down to jurors.

It is important to keep in mind that the majority of registered voters who make up today's jury panel are informed citizens. Over eighty-nine percent of registered voters indicate that they watch an evening news broadcast, and over seventy-two percent indicate that they read a daily newspaper. It is to be expected, therefore, that the average juror will have a familiarity with legal terms that have been picked up by the media. Also, certain courtroom dramas on prime time television have made people feel they have a better sense of the legal system than people did perhaps ten or fifteen years ago.

Occasionally the attorney will have to adjust his or her language to a particular juror. Even though most adults converse

[2]Bailey & Rothblatt, Successful Techniques for Criminal Trials 85-86 (1971).

[3]See Estes, The Psychology of Jury Selection, 1978 Personal Injury Annual 551, 569-579.

on an adult-adult level, a juror occasionally will try to converse on a parent-child level, with the attorney serving as the parent and the juror as the child. The attorney will be alerted to this occurrence by the juror's uncertain or confused answers to relatively simple questions. For example, jurors are asked, "What do you do at work?" Most jurors will respond with a job description. The juror conversing on a child level will hem and haw and perhaps ask for a clarification of what the attorney wants. The attorney should respond with a leading question so that a compatible level of conversation can be established. The attorney should not use a juror's child-like responses to an advantage because other jurors will pick up on this and the attorney will lose credibility.[4] Additionally, the attorney will lose credibility if put in the role of a child. If the attorney notices that a juror is responding as a parent, the attorney should determine whether the juror also treats the opposing counsel as a child. If that is not the case, then the "child" attorney should exercise a challenge to the juror because otherwise the juror will provide the "adult" attorney with an advantage.

§10.3.3 Choosing the Right Words

Not only is the conversation level important but the individual words used also play a significant role. The attorney and judge need to carefully choose their words to elicit open and honest responses from jurors. For example, if the judge tells the jurors that voir dire is aimed at obtaining a "fair and impartial" jury, then a juror's answers may be inhibited due to the juror's desire to be considered a fair and impartial person. However, if the judge stresses that "open and honest" responses are the aim of voir dire, then jurors will be more likely to respond in an open and frank manner.[5] The choice of words

[4] Id. at 571.

[5] See National Jury Project, Amicus Curiae Brief, State v. Williams, Crim. No. 21477 (Cal. Sup. Ct. 1980).

is also important when jurors are struck from the panel. For example, after a juror has been successfully challenged, the judge should say that the juror is "excused" and thank him or her for being honest.[6] Not only will this help the dismissed juror feel better about participating in the process, but it will prevent the remaining jurors from being offended by the treatment of their fellow juror.

The attorney should also carefully consider the phrasing of each question. Questions must be phrased to elicit useful information while minimizing offense to jurors. Regardless of whether the question is forced-choice or open-ended, the phrasing needs to be thoroughly thought out before the attorney speaks.

Jurors will respect an attorney who pauses thoughtfully to ask a well-worded question. They will not respect an attorney who blurts out an inappropriate or incomprehensible questions. For example, if the case involves a schoolteacher, and it is discovered that a juror is a schoolteacher, the attorney may be tempted to ask, "Can you as a schoolteacher be fair and impartial?" Such a question has the potential to cause trouble in two ways. First, the attorney has just questioned the juror's ability to be fair. No one likes being asked if he or she is a fair person and most people will not admit that they are not always fair. Second, the attorney has implicitly maligned the individual's occupation. Studies have indicated that jurors find these kinds of questions especially distasteful. The attorney should take the time to develop a more discreet line of questioning for eliciting the same information.[7]

Finally, the lawyer should remember to use basic communication skills to relax jurors and for increased effectiveness. These skills include reflection, clarification, and limited self-disclosure.

[6]See T. Mauet, Fundamentals of Trial Techniques 29-30 (1980). (For example: "Your Honor, at this time we would ask that Mr. Smith be excused." or "Your Honor, plaintiff would thank but excuse Mr. Smith." Id. at 29.)

[7]See Broeder, Voir Dire Examinations: An Empirical Study, 38 S. Cal. L. Rev. 503, 527 (1965).

Reflection consists of repeating part of a juror's answer with another question. For example, if a juror responds to a question about his health by mentioning that he has had trouble with his back, the attorney could respond, "With your back?" This reinforces the juror's answer and can elicit additional information from the juror.

Clarification is the explaining of a response to a question or the asking of a more specific question following a short answer to a broad question, such as, "Have you or a family member ever been involved in a car accident?" The juror answers, "Yes." The attorney then asks, "Could you tell us about it?" This results in the juror's expanding on the previous affirmative response.

Self-disclosure is the attorney's revealing certain things about himself to put the jurors at ease. These disclosures should be few and never too personal in nature. They should be limited to such things as, "I'm nervous too but . . ."[8] Through the effective use of these basic techniques and through the use of carefully chosen words and phrases, the attorney can conduct a meaningful, thorough voir dire without alienating, embarrassing, or offending prospective jurors.

§10.3.4 Avoiding Misrepresentations

Trial simulations and posttrial juror examinations indicate that there are three sins for which there is no forgiveness from jurors: (1) if they feel that the lawyer has lied to them; (2) if they feel that the lawyer has overstated the facts or the law; and (3) if they feel that exaggerations have been made. This is especially true in civil cases when they feel that the damages have been overstated.

Thomas F. Bridgman, past president of the Illinois Defense Council, made the following statement at the Defense Research

[8]McLaughlin, How to Read a Juror, Personal Injury Annual 623, 628-29 (1979).

Institute in September 1977, while discussing jury selection and opening statements:

> The most significant advantage an advocate can have over his opponent can be related to any misstatement contained in his opponent's opening statement. Such misstatements can be effectively used to demonstrate a lack of credibility which would very well color the jury's determination as to the entire case.

§10.3.5 Disclosing Weaknesses

It is essential that the attorney disclose all weaknesses in his or her case before the opponent has the opportunity to do so. Many attorneys want to hold back damaging information in the hope they can persuade jurors to like the client. Some hope to set the stage so the damaging information will appear to be less damaging than it would be if brought out earlier in the presentation. Some attorneys even advocate waiting at least until the opening statement before disclosing weaknesses in the case. During a trial, however, it is always better to be on the offensive than the defensive.

In an address to the Association of Trial Lawyers of America, Stanley Preiser stated, "The only damaging information in your case is the information you don't reveal." Bailey and Rothblatt concur:

> No matter how damaging the evidence against the accused is, expose it. You can be sure that the prosecutor will! If he explodes it on an unsuspecting jury during the presentation of his case, you might be unable to undo the harm. Besides, the evidence sounds a lot less damaging if it comes from you. The jury will feel that it cannot be too bad if the defendant's own attorney tells us about it.[9]

[9]Bailey & Rothblatt, Successful Techniques for Criminal Trials 120-121 (1971).

Alan E. Morrill, who was a highly respected trial lawyer in Chicago and is now a judge, has made the following observation:

> The jury is going to be unquestionably shocked by this information [the unfavorable explosive material] and you can be quite sure that there will be some prejudice against your client. Nothing, however, softens the blow so much as the guilty party's confessing his sins. As evidence of this, we have only to search our own memories to recall the impressions that were created in our own minds when we learned of the indiscretion of a person through others [as opposed to learning it from the person himself]. No amount of wishful thinking will prevent a jury from learning of it. The inclination is to avoid talking about it because of the obvious prejudice that is going to be created against your client. By confessing, if nothing else, the jury cannot accuse you of being less than sincere and candid with them. This certainly could not be true if you gave the other lawyer the opportunity to disclose this information. To permit the other lawyer to enlighten the jury as to substantial unsavory facts would be tantamount to handing your opponent a bomb so that he can blow you up.[10]

§10.3.6 Explaining the Limits of Rapport

While establishing rapport between the attorney and the jury is important, the lawyer must never forget that any social contact between attorneys and jurors outside the courtroom could be interpreted as tampering with the jury. While all lawyers know this, not all jurors do. So while the lawyer is building a relationship with the jury during voir dire, the jurors must be made aware that once the voir dire is completed, this somewhat informal relationship with the lawyer ends.

An experienced judge will admonish the jury that there must not be any communication by jurors, no matter how innocent, with the attorneys, the client, or the witnesses. But the lawyer

[10] A. Morrill, Trial Diplomacy 9-10 (1972).

should not depend on the judge to convey the importance of this warning. He or she should directly address the issue at the end of voir dire with the following:

> Members of the panel, I am certain that you are aware that there are rules and regulations that govern the actions of all of us in this courtroom. One of those rules is that we lawyers are not permitted to talk to you once you have been selected as members of the jury. I am certain that if you stop to think about it, you can think of some very good reasons why this rule is necessary. We attorneys may not exchange even the simplest hellos with you outside this courtroom. In fact, the judge has advised us that we are not even to ride in the same elevator with you. Is there any one of you who questions the wisdom of such a rule of the court? Is there anyone who will take it as a personal affront if my opponent or I do not say hello to you when we meet you in the morning or do not nod at you if we pass you in the hallway? Is there any one of you who will have any difficulty understanding why these rules of conduct must be observed from the time that you are selected as a member of the panel until the end of trial?

If the trial is expected to be especially long, the attorney might want to add the following:

> And if any of you should observe another juror attempting to speak to a client or a witness or an attorney, of if you should see one of us attempting to speak to a juror, would you call it to the attention of the bailiff so that you will be certain that the rules of the court are being honored? After all, each of us is an officer of the court once we take the oath of duty as a juror and become involved in this courtroom process.

§10.3.7 Anticipating Juror Note-Taking

There is no consensus about whether jurors should be permitted to take notes during a trial. Advocates of the practice point out that notes serve as a "legitimate aid to memory," especially in complex trials.[11] It is also said that notes will allow jurors to improve the quality of their deliberations.[12] Opponents of the practice fear that jurors will take inaccurate or incomplete notes. They state that note-taking is a skill that requires practice and training, which most people lack. Critics also fear that the jurors will become too involved in their note-taking and be distracted from hearing all the evidence presented.[13] While there is disagreement regarding note-taking by jurors, the practice is becoming more widely accepted.

The acceptability of juror note-taking can be raised in a trial in one of three ways. The judge may inform jurors that they may take notes, the attorney can make a motion to the judge to allow jurors to take notes, or the juror on his or her own initiative may begin taking notes. The first two methods are preferred. If counsel notices that a juror is taking notes on his or her own initiative, the attorney should point this out to the judge, who can then instruct the juror about the practice. If the juror continues to take notes even after being warned by the court not to, counsel should make an objection since continued note-taking may be grounds for reversal.[14] Most authorities agree that the decision whether to allow jurors to take notes is within the discretion of the trial judge.[15]

If note-taking is permitted, then certain precautions should be taken to ensure that the problems pointed to by its critics do not arise. First, jurors should be told by the judge that the notes are to serve only as an aid to their memory, not as a transcript of the proceedings. Jurors should be advised against trying to

[11] Flango, Would Jurors Do a Better Job if They Could Take Notes?, 63 Judicature 436, 437 (1980).

[12] Ibid.

[13] Id. at 437. See also Dombroff, Civil Litigation, 4 Natl. L.J. 21 (No. 52, Sept. 6, 1982).

[14] See Cheek v. State, 35 Ind. 492 (1871). (Generally courts are lenient when it is discovered that jurors have been taking notes on their own initiative. Often appellate court decisions discuss note-taking in dicta, commenting that "spontaneous juror note-taking does not warrant declaring a mistrial due to juror misconduct." Parry, Taking Note of Note-Taking, 10 Colo. J.L. and Soc. Probs. 565, 568 (1974)).

[15] See Miresso v. State, 163 Ind. App. 231, 233, 323 N.E.2d 249, 251 (1975).

write down every little detail.[16] They should be told whether they can have important testimony be reread to them. The court should also supply pads and pencils, and then each juror should put his or her name on a pad. The pads should be collected by the court clerk at the end of each day and returned to the appropriate jurors the next morning. After jury deliberations, the notes should be collected and destroyed.[17] If these steps and precautions are followed, note-taking can be a valuable aid to jurors and the litigants can still be assured of a fair trial.

§10.4 Exercising Challenges

The two relevant kinds of challenges involved in the voir dire process are challenges for cause and peremptory challenges. Because challenges for cause are exercised in the presence of the challenged person and frequently in the presence of other panel members, they must be delicately handled. A strategy for exercising peremptory challenges must also be carefully formulated.

§10.4.1 Grounds of Challenges for Cause

Challenges for cause are unlimited in number and are made to individual jurors. They are usually exercised after the chal-

[16] Id. at 250, 163 Ind. App. at 232. (The following instruction was deemed appropriate: "During the trial you may, if you wish, make brief notes to assist your recollection as to things which might be difficult to carry in your mind. However, you should not engage in continuous note-taking, which would hamper you in listening to the evidence and observing the witnesses as they testify.")

[17] See Dombroff, Civil Litigation, 4 Nat. L.J. 21 (No. 52, Sept. 6, 1982). (The ABA standards also seem to support the contention that the notes should be destroyed by stating that "[s]uch notes should be treated as confidential between the juror making them and his fellow jurors." ABA Standards, Trial by Jury §4.2 (approved draft 1968). The commentary following the standard notes that one judge recommended the notes be destroyed. Id. at 100.

lenge to the array and before peremptory challenges. It is the general practice that challenges are made before the jury is sworn to try the case, although the judge may permit challenges after the swearing in but before jeopardy has attached.[1]

Challenges for cause are granted on a "narrowly specified, provable and legally cognizable basis of partiality."[2] Even when it appears that a challenged potential juror has a biased view of the case, the person may be allowed to serve on the jury if the judge is convinced that the person could still be a fair and impartial juror. After the juror has said he or she can and

§10.4 [1]ABA Standards, Trial by Jury, §2.5 (approved draft 1968).

[2]Swain v. Alabama, 380 U.S. 202, 220, 85 S. Ct. 824, 836, 13 L. Ed. 2d 759, 772 (1965). See Hopt v. Utah, 120 U.S. 430, 433, 7 S. Ct. 614, 615, 30 L. Ed. 708, 709 (1887) that lists several reasons for which a challenge for cause can be granted. The reasons are as follows:

"1. Consanguinity or affinity within the fourth degree to the person alleged to be injured by the offense charged, or on whose complaint the prosecution was instituted, or to the defendant;
2. Standing in the relation of guardian and ward, attorney and client, master and servant, or landlord and tenant, or being a member of the family of the defendant, or of the person alleged to be injured by the offense charged, or on whose complaint the prosecution was instituted, or in his employment on wages:
3. Being the party adverse to the defendant in a civil action, or having complaint against or being accused by him in a criminal prosecution;
4. Having served on the grand jury which found the indictment, or on a coroner's jury which inquired into the death of a person whose death is the subject of the indictment;
5. Having served on a trial jury which has tried another person of the offense charged in the indictment;
6. Having been one of the jury formerly sworn to try the same indictment, and whose verdict was set aside, or which was discharged without a verdict, after the case was submitted to it;
7. Having served as a juror in a civil action brought against the defendant for the act charged as an offense;
8. Having formed or expressed an unqualified opinion or belief that the prisoner is guilty or not guilty of the offense charged;
9. If the offense charged is punishable by death, the entertaining of such conscientious opinion as would preclude his finding the defendant guilty; in which case he must neither be permitted nor compelled to serve as a juror."

See also the ABA Standards, Trial by Jury (approved draft 1968) at 68-69 (where both traditional and additional grounds for granting the challenges are listed in the commentary to §2.5).

will be impartial, the court is usually reluctant to call into question the juror's credibility by dismissing the juror for cause. If through further questioning, however, it becomes apparent that the juror has made up his or her mind about the case, then the court may dismiss the juror regardless of any claim of impartiality. The challenger must show that a pervasive bias exists that violates the parties' "right to an impartial jury."[3] Sometimes, however, even the implication of bias may satisfy the court. Once the court has exercised its discretion to grant or deny the challenge, the decision becomes almost unreviewable.[4]

Challenges for cause can be used to a lawyer's advantage and his or her opponent's disadvantage. Challenges are exercised against jurors who cannot be fair and impartial because of their beliefs, previous exposure to the case, or for other reasons. The lawyer's goal is to keep favorable jurors from being dismissed, while forcing the opponent to use peremptory challenges rather than challenges for cause. In order to accomplish this, the lawyer should avoid overstating the case during the early part of voir dire, especially if he or she is representing the plaintiff. Overstating the case may cause some jurors to become convinced that they cannot fairly respond to the issues, something they may readily admit to the opponent, allowing the opponent to exercise a challenge for cause.

At the same time, the lawyer should try to dismiss as many unfavorable jurors as possible with challenges for cause. This can be accomplished by appealing to the jurors' sense of fairness. Explain to a juror who appears to be harboring a bias that as the trial progresses his or her bias may be intensified by the evidence. For example, if the case involves a plaintiff who was hit by a truck driver and the juror's husband is a truck driver, then the lawyer should get the juror to admit that she cannot help but have preconceived ideas about truckers. Finally, any juror who has personality traits that would cause

[3]United States v. Dellinger, 472 F.2d 340, 367 (7th Cir. 1972).

[4]See Babcock, Voir Dire: Preserving "Its Wonderful Power," 27 Stan. L. Rev. 545, 550 (No. 18, 1975).

problems should be challenged for cause. Usually such jurors are undesirable for both sides of the case, so the opponent will likely allow the challenge for cause without dispute.[5]

The right to challenge for cause is not inviolate, and it can be forfeited by an attorney who fails to examine a juror objected to,[6] or by failing to exercise a challenge after examination and acceptance of a juror by the other party.[7] Each state varies somewhat as to when the right to make a challenge for cause will be deemed to have been waived; therefore, the attorney should be sure to comply with the applicable law in order to protect the right.[8]

§10.4.2 Methods of Challenging for Cause

Sometimes the basis for a challenge for cause arises from a single response from a juror. The adversary may choose to resist the challenge, however, and successfully rehabilitate the juror. Usually it is wiser to establish a basis for challenge for cause through a building process. This approach can establish a firm foundation for the challenge and may help persuade not only the judge but also the other panel members that the person would not be a fair and impartial juror.

For example, say a defective products case is brought by a divorced truck driver who has not worked for two years because of a traumatic back injury claimed to have been received while working on a car with a defective jack. A suit has been filed against both Acme Motors and the manufacturer of the

[5] Ibid.

[6] See State v. Matheson, 130 Iowa 440, 103 N.W. 137 (1905).

[7] See Leach v. State, 132 So. 2d 329 (Fla.), *cert. denied*, 368 U.S. 1005 (1961).

[8] For example, some jurisdictions hold the challenge waived if it is denied and the juror is struck by use of a peremptory challenge. Spies v. Illinois, 123 U.S. 131, 8 S. Ct. 21, 31 L. Ed. 80 (1887). Other jurisdictions have held that the denial of a challenge for cause is not prejudicial error if the challenger did not use all of his peremptory challenges. Hopt v. Utah, 120 U.S. 430, 7 S. Ct. 614, 30 L. Ed. 708 (1887). A challenge for cause may also be deemed waived if it is used after the peremptory challenges have been made. See M. Belli, Modern Trials 400 (2d ed. 1982).

jack, M & G Manufacturing. On the list of prospective jurors, the attorney notes a Mrs. Brown, housewife, 52, whose spouse owns an auto supply outlet. The attorney knows that Mr. Brown is active in fighting a closed shop and is very anti-union. Mrs. Brown is therefore a probable target for exclusion by challenge for cause. When voir dire begins, the plaintiff's attorney elicits this information in a pleasant and friendly manner. Further questioning reveals additional information:

Q: Mrs. Brown, do you know the attorney for Acme Motors?
A: Yes, I do.
Q: And what is the nature of that knowledge?
A: Mr. Peterson and I attend the same church and his wife and I are on the reception committee for that church.
Q: Have you ever visited in their home?
A: No, I haven't.
Q: Would you say that your relationship with him and his wife is of the nature of a friendship or more of an acquaintanceship?
A: I guess I would have to say that it would be more toward being an acquaintanceship.
Q: Is there anything about your relationship with that attorney that would lead you to favor his side more than it would any other side?
A: No, I don't think that would happen.
Q: In other words, your knowledge of that attorney would not color your views in any way and your friendship or acquaintanceship with him would still allow you to be a fair and impartial juror?
A: Yes, I think it would.
Q: Is there anyone on the panel who knows Mr. Jackson, the attorney for M & G Manufacturing? Please raise your hand. (Pause.) Mrs. Brown, I see that you have raised your hand to indicate that you know Mr. Jackson. Is that right?
A: Yes, I know Mr. Jackson.
Q: What is the nature of your knowledge of Mr. Jackson?

A: Well, he lived in our neighborhood, just a couple of blocks away.
Q: And do you know his wife and family?
A: Yes, I do.
Q: Is there any member of that family that you know better than another?
A: Well, I know his son, Bill, pretty well.
Q: And how is it that you know Bill?
A: Well, Bill dated my daughter when they were in high school. They are about the same age.
Q: And how many years ago was that?
A: Oh, my daughter has been married for well over 12 years, so I guess it has been quite some time. (General laughter from other jurors.)
Q: Have you visited in Mr. Jackson's home?
A: I don't recall. If I have, it hasn't been recently.
Q: Would you have visited in their home within the last three or four years?
A: I don't think so. My husband has been somewhat ill and we cannot go out as much as we used to.
Q: Is there anything about your knowledge of Mr. Jackson and of Mr. Jackson's family or of his son, Bill, that would make you tend to lean more toward favoring his side than any other side in this law case?
A: No, I think I can be fair.

Q: Is there anyone here, either personally or through a member of their family, who has had dealings with M & G Manufacturing? Please raise your hand. (Pause.) I see, Mrs. Brown, that you indicate that you had dealings with M & G Manufacturing. Could you tell me what the nature of those dealings were?
A: My husband owns an auto supply store and I know that he has bought some jacks that were manufactured by that company.
Q: Is that the only brand of jacks that he carries?
A: I don't know.

Q: How is it that you know that he carries jacks that have been manufactured by M & G Manufacturing?
A: I have accompanied my husband to merchandise shows and we visited the booth that M & G Manufacturing had set up.
Q: Have you ever observed any of their demonstrations that they have made at those booths of the jacks or of the quality of the jacks?
A: I probably have, I don't remember for sure. If I have, I don't remember anything specific about them.
Q: Have you met any of the sales personnel from M & G Manufacturing?
A: Yes, I have.
Q: An under what circumstances did you meet these sales people?
A: They took us — that's my husband and me — out to dinner a few times.
Q: Have you ever had them as guests in your home?
A: No, I have not.
Q: Have you ever met the company's owners, Mr. Owens or Mr. Tucker?
A: Not really. I mean, I may have met them in passing but I don't remember engaging in any long conversations with them. Mr. Owens and Mr. Tucker are members of the Windsor Heights Country Club.
Q: What country club do you belong to?
A: The Windsor Heights Country Club.
Q: And do you remember meeting Mr. Owens or Mr. Tucker or any member of their families there?
A: I may have. I don't really remember. Although I am certain, since it is a fairly small country club, that we have probably both been there at the same time.
Q: Would your husband know Mr. Owens and Mr. Tucker?
A: Yes, I suppose he would. He has a lot more business lunches at the club than I do.
Q: Mrs. Brown, is there anything about the nature of your acquaintance with Mr. Tucker or Mr. Owens and being members with them of the Windsor Heights Country Club

and having met their salesmen and knowing that your husband has purchased jacks from them that would lead you to be prejudiced against my client and would lead you to favor the side of M & G Manufacturing?

A: I'm not sure.

Q: Do you think it might be possible that because of this friendship and because of your husband's business relationship with this company and with the owners of this company that you might be less likely to be objective in viewing the facts of this case?

A: That's possible. I might be.

Attorney for Plaintiff to Judge: I would ask that this person be removed for cause.

Attorney for Defense: Do you mind if I ask just a few questions of this juror, Your Honor?

Judge: Go ahead.

Attorney for Defense to Mrs. Brown: How many items does your husband stock in his auto supply outlet?

A: I don't know.

Q: Would you say that it would tend to be over a hundred?

A: I would say that it would tend to be over several thousands.

Q: Would you say that your husband deals with many companies?

A: Oh, yes, many companies, I couldn't begin to name all of them.

Q: And have you met the salesmen for some of these other companies?

A: Of course, many of them.

Q: And you have no special friendship with Mr. Owens or Mr. Tucker, do you?

A: No, no special friendship.

Q: You look upon them as business acquaintances primarily, isn't that true?

A: Yes, that's true.

Q: And there are many members of your country club, aren't there?

A: Many. It's a small club but there are still many members.

Q: And the fact that they are members of that club doesn't mean that they are right or that you are going to believe that they are always in the right, isn't that so?
A: Yes, that's true.
Q: And it would be possible for you to set aside all of your knowledge of Mr. Owens and Mr. Tucker and put aside the small acquaintance that you have with them and sit here in this courtroom and listen to the evidence and bring in a verdict that would be fair and that would not be one that you had decided just because you knew Mr. Owens or Mr. Tucker or because your husband had done business with them?
A: No, no, of course not. I would try to be fair and I would decide and bring in my verdict based on the evidence that I heard in this courtroom.
Attorney for Defense to Judge: We resist the challenge.
Judge: Challenge denied.

Attorney for Plaintiff to Mrs. Brown: Is there anybody who drives an Acme Motors car? Please raise your hand. (Pause.) I see, Mrs. Brown, that you drive an Acme Motors car.
A: Yes, I do. My husband wouldn't buy anything else. We've had an Acme Motors car ever since we've been married.
Q: And why is that, Mrs. Brown?
A: Because we like them the best and we think they're the safest and easiest to drive.
Q: Mrs. Brown, you know that one of the charges in this case is that Acme Motors commissioned a defective jack and placed a defective jack in one of their cars. You are aware of that, aren't you?
A: Yes, I am.
Q: And do you have any opinion about that statement at this time?
A: No, I wouldn't have any opinion. I would have to wait and see what the evidence shows.

Q: Would those of you who own any stock in the automotive industry please raise your hand? (Pause.) Mrs. Brown, it seems that you tend to answer a lot of my questions in the affirmative. (General laughter from other jurors.) Mrs. Brown, do you or your husband own any stock in Acme Motors?
A: I don't know.
Q: Do you or your husband own any stock in M & G Manufacturing?
A: I don't know. Not in my name, I'm pretty sure of that.
Q: Is it possible that you own Acme Motors stock or that you own stock in M & G Manufacturing?
A: I don't know. I just don't know.
Q: If you were to go home tonight and find out after discussion with your husband that you did own stock in Acme Motors or in M & G Manufacturing, what effect would that have for you in serving as a juror on this case?
A: None. I don't think it would have any effect at all.

Q: There is going to be some controversy in this case about the nature of the injury that my client has suffered. Some of the physicians and psychologists will say that he is totally disabled and that he will never be able to do a full day's work again if it requires physical labor. There will be one physician and one psychologist who will indicate that it is possible that my client could possibly work again but that it is a psychological condition more than a physical condition that keeps him from working. Is there anyone on the panel who feels that in order to find for the plaintiff, you would have to find that my client is totally disabled and incapable of returning to work? Please raise your hand. (Pause.) Ah, Mrs. Brown, and how do you feel about this?
A: Well, I just have some reservations.
Q: And on what do you base those reservations?
A: I know my husband has a lot of trouble in getting his truckers to work sometimes.

Q: If I were to ask you whether you felt that a trucker were more likely to be right or whether you thought a businessman were more likely to be right, which one do you think you would tend to favor?
A: I guess I would tend to favor the person who wasn't a trucker.
Q: You know that my client is a truck driver?
A: Yes, I do.
Q: Do you think that the opinion that you have just shared with this court would lead you not to find credibility when he takes the stand?
A: No, no. I feel that I could listen to him and judge on the evidence.

Q: Mrs. Brown, I feel that I must ask you how you feel about returning a substantial verdict in this case.
A: I think I could do that.
Q: Could you return a verdict, if the evidence were to support such a verdict, to my client for an amount in excess of $1 million?
A: In excess of $1 million? (Long pause.) That's a lot of money.
Q: In other words, you are indicating that you might have trouble returning a verdict that would be that high even if the evidence were to support a verdict that would be that substantial?
A: I--might have difficulty, but I would try to keep an open mind.
Q: Just how much difficulty do you think you might have?
A: I don't know.
Q: Mrs. Brown, let's review the information that you have shared with us this afternoon. You say that you know the attorney for Acme Motors, that you go to the same church with him and with his wife and that you serve on committees with her. You also know the attorney for M & G manufacturing. In fact, your daughter dated his son. You have told us that your husband owns an auto supply out-

let and that he stocks jacks that were made by M & G Manufacturing, that you have met sales personnel from that company, that you have gone out to eat and drink with them. Furthermore, that you have not only met the owners of M & G Manufacturing, Mr. Owens and Mr. Tucker, but that you are also a member of the same country club and possibly know them socially. You tell us that you only drive an Acme Motors car because you believe that they are the easiest and safest cars to drive. You indicate that you don't know whether or not you own stock in Acme Motors or in M & G Manufacturing, but that it is possible that you do. Furthermore, you indicate that it is possible that you might have a tendency to find the owners of companies more credible than truck drivers. And now, Mrs. Brown, you indicate that you would have difficulty in returning a substantial verdict, one which might be in excess of $1 million, even if the evidence were to support that kind of verdict. Is all this true, Mrs. Brown?

A: I guess I said all those things. Yes.

Q: Mrs. Brown, in view of all of these areas that we have just covered, do you think that you would have a tendency to be more responsive to the arguments that would be made to you by the attorneys for Acme Motors and by the attorneys for M & G Manufacturing than you would be responsive to the case as presented to you by me for my client? I want you to think very carefully about that, Mrs. Brown, because it is you and only you who knows exactly how you feel and how you might respond when you go back to the jury room and you make a decision that is very important, not only to M & G Manufacturing, and to Acme Motors, but also very important to my client. Mrs. Brown, do you think that you could put aside all of these tendencies and give my client a fair trial?

A: It looks like I'd have some problem, doesn't it?

Q: Mrs. Brown, only you know whether you could be fair. Can you?

A: I guess I would have great difficulty in some places.

Attorney for Plaintiff to Judge: We challenge for cause.
(Comment: In spite of the defense attorney's attempts to rehabilitate Mrs. Brown, the judge excused her for cause.)

When this kind of follow-up questioning is utilized, so that the juror is not placed under intensive cross-examination or made by the other jurors to feel that she is the victim of a lawyer determined to show that she is not fair, the juror can be excused for cause without contaminating the remaining jurors. Such follow-up questioning takes planning, patience, and sincere good humor. If the potential juror begins to feel threatened or attacked, the outcome will not be positive nor will it be well received by the other jurors.

§10.4.3 Peremptory Challenges

The major function of the peremptory challenge is to "eliminate extremes of partiality on both sides, [and] to assure the parties that the jurors before whom they try the case will decide on the basis of the evidence placed before them, and not otherwise."[9] In addition to this primary function, the peremptory challenge serves several subsidiary functions. First, the challenge demonstrates that the jury trial system is a just mode of dispute resolution because it allows the litigant to be involved in selecting an impartial jury by dismissing the jurors he or she does not like.[10] Second, the challenge allows the attorney to avoid interrogating persons whom he or she feels fit common stereotypes. The attorney can peremptorily dismiss the juror without making a generalized statement about a class or group, even though the lawyer may be thinking of the generalization.[11] Finally, the peremptory challenge can act as a shield for challenges for cause. Occasionally an attorney will question a

[9] Swain v. Alabama, 380 U.S. 202, 219, 85 S. Ct. 824, 835, 13 L. Ed. 2d 759, 772 (1965).

[10] See Babcock, Voir Dire: Preserving "Its Wonderful Power", 27 Stan. L. Rev. 545, 552 (1975).

[11] Id. at 553.

juror on various topics in anticipation of exercising a challenge for cause. Sometimes the juror will become alienated because of this intensive questioning and may even become hostile toward the attorney and client. If the challenge for cause is not granted and the attorney feels that the juror has become alienated or hostile, then the attorney can still choose to dismiss the juror with a peremptory challenge. Thus, the peremptory challenge can make the lawyer feel more at ease and willing to question jurors about sensitive subjects when the situation calls for such questioning.[12] These various functions of the peremptory challenge make it a very important tool for the attorney.

§10.4.4 Exercising Peremptory Challenges

Peremptory challenges are generally exercised after challenges to the array and challenges for cause, but before jurors are sworn. Because no reason need be given for the striking of jurors through a peremptory challenge, the challenge is an important right. However, the right is not inviolate and can be forfeited in both criminal and civil cases. Generally if there has been a fair opportunity for the exercise of peremptory challenges and none are exercised, then the right to use the challenges is deemed waived. Not all courts follow the same rules and the attorney must become familiar with the rules of the jurisdiction.

Peremptory challenges should be exercised intelligently. Their use should be aimed at the juror who is suspected of a bias or prejudice that will harm the attorney's case, but who cannot be successfully dismissed for cause. In order to exercise the peremptory challenges in an intelligent fashion, the attorney needs to listen carefully to each juror's answers throughout the voir dire. A potential juror's answers, body movements, and other nonverbal signals will allow the attorney to develop

[12] Id. at 555.

an opinion about whether the person would be a desirable juror. As with challenges for cause, peremptory challenges should be exercised tactfully to avoid alienating the rest of the jury panel.

§10.4.5 Requesting Additional Peremptory Challenges

Additional peremptory challenges may be granted by the court under special circumstances in some jurisdictions. For example, in criminal cases a defendant may request a change of venue due to the publicity his or her case has received. If such a motion is denied and the attorney feels that public sentiment is running high against his or her client, he may want to request additional peremptory challenges to assure the client a fair trial. If the court is aware of public opinion and sees that there has been a considerable amount of one-sided pretrial publicity, then the court may allow the defendant additional peremptory challenges. The logic behind this allowance by the court may be that a charge of murder or rape is more likely to bring forth prejudices or biases in people than a charge of petty larceny.

The existence of multiple parties is perhaps one of the most common grounds for granting peremptory challenges in both criminal and civil cases. In civil cases the extra peremptories are sometimes governed by statute where the general rule is that each party is entitled to a set number of challenges, with multiple parties being treated as one party. However, if it is determined that the multiple parties have conflicting interests, then usually each individual member of the party will be given the full statutory number of challenges.[13]

The request for additional peremptory challenges should be made in the form of a pretrial motion accompanied by a memorandum in support of the motion. The information given the court should be pertinent to the basis for the motion. For

[13]See generally Annot., 32 A.L.R.3d 747 and Annot., 50 A.L.R. Fed. 350. Concerning criminal cases see Annot., 21 A.L.R.3d 752.

example, a motion based on pretrial publicity could include statistics on the pretrial publicity, summaries of an opinion poll showing community attitudes along with the questions asked in the survey, and a compilation of news clips about the case. In addition, the motion should be supported with citations to any similar cases where additional challenges were allowed. The court will be more willing to grant peremptory challenges if it is supplied with good reasons for doing so. Generally, additional peremptories can play an important role in choosing a fair tribunal and, if circumstances require, the attorney should not hesitate to request them.

PART IV

Nonverbal Communication

CHAPTER
11

Nonverbal Communication in General

§11.0 Introduction

In the last 25 years, there has been a steadily growing appreciation for a relatively new field of study called nonverbal communication. While no systematic approach has yet been outlined for improving or even assessing nonverbal communication skills (such as exists for spoken or written communication), professionals, especially those who assess human behavior, are increasingly becoming more attuned to the desirability, even the necessity, of being able to understand nonverbal messages that they both send and receive.

There are five major reasons for nonverbal communication having generated so much interest both in and out of the courtroom in recent years. First, nonverbal communication is considered to be more reliable than verbal communication because people tend to believe communications they perceive to be less under the message sender's direct control. In an experiment, 310 persons were shown a videotape of a young man stating, "After I have examined all the materials, I am confident that my analysis is the right one. In fact, I am willing to make that statement unequivocally!" While uttering these words, the young man pulled at his tie, sat on the edge of his chair, interrupted eye contact with his supervisor, and sounded nervous.

There was a quiver in his voice that participants in the experiment described as sounding "hesitant" or "unsure." Not one of the 310 persons believed the verbal statement, nor did they believe that the speaker had any real confidence in his own statement.

Second, nonverbal communication is recognized as being inseparable from the psychological makeup of humans. C. David Mortensen, professor of speech communication at the University of Wisconsin, notes the following:

> It is often said that communication is not something which is done to a person; rather it is an interchange which is engaged in by consenting parties. To respond openly to another person is to react to the total dynamic of his behavior, not simply to the words that accompany his presentation. Moreover, each gesture, facial expression, and body movement is a potentially rich source of information about internal emotive states. Nonverbal cues also have a special symbolic value. They invariably reveal, sometimes unconsciously, impressions of self, feelings of worth, denial, esteem, guilt, doubt, confidence, status, social power and so on. Furthermore, the nonverbal lexicon is a gauge to the status of interpersonal relationships; the stream of behavior constitutes a visible record of each party's impressions toward the objects of their coorientation. Finally, and most importantly, nonverbal cues form a large part of the meaning that is assigned in any face-to-face encounter.[1]

Third, the major determinants of meaning in any message derive from nonverbal rather than verbal factors. Anthropologist Ray Birdwhistell, founder of the science of kinesics, the study of the relationship between speech and body movement, states that "probably no more than 30% to 35% of the social meaning of a conversation or an interaction is carried by the words."[2] Albert Mehrabian, a research psychologist, makes an even stronger claim when he estimates that 93 percent of a

§11.0 [1]C. D. Mortensen, Communication: The Study of Human Interaction 210 (1972).

[2]R. L. Birdwhistell, Kinesics and Context 158 (1970).

message lies in nonverbal factors.[3] Even the court recognizes the importance of the nonverbal channel of communication in arriving at the meaning of a message, especially in regard to credibility. The general instruction to jurors on assessing a witness's credibility stresses the need to examine how the witness looks and sounds in addition to listening to the words he or she utters from the stand.[4]

Fourth, it is generally believed that the nonverbal channel of communication is relatively free from conscious deception. Professor Dale Leathers, author of *Nonverbal Communication Systems* asserts the following:

> Nonverbal cues such as gestures are rarely under the sustained, conscious control of the communicator. For this reason, communicators can rarely use nonverbal communication effectively for the purpose of dissembling. In contrast, the verbal dimension of communication seems to conceal or obfuscate the communicator's true intentions more frequently. . . .
>
> In an age that places a very high priority on trust, honesty,

[3]See Mehrabian, Communication Without Words, 2 Psychology Today 52 (Sept. 1968).

[4]The instruction generally is worded as follows:

> You are the sole judges of the weight of the evidence, the credibility of the witnesses, the conclusions to be drawn from the facts and circumstances proved.
>
> If the testimony or any part of it is conflicting, you will reconcile it, if you can, that it may all have weight and effect, but if you cannot, you will then give credit to the testimony and those witnesses that to you, as fair-minded persons, seem most entitled thereto.
>
> In passing on the credibility of the witnesses and weighing their testimony, you should consider their appearance and conduct on the witness stand; their age, intelligence, their interest or lack of interest in the result of the trial, their relation or feeling, if any, toward the parties; the motives, if any, actuating them as witnesses; their candor, fairness, bias or prejudice; the time that has elapsed since the occurrence of which they testify; the reasonableness and probability of their statements or the want thereof; whether their testimony is corroborated or contradicted by other witnesses or by facts proven; and every fact and circumstance proved, thus giving to the testimony of each witness and to every fact and circumstance proved, such weight, and only such weight as it ought reasonably and justly to be given in view of all the evidence.
>
> You should consider and compare the proofs which tend to support the claims of the respective parties, reason upon the same as men and women of intelligence and common sense, and return a true verdict according to the evidence and the instructions now given you by the Court.

> and candor in interpersonal relationships, nonverbal communication takes on added importance. . . . Not only do nonverbal cues typically convey a communicator's real meaning and intent, but they also suggest rather precisely what the communicator thinks of us.
>
> Even such nonverbal cues as gestures, posture, and facial expression may of course be under the conscious control of the communicator. For all but the consummate actor and possibly a few legendary used-car salesmen, however, such conscious control is a temporary phenomenon. In most cases nonverbal cues are not consciously controlled for such extended periods of time as verbal cues, nor do they serve as frequently to transmit deception, distortion and confusion.[5]

Fifth, as society has become dominated by visual aspects of human interaction, nonverbal communication has grown in importance and acceptance. Anthropologist Margaret Mead wrote the following about this trend:

> The young are expressing themselves bodily, in forms designed to be viewed on TV rather than read about in magazines. Demonstrations characterized by strange and conspicuous body positions — sit-in, lie-in, sleep-in, bleed-in, be-in, love-in (in ice-cold ponds on the edge of spring) — have replaced the poster and the handout. Clothes and hairdos have become vitally important indications of ethical and political attitudes. We have moved to a more visual period, where what is seen is more important than what is read, and what is experienced directly is valued over what is learned secondhand.[6]

As the youth of the 1960s and 70s become the young and not-so-young adults of their communities and become increasingly visible in the composition of local jury panels, lawyers will have to be more attuned to the visual, namely, the nonverbal.

A trial lawyer needs to be vitally concerned in both the office and the courtroom with identifying the psychological makeup

[5]D. G. Leathers, Nonverbal Communication Systems 5 (1976).

[6]M. Mead, Male and Female, a Study of the Sexes in a Changing World, (quoted in F. Davis, Inside Intuition 193-194 [1975]).

of witnesses and potential jurors. Therefore, lawyers are becoming aware of their need to be competent in both sending and receiving accurate nonverbal messages.

§11.1 Misconceptions about Nonverbal Communication

To try to define nonverbal communication is to attempt the impossible. At present, the best that can be done is to state what such a definition would exclude. Nonverbal communication is *not* communication that is contained in the value of the spoken or written word. This leaves all other sources of communication, or exchange of meaning, as a form of nonverbal communication.

§11.1.1 Nonverbal Communication v. Body Language

There is a common misconception that nonverbal communication is body language. Such a definition is far too limiting. While it is true that body movement communicates meaning, it is not the only source of nonverbal meaning. Furthermore, while certain bestsellers have touted the concept of a body language, nonverbal communication scholars are in clear agreement that a body *language* does not exist. If it did, a dictionary of body movements and gestures could be written. Then the observer could look up body movement X and find that it means Y_1, Y_2, or Y_3. It could then be generalized that when we observe $X_1 + X_2 + X_3$, we would know that the transmitter of those body movements meant Y_1 or Y_2. This is simply not the case, nor is it expected that it ever will be. People move their bodies according to a variety of socialization patterns, past experiences, and personality characteristics, all of which are far too complex to be reduced totally to several simple formulas. The body and personality, however, are not disassociated. Each person puts together a pattern of movement that expresses his or her personality, activity level, and general attitude at a given time in a given situation. These body *codes* form certain predictable patterns that have meaning in a particular context. If an observer is knowledgeable about general body codes, as well as about how an individual might adapt those codes in keeping with a particular lifestyle or personality type and how those codes might be affected by stress, then the observer could make certain general conclusions about the attitudes and personality traits of an individual.

§11.1.2 *Interpreting Nonverbal Communication Is Not Mind Reading*

Another common misconception about nonverbal communication is that it allows those familiar with its patterns to read minds. Nonverbal communication deals with public behavior. Even if after watching an individual for several minutes a knowledgeable observer has discovered that the person is warm, friendly, compassionate, highly verbal, and a leader type who makes decisions quickly, his or her reactions to a particular case could not be predicted — at least not with absolute accuracy. The observer might have a fair idea of the person's propensity to react to the case issues in a certain way, especially if it is known how people of that general type react to the kind of information that will be presented in court. Based on that assessment, it might be possible to make a prediction about how he or she is likely to react. But improved skill in sending, receiving, and interpreting nonverbal messages does not provide a crystal ball that allows the viewer to look into the future and *know* how a person will react.

§11.1.3 *Nonverbal Communication and Verbal Communication*

Finally, it is important to realize that the nonverbal channel of communication is not separate and distinct from the verbal channel; rather, the nonverbal and the verbal should be evaluated and considered as two complementary elements that make up an indivisible whole. Michael Argyle, the British psychologist, cautions, "Some of the most important findings in the field of social interaction are about the ways that verbal interaction needs the support of nonverbal communication."[1] Professor Mark Knapp, a communication researcher, warns, "There is a danger that the reader may forget that nonverbal communication cannot be studied in isolation from the total communication process. Verbal and nonverbal communication should be treated as a total and inseparable unit."[2] In order to understand what is truly occurring at any particular time in any situation, it is important to *look* at the messages being sent as well as to *listen* to the words being spoken. The combination will contain the totality of the communication's meaning.

When communication is discussed, one of the major considerations in weighing the difference between a verbal communication and nonverbal behavior is the person's intent. When a person intends to send a message, then the person is clearly communicating. But what happens when a message is sent without the conscious intention of the person sending it? Is the perception of that message part of the communication? A person could easily declare that he or she had no intention of sending any particular message about his or her status by wearing a navy pinstriped suit or by assuming an erect, space-using posture. Is there still a message? Has communication occurred? Should the clothing and posture of a person be perceived by others as part of the context of a communication?

Messages are contained in both verbal communications and nonverbal behavior. Both contain valuable information that has shared meaning for members of a common culture. It is important, therefore, to be able to decode all the messages whether or not they are intended. While the difference between verbal

§11.1 [1]M. Argyle, Social Interaction 70-71 (1969).
[2]M. Knapp, Nonverbal Communication in Human Interaction 8-9 (1972).

and nonverbal communication might be a fascinating topic of debate among psychologists and communication researchers, most people simply want to know the significance of intent in interpreting a message.

Most people will place greater reliance on messages that they perceive to be unintentionally sent or that they believe were not specifically intended for them to receive. This is one reason why nonverbal cues are received with a greater degree of credibility than verbal cues, which are generally perceived as intentional. The court's admonition to jurors that they concentrate on the demeanor of witnesses when deciding on the veracity of testimony illustrates the importance placed on nonverbal communication by the legal system.

Whether one considers a nonverbal message to be intentional or to be unconscious behavior that happens to convey information, nonverbal messages affect the conclusions one makes about a communication. All humans follow a three-step process in decoding nonverbal messages. We *observe* a person's behavior (John arose from his chair and left the room during the lecture). Based on our knowledge of the individual, the situation, and the context, we *interpret* that behavior (John left the room because he remembered an important phone call he needed to make, he became upset with the speaker's comments, he was bored with the speaker and decided not to waste time, or he became aware of a physiological need and left to take care of it). Based on our system of values, we *judge* that behavior (John was responsible or sensitive or rude or unorganized). In conversation with others, we might report John's behavior without interpreting it ("John is the type of person who walks out of lectures") or we might report our interpretation ("John is a sensitive person"). Seldom do we engage in an explanation of how we arrived at an interpretation of certain behavior. Regardless of our intentions, behavior will be observed, interpreted, and judged. In the courtroom, we may attempt to limit a witness to reporting only the behaviors observed, but we certainly require the jury to interpret and make judgments about the reported behaviors.

§11.2 Basic Characteristics of Nonverbal Communication

Nonverbal communication deals with that part of the communication process that is not verbal. This does not mean that it is not vocal, since there is an area of nonverbal communication that deals with *how* something is said. In broad terms, nonverbal communication falls into three categories: 1. *Sign language* includes all forms of communication in which words, numbers, and punctuation signs have been substituted for by gestures. These range from the simple gesture of a hitchhiker to such complex systems as sign languages used by deaf persons. 2. *Action language* embraces all movements that are not used exclusively as signals. Walking and drinking, for example, have a dual function. On one hand, they serve personal needs, and, on the other, they constitute statements to those who may perceive them. (Consider the effect on the jury when a key witness pauses, leans forward, picks up a glass of water and slowly drinks.) 3. *Object language* comprises all intentional and nonintentional displays of material things, such as implements, machines, art objects, architectural structures, and, most important, the human body and whatever covers it.[1]

More specifically, nonverbal communication can be classified into seven types:

1. *Physical characteristics,* such as physique, general attractiveness, body or breath odors, height, weight, hair, and skin color or tone, can reveal certain things about a person. These characteristics usually do not change during a period of interaction and are unrelated to movement.

2. *Kinesics* is the study of the relationship between body movement and speech. Ray Birdwhistell, who originated the term kinesics, says that it is "concerned with abstracting from the continuous muscular shifts which are characteristic of liv-

§11.2 [1]See J. Ruesch & W. Kees, Nonverbal Communication: Notes on the Visual Perception of Human Relations (1956).

ing physiological systems those groupings of movements which are of significance to the communication process and thus to the interactional systems of particular social groups."[2] He identifies the eight sources of potentially significant body movement as the head, face, neck, trunk, shoulder-arm-wrist, hand, hip-leg-ankle, and the foot.[3] The major areas of study in kinesics include facial expression, gestures, and posturals.

3. *Haptics* is the study of touching behavior, which includes the meaning derived from actual physical contact between persons. This contact could include stroking, pinching, rubbing, hitting, holding. Touch is frequently used to define the nature of a relationship. The lawyer can use it to relay subtly but definitely to the jury the kind of feelings he or she has for a client.

4. *Proxemics* is generally considered to be the study of an individual's use and perception of his or her social and personal space. There is an area of research called small group ecology included in proxemics that is concerned with how people use and respond to spatial relationships in formal and informal group settings. It involves such variables as seating arrangements; spatial arrangements related to leadership, communication flow, and a task at hand; the impact of crowding on human interaction and emotive display; and the influence of architectural features on residential living units. Space orientation during personal conversation is sometimes studied in terms of how it varies according to sex, status, roles, and cultural orientation. The term space bubble has frequently been applied to the space orientation as defined by these variables. The term territoriality is also frequently used in the study of proxemics to denote the human tendency to stake out personal territory as an untouchable space, at least without invitation.

5. The use of *artifacts* as they are manipulated in self-advertisement to relay certain messages of status, role, and personality can also be revealing. Artifacts include clothing,

[2] R. L. Birdwhistell, Kinesics and Context 192 (1970).
[3] Id. at 17.

makeup, jewelry, adornments or accessories, eyeglasses, hairpieces, and perfumes or aftershave lotions.

6. *Environmental factors* are also studied for nonverbal communication. There is much debate as to whether this category should even be included, since it is so general. It relates to such factors as furniture, interior decorating, lighting conditions and controls, odors, colors, temperature, outside noise, music, and variations in shapes and textures.

7. The last type of nonverbal communication deals with *how* something is said and not *what* is said. It deals with a nonverbal vocal cues associated with speech behavior, such as rate, pitch, tone, accents, rhythm, and pausing.

§11.3 Interpreting Nonverbal Communication

There is no question that everybody sends and receives nonverbal communications all the time. Nor is there any question as to how much importance nonverbal communication can have for the receiver when it is decoded. There is, however, a primary contradiction contained in nonverbal communication: How is it that nonverbal communication is so important and yet so misunderstood?

The answer is somewhat obvious. We all know nonverbal communication even if we do not know the technical terms or are familiar with research on the subject, in the same way as a child knows and uses language before going to school and receiving formal instruction. We accept the fact that everyone learns how to talk but that some people later learn to talk more effectively and in more diverse situations. The same is true of nonverbal communication. We learn about nonverbal communication as we use it. Each of us knows that eye contact is important, that a touch can define a relationship, that how we dress carries a message about who and what we are. However, there are aspects of nonverbal communication in which we are not as successful simply because we haven't become familiar with them or we haven't been made aware of their effectiveness. The person who has a trained awareness, who has been taught what to look for and where to look for it, will be a quicker, more efficient interpreter of nonverbal messages than the untrained or unaware.

We must not overlook the research that demonstrates that certain people are more sensitive to receiving nonverbal messages than others. A team of British psychologists, headed by Michael Argyle, found that women are more affected by the nonverbal channel of communication than men.[1] Robert Rosenthal, professor of social psychology, while heading a research team that devised a test for measuring sensitivity to nonverbal messages, made the following conclusion:

> The [Profile of Nonverbal Sensitivity] PONS has corroborated the popular opinion (and some previous experimental evidence) that females are better than males at detecting nonverbal cues. Females of all ages, from third grade through adult, showed a small but reliable advantage over males. . . .
>
> It's worth noting that this difference between the sexes narrowed significantly, and even reversed itself, among men in occupations, or training for occupations, that we considered to require "nurturant," artistic, or expressive behavior. Actors, artists, interior and industrial designers, psychiatrists, clinical psychologists and the staff of mental hospitals, college students in visual-studies courses, and schoolteachers — among such people the men tended to score "like women." . . .
>
> Other analyses indicate that females perform particularly well compared to males when body cues are included in the nonverbal stimuli. It's hard to know just why . . . perhaps males become sexually distracted by the sight of a woman's body and thus miss the intended message. . . .
>
> So far we haven't discovered the earliest age at which females become more sensitive than males. Our third grade girls were already better than boys. . . ."[2]

§11.3 [1]See Argyle, The Communication of Inferior and Superior Attitudes by Verbal and Nonverbal Signals, 9 Brit. J. of Soc. and Clinical Psychology, 222, 231 (1970).

[2]Rosenthal, Body Talk and Tone of Voice: The Language Without Words, 8 Psychology Today 64, 66 (Sept. 1974).

Not only are females more sensitive than males to nonverbal stimuli, but blacks also appear to be more sensitive than whites. Researchers in a study in Boston found that blacks were more sensitive to the nonverbal messages not only from members of their own race but from whites as well.[3] Chroniclers of slavery referred to blacks' "accurate judgment in discriminating the character of others,"[4] which probably derived from their ability to interpret nonverbal signals.

Why this difference between females and males or blacks and whites? No one knows for sure, although several different theories have been offered in possible explanation. The following has been suggested:

> There are several possible explanations for why women are more sensitive. Perhaps motherhood requires nonverbal skills. Such skills might be part of their genetic make-up, selected during the course of evolution. On the other hand, if the traditional requirements for motherhood are somehow learned rather than inborn, the nonverbal sensitivity could be one of these learned abilities, acquired at a very early age and in many cultures. . . .
>
> One purely social explanation would derive from the premise that women are socially oppressed. If women, as well as other oppressed groups, must "read" the expressions of others with great accuracy in order to advance or even survive, then they could become nonverbally sensitive at an early age. Some commonplace support for this hypothesis is the stereotype of the designing or conniving woman who can engineer social situations to her advantage and manipulate her spouse so that she can get her way while he thinks he's getting his. When one is powerless, one must be subtle.[5]

The operative words here are "powerless" and "oppressed," words that would form a connection between females and blacks. Nancy Henley supports this second view:

[3]See Gitter, Black & Mostofsky, Race and Sex in the Communication of Emotion, 88 J. of Soc. Psychology 273, 276 (1972).

[4]P. English, Behavior Concomitants of Dependent and Subservient Roles, (1972) (unpublished paper, as cited by N. Henley, Body Politics 14 (1977)).

[5]Rosenthal, Body Talk and Tone of Voice: The Language Without Words, 8 Psychology Today 64, 66 (Sept. 1974).

> There is no reason to assume that the sex differences we will discuss here are immutable, or more specifically, that they are innate and gender-linked. Women's greater sensitivity to people, for instance, can easily be traced to their socialization to a sex role which carries rewards for social awareness and punishments for the lack of it. Likewise, body language like vocal language is learned, not innate. There are aspects of body movement and vocal pitch that are related to anatomical differences between individuals and between the sexes, but they are greatly overshadowed by the learned aspects.[6]

The idea that improved nonverbal communication skills can be learned is supported by social psychologist Rosenthal's own work. He found that practice improved a person's ability to interpret nonverbal communication; however, this seems to true only for general nonverbal cues.[7]

Therefore, one might conclude that the greater the number of women or blacks on a panel, the greater the possibility that nonverbal cues will carry more weight than verbal messages. Also, if the trial lawyer is male — particularly if he has not tested or attempted to improve his skill in reading nonverbal messages — he might do well to consider adding a person skilled in reading nonverbal cues to his trial team to assist him in jury selection.

§11.4 Relating Nonverbal Communication to Verbal Communication

There are basic ways in which the nonverbal system relates to the verbal.[1] In each of these the two modes become so inter-

[6]N. Henley, Body Politics 17 (1977).

[7]See Rosenthal, Body Talk and Tone of Voice: The Language Without Words, 8 Psychology Today 64, 68 (Sept. 1974).

§11.4 [1]Much of this section is based on Paul Ekman and W. V. Friesen's article The Repertoire of Nonverbal Behavior: Categories, Origins, Usage and Coding, 1 Semiotica, 49, 98 (1969).

related and dependent on one another that they must be viewed together to form the coherent whole.

For instance, nonverbal communication may merely *repeat* what is being said verbally. If a witness declared, "That is the man I saw, the one sitting there at that table," while pointing his index finger in the direction of the defendant, the gesture would be considered a repetition of the verbalization.

The nonverbal channel can also *contradict* the verbal. If the client yells, "I *am* calm!," most lawyers would conclude that the contrary state was true. Since it is assumed that nonverbal cues are more difficult to fake, when a person is exposed to an incongruous message the nonverbal message is generally perceived to be more reliable.[2]

§11.4.1 Nonverbal Communication as a Substitute for Verbal Communication

Nonverbal behavior can be employed as a substitute for the verbal message. This is especially true with emotive displays. Sometimes it is inappropriate or difficult or even presumptuous to verbalize a statement; sometimes it is merely quicker and more effective to use the nonverbal mode rather than the verbal. The juror who, on returning to the jury box after deliberation, looks at the lawyer confidently and then smiles and nods his head would seemingly be communicating that the verdict about to be read is favorable. Similarly, consider how much easier it is to show rather than tell a significant person how much he or she means. A touch or a glance can show anger or love much more effectively than words, even though words may sometimes be a desirable form of communication. Many persons choose to use the nonverbal channel of communication to *say* something they might prefer not to say verbally.

[2]The incongruous message is of special interest to the trial lawyer. For more discussion of this see §14.8 infra on deception cues.

§11.4.2 *Nonverbal Communication as a Complement to Verbal Communication*

Nonverbal communication can be used to complement verbal communications by modifying or elaborating on it. Professors Burgoon and Saine, communication researchers, state that nonverbal communication can add details to a verbal communication that could not substitute for the verbal message itself.

> [Nonverbal messages] serve to expand on the message being conveyed. A good example is the person who reports an accident he or she has witnessed. While telling the narrative, the individual animatedly recreates the scene through gesture, posture, and voice. All these elements make the story more vivid. They also reveal how that individual feels about the accident. . . . The nonverbal complement is generally important in clarifying both the verbal message itself and the nature of the relationship between speaker and receiver.[3]

Similarly, nonverbal communication can emphasize or accent verbal messages by adding an intensity of meaning that would otherwise be missing. Every speaker has learned the value of moving his or her hands, arms, shoulders, and head in a way that builds interest in a message. The use of the dramatic pause or the sudden turn-about in the courtroom are well-worn nonverbal devices used by every trial lawyer to notify jurors that a key point is about to be made.

§11.4.3 *Nonverbal Communication as a Regulator of Verbal Communication*

Nonverbal communication can also be used to regulate the flow of communication among participants. A communicator might signal with eye contact or a hand motion when it is

[3] J. Burgoon & T. Saine, The Unspoken Dialogue: An Introduction to Nonverbal Communication 12 (1978).

appropriate or inappropriate for another person to enter a conversation. Major occasions for using nonverbal regulators include inviting another interactant to listen and participate with a group, inviting another person to take the floor verbally, shutting off the verbal communications of another, holding the floor, indicating understanding or lack of understanding, and controlling interruptions from other speakers. The use of nonverbal communications to regulate the flow of conversation is particularly useful to the trial lawyer in the examination of witnesses. Anthropologist William J. O'Barr, in his studies on language and the law, found that jurors judge the effectiveness of a trial lawyer largely on his or her ability to control the testimony of witnesses.

> [W]e focused on the relative tendency of the lawyer and the witness to persist in speaking when the other party interrupts or begins to speak at the same time. . . . Findings from this study . . . show significant effects on the perception of the lawyer. Subject-jurors rate the lawyer as maintaining most control when no overlapping speech occurs. The lawyer's control over the examination of the witness is perceived to diminish in all those situations where both lawyer and witness talk at once.
>
> Comparing the situation in which the lawyer persists to the one in which the witness persists, interesting results also emerge. When the lawyer persists, he is viewed not only as less fair to the witness but also as less intelligent than in the situation when the witness continues. The lawyer who stops in order to allow the witness to speak is perceived as allowing the witness significantly more opportunity to present his testimony in full.[4]

Nonverbal regulators are actively employed, generally both deliberately and consciously, to indicate how a message is being received. Skilled trial lawyers are very attuned to the faces of jurors and witnesses. Whenever a juror indicates with a quick frown that there is a lack of understanding, such a lawyer will quickly attempt to alter the communication so that it is more understandable.

[4] O'Barr & Conley, When a Juror Watches a Lawyer, 3 Barrister 8, 11 (1976).

§11.5 A Preview of Nonverbal Communication and Jurors

It is by virtue of their decisions about behaviors and appearances that the jurors reach their decisions about the credibility of each participant in the courtroom drama. Each one is judged by the following:

1. what he or she says,
2. how he or she looks,
3. how he or she sounds,
4. how he or she moves, and
5. how he or she interacts with others.

The verbal means of communicating with the jury has already been discussed at some length in earlier chapters of this book. The remaining four means by which jurors receive and convey information — through nonverbal means — are examined in chapters 12 through 15.

CHAPTER

12

Learning Nonverbal Communication: Appearance

§12.0 Introduction

When an attorney enters a courtroom and encounters a variety of people — courtroom personnel, jurors, witnesses — it is impossible for him or her not to notice how certain ones look and to make judgments, consciously or subconsciously, based on their appearance. It is important that the attorney reach accurate judgments based on knowledge rather than ones colored by bias or false expectations.

How we "look" depends on two aspects of physical appearance — first, natural features that include the body, hair, and skin; second, the artificial features that include all those "things" that humans use to cover up or increase the attractiveness of the body, such as clothing and cosmetics. Each of these aspects of appearance will be explored thoroughly in the following discussion.

§12.1 The Power of Attractiveness

Most of us would like to deny that appearance affects our first impressions of people as well as our subsequent behavior toward them. "Beauty is only skin deep" and "You can't judge a book by its cover" are caveats about appearance that most of us have been taught from early on. But research has demonstrated that attractiveness helps people to be more persuasive,[1] obtain higher salaries,[2] look more credible,[3] be seen as better marital partners,[4] and be more desirable as friends.[5]

Physical attractiveness also counts in the courtroom. Since people are generally more willing to forgive an attractive persons, jurors return more not guilty verdicts for attractive persons than for unattractive persons. Similarly, judges are more apt to offer probation or a reduced sentence to an attractive person. Psychologists Francis Dane and Lawrence S. Wrightsman documented this tendency:

> By combining a variety of defendants' and victims' characteristics, we were able to determine from Kalven and Zeisel's [1966]

§12.1 [1]See Mills & Aronson, Opinion Change as a Function of the Communicator's Attractiveness and Desire to Influence, 1 J. of Personality and Soc. Psychology 173, 1977 (1965). See also M. Knapp, Nonverbal Communication in Human Interaction 73 (1972).

[2]Doctoral dissertation by Starr, A Study of Perceptions of the Communication of Power Among Persons Varying in Organizational Position (University of Iowa 1979).

[3]See Wilson, Perceptual Distortion of Height as a Function of Ascribed Academic Status, 74 J. of Soc. Psychology, 97, 102 (1968); C. W. Mills, The Power Elite (1956). See also Widgery & Webster, The Effects of Physical Attractiveness Upon Perceived Initial Credibility, 4 Mich. Speech J. 9, 15 (1969).

[4]See Singh, A Study of Certain Personal Qualities as Preferred by College Students in Their Marital Partners, 8 J. of Psychological Researchers 37, 48 (1964); Walster, Importance of Physical Attractiveness in Dating Behavior, 3 J. of Personality and Soc. Psychology 73 (1966); Brislin & Lewis, Dating and Physical Attractiveness: Replication, 22 Psychological Reports 966, 976 (1968); Murstein, Gadpaille & Byrne, What Makes People Sexually Appealing? 1 Sexual Behavior 75, 77 (1971); Berscheid & Walster, Beauty and the Beast, 5 Psychology Today 43, 43 (March 1972); R. E. Baber, Marriage and Family, (1939).

[5]See Byrne, London & Reeves, The Effects of Physical Attractiveness, Sex and Attitude Similarity on Interpersonal Attraction, 36 J. of Personality 259, 272 (1968); E. Berscheid & E. H. Walster, Interpersonal Attraction (1969); and N. N. Henley, Body Politics (1977).

> data that in about 14% of those cases in which the jury acquitted when the judge would have convicted, the acquittal was the result of either the defendant being attractive, the victim being unattractive, or both. A similar percentage of cases in which the jury convicted when the judge would have acquitted appeared to owe their outcomes to the unattractiveness of the defendants, attractiveness of the victims, or both.[6]

They backed up their findings with those of two other researchers who in 1973 "examined the reasons given by jurors for sentences and concluded that retribution, rather than utility, better described the jurors' motivations for assigning punishment. That is, the jurors were more interested in punishing the defendant than in using sentence as a general deterrent to crime, especially when the defendant was unattractive."[7]

Research indicates that not only does the attractiveness or unattractiveness of the defendant influence the jurors, but that the victim's attractiveness or unattractiveness also has a tremendous impact on verdicts. It is obvious that one of the worst possible combinations that can be presented to a defense attorney is to have an unattractive defendant and an attractive victim.

Attractiveness has an effect on people in and out of the courtroom because of the way society teaches us to perceive attractive people. We assign more desirable characteristics to attractive people: attractive people are generally considered warmer, more likable, more well-rounded, happier, more socially involved and socially aware. We tend to forgive attractive persons for behavior we would criticize in someone less attractive. We assign more acceptable motives for the actions and behaviors of attractive persons.

In an experiment performed in the Midwest, simulation jurors were given basic facts concerning a civil case in which

[6] F. C. Dane & L. S. Wrightsman, Effects of Defendants' and Victims' Characteristics on Jurors' Verdicts, in The Psychology of the Courtroom 101 (1982).
[7] Ibid.

compensation for property damage was being sought. The jurors were told that a woman had gone into a man's apartment while he was out and had fired a shotgun into his closet and at his furniture, then went outside and shot at his car windshield. The jurors were asked what they thought was the motive behind the woman's actions and how much she should be made to pay in damages, if anything. They were shown a picture of the simulation defendant — half of the jurors were shown an unattractive woman while the other half were shown an attractive woman. Actually, the pictures were of the same person. In one of them she had messy hair, no makeup, a trace of a mustache on her upper lip, circles below her eyes, and unattractive clothing. All her assets were maximized in the other.

The jurors surmised that the attractive woman took such violent actions only because she had been driven to it by the man, who must have previously treated her badly. They wanted to know what he had done to her, what had he promised her, what was the nature of their relationship, and how had he obtained his possessions. They were especially interested in knowing if he had taught her how to shoot or had ever taken her hunting. The attractive woman was given every opportunity to present an explanation of her activities and to place the blame "where it belonged," according to one juror — on the insensitive, cold-hearted man who had obviously mistreated her.

The unattractive woman did not fare as well. The jurors saw her as a "sick and sullen woman" who was upset because men never looked favorably on her. She was acting out on this man her hostilities toward the whole world. According to this theory, the man was assumed to be an innocent bystander — "probably just someone she worked with who made the mistake of being nice to her" or "someone she worked with who never paid her much attention". The jurors felt the defendant was a "misfit" or "a sick person" with a "really hostile, negative outlook on life" who needed the "shock treatment of jail" so that she could learn that "she can't get away with taking her hate out on others." The male victim, they felt, should receive total compensation for the property damage he suffered. Not only did the jurors want to award compensation, they felt the defendant should be punished as well. All hoped she received a criminal trial for her actions. Conversely, none of the jurors who saw the picture of the attractive defendant felt that she should have to face a criminal trial, and, if she did, they would recommend leniency in sentencing. They felt that she shouldn't have to spend any time in jail since "that would just add to her problems, poor child."[8]

The trial attorney who must work with an unattractive client should not readily accept that there will be negative results. Although it apparently has never been done in an actual courtroom, research with simulation jurors suggest that instructions from the judge to ignore the attractiveness or unattractiveness of a victim or defendant have positive results. The ground work for such an instruction would have to be carried out during the trial. Perhaps an expert witness could be called to testify on research concerning attractiveness in an effort to educate the jurors about the reason for the judge's instruction.[9]

As much as one might hope for democratic acceptance of all physical appearances, one cannot deny the abundant evidence to the contrary. Often, an attorney is inclined to have a favorable reaction to a prospective juror for no other reason than that she or he is attractive. Conversely, trial attorneys often have a highly negative gut reaction to an unattractive juror whom background research has identified as possessing desirable attitudes toward the attorney's case. The trial attorney must be wary of such stereotypes of attractive and unattractive persons, both in accepting clients and in selecting prospective jurors.

[8]Unpublished research, V. Hale Starr, Ph.D. (trial simulation with four eight-person juries).

[9]This recommendation is based on research by Friend & Vinson, Leaning Over Backwards — Jurors' Responses to Defendants' Attractiveness, 24 J. of Communication 124, 129 (1974).

§12.2 Body Shape

That there is a relationship between personality and body shape is not necessarily a new idea. Shakespeare's Julius Caesar was one who made the connection early on.

> Let me have men about me that are fat;
> Sleek-headed men, and such as sleep o' nights.
> Yond Cassius has a lean and hungry look;
> He thinks too much: such men are dangerous. . . .
> Would he were fatter.[1]

Yet it was not until 1925 that Ernst Kretschmer, a professor of psychiatry and neurology, became the first to offer a classification system utilizing three body types and their corresponding personality characteristics. His three classes are the asthenic (the skinny and narrow body), the athletic (the well-muscled, well-developed body), and the pyknic (the fat body).[2] Using similar but refined classifications, W. H. Sheldon considerably influenced psychological investigations into the relationship between personality and body build. Sheldon maintains that there are biologically determined associations between body build and personality or behavior.[3] Further investigations have generally verified his thesis.[4]

§12.2.1 Somatotypes

Sheldon's "somatotyping" involves classifying people according to their body type. Like Kretschmer, Sheldon uses

§12.2 [1]Shakespeare, Julius Caesar, Act I, Scene ii, Line 191.

[2]See generally E. Kretschmer, Physique and Character: An Investigation of the Nature of Constitution and of the Theory of Temperament (2d ed. 1970).

[3]See W. H. Sheldon, The Varieties of Human Physique (1940); The Varieties of Human Temperament (1942).

[4]See Child, The Relationship of Somatotype to Self-Rating on Sheldon's Temperamental Traits, 18 J. of Personality 440, 453 (1950); S. Glueck & E. Glueck, A Study of Norms for Body Form-Behavior Relationships (1954).

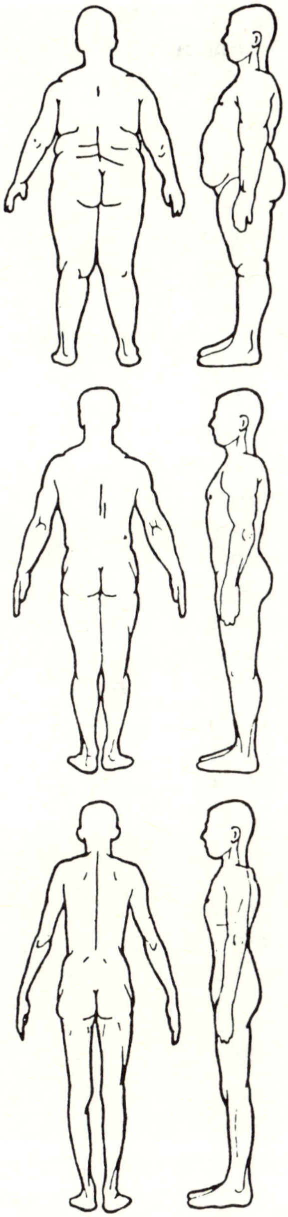

Figure 12-1. Three Basic Somatotypes
Drawings by Linda Andeberg, Penguin Studio, Inc.

Table 12-1
Personality Traits Commonly Associated with the Three Somatotypes

Endomorph	*Mesomorph*	*Ectomorph*
affable	active	afraid of failure
affected	adventurous	aloof
affectionate	argumentative	anxious
calm	assertive	awkward
complacent	attractive	cautious
contented	cheerful	conforming
cooperative	competitive	considerate
dependent	confident	cool
eager to please	courageous	detached
even-tempered	determined	gentle-tempered
extroverted	dominant	introspective
forgiving	domineering	jealous
generous	efficient	low need to achieve
kind	energetic	meticulous
leisurely	enterprising	moody
placid	enthusiastic	nervous
relaxed	high need to achieve	pessimistic
sluggish	hot-tempered	precise
sociable	impetuous	quiet
soft-hearted	nonconforming	reflective
soft-tempered	optimistic	reticent
sympathetic	outgoing	self-conscious
tolerant	reckless	sensitive
unenergetic	self-reliant	serious
warm	strong	shy
	talkative	stubborn
		suspicious
		tactful
		tense
		thoughtful
		uncooperative
		unpredictable
		withdrawn
		worried

three basic classifications: the endomorph (soft, round, fat), the mesomorph (athletic, bony, muscular), and the ectomorph (tall, thin, fragile). These basic shapes are shown in figure 12-1. Personality traits commonly associated with these three somatotypes are listed in table 12-1.

§12.2.2 *Using Somatotyping in the Courtroom*

What does somatotyping mean for the lawyer in the courtroom? Communication researcher Mark Knapp responds to this question by saying, "Simply this: If a case can be made that there are clearly defined and generally accepted physique-temperament stereotypes, we can reason that they will have a lot to do with the way you are perceived and responded to by others."[5] Psychologists Wells and Siegel argue, "[i]t is equally reasonable to assume that stereotypes of somatotypes represent a distillation of ages of social experience; that even if they are not determined by developments in the embryo, they are self-perpetuating and effective forces in the social environment."[6] Knapp makes the following conclusion:

> In other words, a stereotype may be more accurate than we wish to admit — there may be some reason for the stereotype other than prejudicial whims. Clearly, the evidence shows we do associate certain personality and temperament traits with certain body builds. These expectations may or may not be accurate, but they do exist; they are a part of the psychological mortar in interpersonal communication. We must recognize these stereotypes as potential stimuli for communication responses, so we can deal with them more effectively.[7]

It is to the trial attorney's advantage to become familiar with the somatotype stereotypes; not only can he use them as a basis

[5]M. Knapp, Nonverbal Communication in Human Interaction 72 (1972).
[6]Wells & Siegel, Stereotyped Somatotypes, 8 Psychology Rep. 77, 78 (1961).
[7]M. Knapp, Nonverbal Communication in Human Interaction 73 (1972).

for judging potential jurors, but they will, without doubt, be used by jurors to judge the lawyer, clients, and witnesses.

§12.3 Hair

The amount and location of hair on the human body is often a measure of attractiveness. Its styling, length, and cleanliness has long been a measure of societal norms and beliefs. Samson reportedly lost his strength when Delilah cut his hair. Ancient seamen were warned that the gods of the cold would "steal their faces" unless they were shielded from view by heavy beards and mustaches. Hair has often been used to advertise that a person is a member of a particular social group with distinct social values. The 1960s and '70s clearly demonstrated the importance a culture can place on hair. Businesses, schools, homes, families, marriages, law enforcement agencies, religions, the military were all affected by the conflict over questions about how hair should be worn: How long should hair be? Who has the right to make rules and set norms governing hair? One New York City billboard proclaimed, "Beautify America. Get a haircut!" which inspired a reply in black spray-paint: "God had long hair!"

Hair style is usually chosen by the wearer and therefore sends a definite message about the person's self-image. Figures 12-2 and 12-3 illustrate the impact on one's perception of personality, professionalism, and attractiveness that result from drawing various hair styles onto the same basic drawing of a face. Without altering the hair color, the artist has produced vastly different types of individuals. Even the perception of age is altered with the change in hairstyle. While studying the different hair styles, think about which style would be most appropriate for a lawyer, a member of the military, a blue-collar worker, a business person, a fashion model, or a spouse. Generally, people reflect the norms of their community and agree on the hair styles that are most fitting for each of these occupations.

Figure 12-2. Impact of Hair on Image (Male)
Drawings by Linda Andeberg, Penguin Studio, Inc.

Figure 12-3. Impact of Hair on Image (Female)
Drawings by Linda Andeberg, Penguin Studio, Inc.

§12.4 Cosmetics

Next to clothing, cosmetics are probably the most important medium of self-expression in nonverbal communication. Communication researcher Dale Leathers, while investigating the impact of physical appearance, spent an afternoon with the owners of a cosmetic studio in California who specialize in designing corrective cosmetics for people with facial blemishes and skin diseases. "Virtually all of [our] clients had a deficient self-image. 'The major need these people come in with is an enhanced self-image,' "[1] they told Leathers. These cosmetics specialists believe that each person carries with him or her a "reflective image" that they define as "the physical image that [the] client reflects or conveys to others and it may deviate significantly from the client's own image of himself. They emphasize that they are 'interested in the impact of the reflective image of the self-image. And the self-image relationship with social intercourse.' "[2] They contend that since this self-image "determines our place in society,"[3] a significant change in the reflective image will produce a "significant and highly beneficial change in [the] self-image and, consequently, in [the] behavior" of the individual.[4] The cosmetics studio owners cited the case of a young woman who experienced a dramatic and attractive alteration in her behavior as her appearance was likewise dramatically and attractively altered through the skillful use of cosmetics. She became confident, active, and socially accepted where once she had been withdrawn, socially shunned, and uncommunicative.[5]

When a person appears on the jury panel who has taken special care in applying cosmetics, the trial lawyer must ascertain whether the person has a negative self-image that possibly

§12.4 [1] D. G. Leathers, Nonverbal Communication Systems 99 (1976).
[2] Ibid.
[3] Ibid.
[4] Id. at 101.
[5] Id. at 99-101.

has not been alleviated by their use or whether the person has achieved a new, more positive self-image. If the person is of the first type, attorneys may be able to gauge with little difficulty whether to include this person on the panel for a personal injury case. If, however, the person is of the second type, attorneys will form a favorable first impression but then will want to have a closer look at the person's suitability for jury service in this type of case.

§12.5 Clothing and Accessories

Once a person's body shape and posture have been analyzed, the next step is to examine the person's clothing for possible nonverbal information. Clothing and the accompanying accessories are a product of culture and custom, signifying how a particular society views the role and status of its members. Clothing is probably the most easily manipulated variable in a person's appearance.

In daily life, clothing is worn for a variety of reasons and people perceive the choice of clothing as more purposeful in some situations than in others. In the courtroom this is true not only in regard to the robe of the judge, the suit of the attorney, and the defendant's or plaintiff's mode of dress, but also for the clothing selected for their courtroom appearance.

The observer of human behavior must at all times bear in mind that the individual is sending a multitude of nonverbal signals, each one potentially revealing something about personality, character, or attitude. Since dress is planned, it might very well be that inappropriate clothing has been consciously chosen. Wearing inappropriate clothing can be the most effective way to get attention, create a contrast, or emphasize a point. Such contradictory dress in the courtroom should be studied closely.

§12.5.1 *Clothing and Accessories as Indicative of Role*

Dress is self-advertisement of role, status, and personality. A person's role in society is generally demonstrated by the type of dress that he or she selects. A suit, for instance, often connotes a business look; similarly, a uniform tends to identify the wearer immediately with a particular occupation. Our expectations about how a waitress, farmer, doctor, nurse, teacher, librarian, or sex symbol should look is based primarily on the type of dress people in those roles often wear. Status is revealed through the texturc and style of the garment, with higher status associated with name brands and expensive materials. Personality variables are associated with the wearing of particular colors and designs and their appropriateness for specific occasions.

For most people dress is a matter of personal choice; however, dress is also dictated by conformity to fashions. Belonging to a group generally means that all members of a group will dress similarly. Even when a group is supposedly nonconformist, such as the hippies and yippies of the 1960s, the members of the group will conform to a certain mode of dress. Dress, therefore, will indicate group association and membership.

So strong is the association of clothing with group membership, that when a person removes the garments of a particular group, he or she may well lose his or her identification with that group. For instance, the policeman who removes his uniform loses his implicit authority.

To emphasize the significance of dress, author Flora Davis points to the experience of a group of psychology students on the West Coast who went shoplifting as part of an experiment in how dress affects expectations. Those students who were dressed in suits and ties were not watched by store personnel. When other customers observed the acts of pilferage by these well-dressed thieves, they looked the other way. The students wearing clothing identified with the hippie movement, however, were watched suspiciously. Davis concludes, "Dress can alienate or it can persuade."[1]

Alienation caused by dress was further demonstrated by a study of the relationship between acceptance and clothing with high school students. The authors of the study concluded that students who wore unacceptable dress (1) were more consistently in conflict with other members of the class, (2) received lower grades from their instructors (even those who had significantly higher achievement and Intelligence Quotient scores), (3) were less popular and held fewer student government offices, and (4) were less active in extracurricular activities.[2] Trial simulations have shown similar negative reactions to defendants in criminal trials. Prospective jurors tend to more readily believe that a person is deviant and capable of criminal acts if the person favors a style of dress that is viewed as unacceptable by the average member of society.

§12.5.2 Clothing and Accessories as Indicative of Age

Clothing may reflect the age and marital status of an individual. A young single person, for instance, may favor a wider, more extravagant display of color and design in a greater variety of garments than an older married individual. If that older person became single again, however, either because of a divorce or the death of his or her spouse, he or she might buy a whole new wardrobe reflecting the style popular with other single people. Clothing also may reflect the psychological age of a person more than the physical age. The young person who always wears conservative, somber garments will appear to be prematurely old, while the older person who wears youthful styles will often appear younger than his or her years.

§12.5 [1]F. Davis, Inside Intuition 177 (1975).
[2]See Hamilton & Warden, Student's Role in a High School Community and His Clothing Behavior, 58 J. of Home Econ. 789, 791 (1966).

§12.5.3 *Clothing and Accessories as Indicative of Personality*

Personality correlates with color and design choices in clothing. Outgoing women who like to socialize often choose deep shades and saturated colors, while quiet, passive women tend to choose pastels and tints.[3]

Jurors consider women lawyers to be more professional and capable if they are dressed in gray, brown, navy, or camel; they are seen as more excitable, uncontrolled, and emotional when red, green, yellow, light blue, or prints are worn. Lavender, violet, orange, bold splashy prints of any color, wide horizontal stripes, and black velvet is considered inappropriate, even offensive, courtroom attire by jurors.[4]

Clothing leaves a definite impression about the personality, status, and role of the wearer. A general rule concerning clothing, one endorsed by the best tailors and dress designers, is that the garment or accessory should never make so bold a statement that it overshadows the personality of the wearer. Clothing should complement, not dominate, the person; the viewer should remember the person, not just what the person wore. If anyone remembers what the President of the United States was wearing when he made his last address to the nation, his clothing consultant has failed.

§12.5.4 *Color Choice*

While style and garment type are the primary indicators of role, status, and personality, traits and moods are revealed most clearly by color. A three-piece suit in navy, for example, sends a much different message than that identical suit in peach.

[3]See Compton, Personal Attributes of Color and Design Preferences in Clothing Fabrics, 54 J. of Psychology 191, 195 (1962).

[4]Unpublished research, V. Hale Starr, Ph.D.

Colors are associated with moods, but they are also identified with personality traits, and are connected with certain symbols. Consider the following associations between colors and personality, colors and moods, and colors and their symbolic significance.

Red is associated with the personality characteristics of being extroverted, competitive, sensual, dramatic, impulsive, and athletic. The moods associated with red are those of being loving, angry, defiant. Red is symbolic of fire, blood, and royalty.

Blue is associated with being introverted, relaxed, empathetic, and loyal. The moods associated with blue are those of being calm, soothing, and transcendent. Blue is symbolic of masculinity, truth, and nature.

Yellow is associated with being intellectual, idealistic, industrious, serious, and cheerful. Yellow moods are those of being excited, hostile, and joyful. Yellow symbolizes the sun and wisdom. Yellow presents the most complex and potentially conflicting message.

Orange is associated with being sympathetic, extroverted, and athletic. The moods associated with orange are those of being distressed, contrary, and stimulating. Orange symbolizes the sun, harvest, and at times womanhood.

Purple is associated with being affectionate, solemn, creative, and insecure. The moods associated with purple are those of being depressed, dignified, and stately. Purple symbolizes wisdom, wealth, and tragedy.

Green is the color of life and is associated with being fair, frank, and stable. Moods associated with green include being cool and pleasant. Green symbolizes growth and peace.

Black is associated with being formal, sophisticated, mysterious, and solemn. The moods associated with black are those of being serious, intense, and melancholy. Black symbolizes power, fear, and death.

Brown is associated with being responsible, earthy, parsimonious, conservative, and kind. The moods associated with brown include being sad, neutral, and complacent. It symbolizes protection, decay, and atonement.

White is associated with being virginal, flirtatious, sterile, and venal. Coldness, joy, and neutrality are the moods associated with white. The symbolic meanings for white are solemnity, purity, humility, and light.

Recently, research has focused on the peculiar calming effects on violent behavior that are produced by exposure to a hot pink color, known in corrections circles as "Baker-Miller Pink."[5]

Naturally, people do not go around wearing a single color, making clear and simple statements about themselves. Most people have more depth to their personalities than that and, therefore, use color to signal the full range of their personality characteristics. But people do follow color patterns.

People attempting to decode color messages often complain that meanings appear to be contradictory. For instance, if a woman is wearing passionate red, calm blue, and sterile white, what is the message? The decoder must answer the following questions: Which color is dominant? Which color enhances the outfit?

§12.5.5 Impact on the Jury of Clothing and Accessories

John Molloy, the clothing consultant, contends that "it is possible, through the skillful manipulation of dress in any particular situation, to evoke a favorable response to your personality and your needs."[6] He would have advised Haldeman, Ehrlichman, and Mitchell to wear pinstripe suits when they appeared for the Watergate hearings since it "has been traditionally the most credible apparel for a man to wear when selling something important."[7] However, Molloy no longer thinks the pinstripe suit is appropriate for trial since its credibility was diminished during the Watergate episode. Molloy as-

[5]See 'Pepto' Cells Take Pep Out of Potential Violence, The Tribune (Hastings, Neb.), Aug. 29, 1981 at 2 (where corrections officers report that combative prisoners placed in pink cells become calm).

[6]J. Molloy, Dress for Success 12 (1975).

[7]See Kunz, Clothes Made the Defendant, Boston Globe, Oct. 12, 1974 (quoting Molloy).

serts, "If you are representing a client who is accused of having power and misusing it in any kind of so-called white-collar crime, diminish his look of authority by having him wear a pale beige suit, a pale shirt (not light blue), and a pale tie. This combination suggests to a jury that this is not really a man of authority and raises the question of how he could have abused what he obviously didn't have."[8]

Haldeman and Ehrlichman considerably altered their appearance before their trials. Haldeman let his hair grow out from his formerly brisk, militaristic crew cut to a softer, longer hairstyle in keeping with the look favored by businessmen of the day. Ehrlichman adopted a wardrobe that replaced his customary dark suits with lighter blue suits. His newly tanned complexion contrasted with the pale look of the harried Washington government official. He also sported new gold wire-rimmed glasses instead of the dark-rimmed half-glasses he had formerly favored. While the half-glasses would have conveyed the worst possible image under the circumstances because they can imply superiority, the wire-rims may not have been the best substitute. Wire-rims give the impression of inflexibility and rigidity. Soft warm brown plastic rims on full, rounded glasses could have generated the image of a thoughtful, intelligent, even sensitive person.

In sum, mode of dress advertises how a person sees his or her role in life and status within that role. It also yields messages about a person's personality.

§12.5.6 Assessing Juror Dress

There can be little doubt that jurors select with care their wardrobe for the jury selection process. Mary Timothy, jury foreperson in the Angela Davis jury, writes about how consciously she dressed for court in her book, *Jury Woman*:

[8]J. Molloy, Dress for Success 193 (1975).

> What should I wear? . . .
>
> At work I wore pant-suits almost exclusively. Would pant-suits at a time like this really represent the "true" me? Even though that was what I usually wore, I really felt that I was more a conservative-suit-and-low-heels type. I didn't want to go into court on Monday morning and have the attorneys look at me and mis-categorize me.
>
> What was my category anyhow? I tried to think of what role I fit into in today's society.
>
> I had a job, a husband and three children. . . . Politically, I had been a Democrat since the summer of 1952. . . . In recent years, as my distress over the war in Southeast Asia increased, I found I was aligning myself with the liberal wing of the Democrat Party.
>
> Socially and morally, I was pretty conservative — by the standards of the day. I had been raised strictly in a middle-class, small-town environment — a Catholic — and I accepted the mores of that time and place. I like people on a one-to-one basis, I do not like organizations and clubs, I am not a "joiner."
>
> I was just becoming aware of the Women's Movement. . . .
>
> So, in an effort to stereotype myself, I decided the night before on a tailored cashmere suit and flat walking shoes.[9]

This woman wanted to convey all this information to the attorneys involved in jury selection by wearing a tailored cashmere suit and flat walking shoes.

When looking over a prospective jury panel, the following questions should be considered:

1. Who is dressed inappropriately for the courtroom? Why is it inappropriate? Does that tend to advertise that this person is anti-establishment? Or is it more likely that this person's financial situation has prevented an appearance more in keeping with the courtroom look?
2. Who is dressed in the darkest, most conservative clothing? Does it lend an authoritarian look to the wearer?

[9]M. Timothy, Jury Woman 9-10 (1974).

3. Who is brightly attired, suggesting that he or she is outgoing?
4. Who is professionally dressed and, therefore, potentially a leader?
5. Who is dressed with unusual color combinations or role-type combinations?
6. What does the color and design of a person's clothing indicate about the personality of the wearer?

Of course, the answers to these questions must be considered in conjunction with other nonverbal information about the person. It should be remembered, however, that the mode of dress is often a conscious choice and therefore tends to make a deliberate statement, unlike some other nonverbal messages.

CHAPTER

13

Learning Nonverbal Communication: Voice

§13.0 Introduction

How something is said affects the final interpretation of what is said. Consider the following analysis of how members of the media construed the meaning of a presidential spokesperson's response to questions:

> McCloskey, a major spokesperson during President Nixon's administration for the Department of State, has three distinct ways of saying, "I would not speculate": spoken without accent, it means the department doesn't know for sure; emphasis on the "I" means "I wouldn't, but you may — and with some assurance"; accent on "speculate" indicates that the questioner's premise is probably wrong.[1]

During a trial only the words spoken are recorded; the court reporter does not record the manner in which the words are spoken. The reporter would not interject, for instance, "spoken with contempt," "exclaimed in anger," or "stated in boredom and disgust" when recording testimony. Yet these observa-

§13.0 [1]Newsweek, Oct. 5, 1970, at 106.

tions might alter considerably the interpretation of a simple "no" response given by a witness. While the way in which something is said is not included in the court record, it is likely to have an effect on the jury.

§13.1 Vocal Cues in General

Social psychologist Albert Mehrabian examined three sources of information used by listeners to understand a verbal communication: the words, the sound of the voice, and the facial expressions. He determined that 7 percent of meaning is dependent on words, 38 percent is dependent on the sound of the voice, and 55 percent is dependent on facial cues. In other words, the sound of the voice is over five times more important than the words used.

The vocal cues that assist the listener include (1) level of sound (loudness v. softness), (2) pitch, (3) tempo, (4) speech duration, (5) voice quality, (6) articulation, (7) pronunciation, (8) rhythm, (9) range, (10) resonance, and (11) silence. Each of these cues is processed by the listener in reaching judgments of personal information, personality, emotional display, and credibility.

§13.1.1 Revealing Speaker Origins

Even when the speaker is unseen, the listener does not have to rely solely on the words spoken for information about that individual. Five pieces of personal information are often immediately apparent: the speaker's sex, age range, geographic origin (not to be confused with race), intelligence or cultural background, and mood or temperament. These judgments are often made almost automatically and with considerable accuracy after listening to only a few statements by the speaker.

The voice can usually be identified as masculine or feminine according to the stereotypes of how men and women in our culture sound. If a man is considered to have a feminine voice, then he is often judged as possessing other feminine characteristics. A woman with a masculine voice is viewed as a better decisionmaker but as a colder person. Judgments about a person's sex identification that are based on voice tend to be very difficult to overcome.

Age range is tied to certain vocal qualities relating to tone and texture of voice. The voice becomes heavier with age. Although one can seldom identify the exact age of a speaker from vocal cues, it is usually possible to be accurate to within ten years. Older persons who have young sounding voices are frequently viewed in a more positive light and are less likely to be considered elderly.

Intelligence or education is judged primarily by four factors: accuracy of pronunciation, precision of articulation, vocal quality, and voice smoothness. Judgments as to social class are also determined primarily by attention to these vocal cues.

Quality is difficult to define but something easily agreed on by listeners. If the speaker possesses a positive vocal quality, then he or she will be judged more intelligent, more persuasive, more honest, and more cultured. Lawyers who have a positive vocal quality are sometimes associated with the judge, implying more authority in the courtroom. Vocal quality is also said to be the peculiar combination of cues that identifies the voice with the speaker. The smoother, clearer, cleaner, and more precise vocal style is associated with higher levels of education and intelligence and higher levels of cultural exposure.

Mood or temperament is perhaps the easiest judgment to make about a speaker. It is with relative ease that the listener determines whether the speaker is angry, businesslike, happy, or bored.

§13.1.2 Revealing Emotions through Speech

There are considerable variations in people's ability to decode emotions indicated by vocal cues. Research generally supports the following conclusions: females are more accurate than males; artistic or creative people are more accurate than people trained in the hard sciences or mathematics; intelligent people are more proficient; and people who are required to be proficient become more proficient. People also have different abilities in conveying messages of emotion using vocal cues.

Generally, despair, impatience, contempt, grief, anger, fear, indifference, determination, doubt, and disgust can be communicated by vocal cues alone with at least 80 percent accuracy.[1] Amazement, pity, amusement, nervousness, sadness, happiness, sympathy, satisfaction, love, pride, affection, dislike, surprise, joy, cheerfulness, and admiration can be communicated with only 30 to 40 percent accuracy. One of the reasons these particular emotions are so difficult to read with a high level of accuracy is because they are so easily confused with each other. Love, for instance, is frequently confused with pity, sadness, sympathy, and admiration.

It is useful for trial attorneys to be tested on their ability to send or interpret emotions communicated in vocal cues (see §13.3 infra).

Factors that influence the communicating of vocal cues are rhythm, tempo, pitch, loudness, pause, and variation. *Happiness* is communicated through irregular rhythm, quick tempo, a high pitch that shifts downward, pitch variation, and few pauses. *Anger* has a fast tempo, great variation in pitch, and short duration of phonations (the length of time it takes to produce a vocal sound). *Fear* has a fast tempo, high pitch or upward shifting pitch, irregular rhythm, and few pauses within phrases in which the pitch did not shift. *Indifference* is communicated by low pitch (probably the lowest pitch produced by the voice), regular rhythm, moderate tempo, moderate loudness, and little variation in pitch levels. *Grief* is associated with a very slow tempo, much vibrato (a slightly tremulous effect imparted by slight and rapid variations in pitch), regular rhythm, short duration of sound, and much silence. *Contempt* is also associated with slow tempo but this

§13.1 [1]See R. G. Harpter, A. N. Wiens, & J. D. Matarazzo, Nonverbal Communication: The State of the Art 39-44 (1978).

slowness is caused by silences and phonations that are of equal duration. Contempt has great variation in inflection at the ends of phrases, and a wide range of pitch levels that tend to shift downward. Contempt tends to have a fairly regular rhythm. *Satisfaction* has great pitch variation, a moderate to fast tempo, and few pauses. *Nervousness* is associated with a fast tempo accompanied by vocal hesitations and word flow interruptions. Pitch tends to be high and strained, rhythm is irregular, and loudness is uncontrolled, frequently being too loud or too soft for the speech situation. *Surprise* is communicated through a fast tempo, many alterations in pitch that tend to shift upward, and irregular rhythm. *Sadness* is associated with a slow tempo, pitch that tends to shift downward, a regular rhythm, and a moderate number of pauses. Sadness tends to be communicated in a low, soft tone with little variation. *Despair* is an intensification of sadness; the tempo is even slower but it is more irregular and strained. *Impatience* is communicated through a fast tempo, clipped sounds at the end of words or phrases, and little variability in pitch range. *Admiration* is communicated through a higher than normal pitch, but the tempo is smoother and does not carry the clipped, emphatic quality of impatience. The rhythm is regular, the tempo and loudness is moderate.[2]

§13.2 Determining Credibility from Vocal Cues

Probably the single most important element in communication, especially in the courtroom, is the perception of the speaker's

[2]This summary of vocal characteristics of emotion was based on the following research: Fairbanks & Pronovost, An Experimental Study of the Durational Characteristics of the Voice During the Expression of Emotion, 6 Speech Monographs 8, 106 (1939); Fairbanks & Hoaglin, An Experimental Study of the Durational Characteristics of the Voice During the Expression of Emotion — II,8 Speech Monographs 85, 96 (1941); Scherer & Oshinsky, Cue Utilization in Emotion Attribution from Auditory Stimuli, 1 Motivation and Emotion 340 (No. 4, 1977).

credibility. Speaker credibility refers to the listener's perception of how trustworthy and expert the speaker is.

Several dimensions affect the perception of speaker credibility: (1) the speaker's expertise on the topic of concern, (2) the listener's evaluation of the speaker's reliability as a source of information — this judgment depends on the listener's perception that the speaker is dependable, predictable, and consistent, (3) the listener's perception of the speaker's intention in sending a particular message at a particular time, (4) the listener's perception that the speaker possesses warmth and friendliness, (5) the listener's evaluation of the speaker's dynamism — this judgment depends on the listener's perception that the speaker is assertive, emphatic, forceful, and lacking in passive behavior, and (7) the opinion of the majority of the listeners. Unfortunately, most persons do not rely solely on their own analysis of credibility but tend to check their perceptions against those of other listeners. If they are in the minority, they tend to alter their views to be in keeping with the majority.

The first element of credibility, the speaker's expertise, is related to content, credentials, and manner of presentation. Merely because the speaker is considered an expert on a topic doesn't guarantee that he or she will look or sound like an expert.

If the speaker's voice sounds nasally or throaty, he or she will be perceived as lacking credibility. Since these qualities are inherent in some voices, they are difficult to alter. If a witness has one of these negative vocal qualities, the attorney should try to offset its effect on potential jurors during voir dire. The lawyer should solicit a promise from jurors that they will listen to the content of the testimony and try not to be influenced by the quality of the speaker's voice. Of course, if there is no need to present the witness in person, the best way to handle the problem is to use a deposition.

For the final assessment of speaker credibility, the vocal cues discussed in this chapter should be considered in conjunction with the face and body movement cues discussed in chapter 14.

§13.2.1 *Cues that Negate Credibility*

There are basically nine vocal cues that interfere with the perception of credibility: (1) disfluencies in the speech pattern, (2) inappropriate speech tempo, (3) inappropriate range of pitch, (4) faulty articulation, (5) nonstandard speech, (6) inappropriate intonation, (7) lack of warmth and friendliness, (8) inappropriate amplitude, and (9) lack of dynamism in the speaker's voice.

Disfluencies are interruptions in word flow that result in breaks in the thought process. Disfluencies may be fillers ("you know," "oh, like that," "okay," "and like that," or "and such like that, you know what I mean"), repetitions of sounds and phrases ("I was, was go – going to but I, I just kinda, kinda forgot"), and vocalized pauses ("ah," "uhn," "and – ah," or "a – a – a – a"). When a listener hears a disfluency, he or she judges that the speaker is (1) ill-prepared, (2) unknowledgeable, (3) nervous, or (4) lying. Jurors tend to omit nervousness as a justification for word flow interrruptions and are inclined to think a disfluent witness is lying, ill prepared, or unknowledgeable. The conclusion most jurors jump to is that the witness is attempting to hide the truth.

How many disfluencies is a speaker allowed by a listener before losing credibility? That depends on the context of a spoken communication. In a formal situation, if the listener believes the speaker has had ample opportunity to prepare his or her comments, the speaker will lose credibility with the first disfluency. Each additional disfluency will further diminish the speaker's credibility. In an informal situation where the speaker is not expected to be highly prepared and the listeners are nonjudgmental (as in conversations with peers, family, and friends), more disfluencies are allowed. However, when there is a sudden increase in the number of disfluencies that is uncharacteristic of the person's normal speech pattern, the listener will tend to judge the speaker as unknowledgeable, nervous, or lying. In a courtroom, the judgment made by the jurors will probably be that the individual is lying.

The *tempo* of speech needs to fit the occasion. When the

speech rate exceeds 280 words per minute, intelligibility declines and, consequently, so does listener comprehension. A person talking this fast will likely be considered a "fast-talker" — someone not to be trusted. When a person speaks at a sustained fast tempo, the listener will judge that what is being said has not been thought out beforehand.

Conversely, if a slow tempo is utilized, the speaker needs to exhibit intensity of emotion to hold the attention of the listener. Long pauses by the speaker will give the impression of great concern, deep thought, and unexcitability. At the same time, he or she will be perceived as not having much energy, activity, or potency. The effectiveness of speech tempo depends on the purpose for the speech. If the speaker wants to motivate the listener, he or she should use a fairly fast tempo. To portray deep emotion or pain, however, the tempo should be relatively slow. For persuasion, a normal to quick tempo should be used along with pauses that will give the impression of thoughtfulness as well as accommodate listener comprehension.

In the United States, listeners have become accustomed to the controlled, moderate *range of pitch* used by media broadcasters. Greater fluctuation in pitch will make a verbal communication more dynamic and make the speaker seem more outgoing. However, speakers who frequently alter their pitch are sometimes considered excitable, out of control, and tense. In contrast, a speaker with a flat, monotone voice will be perceived as sluggish, cold, and withdrawn.[1] Therefore, a moderate, controlled range is considered most desirable for credible speech. Factual speech is judged to have a more limited range than emotional speech.

Faulty articulation is judged to be the product of a sloppy, unconcerned, ill-controlled, and unintelligent individual. As articulation worsens, the listener will have to work harder to hear and understand the verbal message and will likely become impatient and resentful. This results in increasingly negative

§13.2 [1]Doctoral dissertation by Addington, The Relationship of Certain Vocal Characteristics with Perceived Speaker Characteristics (University of Iowa 1963).

judgments about the speaker. Faulty articulation should not be confused with accent or dialect — speakers who are not using their native language or mode of speech are judged on a different basis.

Nonstandard speech will cause confusion and lack of understanding and will result in listeners making negative judgments about the speaker. Nonstandard speech includes dialect, accented speech, jargon, and technical speech. Clearly, the use of standard speech is superior for achieving high credibility. Consider the following conclusions concerning standard and nonstandard speech and its effect on credibility:[2]

1. Judgments concerning the credibility of an accent or dialect depend on how the mode of speech is generally regarded. The greater its general acceptance, the higher its credibility.
2. The type of speech commonly used by radio and television commentators, now called General American speech and associated with the Midwest, tends to have the highest rating of credibility.
3. Speakers of standard English will be perceived as more credible than speakers of nonstandard English regardless of the listener's race.
4. Standard speech tends to be rated as more dynamic, more aesthetically pleasing, and reflective of a higher socio-economic status.
5. Judgments of credibility are affected by the listener's prejudices, biases, and prejudgments.
6. Speech patterns common to a particular region will be perceived as more sincere and trustworthy to a listener from that region.
7. When a person listens to a dialect or accent for a long

[2]This summary of vocal cues and their association with credibility is based on the survey of literature presented in H. Giles and P. F. Powesland's book Speech Style and Social Evaluation (1975) and from the summary of vocal cues in J. Burgoon & T. Saine, The Unspoken Dialogue: An Introduction to Nonverbal Communication 209-213 (1978).

time, its effect on the listener's judgment of the speaker may begin to diminish. This may happen, for instance, when a witness is on the stand for a long time.

Inappropriate intonation creates the impression that the speaker is powerless. The most common is the use of rising intonation at the end of a declarative sentence causing a statement to sound like a question. For instance, if a witness is asked how far he was from the accident, and he answers, "thirty feet" but says it with rising intonation, the listener will conclude that his meaning is "I think it was thirty feet — am I right?" This speech pattern is most frequently used by persons who are not accustomed to making and implementing decisions, namely, speakers who are not accustomed to exercising power. To correct this, the speaker's self-confidence must be improved, a difficult task.

It is difficult to determine exactly what vocal cues are present or missing when a voice is perceived to be *lacking in warmth and friendliness.* However, listeners tend to readily pick up on whether a speaker is cold and aloof or warm and friendly. While listening to a potential juror answer questions during voir dire, the attorney will likely form a highly accurate impression about whether the individual is inclined toward friendliness. The warmth and friendliness of a person may vary: a speaker may address one person very warmly and turn cold and aloof when speaking to another individual. The plaintiff's witness, for example, may be friendly toward the plaintiff's attorney but cold to the defense attorney. Such differences will be judged by listeners as indications of personal preference and bias.

Inappropriate amplitude creates problems both in listener comfort and perceptions of personality. Naturally, if the speech is delivered at such a low volume that it cannot be heard, the speech will have no credibility. If the delivery is too loud, however, the speaker will be considered pushy, demanding, obstreperous, or defensive. It is not uncommon that as a speaker experiences anxiety or stress, his or her voice will diminish to a whisper. While listeners may have empathy for a stressed or anxious speaker, the information will have no credibility if it cannot be heard. Again, the most credible level of amplitude is that which is normal and controlled.

If a speech pattern is too controlled, however, the speaker will be perceived as *lacking in dynamism*. For this reason rehearsed speech is often judged to be lacking in credibility. A speaker must have spontaneity of expression and a variety of sound cues, or he or she will be perceived as apathetic, uninteresting, and unemotional.

In conclusion, the speaker needs an overall good speech delivery to be perceived as credible. Credibility seems to fall into two basic categories that appear almost to contradict each other: (1) competency and expertness, which is associated with dynamism, high-status vocal cues, and an authoritarian mode of speech, and (2) trustworthiness and friendliness, which is associated with a calm and low mode of speech. To be persuasive, a speaker must rate high in both categories.

§13.2.2 Application at Trial

Fortunately for the trial attorney there is ample opportunity for displaying both of these credibility factors before and during trial. During both voir dire and examination of witnesses, the attorney might employ a conversational style very effectively, and then speak in a dynamic, competent, and expert mode during cross-examinations and the closing argument. Successful trial attorneys use a wide range of vocal styles during a trial. While it is important to be true to one's self-image, different styles can signal the jury as to the lawyer's purpose. Variation can also build interest. Communication specialist Addington, who studied how vocal cues are associated with personality cues, made the following conclusion:

> [T]his study has made it quite evident that it is possible for a speaker, through a variety of vocal changes, to make gross or subtle alterations in his personality as it is perceived by listeners cued only by a sample of the speaker's speech. . . . For those

speakers interested in creating a perceived personality they would be pleased to claim as their own, and for those interested in character interpretation, vocal dexterity is a mandatory skill.[3]

§13.3 Sending and Identifying Emotions in Vocal Communications: Practice

It is useful for trial attorneys to be tested on their ability to send and interpret emotions in verbal communications. To test his or her proficiency in sending vocal cues, the lawyer is asked to read a statement several times, each time attempting to communicate a different emotion. A statement like the following might be used:

> I don't understand. You've asked me that before. The answer is the same. I don't understand.

Table 13-1
Vocal Cues for Emotional Meaning — Checksheet

Message number one:

____despair	____impatience	____grief	____indifference
____contempt	____nervousness	____anger	____happiness
____sadness	____admiration	____fear	____satisfaction

Message number two:

____despair	____impatience	____grief	____indifference
____contempt	____nervousness	____anger	____happiness
____sadness	____admiration	____fear	____satisfaction

Message number three:

____despair	____impatience	____grief	____indifference
____contempt	____nervousness	____anger	____happiness
____sadness	____admiration	____fear	____satisfaction

(Repeat table for all 12 vocal cue messages.)

[3] Addington, The Relationship of Selected Vocal Characteristics to Personality Perception, 35 Speech Monographs 151 (1968).

The lawyer is asked to affect despair, impatience, contempt, grief, anger, fear, indifference, nervousness, sadness, happiness, admiration, and satisfaction (see §13.1.2 supra).

After the lawyer has practiced, the statements are repeated again and tape-recorded. The order of the statements is then altered and each statement is introduced by a neutral voice identifying them by number. The tape is then played to persons who have been asked to identify the emotions being conveyed.

Experienced trial attorneys generally perform well in sending emotional messages with vocal cues as long as they are not the victims of vocal inflexibility. Most attorneys who are limited in their vocal abilities compensate by using enhanced body movement or additional facial expression.

To test the lawyer's ability to interpret vocal cues, he or she is asked to identify emotions being communicated on a tape recording made by professionals. A checksheet like the one in table 13-1 can be used to track the emotions the lawyer identifies.

The listener should listen carefully but not try to force his or her perceptions of the message to fit a corresponding emotion. It is as valuable to know which emotions are consistently misinterpreted as it is to know which emotions are identified correctly. The testing situation should not be allowed to become tense. If the lawyer maintains a relaxed, businesslike attitude, he or she will be performing at the same level as he or she would in the courtroom. Still, the goal is to develop one's skills such that it will be possible to identify vocal cues almost instantaneously.

After completing the test, compare responses on the checksheet with the correct identifications. Attorneys vary widely in their initial attempts to correctly identify vocal cues. A recommended rating system follows:

Emotion	*Correct response*
one	8%
two	17%
three	25%

four	33%
five	42%
six	50%
seven	58%
eight	67%
nine	75%
ten	83%
eleven	92%
twelve	100%

A score of 75 percent or above should be considered excellent; 67 percent to 74 percent, above average; 42 percent to 65 percent, average; and below 41 percent, poor. Generally, the attorney will improve by 14 to 20 percent with each additional testing, eventually achieving an excellent score.[1]

Attorneys tend to be quite proficient in producing vocal cues correctly. In fact, they tend to be about twice as good at communicating emotions as they are at identifying them.

§13.3 [1]Unpublished research, V. Hale Starr, Ph.D. (Based on percentages from testing conducted with attorneys during a series of continuing legal education seminars in Iowa and South Dakota in 1978).

CHAPTER

14

Learning Nonverbal Communication: Movement

§14.0 Introduction

Judgments about people based on the way they look are made on a static level — they can be made merely by viewing a photograph of a person. However, people are not one-dimensional or cast in stone. They move, and the way they move creates impressions that can result in judgments about their personality, emotional level, attitudes, and social status. There is meaning in movement. Interest in nonverbal communication through movement, those that are both intentional or unintentional, was triggered by Ray Birdwhistell's early work. Many body movement studies have been carried on according to guidelines set out by Birdwhistell. The study of movement centers around the messages communicated by facial expression, posture, and gestures.

§14.1 Facial Expression

Most people readily associate effective display of emotion with facial expression. "Look happy," it is demanded of someone, and immediately the person sports a bright smile and bright, alert eyes.

The face is the part of the body most readily and consciously controlled by a person. It is only the naive or innocent person who lets emotions flow across his or her face so that others know what is being thought or felt. While the "poker face" — a face that reveals little about what the person is thinking — is considered a definite asset by trial lawyers, diplomats, business people, and decisionmakers, not being able to "read" a person's face can be a liability.

Most people do not want to conceal all emotion. They want to display the emotions they enjoy sharing while concealing those that make them seem vulnerable or undesirable. Since this is an almost universal tendency, it would seem that the majority of people would be skilled in both their ability to display emotion on the face as well as their ability to read the emotive displays of others. However, research has demonstrated (1) that some emotions are easier to read than others, and (2) that some people are more skilled in reading others' emotional displays.

In an experiment using photographs of one woman's display of 6 emotions, 390 people were asked to link the photographs with the appropriate emotion. The results were as follows: happiness was correctly identified by 366 people, suffering by 325, determination by 310, surprise by 304, disgust by 294, and contempt by 190 subjects.[1]

Facial expressions of emotions are often only fleeting; often as soon as an emotion appears on an individual's face, the individual moves to control it. Some facial emotions last only a second, as with an expression of surprise. Since most testing of people's ability to interpret facial emotions has involved still pictures that can be viewed for as long as desired, results would seem to be less accurate than if participants were tested on the fleeting expressions encountered in real life. Participants in much of this research were also asked to identify only a limited number of emotions. They were generally given ten or

§14.1 [1]See Ekman, Friesen & Tomkins, Facial Affects Scoring Technique: A First Validity Study, 3 Semiotica 37, 58 (1971).

twenty photographs and asked to associate them with ten different emotions. The natural assumption would be to think that there are one or two pictures for each emotion, which was indeed the case. In real life, however, no such assumption is reasonable. "Physiologists estimate the facial musculature is capable of producing some 20,000 different facial expressions."[2] This doesn't mean that there are that many different expressions of emotion. Birdwhistell reported that his five assistants who identified twenty-three different eyelid positions all agreed that only four different emotions were communicated.[3] Of the vast number of expressions that the face is capable of producing, each culture applies meaning to only a few.

Psychologists Paul Ekman and Wallace V. Friesen, who have been studying the meaning of facial expression since 1965, have devised a system that divides the face into the three primary regions that display emotion. The three planes of the face according to this Facial Affect Scoring Technique (FAST), are (1) the forehead and eyebrows, (2) the eyes, eyelids, and bridge of the nose, and (3) the cheeks, nose, lips, mouth, chin, and jaw.[4] Ekman and Friesen characterized the temporary rapid facial movements that correspond with each of six basic emotions: surprise, fear, disgust, anger, happiness, and sadness. Attorneys should be able to identify these expressions with accuracy and immediacy.

§14.2 Posture

Of all nonverbal cues, posture is the easiest to learn to interpret. Posture is so characteristic of a person that we learn to

[2] M. Knapp, Nonverbal Communication in Human Interaction 94 (1972).

[3] See Birdwhistell, Communicative Signals and Their Clinical Assessment, 2 Voices: The Art and Science of Psychotherapy 37-42 (1965).

[4] See P. Ekman & W. V. Friesen, Unmasking the Face: A Guide to Recognizing Emotions in Facial Clues 8-15 (1975). (See book generally for descriptions of facial expressions.)

identify and recognize others by how they carry themselves. Behavioral scientists report that a person even assumes different positions while sleeping that are indicative of personality and mood.

Primary posture cues are those that indicate (1) energy level, (2) immediacy, (3) actions of appeal, (4) interest and involvement, and (5) attitude.

Energy level is associated with the degree of relaxation or alertness and is viewed in relation to the body's erectness, quickness and smoothness of movement, and the amount of tension. When movements are slow, halting, pulled downward by gravity, or nonexistent, the actor is regarded as being tired, bored, despondent. Conversely, frequent quick, smooth, and controlled movements are associated with confidence, capability, and with the high energy leader type. When movements are excessive, too quick, jerky, or uncontrolled, the actor will be considered nervous, irritated, or ill.

Immediacy is the combination of physical distance between people and body orientation. It indicates involvement, interpersonal trust, attraction, and reaction to a particular situation. While it is often true that physical proximity and eye contact signal involvement, trust, and attraction, occasionally the particular situation affects immediacy. For instance, a judge in the courtroom is physically removed from others but does not intend to signal disapproval by his or her place at the bench.

Attitude is shown by many different body postures but is most easily identified by movements that indicate interest and involvement. During the trial of the Chicago Seven, defense attorney William Kunstler felt that Judge Julius Hoffman was adversely influencing the jury by communicating his opinion of the parties. Kunstler objected to the extreme forward lean demonstrating attentiveness and interest adopted by Judge Hoffman during the prosecutor's closing argument, that contrasted with his leaning so far back during the defense' final argument that he looked as if he were sleeping.[1]

§14.2 [1]See F. Davis, Inside Intuition 93 (1975).

§14.2.1 Juror Movement and Posture in the Courtroom

For a better understanding of how posture communicates in the courtroom, this section includes photographs of models for purposes of illustration. (The photographs, labeled photograph 14-1 through photograph 14-15, appear at the end of this section at pp. 388-402.) Since the jury is primarily observed while seated, that is the posture that is examined.

§14.2.2 Sitting on the Edge of a Chair

Photograph 14-1 demonstrates sitting on the edge of a chair. Whenever a potential juror is seen in this position in the courtroom, it is likely the person doesn't expect to occupy the seat for long. Either the person wants to be excused from jury service or doesn't expect to be chosen.

When examining photographs like these, one's attention is frequently drawn to facial expression as well as posture. Both message sources contain meaning for the observer, but posture is the element of meaning for the purposes of this section. In assuming the following postures, the models were instructed to maintain neutral expressions. Posture affects attitude, however, so there is some alteration of facial expression. For this reason a black bar has been placed across the upper face of the models so that the reader's attention will be focused on the models' posture. Of course, in actual analysis during jury selection, *all* message sources should be examined.

Reexamine photograph 14-1 — where the models' upper face has not been covered over — to see how much of the message was read from the facial expression, then block out the face and see if the message is altered.

§14.2.3 Sitting Up Straight in a Chair

Sitting on the edge of a chair should not be confused with sitting very straight with a rigid back as shown in photograph

14-2. People who sit with a rigid back will continue to provide their own body contour, without submitting to the contours of the chair. The rigid back of this individual is probably also reflected in the legs, which are primly crossed at the ankle or are positioned with both feet planted flatly on the floor. This individual doesn't allow the body to relax and be comfortable. The observer can interpret that if this person is going to be this hard on himself or herself, than he or she will be equally hard on others. The rigidity of this individual sends a message indicating the following attitude: "I will follow the rules and regulations of our society and our culture in a precise way. What the judge instructs, I will carry out to the letter." This person would not be interested in what is convenient or humanly probable but rather in what is "right."

What can be called the solid citizen sitting posture is illustrated in photograph 14-3. This is the position often recommended that witnesses assume while testifying, since it conveys the image of a conscientious citizen. It is a posture, however, that is not always appreciated when displayed by someone on the jury panel. Notice that each person's arms are comfortably spread to the arms of the chairs, each is occupying the full space provided, and that the two taller models have both feet planted solidly on the floor. The two women differ in height by twelve inches; Lin, the taller woman, can easily place her feet on the floor, while Donna, who does not have long enough legs to do this, has tucked her left ankle beind her right ankle. Obviously, the observer must always take into consideration the environment provided, plus the size of the individual who occupies that space. The fact that Donna, due to her shortness, must tuck her left ankle behind her other does not diminish the overall message of the posture. A person who is so seated with his or her spine resting against the back of the chair, in an upright but not a rigid position, conveys the solid citizen message. Generally, the person's head is not tilted but faces so that she or he can look directly and evenly into the eyes of the questioner. This solid citizen posture transmits the message that the individual is comfortable, at ease, and confident.

§14.2.4 Sitting Leaners

In photograph 14-4, the models have slid their buttocks slightly forward to the middle of the chairs while leaning their backbones against the chairs' backrest — the slight backward lean. As a backward lean is introduced into the posture, the message transmitted is that the person is experiencing greater relaxation and confidence, but also greater indifference. A potential juror who assumes this position is not completely involved in the process yet but is listening and is capable of becoming involved. It is likely that if the voir dire questioning suddenly shifted to him or her, a more upright position would be assumed. If the juror should remain in this position while being questioned, he or she would be conveying the message that the topic carries no stress or interest.

The people shown in photograph 14-5 employ a moderate backward lean, indicating to all that nothing is currently occurring in the courtroom that is of interest. Moderate boredom is the major message here, even though they all are still listening (this is indicated by the tilt of their heads and the straightness of their postures). These people are certainly not being challenged or informed of vitally important information, nor are they being presented with any activity that holds their interest. This posture is not often seen during voir dire unless the examination runs extremely long or is poorly conducted. Again notice the difference in posture that results from the difference in height. Lin (on the left) does not appear to be as relaxed or indifferent as Donna since, due to her height, she must keep her legs at a sharper angle in order to occupy the same amount of physical space. While this position would not be as comfortable for Lin as for Donna, the overall message is the same.

The postures demonstrated in photograph 14-6 illustrate the extreme backward lean along with the hands clasped behind the neck. Anyone who assumes this position is feeling superior and totally in control of the situation. While this position is frequently assumed by judges and lawyers, it is seldom displayed in the jury box. However, a juror who does assume this position is likely to take on a leadership role during deliberations. Jurors who tend to be subordinates will strike a more upright — though not necessarily rigid — position in the presence of those whom they consider their superiors.

Lawyers will feel more comfortable with jurors who respond to them with the postures demonstrated in photographs 14-7 and 14-8. The slight forward lean, best illustrated by photograph 14-7, indicates that the person is listening intently and is therefore involved and interested. There is a slight tension indicated in such a posture that indicates limits to the juror's degree of involvement. As the juror's interest and involvement increase, in all likelihood so will the forward lean. An extreme forward lean, as shown in photograph 14-8, is not often displayed under the formal and controlled situation of the courtroom, unless the juror is expressive, demonstrative, and uninhibited. When this posture is observed, the person displaying it is interested, involved, and in control. This person is following the events or arguments with great intensity and concern. Whether that concern is favorable or unfavorable may be indicated by the juror's facial expression; however, most often the attitude is masked. This position is one that is affected by the height of the person. In order to assume the full expression of this position, Donna (on the right) is placed in much greater tension than the taller models. Therefore, since the position lacks the ease and comfort for her that it holds for the others, it is unlikely that she would assume this full leaning-forward position. More probably, she would assume a modification of this position using the arm of the chair instead of her knee as a resting place for her elbow.

Photograph 14-9 illustrates a position that, even though it includes an extreme forward lean, is not an encouraging one for the lawyer. Instead of one arm crossed over a knee in a resting position with the other arm cradling the chin so that the head is forced upright and alert, as in photograph 14-8, this position allows the chin to be cradled by having both arms resting on the knees. This head-down-and-cradled position indicates that the juror is experiencing a high degree of interest and involvement, but also that he or she is confused and torn by the various options; the necessity to reach a decision is seeming burdensome. At the end of closing arguments, jurors who have not really made up their minds might assume this position if they are not trying to mask their uncertainty.

§14.2.5 Sitting with Feet on the Ground

Most of the previous photographs have shown postures in which the feet are flat on the floor. It is more common for both males and females to cross their legs, especially when informal attire is worn. The crossed legs by themselves carry no particular message; however, the degree of tension shown in a juror's leg muscles will be revealing. The greater the muscle tension, the more negative the emotion that is being experienced, whether it be anxiety, apprehension, nervousness, or simply stress.

There are basically two fashions for crossing the legs: (1) the European mode as shown in photograph 14-10 and (2) the American mode as shown in photograph 14-11. The European mode shows one leg casually thrown over the other. This style is favored by most females, European males, and males who tend to be highly cultured or educated. In the United States, many men, and some women who wear slacks, cross their legs with the ankle of one leg placed on top of the knee of the other leg. This leg cross, sometimes referred to as the "figure four" leg cross, requires more space and is generally assumed by people who tend to be relaxed. At one time, it was believed that opinion leaders were more likely to sit in the American rather than the European mode. However, evidence now seems to indicate that the type of leg cross one prefers is more a reflection of body size and cultural orientation.

It is also important when observing the manner in which a person's legs are crossed to analyze what it means when it is done in conjunction with the torso lean. The legs often contradict the message that the torso is giving; the legs will indicate stress or tension not shown by the trunk. This is also true of the hands. A person's hands folded primly and passively in his or her lap indicates that the person ascribes to societal norms. As the person moves his arms away from the center of his or her lap and toward the arms of the chair, the person will take up more space, generally demonstrating a greater degree of confidence and relaxation. If a hand should become clenched or formed into a fist, even while resting on the arms of the chair, tension will also be revealed in other parts of the body, most frequently in the upper chest. These signs of tension should be monitored since they indicate the person is losing control, feeling increased stress, or feeling a need to express greater self-control. Whenever signs of tension are seen in the limbs, the questioner can be certain that a topic has been approached that the potential juror or witness considers sensitive.

§14.2.6 Carried Items

It is always interesting to notice how people handle items they carry into the jury box with them. The most common items carried into a jury box are books or magazines, newspapers (except in courthouses where potential jurors are forbidden access to news reports), purses, coats, hats, or handicraft supplies (generally knitting, crocheting, or other forms of needlecraft). How these possessions are handled by the prospective juror indicates his or her attitude toward possessions in general. Women's attitudes are most easily observed since almost all women carry purses into the jury box with them. Basically, there are two types of purses: the shoulder bag and the handbag. Women who want to have the freedom to use their hands at will favor the shoulder bag. These women are usually a little more outgoing and confident than their counterparts who favor the handbag.

What can be called the perfect lady sitting posture is illustrated in photograph 14-12. Both Donna and Lin have placed their bodies neatly in the chairs with backs somewhat rigid, feet flat on the floor, and purses firmly placed in the center of their laps where each has a hand or both hands ready to protect it. Donna (on the right) favors a more conservative posture with her hands quietly folded over the purse. This issues the unequivocal message that she knows how to hold tightly to her possessions, in a manner that is protective rather than aggressive or demanding. Lin shows a slightly less formal posture although she too shows that she is very aware of her possessions. She is more at ease with herself and her possessions, which she would keep in sight but not necessarily firmly locked and guarded. Such a woman would be less fearful, more confident, and less conscious of her possessions or the possessions of others. She heeds warnings about strangers and strange places somewhat less conscientiously than the perfect lady.

What can be called a tucker is illustrated in photograph 14-13. Donna (on the right), who tucks the purse beside her in the chair, indicates that she is aware of her possessions and guards them. Lin, favoring what can be called the setting hen tuck, has placed her purse carefully under the chair where it is guarded by her body and feet. While her possession is out of sight, it is not out of mind nor unguarded. The tucker is not as uptight about making sure that her possessions are under lock and key and protected at all times, but she is just as concerned about the safety of her possessions as the perfect lady. The tucker will tend to be more critical, for instance, of the person who has stolen a car, regardless of the circumstances, than she will be of the person who left the keys in it.

Some women might not place a purse in their lap or under the chair, but rather place it beside the chair or even toss it aggressively to the floor and allow it to stand wherever it lands. It is less important to notice the purse's location than it is to observe the manner by which it got there. If the woman has carefully placed and adjusted the purse, she is no less neat than the perfect lady or tucker but simply believes in using more space. Therefore she is more apt to be a social leader or opinion leader than the other two women. If the purse has been casually tossed to the floor, the woman would be more casual, less formal, and more relaxed in her attitude toward herself and her possessions than any of the women so far pictured.

Men are more likely to toss their possessions casually aside, unless they are of a precise, prim, or controlled personality type. Men tend to be space-users, taking up floor space to the side or front of the area occupied. This corresponds to the role of decisionmaker or head-of-household that society has traditionally assigned to men.

The woman who carries a shoulder bag or briefcase has all of the choices illustrated above with the handbag. In addition, she can hang the bag somewhere. Most commonly, this type of purse will be hung either from the back of the chair or the chair's arm, as illustrated in photograph 14-14. Usually, the woman who chooses a shoulder purse is a freedom-lover and space-user. The woman who has a briefcase or attaché case is often a leader type employed in a professional occupation. She is used to occupying more space than is needed. This woman will be confident and assured in her approach to decisions that she would be faced with as a juror. She will be more action oriented and possess a higher energy level.

The business woman or man who opts for a portfolio or folder places less stress on freedom and more on utility. Since these must be clutched, this person is likely to be possession oriented.

The purse or briefcase is also of interest for its color (see §12.5.4 supra) and size. The size of the purse indicates the person's feelings about personal space. The larger the purse, for instance, the greater the likelihood that the person will perceive himself or herself entitled to a lot of space, indicative of a decision maker.

§14.2.7 Seated Listening Position

All of the above illustrations have depicted persons sitting squarely in their chairs and facing forward. However, people often sit otherwise. A common variation is pictured in photograph 14-15; all three people are seated sideways in the chairs. This position indicates that the listeners are not directly involved in what is taking place. Lin (on the left) is the most interested listener, while Donna is more passive. Jim approaches being bored; he is relaxed and experiencing little or no tension or stress. If a potential juror assumes one of these sideways postures during voir dire, it would indicate that the individual is not directly concerned. Maintaining this position while being questioned would indicate that the individual is unwilling to become personally involved in the proceeding. The sideways positioning is more appropriate to discussion of casual, impersonal, or uninvolving topics.

Photograph 14-1
Photograph by Dana Downie

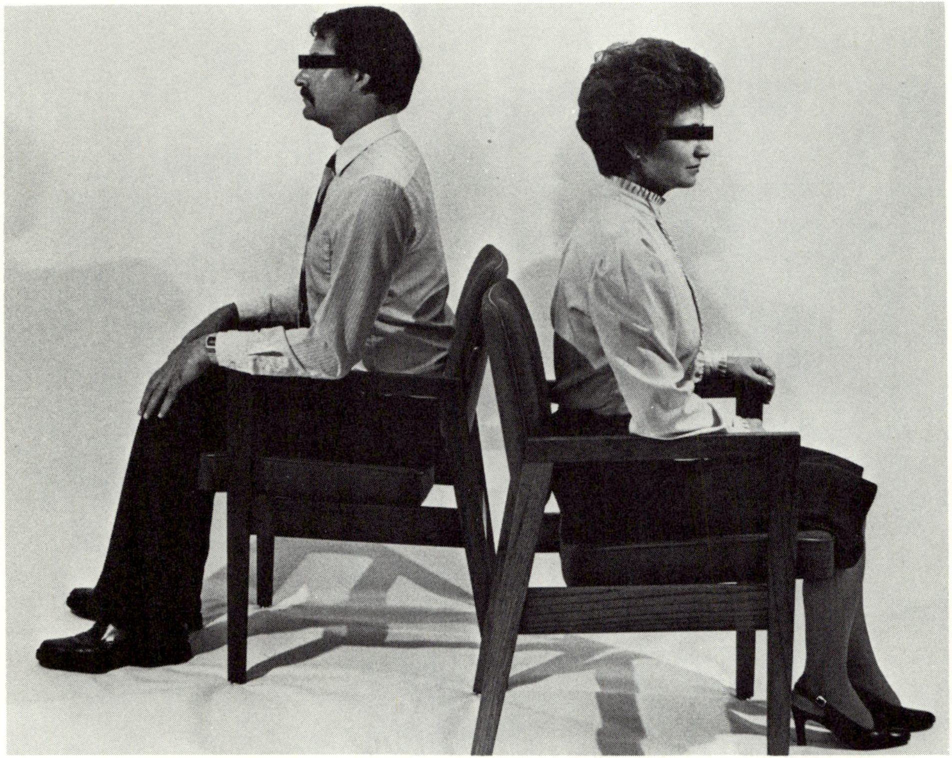

Photograph 14-2
Photograph by Dana Downie

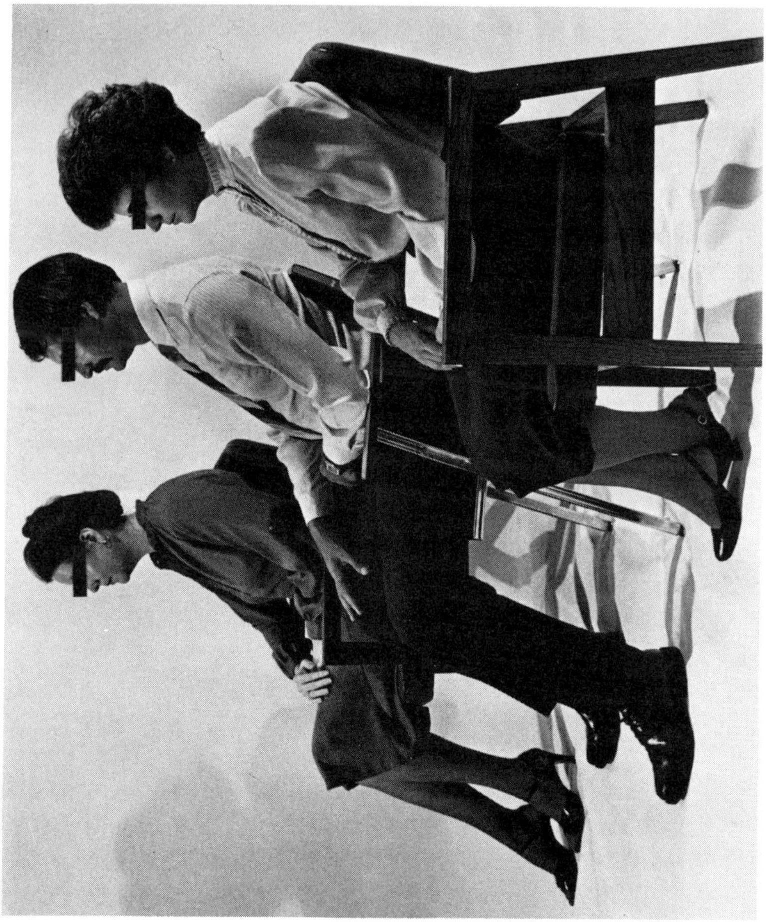

Photograph 14-3
Photograph by Dana Downie

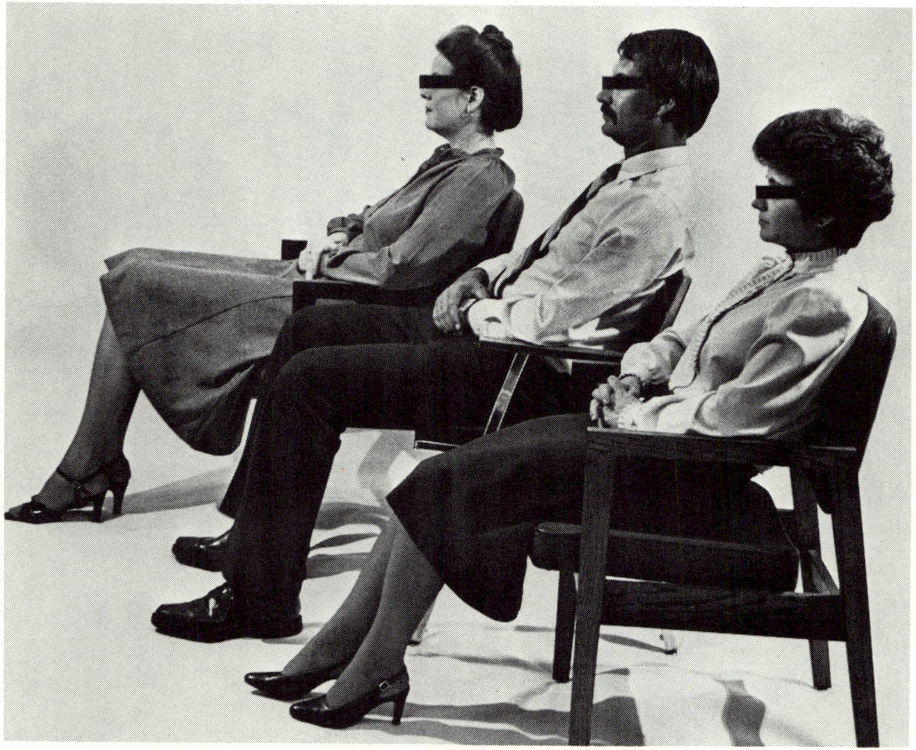

Photograph 14-4
Photograph by Dana Downie

Photograph 14-5
Photograph by Dana Downie

Photograph 14-6
Photograph by Dana Downie

Photograph 14-7
Photograph by Dana Downie

Photograph 14-8
Photograph by Dana Downie

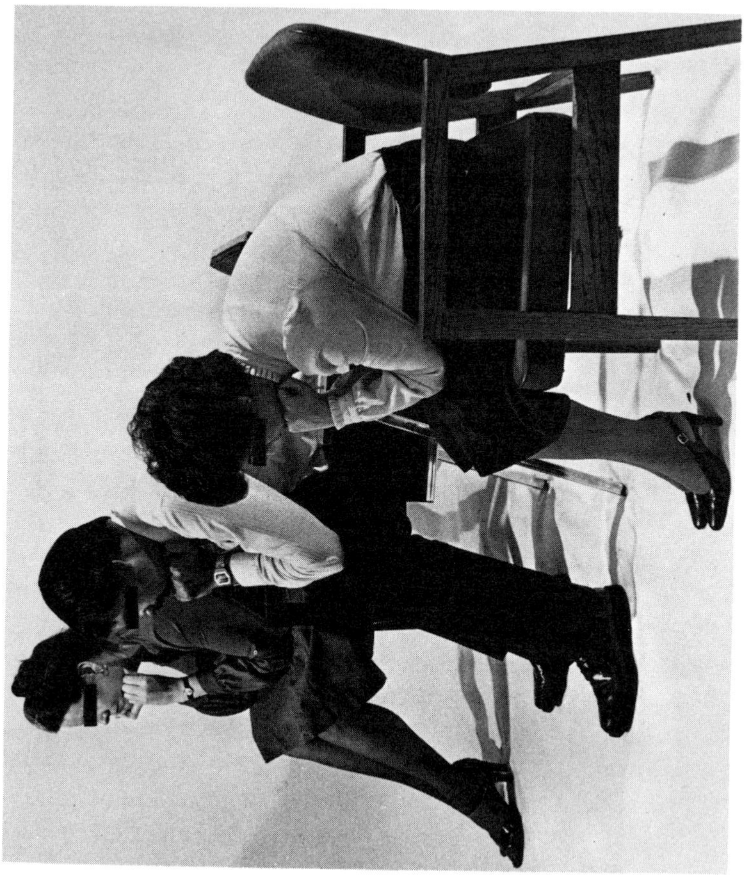

Photograph 14-9
Photograph by Dana Downie

Photograph 14-10
Photograph by Dana Downie

Photograph 14-11
Photograph by Dana Downie

Photograph 14-12
Photograph by Dana Downie

Photograph 14-13
Photograph by Dana Downie

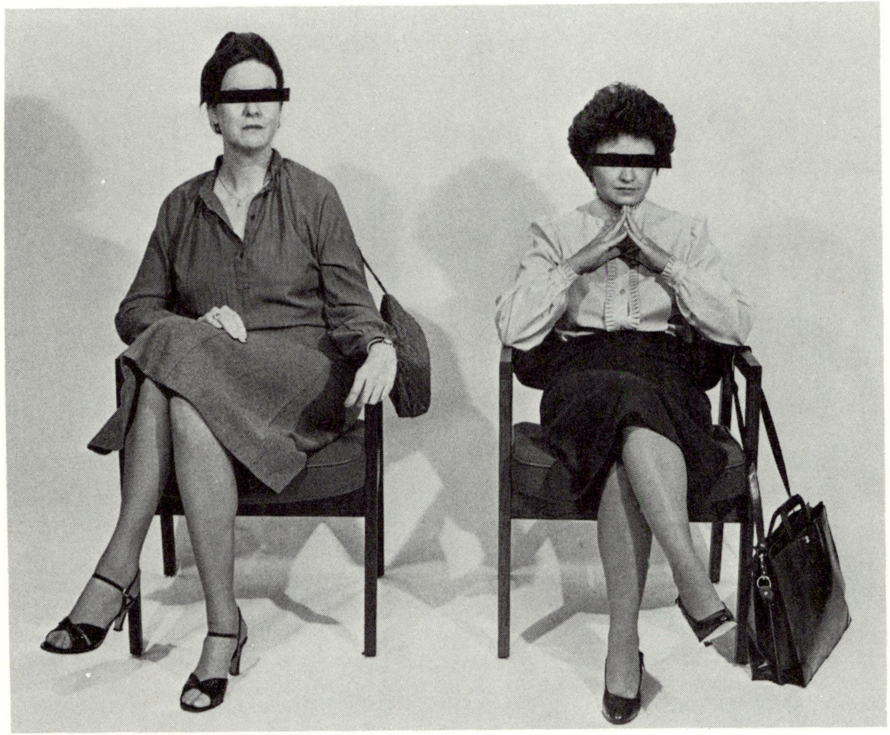

Photograph 14-14
Photograph by Dana Downie

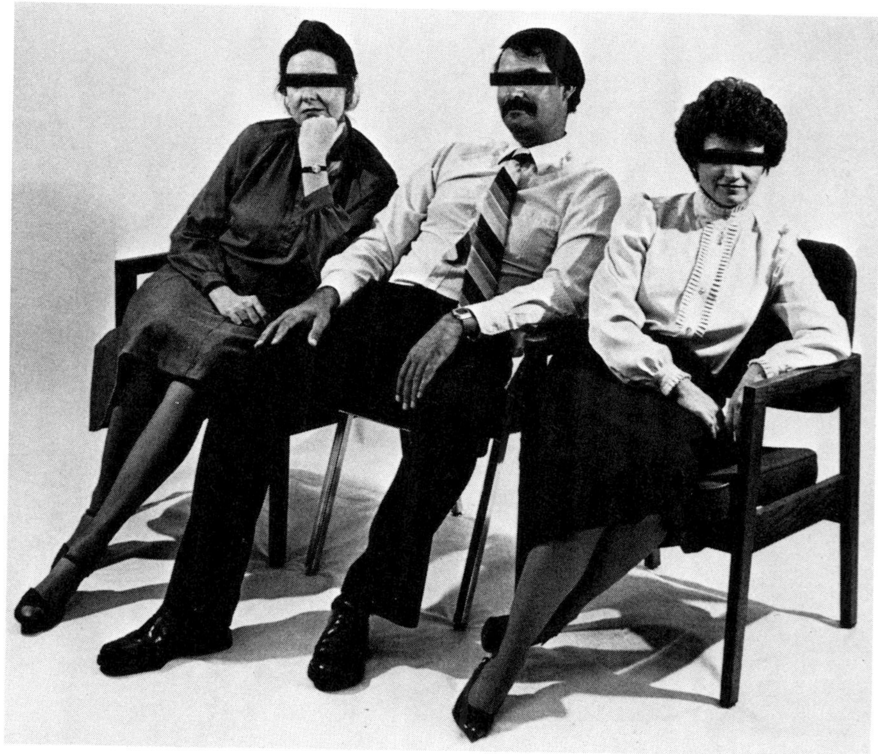

Photograph 14-15
Photograph by Dana Downie

§14.3 Gestures

Postures and gestures are differentiated by how much of the body is involved. The entire body is involved with posture, while only part of the body is involved in a gesture. We often think of a gesture as involving only a hand; however, the head, legs, and feet are also utilized in gesturing. Gestures include actions that are functional as well as actions that express emotion or attitude.

Personality, sex, race, culture, age, body type, health, transitional moods, and education (particularly in dance, drama, athletics, or religion) influence the type of gestures a person exhibits.[1] Generally, fat people tend to move less rapidly than thin people, and tall people move differently than short people. Calm, determined people will display more controlled and deliberate movement than will anxious, frantic ones. While each of these characteristics raises certain expectations for gesture display, the individual still has a wide range of acceptable behavior from which to choose. This increases the difficulty of predicting behavior.

A gesture can be appropriate at one moment and then inappropriate the next. For instance, when a judge is away from the bench and court is not in session, the jurors can freely talk to each other, laughing and joking, sitting in a relaxed manner, gesturing freely with their hands and eyes. When the judge enters the courtroom, these gestures are likely to cease, with the joking brought to an end and a serious deferential demeanor adopted by all.

§14.3.1 Illustrators, Adaptors, and Regulators

Illustrators are movements that add to the meaning of a verbal message by expressive action. Illustrators do not always

§14.3 [1] See G. W. Allport & P. E. Vernon, Studies in Expressive Movement (1937).

agree with the verbal message; on occasion, the action will contradict the meaning of the words being used.

When attempting to become more aware of body language, it is easy to confuse illustrators with adaptors. An adaptor is a movement that provides personal comfort. Adaptors include itching, scratching, and rubbing oneself. Some adaptors, however, are simply the result of nervous habit.

Movements that maintain and regulate interaction between people are called regulators. Eye contact, head dipping, smiling, and hand motions are frequently used to control communication and interaction between participants.

§14.3.2 Cultural Influence

Culture greatly influences the gesture style of an individual. Author Flora Davis notes that some people who are multilingual use more than one set of body gestures.[2] Observations of people who speak two or more languages have revealed that the gesture pattern that accompanies each language is dramatically different. Davis states, "An expert in kinesics can actually tell a European from an American just by the way they move their eyebrows in conversation!"[3]

Jurgen Ruesch and Weldon Kees, early nonverbal behavior researchers, have described the gesture styles of the French, Germans, and Americans. They found the French to be spare in movements, which were elegant, precise, or stylized. "The French [are] not as expansive as Italians, . . . as angular and incisive as Germans, nor as casual as Americans."[4] Germans tend to have particularly expressive faces, according to their research. Americans appeared to Ruesch and Kees to have no general gesture style, rather, their gestures seemed to reflect regional differences.[5]

[2]See F. Davis, Inside Intuition 22 (1975).
[3]Ibid.
[4]J. Ruesch & W. Kees, Nonverbal Communication 75 (1956).
[5]Id. at 75-77.

Attorneys who become sensitive to these various gesture differences will be able to read the meaning and attitude of prospective jurors more accurately.

§14.4 The Walk

Every individual has a distinctive walk that is often recognizable by others. Walking style is a combination of posture and gesture in movement. The style of walk that is presented by an individual is affected by his or her body type and body structure. Pace, length of stride, and overall posture are other walking style factors that change with energy level, mood, and emotional state.

The trial attorney will want to watch jurors as they enter and leave the jury box so that he or she can determine which one is setting the pace. This person is apt to be one of the leaders of the group. He or she is easiest to identify when jurors are called to return from a recess. It is likely that the leader type will not only set the pace, but will round up and direct other jurors back to their seats.

§14.5 Eye Contact

According to the folklore of some cultures, the eyes carry the message of the soul. Today many people feel that if they look deeply into the eyes of another person, they can discern the true character of that individual.

There is no question that eye contact is vitally important in dealing with others. Consider the bank robber who, hoping to conceal his or her identity, simply wears a mask that covers the eyes.

Psychologist Michael Argyle has observed that while conversing two people will look at each other between 30 and 60 percent of the time. If they make eye contact more than 60 percent of the time, they are probably more interested in each other than they are in the topic of conversation. Argyle also says that abstract thinkers make more eye contact than people who think in concrete terms. He reasons that abstract thinkers have a greater ability to process communication cues and are therefore less likely to be distracted by eye contact.[1]

§14.5.1 Eye Contact in the Jury Box

The trial attorney will observe some prospective jurors in the jury box who act as if they are at a tennis match: their eyes will continually go from the questioner to the witness and back to the questioner. This type of concentrated listener is apt to be an abstract thinker, who can process data as it is received without a great need to ponder the various fine points. Conversely, the individual who sits in the jury box with eyes averted either to the ceiling or to floor, may well be processing the information and will need to think in concrete terms about its meaning. In a criminal trial, the defense attorney will wonder what it means if certain jurors fail to establish any eye contact with the defendant. Since eye contact requires an individual to admit recognition of another, the message in respect to the defendant may be, "I'm not going to deal with you as an individual but as an object."

§14.5.2 Gaze Awareness

Michael Argyle and Mark Cook, English social psychologists, attempt to clarify individual differences in gaze to correct some popular misconceptions. They state that gaze is a function of personality, situation, and interaction. People have predictable gaze patterns that do not change much in different situations.

§14.5 [1]See M. Argyle, Psychology of Interpersonal Behavior 105 (1972).

Females tend to gaze at others more than men do with the level of gaze being especially high during childhood, falling off during adolescence, and increasing again in early adulthood. Friendly and self-confident people tend to gaze at others more than people who are dishonest or disinterested. People gaze or look a lot at others when (1) placed far apart, (2) discussing impersonal or easy topics, (3) there is nothing else to look at, (4) they are interested in each other, (5) they like or love each other, (6) they are extroverted. A person of a low social status will look more at a superior than the superior will look at the subordinate.[2]

People who look more at others are generally perceived as being more truthful and more credible. When a speaker maintains high contact with his or her audience, the audience will judge the speaker as being more effective and will allow that speaker to have a more persuasive effect. When gaze between speaker and audience is regular, the speaker is usually rated as more skillful, informed, experienced, friendly, kind, and honest. When gaze approaches a stare, it becomes offensive and can result in a negative impression of the speaker. However, it is generally true that a speaker who looks more at an audience with longer glances will be perceived in a favorable manner and will be liked more by the audience.[3]

Looking too much or staring may be used deliberately by an attorney to unnerve a witness (or vice versa). It may also be used by witnesses, defendants, judges, or jurors, who, intending to perform in an expected way — knowing that eye gaze generally has a positive connotation — simply look too much.

As communication researcher Mark Knapp has noted, there are many reasons why jurors may or may not follow courtroom exchanges with eye contact. People will tend to follow their natural conversational tendency. People who are curious will look more. Eye contact is invited more when someone says something provocative. People who have a tendency to rely on

[2]See M. Argyle & M. Cook, Gaze and Mutual Gaze 173, 176-177 (1976).

[3]See Tomkins & McCarter, What and Where Are the Primary Affects? Some Evidence for a Theory, 18 Perception and Motor Skills 119, 158 (1964).

visual cues to obtain the meaning of an interaction will look more. Each of these reasons could provide another interpretation of the meaning of jurors' eye contact (or lack of it) in the courtroom. The person who is looking for meaning in the nonverbal communication of jurors must always ask what else a gaze may mean and avoid the glib assumption of the single-meaning approach.

§14.6 Smiles

It is not uncommon to hear a young defense attorney complain, "The jury had just filed into the box to return the verdict when the foreman turned to me and smiled. It really made me feel good because I believed then that the verdict would be not guilty — and then he stood up and announced to the court that my guy was 'guilty!' "

This attorney was the victim of the appeasing smile. He should have remembered Hamlet's realization "That one may smile, and smile, and be a villain. . . ."[1] There are smiles, and then there are *smiles,* and it is important for the trial attorney to determine what kind of smile he or she is observing.

Consider first the mechanical smile or socially-conditioned response. This is the response that a well socialized individual automatically delivers on social demand. When a person is introduced to someone, the automatic smile is delivered as a graceful acknowledgment of the other person. If someone is caught in another person's territory and that person returns, the invader may flash a mechanical smile to indicate that no harm was meant. The mechanical or appeasing smile is one that involves only the mouth and does not engage the eyes or the muscles of the cheeks. It is a conditioned response and in no way indicates happiness or humor. The other extreme is the

§14.6 [1]Shakespeare, Hamlet, Act I, Scene v, Line 106.

broad smile, with which a person displays genuine pleasure or excitement or both.

There have been many attempts to categorize smiles according to whether they are sincere, mechanical, or indicating pleasure; however, it appears that smiling is a highly individualistic trait. Smiles between the two smiles categorized above depend on a person's dental structure, self-confidence, social conditioning, and other factors. For a smile to be evaluated and its message to be clearly understood, it must be taken in conjunction with all other cues displayed by gesture, posture, and other aspects of facial expression. The attorney who practices in various jurisdictions should be concerned that within the United States there are different norms for smiling.

> In the Great Lakes region, a person who does a lot of smiling may be asked, What's so funny?; in Georgia, someone who doesn't smile much may be asked if something is wrong. It's not that those who smile a lot are simply happier, but rather that as children all of us learn in which situations we are expected to smile and in which ones we're not expected to smile, and we learn differently in different parts of the country.[2]

§14.7 Physical Space

Space is associated with power. The more space allotted to a person, the more powerful that person is perceived to be. Similarly, if a person claims more space, that person is perceived by others to be a leader.

Territoriality is a somewhat new topic of study, but it has been well researched in recent years. It refers to behavior associated with the staking out an area, marking it as one's own, and defending it against invasion by others. Territoriality goes along with dominance — that is, a person who is dominant will possess more territory than submissive persons.

[2]F. Davis, Inside Intuition 23 (1975).

It is easy to observe human beings claiming territory when they go into unknown space, that space which is unmarked or undesignated. For instance, as a juror enters the courtroom, she or he will claim a seat. If later the juror has to leave that seat temporarily unattended, he or she may leave a marker, some small item that identifies that the space is occupied and will be reclaimed. Even if a marker is not left, when the person returns, he or she is likely to return to the same seat. If someone else is seated there, that person will probably be informed, "This is my seat." The "invader" will in all likelihood select a new seat. The concept of territoriality is so ingrained in people that a person may become very upset if the social rules that govern territory are not honored. Consider the disruption that can result from overlooking jurors' sense of territory, as observed by one of the authors of this book at a recent trial. Four days into the trial a woman seated in a back row of the jury box informed the judge that because of a hearing impairment she was having difficulty following the proceedings. The next day the woman took a seat in the front row, telling the former occupant that she had been instructed to do so by the judge. The entire jury protested and refused to allow the trial to continue until the "personal comfort" of both jurors had been seen to in keeping with "common courtesy." The matter was finally resolved by adding another chair to the front row for the woman from the back of the jury box. It was acceptable, therefore, for new territory to be established, but not for someone else's territory to be invaded.

There are five basic rules relating to space use by humans: (1) The most dominant persons will be awarded the most and best territory. (2) Dominant persons will be allowed to move freely in territory that they do not claim. (3) Subordinate persons will yield space in passing or approaching dominant persons. (4) Dominant persons will occupy a position that is held in reverence by others and from this position they will be allowed to control others and their resources. (5) Dominant persons will be accorded a greater amount of personal space for themselves and their possessions. It is this last rule that marks the leader in the courtroom. When the leader takes a position in the jury box, he or she will claim more space than is normally allotted for the seat. Frequently this is done by draping an arm across the back of an adjoining chair, by placing a coat or some other possession on the rail or in front of the chair space, or by sticking one's feet out to cover space that is normally considered aisle space.

§14.8 Deception Cues

One of the major reasons lawyers tend to be interested in nonverbal communication is that it helps them identify deception on the part of witnesses, clients, and potential jurors. They realize verbal communication is more conscious and deliberate and, therefore, more easily controlled and monitored. It is for this reason that at the end of trial judges admonish jurors to weigh verbal testimony against witnesses' demeanors.

Skill at interpreting deception cues is closely associated with the degree of sophistication that is used in the cognitive process (perception, memory, reasoning or judgment). Agnes Hankiss of the Research Center for Mass Communication in Budapest, Hungary, states the following:

> Emotional patterns, motives of interest, defense mechanisms, and so on are all involved in the act of interpretation. The most important principle of this type is the process of *projection.* It is based on the circumstance that people, in their approach to reality, are not impartial. They believe what they would like to believe, and judge as genuine something that they would not credit in a neutral situation.[1]

She also contends that one of the most important principles of the rational construction of meaning in the interpretation of deception is the presumption of normality:

§14.8 [1]Hankiss, Games Con Men Play: The Semiosis of Deceptive Interaction, 30 J. of Communication, 104, 109 (No. 2, Spring 1980).

> Let us start from the assumption that our everyday lies are characterized basically by restraint. This restraint is manifest at three points: (1) when telling a lie, one is convinced that there is no other choice, and with this sense of compulsion alleviates any guilt; (2) the quantity of false information is kept to a minimum as indicated by the circumstance; and (3) elements of truth are laced throughout to lessen the severity of a lie. The common result of the conflict of values created by the act of lying and of the above three forms of restraint is that people usually do not lie strategically. Their lies are not premeditated and well-planned but instead are born out of momentary reasons with their objective being to ease the tensions of a given situation.[2]

Depending on practice and frequency, the person who lies from necessity rather than from strategy will probably have more tension and, therefore, will display more verbal and nonverbal stress cues. The strategic liar is careful to plan statements that appear sincere and honest and to weave as much truth as possible into the fabric of the untruth.

§14.8.1 The Hierarchy of Deception Cues

While people vary in their ability to interpret deception cues, they are almost unanimous in their choice of what kinds of stimuli they would like to observe if they were to be asked to make a judgment as to whether a person is lying. Unfortunately, they make the mistake of wanting the most cues possible. To judge whether a person is lying or not, is it better to (1) listen to the voice only, (2) observe the body (gesture and posture) and facial movements, or (3) observe both voice and movement? Those who are most accurate in detecting deception choose to listen to the voice only. While most people tend to believe that seeing is believing, the more accurate statement is hearing is believing. "Research shows that voice pitch is a more dependable indicator than facial expression — thus

[2] Id. at 108.

confirming the wisdom of the artist who depicted Justice as wearing a blindfold."[3]

A review of research in nonverbal communication suggests that the following list of cues would be helpful to the untrained observer attempting to identify deception:

1. *Appearance* — sloppy or garish dress; presence of facial hair; hair style inappropriate for the social norms of the local community.
2. *Posture* — sudden shifts in posture or slumped posture.
3. *Voice* — stammering, brevity of responses, or disfluencies in speech; overly expressive pitch variation, monotone voice, or antagonistic tone; responses that are vague, implausible, or too detailed; long pauses or deviation from normal speech pattern; responses that are too quick or too slow in answering questions.
4. *Eye contact* — avoidance of eye contact, shifting of eyes, or sudden widening of the eyes while looking into the eyes of the questioner.
5. *Movement* — touching the self, especially stroking one's hair, skin, or clothing; smiling too much or too little; nervous hand gestures; shielding one's face with one's hands.

While one might be reluctant to adopt the cynical conclusion of *Psychology Today* editor Daniel Goleman that "[a]s a matter of fact, there are no foolproof signs of lying,"[4] it is easy to accept his conclusion that "detecting a lie is not as easy as we might think."[5] The attorney, the judge, and the jurors might all benefit from careful instruction on determining the credibility of witnesses, particularly witnesses testifying under stress. The ease with which deception can be confused with other stress cues necessitates that every cue be carefully processed.

[3]Id. at 18.

[4]Goleman, Can You Tell When Someone is Lying to You, 16 Psychology Today 14, 18 (1982).

[5]Ibid.

§14.9 A Lawyer's Perspective on Utilizing a Specialist in Nonverbal Communication — Dwight James, Des Moines, Iowa

By the time the trial commences, the carefully prepared lawyer knows the judge, the course that the testimony will take, the documents, and how the case is to be presented. All of the parties, witnesses, and exhibits are known. The jury is the unknown. Suddenly, people are being called to take their places in the jury box. The lawyer's eyes and mind try to keep up with the flood of names, addresses, facts, body shapes, movements and posture of the jurors. The skillful trial lawyer attempts to catalog all of these things, relating to some twenty people, all at the same time.

There are prominent trial lawyers who claim to be able to take in all of the movements, conversation, and other data relating to all of the jurors involved in the jury selection process, while examining a single prospective juror. Some may be able to do that; most people cannot.

The thought of anyone knowing more about the jury selection process than the litigator is threatening to most lawyers. Litigators are skeptical about the ability of a person to "read" the jury when they have been doing that through intuition for years. Have you ever had a hunch that a person doesn't like you, only to have someone say to you, "That person doesn't like you, she turned her head when you were talking to her, she turned her body so that it didn't face you"? Sometimes we are so involved in the process of selecting the jury that we cannot see the actions that give rise to our feelings. A courtroom observer may be able to observe conduct that would make the lawyer uneasy about having such a person sit as a juror if he or she saw the conduct.

How can a lawyer learn how to observe the leaders, the potential foremen, the followers, and the loners? A nonverbal communications specialist should be able to enable one to increase the chances of identifying these people.

Through trial lawyer associations, other trial lawyers, or trial publications, people with advanced degrees in psychology or communications research, who have done work in nonverbal communication and interpretation, can be identified. Engage a well-qualified person to work with you in jury selection. Have that person work with you and train a legal assistant, paralegal, or secretary from your staff in basic skills. Read the literature on nonverbal communication and have your staff members do likewise.

Review your entire case with your expert. Point out the problems that you believe may prevent a jury from deciding in your client's favor. Develop questions that will be designed to make the juror express his or her thoughts verbally and in sufficient length to let your observer see whether the prospective juror's response is an honest one. If a juror just answers yes or no, you have little opportunity to accurately weight the response. Some lawyers are afraid to get truthful answers because it may leave them feeling stuck with a bad jury. If the lawyer knows the state of the juror's mind, however, he or she can work to offset any prejudice, strike the juror, or settle the case out of court. Eliciting a full response is done by asking open-ended questions.

The expert in nonverbal communication can help you in many ways in the jury selection process. Usually, the attorney's attention is fixed on individual jurors while trying to develop a bond of sincere, open communication that will lead to a trusting relationship during the trial. The attorney's eyes cannot be darting all over the courtroom during such a process of examining one juror at a time. When a juror is responding favorably to a question, an assistant may be observe another juror turn to her neighbor in disgust. That event should be recorded. It is one that the attorney will miss if he or she is paying attention to the juror being questioned, but it is an event that is important to the selection process.

Jury selection is often interrupted by challenges or breaks when the judge and the attorneys confer in the judge's chambers. This is the time that your observer will be casually, anonymously, and accurately reading the jury. One juror may lean over and talk on separate occasions to the jurors around her. They may respond in a friendly way. Or one of the other jurors may not respond at all. It may be that none of the other jurors initiate conversation. Such information might be important for identifying leaders and followers. During this time, it may also be possible to observe that certain jurors are loners.

During breaks the jurors may be observed in the halls of the courthouse. An assistant may be able to relate to you how the jurors interact with one another and identify your potential foreman, your followers, and your loners. Now you can attempt to make a leader your leader. How does that person respond to you and to your questions? Is there an appeasing smile? Is there honest agreement with your philosophical position? Is the person thin lipped, unsmiling, and stiff? Does the person seem to have a sense of self-worth? How many leaders can you have on the jury? Will there be a challenge for leadership? The trial lawyer must make very quick decisions regarding all of these matters. The time allowed for decision is short.

While you are questioning jurors, your trial assistants can make an independent study of who should be a leader based on demographic information, who the followers are, who the loners are, and how the jurors will relate with one another. The assistants can analyze similarities between you, your client, and the jurors. If you are in a rural community and faced with a small panel of jurors, you may find that it is possible to do a demographic study in advance of the trial. You may be able to make some tentative conclusions about the people you will be questioning before you actually see them. If you have occasion to review that information in advance, you will find that it is easier for you to associate jurors with their names. You will have already catalogued some information about each person. The juror is likely to appreciate that instant identification and feel more comfortable about the process. If the case is to be tried in a court that does not use juror questionnaires, it is suggested that you encourage this practice.

You and your expert should talk about what kind of person will be helpful to your cause. Discuss the kind of attitude that the person you want as a juror will exhibit. What kind of body type will most likely be sympathetic to your cause? What occupational groups should be excluded? Will nationality play a role? Perhaps more important, how does the juror react to you, your client, and your questions during the selection process? One inviolable rule is that if you feel strongly that a person should be stricken from the jury, never let someone convince you otherwise. Strike that person. Your instincts are better than the observations of others.

An expert can help you in other nonverbal communication areas. Is your manner of dress giving messages that will detract from your client's cause or your trustworthiness? Does your dress tell the jury you are cocky, arrogant, a mover with the women, or that you are stable, trustworthy, and helpful? Are you wearing jewelry that will give a negative message to the jury? It is helpful to videotape your client and your chief witnesses to test their credibility. It is important that you videotape yourself doing an opening statement or a mock voir dire to see if you are comfortable with your own credibility. Have others watch the tape. See what they think. Have your nonverbal expert do a credibility check based on your presentations of the facts in your case. Have the videotape shown to impartial observers. What messages are you projecting? A different choice of words, hair style, dress, or jewelry may make a difference in how your client's case is received by the jury.

If you videotape your opening statement and your final argument prior to trial and listen to them yourself, you may make some interesting observations of what can be done to improve your effectiveness as a trial lawyer. You should be aware that it can be difficult to perform as well for a camera as you might for a jury. However, you can videotape the presentation with low, medium, or high energy. You can use few gestures or many. Your gestures can be dramatic or soft. You can then make some determination about the most effective way for you to communicate.

Perhaps more important than how *you* communicate is the way your chief witnesses testify. You have training. Don't let your client assume the witness stand or have a deposition taken without training. His or her nonverbal messages are critical to good communication. Videotape is the most effective means of training your client to effectively convey his or her message. Some people will not want to view themselves on film. People who have been badly disfigured by burns, for instance, do not need to be punished by seeing themselves on videotape. One can work on verbal messages by use of a tape recorder and suggest nonverbal changes orally.

The videotape process is helpful in showing clients that they will communicate more effectively with appropriate dress, jewelry, or hair style. Some clients interject filler words in their sentences. The client who ends every other sentence with "you know what I mean?" will see and hear the effect of that kind of communication on videotape. Other problems, such as pauses in speech, fidgeting, and poor posture can be addressed. It is likely that your client will be grateful for the opportunity to improve his or her testimony.

The communication specialist can help with other aspects of trying a case as well and may prove instrumental to your client's cause.

§14.10 Concluding Remarks on Nonverbal Communication

In this part of the book on nonverbal communication, detailed information has been supplied that would allow the careful, trained observer to reach judgments that may be considered to have a high probability of accuracy. These judgments include determinations of personality, character, and attitudes of individuals, all of which are based on the nonverbal messages of how a person looks, sounds or moves. A section has been devoted to the specifics of each variable. The real challenge occurs when the observer puts all the information together, identifying variables that are consistent or inconsistent, and arrives at a final judgment.

Of course, this is only an introduction to the variables of interest in understanding people and their attitudes and behaviors. Often, when people first concentrate on reading nonverbal cues, there is a tendency to want to find meaning in every movement and every modification of sound. This should be avoided since it is the *pattern* of behavior that is generally most important.

Also, the context is particularly important when interpreting cues. For instance, what effect does the swearing in, the presence and activity of the court reporter, the solemnity of the courtroom have in modifying a juror's behavior patterns?

How does one decide which message is the "right" one when, for instance, a person's appearance indicates primness, while his or her movement is sloppy and uncontrolled? Generally, various messages will be consistent and will reinforce each other. However, when there are inconsistent messages, then one looks for "leakage" of meaning. Usually, people are aware of the displays they make with their faces, bodies, or hands and so they will attempt to control these expressions. Therefore, these parts of the body become the least valuable for accurate judgments. A good general guide is, the smaller the message source the more accurate the cue that is being sent and the greater importance its meanings should be given.

There are a few other guidelines that are helpful for reaching a final conclusion about an individual:

(1) When determining credibility, the voice is the best clue source and should be given dominance in reaching any conclusion about whether a person is deceptive.
(2) The posture reflects overall attitude, while the facial expression is the best indicator of emotional display.
(3) The face is the easiest area to control and, therefore, the least likely to "leak" a true message of the emotion being experienced. Conversely, the hands, arms, feet, and legs are the most difficult to control and so, are the best sources of leaked information; as such, their message should be given greater credence.
(4) Personality clues (dress, artifacts, color, and ease of

movement) should receive less emphasis than those of attitude and beliefs when determining whether the person should be considered a desirable juror. A likable person who holds views that are in direct opposition to a major contention of the case is just as undesirable as an unlikable person.

(5) Clues of stress and tension in voice and movement should receive primary consideration when identifying beliefs and attitudes.

Each observer soon identifies which clues she or he reads most easily and most accurately. Constant practice enhances this skill. Giving attention to the least well interpreted clues and continuing to practice reading them will prevent the observer from depending on only a few of the available messages.

PART V

At Trial

CHAPTER

15

Jury Selection in the Courtroom

§15.0 Introduction

Finally the day arrives when the case goes to trial and jurors must be selected or, in reality, eliminated. The well-prepared attorney approaches the courtroom ready to present the case to the citizens of the community who have been summoned to jury duty.

Pretrial steps may have included any or all of the procedures outlined in chapters 1 through 10 of this book. The attorney may have commissioned a community attitude study to profile the most desirable or undesirable juror; if that step has not been taken, possibly a demographic analysis has been conducted during which the trial team met in conference to list criteria that could be used to evaluate prospective jurors. Information that was obtained from trial simulation has been incorporated into desirable and undesirable juror profiles as well as into the trial strategy. In cooperation with other members of the trial team, the voir dire has been designed so as to meet time constraints and the primary needs of the case. If it had been deemed desirable, the investigation into the background of the jurors has been completed and the information provided has been incorporated into a pretrial evaluation of the prospective jurors. The attorney has attained a general knowledge of nonverbal communication and is prepared to work with the team specialist in analyzing prospective jurors during voir dire. All in all, the trial team has completed every step possible to assist in their selection of the best jury possible.

§15.1 The Trial Team

Now the trial team has been assembled and each member has been assigned specific duties. The in-court trial team consists of the trial attorney or attorneys plus personnel who will assist in the analysis of verbal and nonverbal messages. Depending on the complexity of the case and the budget available, this team could include several experts, each with a particular expertise.

Ideally, there should be a minimum of three members on the courtroom team, although obviously two people may perform all of the tasks if the attorney takes responsibility for conducting voir dire and recording the factual and experiential information. A third important task is analysis of the personality and attitude profiles. The team member assigned the task of the personality and attitude profile should not be seated at the counsel table but behind the bar, even if this person is a professional jury worker (a psychiatrist, psychologist, sociologist, or communication researcher). The position behind the bar will allow that person to work without the necessity of being introduced to the court or jury. More important, it places this observer in a better position from which to record all behaviors in the courtroom. Being seated at the counsel table would involve the person too heavily in the interaction, lessen the likelihood of that person making independent observations, and decrease the overall objectivity of the analysis. Sitting outside the action area allows *all* interactions, including those between the adversaries and the judge and those that occur during the absence of the judge and attorneys, to come within the sphere of analysis.

Every attorney, however, should be assisted by at least one other individual. The attorney has the responsibility to ask the questions, record the verbal responses, and maintain the trial record. It is not rational to expect that the attorney can perform all these tasks and also be attentive to an analysis of attitudes and personality that is highly dependent on attentiveness to nonverbal cues. Additionally, the attorney can only analyze those cues that are visible or audible to him or her. If the observer is not seated behind the bar, many interaction cues will be concealed from observation. Furthermore, the observer should be an individual who is not involved in the courtroom interaction since this provides a basis for establishing a baseline of behavior, which is most conducive to accurate and meaningful interpretation. This observer need not be a professional jury worker; a trained, skillful paralegal, a legal secretary, a law student, or a spouse could serve the function.

In any event, the trial team, whether it includes two or several persons, is assembled and ready for the jury selection process. An evaluation technique has been agreed on and the necessary forms have been provided to the team.

§15.2 Jury Selection Forms

Attorneys have a wide choice of forms from which to select one for use in the courtroom. The most typical form is a sheet of paper divided into the same number of squares as there will be jurors seated for voir dire. For example, if sixteen jurors are seated from which eight will be struck and eight left, then the paper would be divided into sixteen squares according to the seating arrangement. For instance, if six people occupy each seat in two rows in the jury box and four people sit in chairs in front of the box, the form could be like the one illustrated in form 15-1.

Another form uses this basic format but each square of the divided sheet contains printed information that the attorney uses as a check list to make certain that certain demographic information is obtained from each juror. If one of the items on

<table>
<tr><td>J #1</td><td>J #2</td><td>J #3</td><td>J #4</td><td>J #5</td><td>J #6</td></tr>
<tr><td>J #7</td><td>J #8</td><td>J #9</td><td>J #10</td><td>J #11</td><td>J #12</td></tr>
<tr><td>J #13</td><td>J #14</td><td>J #15</td><td>J #16</td></tr>
</table>

Form 15-1. Jury Selection Form

#______ N____________________________

Sx_____ MS_____ Ag_____

Occ____________________________________

SOcc___________________________________

ChOcc__________________________________

PJS_____ Cv_____ CR_____ P/D

Abbreviation code:

\# — Juror name
N — Name of juror
Sx — Sex of juror
MS — Marital status
In this space, the attorney would record the following:
s — single
m — married
d — divorced
w — widowed
Occ — Occupation of juror
SOcc — Spouse's occupation
ChOcc — Occupation of children of juror
PJS — Prior jury service
Cv — Number of civil cases on which juror served
Cr — Number of criminal cases on which juror served
P/D — If the juror had been a defendant in a lawsuit, the "D" would be circled; if a plaintiff, the "P" would be circled.

Form 15-2. Jury Selection Form

Form 15-3
Jury Selection Form

Juror Name____________________ **Juror Number**________ **Rater** __________________

NEGATIVE FACTORS:

_____Emotionally unstable
_____Intolerant
_____Narrow-minded
_____Prejudiced
_____Dissimilar other
_____Pessimistic
_____Fatalistic
_____Rigid
_____Opinionated
_____Selfish
_____Stingy
_____Critical
_____Snobbish
_____Stubborn
_____Willful
_____Defiant
_____Aggressive
_____Impatient
_____Temperamental
_____Sarcastic
_____Resentful
_____Lacks understanding
_____Domineering
_____Compliant
_____Argumentative
_____Moralistic
_____Other:

LEADERSHIP ROLE:

_____Leader _____structural
_____opinion
_____social
_____Opinion generator
_____Follower
_____Independent
_____Loner

INTELLIGENCE:

_____Quick to learn
_____Slow
_____Skeptical
_____Reflective
_____Intuitive
_____Poor/hasty conclusions
_____Other:

POSITIVE FACTORS:
- _____Emotionally stable
- _____Assertive
- _____Outgoing
- _____Likes people
- _____Similar other
- _____Open-minded
- _____Empathetic
- _____Likes self
- _____Generous
- _____Giving
- _____Helpful
- _____Sincere
- _____Idealistic
- _____Tolerant
- _____Patient
- _____Initiates interaction
- _____Determined
- _____Optimistic
- _____Good sense of humor
- _____Responsive
- _____Other:

RESPONDS TO:
- _____Logic/Reason
- _____Feelings/Emotions
- _____Facts/Technical information
- _____Medical views

PRIORITIES:
- _____Principles/"Right"
- _____Materialism
- _____Societal expectations
- _____Helping others
- _____Other:

ORIENTATION: _____Toward people _____Toward self _____Away from people

FEARS: _____Failure _____Ridicule _____Rejection _____ Expression Other:

SELF-PERCEPTION: _____Vanity _____Inferiority _____Good esteem Other:

VIEWPOINT: _____Conservative _____Moderate _____ Permissive _____Liberal

OBSERVATIONS AND COMMENTS ON REVERSE SIDE

the check list is not covered by the previously completed juror information sheets or if there is some question as to how the information should be interpreted, that information can be solicited during voir dire. Each square of the form would be printed in the way illustrated in form 15-2. The space under the printed information provides room to record additional factual or experiential information that is obtained from prospective jurors during voir dire. Frequently, lawyers elect to record responses elicited during the plaintiff attorney's voir dire in one color ink, such as black, while the defense attorney's voir dire information is recorded in another color, such as blue or green. This not only helps the team to analyze the information obtained in exercising the peremptory challenges but also allows the trial team to analyze which elements the opposition considered relevant or important in the jury selection process. Often, careful analysis of these points provides valuable cues concerning attitudes or biases the opposition expects to rely on in opening statements or closing argument.

A form favored for use in performing a personality profile emphasizes factors other than the demographic or experiential ones (see form 15-3). This form is used by the trial team member seated behind the bar.

§15.3 Three Types of Jurors

When observing potential jurors, the trial team should try to identify the interaction style that each individual juror might adopt during deliberations. Jurors' interaction styles will generally fall into three categories: leaders, followers, and loners.

§15.3.1 Leaders

A leader is a person who will want to take charge of the jury in an effort to determine the outcome of the deliberation process. Jurors who are likely to take on this role should be studied closely for their probable leadership style during deliberations. A leader may be categorized as a structural leader, an opinion leader, or a social leader.

The *structural leader* will be most interested in providing the framework within which the jurors will deliberate. This person will be concerned about order, process, and timing. He or she will want to establish the order of events or the voting sequences. This type of leader might also be concerned about whether voting should be performed by ballot or voice or raised hands. Process is a major concern of the structural leader; he or she will want to be certain that everyone is offered an opportunity to express himself or herself and that everyone understands the procedures being followed. The structural leader is concerned with accomplishing the assigned task as efficiently as possible, namely, in the case of jury deliberation, the reaching of a verdict. Whether the structural leader is democratic or authoritarian, the satisfaction level of the jury will be highly dependent on how well members identify with the particular leader's style. If the structural leader is a man it is likely that he will be the best candidate for foreperson of the jury. The structural leader can often be identified during the voir dire process. At that time he or she will often favor an upright position, gestures that are contained and controlled, a voice that is strong as well as determined and brisk, and a very orderly mode of dress. The structural leader's answers to voir dire questions will be complete but tending toward economy of speech. The structural leader will not be adverse to questioning the judge or lawyer about the trial process.

The *opinion leader* will be a primary contributor of ideas and arguments during deliberations and will actively attempt to persuade others to share his or her view of the case. It is not unusual to have more than one opinion leader on a jury. This becomes troublesome if one of the opinion leaders is more interested in the deliberation process than the goal of reaching a verdict. The opinion leader is recognizable by his or her willingness to express an opinion during voir dire. Also, this person tends to be more extroverted and determined than the others. The opinion leader generally offers a rather strong display of self-image in voice, posture, and gesture. The opinion leader is not likely to be adverse to interrupting the attorney to demand an explanation or clarification, or to disagree with certain wording of an idea. This type of leader is frequently a source of humor during the voir dire, even in interactions with the judge, enjoying the opportunity to display verbal skills.

Interestingly, opinion leadership appears to be a function of interaction rather than a personality constant. That is to say, the person with the strongest personality within a group will assume this leadership role. Therefore, a person who might be an opinion leader in a group where he or she feels equal or superior to others, might assume the role of an opinion generator or a follower when grouped with persons who have stronger personalities or higher social standing. An opinion generator will voice an opinion but will not take on the work of persuading others within the group to accept that opinion.

The *social leader* will be concerned with the emotional climate of the jury deliberations. This person will be concerned that group maintains social order and a positive balance of interaction. The social leader emerges when there is a need for someone to minimize friction in a group that is attempting to accomplish a certain task. The social leader seeks to maintain good cheer and to develop group members' sense of emotional satisfaction from involvement in the group process. Frequently, this position of social-emotional leader is assumed by a woman, although men who are attuned to the emotional needs of others might also be candidates for this role. Interestingly, studies have shown that the person most liked by other members of a group is the one who usually takes the social leader role, while the least liked person often fills the opinion leader role.[1]

A person's social status has a significant effect on determining the role the individual will have within a group. Sociologists Strodtbeck and Mann found that professional persons

§15.3 [1]Bales, The Equilibrium Problem in Small Groups, Working Papers in the Theory of Action 111-161 (1954).

appear to have a greater influence on jury verdicts than persons who have occupations with less prestige. Similarly, they found that men are more likely to be chosen to serve as jury forepersons than women. They concluded that the jury reflects the values the community places on various roles and occupations.[2]

§15.3.2 Followers

While it is important to identify the potential leadership roles of various panel members, it is also very useful to identify probable followers and to note with which leader they are likely to identify. Hopefully, at least half of the panel members will assume the role of followers, otherwise the deliberation process will become as much of a power struggle as it will be an attempt to reach a verdict. Followers tend to speak in less than definite tones, to be more hesitant in their responses, to have nonassertive postures, to use indecisive gestures, and to have occupations that do not require decision-making skills. The follower tends not to initiate interaction with other jurors during breaks, although the follower may be quite gregarious and responsive to the overtures of others. Followers tend to identify with leaders who recognize their needs, seek them out for discussion, have similar occupations, live in similar neighborhoods, or who share their attitudes. Of course, followers will identify the more attractive leader as a more desirable person to associate with when competition develops between two like leaders.

§15.3.3 Loners

The loner is the most difficult individual to identify or to make predictions about. This individual is not at all interested

[2]Strodtbeck & Mann, Sex Role Differentiation in Jury Deliberations, 19 Sociometry 3, 11 (1956).

in persuading others to share opinions or attitudes, nor is he or she open to persuasion. The loner neither identifies with a group nor cares about others reaction to his or her style. Yet, a loner may decide to take a particular view of a case and hold to it firmly. He or she will not feel any compulsion to explain to other jurors how certain conclusions were reached or help the group arrive at a consensus. Obviously, this is the type of individual who could bring about a hung jury. The loner tends to be an unsocialized member of the community who will sit alone as much as possible in order to avoid interaction with others on the jury. This person would be quite capable of walking away from a social leader's invitation to be included in the jury society. The loner does not often turn up on a jury panel. When such a person does appear on a panel, it is generally best to allow him or her to be excused or to exercise a challenge.

§15.4 Sample Jury Selection

The remainder of this chapter provides an example of how the techniques discussed in this book have been used to select a jury scientifically. The process is illustrated by using photographs of simulation jurors.

The jurors used to illustrate the following jury selection procedure were participants in a trial simulation for a civil case. The simulation was conducted for the plaintiff in Des Moines, Iowa, in the summer of 1982. The plaintiff's attorney in the simulation was the senior member of the actual trial team, while the role of the defense attorney was performed by his law partner.[1] The plaintiff's trial team was composed of the attorney who conducted the voir dire, a paralegal who recorded

§15.4 [1]The law firm of James and Galligan of Des Moines, Iowa, authorized the use of information from a products liability case which went to court in Council Bluffs, Iowa in 1982. Dwight W. James acted the part of the plaintiff's attorney while Michael J. Galligan acted the part of the defense

factual information, and a communication researcher who did the personality and attitude analysis. The jurors were citizens from the area who qualified for jury service and who had agreed to participate in the simulation.[2] (Information concerning the facts of the case can be found in §15.4.2 infra.)

The jury selection procedure used was the strike system, which involves sixteen jurors seated in the jury box. Voir dire is conducted by the attorneys (plaintiff's attorney first, followed by the defense attorney), and then each side exercises four strikes alternately until there are eight jurors remaining. Alternates are selected by the same procedure: if two alternates are to be used, then six jurors are called to the box, they are questioned, and then each side alternately strikes two jurors. The two jurors remaining serve as alternates.

Jurors' names are not available until the attorneys are present in the courtroom and the jury is ready to be seated. This means that no information is available about the prospective jurors prior to the date of trial, thus eliminating any opportunity for performing a pretrial investigation into their backgrounds. Therefore, the only information about jurors available to attorneys at voir dire is that which is included in jury information sheets and that which can be observed in the courtroom.

§15.4.1 Preselection Procedure

The jury for this case came from a panel that was called for service for a 30-day period. On the first day of service, jurors were shown a film that explained legal terms to which they

---

attorney. Judge Lou Lavorato served as the judge for the trial simulation, which was held in his courtroom on June 29, 1982. Starr and Associates, Inc. also assisted. The purpose of the trial simulation was two-fold: (1) to study this particular civil case and (2) to secure photographs and videotapes of the proceedings for any reasonable educational, commercial, or informational purpose.

[2] All participating jurors signed a release that allows use of the photographs, data, and videotapes for any reasonable educational, commercial, or informational purpose.

would be exposed and demonstrated a typical voir dire so that they had an idea of what to expect. Also, a judge discussed the current court calendar with them and ruled on requests from jurors who wished to be excused from service due to hardship. It is not unusual for jurors to serve on three or four cases during the course of their month-long duty.

Generally, when the judge has notified the bailiff that the case is ready for the jury, the bailiff informs the jury clerk, who then randomly selects jurors from the jury room. Unless the case has some unusual feature, a total of 32 people are sent to the courtroom: The first 16 will be sent to the jury box and when a juror is excused for cause, the next in line will be seated. Impaneling thirty-two people generally suffices for providing the eight jurors and two alternatives necessary for trial.

Once the jurors are seated in the jury box according to the order in which they were called, the bailiff hands the first sixteen jurors' information forms to the attorneys. The attorney is allowed approximately twenty minutes to examine the forms and to record the information from them on whatever form chosen for use in the jury selection process. As jurors are excused, the attorneys give the information forms to them to take back to the jury clerk in the main jury pool room. The bailiff then gives the attorneys the information form for the juror who is replacing the excused juror. Therefore, an attorney never has more than sixteen juror forms at any one time.

The plaintiff's attorney can use the twenty-minute period to memorize each juror's name and occupation so that he or she can call the jurors by name during voir dire even when asking questions in random order.[3] Both trial teams can use this time

[3]No specific research has studied the effect that an attorney's calling jurors by name without referring to notes has had on jurors' evaluation of the effectiveness or personality of the attorney. It seems to creates a strong positive initial evaluation. Ingratiation theory, which finds that there is a positive effect in persuasion when some expression of appreciation is given to jurors for having fulfilled their function, would support the desirability of taking the time and effort to memorize jurors' names. A major problem with ingratiation is that it backfires if it is obvious. Memorizing the jurors' names accomplishes the ingratiation in a subtle way that can have a positive payoff in jury deliberations. For research on ingratiation theory, see E. E. Jones & C. Wortman, Ingratiation: An Attributional Approach (1973).

to record the demographic information so that a demographic analysis can be performed (see §15.4.4 infra). Before the demographic analysis can be done, of course, one must understand the case's issues and consider how jurors of differing backgrounds will react to them.

§15.4.2 *Outline of the Case*

The trial simulation involves a products liability case concerning the following issues:

The plaintiffs, a late-middle-aged couple working a farm in western Iowa, had had a new water heater installed in the basement of their farmhouse when they moved in. Twenty-seven years later on a fall day in 1980, the water heater's pilot light went out. When the wife's husband came in from the fields that day she told him that she thought that she had smelled gas and that the pilot light had apparently gone out; he would have to relight before taking his shower, she told him.

While the husband went to the basement to check the heater the wife stood at the top of the stairs. He knelt down by the heater and smelled for gas; having smelled none he then struck a match on the basement floor. There was an explosion and flames shot up the basement stairwell engulfing both the husband and wife. The couple ran out of the house and rolled in the grass until the flames were extinguished. They were both seriously burned.

Engineering testimony established that the fail-safe control valve for the pilot light was stuck open when it went out, permitting the propane gas fumes, which are heavier than air, to leak out and settle at floor level. The jury found the defective valve to be unreasonably dangerous and awarded substantial damages to the injured couple.

§15.4.3 *Juror Specifics*

The factual information for the sixteen jurors is presented in the following order: juror number, juror name, age, marital status, education, residence, occupation, and, when appropriate, spouse's occupation. (To associate jurors with jurors' identification numbers for the purposes of the discussion in this chapter see captions for photographs 15-1 and 15-2.)

Juror 1 Jo Nelson, 47, divorced, bachelor of arts degree, owns home in urban area, disability examiner for the Social Security Administration.

Juror 2 Ray Gosselink, 69, married, high school degree, owns home in small rural town, insurance agent. His wife is a retired bookkeeper.

Juror 3 Art Fine, 35, married, master of science degree, owns home in urban area, the administrator/director of a private non-profit organization called the Prescribed Activity Center for Handicapped Children. His wife is an administrator "in the same field."

Juror 4 Mary DeJong, 33, divorced, master of public administration, rents a house in urban area, research analyst.

Juror 5 Paul Kurtz, 18, single, college freshman, lives with parents in urban area house, student.

Juror 6 Dorothy Sloma, 63, married, registered nurse degree, owns home in suburban area, works as an office clerk. Her husband, the former executive director of the Iowa Medical Society, is retired.

Juror 7 Mary Miller, 60, widow, high school degree, lives in suburban home, marketing administrator.

Juror 8 Marsha Irwin, 22, single, bachelor of science degree, lives in rented duplex in suburban area, elementary school teacher.

Juror 9 James D. Calvert, 35, married, two years of college, lives in suburban home, real estate salesperson. His wife is a store manager.

Juror 10 Yvonne B. Chadek, 66, divorced, master of arts degree, lives in urban home, retired teacher who now lectures on nutrition.

Juror 11 Abe Binder, 64, married, two years of college, lives in suburban home, sales representative, wife does not work outside the home.

Photograph 15-1. First View of Jury

Back row: Jurors 1, 2, 3, 4, 5, 6. *Middle row:* Jurors 7, 8, 9, 10, 11, 12. *Front row:* Jurors 13, 14, 15, 16.
Photograph by Dana Downie

Photograph 15-2. Jury Listening to Judge
Back row: Jurors 1, 2, 3, 4, 5, 6. *Middle row:* Jurors 7, 8, 9, 10, 11, 12.
Front row: Jurors 13, 14, 15, 16.
Photograph by Dana Downie

Juror 12 Jo Robertson, 34, married, some college work, lives in rented urban home, secretary. Her husband is a student.

Juror 13 Sandi J. Schultz, 29, single, bachelor of arts and bachelor of science degrees, lives in an apartment, cashier.

Juror 14 Jean P. Crook, 41, separated, one year of college, lives in apartment in urban area, a babysitter.

Juror 15 Andrea J. Acivedo, 25, married, two years of college, lives in suburban home, a student and homemaker. Her husband is the executive director for an employment and training firm (government supported).

Juror 16 John Roemer, 18, single, freshman in college, lives with parents in suburban home, student.

§15.4.4 Assigning Demographic Ratings

At this early stage of the jury selection process demographic ratings can only reflect the reactions one would expect based on the life experiences and education of the potential jurors. (Review chapter 7 which describes the process by which a juror is evaluated by his or her demographic background.) Using the following rating system, what would be the rating for each of the 16 jurors?

+ + +	Best possible plaintiff's juror
+ +	Good plaintiff's juror
+	Acceptable plaintiff's juror
0	Neutral juror
X	Acceptable defense juror
XX	Good defense juror
XXX	Best possible defense juror[4]

[4]Demographic ratings assigned by the professional jury worker were as follows:

1 XX
2 XXX
3 + + +
4 X

Jurors who would likely favor the opposition should be closely observed and questioned during voir dire. It can be expected that some of the ratings will change after jurors are observed in person, however, the initial demographic ratings should always be used as warning points. It is highly unlikely that a potential juror would rate XXX on demographics and then move to + + + by the end of voir dire. If this should occur, careful review of behaviors and verbal responses should be made to determine why the individual appears to be at variance with his or her life experiences.

Working quickly within the limited time allowed, each team member assigns a demographic rating to each juror. If the ratings differ greatly, a brief discussion is held so that each rater can explain his or her reasoning. For instance, juror 2 was rated by one team member as + +, by another as + and by the third as XX. The + + was assigned based on the idea that this man is a "similar other" to the plaintiff and, as such, would identify with him and be sympathetic to his cause. After all, they share the same occupations, educational backgrounds, similar marital situations, and general neighborhood. The team member who rated him as being firmly in the defense's camp believed that the juror's insurance background and age were

---

# 5	XX
# 6	XXX
# 7	X
# 8	X
# 9	+ +
#10	X
#11	+
#12	0
#13	X
#14	+
#15	X
#16	XX

Obviously, this panel favors the defense, if these ratings are accurate. At this point, the trial attorney might examine the case issues and reconsider any settlement offers that had been made before continuing with the jury selection process. With 11 of the 16 jurors assigned defense ratings, the defense should be in the stronger position based on the attitudes and expectations that the jurors bring with them into the jury box.

dominant factors that would likely lead to an attitude detrimental to the plaintiff. Therefore, juror 2 is one of the potential jurors who will be examined both verbally and nonverbally with special attention.

§15.4.5 First Look at the Jury

At this point, the bailiff ushers the jurors into the room and shows them into the jury box. The courtroom team gets their first look at them (see photographs 15-1 and 15-2). Skills involving voir dire and nonverbal communication will now be called on by team members. The judge reads the complaint and then checks to see if anyone desires to be excused for hardship. Even after being informed that the case is expected to last two weeks, none of the jurors seeks to be excused.

Observation of the jury during their interaction with the judge establishes the baseline of behavior by which the trial team will assess the jurors. The attitudes and personalities shown at this time will be compared to the reactions of jurors to the plaintiff's attorney and defense attorney during voir dire. Also, by following basic guidelines concerning how people look and sound (see chapters 13 and 14), general observations can be made of each individual juror.

Dress is examined to see how it matches expectations for the time of year (in this instance, the end of June), weather (hot), and the specific environment and circumstances (sitting in an air conditioned courtroom waiting to be chosen or eliminated from this jury). First, notice in the photographs that none of the men are wearing suit jackets, while five of the women are wearing jackets (jurors 4, 6, 7, 8, and 12), although jurors 4 and 8 have a basically casual look to their dress. All of the men are wearing casual and comfortable attire. Jurors 6, 7, and 12 have a conservative, conforming, and professional appearance that demonstrates the seriousness they assign to jury duty. None of the jurors displays a precision of dress that would lead one to expect the person to demand a precise, technical case. On the other hand, none of the jurors is brightly attired; rather, all seem to favor a more conservative self-display. Most of the jurors are wearing dark or subdued colors and none is sporting bold, assertive stripes or patterns. Overall, the jury's mode of dress would indicate that the group is more apt to respond to factual, though not necessarily technical, information and will be relatively unresponsive to emotional appeals.

Space use patterns displayed by jurors 3. 4, 9, and 11 establishes them as potential leaders. Jurors 6, 7, 12, and 16 are occupying less space, which would leads one to suspect they might be followers or, at most, opinion generators.

§15.5 Sample Jury Selection: Observing Juror Interaction

Other observations can be made about each individual using general nonverbal behavior guidelines. The observer who concentrates on nonverbal factors will be able to track the behaviors of each prospective juror (every three minutes or so) by noting posture, facial expression, and general response patterns. Naturally, during the time a prospective juror is answering questions, the observer will obtain more information since the speech channel is open, which adds to other message sources. At the same time, however, other jurors should not go unobserved since the most telling observations frequently occur when a juror doesn't feel that he or she is the focus of attention. At these times, the juror is more likely to act in an unguarded manner, revealing feelings and attitudes that under direct questioning would be masked or responded to according to what he or she feels is expected by the court.

§15.5.1 Observations during the Plaintiff's Voir Dire

Photographs 15-3 through 15-5 were taken during the voir dire session conducted by the attorney for the plaintiff. Each photograph is taken approximately four minutes apart. By tracking the movements of the jurors, it is possible to obtain a reading on their reactions to the plaintiff's case as it is revealed

Photograph 15-3. First Reaction to Plaintiff's Attorney
Photograph by Dana Downie

Photograph 15-4. Second Reaction to Plaintiff's Attorney
Photograph by Dana Downie

Photograph 15-5. Last Reaction to Plaintiff's Attorney
Photograph by Dana Downie

by the questions asked during voir dire. Juror 1, for instance, has a fairly positive initial response (see photograph 15-3), but becomes skeptical (see photograph 15-4) and finally unresponsive and distant (see photograph 15-5). Juror 2 shows a similar pattern except that he is never as open to the attorney for the plaintiff as is Juror 1. He begins with a "show me, I'm listening" attitude (see photograph 15-3), moves to disbelief and disapproval (see photograph 15-4), and ends with rejection and coldness (see photograph 15-5). Conversely, juror 11 demonstrates a more positive pattern in reaction to the plaintiff's attorney. Beginning with a fairly neutral listening attitude (see photograph 15-3), he becomes concerned, serious, and involved (see photograph 15-4) and then openly responsive and approving (see photograph 15-5).

Photograph 15-5 reveals an interesting phenomenon. Often attorneys are reluctant to use humor in voir dire, fearing that it might generate negative reactions in some jurors. This photograph captures the responses of the jurors to a mildly humorous remark concerning the weather and the time of year. Jurors 10, 11, 12, and 15 are openly responsive and appreciative of the remark, indicating full approval of the attorney and his comment. Conversely, jurors 1, 2, 6, and 7 seem to find nothing humorous in the remark and respond with disdain and coldness. Jurors 8, 13, and 14 apparently do find some humor in the remark but are obviously holding back a full, free response. These reactions correlate exactly with the verdicts they eventually decided on.

§15.5.2 Observations during the Defendant's Voir Dire

Photographs 15-6 through 15-8 were taken during the defense attorney's voir dire at approximately four minute intervals. Movement is definitely more restricted in this sequence. Some jurors, such as jurors 5, 6, 11, and 12, reveal only minute movement. None of the jurors displays significant movement patterns like those discernible during the plaintiff attorney's presentation. This would indicate that the range of emotions, attitudes, and ideas generated by the attorney was limited.

Photograph 15-6. First Reaction to Defendant's Attorney
Photograph by Dana Downie

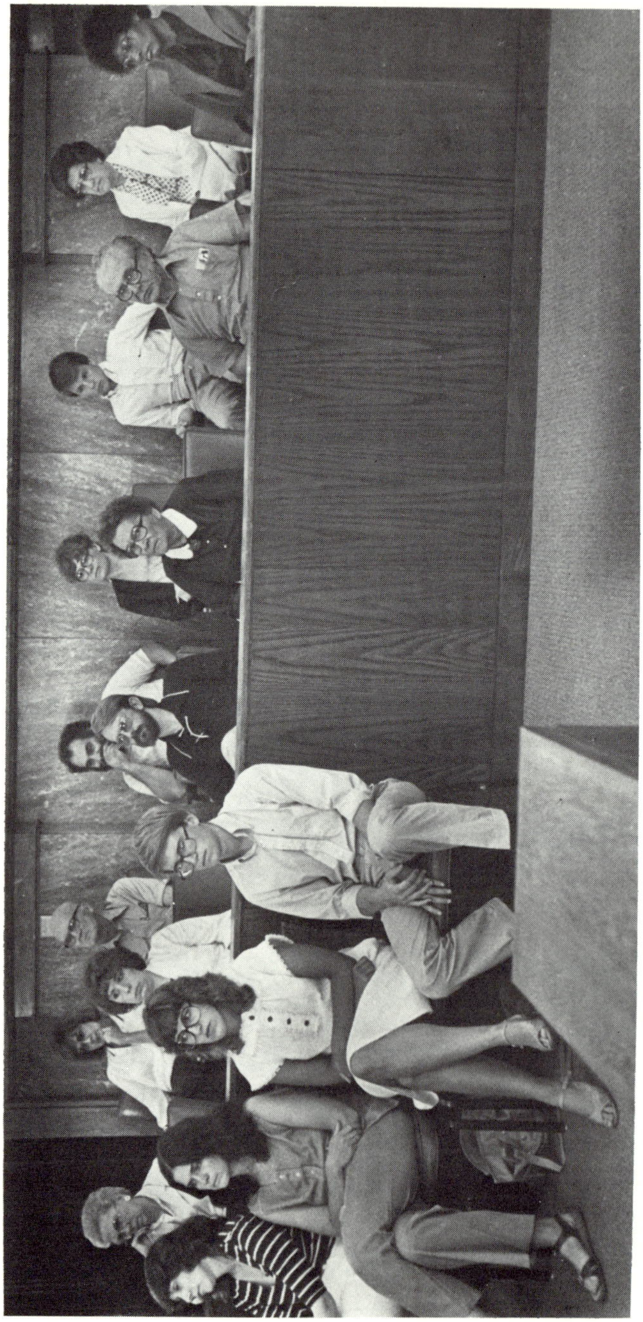

Photograph 15-7. Second Reaction to Defendant's Attorney
Photograph by Dana Downie

Photograph 15-8. Last Reaction to Defendant's Attorney
Photograph by Dana Downie

Most of the movement occurs between photographs 15-6 and 15-7, where the jurors move from positions evincing a skeptical and questioning attitude into positions that indicate acceptance (specifically jurors 7 and 14). The questions that were asked between photographs 15-6 and 15-7 concerned the jurors' ability to accept that each person has a responsibility for his or her actions, even if the person's actions result in harm to another or others. The attorney was asking such questions in order to determine whether the jurors could accept the concept as the law of the case.

When jurors do not deviate from a baseline of behavior, it is more difficult to learn about their attitudes, beliefs, and feelings. However, it does not preclude the observer from reaching valid conclusions about jurors' reactions to the attorney and his or her position on the issues.

§15.5.3 Determining Juror Leadership

Observing interaction between jurors is of tremendous value in determining who has leadership qualities. Jurors are most likely to mingle when the judge and attorneys are busy at the bench or in the judge's chambers. This is one of the major reasons it is recommended that the nonverbal analysis be performed by someone other than the attorney. Obviously, the attorney cannot analyze what is taking place while his or her back is turned to the jury or he or she is out of the room. Someone seated behind the bar can observe all of the interactions and make determinations about what each potential juror would be like as a member of a small decision-making group. Not only must the personality and attitudes of each individual be assessed, but also some determination must be made about how each individual would relate to others on a jury. If it comes to a choice of eliminating a follower, an opinion generator, or an opinion leader, the interaction of jurors becomes one of the most important considerations. Even a follower who is considered the worst possible choice might be left on the jury if all of the leaders are considered desirable. Similarly, it might be wise to eliminate a leader, even though she or he has a neutral to positive rating, if it is likely that she or he will not get along well with other leaders. It is possible to have too many leaders and not enough followers, resulting in an unpredictable situation. In such circumstances one individual may decide to play the devil's advocate just to demonstrate the effectiveness of his or her leadership skills.

Photographs 15-9 through 15-16 track interactions that occurred during a brief break called by the judge at the end of the plaintiff's voir dire and before the defense's voir dire. The judge gave the jurors five minutes to stretch and talk quietly in the jury box, while he and the attorneys went into his chambers. Photograph 15-9 was taken 30 seconds after the judge left the room. Every thirty seconds thereafter, another photograph was taken producing this series.

It is interesting to note that within 30 seconds a majority of the jurors had assumed either a standing or sitting position. Only juror 9 starts out seated and then stands, evidence of his adaptive personality, indicating a willingness to alter positions to achieve a desired end. Initially he makes self-identifying movements (see photograph 15-9) then discovers there is no one in his row with whom he can interact. He then twists his head to see who is available in the back row (see photograph 15-10) or in his own row (see photograph 15-11) before he stands (see photograph 15-12). Once standing, he turns toward the two men in the back row, jurors 2 and 3, but juror 2, although responsive, does not orient his body to indicate that he would like to converse with jurors 3 and 9 (see photograph 15-13). Juror 9 then turns the other way to become part of the group formed earlier by jurors 3 and 4 (see photograph 15-14). Juror 9 shows a certain amount of social courage by being willing to risk rejection from the jurors in the back row. From these interactions we can determine that juror 9 is an opinion leader.

Interaction within the group that juror 9 eventually joined also is interesting to track. At the beginning (see photograph 15-9), juror 3 looks at juror 9 as if he would like to initiate a conversation, but the distance created by being in different rows and in different postures is too great. Juror 4 is holding to a strictly noninteractive posture and expression. Juror 3 initiates a strong turn toward juror 4 (see photograph 15-10) to

Photograph 15-9. Interaction (First) during Recess
Photograph by Dana Downie

Photograph 15-10. Interaction (Second) during Recess
Photograph by Dana Downie

Photograph 15-11. Interaction (Third) during Recess
Photograph by Dana Downie

Photograph 15-12. Interaction (Fourth) during Recess
Photograph by Dana Downie

Photograph 15-13. Interaction (Fifth) during Recess
Photograph by Dana Downie

Photograph 15-14. Interaction (Sixth) during Recess
Photograph by Dana Downie

Photograph 15-15. Interaction (Seventh) during Recess
Photograph by Dana Downie

Photograph 15-16. Interaction (Eighth) during Recess
Photograph by Dana Downie

which she responds with a turn of the head that simply acknowledges him (see photograph 15-11). As juror 9 makes his move to engage juror 3, she watches without resentment (see photograph 15-12), apparently accepting that it is to be expected that men will engage each other in conversation. However, when juror 9 turns to include her in the group, she responds with ease (see photograph 15-14) and becomes an active participant (see photographs 15-15 and 15-16). This indicates that she tends to conform to society's norms in public interaction, but that she can become an assertive and active participant in a group once she is granted entry. If selected for the jury, she would likely feel that she had been granted such entry and would, therefore, be a vocal and active group member. At the least she is an opinion generator who would move into the position of an opinion leader if she felt that no one else was doing a good job of representing her views.

Some of the jurors maintain a passive, noninteractive role throughout the break. The confines of the jury box are partly responsible for this. Jurors on the ends of rows (jurors 1, 6, 7, 12, 13, and 16) have limited options for interaction. By necessity they must interact with the person at their side. Interaction with someone in another row, a difficult social task, would call for a person who is outgoing and mobile. The fact that none of the persons is able to overcome the limitation of his or her seat location indicates that all of those on the ends of rows are followers or, at best, opinion generators.

Juror 12 is the most deliberate about maintaining a passive, noninteractive role. Tracking her movements through the eight photographs, very little alteration of posture or eye gaze can be seen. She is limited by her seat location, but it is also possible that as the only black on the panel she feels isolated. Her posture and expression seem to indicate that she is consciously setting herself off from the group. While her nonverbal message indicates a sense of self-worth, she is obviously unwilling to push herself onto others.

For the young juror 16, the natural choice for conversation would be the woman to his right; however, his timing is off and he never looks at her when she is looking at him (see photographs 15-10 through 15-13). Instead, he resorts to acting as if centered on his own concerns, becoming inner directed in his actions (see photographs 15-12 through 15-14). He eventually settles into a constant gaze outward and to the left, much like juror 12. His uncertainty and lack of assertiveness indicate that he will play the role of follower during jury deliberations.

Juror 7 is another of those limited by an end seat. Her natural choice for interaction is juror 8 on her immediate left. Juror 8 maintains a stationary but open position that is oriented primarily to those on her left. While it is apparent that she is not going to initiate interaction, she does maintain a pleasant demeanor that indicates she would not rebuff anyone who initiated conversation with her. Yet juror 7 chooses not to begin a conversation and the two remain in passive, noninteractive postures throughout the break. This raises questions about the criteria used by juror 7 in deciding not to interact (Status or age difference? Fear of rejection?). The interpretation of this sequence would be important in determining juror 7's attitudes and biases. It also raises a question concerning her leadership abilities. She has the assertive posture and dress of an opinion leader, yet she opts out of a leadership role. Is she a loner? Or is she a leader when she is convinced of the importance of the situation? Additional observation should provide the answer. On the other hand, juror 8 is a follower with potential for becoming a social-emotional leader in a subgroup of the jury.

An interesting phenomenon occurs with jurors 6 and 7: They are both high energy types but neither initiates any conversation. It is obvious that both of these women are curious, active, and capable of being quite outgoing. In tracking their actions through the eight-photograph sequence, it is easily seen that they are interested in their roles as potential jurors and take notice of those around them. Yet they do not become involved in conversation with anyone on the jury. This is partly due to the lack of natural choices for interaction. It might easily be hypothesized that if these two women had been placed next to each other, they quickly would have become involved with each other. Despite the disadvantages of their locations in the jury box, neither woman overcomes her tendency not to interact. It could therefore be concluded that these women would not take much pressure from the group if to do so would make them appear unlikable. They would be opinion generators but not leaders.

The interaction between jurors 10 and 11 is interesting to track through the sequence. Both jurors readily interact. Just before the first picture, after the judge had left the bench, the two turned toward each other quite naturally and engaged in conversation at once. The man stopped and let the woman speak while he listened attentively, a courtesy that she then reciprocated when it was his time to talk. They allowed periods of silence (see photographs 15-11 and 15-14) with all the ease of skilled communicators, apparently feeling no pressure about maintain constant attention. The ease with which they interact indicates that either of them could be a candidate for foreperson or social-emotional leader. Also, the ease with which they accommodate each other's interaction styles would indicate that they would not play devil's advocate during deliberations.

A second break was given to the jury at the end of voir dire, immediately prior to the exercise of the strikes, while the attorneys and judge held a discussion at the bench. The judge told the jurors that they could quietly converse, but asked that they remain seated. This break lasted only about two minutes, during which time the jurors assumed the positions shown in photographs 15-17 and 15-18. Notice how the jurors divided up into groups of four members each. Some of the groups were highly interactive, others less so; still, all the groups showed some degree of involvement.

Group one, which included jurors 1, 2, 7, and 8, is fairly limited in its interaction. Only jurors 1 and 2 engage in conversation, with juror 1 primarily listening to juror 2 without adding much. Juror 2 appears to be making some point about which he has a high degree of concern. Meanwhile, juror 7 remains isolated although she actively observes the behavior of those around her. Juror 8 seems at first to be resigned to not having an opportunity for interaction (see photograph 15-17) but then becomes an open and appreciative audience for group two.

Group two, composed of some of the strongest personalities on the panel, falls into an easy and natural interaction relatively unrestrained by the formality of the courtroom. Juror 10 shows her high self-esteem and conversational comfort by actively

Photograph 15-17. Interaction (First) during Second Recess
Photograph by Dana Downie

Photograph 15-18. Interaction (Second) during Second Recess
Photograph by Dana Downie

interacting with a group dominated by younger persons with professional backgrounds unlike her own. That she wisely chose to join the group is shown by the attentive and responsive actions that take place. Her skill in interaction would make her another candidate for foreperson, unless she was one of only a few women on the jury. Jurors 3 and 9 also demonstrate leadership qualities; both of these young men possess attributes that would lead them to seek out positions of responsibility. Both will be highly vocal about offering opinions and interpretations of the facts presented during the trial. While juror 4 does not initiate as much interaction as others of this group, she too would be an active participant during jury deliberations. It is likely that she would be an opinion generator.

Group two includes jurors that could be considered desirable companions for the younger jurors. This is evidenced by the admiring attention given the group by jurors 8 and 5. It is evident that these two jurors would like to be part of group two. In fact, juror 5 has opted for the role of an observer of that group rather than choosing to be an active participant in his own group.

The group that juror 5 has disregarded is dominated by older jurors, led by juror 11. While he was actively involved with juror 10 during the previous break, during the second break juror 11 demonstrates his awareness of social responsibility by turning his attention to the two women who did not previously interact. Using his well-developed social skills, he initiates group interaction that is active and obviously satisfying to him without his having to dominate. In all, his interactions demonstrate his natural leadership skills. He is obviously a candidate for foreperson. Jurors 6 and 12 respond eagerly to this opportunity to be expressive and active, which yields an opportunity to more fully interpret their behaviors. With solicitous leadership, both jurors would become active participants in jury deliberations, although neither demonstrates that she would be more than a follower.

Group four never forms into an actual group, since none of these potential group members has the initiative to break from the courtroom formality and position his or her chair to accommodate interaction. Only jurors 13 and 14 manage to engage in some limited conversation, leaving jurors 15 and 16 to maintain self-tending, noninteractive behavior. All of these jurors would be followers.

§15.6 Sample Jury Selection: Making the Choices

Based on observations of the jurors' interactions and their responses offered during voir dire, a base of information has been obtained about each prospective juror. Now is the time to make the final decisions about the desirability of each juror for service on this particular case.

During voir dire, the attorney for the plaintiff obtained the following responses to his questions:

1. All jurors have gas water heaters in their homes;
2. None of the jurors has an engineering background nor does any family member;
3. All jurors admitted that there have been occasions when they smelled gas around their homes and they were not able to identify the source of the smell; furthermore, all jurors stated that on such occasions the smell of gas dissipated without causing any harm;
4. None of the jurors has replaced a water heater because it was "too old";
5. None of the jurors has any awareness of safety devices on his or her water heater, athough all assume they are on the heater;
6. None of the jurors has any special concern about gas or the safety of gas water heaters; and
7. None of the jurors has had any prior experience as a juror in either civil or criminal cases.

Additional information of an individual nature obtained from the plaintiff's attorney's voir dire is listed on fact sheets that accompany jurors' photographs (see pp. 470-501 infra).

Information that was elicited from the prospective jurors by the defense attorney is as follows:

1. No one would find it difficult to say no to the plaintiffs if the defendant was not responsible for their injuries; all jurors agreed that the plaintiffs were not entitled to compensation merely because they had suffered pain and injury;
2. All jurors admitted that there have been occasions when they suffered injury and pain do to their own negligence;
3. None of the jurors has tried to blame others on those occasions;
4. None of the jurors would have tried to blame others for his or her own negligence even in a case of severe injury;
5. All jurors admitted having smelled gas in their homes;
6. All jurors agreed that the smell of gas indicates danger;
7. None of the jurors would strike a match in a place that had an odor of gas;
8. All jurors believe that smelling gas signals the potential for an explosion or fire; and
9. All jurors believe the owner of a house that has a gassy smell has the duty to be careful and to take all reasonable precautions to avoid an explosion or a fire, and that this certainly included not lighting matches.

Additional information of an individual nature obtained from the defense attorney's voir dire is listed on the fact sheets that accompany jurors' photographs (see pp. 470-501 infra).

Judgments about each prospective juror's desirability for service on this particular case would now be made. In order to reach these judgments, each juror would be evaluated according to his or her *probable* reaction to (1) liability and (2) compensation. Each juror's leadership style would also be predicted.

Photographs of individual jurors are examined and information elicited on voir dire is reviewed before a rating is assigned. No doubt there will be times when additional information would be helpful; however, since voir dire will have been completed, no more information will be forthcoming.

Photographs and information forms for trial simulation jurors follow.

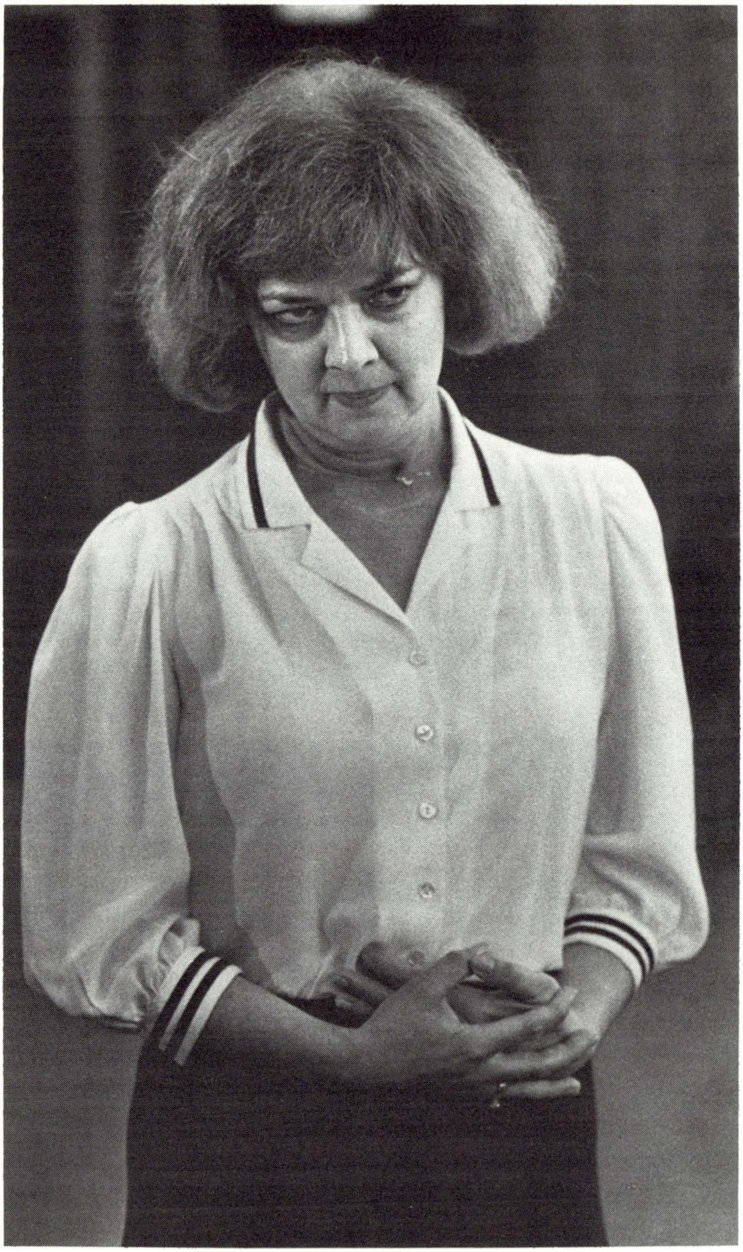

Photograph 15-19. Juror One
Photograph by Dana Downie

Form 15-4
Juror 1

JUROR'S NAME: Jo Nelson

AGE: 47 **MARITAL STATUS:** D

EDUCATION: Bachelor of Arts Degree

NUMBER OF CHILDREN: 3

CHILDREN'S AGES: 27, 25, 22

OCCUPATION: Social Security Administration employee

SPOUSE'S OCCUPATION: N/A

INFORMATION ELICITED BY PLAINTIFF'S ATTORNEY: (1) When asked about her duties as a Social Security disability examiner, she explained, "We only decide if someone is disabled. Social Security decides the benefits and we pretty much follow what the doctor reports." (2) Had a pilot light that went out that she called gas company to have relit; "I'd never try to light the pilot myself!"

INFORMATION ELICITED BY DEFENSE ATTORNEY: The attorney called her "Mrs. Nelson," she corrected him by saying it was "Ms."

JUDGMENTS: (Please check your preferred answer.)

Leadership style:

____Structural Leader	____Social Leader	____Opinion Leader
____Opinion Generator	____Follower	____Foreperson

PROBABLE LIABILITY VERDICT:

____for the plaintiff ____for the defense

PROBABLE COMPENSATION VERDICT FOR BOTH PLAINTIFFS:

____Very high ($1,500,000 as plead or more)
____High ($750,000 to $1,499,000)
____Moderately high ($500,000 to $749,000)
____Moderate ($100,000 to $499,000)
____Low (less than $100,000)
____Nothing

OVERALL RATING AS POTENTIAL JUROR: (Please check one answer.)

____XXX ____XX ____X ____0
____+ + + ____+ + ____+

Photograph 15-20. Juror Two
Photograph by Dana Downie

Form 15-5
Juror 2

JUROR'S NAME: Ray Gosselink

AGE: 69 **MARITAL STATUS:** M

EDUCATION: High School Diploma

NUMBER OF CHILDREN: 4

CHILDREN'S AGES: 46, 43, 39, 34

OCCUPATION: Insurance Agent

SPOUSE'S OCCUPATION: Retired nurse's aide

INFORMATION ELICITED BY PLAINTIFF'S ATTORNEY: (1) Experienced in "all kinds" of insurance. (2) "Possibility" that too many people go to court. (3) "I could conceive of a situation where no amount would be enough compensation." (4) "You must prove negligence, real negligence, to obtain compensation."

INFORMATION ELICITED BY DEFENSE ATTORNEY: Was in a "serious" car accident and settled out of court; however, he served as "an unfriendly witness for the insurance company" in its suit against the driver.

JUDGMENTS: (Please check your preferred answer.)

Leadership style:

____Structural Leader	____Social Leader	____Opinion Leader
____Opinion Generator	____Follower	____Foreperson

PROBABLE LIABILITY VERDICT:

____for the plaintiff ____for the defense

PROBABLE COMPENSATION VERDICT FOR BOTH PLAINTIFFS:

____Very high ($1,500,000 as plead or more)
____High ($750,000 to $1,499,000)
____Moderately high ($500,000 to $749,000)
____Moderate ($100,000 to $499,000)
____Low (less than $100,000)
____Nothing

OVERALL RATING AS POTENTIAL JUROR: (Please check one answer.)

____XXX ____XX ____X ____0
____+ + + ____+ + ____+

Photograph 15-21. Juror Three
Photograph by Dana Downie

Form 15-6
Juror 3

JUROR'S NAME: Art Fine

AGE: 35 **MARITAL STATUS:** M

EDUCATION: Master of Science Degree

NUMBER OF CHILDREN: 1

CHILDREN'S AGES: 2

OCCUPATION: Administrator/Director of the Prescribed Activity Center for Handicapped Children

SPOUSE'S OCCCUPATION: Administrator "in the same field."

INFORMATION ELICITED BY PLAINTIFF'S ATTORNEY: (1) Had trouble with the water heater and the service man told him it was "old but okay." No, he didn't check the safety device, he replied, "I have more trust in the service man."

INFORMATION ELICITED BY DEFENSE ATTORNEY: (1) His wife was a plaintiff in an automobile accident case where she suffered soft-tissue damage after being hit from behind at a stoplight. He was satisfied with the outcome.

JUDGMENTS: (Please check your preferred answer.)

Leadership style:

_____Structural Leader	_____Social Leader	_____Opinion Leader
_____Opinion Generator	_____Follower	_____Foreperson

PROBABLE LIABILITY VERDICT:

_____for the plaintiff _____for the defense

PROBABLE COMPENSATION VERDICT FOR BOTH PLAINTIFFS:

_____Very high ($1,500,000 as plead or more)
_____High ($750,000 to $1,499,000)
_____Moderately high ($500,000 to $749,000)
_____Moderate ($100,000 to $499,000)
_____Low (less than $100,000)
_____Nothing

OVERALL RATING AS POTENTIAL JUROR: (Please check one answer.)

_____XXX _____XX _____X _____0
_____+ + + _____+ + _____+

Photograph 15-22. Juror Four
Photograph by Dana Downie

Form 15-7
Juror 4

JUROR'S NAME: Mary DeJong

AGE: 33 **MARITAL STATUS:** D

EDUCATION: Master's in Public Administration

NUMBER OF CHILDREN: 1

CHILDREN'S AGES: 12

OCCUPATION: Research analyst

SPOUSE'S OCCUPATION: N/A

INFORMATION ELICITED BY PLAINTIFF'S ATTORNEY: (1) She rents a home that has a new water heater. (2) When married, the water heater went out once and she waited for her husband to re-light it. (3) She stated she is "afraid" of gas.

INFORMATION ELICITED BY DEFENSE ATTORNEY:

JUDGMENTS: (Please check your preferred answer.)

Leadership style:

Structural ____Leader	Social ____Leader	Opinion ____Leader
Opinion ____Generator	____Follower	____Foreperson

PROBABLE LIABILITY VERDICT:

____for the plaintiff ____for the defense

PROBABLE COMPENSATION VERDICT FOR BOTH PLAINTIFFS:

____Very high ($1,500,000 as plead or more)
____High ($750,000 to $1,499,000)
____Moderately high ($500,000 to $749,000)
____Moderate ($100,000 to $499,000)
____Low (less than $100,000)
____Nothing

OVERALL RATING AS POTENTIAL JUROR: (Please check one answer.)

____XXX ____XX ____X ____0
____+ + + ____+ + ____+

Photograph 15-23. Juror Five
Photograph by Dana Downie

Form 15-8
Juror 5

JUROR'S NAME: Paul Kurtz

AGE: 18 **MARITAL STATUS:** S

EDUCATION: College freshman

NUMBER OF CHILDREN: 0

CHILDREN'S AGES: N/A

OCCUPATION: Student

SPOUSE'S OCCUPATION: N/A

INFORMATION ELICITED BY PLAINTIFF'S ATTORNEY: All questions were responded to with a nod or shake of the head. He did not add any information.

INFORMATION ELICITED BY DEFENSE ATTORNEY:

JUDGMENTS: (Please check your preferred answer.)

Leadership style:

Structural	Social	Opinion
_____Leader	_____Leader	_____Leader
Opinion	_____Follower	_____Foreperson
_____Generator		

PROBABLE LIABILITY VERDICT:

_____for the plaintiff _____for the defense

PROBABLE COMPENSATION VERDICT FOR BOTH PLAINTIFFS:

_____Very high ($1,500,000 as plead or more)
_____High ($750,000 to $1,499,000)
_____Moderately high ($500,000 to $749,000)
_____Moderate ($100,000 to $499,000)
_____Low (less than $100,000)
_____Nothing

OVERALL RATING AS POTENTIAL JUROR: (Please check one answer.)

_____XXX _____XX _____X _____0
_____+ + + _____+ + _____+

Photograph 15-24. Juror Six
Photograph by Dana Downie

Form 15-9
Juror 6

JUROR'S NAME: Dorothy Sloma

AGE: 63 **MARITAL STATUS:** M

EDUCATION: Registered Nurse

NUMBER OF CHILDREN:

CHILDREN'S AGES:

OCCUPATION: Office clerk

SPOUSE'S OCCUPATION: Retired Executive Director of Iowa Medical Society

INFORMATION ELICITED BY PLAINTIFF'S ATTORNEY: (1) The current water heater is two years old and works fine. The previous one was about thirty years old and they replaced it when it "made lots of noise." The pilot light went out once and they called a service man to re-light it.

INFORMATION ELICITED BY DEFENSE ATTORNEY:

JUDGMENTS: (Please check your preferred answer.)

Leadership style:

Structural	Social	Opinion
____Leader	____Leader	____Leader
Opinion	____Follower	____Foreperson
____Generator		

PROBABLE LIABILITY VERDICT:

____for the plaintiff ____for the defense

PROBABLE COMPENSATION VERDICT FOR BOTH PLAINTIFFS:

____Very high ($1,500,000 as plead or more)
____High ($750,000 to $1,499,000)
____Moderately high ($500,000 to $749,000)
____Moderate ($100,000 to $499,000)
____Low (less than $100,000)
____Nothing

OVERALL RATING AS POTENTIAL JUROR: (Please check one answer.)

____XXX ____XX ____X ____0
____+ + + ____+ + ____+

Photograph 15-25. Juror Seven
Photograph by Dana Downie

Form 15-10
Juror 7

JUROR'S NAME: Mary Miller

AGE: 60 **MARITAL STATUS:** W

EDUCATION: High School Diploma

NUMBER OF CHILDREN: 3

CHILDREN'S AGES: 37, 35, 30

OCCUPATION: Marketing administrator

SPOUSE'S OCCUPATION: N/A

INFORMATION ELICITED BY PLAINTIFF'S ATTORNEY: The first water heater was "original equipment with the house in 1945 and my husband replaced it in 1966."

INFORMATION ELICITED BY DEFENSE ATTORNEY: "If the pilot light went out, which it never had, I would never try to re-light it myself. I'd always call a professional."

JUDGMENTS: (Please check your preferred answer.)

Leadership style:

____Structural Leader	____Social Leader	____Opinion Leader
____Opinion Generator	____Follower	____Foreperson

PROBABLE LIABILITY VERDICT:

____for the plaintiff ____for the defense

PROBABLE COMPENSATION VERDICT FOR BOTH PLAINTIFFS:

____Very high ($1,500,000 as plead or more)
____High ($750,000 to $1,499,000)
____Moderately high ($500,000 to $749,000)
____Moderate ($100,000 to $499,000)
____Low (less than $100,000)
____Nothing

OVERALL RATING AS POTENTIAL JUROR: (Please check one answer.)

____XXX ____XX ____X ____0
____+ + + ____+ + ____+

Photograph 15-26. Juror Eight
Photograph by Dana Downie

Form 15-11
Juror 8

JUROR'S NAME: Marsha Irwin

AGE: 22 **MARITAL STATUS:** S

EDUCATION: Bachelor of Science Degree

NUMBER OF CHILDREN: 0

CHILDREN'S AGES: N/A

OCCUPATION: Elementary school teacher

SPOUSE'S OCCUPATION: N/A

INFORMATION ELICITED BY PLAINTIFF'S ATTORNEY: Was an elementary school teacher but is now studying to be a nurse anesthetist.

INFORMATION ELICITED BY DEFENSE ATTORNEY: She has worked in a nursing home.

JUDGMENTS: (Please check your preferred answer.)

Leadership style:

Structural _____Leader	Social _____Leader	Opinion _____Leader
Opinion _____Generator	_____Follower	_____Foreperson

PROBABLE LIABILITY VERDICT:

_____for the plaintiff _____for the defense

PROBABLE COMPENSATION VERDICT FOR BOTH PLAINTIFFS:

_____Very high ($1,500,000 as plead or more)
_____High ($750,000 to $1,499,000)
_____Moderately high ($500,000 to $749,000)
_____Moderate ($100,000 to $499,000)
_____Low (less than $100,000)
_____Nothing

OVERALL RATING AS POTENTIAL JUROR: (Please check one answer.)

_____XXX _____XX _____X _____0
_____+ + + _____+ + _____+

Photograph 15-27. Juror Nine
Photograph by Dana Downie

Form 15-12
Juror 9

JUROR'S NAME: James D. Calvert

AGE: 35 **MARITAL STATUS:** M

EDUCATION: Two years of college

NUMBER OF CHILDREN: 0

CHILDREN'S AGES: N/A

OCCUPATION: Real estate salesperson

SPOUSE'S OCCUPATION: Store manager

INFORMATION ELICITED BY PLAINTIFF'S ATTORNEY:

INFORMATION ELICITED BY DEFENSE ATTORNEY: "I'd have trouble understanding lighting a match around leaking gas."

JUDGMENTS: (Please check your preferred answer.)

Leadership style:

Structural _____Leader	Social _____Leader	Opinion _____Leader
Opinion _____Generator	_____Follower	_____Foreperson

PROBABLE LIABILITY VERDICT:

_____for the plaintiff _____for the defense

PROBABLE COMPENSATION VERDICT FOR BOTH PLAINTIFFS:

_____Very high ($1,500,000 as plead or more)
_____High ($750,000 to $1,499,000)
_____Moderately high ($500,000 to $749,000)
_____Moderate ($100,000 to $499,000)
_____Low (less than $100,000)
_____Nothing

OVERALL RATING AS POTENTIAL JUROR: (Please check one answer.)

_____XXX _____XX _____X _____0
_____+ + + _____+ + _____+

Photograph 15-28. Juror Ten
Photograph by Dana Downie

Form 15-13
Juror 10

JUROR'S NAME: Yvonne B. Chadek

AGE: 66 **MARITAL STATUS:** D

EDUCATION: Master of Arts Degree

NUMBER OF CHILDREN: 5

CHILDREN'S AGES: 35, 33, 31, 26, 24

OCCUPATION: Retired teacher who now lectures on nutrition

SPOUSE'S OCCUPATION:

INFORMATION ELICITED BY PLAINTIFF'S ATTORNEY: (1) No idea of age of water heater but "not new." (2) Pilot light went out once but her husband re-lit it and "I didn't worry about that."

INFORMATION ELICITED BY DEFENSE ATTORNEY: She was a defendant in a lawsuit over a car accident; "nothing serious, just an icy road."

JUDGMENTS: (Please check your preferred answer.)

Leadership style:

Structural ____Leader	Social ____Leader	Opinion ____Leader
Opinion ____Generator	____Follower	____Foreperson

PROBABLE LIABILITY VERDICT:

____for the plaintiff ____for the defense

PROBABLE COMPENSATION VERDICT FOR BOTH PLAINTIFFS:

____Very high ($1,500,000 as plead or more)
____High ($750,000 to $1,499,000)
____Moderately high ($500,000 to $749,000)
____Moderate ($100,000 to $499,000)
____Low (less than $100,000)
____Nothing

OVERALL RATING AS POTENTIAL JUROR: (Please check one answer.)

____XXX ____XX ____X ____0
____+ + + ____+ + ____+

Photograph 15-29. Juror Eleven
Photograph by Dana Downie

Form 15-14
Juror 11

JUROR'S NAME: Abe Binder

AGE: 64 **MARITAL STATUS:** M

EDUCATION: Two years of college

NUMBER OF CHILDREN: 2

CHILDREN'S AGES:

OCCUPATION: Sales representative

SPOUSE'S OCCUPATION: Does not work outside home

INFORMATION ELICITED BY PLAINTIFF'S ATTORNEY: (1) Has been a manufacturer's representative with farm products. (2) Used to live in New York City before moving to Iowa about six years ago. (3) Current water heater is about six years old; "I've never paid much attention to the water heater as long as it was working." (4) They smelled gas once and called the gas company; "they fixed it."

INFORMATION ELICITED BY DEFENSE ATTORNEY: "I would listen to all the facts before deciding. That would only be fair.

JUDGMENTS: (Please check your preferred answer.)

Leadership style:

Structural	Social	Opinion
_____Leader	_____Leader	_____Leader
Opinion	_____Follower	_____Foreperson
_____Generator		

PROBABLE LIABILITY VERDICT:

_____for the plaintiff _____for the defense

PROBABLE COMPENSATION VERDICT FOR BOTH PLAINTIFFS:

_____Very high ($1,500,000 as plead or more)
_____High ($750,000 to $1,499,000)
_____Moderately high ($500,000 to $749,000)
_____Moderate ($100,000 to $499,000)
_____Low (less than $100,000)
_____Nothing

OVERALL RATING AS POTENTIAL JUROR: (Please check one answer.)

_____XXX _____XX _____X _____0
_____+ + + _____+ + _____+

Photograph 15-30. Juror Twelve
Photograph by Dana Downie

Form 15-15
Juror 12

JUROR'S NAME: Jo Robertson

AGE: 34 **MARITAL STATUS:** M

EDUCATION: Some college work

NUMBER OF CHILDREN: 3

CHILDREN'S AGES: 13, 11, 10

OCCUPATION: Secretary

SPOUSE'S OCCUPATION: Student

INFORMATION ELICITED BY PLAINTIFF'S ATTORNEY: (1) When she was ten years old, her mother was injured and two brothers died in a fire. "The furnace blew up, I think." There was no lawsuit. (2) The water heater "went out the other day. I called a service man." Why? "I just wanted hot water."

INFORMATION ELICITED BY DEFENSE ATTORNEY: "I have no special fear of gas or fire."

JUDGMENTS: (Please check your preferred answer.)

Leadership style:

_____Structural Leader	_____Social Leader	_____Opinion Leader
_____Opinion Generator	_____Follower	_____Foreperson

PROBABLE LIABILITY VERDICT:

_____for the plaintiff _____for the defense

PROBABLE COMPENSATION VERDICT FOR BOTH PLAINTIFFS:

_____Very high ($1,500,000 as plead or more)
_____High ($750,000 to $1,499,000)
_____Moderately high ($500,000 to $749,000)
_____Moderate ($100,000 to $499,000)
_____Low (less than $100,000)
_____Nothing

OVERALL RATING AS POTENTIAL JUROR: (Please check one answer.)

_____XXX _____XX _____X _____0
_____+ + + _____+ + _____+

Photograph 15-31. Juror Thirteen
Photograph by Dana Downie

Form 15-16
Juror 13

JUROR'S NAME: Sandi J. Schultz

AGE: 29 **MARITAL STATUS:** S

EDUCATION: Bachelor of Arts and Bachelor of Science Degrees

NUMBER OF CHILDREN: 0

CHILDREN'S AGES: N/A

OCCUPATION: Cashier

SPOUSE'S OCCUPATION: N/A

INFORMATION ELICITED BY PLAINTIFF'S ATTORNEY: "I have no idea how old the water heater is!"

INFORMATION ELICITED BY DEFENSE ATTORNEY: Would she blame someone for an injury that was her own fault? "I would hope not." (Loud laugh.)

JUDGMENTS: (Please check your preferred answer.)

Leadership style:

Structural	Social	Opinion
____Leader	____Leader	____Leader
Opinion	____Follower	____Foreperson
____Generator		

PROBABLE LIABILITY VERDICT:

____for the plaintiff ____for the defense

PROBABLE COMPENSATION VERDICT FOR BOTH PLAINTIFFS:

____Very high ($1,500,000 as plead or more)
____High ($750,000 to $1,499,000)
____Moderately high ($500,000 to $749,000)
____Moderate ($100,000 to $499,000)
____Low (less than $100,000)
____Nothing

OVERALL RATING AS POTENTIAL JUROR: (Please check one answer.)

____XXX ____XX ____X ____0
____+ + + ____+ + ____+

Photograph 15-32. Juror Fourteen
Photograph by Dana Downie

Form 15-17
Juror 14

JUROR'S NAME: Jean P. Crook

AGE: 41 **MARITAL STATUS:** Sep.

EDUCATION: One year of college

NUMBER OF CHILDREN:

CHILDREN'S AGES:

OCCUPATION: Babysitter

SPOUSE'S OCCUPATION:

INFORMATION ELICITED BY PLAINTIFF'S ATTORNEY: (1) "I have some trouble understanding what you mean when you talk about compensating for pain and suffering." (2) "I don't know how old the water heater is."

INFORMATION ELICITED BY DEFENSE ATTORNEY: "I couldn't make up my mind yet. I need to hear all the facts."

JUDGMENTS: (Please check your preferred answer.)

Leadership style:

_____Structural Leader _____Social Leader _____Opinion Leader

_____Opinion Generator _____Follower _____Foreperson

PROBABLE LIABILITY VERDICT:

_____for the plaintiff _____for the defense

PROBABLE COMPENSATION VERDICT FOR BOTH PLAINTIFFS:

_____Very high ($1,500,000 as plead or more)
_____High ($750,000 to $1,499,000)
_____Moderately high ($500,000 to $749,000)
_____Moderate ($100,000 to $499,000)
_____Low (less than $100,000)
_____Nothing

OVERALL RATING AS POTENTIAL JUROR: (Please check one answer.)

_____XXX _____XX _____X _____0

_____+ + + _____+ + _____+

Photograph 15-33. Juror Fifteen
Photograph by Dana Downie

Form 15-18
Juror 15

JUROR'S NAME: Andrea J. Acivedo

AGE: 25 **MARITAL STATUS:** M

EDUCATION: Two years of college

NUMBER OF CHILDREN: 2

CHILDREN'S AGES:

OCCUPATION: Student

SPOUSE'S OCCUPATION: Executive director of an employment training firm

INFORMATION ELICITED BY PLAINTIFF'S ATTORNEY: (1) The water heater is ten years old. A rusty water pipe was replaced one year ago. "There never has been an occasion when the pilot light went out so I don't know for sure what I'd do then." (2) "I don't fear gas but I sure respect it."

INFORMATION ELICITED BY DEFENSE ATTORNEY:

JUDGMENTS: (Please check your preferred answer.)

Leadership style:

____Structural Leader	____Social Leader	____Opinion Leader
____Opinion Generator	____Follower	____Foreperson

PROBABLE LIABILITY VERDICT:

____for the plaintiff ____for the defense

PROBABLE COMPENSATION VERDICT FOR BOTH PLAINTIFFS:

____Very high ($1,500,000 as plead or more)
____High ($750,000 to $1,499,000)
____Moderately high ($500,000 to $749,000)
____Moderate ($100,000 to $499,000)
____Low (less than $100,000)
____Nothing

OVERALL RATING AS POTENTIAL JUROR: (Please check one answer.)

____XXX ____XX ____X ____0
____+ + + ____+ + ____+

Photograph 15-34. Juror Sixteen
Photograph by Dana Downie

Form 15-19
Juror 16

JUROR'S NAME: John Roemer

AGE: 18 **MARITAL STATUS:** S

EDUCATION: Freshman in college

NUMBER OF CHILDREN: 0

CHILDREN'S AGES: N/A

OCCUPATION: Student

SPOUSE'S OCCUPATION: N/A

INFORMATION ELICITED BY PLAINTIFF'S ATTORNEY: His father owns a manufacturer's representatives company and is considered to be successful, financially and socially. His mother does not work outside the home.

INFORMATION ELICITED BY DEFENSE ATTORNEY: "At age 15, I was riding my bike when I shouldn't have. I'd been told by my parents not to. I was doing it anyway and fell off. I ended up with several stitches and a concussion. It was all my own fault."

JUDGMENTS: (Please check your preferred answer.)

Leadership style:

____Structural Leader	____Social Leader	____Opinion Leader
____Opinion Generator	____Follower	____Foreperson

PROBABLE LIABILITY VERDICT:

____for the plaintiff ____for the defense

PROBABLE COMPENSATION VERDICT FOR BOTH PLAINTIFFS:

____Very high ($1,500,000 as plead or more)
____High ($750,000 to $1,499,000)
____Moderately high ($500,000 to $749,000)
____Moderate ($100,000 to $499,000)
____Low (less than $100,000)
____Nothing

OVERALL RATING AS POTENTIAL JUROR: (Please check one answer.)

____XXX ____XX ____X ____0
____+ + + ____+ + ____+

§15.7 Sample Jury Selection: The Results

After voir dire was completed, the attorneys exercised their strikes. Each side was allowed to strike four people. They alternately exercised the strikes with the plaintiff having the first opportunity. The jurors were then divided into two groups: the eight jurors who were eliminated and the eight who were kept.

All sixteen jurors then listened to twenty minute of opening statements from each side. At the end of that time, the jurors were called before the judge, one at a time, to answer three questions based on information presented up to that point in the proceedings.

1. Would you find for the plaintiffs, Joanne Junct and Carroll Junct or would you find for the defendant, Robert Shaw Controls, Inc.?
2. If the jury were to favor awarding compensation to the plaintiffs, what amount of compensation do you feel would represent a fair verdict?
3. What fact or facts would be most important to you in reaching your verdict?

The sixteen jurors responded with the following *verdicts:*

JUROR 1, JO NELSON:

1. For the defendant.
2. $1.5 million for him and $750,000 for her.
3. "It's unclear if this reset valve actually failed at the time and if the gas leaking through would be an expected thing or a normal thing on most water heaters of this type."

JUROR 2, RAY GOSSELINK:

1. For the defendant.
2. If we eliminate our sympathy, there wouldn't be any compensation. If it's a matter of human sympathy -- why, possibly the doctor bills. That's $40,000.

3. "I don't feel they took reasonable precautions with the amount of warnings that he had. I would not have the slightest inclination to light a match under those conditions."

JUROR 3, ART FINE:

1. For the plaintiff.
2. About $1 million.
3. "I believe the valve failed. In the literature put out by the company, they claimed it was 100 percent effective and it appears to me that it may have been 99 percent effective, but not 100 percent effective."

JUROR 4, MARY DeJONG:

1. For the defendant.
2. $750,000 for both.
3. "The major reason was that the experts didn't immediately look at the little pin that supposedly was the cause of the accident. Also, the fact that they had smelled gas all the time and still lit a match."

JUROR 5, PAUL KURTZ:

1. For the defendant.
2. $1.5 million.
3. "Their carelessness. The evidence given that they did smell the gas and she indicated to him she had smelled it twice. She indicated that to him."

JUROR 6, DOROTHY SLOMA:

1. For the defendant.
2. $20,000 pus their $40,000 medical expenses.
3. "They smelled gas all day and hadn't done anything about it. I don't think that much gas would come out if just a pilot light may have been out."

JUROR 7, MARY MILLER:

1. For the plaintiffs.
2. $750,000.
3. "The fact that there was an explosion. Normally, if you thought the pilot light was off and you were not

smelling gas right at the time, you'd probably attempt to light it, especially the man of the house. And they were badly burned. And it was the fault of the safety control."

JUROR 8, MARSHA IRWIN:

1. For the defendant.
2. Two-thirds of what they asked for, one million and fifty thousand dollars.
3. "The smell of the gas. They should have known."

JUROR 9, JAMES D. CALVERT:

1. For the plaintiffs.
2. $1.5 million for him and $750,000 for her.
3. "It was pointed out that how the valve was used after the accident happened, with the gas being completely shut off and then being turned back on and the fact that the experts for the defendants also said that there was no foreign matter in the valve even though it had been sitting outside. And it appeared as though this pin was sticking."

JUROR 10, YVONNE B. CHADEK:

1. For the plaintiffs.
2. $1.5 million.
3. "The fact that there was an explosion proved that the device did not work."

JUROR 11, ABE BINDER:

1. For the plaintiffs.
2. About $1 million.
3. "The fact that the item was advertised as 100 percent safe and the fact that the experts who testified it was defective were more credible."

JUROR 12, JO ROBERTSON:

1. For the plaintiffs.
2. $500,000 each.
3. "There was the explosion. I mostly centered on the pain and suffering and the fact that he will not be

able to work and make the money that he's used to."

JUROR 13, SANDI J. SCHULTZ:
1. For the defendant.
2. Maybe $200,000.
3. "I don't believe there was a risk of danger on the part of the defendant in making the water heater, and the plaintiff did not prove the defendant caused the accident or whatever."

JUROR 14, JEAN P. CROOK:
1. For the defendant.
2. $250,000 for him and $25,000 for her.
3. "The fact that so many people smelled gas in the house. Both Mr. and Mrs. and a friend and a relative all smelled gas in the house."

JUROR 15, ANDREA J. ACIVEDO:
1. For the plaintiffs.
2. $500,000.
3. "The fact that the apparatus, the control, was not found to be debris laden. It was in good condition when the engineers took it apart and put it back together again."

JUROR 16, JOHN ROEMER:
1. For the defendant.
2. Close to $600,000 for both.
3. "I think the plaintiffs were more negligent than the defendant."

§15.7.1 The Effect of Individual Jurors on the Verdict

Jurors 5, 8, 9, 10, 11, 13, 14, and 15 were selected for the simulation jury. They divided evenly into two groups of jurors each favoring a party (jurors 9, 10, 11, and 15 favored the plaintiff; jurors 5, 8, 13, and 14 favored the defendant). The panel chose juror 11 (Abe Binder) as the foreperson. Jurors 9

(James Calvert), 10 (Yvonne Chadek), and 15 (Andrea Acivedo), were opinion leaders, though juror 10 also served the role of social-emotional leader. Juror 13 (Sandi Schultz) became the opinion generator for the defendant. The other jurors from the group that favored the defendant, however, took on the role of followers and in the end this group returned a verdict favoring the plaintiff, with compensation in the amount of $1,250,000 for both.

The eight jurors who were eliminated by the two attorneys formed a second deliberating panel. Of this group, five favored the defense (jurors 1, 2, 4, 6, and 16) and three favored the plaintiff (jurors 3, 7, and 12). They selected one of the plaintiff's jurors, 3 (Art Fine), as the foreperson, but since the other plaintiff's jurors were followers he was alone in his arguments against the three very strong opinion leaders favoring the defense. Jurors 1 (Jo Nelson), 2 (Ray Gosselink), and 4 (Mary DeJong) formed a solid block for the defense. Jurors 6 (Dorothy Sloma) and 16 (John Roemer) were given little opportunity to do anything more than nod in agreement. Before long, juror 7 (Mary Miller) was persuaded to join those who favored the defendant; however, the other two jurors did not alter their views. When time was called, the final vote was 6 to 2 in favor of the defendant. Compensation was never discussed.

The preceding exercise demonstrates how the jury team can work together to evaluate jurors and exercise the peremptory challenges more intelligently and skillfully. Naturally there is nothing that replaces the courtroom atmosphere and certainly a paper-and-pencil exercise does not really give the flavor of working on an actual court trial.

§15.8 A Lawyer's Perspective on the Application of Scientific Jury Analysis — Browne Greene, Los Angeles

It is my experience, having used a vital and successful jury consultant, that indeed juror stereotypes do not necessarily hold. The key is to remember that it is individuals that you are assessing. The assessment of an individual's background as well as body language in the courtroom should be the primary focus of a lawyer picking a jury.

How do you best get at the background of a juror to determine what it is that he or she has to offer to your particular case? In the past, we have all had to rely primarily on our own particular ability to "play hunches" concerning the responses of jurors to questions asked during voir dire. In most locales, very little information is provided to lawyers about to select a jury. Limitations on voir dire in many jurisdictions keep the lawyer in a civil case from inquiring, for example, into whether a prospective juror is a Democrat or Republican. What can you do to bring order and effectiveness to this process? It has been suggested that when picking a jury, lawyers should not merely listen to what is said by prospective jurors, but should also watch their body language and reactions because although words can lie body actions cannot. There is a great deal of wisdom in that advice. In my own personal use of evaluations and assessments of jurors' behaviors and verbal responses, I have found that effectiveness can be brought to jury selection.

The jury consultant I use assists me in planning the voir dire as well as working with me in the courtroom. When I have a case that presents special problems, the jury consultant is especially valuable.

One such case concerned an action by a 71-year-old man who, along with his wife, had been injured in an accident involving a two-month-old luxury automobile. The man had sued the car manufacturer charging defective design and the first trial had ended in a hung jury. My jury consultant had conducted a postverdict interview with jurors who were willing to discuss the case.

In picking the jury for the second trial, I again used my jury consultant. I learned from this experience that it is as important to determine how jurors are acting out in the hallway during recesses as it is to find out what they are doing in the courtroom.

I found that the use of a consultant was not only beneficial in giving me an extra pair of ears and eyes during jury selection, but also was extremely beneficial in bolstering my own confidence during this all-important process. Most lawyers have felt that he or she was operating on hunches and supposition rather than utilizing knowledge. But my jury consultant was helpful in analyzing linguistic and nonverbal communication for indications of attitude, character, and bias. The consultant then prepared a final report that analyzed each juror's character and attitude and projected his or her reaction to various case issues. This analysis was then used in finalizing our trial strategy. This report was shared with key witnesses that we felt would benefit from having a better understanding of their audience, the jury. We found that as a result the witnesses, especially the experts, were able to structure their testimony in terms that had relevance to the jury.

A sample of the information contained in this report follows (one plaintiff's juror and one defendant's juror is profiled):

Juror No. 1

Demographics: A young black female, single, works as a collections clerk for the City of Los Angeles. Has had prior jury duty. She drives a Ford Pinto and has a brother and sister who drive Chevy Chevettes. She has cared for a grandfather who has memory problems due to old age.

Personality: Fairly intelligent, very attractive, critical, self-confident, certain of her own ability (she is a supervisor who is responsible for four workers), open, friendly, strong-minded, not a compromiser, deliberate, likes organization and neatness. Will probably find the plaintiff's wife a similar other. Probably drives fast.

Analysis: Responsive to the plaintiff's lawyer, will be moderate in amount of compensation and have questions about liability, but not extremely difficult to convince. Medical considerations will not be a major problem area on questions of liability, but questions as to how the defect actually affected this particular collision will be a stumbling block to her (she would accept human frailty — i.e., foot slipping off brake, jamming onto accelerator — as an "excuse" for not holding the defendant liable). She will be an opinion leader who will try to persuade others to hold her view.

Final Rating: Probably plaintiff-minded juror.

Final Result: This juror voted for the plaintiff, was very favorable on liability and was an opinion molder in determining the amount of damages for the plaintiff and was especially sympathetic in her claim for loss of consortium.

Juror No. 3

Demographics: White male, 35 years of age, personnel analyst. Lives in Glendale. Drives a 1978 Volvo and a Honda. His father gave him a 1947 Cadillac when he was 13 to "bang around on." Has a degree in Social Studies from Berkeley. His father was a mechanical engineer who worked with textiles. (Worked in design as well as engineering aspects.) He works on his own cars. Calls himself a "shade tree mechanic." Just finished jury duty on a case involving installation of a fireplace and vents for it along with two other jurors, Jurors No. 2 and No. 4 on your case. (From tone of voice, I believe that verdict on that was for the defense. He said it involved the fact that the plaintiffs "alleged" improper installation.)

Personality: Pouts, defensive, judgmental, critical, a law-and-order type who will be very responsive to the judge's instructions and will do his best to apply the law, even if he personally does not like the law. He can be a whiner and a complainer. He likes to take the "other view." He has read Ralph Nader's book *Unsafe at Any Speed,* which was "critical of [another make of car by defense]" (so he remembers), but he feels that he would be more critical of Nader than American car manufacturers. He feels he is capable of superior judgment — he was willing to challenge the defense lawyer during that attorney's voir dire of him.

Analysis: Fairly responsive to plaintiff's lawyer. Most responsive to judge and will identify with him most of the time — he will see himself as an extension of the judge's opinion, i.e., an extension of the "law." He will be good on single liability issues, but will be low on the amount of compensation that he views will be adequate (conservative type). Possible foreman material.

Final Rating: Neutral to negative. Some things good, some bad, so that the final effect is that each cancels out the other. It will depend upon how the trial develops as to how he will react.

Final Result: This juror was the strongest defense juror that was left on the jury. He was an adamant juror against the plaintiff on the issue of liability and on the issue of damages he did not want to award substantial damages.

The following is a final analysis of the jury of ten women and two men that included five blacks, four Latinos, three whites.

Liability:
Poor — Jurors 2, 3 and 8
Moderate — Juror 6
Good — Jurors 9 and 10
Remaining unrelated

[Note: The final ballot showed jurors 3 and 8 for the defense with the remaining ten for the plaintiff, which produced a winning ballot for the plaintiff.]

Compensation:
Low — Juror 8
Moderate — Jurors 1 and 6
High — Jurors 4 and 11
Remaining unrelated

[Note: Most persuasive jurors on compensation in favor of plaintiff were 4, 7, 10, and 11. The verdict was a seven figure amount.]

Possible Forepersons:
Jurors 3, 4 and 5

[Note: No. 4 was the foreperson.]

Suggested Areas and Means of Persuasion
Jurors who would like emotional appeal:
— Jurors 5, 8 and 12
Jurors who would like pure logic:
— Jurors 3 and 11

[The rest will want a mixture of both emotion and logic with the primary emphasis on logic and reason.]

The plaintiff's wife needs to make these jurors like her and believe that she is warm and compassionate:
— Jurors 1, 3, 4, 5 and 11

The plaintiff needs to impress these jurors that he is worthy of compensation and capable of producing income had it not been for this occurrence:
— Jurors 3, 4 and 11

Your expert witness on liability should concentrate on:
— Jurors 1, 3, 4, 10 and 11.

Eyewitness testimony should center on:
— Jurors 2, 3, 5, 10 and 11

The plaintiffs in this action received a seven figure plus verdict. The types of jurors we selected had many of the qualities of human compassion, warmth, openness, and empathy that we were looking for. I am sure that certain critics of jury consultants would say that one could pick a jury without a jury consultant and obtain favorable results, as indeed lawyers have done and still do. It is my feeling that the jury consultants and their efforts can not only advise you how to win a case, but when to settle a case rather than go to trial with the jury panel presented to you. That, probably, is at least as important a bit of advice as one could ever hope to obtain.

Afterword

This book has attempted to present the techniques of scientific jury selection as a supplement to rather than a substitute for an attorney's experience and intuition. Just as trial preparation generally has become more careful, deliberate, and thorough, so has the approach to jury selection become more purposeful. The goal of choosing a good jury is nothing new, but the means offered here for achieving that goal are more sophisticated and thorough. Because the jury will decide the outcome of the case, jury selection is the single most important procedure in the trial. An attorney familiar with those techniques can therefore go to trial with more confidence.

Preparing for jury selection involves obtaining as much information about potential jurors as possible before the process commences. This means using information from jury questionnaires when they are available. It sometimes means conducting pretrial investigations of potential jurors. This is a sensitive task that must be done carefully and properly. Precautions should be taken to ensure that the information is gathered by qualified people in a lawful manner. In addition, the information must be organized so that it is accessible during voir dire. Above all, the information must be both reliable and relevant.

Community attitude assessments are an invaluable tool for constructing a profile of potential jurors. Such assessments are generally helpful when selecting a jury, but they can also be used for more specific objectives such as supporting a motion for change of venue, seeking a change in voir dire procedures, and in making trial strategy decisions. When a litigant's financial resources limit the type of assessment that can be conducted, a behavioral scientist can often be helpful in designing a study that will be cost effective in producing an accurate profile of potential jurors. A poll, survey, community attitude study, or psychological interview each has its own proven benefits. The community attitude study offers the best opportunity for determining community prejudice or bias, but because of its administrative and analytical complexity it demands the greatest skill in its use.

The trial simulation is another technique designed to assist in selecting a good jury. Its general purpose is to gauge the reactions of prospective jurors to the evidence and argument for a specific case. It is also helpful for developing a trial strategy. Because it is an elaborate procedure that involves a substantial investment of time and expense, it is a technique that is generally reserved for cases that are particularly complex or involve high stakes.

When the time for voir dire arrives the lawyer must be ready to take advantage of the opportunity it provides. Being prepared means being aware of the potential of voir dire as a means to identify and expose prejudice. It also means having an understanding of the mechanics of the process. Before entering the courtroom the lawyer should be prepared to follow the procedures mandated by the particular judge. Arrangements should have been made to have the proceeding on the record in anticipation of an appeal.

If the attorney is to be given a role in determining how voir dire is to be conducted, he or she must be prepared to request procedures that will facilitate selecting the best jury for the case. Morever, the lawyer should know in advance how many and what kind of questions to ask each juror and must be ready to confront sensitive topics as well as unanticipated responses.

The time for exercising challenges is a time for decision. Challenges for cause involve strategic choices. They must be carefully and tactfully exercised. Exercising peremptory challenges will involve marshalling information from pretrial studies, courtroom observations, and the intuition and past experience of all trial team members. While no substitute exists for the experience, intuition, and skill of the lawyer, the ability to educate and gain rapport with jurors will depend to a large extent on the application of the teachings of the behavioral scientist's methods.

Perhaps the most important teaching is an understanding of nonverbal communication. There is nothing new to most people about the idea that nonverbal cues are more of an indicator of a person's feelings and beliefs than verbal communication. Empirical studies and objective data have verified much of what was previously guessed at or intuitively felt. With a better understanding of nonverbal communication more confidence in its reliability can be gained. Such an understanding of nonverbal communication is indispensable to careful and accurate decisions during jury selection. Even if the lawyer defers to the professional in the courtroom for assistance in using nonverbal communication techniques, the lawyer's understanding will add to its utility in making decisions only the lawyer can make in the jury selection process.

This book is offered as a reference tool. Its suggestions are conveyed by explanation and example. It is intended to be as informative for a general practitioner preparing for the trial of a routine case as it would be for a specialist anticipating a complex trial. The techniques of scientific jury selection may be applied selectively depending on the particular case. Although it is often helpful to have the assistance of an expert in applying these techniques, such assistance is not indispensable. The ordinary lawyer with an understanding of the techniques discussed in this book should be able to take advantage of them without undue expense. When the lawyer wishes to employ an expert, an understanding of scientific jury selection will not only help him or her decide whom to employ, but will also be useful when deciding how to use the information provided by the expert.

Appendices

APPENDIX

1

Sample Juror Questionnaires

FEDERAL COURT

JUROR QUALIFICATION QUESTIONNAIRE

PRINT OR TYPE YOUR ANSWERS
PLEASE READ LETTER ON OTHER SIDE

AO 178D

A. IDENTIFICATION

NAME

MR. ☐ MRS. ☐ MISS ☐

(1) ARE YOU A U.S. CITIZEN ☐ YES ☐ NO

(2) BIRTH DATE — month — day — year (3) AGE

(4) PLEASE INDICATE YOUR RACE ON THE LIST BELOW

FEDERAL LAW REQUIRES YOU AS A PROSPECTIVE JUROR TO INDICATE YOUR RACE. THIS ANSWER IS REQUIRED SOLELY TO AVOID DISCRIMINATION IN JUROR SELECTION AND HAS ABSOLUTELY NO BEARING ON QUALIFICATIONS FOR JURY SERVICE. BY ANSWERING THIS QUESTION YOU HELP THE FEDERAL COURT CHECK AND OBSERVE THE JUROR SELECTION PROCESS SO THAT DISCRIMINATION CANNOT OCCUR. IN THIS WAY THE FEDERAL COURTS CAN FULFILL THE POLICY OF THE UNITED STATES WHICH IS TO PROVIDE JURORS WHO ARE RANDOMLY SELECTED FROM A FAIR CROSS SECTION OF THE COMMUNITY.

☐ INDIAN (American)
☐ ORIENTAL
☐ BLACK (or Negro)
☐ WHITE
☐ OTHER (Specify)

B. OCCUPATION

Federal Law requires that you answer No. 5, 6, 7, & 8 so that the Federal Courts may determine promptly whether you fall within an excuse or exemption category (See "G" & "H").

(5) ARE YOU NOW EMPLOYED? ☐ YES ☐ NO

(6) YOUR EMPLOYER'S NAME

(7) YOUR USUAL OCCUPATION, TRADE OR BUSINESS

(8) BUSINESS ADDRESS OR EMPLOYER'S ADDRESS

Street

City

State — Zip

C. HEALTH

(9) DO YOU HAVE ANY PHYSICAL OR MENTAL INFIRMITY IMPAIRING YOUR CAPACITY TO SERVE AS JUROR? (IF "YES", PLEASE EXPLAIN AND GIVE EVIDENCE OF YOUR INFIRMITY IN AN ATTACHED LETTER). ☐ YES ☐ NO

NOTE: *DO NOT ASK THE COURT TO CALL YOUR DOCTOR.* ANY DOCTOR'S STATEMENT YOU OBTAIN REGARDING YOUR PHYSICAL CONDITION MUST BE SENT TO THE COURT BY YOU RATHER THAN BY THE DOCTOR.

D. RESIDENCE

(10) HAVE YOU LIVED FOR THE PAST FULL YEAR IN

• THIS STATE ☐ YES ☐ NO • THE SAME COUNTY ☐ YES ☐ NO

IF "NO" GIVE NAMES OF OTHER COUNTIES OR STATES IN WHICH YOU LIVED DURING THE YEAR AND SHOW DATES. (USE REVERSE IF NECESSARY.)

(11) PHONE — HOME — WORK (INCL. EXTENSION)

E. EDUCATION

(12) CAN YOU . . .

• READ ☐ YES ☐ NO
• WRITE ☐ YES ☐ NO
• UNDERSTAND AND SPEAK ☐ YES ☐ NO
} THE ENGLISH LANGUAGE?

(13) SHOW THE EXTENT OF YOUR EDUCATION BY GIVING THE NUMBER OF FULL YEARS COMPLETED

In Grade School ___ In High School ___ Trade Vocational School ___ Above High School ___

F. CRIMINAL RECORD

(14) HAVE YOU EVER BEEN CONVICTED, EITHER BY YOUR GUILTY OR NOLO CONTENDERE PLEA OR BY A COURT OR JURY TRIAL, OF A STATE OR FEDERAL CRIME FOR WHICH PUNISHMENT COULD HAVE BEEN ONE YEAR OR MORE IN PRISON? ☐ NO ☐ YES

(15) (IF "YES") WERE YOUR CIVIL RIGHTS RESTORED? ☐ NO ☐ YES
(IF "YES", EXPLAIN ON REVERSE SIDE)

(16) ARE ANY CHARGES NOW PENDING AGAINST YOU FOR A VIOLATION OF STATE OR FEDERAL LAW PUNISHABLE BY IMPRISONMENT FOR MORE THAN ONE YEAR? ☐ NO ☐ YES

NOTE
If your answer to either question 14 or 16 is YES, please state on the reverse side of this form: a) date of the offense, b) date of the conviction (or date of pending charge), c) the sentence imposed (if a conviction), and d) the name of the court. One is disqualified from jury service only for criminal offense punishable by imprisonment for more than one year, but it is the maximum penalty, and not the actual sentence, which controls.

G. EXEMPTIONS

(17) CHECK IF YOU ARE EMPLOYED ON A FULL-TIME BASIS AS ONE OF THESE:

PUBLIC OFFICIAL OF THE UNITED STATES, STATE, OR LOCAL GOVERNMENT WHO IS ELECTED TO PUBLIC OFFICE OR DIRECTLY APPOINTED BY ONE ELECTED TO OFFICE. ☐ YES ☐ NO

MEMBER OF ANY GOVERNMENTAL POLICE OR REGULAR FIRE DEPT. (NOT INCLUDING VOLUNTEER OR COMMERCIAL DEPTS.) ☐ YES ☐ NO

MEMBER IN ACTIVE SERVICE OF THE ARMED FORCES OF THE UNITED STATES. ☐ YES ☐ NO

H. GROUNDS FOR REQUESTING EXCUSE

You MAY be excused by the court from service as a juror if you are within a category shown below. If you request to be excused for that reason, mark the category which applies to you. HOWEVER, IF YOU WISH TO SERVE DO NOT MARK YOUR CATEGORY.

I am

☐ Over 70 years of age

☐ A person who has served as a grand or petit juror within the last 2 years (give name of court and dates you served on reverse side).

☐ A person having active care and custody of a child or children under 10 years of age whose health and/or safety would be jeopardized by my absence for jury service; or a person who is essential to the care of aged or infirm persons. (Explain fully on reverse side.)

☐ A person whose services are so essential to the operation of a business, commercial, or agricultural enterprise that it must close or cease to function if I am required to perform jury duty (Explain on reverse side.)

☐ Actively practicing or engaged full-time in one of these occupations | attorney, | physician, | dentist, | registered nurse. | XXXXXXXX

FULL TIME STUDENT OR TEACHER

PLEASE READ LETTER ON OTHER SIDE

FOLD

A

FROM

RETURN THIS FORM IN THE ENCLOSED ENVELOPE TO:
UNITED STATES DISTRICT COURT

(18)

TO

IF YOUR NAME OR PERMANENT ADDRESS IS NOT CORRECT, PLEASE CHECK ☐ AND SHOW CORRECTIONS ON REVERSE.

(19)

COUNTY YOU NOW LIVE IN →

(20) I declare under penalty of perjury that all answers are true to the best of my knowledge and belief

SIGN HERE ➡ .... DATE ....

If another person filled out the above form, please indicate your name, address and reason why on other side of form.

YOU MUST ANSWER ALL QUESTIONS THAT APPLY TO YOU. PLEASE MAKE SURE YOU HAVE DONE SO

REMEMBER, ALL CITIZENS HAVE AN OBLIGATION TO SERVE AS JURORS WHEN CALLED UPON

Form A-1. Federal Juror Qualification Questionnaire

UNITED STATES DISTRICT COURT

PLEASE NOTE: Unless shown elsewhere, the address of the U.S. Court which sent you this questionnaire is shown on reverse side at box 18.

Dear Prospective Juror:

Your name has been drawn by lot, and you are being considered for jury service in the United States District Court. Trial by jury is a keystone of our system of justice. Jury service is therefore both an opportunity and an obligation of every American. Jurors will receive mileage and, unless they are Federal Government employees, $30.00 per day for each day of service.

This is not a summons for jury service. It is a way of obtaining some information about you from which we can objectively determine whether you are qualified to serve pursuant to federal law. Please answer each question, sign and return the form within ten days. If we find you qualified, you may be summoned at a later date.

If you are unable to fill out this form, someone else may do it for you provided that person indicates below why it was necessary for him to do it instead of you.

If you do not return this questionnaire form, fully completed, within ten days you are liable to be summoned to report at your expense for completion of the questionnaire at this office.

There are certain grounds for excuse or exemption from jury service. If you are exempt or claim a right to be excused, give us that information under sections G and H. The right to request excuse is automatically extended only to those categories of persons, if any, that are listed in Section H. Others may be excused only by showing at such time as they may be summoned that jury service would cause them undue hardship or extreme inconvenience. If you show under Section C that you have a physical or mental infirmity, please attach evidence of your infirmity. **Do not ask to be excused by telephone.**

If your address changes after you have returned this questionnaire, please notify us promptly by letter or post card, addressing it to "Attention: Jury Clerk".

CLERK,
UNITED STATES DISTRICT COURT

SPACE FOR OFFICIAL USE ONLY

QUALIFIED	EXCLUDED	EXCUSED	EXEMPT	DISQUALIFIED
☐	☐	☐	☐	☐

Additional space for jurors to complete answers to any items on questionnaire. Indicate number of question(s) to which you are further responding:

Form A-1 (continued)

JUROR QUESTIONNAIRE

Please complete and promptly return to Clerk of Court in enclosed envelope.

Name____Age_____
(First) (Middle initial) (Last)

Spouse's Name____
(If widowed, name of late spouse.)

Home Address:______________________CITY____________________Phone__________

Years of Residence: In Iowa______________In your County________________

Highest school grade completed and college degrees:____________________

Marital Status:________________________Number of Children:______________

Occupation:_____________________________Employer — BUSINESS PHONE —________________
(If retired, check here____and list above last occupation and employer.)

Spouse's Occupation_____________________Employer______________________
(If widowed, insert last occupation and employer of late spouse. If spouse is retired, check here____ and list above last occupation and employer.)

Have you previously served as a juror?____When?__________What kind of case or cases?____
Was prior jury service in State or Federal Court?_____________

Have you or any near relative ever suffered serious bodily injury. Has any near relative been killed in an accident of any kind?______If so, state who was injured or killed, when, the type of injury, and the type of accident__________
____
____

Have you or any near relative ever been a party to a lawsuit other than divorce?
_____If so, who?________________________Nature of lawsuit?_______________
______________________________________Was the lawsuit tried or was it settled before trial?____
If tried, what was the result?____

Have you or any near relative ever made a claim for damages for personal injury?
_____Has such a claim ever been made against your or any near relative?______

Are you or any near relative a stockholder, director, officer, employee or agent of any casualty insurance company?______Who?_____________________________
What company?____

Do you drive an automobile?_________

Are you or any near relative a law enforcement officer?_____Who?____________
___________________What law enforcement agency?_________________________

Have you or any near relative ever been the victim of a serious crime?__________
Who was the victim?____
Nature of crime?____

Have you or any near relative ever been a defendant or witness in a criminal case?
_____Who?___________________________Defendant or witness?_______________
Nature of case?____

Have you or any near relative ever been convicted of a felony?______When?________
_____________State nature of offense___________________________________

How is your: Health?___________________Eyesight?_____________Hearing?__________

I hereby certify that the foregoing information is true and correct.

Date________________ Signature____

Form A-2. Supplementary Federal Juror Qualification Questionnaire

State of Indiana **JUROR NO. ______**
Allen Circuit Court
Indiana 38th Judicial Circuit

JUROR PERSONAL HISTORY QUESTIONNAIRE

TO THE JUROR: You have already been found generally qualified to serve as a juror. However, you may not be suitable for service in a given case. In order to find out whether you are suitable for service in each case, you will be questioned by the Judge or attorneys. Certain questions are asked in most cases, and to save time you are being required to fill out this questionnaire, so that these questions do not have to be asked in Court. You can appreciate the time and money this questionnaire will save.

The questions asked in this questionnaire are questions which could be asked of you in open court. You are therefore given more privacy by having you answer them in this questionnaire.

You are required to answer the questions truthfully. As you answer the questions it will become obvious to you why such questions must be asked.

ANSWERS MUST BE WRITTEN OR PRINTED BY THE JUROR HIMSELF.

JUROR QUESTIONNAIRE

PLEASE READ CAREFULLY AND COMPLETELY ANSWER EACH OF THE FOLLOWING QUESTIONS:

1. Name____________________________________ Age:______
   (First) *(Middle Initial)* *(Last)*
2. Home Address:____________________________________

   Home Phone No.:__________ Business Phone No.:__________
3. Years of Residence:

   At Present Address:____ In Allen County:____ In Indiana:____

Form A-3. State Juror Questionnaire

4. Prior place(s) of residence (Last five (5) years):______________

____

5. Current marital status: Married____ Separated____ Widow____
(check one) Single_____ Divorced_____ Widower__

6. Number of children (total)________ Children at home________

7. List *all* members of your family residing in your home (omit names):

Relationship	*Age*	*Occupation*	*Employer*

8. (a) Your present occupation and employer:

____

(b) Years employed by present employer:

____

(c) Your prior occupations and employers (last 3 years):

____

____

9. If retired, give last occupation and employer:

____

____

____

10. If you are a widow or widower, give occupation and employer of deceased spouse:

____

____

11. (a) Have you served as a juror prior to this year? Yes____No____

    (b) If yes, when and where?____________________

12. (a) Have you or any member of your immediate family been a party to a lawsuit? Yes____No____

    (b) If yes, when and where?____________________

13. (a) Have you or any member of your immediate family been a *witness* to a lawsuit? Yes____No____

    (b) If yes, when and where?____________________

14. (a) Have you ever made a claim for damages to your person or property? Yes____No____

    (b) Have any members of your immediate family ever made a claim for damages to their persons or property? Yes____No____

15. Has any claim for damages to person or property ever been made *against* you or any member of your immediate family? Yes____No____

16. Have you or any member of your immediate family ever been involved in an automobile collision? Yes____No____

17. (a) Have you ever been *charged* with a serious crime? Yes____No____

    (b) Has any member of your immediate family ever been charged with a serious crime? Yes____No____

18. (a) Have you ever been convicted of a serious crime? Yes_____No_____

(b) If yes, specify date_________Court_________Crime_________

19. Have any members of your immediate family ever been convicted of a serious crime? Yes_____No_____

20. (a) Do you now hold a license to operate a motor vehicle? Yes_____No_____

(b) Type of license (check):

Beginners_________Operators_________Chauffeurs_________

(c) Years of driving experience:___________

21. (a) Are you a resident voter of Allen County, Indiana? Yes_____No_____

(b) Are you a freeholder, householder or the spouse of a householder? Yes_____No_____

22. Do you have any uncorrected defects of sight or hearing which prevents you from reading ordinary newsprint or hearing an ordinary conversation? Yes_____No_____

23. (a) Do you have any other physical or mental impairment or disability which would disqualify you for jury service? Yes_____No_____

(b) If yes, name and address of physician_________________

____

24. Do you have religious convictions or conscientious scruples which would prevent your sitting in judgment on another person? Yes_____No_____

25. (a) Do you know of any other valid and legal reason for your disqualification for jury service or why you could not serve as a fair and impartial juror? Yes_____No_____

(b) If yes, please explain fully:____________________________

____

____

____

26. Are you or any member of your immediate family employed by or have any interests in or own any stock of any insurance company? Yes_____No_____

27. Are you an employer, landlord, or tenant? (Specify)

____

28. How long have you lived in Allen County?

____

29. Have you ever studied law? (Explain)

____

____

30. Have you ever studied medicine? (Explain)

____

____

31. How far did you go in school? (Indicate highest grade completed or degrees received): ______________________________

____

32. Have you ever served as a juror?________________________

If so, when and in what courts?________________________

33. Have you ever been discharged (not excused) from jury service?____

If so, for what cause?________________________________

34. Do you drive a car?___________________________________

Do you (or your spouse) own a car?______________________

35. If so, is it insured?_______With what company?_______________________

36. Have you ever been in an accident? (Explain)_______________________

37. Were you injured?_______________________

38. Was anyone else injured? (Explain)_______________________

39. Has any member of your family, or a close friend ever been in an accident?_______________________
If so, explain:_______________________

40. Are you a director of, or do you own stock in, any insurance companies?_______________________

41. What companies?_______________________

42. Were you ever an inmate in a state or county institution? (Explain)_______________________

43. Have you ever been convicted of a crime or misdemeanor (other than for a non-moving traffic violation?)_______________________

44. If so, explain:_______________________

45. Have you ever been arrested and charged with any crime? (Explain):_______________________

46. If so, is that charge pending?_______________________

47. Have you ever been a party to any suit, either civil or criminal?

48. If so, state the nature and number of each suit and in what court:______________________________________

49. Please state the number of miles from your house to the Court House______________________________________

This information is NOT for the public. Only the judge and the attorneys who will be involved in the jury cases during your term on a jury will see this. Please answer all questions the best you are able to — but answer them all, if you will please, to the very best of your information.

I hereby certify under the penalties of perjury that the answers to all questions herein are true and correct.

Date:____________________, 19____ ____________________________
(Signature)

NOTE: PLEASE COMPLETE AND RETURN THIS QUESTIONNAIRE IN THE SELF-ADDRESSED AND STAMPED ENVELOPE ENCLOSED HEREWITH WITHIN SEVEN (7) DAYS.

JUROR PROFILES FORM*

NAME & ADDRESS	ID NO.	AGE	OCCUPATION/ EMPLOYER	EDUCATION COMPLETED	MARITAL STATUS/ SPOUSE'S NAME	SPOUSE'S OCCUPATION/ EMPLOYER	OTHER MEMBERS OF IMMEDIATE FAMILY	YEARS OF RESIDENCE STATE/COUNTY	VICTIM OF CRIME	ACCUSED OF CRIME	FELONY CONVICT OR UNDER INDICTMENT	FRIEND OF LAW OFFICER	CIVIL CLAIMS	SERVE AS JUROR

*Demographic information for this form is often available before or at trial from court records on potential jurors.

Form A-4. Juror Profiles Form

APPENDIX

2

Community Attitude Study Training Manual

WELCOME

I'm very happy you could find the time to work with us. I think you will find the overall process of conducting a community attitude survey exciting, even if you sometimes become a bit weary conducting the individual interviews.

Do remember that this is dedicated to the concept that justice is best served when truth and accuracy are served.

The project director, ___*(name)*___, will be responsible for the following:

1. assigning your duties,
2. training you in the requirements of this particular interview process,
3. determining your salary and expenses,
4. taking care of any major or minor problems that you encounter while performing your duties. (Do contact him or her immediately if you have any problem or if anything unusual occurs. He or she will have the answer or will secure it for you.)

Thank you. I do appreciate your cooperation. I hope that all goes smoothly for you. If for some reason ___*(project director)*___ is not available to assist you, please call on me. If I am out of the office, someone there will know how to reach me.

My phone numbers are as follows:

Home: *(number)*
Office: *(number)*

(name)
Principal Investigator

Materials List:
(Be certain to have these supplies with you daily.)

1. thirty interview schedules
2. a red pen
3. a black pen
4. a yellow legal pad
5. your call sheets (also called Telephone Dialing Records)
6. your list of instructions
7. *(Name of principal investigator's)* telephone number is ______.
8. *(Name of project director's)* telephone number is ______.

What Counts as an Interview

We need to complete the full schedule of interviews — 150 in all — in order to conduct a useful survey. Everything possible has been done to make sure that preparation for the interviews is complete. Now it is up to you, the interviewer, to continue the process. You will only be paid for completed interviews. So what counts as a completed interview? Those that meet the following criteria:

1. Interviews must be complete from beginning to end — that means that a response is indicated on the answer

sheet for EVERY question. If someone breaks off in the middle of an answer, it will be considered an incomplete response. If there are more than two unanswered questions, the interview will be considered incomplete. IN OTHER WORDS, SEEK AND RECORD RESPONSES TO EVERY QUESTION.

2. It is particularly important that each interview be conducted with a *qualified* respondent:
   a. A person at the specified phone number,
   b. A person who is 18 or older, but who is not older than 70,
   c. A person who is *not* an elected or appointed governmental official or actively serving in the armed forces,
   d. A person who is *not* an attorney, a police officer, or a firefighter.

The Interview Telephone Dialing Record

It is important that each interviewer fill out the interview telephone dialing record accurately and completely.

You will be given an interview telephone dialing record that will contain telephone numbers that have been randomly selected for a community. THESE TELEPHONE NUMBERS, AND ONLY THESE NUMBERS, WILL BE THE ONES YOU WILL CALL. Each number should be called three times before considering it an "exhausted" number. This means that if a call results in a busy signal or if there is no answer, you should call that number again. You should attempt to reach the party *three* times.

There are six possible responses for recording on the dialing record:

busy — line is busy
n.a. — no one answers the phone

Interviewer name ____________ Interviewer number ______ Community code _____ Date ____________

#	Telephone number	Completed	First contact					Second contact					Third contact					Comment
			busy	n.a.	refuse	n.el.	bsn#	busy	n.a.	refuse	n.el.	bsn#	busy	n.a.	refuse	n.el.	bsn#	

Form A-5. Interview Telephone Dialing Record

refuse — The person who answered the phone refused to begin or continue the interview. (If the person *begins* to respond and then breaks off the interview, record the number of the last item responded to in the "comment" column.)

n.el. — This means "no eligible respondent" at the number. NOTE: Record why the respondent was not eligible in the "comment" column.

bsn. — business number (No interviews are to be conducted using a business number.)

completed — If the interview is completed, mark the interview number in the completed column. (If you think this completed interview will need special attention for coding purposes, note that in the "comment" column by marking "code check.")

If a person indicates that he or she is busy now but would have time later, make an appointment for a call-back. Put the time for this call in the "comment" column and place the initials "C.B." under the "busy" column. Be sure to keep your appointment to call the person back.

For completing the questionnaire, note that you are to indicate the date of the contact and whether the contact was made in the morning (a), afternoon (p), or evening (e).

Basic Instructions

1. When you begin a new interview schedule, be sure that you fill in the coding information at the top of the sheet. This will include your interviewer number (the code that identifies you to the computer), the number of the interview you are conducting, and the community code.
2. Be sure to follow through the questionnaire exactly as it is constructed. DO NOT REPHRASE ANY OF THE

QUESTIONS. Proceed through the questions according to the design of the form. Even if you think that something would work better for you, *do not* make any changes. This is important in order for the final analysis of the survey is to be accurate.

3. If the question is not open-ended, you must record one and *only one* response in the blanks provided on the questionnaire. If you are not sure how to record a response, ask the participant "How should I record this?" and then read back the responses as you have them written on the questionnaire.
4. ALWAYS BE FRIENDLY.
5. If a person says that he or she is too busy to answer your questions right now, ask if you can call back at a more convenient time. Make an appointment for the call-back and keep that appointment.
6. No matter how antagonistic a respondent becomes, it is important that you do not become aggressive or antagonistic. Keep your cool. Refer all questions to the principal investigator, *(name)*. Tell such persons that they can call collect if they identify themselves with the *(location name)* community attitude study. Notify *(name)*, the project director, if you have someone who is troublesome. (The project director will define what should be considered troublesome.)
7. Try to keep the interview as short as possible without losing accuracy of response. You will, of course, want to complete as many interviews as possible in the time allowed. Also, you should careful not to intrude too much on the respondent's time.
8. Be sure to tell the respondent how much you appreciate his or her cooperation. Do not act secretive. Give full and accurate answers to questions about the survey.
9. In order to keep an accurate record of incomplete questionnaires, code them alphabetically. For instance, if during interview number 12 the respondent stops on the second page, place an *A* after the interview number

at the top of the page. You would designate the next completed interview 12*B*.

10. BE SURE TO WRITE THE PHONE NUMBER IN THE BLANK SPACE PROVIDED FOR THE FIRST QUESTION.
11. The questionnaire has been designed in such a way that you probably will not have to read the response choices to the respondent. Note the specific places where you may need to use capital letters.
12. COMPLETE ONLY THE NUMBER OF INTERVIEWS SPECIFIED IN THE UPPER RIGHT-HAND CORNER OF THE TELEPHONE DIALING RECORD/CALLING SHEET. THIS IS CRITICAL FOR ACCURATE RECORD KEEPING.
13. If you must stop an interview because you have discovered that a participant is on the list of persons to be excluded from the survey, use this statement: "Thank you for this information concerning your employment background. We appreciate your assistance very much. Goodbye."
14. Communities that will be contacted during the interviewing process have been assigned a code number. This number appears at the top of the first page of each set of callsheets. SOME COMMUNITIES WILL SHARE A CODE NUMBER, SO IT IS IMPORTANT THAT YOU COPY DOWN THE NUMBER PROVIDED ON THE TOP OF THE CALLSHEET.
15. If the phone line is busy or if no one answers on the first contact, try that number again during the next calling period. For instance, if you dial the number during the afternoon period (p), try the number again during the evening period (e). If you are still unable to get through to the party, dial the number a third time the following morning (a). EACH NUMBER MUST BE TRIED THREE TIMES BEFORE IT IS CONSIDERED AN "EXHAUSTED" NUMBER.
16. Your telephone area code is <u>*(number)*</u>. The tele-

phone area code has nothing to do with the blank space in the box at the head of the questionnaire that is reserved for an area code.

Recording the Responses on the Questionnaire

You are being supplied with both a black pen and a red pen. Use the black pen to record the responses of the interviewee when they clearly fall within the anticipated response pattern. Use the red pen to highlight an unexpected or unusual response. This will alert the coder that the response needs special attention.

Record the responses accurately. The coder can only decode that which is on the interview form. Be sure that every question is marked with an appropriate response. DO NOT LEAVE ANY BLANKS. Also, do *not* mark more than one response. If you have a question about a respondent's answer, repeat the response you think you heard and ask the respondent to verify that answer. DO NOT BE VAGUE.

BE CAREFUL NOT TO SUPPLY INFORMATION beyond that which a question provides. Do not lead the response in any way.

BE CONSERVATIVE IN YOUR RECORDING. DO NOT INTERPRET THE RESPONDENT AS BEING MORE NEGATIVE OR POSITIVE THAN THE RESPONSE INDICATES. If you feel the response is ambiguous, repeat the question and the response you are thinking of marking, then ask if the response was recorded accurately. For example, the last question before the section on demographics reads, "Do you think your insurance costs today are higher because of large jury awards?" If the respondent answers with "Oh, well, that could be, I guess," do *not* mark that as a *yes* response. Repeat the question and add, "You seemed to indicate a *yes* response. Is that how you would like me to record your answer?" If the respondent answers "yes," then leave the response as recorded. If he or she answers "no," then ask how he or she wants the answer recorded. Provide three choices: *yes, no* or *I don't know.* Pin the person down to one of those three responses.

The Introduction Statement

The introduction statement is contained in the first five lines of the questionnaire beginning with the statement, "My name is ________________." (You should have written your own *true* name in this blank.)

Read the introduction statement *slowly* and clearly, emphasizing the words "citizen survey association" and the part about anonymous nature of the responses.

If at the end of this introduction the person responds negatively, thank him or her and HANG UP. Don't waste time trying to talk the person into participating in the interview.

HOWEVER, if the person says something like "I don't have time right now," ask if he or she will have time later on and try to set up a call-back appointment.

IF at the end of the introduction the person is curious and wants more information ("What is this all about?" or "Could you give me an idea of who is going to be using this information?"), supply them with the following:
PROBE INFORMATION:

> This is a study being conducted by *(name)*, a *(title)*, in *(city, state)*. I work as a research assistant for *(name)*. *(Name)* is interested in current social, legal, and economic issues. The research attempts to determine what attitudes you have about certain questions and how you formed those opinions. In particular, this questionnaire explores the community's assessment of the value of life. If at the end of the interview you still have questions, you can call *(name)* directly at *(number)* and one of the persons in that office who is involved in this research will try to answer your questions more fully.

In general, answer such questions fully and freely but do not waste time. If the person is especially inquisitive, ask the person to contact the office — calling collect if necessary. Call the person back later if you are instructed to complete the contact.

Do not give out the number of the telephone that you are using to conduct the interviews. Explain that the phone is constantly in use and that the individual would only suffer frustration in trying to reach you at that number.

Special Instructions Relating to the Community Attitude Study

Note: Use this form for any specific instructions relating to the particular community involved in the study. Some special instructions might be as follows:

Questions 8, 9, and 10 refer to the scale of one to ten first mentioned in question 7.

Ask question 10 only if the respondent indicates in question 6 that he or she has a license.

In the comments section of question 20, the respondent may think aloud. Record any such statements as accurately as possible. We are particularly interested in such overriding comments as "There's no way to pay for a life, but more money should be given to a young, educated breadwinner."

On open-ended questions, please record responses in detail and as true to the original language as possible, even if it is not grammatically correct.

APPENDIX

3

Civil Case Voir Dire

This appendix includes a basic outline of voir dire subjects for a civil case, followed by examples of basic questions that might be relevant for a particular civil case. All of these questions are merely illustrative. Each lawyer should design voir dire questions in accordance with his or her own style and in keeping with the needs of the particular case.

A. Basic Topic Outline

1. Introductory statement
2. Relationship with persons in the case
   a. Attorneys
   b. Plaintiffs
   c. Defendant
   d. Witnesses, both lay and expert
3. Connection with insurance agencies
4. Organizational affiliations
5. Prior jury experience and attitude toward current jury service
6. Attitude toward the liability alleged
   a. Experience with such areas of liability
   b. Attitude toward such areas of liability
   c. Special interest in such areas of liability
   d. Most damaging features of the case

7. Attitude toward compensation
   a. Acceptance that money is the only viable form of compensation recognized in the American court system
   b. Acceptance of substantial compensation verdicts
   c. Influence of insurance advertising on jury verdicts in compensation cases
8. The question of punitive damages (when applicable)
9. Pretrial publicity
   a. Influence of media (radio, television, and newspapers)
   b. Knowledge of the case as covered by the media
   c. Prior discussions of the case
   d. Hearing opinions of the case by others
   e. Expressions of opinions by the potential juror about what the probable verdict should be
10. Burden of proof
11. Special problems of the case
    a. Prejudgments and prejudices that might apply to the case
    b. Similar unfortunate experiences
    c. Feelings of expertise on the part of the potential jurors that would make them unacceptable or would make them disregard expert testimony
12. Attitude toward plaintiff
    a. In general
    b. Toward the plaintiff's personality
    c. Toward the plaintiff's suffering or damages
13. Attitude toward the attorneys
    a. Acceptance of objections that will be made in the courtroom
    b. Acceptance of discussions that will take place between the attorneys and judge outside the hearing of the jury
14. Attitude toward the verdict
    a. Acceptance of the concept of the two-stage verdict
       1. Determination of liability

2. Determination of compensation for damages or for pain and suffering, etc.

b. Willingness to arrive at a decision on both levels of the case

c. Willingness to vote own convictions

d. Willingness to be a participant in a verdict that might be unpopular with certain groups or with certain members of the community

e. Acceptance of willingness to raise insurance rates if that should be a consideration in the case

B. Examples of Basic Civil Case Voir Dire Questions

Association with the Medical Field[1]

1. Have you ever been trained in a medical area? If so, would you please explain the nature of that training and the extent of that training.
2. Have you or has anyone close to you ever worked for a hospital or for a doctor or had any association with the medical field? Would you please explain to us what that association was?
3. Have you ever studied medicine or gathered medical knowledge on your own? Would you please explain to us the reason for that study and the areas of study?
4. Is there any occasion when you would superimpose your own personal medical knowledge on the testimony that you heard from expert witnesses?
5. Is there anyone here who feels that he or she is a qualified instructor in first aid or in emergency aid of a medical nature? Furthermore, have any of you ever been called on to personally apply medical first aid or to act in a medical emergency?

[1]Questions of the type in this group would be asked when damages are medical in nature.

Fate

1. Do you believe in fate? That is, do you think that some things happen because it is time for them to happen or that they are predestined to happen at that time?
2. Do you believe that when common safety and responsibility standards are followed, many tragic occurrences can be prevented?
3. When something is termed an accident, do you tend to think of it as something that has occurred because of fate, or do you think that it has occurred because someone was careless or did not live up to his or her responsibilities in following common safety procedures? That is, do you feel that the term accident means that there is no fault or liability involved?
4. Do you realize that we as individuals frequently refer to an occurrence as "an accident" when in fact it was not an accident, but rather something that could have been prevented, and that it was, therefore, "an act of irresponsibility" or "an act of fault"?

Negligence

1. The defendants are being charged with negligence and not with any criminal behavior. Is there any juror who does not understand this or who has any questions about what the statement means?
2. Many times when I have heard jurors discuss the facts of a civil case, they will say that the defendant was guilty or not guilty. Do you understand that there is no question of guilt in this case — guilt has to do with criminal cases. In this case we are talking about negligence or the liability that arises from negligence. Do you understand the difference?
3. How do you feel about negligence — that is, is there ever a time when negligence is permissible or understandable? If so, when, in your mind, do you feel that negligence is permissible or when do you feel it is understandable?

4. What does negligence imply to you? Does it mean *committing* an act because of inattention or inexperience or does it mean committing an act that the person knew better or should have known better than to do?

Specific Case Injuries[2]

1. Have you or has any member of your family or a close friend ever suffered a back or leg injury? If so, would you share with us the details of that injury — what was the cause, extent and permanency?
2. Have you or has any person close to you ever spent more than three weeks in a hospital? If so, would you give us full information about that experience?
3. Have you or has any person close to you ever had surgery on his or her spine, neck, or legs?
4. Have you or has any person close to you ever been treated by a physical therapist or occupational therapist? Was there anything about that experience that caused you to form any lasting impressions about either physical therapists or occupational therapists? If so, would you please share those options with us?
5. Have you ever suffered an injury that, though healed, still causes you discomfort or pain? If so, please tell us about it.
6. Have you or has anyone close to you ever been through a series of operations, one after the other, all relating to the same part of the body or the same cause? If so, would you give us full information relating to this?
7. Do you accept the idea of psychological injury or damage that can accompany a physical injury? If not, why not?
8. Do you believe that a physical disorder may result in a personality change or in an alteration of the personality?

[2]These questions are phrased for a case involving a back or leg injury. They should be modified according to the injuries involved in a particular case.

9. Have you ever seen or experienced such an alteration in either your own personality or in the personality of a close friend or relative? Let me also ask that in the reverse: Have you ever seen or known of a person who has suffered severe physical injury who has not also experienced or undergone a personality change or personality alteration?

Attitude Toward Bringing Suit and Compensating For Damages

1. Are you aware that money is the only form of compensation a person can seek under our system of justice?
2. Though money may not be capable of restoring a physical or emotional loss, would you feel justified in determining an amount of money to be paid to a person who has suffered a loss?
3. Do you have any feeling against a person's coming to court and asking monetary compensation[3] for injury and damage done to him or her?
4. Do you believe in making compensation through a fair, just, and adequate verdict to a person who has been injured and damaged entirely through the fault of another person or corporation?
5. If you were injured solely by the negligent conduct of another, would you expect that person to compensate you for those damages?
6. Let me ask that another way: If someone broke into your office and damaged your computer so that it no longer functioned adequately, would you expect that person to pay for repairing the computer or for replacing it? Furthermore, would you expect that person to be responsible for any losses that you incurred while waiting for the computer to be fixed?

[3]The word award should be avoided since it connotes something that a person either wins or is given. It is recommended that the word compensation be used because it connotes something that a person deserves to make up for losses or damages.

7. Do you see any difference in the person who broke your computer having to pay for it and the person who broke part of your body having to pay for it? If you see such a difference, please share your thoughts with us at this time.
8. Under our system of jurisprudence, people like you, the members of this jury, are not only permitted but are required to determine what amount of money in a given case constitutes a fair, just, adequate, and reasonable compensation for a given injury. Do you find any quarrel whatsoever with that system?
9. Naturally, you will want to hear all of the evidence first, but after you have heard all the evidence, if, in your opinion, it would take a very substantial sum of money to make fair compensation to the plaintiff, would you hesitate to bring in a substantial verdict in this case?
10. By adequate, I mean that the amount of money would be sufficient to compensate for all of the elements of damage, whatever they may be, small or large. Do you understand my meaning and do you have any quarrel with that?
11. I want to be certain that you do not have some artificial financial limits that you carry around in your head beyond which you would not make any compensation in money. I say this because some people, no matter how badly they think the plaintiff may have been treated or how much money he or she may have lost or how much damage he or she may have suffered or how much pain and suffering he or she may have endured, will, in their own mind, without telling anyone else, just simply say, "I would not compensate with more than *X* dollars," whatever that figure may be. Do any of you feel that way?
12. Is there anything in your background or in your beliefs that would keep you from making a substantial monetary compensation to the plaintiff for his or her loss and enjoyment of life or for interference with enjoyment of life if he or she proves under the law and by the evidence that he is entitled to recover for such loss?

13. Is there anything in your education, background, experience or belief system that leaves you with any preconceived bias against a person's seeking to recover damages for more than just the expenses incurred? If the evidence shows that the plaintiff was seriously and permanently injured and is therefore entitled to a verdict compensating for those injuries, would you be able to give him or her a firm measure of justice in keeping with the injuries received?
14. Is there anything in your education, background, experience or belief system that makes you feel that a person cannot be compensated with money for pain and suffering? Would you feel this way even if the court instructed you that the plaintiff has the right, under our law, to be compensated for any and all pain and suffering that he has felt or will continue to feel?
15. Let me ask all this from another perspective: Does $1 million in actual damages sound like a high jury verdict to you?
16. How many of you would say to yourself, $1 million is a lot of money? Would you please raise your hand.
17. Can you imagine as you sit here prior to trial and prior to hearing any of the real facts of this case, a set of circumstances and facts that could be presented to you as a juror that would make you say to yourself that this plaintiff deserves $1 million?
18. Let me put that in another way: Are there any of you who feel that $1 million in the verdict is just too much money and that no matter what the facts are, no matter what the evidence shows, it would be impossible for you to return a verdict of $1 million?
19. Is there any one of you on this panel who would sit and look at my client and say, "There's just no way that this person would ever earn or would ever receive $1 million except through some kind of a fluke like this — that is, through some kind of a lawsuit against a person with a lot of money or a corporation with a lot of money"? Is there any one of you who would feel like that?

20. Is there any member of this panel who feels that a person is not fully entitled to recover for the damages that he or she has received when those damages have been great and extensive and have caused major lifestyle changes?
21. In other words, does the word reasonable, when it is used in relationship to the concept of damages in a court case, imply to you a certain amount of money, or an amount of money that has a certain dollar ceiling on it?
22. If a certain dollar amount seems "reasonable" to you in most cases, what amount is it?
23. Is that amount the ceiling that you have in compensating for damages in a case?
24. The court will instruct you that there are certain elements of injury for which the plaintiff is entitled to receive compensation. Will you, as a member of the jury, examine each element to determine the full amount of compensation to which the plaintiff is entitled for that one element and then go on to the next element and make the same determination in order to arrive at the total amount of compensation to which this client is entitled?
25. Once you have reached the sum of the reasonable amounts to which the client is entitled as compensation, will you award that total amount, or will you be a "K-Mart jury" or a discount jury? By that I mean, would you feel it necessary to "knock a little off the top" so that the jury verdict won't be too high or beyond that ceiling you might carry around in your head?

Punitive Damages

1. One question you as jurors on this case will be asked to decide is whether punitive damages should be assessed against an insurance company for not treating its policyholders fairly. If the jury chosen this morning finds against the insurance company on this question,

the jury will *have to recommend* an amount that will serve to punish the company for its unfair treatment and to seriously discourage it from repeating that kind of conduct. Have any of you ever heard of punitive damages?

2. If your child, Johnny, deliberately chose to throw his baseball through a plate glass window, you as a parent would have to decide whether tapping Johnny on the wrist and saying "Now, Johnny, please don't do that again" is really adequate punishment to seriously discourage Johnny from doing something like that again. What you as a juror will be called on to do in this case, if the law and the evidence indicate that you *must recommend* an amount of punitive damages, is to take on a role just like the parent who must determine what to do about Johnny. Is there any reason why you could not take on this responsibility for determining the issue of punitive damages?
3. Those of you familiar with the term punitive damages may realize that if you as jurors *have to recommend* an amount of punitive damages, those damages will go to the plaintiffs. Is there any reason why you could not return a recommended verdict on punitive damages?
4. In your deliberations if you decide that you *have to recommend* an amount for punitive damages, do you think it would make any difference to you in your approach to the law and the evidence on punitive damages if instead of Mrs. Jones who represents the four Jones children, I was representing the American Cancer Society seeking an assessment of punitive damages against this insurance company?
5. What I'm really asking is whether you could approach the responsibilities of deciding the issue of punitive damages, including the amount, just as if I represented the American Cancer Society?
6. If under the law and the evidence you as jurors arrive at the conviction that the recommended verdict on punitive damages should be millions of dollars, would you be reluctant to vote that conviction?

Burden of Proof

1. Are you aware that there is a difference between the burden of proof in a criminal case and the burden of proof in a civil case?
2. How many of you have served in a jury trial in a criminal case? How many in a civil case?
3. The court will instruct you that the plaintiff has the burden of proof in a civil case. Since this is a civil case, we must prove by a preponderance of the evidence that the defendant is liable for our damages. Now, I know that sounds like a lot of technical and legal language. What that means simply is that if we had a scale and if the scale were evenly balanced, as it is in your minds right now at the beginning of the trial, all we would have to do as the plaintiff in this case would be to tip that scale slightly so that the evidence would tend to show that the defendant is liable for the damages. Do you understand the concept that I am discussing with you?
4. Do any of you have any difficulty in differentiating between these two concepts: (1) that there is a burden of proof by a preponderance of the evidence, which is the burden of proof we have in this civil case; (2) that there is also a burden of proof beyond a reasonable doubt, which is the burden of proof that exists in a criminal case? If you have difficulty in understanding this, please raise your hand and we will try to explain in greater detail what the differences are.
5. Do you have any difficulty in understanding the standard of "preponderance of the evidence"?
6. Would you have any difficulty applying the standard of "preponderance of the evidence" rather than the standard of "beyond a reasonable doubt" in this case?

APPENDIX

4

Criminal Case Voir Dire

This appendix includes a basic outline of voir dire subjects for a criminal case, followed by examples of basic questions that might be relevant for a particular criminal case. All of these questions are merely illustrative. Each lawyer should design voir dire questions in accordance with his or her own style and in keeping with the needs of the particular case.

A. Basic Topic Outline

1. Introductory statement
2. Relationship with persons in the case
   a. Attorneys
   b. Defendants
   c. Victim
3. Connection with law enforcement agencies or personnel within those agencies
4. Organizational affiliations
5. Prior jury experience and attitude toward current jury service
6. Attitude toward crime alleged
   a. Experience with crime alleged
   b. Opinion toward crime charged
   c. Nature of the defense and attitudes of potential jurors toward that defense
   d. Most damaging features of the case

7. Pretrial publicity
   a. Influence of media (television, radio, or newspapers)
   b. Knowledge of media coverage
   c. Discussions of the case with others
   d. Hearing of opinions or statements of knowledge of the case in discussions with others
   e. Expression of opinion by potential juror
8. Burden of proof and presumption of innocence
   a. Assurance of jurors' understanding of these concepts
   b. Special problems that might arise under this particular type of defense
9. Special problems with prejudice or prejudgment
   a. Racial prejudice
   b. Prejudice in favor of police officers or against police officers
   c. Prejudice toward a particular group, organization, or affiliate group
   d. Unfortunate experiences with any such group that might lead to prejudgment
   e. Ability to accept prejudgment or prejudice and to deal with the case in spite of such prejudgment or prejudice
10. Attitude toward the defendant
    a. In general
    b. Toward possible prior criminal record
    c. In case the defendant will not take the stand in his or her own behalf
11. Attitude toward the attorneys and the judge or the justice system in general
    a. Attitude toward objections
    b. Attitude toward conferences that will occur out of hearing of the jury
12. Attitude toward the verdict
    a. Willingness to reach a decision
    b. Willingness to vote their consciences
    c. Willingness to participate in a verdict that would be

unpopular in the community or that would be unpopular to certain groups of people

B. Examples of Basic Criminal Case Voir Dire Questions

Presumption of Innocence

1. My client, Mr. Thomas, has been charged with a crime by means of an indictment. Do you all realize that an indictment is merely a piece of paper used to bring a defendant into court in the same way that a complaint is used in a civil case? Is there anyone who does not realize that?
2. Is there anyone who does not realize that an indictment is merely a formal legal pleading, a piece of paper that is filed by the prosecutor simply in order to start these proceedings and that it has no weight of evidence or testimony? Do you all realize that?
3. Of course, you have all heard many times that a person is presumed innocent until proven guilty beyond a reasonable doubt. Now, let's examine that statement and see if it is one that you, as prospective jurors, really believe. How many of you think that the police tend to arrest innocent people? Please raise your hand.
4. How many of you think that innocent people are, indeed, arrested by the local police? Please raise your hand.
5. How many of you believe that if an innocent man is arrested by the police, then hires an attorney, and then has the prosecutor's staff look over the charges leveled against him by the police, that there still would be a possibility, a strong possibility, that that person would sit in court and not be guilty of the crime as charged? Please raise your hand.[1]

[1] If you have people who do not raise their hand in response to this question, then pick out individual jurors and ask them the same series of questions and see whether they actually know of an instance when the local police

6. Now, members of the jury, we are asking you to follow the concepts of justice that are guaranteed to defendants in this country, to give to the defendant all of the rights guaranteed by the law of our nation and by the Constitution. We are asking you as jurors in this case to give the defendant the benefit of the presumption of innocence without any mental reservations whatsoever. Is there anyone on this panel who feels that that is asking too much? Please raise your hand.
7. Furthermore, under our American system of justice, you, as jurors, are to consider this presumption of innocence as actual proof of innocence until this presumption is overcome by proof of guilt — proof of guilt that has been presented by the state and that reaches beyond a reasonable doubt. Is there anyone who feels that that is asking too much? Do you realize, then, that it is your duty as a juror to believe the explanation or the statement of denial offered by the defendant, Mr. Thomas, at this time? That it is your duty to believe him when he says that he is not guilty and to continue to believe him and to accept his explanation of what happened until such time as the state can move you to believe in his guilt beyond a reasonable doubt? Are there any of you who would have trouble with being that fair to the defendant or in following the dictates of the system of American law as so ordered?
8. Do all of you now have an understanding of what the presumption of innocence actually means? Is there anyone who could not give me his or her promise that he or she would give the defendant the full benefit of the presumption of innocence?

---

have arrested innocent people. Drive home the fact that, generally speaking, most people believe that when a person is arrested and brought to trial — that is, when a person has been indicted, arrested, and has had his or her case reviewed by the prosecutor — that that person is considered guilty as charged. Ask the prospective jurors the basis for their disagreement with this concept.

Burden of Proof

1. You know, don't you, that the state and the prosecutor have the burden of proof in this case?
2. That means that the state must prove its case to your satisfaction beyond a reasonable doubt and to a moral certainty. Do you think that that places too much of a burden on the state?
3. Your understand, do you not, that the burden of proving my client guilty beyond a reasonable doubt rests totally with the prosecutor and the state and that the accused, my client, need not introduce any evidence whatsoever, at any time during this case?
4. Knowing that, would you require my client at any time to show to you that he or she is innocent or to prove to you that he or she is innocent?
5. I want to be certain that you understand the principle of burden of proof. Will you, at any time, expect me, as the lawyer for my client, to prove to you that my client is innocent rather than placing the burden of proof on the prosecutor and the state, so that they must prove to you that my client is guilty beyond a reasonable doubt?
6. Let us examine some of the other rights and privileges that a defendant has under the American system of government. You do understand, don't you, that the burden of proof is always on the prosecution and that the defendant need never present any evidence on his behalf? Let me explain to you what that means. We, the defense, can cross-examine the witnesses or can cast doubt on the evidence as presented by the state and when the state rests — that is, when the state says that it is finished with its case — we can stand up before you, the jurors, and the judge and we can say that we do not feel that the state has presented a case that is strong enough to cast reasonable doubt on the statements that have been made by our defendant, Mr. Thomas. Do you understand that that is our right?
7. Furthermore, do you understand that it is the right of

the defendant not to testify in his own behalf? That he need never take the stand and tell anything at all to the jury?

8. Let us talk a little bit more about the burden of proof, which rests solely on the shoulders of the prosecution. Do you understand that all the elements of the crime charged must be proven beyond a reasonable doubt and that if even one element is not proven, then you should vote not guilty?
9. If the prosecution fails to prove the guilt of the accused — that is, the guilt of our client, Mr. Thomas, who is seated here in the courtroom with you — if it cannot prove his guilt beyond that degree of moral certainty that amounts to proof beyond a reasonable doubt, then you realize that you would have to vote not guilty if you are going to carry out your oath as a juror. Do you understand that?
10. When I was talking with my daughter last night, she asked me how I was going to prove Mr. Thomas innocent. Now, I find all too often when I go into court that that is the attitude, not only of a six-year-old child, but also of many adults. Is there anyone on the panel who does not now understand that my client does not have to prove that he is innocent, but that he is presumed to be innocent — in fact, that presumption is the proof of his innocence and he does not have to prove anything to anybody but all of the proof instead must come from that side of the table, from the prosecutors who represent the state. Is there anyone who does not now understand that my client does not have to prove his innocence but that the state must prove beyond a reasonable doubt that he is guilty as charged?

Reasonable Doubt[2]

1. Mrs. Jones, you have indicated that you know that the defendant, Mr. Smith, is innocent as he sits in this chair

[2]This series of questions would follow questions on presumption of innocence and burden of proof and would be asked by the defense.

today, or at least that he is presumed to be innocent, isn't that right?

2. Mrs. Jones, if you were to vote right now before any evidence were presented or before any testimony were heard, how would you have to vote?
3. (NOTE: If the prospective juror responds that she would have to hear the evidence first, ask the following question.)

   If you had to vote, even though it would be unreasonable or unlikely that you would have to vote at this time, what would you have to vote under the law of the American system of justice? (If the prospective juror says that she simply couldn't vote at this time, ask the following question.) Is the reason that you couldn't vote because somewhere in the back of your mind, you feel that Mr. Smith is in court for a reason and you have a suspicion that Mr. Smith might be guilty or he wouldn't be in court?

   Mrs. Jones, don't you believe that where there is smoke, there is probably fire or at least there is some kind of a smoke bomb?

   (NOTE: It is important that the juror eventually answer that by the law of the United States, if he or she were asked to cast a vote before hearing the evidence, he or she would have to cast a vote of not guilty.)
4. Knowing that the defendant, Mr. Smith, is presumed innocent at this time, do you understand that whatever explanation he has to offer as to why he was present at the scene or why circumstances led to his arrest, you, as jurors, would have to accept that explanation unless the state is able to give you proof beyond a reasonable doubt that the story is not true? Is there anybody who has any problem with that or who doesn't understand that aspect of the law?
5. Now, let's say that you have sat through the trial and you have heard the testimony and you have seen the evidence and now you are going back into the jury room and you are going to be required to cast a vote. Now, Mrs. Jones, when you get back into the jury room, you

just say to yourself, "I *suspect* that maybe Mr. Smith committed the crime in the way the State said that he did. I just have a *suspicion* that it could have happened that way." How are you going to vote, Mrs. Jones?

(NOTE: Obviously, the juror must be led to say "not guilty." It should also be noted that the more often you can get the jurors to actually say the words "not guilty," the more strongly you will instill in their minds that this is, indeed, a realistic verdict that can be brought in. Therefore, as often as possible, have as many of the jurors as possible utter the words "not guilty.")

6. Now, Mrs. Jones, let's say that rather than just having a *suspicion* that Mr. Smith committed the crime in the way that the State said he did, you say to yourself, "You know, I think he *possibly* committed the crime that way." Now, Mrs. Jones, how are you going to vote?

   (NOTE: And of course, again the juror will have to respond "not guilty.")

7. Now, Mrs. Jones, let's say that the evidence and the testimony were stronger so that when you went back into the jury room you said to yourself, "I don't know, but I think Mr. Smith *probably* committed the crime just the way the state said. I'm pretty sure he probably did it in that fashion." Now, Mrs. Jones, how would you vote?

   (NOTE: And of course, once more the prospective juror must answer "not guilty."

8. Now, Mrs. Jones. Let me just be clear that we both have the same understanding. If you have just a *suspicion* that Mr. Smith committed the crime in the way that the state says he did, you are going to vote how? (Again the juror must say "not guilty.") And if you think that he *possibly* committed the crime that way, how are you going to vote? (Again the juror would have to say "not guilty.") And if you say that he *probably* committed the crime in the way that the state says, how are you going to vote? (The juror would again have to say "not guilty.")

9. (NOTE: The questions would now be addressed to a

different juror.) Mr. Conway, how do you feel about that? Do you think that it is reasonable to ask the state to prove the case beyond a *suspicion* of guilt, beyond a *possibility* of guilt, and even beyond a *probability* of guilt? Do you think that is too much of a burden to ask the state to bear?

10. This is a very important element of the American criminal justice system, so I am just going to go down the line of prospective jurors and I am going to ask each of you how much evidence it is going to take for you to find Mr. Smith guilty as charged in this crime?

    (NOTE: Each juror at this time should be encouraged to say "beyond a reasonable doubt.")

11. Since this is such an important issue to me, to my client, and to the American system of criminal justice, I want to ask you to raise your hand if you would be willing to find my client guilty just because you *suspected* that he might be guilty? (Pause.) Now, I'm going to ask you to raise your hand if you would be willing to find my client guilty because you think that he *possibly* committed the crime. Please raise your hand. (Pause.) And, finally, I am going to ask you if there is anyone who would be willing to find my client guilty if he *probably* performed the crime in the way the state says. Will you please raise your hand. (Pause.) And now, how many of you would be willing to find my client guilty if the state proved its case *beyond a reasonable doubt*? Please raise your hands.[3]

Defendant's Right Not to Testify[4]

1. You have been told that it is the defendant's right not to take the stand to testify on his own behalf. You have all indicated that you have no problem with that. But, if we

[3] All jurors should raise their hands. If any juror does not raise his or her hand, address that juror and find out why he or she would be unwilling to find your client guilty if the state proved its case beyond a reasonable doubt. Use that juror to demonstrate all over again what is or is not a reasonable doubt.

[4] The reactions of prospective jurors during trial simulations to the refusal of

are looking at this realistically, you would, Mrs. Jones, really want to hear both sides of the story, wouldn't you?

2. If Mr. Thomas decided not to testify on his own behalf, what reasons do you think he might have for not doing so?[5]
3. Mr. Conway, if someone made a charge against you and if that charge was false, would you want to explain to your friends and neighbors, and to jurors sitting in judgment of you, why it is false?
4. Is there any reason that you can see, Mr. Conway, that you would not give or offer an explanation? In other words, Mr. Conway, in your heart of hearts, you would feel that if Mr. Thomas did not take the stand and explain the story, that it must be because he has something to hide or it must be because he is afraid of something?[6]

---

a defendant to take the stand on his or her own behalf are almost always totally negative. If a defendant refuses to take the stand, prospective jurors tend to believe that he or she has done so for one or more of the following reasons: (1) The defendant has something to hide; (2) If the defendant took the stand, information about his or her past would come out that would be detrimental; (3) The defendant is not a good enough liar to take the stand and will, therefore, depend on a "professional liar" (the lawyer) to do the job; and (4) The defendant is too dumb or is insane or has something else mentally or physically wrong with him that prohibits him or her from taking the stand.

It has been determined by conducting trial simulations that if any one of the following obtains, the defendant who does not testify on his or her own behalf will be found guilty: (1) If the defendant is unattractive; (2) If the defendant is from a different part of the country; (3) If the defendant has no weeping or concerned-looking wife, mother, or children present in the courtroom to support him or her; or (4) If the defendant has a prior criminal record, no matter how insignificant or dated.

If the attorney feels that it is important in a particular case that the defendant not take the stand, then this group of questions should be asked during voir dire.

[5]Obviously, most of the jurors are going to volunteer negative statements as to why they feel the defendant wouldn't take the stand. There is no reason to be fearful of this. If they feel that way, they are going to discuss it in the jury room. You might as well deal with it during voir dire so it will not become an issue of contention during deliberations.

[6]If the juror is firm in his or view that a defendant who does not take the stand is guilty by implication, the juror should be challenged for cause.

(NOTE: The questions would now be addressed to a different juror.)

5. Mr. Elliott, do you think that most people want to hear both sides of a story?
6. Now, Mr. Elliott, do you accept the principle of law that says that there is no reason why a defendant has to tell or is required to tell or even should tell his side of the story, so to speak, do you understand that?
7. Do you realize that the only story that needs to be told in this courtroom is the side that is presented by the state and that that side must contain evidence and must contain statements that are so strong that they go beyond a moral certainty, that they go beyond a reasonable doubt in convincing you that Mr. Thomas actually committed the acts with which he is charged?
8. Do you realize that there are other ways of showing that the side presented by the state is unworthy: That might be by cross-examining its witnesses and establishing that their testimony is so confused and so weak that it will not raise the level of evidence above a suspicion, a possibility, or a probability that Mr. Thomas committed the crime? Can you accept that as a possibility of what could happen in this courtroom? Is there anyone who could not? Please raise your hand so that we can discuss it at this time.
9. Again, let me ask, would any of you require in your own heart or in your own mind that the accused take the stand to satisfy you that he is innocent?
10. Is there any one of you who will feel that the accused has not shown full cooperation by failing to take the stand or who will hold it against him for any reason at all? Is there any one of you who feels that you would deliberately deny him his right not to take the stand and that you would not only deny him his right not to take the stand but that you would hold it against him and would use it as proof against him?
11. One last time I would like to ask you if there is any one of you who would consider the defendant's failure to

testify as an indication of his guilt or of his unwillingness to fully cooperate in defending his own case. If so, please raise your hand.[7]

Prior Conviction of the Defendant: Murder[8]

1. Mr. Jones, I want to tell you something right up front. I don't know whether you have read it in the newspaper or heard it on television, but I want to be certain you know something about Pat Murphy. Pat Murphy has been previously convicted of murder. Pat Murphy has served time for that murder that occurred ten years ago. Have you ever known a convicted murderer?
2. Do you have any expectations about what a convicted murderer is like or any expectations about how a convicted murderer would act?

   (NOTE: Almost always, the prospective juror will answer this series of questions in the negative.)
3. I haven't told you anything about the situation of the murder that Pat Murphy committed when he was 32 years old. Do you feel that knowing the details of that murder that occurred ten years ago would help you determine whether Pat Murphy is guilty of this murder that occurred on September 12, 1980?

   (NOTE: The answer that the juror should give to this question is obviously "no.")

[7]There are generally two reasons for not putting the defendant on the stand: (1) The fact that he or she could be impeached through the showing of prior convictions; (2) Fear that the defendant cannot withstand a vigorous cross-examination.

If prior convictions are admitted up front during voir dire, and if the defendant has received the proper kind of pretrial work in preparation for testimony, neither one of these considerations are as potentially damaging as the jurors' negativism toward the absence of the defendant's testimony.

[8]A prior conviction for murder is used as an example here because it is one of the worst felonies that can be submitted to a jury prior to putting the defendant on the stand. Information concerning prior convictions should be presented early in the voir dire. Often it should be the first information given to the prospective jurors after the basic demographic information has been gathered.

4. Does the information that you have just been given shock you or cause you such alarm that you would rather not sit on this case as a juror?
5. Now that you have received this information, do you feel that you are trying two trials here — the murder that Pat Murphy was convicted of ten years ago plus the current case being tried in this court?
6. Is there anyone here who feels that knowing what occurred ten years ago would have any meaning, would lend any validity or credibility to any of the charges that are being brought today?
7. Mr. Harrison, is there any act that you committed ten or fifteen years ago that you wouldn't want your son to commit today?
8. Is there any action or any behavior that you took ten or fifteen years ago that it is unlikely to be committed again by you today?
9. Is there any person on the panel who believes that just because you have done something once, it *necessarily* means that you will do it a second time or a third or a fourth time?
10. Now we know that there are things that can become habits. These are things that we do over and over and over again and frequently as we do them over and over we don't even stop to think about them. Is there anyone on the panel who thinks that committing a crime is something that, generally speaking, becomes a habit and is therefore something that is done over and over and over again without thinking?

    (NOTE: If the defendant is, indeed, a habitual criminal, this line of questioning probably would not be desirable.)
11. I have told you now that Pat Murphy has been previously convicted of murder. How many of you feel that you honestly could put that completely out of your mind and never refer to it again during the whole course of the trial? Of course not, it would be foolish of me to ask you to do that. You have now received that

information and it is information that you will use to evaluate other information that comes your way. But I do not think it is foolish of me to ask you to put that information in its proper place and to evaluate the testimony and the evidence that will be presented to you in this trial, not as a defense of this prior conviction but as a defense or as a standard of proof in this particular case, which is the State of ________________ v. Pat Murphy. Can you all assure me that you will do your best to evaluate Pat Murphy as he sits before you in this courtroom today and not the ghost of Pat Murphy that hovers behind the chair and who was convicted of murder ten years ago?

12. In other words, as you prospective jurors sit here now, do you feel that you could decide the issues in this case irrespective of any actions that occurred ten years ago and that do not directly pertain to this case?
13. The information that we have just shared with you isn't going to disturb you or bother you so much that you will use it greatly to influence your decision, is it? If so, please raise your hand.
14. Is there anyone who feels that the standards of proof or the presumption of innocence or the burden of proof should be different for Pat Murphy just because ten years ago he was found guilty in a trial for murder? Is there any person on this panel who would today say that Pat Murphy is not entitled to every single right that any defendant that is tried in this courtroom is entitled to?
15. Now that you know that Pat Murphy is a convicted murderer, are you going to make it easier for the state to convict him again or are you going to make it just as difficult for the state to convict him on these charges as if Pat Murphy had never done anything wrong in his entire life?
16. Will you all promise me that this prior conviction Pat Murphy has admitted to will have nothing at all to do

with the verdict that you bring in? Please raise your hand if you can give me that assurance.

17. Now, I would like to carry this one step further. We all know that there will be only 12 people deliberating in the jury room when you reach the verdict. Now, if one of you should forget this promise that you have made and if you should say something like "once a murderer, always a murderer," will the other 11 of you remind that juror of his or her assurance, his or her commitment, that has been given, so that Pat Murphy will be tried only on the evidence that is presented in this courtroom and only on the testimony of the witnesses that are present in this courtroom, and that he will not also be tried by the shadows of a prior conviction? Will you all accept that as one of the duties that goes along with your oath as jurors?

Prior Convictions of the Defendant: In General

1. If, during the course of this trial, my client takes the stand and admits that he or she has had previous involvements with the law, how will you respond to the testimony he or she gives at this time as to the facts in this case? What I'm asking is how many of you will give him or her as much credibility as you would if there had not been previous convictions? Please raise your hand.
2. Are you going to say that because he or she was convicted of a crime on another occasion at another time during his life, that he or she is more likely to be guilty of this crime? If you believe that, please raise your hand?
3. Are you going to think that because a person has been found guilty of a crime, he or she cannot be believed under any circumstances?
4. Or are you going to carefully listen to the testimony and determine from the facts and the circumstances surrounding the case whether the testimony presented is reasonable and believable?

5. You would not want to convict an innocent person, would you, merely because that person had a prior conviction? If you feel that way, please raise your hand.
6. Will you assure me that you will not allow the previous record of my client to interfere with your evaluation of the testimony that he or she will give to you from the witness stand in this case?
7. Our system of justice dictates that each case should stand or fall on its own merits. Is there anyone who disagrees with that concept? If so, please raise your hand.
8. If you believe that, then anything that might have happened in another case is not relevant to the question of guilt or innocence in this case. Do you all accept that not only as a principle of law but also as a guideline that you will use in determining the verdict in this case?

Prior Experience with Crime, Especially as a Victim

1. Have you personally ever been a victim of a crime? If yes, please tell us the nature of the crime and when it occurred and what was the final outcome of the investigation of that crime. If there is any reason why you would wish privacy in responding to this question, please raise your hand and ask for permission to approach the bench.
2. Has any member of your family or has a close friend ever been a victim of a crime? If so, where and when and what type of crime?
3. The crime that is charged in this case is ________ ________________. Do you see any similarity between the crime in which you were a victim or in which a friend or relative was a victim and this crime? Would you please tell us where you feel that similarity lies? Is there any reason why your previous experience as the victim of a crime would hinder you from being a fair and impartial juror on this case?

4. Following the crime, were you interviewed by the police?
5. Were you satisfied by the activities and actions that were used by the police in following up?
6. Was there an extensive investigation of that crime?
7. Was that crime ever solved?
8. Is there anything about the investigation of the crime that leads you to have any feelings for or against the police department of your city? Is there anything about those feelings that would make you unable to be a fair and impartial juror in this case, that is, a fair and impartial juror for both the defendant and for the state?
9. After having been a victim of that crime or after having participated in the investigation of that crime, have you developed a special awareness about criminal events in your neighborhood or in your community? Specifically, have you become active in any groups or any organizations that have as a goal the prevention of crime or the reduction of crime in the community? What is the nature of that organization with which you are involved and what activities have you participated in?

Eye Witnesses

1. One of the principal witnesses in this case is a person who claims to be an eye witness. Have any of you ever been an eye witness to an accident or to a criminal event or to any occurrence that you have later been called on to report?
2. Have any of you taken psychology classes in which you participated in experimentation with the amount of memory that an eye witness might have?
3. In weighing the identification of the defendant that will be made by the eye witness, will you consider the witness's capacity for memorization?
4. Will you consider his or her familiarity with the defendant?
5. Will you consider the conditions under which the observations were made?

6. Would you consider any bias or prejudice he or she may have toward the accused?
7. Would you consider the amount of time that the witness had to observe the defendant?[9]
8. Are you aware that much of the psychological investigation of eye witness accounts demonstrates that the manner in which the question is first addressed to the eye witness will determine to a great extent what the eye witness will recall or will remember at a later date?
9. Do you recognize in your own daily experience how difficult it is to remember something with accuracy and with clear mental images?
10. In your own experience have you, yourself, ever mistakenly confused a stranger for a person you know very well?
11. Do you agree that the identity of the defendant as the person who committed the crime must be shown to you with such certainty as to eliminate any possibility of error?
12. Do you feel that one eye witness is sufficient to convict or do you feel that there must be additional information to back up that eye witness account?
13. Do you feel that when someone has observed something during a time of shock that either a mental image is indelibly imprinted on that observer's mind or, because of the emotion occurring at the time, that observer's perception of details is confused or distorted? Are there any of you who strongly favor one theory over the other or will you let the evidence show which of these theories tends to draw more credibility in this particular case?

[9]If, as is frequently the case, the amount of time the eye witness actually had to observe the defendant was very short, then at this time it might be wise to inject a psychological-emotional catchphrase that would be used in identifying and evaluating the witness's credibility; for instance, refer to "the two-second witness" or "the intoxicated observer."

14. Do any of you have any feelings about the reinforcement of impressions? By that I mean that if you have observed a crime and later you are shown photographs of persons by the police, who then ask you to identify the perpetrator of the crime in a lineup, do you think that your original impression of the person might have been affected by the photographs and the lineup?

When a Child Is a Witness: In Anticipation of Cross-Examination by the Defense

1. In this case a child is going to be a witness. In judging the credibility of a child witness, would you take into account his or her age, intelligence, ability to perceive and observe, realizing that life or liberty of the accused is at stake?
2. Do any of you feel that just because a child is going to testify, that whatever the child says has to be the truth?
3. Is there anyone who would quarrel with the concept that as we gain in age, we gain in experience, and that this maturity helps us to absorb situations of shock and therefore be better observers during unusual circumstances or unusual situations?
4. Is there anyone who feels that as a general rule, adults are more susceptible to suggestion than children are?
5. Is there anyone who doubts that it is easier for a child to mix fact with fiction or to allow the imagination greater play than it normally would be for an adult?
6. Furthermore, is there anyone who does not realize that when the child is on the stand we, as defense attorneys, fully realize that this is a stressful situation for the child and that we will not be able to ask some of the more searching and more probing questions that we might put to an adult?
7. We do not want to appear to you to be monsters. Neither do we want to neglect a full defense of our client's case. Can you, as jurors in this case, appreciate

the delicate balance that we must maintain between not traumatizing a child who is already traumatized by being required to appear as a witness in a criminal case and in trying to defend our client to the fullest? We ask in advance that you understand that problem that we have. Is there any one of you on the jury who feels that if we ask any questions in cross-examination at all of the child, that we are being cruel or that we are being inhuman?

When a Child Is a Witness: In Anticipation of Direct Examination by the Prosecution

1. Is there anyone on this panel who feels that just because a person is under the age of what we might call adulthood, that that person is an unreliable source of information?
2. Is there any person on the panel who feels that we are taking unfair advantage of a child by bringing that child into court and asking that child to testify as to what he or she saw or heard under certain circumstances if that is evidence in this court case?
3. We all know that frequently children are not taken into account by adults as fully as other adults are — that is, we know that we have a tendency to neglect the presence of a child. For this reason, children are sometimes in positions where they can see things or hear things without adults being aware of it or concerned about it if they were aware of it. If this were to be the case here, would you understand that the child would be able to come into the courtroom and supply evidence even though he or she might not realize the full implication or the full meaning of what that evidence might be?
4. Is there anyone on the panel who feels that we should avoid presenting a child as a witness? For any reason at all, will you hold it against the state because we have asked a child to come into court and to testify as to what he or she saw and heard?

Innoculation against Personality Defect of a Witness[10]

1. In this courtroom you are going to be asked as jurors to judge the case and to reach a verdict based on what you believe to be the truth from among the facts and the testimony presented to you by the two sides. You have all indicated that you could make decisions concerning the credibility of witnesses. I would, at this time, simply like to determine that the standards you use are those that can easily be applied to all of the witnesses in the case. For instance, one of our witnesses, Mary Jo, is a very shy person. She hesitates to look people in the eye, she talks in a very soft manner, she is easily frightened and she tends not to like to be among strangers. Now Mary Jo is going to be asked to come into court and to do all of those things that she finds very difficult. When you observe Mary Jo on the stand, if she talks softly, if she appears to be highly nervous, or if she gets flustered easily when we ask her questions or when she is cross-examined by the other side, will you be able to distinguish between those manners that result from her shyness and those manners that you might normally attribute to a person who is not telling the truth? If there is anyone who feels that he or she would have any trouble at all in doing this, would you please raise your hand so we can discuss it.
2. I am especially concerned about Mary Jo's lack of eye contact. How many of you believe that a person who is telling the truth tends to look you in the eye?

[10]In this particular case, we will be asking questions about a witness who is shy and who tends not to establish eye contact or to speak up loudly and clearly and who is easily intimidated by cross-examination. The same types of questions should be modeled to fit witnesses with other personality problems, such as stuttering, facial tics, highly nervous habits, or anything else that might be deemed by the jurors to be behavior that is indicative of a lack of credibility. If a witness normally suffers from a speech impediment due to a physical ailment — the slurred speech of a stroke victim, for example — that information should also be presented to the jurors prior to the actual physical presentation of that witness.

3. If Mary Jo never looks anyone in the eye, not even me or a close friend, except under very unusual circumstances, would you feel that she was lying?
4. Is there anyone on the panel who is going to hold it against Mary Jo and who is not going to believe her testimony if she acts in a nervous, shy manner and doesn't establish eye contact with anyone?
5. You realize that there are expert witnesses and lay witnesses. Many of the police officers or the officers who will be representing the government in this case have been on the stand many, many times. Many of our witnesses will be there for the first time and this is going to be a very new experience for them, one that they will find frightening. Will you realize that it is for this reason that Mary Jo is perhaps going to demonstrate some highly nervous and some highly shy mannerisms while she is testifying?
6. Do you further realize that many of the witnesses who are testifying for the prosecution are witnesses who personally have nothing to gain or to lose by their testimony but that Mary Jo considers the defendant to be a very close friend, a person that she admires? Do you realize that her friendship for the defendant adds to her stress and emphasizes, rather than diminishes, her shyness and her nervousness? Can you all understand that and accept that?

Violence[11]

1. How do you feel about violence?
2. Mr. Jones, do you approve of violence?
3. Mr. Jones, is there any time when you feel that violence is justified?[12]

[11] If violence is an issue, especially the violence that might be connected with a self-defense case, the following questions would elicit potential jurors' attitudes and would also serve as conditioning questions.

[12] Generally, potential jurors will indicate that violence would be justified in

4. In order for you to condone violence, would you have to say that the danger was real or perceived?
5. If His Honor (Her Honor), the judge, instructs you that a person who *perceives* that his or her life or property is threatened has the same right of self-defense as the person who actually does have his or her life or property endangered, would you accept that as a valid principle of law? Is there anyone who has a problem with this concept?
6. Does the mere fact that violence occurred or that there was bloodshed connected with the violence so upset you that you would find it difficult to serve as a juror in this case?

Effect of Police Officers in the Courtroom

1. How many of you have not noticed the presence of armed police officers in this courtroom? Please raise your hand.
2. Does the fact that there are armed police officers in this courtroom create in your mind any impression of violence or guilt or innocence or passivity in the defendant?
3. Does the fact that you see these armed guards when you come into this courtroom create in your mind any concept or any impression of guilt or potential violence? Please raise your hand if that is so.
4. When my client, the defendant, Mr. Ames enters this courtroom and receives treatment that is commonly identified as criminal treatment, does that treatment cause you to view my client not only as person who is currently being treated as a criminal but also as a person who must *be* a criminal? What I am really asking, ladies and gentlemen of the jury, is can you observe these behaviors and these actions toward my client, the de-

---

defense of property or life or family. If they do not volunteer on their own one of these responses, then questions that would lead them to respond in this fashion should be addressed to them.

fendant in this case, and still consider him to be potentially not guilty, or do these extreme security measures so color your image of the defendant that you cannot help but wonder if that person is guilty?

5. Do security measures, such as those that you have observed in the hallway and in the courtroom connected with my client, create in you a suspicion of guilt or a suspicion of possible or probable violence?

Different Lifestyle of Defendant[13]

1. How do you feel about people whose lifestyles are vastly different from your own? Do you feel they are strange or different or unusual and that that strangeness or unusualness poses a threat to your own lifestyle?
2. Have you ever expressed any hostility toward people who follow a lifestyle different from your own?
3. Have you ever expressed irritation with persons who drive motorcycles "as if they owned the highway"?
4. How do you feel about persons who use drugs or who recommend or support the use of drugs?
5. When you see someone whose dress is significantly different from the typical business dress of the typical middle-class dress, do you feel that that person is a threat to the American way of life, or that he or she must hold attitudes or opinions that oppose those of middle-class white Americans?

Drug Use

1. Would you please raise your hand if you feel that marijuana should be decriminalized?

[13]These questions would be asked especially when the lifestyle of the defendant is vastly different from that of the average white middle-class American. If the person were a homosexual, a member of a motorcycle gang, or were in any other way significantly different, then questions modeled after these would be highly recommended.

2. Would you please raise your hand if you feel that marijuana should be legalized?
3. Miss Claypool, what do you think about people who use marijuana or who smoke marijuana?
4. Do you consider the use of marijuana to be habit-forming?
5. Do you feel that the use of marijuana destroys the human mind or the human memory or has any other detrimental effects on the human body?
6. Please raise your hand if you have read articles considering the abuse or misuse of drugs.
7. Please raise your hand if you have read articles or newspaper items that connect the use of drugs with an increase in the crime rate.
8. Will you please raise your hand if you feel that there is a direct connection between drug use and the rising crime rate?
9. I cannot ask you how many of you have smoked marijuana, since it is a crime in this state, or how many of you have been around other people who have smoked marijuana. But let me ask you this: How many of you favor the legalization of marijuana in this state? Please raise your hand.
10. How many of you feel that the use of marijuana directly leads to the use of harder drugs or drugs that we would consider to be addictive?
11. How many of you feel that the use of marijuana is addictive?
12. How many of you feel, aside from the fact that the use of marijuana is illegal and the use of alcohol is not illegal, that drinking is a better way of getting high than using marijuana? If that is what you feel, please raise your hand.
13. How many of you feel that a person's use of marijuana or some other drug makes him or her more likely to commit a crime than a person who uses alcohol? Please raise your hand and hold it high.

Right to Bear Arms

1. Do you own a hunting rifle or shotgun?
2. Even if you do not, have you ever hunted?
3. Do you own a firearm of any kind?
4. Do you own a gun that you keep in a certain place, either in your home or in your place of business, for your protection?
5. Do you believe that a citizen has the right to keep arms in his or her home or place of business for self-protection?
6. Do you belong to any group that supports the non-registration of firearms?
7. Do you belong to any group that promotes the registration of firearms?
8. Do you agree that a person has a constitutional right to use reasonable force when attacked or threatened in any way?
9. Do you have any fear of a firearm?
10. Have you ever purchased a bumper sticker with a slogan that expresses an opinion about the use of firearms or other weapons? If so, please raise your hand. What was the nature of the opinion expressed by the slogan on that bumper sticker?
11. Do you now own or have you ever owned a pistol, a shotgun, a rifle, or a gun of any kind?
12. Do you have any quarrel with the constitutional right to bear arms?
13. Have you ever shot at an animal or participated in any kind of target shooting or skeet shooting? Please raise your hand.
14. Do you have any feeling about the type of education a person should have before he or she is entitled to own a gun or to shoot it? If so, please raise your hand.
15. Do you feel that a police officer has a greater right to bear arms or to wear a gun than a store owner or a black citizen in his own home? If so, please raise your hand so that we can discuss it.

Use of Weapons

1. Do you feel that just because a person has a weapon near him, that that person intends to use that weapon? Please raise your hand if you feel that this is the case.
2. You are all aware of the fact that police officers carry guns? Do you feel that just because police officers carry weapons, that they plan on using those weapons during the eight or ten hours of duty that they put in? If so, please raise your hand.
3. Do you feel that a police officer wears a gun with the intention of firing that gun each time it is worn?
4. Do you have a different standard for the defendant's having a weapon present?
5. Would you have a different standard for a person who was a hunter than you would for a person who was simply carrying a gun for protection?
6. How many of you carry a spare tire in the trunk of your car? Please raise your hand if you have a spare tire in your car trunk.
7. Would you consider that that spare tire is there for your protection in case you have a flat tire?
8. Every time you get into your car, do you expect to use your spare tire?
9. How many of you feel that it is more unexpected or more unusual to be required to use the spare tire than not to be required to use it?
10. What criteria do you use in determining when you will use the protection of your spare tire?
11. Is there anyone here who feels that a person who has a weapon for protection might not be using it with exactly the same frame of mind as you would when you have your spare tire in the trunk of your car?

Lewd and Lascivious Acts Charge Brought by Preteen Males

1. Do you think children under the age of 14 are capable of plotting a plan of action to get their own way or to seek revenge for some action?

2. Do you think children below the age of 14 always tell the truth about serious matters?
3. Do you think children over 10 and under 14 generally have excellent or good memories about things that have made an impression on them?
4. Do you think that they would all tell essentially the same story if they shared a common experience? Would you expect that story to agree on major points, such as time, place, and number of participants?
5. Do you have any particular image of the kind of children who come from a broken home, I mean, can you be fair to the state even though these charges are brought by young boys who are suffering from the effects of either their parents currently getting a divorce or their parents recently having been divorced?
6. What effects do you think divorce has on the children involved?
7. Do you think that merely because charges of this kind have been brought by boys of this age that the charges are probably true?
8. Do you think it is possible for a child to bring false charges of this kind of act against an adult? Do you think it is probable?
9. Does discussion about sex in general disturb you?
10. Can you be objective in determining what is a fact when it relates to a charge of a sexual act between an adult and a child?
11. Can you be objective in determining what is a fact when it relates to matters concerning a homosexual act?
12. Can you be objective when it relates to matters concerning a homosexual act between an adult and a child?
13. At what age do you believe young male children begin to have sexual fantasies?
14. Do you believe that sometimes these sexual fantasies can be homosexual in nature?[14]

[14] In over twenty trial simulations on the questions of homosexual acts between adults and teenage or preteen children, the overwhelming result is

Self-Defense[15]

1. Do you have any qualms about the law that states that a person is permitted to protect himself or herself when another person attacks him or her? Do you have any problems with accepting that as the law?
2. Do you have any quarrel with the law that a person can use force equal to the force that another person uses when that person is attacked and feels that he must defend himself or herself?
3. Do you believe a person is justified in killing another human being if he or she believes that he or she is in actual danger of being seriously injured or killed by the attacker?
4. Do you have any feeling against a person who uses a gun or a knife to protect his property, his family, or himself?
5. Do you have any qualms against it being lawful that a person may use a gun to defend himself or herself against another person who has a gun?[16]
6. If His Honor (Her Honor) instructs you that self-defense is a complete defense to the charge of murder, will you accept that as being the law?
7. Even if you yourself do not feel that you would act in such a way, will you use the standard of what the law allows in reaching your verdict?
8. His Honor (Her Honor) will instruct you that a person has a right, and I repeat, a right, to use a knife or a gun or any other weapon that is available or close at hand to protect home and family. Do you have any problems with following such an instruction and will you deter-

---

that adults (1) do not consider that a young person would lie about a question of this nature; (2) believe that the children are far more likely to be telling the truth than the adults; and (3) are very unforgiving about acts of this nature, regardless of background and conservative or liberal attitudes.

[15]The questions on attitudes toward violence, pp. 574-575 supra, are frequently useful as a lead-in to questions on self-defense.

[16]Substitute the type of weapon used in the particular crime.

mine that any violence that occurred under such circumstances is the result of self-defense and therefore also the result of actions that are within the law? Do you promise to heed that information and follow those instructions if they are given to you by the judge?

9. Do you fully appreciate and understand that the question in this particular case is not whether there was a victim who died, but whether the defendant properly acted in proper self-defense?
10. We have talked about the burden of proof being with the state. Do you further understand that the burden of proof in a case where we claim self-defense will be on the prosecution, and that the prosecution must prove to you, as members of the jury, beyond a reasonable doubt, that the accused did not act in self-defense?
11. You realize, of course, that if you, as a juror, have reasonable doubt — that is, if you are not convinced beyond a moral certainty as to whether or not the defendant was justified in acting in self-defense — then you must, as our law demands, resolve that doubt in favor of the defendant and render a verdict of not guilty. Is there anyone who has any problems with that concept?
12. If we prove to your satisfaction that at the time of the shooting my client was in a state of fear and was merely trying to protect his or her own life and liberty, will you consider that in determining the guilt or innocence of my client?
13. If the evidence establishes that the victim approached my client in a menacing manner and threatened to do him harm or threatened to kill him, will you consider those actions in determining the issue of self-defense?
14. If the evidence shows you that the man who died in this case had a history of violence and in the past had threatened to commit violent acts (be as specific as possible), would you take those things into consideration in determining the issue of self-defense in this case?
15. If the judge instructs you that the killing of one human

being by another is justifiable when committed by any person when resisting an attempt to murder such person or such person's spouse or family member, will you accept that as being the law?

16. Even if you yourself feel that the law is wrong and that it should not be the law, will you be able to set aside your own feelings and your own repugnance of violence and follow the instructions of the court?
17. If the judge instructs you that in determining the issue of self-defense, it is not necessary that danger actually exist, but only that the defendant has reasonable grounds for believing that danger exists and then acts to defend himself or herself in such a manner and with such means as may seem to him or her reasonable, will you accept that as being the law?
18. In other words, will you accept the fact that a human being may act in any manner and with any means as may seem reasonably necessary to him or her in view of inherent and imminent danger? Can you accept that as the law and follow that as the law if the judge so instructs you?
19. Some of you have appeared to hesitate over what constitutes perception of threat or what self-defense really means. Will you just state your own opinion of what you think must occur in order to justify one human being killing another human being?[17]

Offsetting Impression of Guilt Due to Arrest

1. How many of you feel that where there is smoke there is probably fire or at least there is probably more smoke?
2. Do you think that just because the state's attorney has charged the defendant with a crime that this is evidence against my client?

[17] Address this question to members of the jury who give either verbal or nonverbal indications that they may have difficulty accepting this concept.

3. Just because my client has been arrested and has been brought to trial here today, does my client start out with a strike or two against him in your mind because the state's attorney has charged him with that crime?
4. Surveys conducted throughout the nation indicate that most people believe that the police do not arrest innocent people. How many of you feel that the police in this community do not arrest innocent people? Please raise your hand.
5. Since you don't have a background in law, let me ask you if you are aware of the method for determining whether a person should be charged with a crime?
6. If you find that the evidence does not support the charge brought by the state's attorney, you will have to find that the police have, indeed, arrested an innocent person and that the state's attorney has tried to convict an innocent person. Would you then find it contrary to your beliefs to vote my client not guilty in view of the fact that he has been arrested, investigated, and brought to trial? If so, please raise your hand.
7. Do we, my client and I, have your complete assurance that your judgment will rest solely on the evidence presented in this courtroom and that you will not consider the fact that he has been arrested and charged by the state's attorney when reaching your verdict?
8. Do you think that it is *possible* that a state's attorney may charge a person with a certain crime just on the basis of suspicion, rather than hard and competent evidence? I am not asking if that is what you think happened in this case. I am asking if you think that such could be *possible.* If you think that is possible, please raise your hand.
9. You understand, of course, that no implication of guilt can be drawn from the fact that my client is charged in an information of a crime and no inference can be drawn against my client, the defendant in this case, simply because there has been such a charge.
10. I do not want to belabor a point, but you understand that my client is absolutely innocent as he sits at this

table today and that there must not be any assumption of guilt merely because he has been charged with the crime. Do you all accept that as the law for this case? Please raise your hand if you do.

Intoxication as a Defense

1. Is there anyone on the panel who does not drink an alcoholic beverage, whether it be wine, beer, or straight alcohol, under any circumstances or at any time? Please raise your hand.
2. Are any of you members of any organization that is trying to stop the sale or distribution of intoxicating beverages? If so, please raise your hand.
3. Is there any person on the panel who does not accept the notion that a person's ability to think or act is altered when he or she is under the influence of alcohol?
4. We do not want to hide anything from you, members of the jury. Our defendant, Mr. Thompson, will admit that he was intoxicated at the time of the alleged crime. Now His Honor (Her Honor) will instruct you that it is up to you, the jury, to determine the extent of the defendant's intoxication and whether that intoxication was great enough to prevent the defendant from forming the intent necessary to constitute the crime. Let me make certain that you understand what we are saying. His Honor (Her Honor) will tell you that it was a crime only if the defendant *intended* to commit the crime as charged. Do you all understand that? Is there anyone who feels that that should not be the law? Will you please raise your hand?
5. Further, if His Honor (Her Honor) charges that should you find that the defendant was too intoxicated to form the intent necessary to deliberately commit the crime, you must render a verdict of not guilty. Is there anyone on this panel who feels that because of his or her background or because of his or her personal beliefs it would be impossible for him or her to follow that instruction?

Insanity Defense

1. Is there anyone here who does not accept psychology or psychiatry as a valid science of the mind or at least an acceptable medical or mental treatment of emotional ills? If so, please raise your hand.
2. Do you accept the fact that there are times when an individual is emotionally disturbed and not in full control of his or her actions?
3. Is there anyone who feels that individuals should be held responsible for their actions no matter what their mental, emotional, or physical condition might be? If so, please raise your hand.
4. Are you aware that under the laws of the United States, a person is not responsible for his actions if he is found to be insane at the time the act was committed?
5. Is there anyone who feels that if that action is a crime the individual should be treated as a criminal rather than an emotionally ill person or as an insane person?
6. Is there anyone on this panel who has ever expressed the opinion that "not guilty by virtue of insanity" is just a clever way to get a person "off," so that he or she will not be held responsible for an act, a crime, that he or she has committed?
7. Is there anyone on this panel who feels that simply because a psychiatrist examines a person after the fact and says that that person was not capable of knowing right from wrong, that that person should be treated as a person who is not guilty rather than a person who is guilty?
8. If His Honor (Her Honor) instructs you that you must find the defendant not guilty if he was incapable of knowing the nature or quality of the act he committed — that is, if he was legally insane — is there anyone who could not follow that instruction? That is, is there anyone who could not find a legally insane person not guilty of the act committed?
9. Now, do you agree that if the accused, the defendant in this case, was insane or was incapable of knowing the

nature and quality of the act or of knowing that what he was doing was wrong, he must be acquitted — that is, found to be not guilty? Do you all agree to that?

10. If you find that the defendant was legally insane when the crime was committed, do you promise to follow the court's instruction and render a verdict of not guilty?

Testimony by Accomplice

1. In deciding whether you are going to believe a witness, would you consider that witness's conduct prior to his taking the stand, his or her opportunity or ability to observe the situation, his or her bias, or the probability or improbability of the story?
2. Would you also consider what this person might have to gain from the story that he or she were to tell?
3. Do you understand what is meant by the term accomplice?

   (NOTE: If the respondents indicate a negative answer, be prepared to explain the term in a manner that is in keeping with the instructions that will be given by the court.)
4. Do you understand that the testimony of an accomplice is considered to be testimony from a tainted source and, therefore, should be scrutinized with greater care and caution than the testimony of other witnesses?
5. At the end of this trial, the judge will instruct that in order for you to convict the defendant, the testimony from the accomplice has to be supported by other evidence that connects the defendant with the crime. Do you understand that?
6. Do you understand that this extends to every material fact necessary for the prosecution to establish the crime?
7. His Honor (Her Honor) will also instruct that this supporting testimony must come from a believable and unimpeached source. Do you understand that if an accomplice makes a claim or relates an incident in a certain way, you, as jurors, have the duty to scrutinize his or her testimony for credibility and believability?

APPENDIX

5

Sample Voir Dire Questions

This appendix contains nine lists of voir dire questions that were used in actual cases. The names of the parties have been changed to protect their identities. Each list is preceded by a statement identifying the nature of the case and the problems associated with it, and the verdicts of cases that have been tried are disclosed. These sample voir dires are offered to illustrate how questions must and can be adapted to the needs of particular cases.

1. Plaintiff's voir dire questions for a products liability case concerning a carbonated beverage bottle that exploded.
2. Plaintiff's voir dire for a civil case concerning the liability of a negligent motorist.
3. Plaintiff's requested questions for judge-conducted voir dire for a medical malpractice case.
4. Plaintiff's voir dire questions for a personal injury products liability case based on an explosion.
5. Defendant's voir dire questions in a personal injury products liability case based on an automobile accident.
6. Defendant's voir dire questions in a case based on a contract dispute.
7. Property owner's voir dire for an eminent domain case.
8. Defendant's voir dire for a rape case.
9. Defendant's voir dire for a murder case.

Sample 1: Plaintiff's Voir Dire for a Products Liability Case

PROPOSED VOIR DIRE: Civil Case
TYPE OF CASE: Products Liability
NAME OF CASE: Tom and Linda Smith, Sr. and Thomas Smith, Jr. v. T & T Bottling Co.
CASE SPECIFIC INFORMATION: A grandmother, 69, who was caring for a 2-year-old boy, was unloading groceries when a pop bottle exploded, injuring the child. The child suffered permanent eye injury.
SPECIAL PROBLEMS OF CASE:

1. Age of the person who was caring for the child
2. The fairly common acceptance by most individuals of carbonated drinks being sold in bottles
3. Proof that the bottle was not dropped but that the explosion was caused by negligence

FINAL VERDICT: Very favorable to the plaintiff

1. Name of potential juror
2. Address
3. Occupation and past occupations for the last ten years
4. Marital status
5. Spouse's occupation: If spouse is currently not working, what was the last paid employment or last employment outside of the home? If retired, what was the last place of employment? If disabled, what is the nature of the disability and what was the last form of employment?
6. What are the ages, sexes, residences, and occupations of your working children, if any?
7. Union membership (both self and spouse)
8. Length of residence in community
9. Highest level of education
10. Activity in service organizations or other community organizations, with special interest in leadership roles in these organizations
11. Knowledge of other persons on the panel — have you

had contact at all with them either as friends, neighbors, church members, co-workers, or relatives?

12. Have you ever been a party to a lawsuit?
13. If so, were you the plaintiff — the person bringing the action, or the defendant — the person defending the case?
14. What was involved in that case?
15. Were you generally satisfied with the outcome of the case? Did it alter your opinion of the court system?
16. Have you ever served on a jury? If yes, was it a criminal or civil case? If civil, did you make any monetary awards? If yes, what was the amount? Are you bothered or concerned about any aspect of your prior jury service?
17. Have you ever been a witness in a lawsuit?
18. Did you testify in court or were you interviewed outside the courtroom with your statement being taken in the form of a deposition?
19. Now, while you have informed us that you have been neither a witness nor a party to a lawsuit in the past, have you had a member of your family or a close friend who was either a party or a witness in a lawsuit? Because of that close relationship to the person, do you have certain thoughts or concepts or feelings regarding the judicial system in this country? If you do, would you please share these with me?
20. I asked you if any of you had your statement taken in the form of a deposition. A deposition, which is a written statement taken under oath before a court reporter, is the same as testimony produced in the courtroom. We will be having such sworn statements, or depositions, read to you in this case. Is there anyone who will find such written testimony less credible or less impressive than if the person were actually here in the courtroom? Would you please raise your hand if you think that would be true for you?
21. Have any of you had any connection, even if it was only as a close friend or a supportive listener, with a prod-

ucts liability case? If yes, would you please tell us the nature of that case and what company was involved?

22. For your information, this case will probably take ________ days. It will require your presence in this courtroom from about 9:00 in the morning until about 5:00 in the afternoon with time out for lunch. Is there anyone here who would find that a hardship for health or personal reasons or for occupational reasons?
23. We are going to be working together on this trial for all of that time. For this reason, I would like to know the following:
    a. Will it cause you any hardship to stay with us for that long?
    b. Will it cause hardship on any member of your family?
    c. To any of your present plans?
    d. Do you daydream sometimes?
    e. Do you get bored easily?
    f. Do you often take a nap during the day? If so, do you think you can function easily without having the opportunity to do so?
    g. Do you get tired easily?
    h. Do you suffer from headache or experience any physical pain from inactivity?
    i. Will your legs bother you from being required to sit still for so long without the opportunity to move around?
24. Is there anyone on this panel who never drinks a soft drink or a carbonated drink of any kind?
25. Do any of you refuse to purchase carbonated drinks that are in bottles?
26. Have you ever been trained in the medical area or studied for any degree in a medical topic? If yes, would you please explain the nature of that training?
27. Have you or has anyone close to you worked for a hospital or a doctor or had any work association with the medical field? What was that association?
28. Have you ever studied medicine or gathered medical knowledge on your own? In what area?

29. Would you superimpose your own personal knowledge of medical issues on the testimony you heard from expert witnesses from the medical field?
30. Have you ever studied chemistry or physics? What was the extent of your studies in these fields?
31. Do you believe in "fate"? That is, do you think that something generally happens because it is time for it to happen or because it is predestined to happen at this time? Or do you believe that when common safety and responsibility standards are followed, many tragic occurrences can be prevented?
32. Have you or any member of your family or a close friend ever suffered an eye injury? If so, would you share with us the details of that injury — what was the cause, extent and permanency?
33. Have you or any person close to you ever spent more than two weeks in the hospital? If so, would you give us full information about that experience?
34. Have you ever suffered an injury that, though healed, still causes you discomfort or pain? If so, please tell us about it.
35. Do you accept the idea of psychological injury or damage? If not, why not?
36. Do you believe that a physical disorder may result in a personality change or alteration?
37. Do you think that a person who has an obvious physical disability is treated any differently than persons who are not so injured?
38. Have you ever witnessed some incident in which a small child was injured? If so, would you describe the cause, extent, and permanency of injury, and who was responsible for supervising the child's activities at the time of the injury?
39. (For potential jurors with children.) When your child or children were young, what child care arrangements did you make? At any time, was the child cared for at a licensed day care center? Did you ever use sitters? Who sat with your child — a relative, a neighbor?
40. Have you been around small children when they were

sick? For instance, did your children ever have the measles or mumps? Did you encounter any problems in caring for them when they were ill?

41. During the course of the trial, you will hear the testimony of several expert witnesses (including medical experts, engineering experts, and accident reconstruction experts . . .) and the testimony of Tommy's parents and grandmothers. Will you be able to place just as much credence in the family's testimony as in that of the experts? That is, how much of a bearing does level of education have on the weight you are likely to give to testimony?

42. The basic task of those who serve on this jury is to listen to the facts and then to reach a verdict based on those facts. That verdict is of grave concern to all the parties involved in this case. The Smiths, plaintiffs in this case, are greatly concerned. T & T Bottling, the defendant, is also concerned about the decision you will make. The reason we are here in court is that we need a third party to make the decision for us. We, therefore, have come to you as that third party, and we will rely on the decision you will make after hearing the evidence presented to you in this courtroom. Now, some people just don't like to make decisions. They would much rather that someone else make their decisions for them and they certainly don't want to make decisions for other people. I can understand that. I have felt that way myself sometimes. But it is important that each and every person on this jury accept the responsibility of considering the facts and only the facts and of reaching a decision based on those facts. Is there anyone here who would rather not have that responsibility? Please just raise your hand and let us know.

43. This suit is a civil suit, not a criminal suit. In a criminal case, you as jurors would be required to make only one decision. Is the defendant guilty or not guilty? In a civil case, you are asked to make two decisions: first, you must determine whether T & T Bottling was at fault;

second, if and only if you find T & T Bottling was at fault, you must determine compensation for Tommy and his parents for the damage done to Tommy as a result of that fault. Do you all understand that you would consider the question of compensation only if you first found fault? Is there anyone who feels that he or she would not be able to distinguish between these two decisions without experiencing difficulty?[1]

44. Fault in this case means two things. First, there is *strict* liability. Strict liability means that, if you have the knowledge to create a safe product and don't, you are to be held accountable. Second, there is negligence. Negligence is *deliberate,* as in the choice *not* to warn of the inherent danger of a product or in the failure to utilize an alternative product in the place of a potentially defective one. Do any of you have any problem in accepting these ideas or concepts regarding fault?
45. You realize that although there are twelve persons on this jury, each of you will have the task of making up your own mind and reaching your own conclusions. Now, that does not mean that you won't listen to other members of the jury and consider what they have to say — that is essential in reaching your final verdict. But it does mean that you have to believe in that verdict and not just vote to go along with the other jurors because eight or ten or eleven of them don't see things the same way you do. Do you all feel that you would vote your own conviction and your own conviction only?
46. Is there any person on this panel who feels that if the decision were to come down to eleven persons voting one way and one person voting the other way, that the one person not voting with the majority would have to be wrong? Do you all accept that one person can be just

[1]You may want to substitute the words liability and negligence for the word fault. It is often very important for the plaintiff's attorney to emphasize the nature of the two-stage decision process.

as right as eleven persons, considering the way he or she views the evidence?

47. The defendant in this case is a company, but a company is made of of individual people. Also, this is a negligence case, and if you should find the defendant guilty of negligence, then damages are assessed against the defendant the same as if he were guilty of injuring the plaintiff personally. Is there anyone on this jury who feels that he or she would have any personal reservations or personal hesitation about finding the defendant liable in this case because the defendant is charged with negligence?
48. Would any of you feel that a company can't be held responsible for its actions?
49. You understand that in this case, a civil case, the plaintiffs, Thomas Smith, Jr., and his parents, Linda and Thomas, have *only* to prove their case by a preponderance of the evidence and *not* beyond a reasonable doubt. Proof beyond a reasonable doubt is the requirement in a criminal case. Is there anyone here who would not be willing to follow the court's instructions that the plaintiffs are entitled to win their case if they prove it by a preponderance of the evidence and that they are not required to prove their case beyond a reasonable doubt?
50. Do any of you have any question about how much proof it takes to establish a "preponderance"? (Give example.)
51. You do all understand that this is a civil case and not a criminal case? We are not charging that the defendant has committed a criminal act for which he is guilty, but that he was negligent and that the negligence resulted in an injury to our plaintiff, Thomas Smith, Jr. Is there anyone who has any problem understanding the difference between being guilty of a criminal act and being responsible or at fault for an injury due to negligence?
52. Do you think that a company bears the burden of the responsibility for manufacturing and designing a product that is safe to use?

53. Do you feel that a company should warn users of its products about the possible dangers inherent in the use of the product?
54. Are you aware that money is the only form of compensation that a person can seek under our system of justice?
55. You must accept the fact that we can't restore things to exactly the way they were in *(month)* of 19__. Even though money will not restore the physical or emotional loss, would you feel justified in determining as a verdict an amount of money to be paid to Tommy in compensation for his suffering and for his lifetime losses?
56. Do you have any feeling against any person coming to court and asking to be compensated with money for an injury or for a damage that has been done to him?
57. Do you believe in awarding a fair, just, and adequate verdict to a person who has been damaged through the fault of another person or company?
58. If you were injured solely by the negligent conduct of another, would you expect to be compensated for damages by that other individual or company?
59. Under our system of jurisprudence, people like you, the members of this jury, are required to determine what amount in a given case constitutes a fair, just, adequate, and reasonable compensation for a given injury. Do you have any quarrel with that system?
60. Naturally, you will want and need to hear all of the evidence first; but after you have heard the evidence, if in your opinion it would take a very substantial sum of money to make fair and adequate compensation to Tommy, would you hesitate to make that compensation?
61. By adequate, I mean that it is sufficient to compensate for all of the elements of damage, whatever they may be, small or large. Do you understand my meaning?
62. I want to be sure that you do not have some artificial financial limits that you carry around in your head beyond which you would not make any compensation in

money. I say this because some people, no matter how badly they think a plaintiff may have been treated or how much money he or she may have lost or how much damage he or she may have suffered or how much pain and suffering he or she may have endured, will, in their own mind, without telling anyone else, just simply say "I will not compensate with more than *X* dollars," whatever that figure might be. Do you feel that way? Do you carry such a figure in your head?

63. Is there anything in your background or beliefs that would keep you from making a substantial compensation to Tommy for his loss of enjoyment of life or the interference with enjoyment of life if he proves under the law and the evidence that he is entitled to recover for such loss?
64. Is there anything in your education, background, experience, or belief system that leaves you with any preconceived bias against the person seeking to recover damages for more than the actual expenses incurred as the result of that injury?
65. If the evidence shows that Tommy was seriously and permanently injured and that he is entitled to a verdict in compensation for these injuries, will you decide on a verdict that allows him a full measure of justice in keeping with the injuries received?
66. Is there anything in your education, background, experience, or belief system that makes you feel that a person cannot be compensated with money for pain and suffering? Would you feel this way even if the court instructed you that the plaintiff has the right to be compensated for any and all pain and suffering that he has felt and will continue to feel throughout his life?
67. Let me ask all this from another perspective: Does $2 million in actual damages sound like a high jury verdict to you?
68. Can you imagine as you sit here prior to this trial, a set of circumstances or facts that could be presented to you as a juror and which would demand that you make

compensation of $2 million to any plaintiff in any lawsuit?

69. In other words, does the word reasonable, when it is used in relationship to the concept of damages in a civil court case, imply to you a certain amount of money? Or an amount of money that has a certain dollar ceiling on it?
70. If you have a dollar amount that seems to be "reasonable" in most cases, what amount is it?
71. Have any of you ever said or felt that a million dollars is an awful lot of money and that there wasn't much that is really worth that much money at one time?
72. Have any of you experienced any extended periods of suffering and pain? If so, please raise your hand. Those of you who have raised your hand, describe for me the circumstances under which you experienced that pain and suffering and the length of time you endured that pain and suffering.
73. Has any member of this jury heard this occurrence discussed or has anyone on the jury read or heard anything about this case in the media? If yes, what is it that you have read or heard? Is what you have read or heard going to affect your ability to sit as an impartial juror in this case?[2]
74. Are you personally acquainted with or to your knowledge is any member of your immediate family personally acquainted with or related in any way to any of the following persons who may testify in this case? (Recite the list of people who will testify.) If any of you are so acquainted, what is the nature of that relationship and what is the extent of that acquaintanceship? Will that acquaintanceship or relationship affect your consideration of the case by giving added weight to the testimony of that witness?[3]

[2]The attorney should request individual voir dire of such jurors out of the presence of the other panel members to determine the accuracy of their knowledge and possible bias.

[3]If the list is longer than seven names, it should be written on a chart.

75. Are you personally acquainted with or to your knowledge is any member of your immediate family personally acquainted with any of the defendants in this case? If yes, what is the nature and extent of that relationship? Is there any reason to feel that you would give more or less weight to their testimony than to that of the plaintiff in this case? Do you feel that it would cause you embarrassment or particular stress if you were required to sit on a jury in a case in which the defendants are involved?
76. Are you personally acquainted with or is any member of your family personally acquainted with the plaintiffs, Thomas Smith, Jr., and his parents, Linda and Thomas, Sr.? If yes, what is the nature and extent of that relationship?
77. Are any of you personally acquainted with or, to your knowledge, is any member of your immediate family acquainted with the Smith family?
78. Are you personally acquainted with or, to your knowledge, is any member of your immediate family personally acquainted with (the owner of T & T Bottling Company, employees, etc? [Listing names on a chart would be appropriate if the list is long.])
79. Are you or, to your knowledge, is any member of your immediate family personally acquainted with or related in any way to any of the attorneys for the defendant or to the attorneys for the plaintiffs? (Give a complete list of the names and firms of each attorney involved in the case.) If the answer is affirmative, please explain the extent and nature of that acquaintanceship and explain whether you have been or have ever contemplated being a client of that attorney.
80. Are you or to your knowledge has any member of your immediate family personally been acquainted with or related in any way to any of the wives, parents, or children of any of the witnesses previously mentioned, any of the plaintiffs, any of the defendants, or any of the lawyers in the law firms mentioned above or any of the employees of any of the law firms?

81. For the information of those of you who have never been a juror or who have never been involved as a party or a witness in any lawsuit, at the conclusion of all of the evidence and after closing arguments by counsel, you will be given instructions by the judge concerning the law. Would you apply the law as given by the judge even though *you might not agree* with it?
82. Will you honestly and to the best of your ability determine each question of fact submitted to you in this lawsuit on the basis of the evidence presented in this courtroom and the law that the judge will give you concerning this question and on that basis only?
83. Will you promise me that if you are chosen as a juror in this case, you will decide this case solely on the basis of the evidence that you hear in this courtroom and on the instructions of the court and that you will not consider any outside source of information or make any independent investigations of your own?
84. If you were the plaintiff in this case, would you be satisfied to have a juror in your present frame of mind sit on your case? If you would not be satisfied to have a juror like yourself on your own case, please raise your hand.
85. I would like to ask you if you have any reason at all, however private, that would make you feel you would not like to serve on this case? If so, please raise your hand and indicate to the court what that feeling is.
86. Would you look at the other panel members, please? Is there anyone you know? How and to what extent do you know them?

Sample 2: Plaintiff's Voir Dire for a Personal Injury Case

PROPOSED VOIR DIRE: Civil Case
TYPE OF CASE: Personal Injury[1]

[1]The trial was divided into two sections. The liability issue was to be tried first and then two months later the issue of damages was to be tried if the first jury had found liability.

NAME OF CASE: Carol Canyon v. Ball Trucking Co. and David Platt (farmer)

CASE SPECIFIC INFORMATION: Carol Canyon was on her way to play bingo in a small town on a country gravel road about 15 miles from her place of residence. Her sister, Barbara Noble, age 19, was with her in the car and was killed instantly at the scene of the automobile wreck. (Her husband, John Noble, settled their case out of court.) Carol Canyon was an unwed mother with no speeding violations and no prior accidents. The wreck occurred as David Platt, the farmer, was using a tractor without lights to push a truck that was owned by Ball Trucking Company off the road from where the truck had stalled. The electric system was also inoperative on the truck so there were no lights of any kind. There was no one to verify the speed at which Carol was driving; Carol claimed to have been observing the speed limit, which was 55 miles per hour. David Platt, the farmer, estimated that she was going "a little faster than that" and according to an initial police report the driver of the truck estimated that she was going 50 miles an hour. At the time of his deposition, however, he had revised his estimation to 65 miles per hour.

SPECIAL PROBLEMS OF CASE:

1. Carol was an unwed mother at the time of the wreck.
2. Carol had not worked nor sought work since the wreck, even though her medical doctor had deemed her ready to return to work.
3. Carol's psychologist was to testify that she has such a fear of being in a car that she finds it impossible to drive to and from work daily and she lives in a neighborhood that would require transportation to any job that she could find.
4. Carol suffered facial injuries and head injuries resulting in four separate surgical procedures. Carol sustained a depressed skull fracture and several facial fractures. She had three surgical procedures performed for plastic repair of her face, especially of her nose and right cheek and chin.

5. The farmer, David Platt, is a highly respected, well liked and moderately well-off farmer who will have high credibility in his community; whereas the Canyon family has been frequently associated with nefarious acts and are obviously from the "wrong side of the tracks."

FINAL VERDICT: Case had not reached the court.

1. Name of potential juror
2. Address
3. Occupation and past occupations for the last ten years
4. Marital status
5. Spouse's occupation. If spouse is currently not working, what was the last paid employment or the last employment outside the home and when was that?
6. Union memberships (self, spouse, family members)
7. Length of residency in community[2]
8. Highest level of education
9. Activity in service organizations or other community organizations, with special interest in leadership roles in those organizations
10. Knowledge of other persons on the panel — any contact at all with them either as friends, neighbors, church members, co-workers or relatives
11. Have you ever been a party to a lawsuit?
12. If so, were you the plaintiff — the person bringing the action, or the defendant — the person defending the case?
13. What was involved in that case? Especially, was it dealing with personal injury or an automobile accident?
14. Were you generally satisfied with the outcome of the case?
15. Have you ever been a witness in a lawsuit?

[2]Since the farmer, David Platt, has lived in the community for so long and is so well respected, it will be of great interest to determine how many other people live there and whether they recognize his name or are aware of his reputation.

16. Did you testify in court or were you just interviewed outside the courtroom with your statement being taken in the form of a deposition?
17. Now, while you have informed me that you have neither been a witness nor a party to a lawsuit in the past, have you had a member of your family or a close friend who was either a party or a witness in a lawsuit? Because of that close relationship to that person, do you have certain thoughts or concepts or feelings regarding the judicial system in this country? If you do, would you please share those with me?
18. I asked you if any of you had ever had your statement taken in the form of a deposition. Now a deposition is a written statement taken under oath before a court reporter that would be just the same as the testimony that would be produced in the courtroom if the person could be physically present. However, since that person cannot be physically present in the courtroom, that deposition or sworn written statement is read to you in the courtroom. We will be having testimony of this nature in this case. Is there anyone who will find testimony that is produced in that way less credible or less impressive than if the person were actually here in the courtroom? Would you please raise your hand if you think that would be true for you?
19. For your information, this case will probably take about ten days. It will require your presence in this courtroom from 9:00 in the morning until about 5:00 in the afternoon with time out for lunch. Is there anyone here who would find that a hardship for personal or health reasons or occupational reasons?
20. We are going to be working together on this trial for all of that time. For this reason, I would like to know the following:
    a. Will it cause you any hardship to stay with us that long?
    b. Will it cause any hardship on any member of your family?

c. To any of your present plans?
d. Do you daydream sometimes?
e. Do you have difficulty getting going in the morning?
f. Do you get bored easily?
g. What will happen in this courtroom may have very little similarity to watching *Perry Mason.* Will that bother you?
h. Do you often take a nap during the day? If so, do you think you can function easily without having the opportunity to do so?
i. Do you get tired easily?
j. Do you suffer from headache or from any physical pain from inactivity?
k. Will your legs bother you from being required to sit still for so long?

21. Have you ever been trained in a medical area or studied to any degree any medical topic?
22. Have you or anyone close to you worked for a hospital or a doctor or had any work association with the medical field? What was that association?
23. Have you ever studied medicine or gathered medical knowledge on your own? In what areas?
24. Is there any occasion where you would superimpose your own personal knowledge of medical issues over the testimony you heard from expert witnesses from the witness stand?
25. Do you believe in "fate"? That is, do you think that something generally happens because it is time for it to happen or it is predestined to happen at that time or do you believe that when common safety and responsibility standards are followed, many tragic occurrences could be prevented?
26. Have you or any member of your family ever been involved in an automobile accident in which there were personal injuries suffered? If so, would you please tell me the details of that occurrence; for instance, who was driving, what was the nature of the accident, what was

the extent of the personal injuries, and were there any lawsuits that arose from that occurrence?

27. Do any of you have special drivers' licenses, such as a truck driver's license or a chauffeur's license?
28. Have any of you ever driven a tractor? If so, how experienced are you and how frequently have you driven such tractors? What kinds of tractors did you use? Are you aware of the slow moving traffic regulations? Did you ever drive a tractor after dark?
29. Have any of you ever driven a farm truck or grain truck? If so, how frequently and for how far?
30. Would you consider the skills required in driving a truck to be different from the skills required in driving a car? If yes, what are the differences in skills that you think would be required to perform as a safe truck driver as opposed to a safe auto driver?
31. How many of you are familiar with the road called County W? If yes, how many times have you driven over that road and how familiar would you say that you are with that road? Do you know the Platt farm driveway that is in the approximate area where this *wreck*[3] occurred?
32. The drivers of the two vehicles, one a tractor and the other a car, that met head on were both teenagers. Is there any person here who would doubt that a teenager could be a responsible and careful driver?[4]
33. There were two other drivers, both adults, present and involved. Is there anyone here who feels that the adults should be held more responsible than the teenagers for what occurred?

[3]Be sure to use the term wreck whenever the collision is referred to, since this is the most powerful word associated with this kind of collision as shown in tests with all ages, both sexes, and all occupation groups. The mental image that "wreck" creates in the mind of the average juror is one of great violence and great impact with someone clearly at fault for the occurrence.

[4]Trial simulations and community attitude studies have shown that there is great forgiveness for teenage drivers. In other words, jurors tend not to hold teenage drivers responsible for their actions. This is especially true when severe injury or death has occurred.

34. Is there anyone on the panel who feels that since this is a gravel road called County W that it should be thought of as a "farm road" and that farm vehicles should be favored or should be given any special treatment rather than vehicles that are being driven for pleasure?
35. There are those people who feel that farm vehicles are not to be held to the same level of responsibility for following the laws of the road, especially in having all of the slow-vehicle warning systems or special lights that are required by the law. There are some people who feel that the laws are too restrictive on the farmer. Is there anyone on this panel who has an opinion of that nature? If you do, do you feel that you would rather abide by your feelings about what the law should be rather than following the instructions of the court as to what the law actually is? What we are really asking is, will you decide the verdict of liability in this case by what you think the law should be or by what the law actually is?
36. Is there any member of this jury panel who never goes for a drive without the use of safety belts? Please raise your hand.[5]
37. This is a negligence case and if you should find the defendant guilty of negligence, then damages are assessed against the defendant the same as if he were guilty of injuring the plaintiff personally. Is there anyone on this jury who feels that they would have any personal reservations or personal hesitation about finding the defendant liable in this case because the defendant is charged with negligence?
38. You understand that in this case, it being a civil case, that the plaintiff, Carol Canyon, has only to prove her case by a preponderance[6] of the evidence and not be-

[5]The law in the state did not require the wearing of safety belts. The reason for this question was to eliminate any attempt by the counsel for the defendant to suggest that the plaintiff was not using careful judgment or was lacking in caution in her driving habits.

[6]The word preponderance may be substituted for with the phrase greater weight.

yond a reasonable doubt. Proof beyond a reasonable doubt is the requirement in a criminal case. Is there anyone here who would not be willing to follow the court's instructions that Carol is entitled to win her case at the point that she proves it by a preponderance of the evidence and that she is not required to prove her case to a point that reaches "beyond a reasonable doubt"?

39. You do all understand that this is a civil case and not a criminal case? We are not charging that the defendant has committed a criminal act for which he is guilty, but only that he was negligent and that that negligence resulted in an injury to our plaintiff, Carol Canyon. Is there anyone who has any problem understanding the difference between being guilty of a criminal act and being responsible for an injury due to negligence?
40. Has any member of this jury heard this occurrence discussed or has anyone on the jury read or heard anything about this case in the media? If yes, what is it that you have read or heard? Is what you have read or heard going to affect your ability to sit as an impartial juror in this case?[7]
41. One of the drivers involved in this case was a truck driver. Is there any one of you who does not feel that a trucker should have full knowledge of all of the laws of the highway, since he makes his living on the highway?
42. It is the law in this state that lights must be used whenever vehicles of any kind are driven after dark. Both the trucker and the farmer will admit in court that there were no lights on their vehicles. The trucker will testify that there were emergency flares in his truck and the farmer will testify that he had special fluorescent

[7]The media coverage was very favorable to Carol Canyon, and very unfavorable to the Ball Trucking Company. For this reason, the plaintiff's attorney could ask this question in open court so that all panel members could hear any damaging information about the defendant that might not otherwise be admissible. The attorney employing this tactic must be prepared to limit responses so as to avoid the risk of mistrial.

warning signals in his pickup truck. None of these was used or placed on the road until after the wreck had occurred. Will you require even well-liked individuals who meant well and who were simply being good samaritans in helping other people out to still obey the laws of the road and to be responsible for any acts that might have resulted from not obeying the laws of the road?

43. Are you personally acquainted with or, to your knowledge, is any member of your immediate family personally acquainted with or related in any way to any of the following persons who may testify in this case? (Recite the list of people who will testify.) If any of you are so acquainted, what is the nature of that relationship and what is the extent of that acquaintanceship? Will that acquaintanceship or relationship affect your consideration of the case or give added weight to the testimony of that witness?
44. Are you personally acquainted with or to your knowledge is any member of your immediate family personally acquainted with any of the defendants, farmer David Platt or the Ball Trucking Company, in this case? If yes, what is the nature and extent of that relationship? Is there any reason to feel that you would give more or less weight to their testimony than to that of the plaintiff in this case? Do you feel that it would cause you embarrassment or special stress if you are required to sit on a jury in a case in which the defendants are involved, especially if you return a verdict against them?
45. Are you personally acquainted with or is any member of your family personally acquainted with the plaintiff, Carol Canyon? If yes, what is the nature and extent of that relationship?
46. Are any of you personally acquainted with or, to your knowledge, is any member of your immediate family acquainted with the family of Carol Canyon?
47. Are you personally acquainted with or, to your knowl-

edge, is any member of your immediate family personally acquainted with Barbara Noble, who was killed in that automobile wreck, or with her husband, John Noble, who is now working as a construction engineer for Roark Construction Company?

48. Are you or to your knowledge is any member of your immediate family personally acquainted with or related in any way to any of the attorneys for the defendant or to the attorneys for the plaintiff? (Give a complete list of the names and lawyers connected with firms for each attorney involved in the case.) If yes, please explain the extent and nature of that acquaintanceship and explain whether you have ever been or ever contemplated being a client of that attorney.
49. Are you or, to your knowledge, is any member of your immediate family personally acquainted with or related in any way to the wives, parents, or children of any of the witnesses previously mentioned, any of the plaintiffs, any of the defendants, any of the lawyers in the law firms mentioned previously or any of the employees of any of the law firms?
50. For the information of those of you who have never been a juror or involved as a party or a witness in any lawsuit, at the conclusion of all of the evidence and after closing arguments by counsel, you will be given instructions concerning the law by the judge. Would you apply the law as given by the judge even though *you might not agree* with it?
51. Will you honestly and to the best of your ability determine each question of fact submitted to you in this lawsuit on the basis of the evidence brought here before you in the courtroom and on the law that His Honor (Her Honor) will give you concerning this question and on that basis only?
52. Will you promise me that if you are chosen as a juror in this case, that you will decide this case solely on the basis of the evidence that you hear in this courtroom and on the instructions of the court and that you will not consider any outside source of information or make

any independent investigations of your own outside this courtroom?

53. If you were the plaintiff in this case, would you be satisfied to have a juror who was in your present frame of mind sit as a juror on your case? If you would not be satisfied to have a juror like yourself on your own case, please raise your hand.
54. As my last question, I would like to ask you if you have any reason at all, however personal or private, that would make you feel that you would not like to serve on this case? If so, please raise your hand and indicate to the court what that feeling is.

Sample 3: Plaintiff's Voir Dire for a Medical Malpractice Case

PROPOSED VOIR DIRE: Civil Case (to be submitted to the judge)

TYPE OF CASE: Medical Malpractice

NAME OF CASE: Edith Mabel George v. Conway Davidson, M.D.

CASE SPECIFIC INFORMATION: Plaintiff claims that she suffered an accidental severing of the nerves that affect the bowel and bladder functions and as a result has experienced a loss of feeling in her sex organs. She claims that this condition is the result of a surgical procedure that was performed by the defendant. Edith George is a married woman, 43, with no children.

SPECIAL PROBLEMS OF CASE: Edith George had suffered a severe personality alteration that made her a very bitter woman, one that the attorneys felt was unpleasant and caused her to be evasive. Also, Edith George had an extensive prior medical history, including a double mastectomy and several other operations for skin cancer. The doctor, Conway Davidson, was a highly respected local physician who had been in the community for more than 20 years and was considered to be a leading surgeon in the area. He also was a department head at a teaching university for medicine and served on many boards for charity and church organizations in the community.

FINAL VERDICT: A settlement was reached prior to the verdict being delivered. The settlement was substantial.

The plaintiff respectfully requests the court to permit a jury voir dire in accord with the following questions.

Plaintiff respectfully requests the court to permit plaintiff's counsel to examine the jury in accord with the proposed questions; however, if this request is refused, in the alternative, plaintiff requests the court to inquire of the jury in accord with the submitted questions and to permit plaintiff to supplement that inquiry with questions that the Court may fail to make.

Plaintiff says that it is impossible at this time to make certain that all proper questions are herewith submitted and would respectfully request that she be granted the right to supplement this list immediately prior to trial.

If the juror gives an affirmative response to any of the questions, the court is respectfully requested to develop in detail all information from that juror relative to the affirmative response in order to permit counsel for plaintiff and defendant to intelligently exercise their challenges for cause and their peremptory challenges.

If a negative response indicates that a juror should be questioned further, then the Court is respectfully requested to explore further with that juror the nature of the matter relating to that response in order to permit counsel to intelligently exercise challenges for cause and peremptory challenges.

Plaintiff further moves that these motions and the requested questions be made a part of the record of this case.

1. Have you or any members of your immediate family ever been hospitalized at The Regional Hospital?
   a. If so, who, when and what for?
2. Are you personally acquainted with or to your knowledge is any member of your immediate family personally acquainted with or related in any way to any of the following persons who may testify in this case? (List witnesses on a chart and also read names.)
   a. If any juror gave an affirmative response, please

inquire whether it is the juror or a member of the juror's family who is acquainted with the witness;

b. Find out which witness they are acquainted with;

c. The extent and nature of the acquaintance; and

d. Thorough examination must be had to make certain that the acquaintanceship or relationship will not affect that juror's consideration of the case or weight that that juror will give the testimony of that witness (asking the juror the conclusionary question whether it would affect his or her judgment cannot enlist a total, complete, and truthful answer).

3. Are you personally acquainted with or to your knowledge is any member of your immediate family personally acquainted with anyone who is employed at The Regional Hospital?

   a. If any juror gave an affirmative response, please inquire whether it is the juror or a member of the juror's family who is acquainted with the employee of the hospital;

   b. The extent and nature of the acquaintance; and

   c. Thorough examination must be had to make certain that the acquaintanceship or relationship will not affect that juror's consideration of the case (asking the juror the conclusionary question whether it would affect his or her judgment cannot enlist a total, complete and, truthful answer).

4. Are you personally acquainted with or, to your knowledge, is any member of your immediate family personally acquainted with anyone who is employed by Dr. Bill Casey, Dr. Charles Nation, Dr. Harold Cole, Dr. Wilmer Banks, Dr. Harvard Sinclair, Dr. Howard Mason, Dr. John Houser, Dr. Louise A. Cellar, Dr. Midas Pancho, Dr. David Palmer, Dr. Samuel Damer, or Dr. Lee Conner?

   a. If any juror gave an affirmative response, please inquire whether it is the juror or a member of the juror's family who is employed by any of the physicians named above;

b. Find out whom they are employed by;
c. The extent and nature of the employment; and
d. Thorough examination must be had to make certain that the employment will not affect that juror's consideration of the case or weight that the juror will give the testimony of that witness (asking the juror the conclusionary question whether or not it would affect his or her judgment cannot enlist a total, complete, and truthful answer).

5. Are you or, to your knowledge, is any member of your immediate family personally acquainted with or related in any way to any of the wives, parents, or children of any of the witnesses previously mentioned?
   a. If any juror gave an affirmative response, please inquire whether it is the juror or a member of the juror's family who is personally acquainted with any of the above listed persons:
   b. Find out whom they are acquainted with and that person's relationship to the witness;
   c. The extent and nature of the acquaintance; and
   d. Thorough examination must be had to make certain that the acquaintance will not affect that juror's consideration of the case or weight that the juror will give the testimony of that witness (asking the conclusionary question whether it would affect his or her judgment cannot enlist a total, complete, and truthful answer).
6. Are you or to your knowledge is any member of your immediate family personally acquainted with or related in any way to Mr. Jack A. Daniel, the attorney for defendant, Conway Davidson, or any members of the law firm of David, Smith, Larger, Hope and Colder, with which he is associated? The lawyers associated with the firm are (list all attorneys).
   a. If any juror gave an affirmative response, please inquire whether it is the juror or a member of the juror's family who is personally acquainted with any of the above-listed persons;

b. Find out whom they are acquainted with;
c. The extent and nature of that acquaintance; and
d. Thorough examination must be had to make certain that the acquaintance will not affect that juror's consideration of the case (asking the juror the conclusionary question whether it would affect his or her judgment cannot enlist a total, complete, and truthful answer).

7. Are you or to your knowledge is any member of your immediate family personally acquainted with or related in any way to anyone who is now or has in the past been employed by any of the lawyers mentioned above or in their law firm?
   a. If any juror gave an affirmative response, please inquire whether it is the juror or a member of the juror's family who is personally acquainted with any of the above listed persons;
   b. Find out whom they were employed by;
   c. The extent and nature of that employment; and
   d. Thorough examination must be had to make certain that that employment will not affect that juror's consideration of the case (asking the juror the conclusionary question whether it would affect his or her judgment cannot enlist a total, complete, and truthful answer).
8. Are you or to your knowledge is any member of your immediate family personally acquainted with or related in any way to the spouse, parents or children or other family member of any of the lawyers in the law firm mentioned above or employees of that law firm?
   a. If any juror gave an affirmative response, please inquire whether it is the juror or a member of the juror's family who is personally acquainted with or related to any of the above listed persons;
   b. Find out whom they are acquainted with or related to;
   c. The extent and nature of the acquaintance or relationship; and

   d. Thorough examination must be had to make certain that the acquaintance will not affect the juror's consideration of the case (asking the juror the conclusionary question whether it would affect his or her judgment cannot enlist a total, complete, and truthful answer).

9. Are you or is any member of your immediate family to your knowledge now a client of any of the lawyers in the law firm representing the defendant, Conway Davidson?
   a. If so, find out who is the client and who is the lawyer; and
   b. Find out the nature and extent of that representation.
10. Have you or to your knowledge has any member of your immediate family ever been a client of any of the lawyers in the law firm representing the defendant, Conway Davidson?
   a. If the answer is yes, find out who was the client and who was the lawyer; and
   b. Explore the nature and extent of that representation.
11. Are your or is any member of your immediate family associated in any way with the defendant's lawyer, Jack A. Daniel, or with any of the members of the law firm with which Mr. Daniel is associated?
   a. If the answer is yes, find out who is associated with whom; and
   b. Find out the full extent and nature of that association.
12. Are you or is any member of your immediate family associated in any way with Dr. Wade Lewis, Dr. Bill Casey, Dr. Samuel Damer, Dr. Conway Davidson of the Medical College or of The Regional Hospital?
   a. If the answer is yes, find out who is associated with whom; and
   b. Find out the full extent and nature of that association.
13. Have you or has any member of your immediate family

ever been operated on for a lumbar or low back disc? A disc anywhere else?

   a. If the answer is yes, find out who was operated on;
   b. Where and when;
   c. Who was the surgeon; and
   d. Describe the operation and its results and where the disc was located.

14. Is there anything in your background, readings or beliefs that would prevent you from awarding substantial damages to Edith Mabel George and against Dr. Conway Davidson, the defendant, if you find from the evidence and the law in this case that she is entitled to recover such damages?
15. Is there anything in your background, readings, or beliefs that would prohibit you from making a substantial award of damages in this case for pain and suffering or mental anguish if under the law and the evidence the plaintiff proves she is entitled to such damages?
16. Is there anything in your background or beliefs that would keep you from awarding plaintiff a substantial verdict for her loss of enjoyment of life or interference with enjoyment of life if she proves under the law and the evidence she is entitled to recover such loss?
17. Is there anything in your background, readings, or beliefs that would prohibit you from awarding the plaintiff judgment in the amount of $2 million if under the evidence and law in this case it is proven to you that the plaintiff is entitled to such an award?
18. Is there anyone in your family who has had damage to the nerves affecting the bowel function, bladder function or causing a loss of feeling in sex organs due to injury to nerves?
    a. If so, find out the full information relating to this, such as who, how, and when.
19. Have you ever been a witness in a lawsuit?
    a. If the answer is yes, was this (1) a criminal or a civil matter; and (2) did you testify for the winning or the losing side?

20. Have you or any member of your immediate family ever been a plaintiff in any lawsuit against another person?
    a. If yes, what kind of lawsuit was it, and what was the result?
21. Have you or any member of your immediate family ever made a claim for personal injuries?
    a. If yes, who was the party involved as plaintiff and what was the result?
22. Have you or any member of your immediate family ever been a defendant in a lawsuit, that is, have you or any member of your family ever been sued?
    a. If the answer is yes, what was the nature of the suit, and what were the details?
23. Have you ever had a claim made against you?
    a. If yes, what was the nature of the claim?
24. Have you ever been involved in a claim or suit made against your employer?
    a. If so, what was the nature of the claim, and the result?
25. If you or any member of your immediate family was injured in any accident caused by the fault of another, would you hesitate to file a lawsuit in order to collect damages for the injury?
    a. If so, would you please raise your hand?
26. Have you ever been a juror?
    a. If so, in what court, and was it civil or criminal?
27. Have you ever heard anything about this case?
    a. If the answer to any of these three previous questions is yes, what is the extent and nature of that association, and what have you heard or read?
28. The court will instruct you at the end of this case on certain legal matters. Is there anyone on this jury that would have a problem in following the law as the Court gives it to you, even though you may not agree with that law?
29. Is there any person on this jury who would refuse to decide the case on the evidence introduced, exhibits introduced, and instructions of the court regardless of

whether you have other information? That is, do you agree to decide this case solely on what you hear in the courtroom?

30. Are you aware that the defendant's license to practice medicine is not in danger in this proceeding, and that no claim is being made that the defendant should be barred from the practice of medicine?
31. If the evidence shows that the plaintiff was seriously and permanently injured and that she is entitled to a verdict, will you award her a full measure of justice in keeping with the injuries that she received?
32. Do any jurors believe that it is wrong in part or in whole for a patient to sue his or her doctor?
33. This defendant is being charged with negligence and not any criminal behavior. Is there any juror who does not understand this?
34. Is there any juror here who feels indebted to the medical profession?
35. Is there any juror or immediate member of their family currently under medical care?
    a. If so, would this have any effect on being able to sit for this case?
    b. Under whose care is the juror or family member?
    c. What is the nature of the malady?
    d. Is it the juror or a family member?
36. Usually in this type of case, the plaintiff must offer expert testimony by another doctor who believes that the defendant did something wrong. It is generally recognized that the plaintiff may have some difficulty in procuring doctors to testify against other doctors. Is there any juror who might be prejudiced against the plaintiff because she does or does not match quantitatively the expert testimony presented on behalf of the defendant or does not have a doctor from this local area to testify on her behalf?
37. Have you or to your knowledge has any member of your immediate family ever been associated with the health care industry in any way? That is, have they ever

been employed by hospitals, physicians, medical schools, dentists, etc.

a. If yes, find out who, where, when, and how.

38. Are any of you presently or have you been in the past an officer or member of the board of directors of The Regional Hospital?
39. Have you ever been an officer or member of the board of directors of any hospital?
40. Have you or, to your knowledge, has any member of your immediate family ever been a patient of or received treatment from (list doctors involved)?
41. Have you ever discussed or overheard anyone else discussing anything concerning malpractice actions against physicians or have you read anything about malpractice actions against physicians?
    a. If yes, find out what was heard and what was read;
    b. When;
    c. Where; and
    d. What opinions have they formed as a result of hearing or reading about malpractice actions?
42. Have you ever undergone any surgical procedure?
    a. If yes, find out where, when, who did it, and what it was for;
    b. Did they have any complications or problems;
    c. Did they make a claim for the problems; and
    d. What were the complications or problems.
43. Do you or any member of your family belong to any church or other organization at which any of the above physicians or their families attend?
44. Do you or any member of your family belong to any club, lodge or fraternal organization at which the above named physicians or their families belong?
45. Do you or any member of your family belong to any church or other organization at which any of the lawyers representing the defendant or their families attend?
46. Do you or any member of your family belong to any club, lodge, or fraternal organization at which any of

the lawyers representing the defendant or their families belong?

47. Do you see anything wrong with a person suing a physician for money damages if the doctor is at fault?
48. Will you deal with this defendant doctor, Conway Davidson, without allowing him special advantage because he is a physician — that is, treat him as your equal in this courtroom but not as your superior?
49. Is there any juror who feels indebted to the medical profession for medical services rendered to you or a loved one in the past?
    a. Would such indebtedness that you feel make it difficult for you to render a verdict in this case against a physician?
50. This is a negligence case and if you should find the defendant guilty of negligence, then damages are assessed against the defendant the same as if he were guilty of injuring the plaintiff with an automobile. Is there anyone on this jury who feels that they would have any personal reservations or personal hesitation about finding the defendant liable in this case because the defendant is charged with malpractice, which is nothing more than negligence?
51. You understand that in this case, it being a civil case, that the plaintiff, Edith Mabel George, only has to prove her case by a preponderance of the evidence and not beyond a reasonable doubt. Proof beyond a reasonable doubt is the requirement in a criminal case. Is there anyone here who would not be willing to follow the court's instructions that the plaintiff is entitled to win her case if she proves it by a preponderance of the evidence and that she is not required to prove her case beyond a reasonable doubt?
52. Is there any member of this jury who would hold it against the plaintiff, Edith Mabel George, that one of her lawyers is from out of state? Do you agree to treat the lawyers for Edith Mabel George in the same way as you would treat the lawyers for the defendant, Conway

Davidson? If there is anyone on this jury who would be unable to treat all the lawyers on both sides equally, please raise your hand.

53. Has any member of the jury heard or read anything in the newspaper or magazines or heard on the TV any articles, stories, reports, or news broadcasts relating to lawsuits that would in any way affect your verdict in this case?
    a. If yes, find out everything that the juror has read or heard; and
    b. Make certain that what they have read or heard would not, in fact, *really* affect their ability to sit as an impartial juror in this case.
54. Has any member of the jury read or been influenced by insurance industry magazine advertisements regarding the size of jury verdicts?
55. Have you or, to your knowledge, has any member of your immediate family ever had bowel or urinary incontinence or inability to control his or her bowels or bladder?
    a. If the answer is yes, find out whom, when, the age and relationship of the person, and what caused the condition.
56. Have you ever been or to your knowledge has any member of your immediate family ever been employed by the Medical College?
    a. If yes, find out who was employed, when, for how long and the nature and extent of that employment.
57. Are you or to your knowledge is any member of your immediate family associated in any way with anyone who is connected with or associated with the Medical College?
    a. If yes, find out who is associated with whom;
    b. The connection or association with the Medical College; and
    c. The entire relationship between the juror or family member and the college or associated with the college.
58. Is there anything about medical malpractice cases that

would bother you or prevent you from returning a substantial verdict in favor of the plaintiff, Edith Mabel George, and against Conway Davidson, if under the law and the evidence the plaintiff proves she is entitled to such a verdict?

59. Do you agree to treat the witnesses for the plaintiff, some of whom are from Pennsylvania and Florida, in the same manner as you treat the witnesses for the defendant? If any of you will be prejudiced in any way against the plaintiff or her medical witnesses because her medical witnesses are from Pennsylvania and Florida, then please raise your hand because all witnesses under the law should be judged in the same manner regardless of the state in which they live or work.
60. Have you or has any member of your immediate family to your knowledge or any of your friends ever been injured or damaged by a doctor's carelessness or negligence?
61. If you were the plaintiff in this case, would you be satisfied to have a juror who is in your frame of mind sit as a juror on your case? If you would not be satisfied to have a juror like yourself on your own case, please raise your hand.

Respectfully submitted on behalf of the plaintiff, Edith Mabel George

By______________________________[1]
Of Counsel

Sample 4: Plaintiff's Voir Dire for a Products Liability and Personal Injury Case

PROPOSED VOIR DIRE: Civil Case
TYPE OF CASE: Products Liability and Personal Injury

[1] Normally firms representing plaintiff would list full name of counsel and full name of firm plus complete addresses at the left hand margin below counsel's signature.

NAME OF CASE: James Pittford v. The Local Gas Co. and Freitag Manufacturing Co.

CASE SPECIFIC INFORMATION: The plaintiff opened the oven door of his stove to place a pizza into the oven. The pizza had been previously prepared for him by his wife, who was absent for the evening. The stove exploded and the plaintiff received severe burns on his upper chest, both arms, and his face. Also, the trailer home in which the stove existed was totally destroyed by fire. The gas company had suffered an outage in that area for a five-hour period. The spouse of the plaintiff had called the gas company and asked them to send someone out to relight all of the pilot lights for the gas heaters and gas stove. There was a pilot light that was at the back of the stove that required the stove to be moved out for that pilot light to be lit. There was no warning on the stove that such a pilot light existed. That pilot light was not lit and that was the cause of the eventual explosion.

SPECIAL PROBLEMS OF CASE: The plaintiff had consumed five beers prior to opening the oven door.

FINAL VERDICT: The verdict was in excess of $1.5 million, equally divided between the defendants.

1. Have you heard or read anything about this case, other than what you have heard here today?
2. If so, what have you heard?
3. Have you ever served on a jury before?
4. If so, when and how many times?
5. In what court?
6. Were the cases civil or criminal?
7. If the cases were civil, what did they concern?
8. In those civil cases, what were the verdicts?
9. In those criminal case, what were the charges and what were the verdicts? Guilty or not guilty?
10. Are you aware that there is a difference in the burden of proof between a criminal and civil case?
11. The court will instruct you that the plaintiff has the

burden of proof in a civil case and in this case. That means we must prove by the preponderance of the evidence that the defendant is liable for our damages. Do you understand that this is a different burden than "beyond a reasonable doubt"?

12. Will you apply this standard rather than the standard of "beyond a reasonable doubt"?
13. (There may be a necessity for more questions in connection with the answers to the previous three questions, depending on each potential juror's prior experience.)
14. Is there anything about your previous experience on a jury, or experience being involved with a panel and being subjected to questioning by the court and lawyers, that makes you feel you would rather not sit again on a jury and, in particular, on this one?
15. Have you ever been a party to a lawsuit?
16. If so, were you the plaintiff — the person bringing the action, or the defendant — the person defending the case?
17. What was involved in the case?
18. Were you generally satisfied with the outcome of the case?
19. (In the event the prospective panel member was a defendant in a lawsuit, the following question should be asked.) Is there anything about the case in which you were the defendant that causes you now to have a feeling against the plaintiff or claimant due to the fact that you have been in the position of the one being sued, the defendant in a case?
20. (In the event the panel member was a plaintiff in a previous case, the following question should be asked.) Is there anything about the situation that would cause you to have a leaning in favor of the plaintiff, because you had once been in the same position in your lawsuit?
21. Have you ever been a witness in a lawsuit?
22. Did you testify in court or were you just interviewed outside the courtroom with your statement being taken in the form of a deposition?

23. Is there anything in particular that you do not like about our judicial system, whether it be with the courts themselves or the lawyers or even jury service? If you have any such thoughts, please explain them.
24. Now, while you have informed me that you have neither been a witness nor a party to a lawsuit in the past, have you had a member of your family or a close friend who was either a party or a witness in a lawsuit? Because of your close relationship to that person, do you have certain thoughts or concepts or feelings regarding the judicial system in this country? If you do, would you please tell me about them?
25. For the information of those of you who have never been a juror or involved as a party or a witness in any lawsuit, at the conclusion of all of the evidence and after closing arguments by counsel, you will be given instructions concerning the law by the judge. Would you apply the law as given by the judge, even though you might not agree with it?
26. Will you honestly and to the best of your ability determine every question of fact submitted to you in this lawsuit on the basis of the evidence brought here and the law that His Honor will give you concerning this question? And on that basis only?
27. Will you promise me that if you are chosen as a juror in this case that you will decide this case solely on the basis of the evidence you hear in this courtroom and on the instructions of the court and not consider any outside source of information or make any independent investigations of your own outside this courtroom?
28. Are you acquainted with or have you ever worked with any of the parties to this case?
29. Have you ever heard of either of the parties or do you know them by reputation?
30. Are you personally acquainted with or, to your knowledge, is any member of your immediate family acquainted with any of the witnesses, lawyers, or parties of this case or any of their spouses, parents, or children?

   a. If yes, inquire whether it is the juror or a member of the juror's family who has this knowledge;
   b. Find out whom they are acquainted with and that person's relationship to the witness;
   c. The extent and nature of the acquaintance; and
   d. Thorough examination must be made to be certain that the acquaintance will not affect that juror's consideration of the case or weight that the juror will give the testimony of the witness.

31. Are you acquainted with any of the lawyers who are representing the parties in this case or with any of the lawyers who are connected with the firms they represent?
32. Have any of these lawyers or any member of their firms represented you or a member of your family or a close friend? If yes, in what way have they done so?
33. In the event that you are acquainted with any one or more of the attorneys here, or with their reputations, would this in any way keep you from being a fair and impartial juror if you were chosen for this jury?
34. Would you, if you are selected as a member of this jury, be able to be as attentive to the reading of depositions of different witnesses as you would if the witness was here in person?
35. Would you be able to give it as much credence when it is a deposition being read in court as opposed to the witness being here in person?
36. If not, could you tell me why?
37. Do you have a problem with seeing?
38. Do you have any problem with hearing? Especially in this courtroom? I know some courtrooms have bad acoustics and it is important that you are able to hear everything all the time. Do you have any problem?
39. Regarding your seeing and hearing, do you think it is easier for you to learn from something you see or from something you hear? Do you need to both see and hear something in order to remember it after several hours?
40. Do you have any feeling against a person coming to

court and asking to be compensated with money for an injury and damage that was done to him or her?

41. Do you believe in making compensation with a fair, just, and adequate verdict to a person who has been injured and damaged entirely through the fault of another person or corporation?
42. If you were injured solely by the negligent conduct of another, would you expect to be compensated by that other individual for your damages?
43. Under our system of jurisprudence, people like you, the members of this jury, are permitted to determine what amount in a given case constitutes a fair, just, adequate, and reasonable compensation for a given injury. Do you find any quarrel whatsoever with that system?
44. Naturally you will want to hear all the evidence first, but after you have heard the evidence, if in your opinion it would take a very substantial sum of money to make fair compensation to the plaintiff, would you hesitate to make that compensation in this case?
45. By adequate, I mean that it is sufficient to compensate for all of the elements of damage, whatever they may be, small or large. Do you understand my meaning?
46. I want to be sure that you do not have some artificial financial limits that you carry around in your head beyond which you would not award any more money. I say this because some people, no matter how badly they think the plaintiff might have been treated or how much money he or she may have lost or how much damage he or she has suffered or how much pain and suffering has been endured, will just in their own mind, withour telling anyone else, will simply say, I would not award more than *X* dollars, whatever that figure may be. Do you feel that way?
47. Is there anything in your background or beliefs that would keep you from awarding the plaintiff a substantial verdict for his loss of enjoyment of life or interference with enjoyment of life if he proves under the law

and the evidence that he is entitled to recover for such loss?

48. Would you have any trouble at all in awarding punitive damages in this case in the event there was evidence to support such an award and the court instructed you as to when punitive damages would be allowed? Would you have any hesitancy in awarding punitive damages?
49. Is there anything in your education, background, experience, or belief system that leaves you with any preconceived notion, bias or prejudice against a person seeking to recover damages for more than just the actual expenses incurred?
50. If the evidence shows that the plaintiff was seriously and permanently injured and that he is entitled to a verdict, will you award him a full measure of justice in keeping with the injuries received?
51. Is there anything in your education, background, experience, or belief system that makes you feel that a person cannot be awarded any money for compensation of pain and suffering? Would you feel this way even if the court instructed you that the plaintiff has the right to be compensated for any pain and suffering that has been or is being felt?
52. Let me ask all this from another perspective. Does $5 million in actual damages sound like a high jury verdict to you?
53. Can you imagine as you sit here, prior to trial, a set of circumstances and facts which could be presented to you as a juror that would allow you to award $5 million to any plaintiff in a lawsuit?
54. In other words, does the word "reasonable" when it is used in relationship to the concept of damages in a court case imply to you a small amount of money? Or an amount of money that has a certain dollar ceiling on it?
55. If you have a dollar amount that seems to you to be "reasonable" in most cases, what amount is it?
56. Have you or has any member of your family ever suf-

fered from being burnt? If so, would you give us full information relating to this?

57. Have you or has any member of your family ever spent more than two weeks in the hospital? If so, would you give us full information relating to this?
58. Have you or has any member of your family ever been through a series of operations, one after the other? If so, would you give us full information relating to this?
59. Have you or has any member of your family or a close friend ever been involved with a beauty school, beauty pageant, or cosmetic business?
60. How do you feel about scars? Are they generally repulsive to you?
61. Do you think that a person who is scarred, especially on the face and other visible parts of the body, is treated any differently than persons who are not scarred?
62. Have you or any member of your family ever undergone minor or major plastic surgery? If so, would you give us full information relating to this?
63. Is there any person who disapproves of plastic surgery for any reason?
64. Have you or any member of you family ever had a skin graft? If so, would you give us full information relating to this?
65. Do you think that in a marriage the absence of touching and being together can have a negative effect on the relationship between the marriage partners?
66. Do you think the presence of extensive scarring is apt to eliminate the desire to touch?
67. Do you think that a company bears the burden of the responsibility of manufacturing and designing a product that is safe to use?
68. When a company has standards of safety that they have defined as essential steps to be followed under certain circumstances, do you think the people who work for that company are bound to know those steps and to follow them?
69. If a person who is employed by a company neglects to

follow the standards of safety set up by the company, would you feel that the company was responsible for any damage that would occur as a result of that neglect?

70. Do you believe in "fate"? That is, do you think that generally something happens because it is time for it to happen or it is predestined to happen at this time? Or do you believe that when common care and responsibility standards are followed, many tragic occurrences can be prevented?
71. Do you feel that a company should warn users of its products about the possible dangers inherent in the use of the product?
72. Is there anyone on this panel who never partakes of an alcoholic beverage?
73. Is there any person on this panel who has ever been a member of an organization that has attempted to stop the sale of alcoholic beverages?
74. The plaintiff will admit to having consumed several beers prior to opening the oven that exploded and caused his burns. Is there any member on the panel who feels that simply because our plaintiff had consumed beer that this, in some way, changes the obligation of the gas company or of the manufacturer of the stove so that they no longer are responsible for the design of a dangerous product or for negligence in performing their duties?
75. Is there anyone who sees relevancy between the consumption of beer by the plaintiff and the opening of the oven and the negligence and unsafe standards of the defendant?
76. One of the highest duties a citizen of this country can be called for is jury service. Will you assure me that you will give it all of the attention and energy that it requires?
77. What is your feeling about jury duty?
78. Do you consider it simply an intrusion on your time?
79. Would you prefer not to be here on this panel? Why?
80. From what you know about this case, and admittedly at

this point you don't know very much, would you like to serve on this jury? If not, why not?

81. For your information, this case will probably take about three weeks. It will require your presence in this courtroom from 9:00 in the morning until about 5:00 in the afternoon, with time out for lunch. Is there anyone here who would find that a hardship for personal or health reasons?
82. Both defendants are being charged with negligence and not with any criminal behavior. Is there any juror who does not understand this or who has any question about what this statement means?
83. How do you feel about negligence — is there ever a time when it is permissible or understandable? If so, when?
84. Has any member of the jury seen or heard or read anything in the newspapers or magazines or radio or television relating to lawsuits that would in any way affect your verdict in this case?
    a. If yes, what effect has this had on your thinking and your expectations of what should happen in a courtroom?
    b. Would this affect your ability to sit as an impartial and fair juror on this case?
85. We are going to be working together on this trial for the next three weeks. For this reason, I'd like to know the following:
    a. Will it cause you any hardship to stay with us that long?
    b. Will it cause any hardship on your family?
    c. To any of your present plans?
    d. Do you daydream sometimes?
    e. Sometimes do you find it easy to go from happy to moody or from moody to happy?
    f. Do you have difficulty getting going in the morning?
    g. Do you get bored easily?
    h. What will happen in this courtroom may have little

similarity to watching *Perry Mason.* Will that bother you?

i. Do you often take a nap during the day? If so, do you think you can function easily without having the opportunity to do so?

j. Do you get tired easily?

k. Do you suffer from headache or from any physical pain from inactivity?

l. Will your legs bother you from beng required to sit still for so long?

86. One of the defendants in this case is the gas company that serves all of your homes if you use gas. Is there anyone who fears that if they bring in a substantial verdict that their own gas bill will go up? Does this worry you? If it does, do you think it might not be fair for you to sit on this jury since such a concern might cloud your perception or acceptance of the testimony and evidence and will affect your final verdict?

87. How many of you use gas supplied by this gas company?

88. Is there any reason that you can think of that would prevent you from being a fair and impartial juror? For any reason, including any that we haven't thought about to ask?

89. If you were the plaintiff in this case, would you be satisfied to have a juror who is in your frame of mind sitting as a juror on your case?

90. Would you just look around at the other members of the panel and tell me if you know any of them, even if just by sight or by reputation? Who are they and how do you know them?

Sample 5: Defendant's Voir Dire for an Automotive Products Liability Case

PROPOSED VOIR DIRE: Civil Case
TYPE OF CASE: Products Liability, Automotive
NAME OF CASE: Karen Mills v. Foreign Car Manufacturer of America, Inc.

CASE SPECIFIC INFORMATION: Karen Mills was thrown from her car in a wreck that involved the drivers of a rental car. The car that Karen was driving was a small car; the rental car was a large car. Karen is now claiming that Foreign Car Manufacturer had placed a defective latch on the car and that that was the cause of her injuries. Karen is now a paraplegic.

SPECIAL PROBLEMS OF CASE: There has been substantial media coverage about recall by this car manufacturer of this particular car but not for a defective latch. The question of a defective latch has been at issue for this manufacturer in only three previous cases.

FINAL VERDICT: Case had not reached the court.

1. Name of potential juror
2. Address
3. Occupation and past occupations for the last ten years
4. Marital status
5. Spouse's occupation: If spouse is currently not working, what was the last paid employment or last employment outside of the home? If retired, what was the last place of employment. If disabled, what is the nature of the disability and what was the last form of employment
6. Union membership
7. Length of residence in community
8. Highest level of education
9. Activity in service organizations or other community organizations, with special interest in leadership roles in those organizations
10. Knowledge of other persons on the panel. Any contact at all with them either as friends, neighbors, church members, co-workers or relatives.
11. Have you ever been a party to a lawsuit?
12. If so, were you the plaintiff — the person bringing the action, or the defendant — the person defending the case?

13. What was involved in that case? Especially, was it dealing with personal injury or an automobile accident?
14. Were you generally satisfied with the outcome of the case? Did it alter your opinion of the court system?
15. Have you ever been a witness in a lawsuit?
16. Did you testify in court or were you interviewed outside the courtroom with your statement being taken in the form of a deposition?
17. Now, while you have informed me that you have neither been a witness nor a party to a lawsuit in the past, have you had a member of your family or a close friend who has been either a party or a witness to a lawsuit? Because of that close relationship to the person, do you have certain thoughts or concepts or feelings regarding the judicial system in this country? If you do, would you please share those with me?
18. I asked you if any of you had your statement taken in the form of a deposition. Now a deposition is a written statement, taken under oath before a court reporter, that would be just the same as the testimony that would be produced in the courtroom if the person could be physically present. However, since that person is not physically present in the courtroom, that deposition or written and sworn statement is read to you in the courtroom. We will be having testimony of this nature in this case. Is there anyone who will find that testimony that is produced in that way is less credible or less impressive than if the person were actually here in the courtroom? Would you please raise your hand if you think that that would be true for you?
19. Have any of you ever been involved in an automobile accident that resulted in injury to any of the passengers or drivers in any of the cars involved in the accident? If so, would you please tell me whether you were the driver or the passenger and what was the nature of the accident and what was the nature of the injury that occurred in that accident?
20. Have any of you had any connection in any form, even

if it was only as a close friend or supportive listener, with a products liability case? If yes, would you please tell me what the nature of that case was and what company was involved?

21. For your information, this case will probably take 14 days. It will require your presence in this courtroom from about 9:00 in the morning until about 5:00 in the afternoon with time out for lunch. Is there anyone here who would find that a hardship for health or personal reasons or for occupational reasons?
22. We are going to be working together on this trial for all of that time. For this reason, I would like to know the following:
    a. Will it cause you any hardship to stay with us for that long?
    b. Will it cause hardship on any member of your family?
    c. To any of your present plans?
    d. Do you daydream sometimes?
    e. Do you get bored easily?
    f. Do you often take a nap during the day? If so, do you think you can function easily without having the opportunity to do so?
    g. Do you get tired easily?
    h. Do you suffer from headache or experience any physical pain from inactivity?
    i. Will your legs bother you from being required to sit still for so long without the opportunity to move around?
23. Have you ever been trained in a medical area or studied to any extent any medical topics? If yes, would you please explain the nature of that training?
24. Have you or anyone close to you worked for a hospital or a doctor or have any work association with the medical field? What was that association?
25. Have you ever studied medicine or gathered medical knowledge on your own? In what area?
26. Is there any occasion when you feel that you would

superimpose your own personal knowledge of medical issues over the testimony you heard from expert witnesses from the medical staff?

27. Do any of you have special driver's licenses, such as a truck driver's license, a motorcyclist's license or a chauffeur's license?
28. Have any of you ever owned or do you now own a small car manufactured by the defendant company?
29. Have any of you ever owned a large car? If yes, what was the model and year of that car? Be specific.
30. Have any of you ever expressed the opinion that you would not purchase a small car because you felt that they were not safe on the highway? If yes, what was the basis for that opinion? Do you feel that you would be prejudiced, in any way, against the owner of a small car who purchased such a small car, and who drove it on the highway?
31. Is there any person on this panel who feels that the mere fact that a car is a small car makes it unsafe or would prejudice you against the manufacturer of that small car?
32. Karen Mills, at the time of this accident, was a teenage driver. Is there any person on this panel who feels that a teenage driver is not a safe driver?
33. Do you all understand that this is a civil case and not a criminal case? Do you all understand that the defendant is not charged with a criminal act for which he is guilty but is charged with negligence in the construction or design of the small car? Is there anyone who has any problems understanding the difference between a criminal act and an act of negligence?
34. Has any member of this jury heard about this specific case in the media or heard it discussed with any of your friends?
35. Has any member of this jury heard, either in the media or through discussion with friends, any references to the general safety of the small car of this manufacturer as it was manufactured prior to 1975? If the answer is

yes, what is it you have read or heard?[1] Is what you have read or heard going to affect your ability to sit as an impartial juror in this case?

36. How many of you have never served on a jury before?
37. Are any of you bothered or concerned about the fact that you are being asked to serve on a jury when you have not had any prior experience as a juror?
38. The basic task of those 12 persons who will serve on this jury is to listen to the facts and then to reach a verdict based on those facts. That verdict is of grave concern to all the parties involved in this case. It is of great concern for Karen Mills who is the plaintiff in this case. Foreign Car Manufacturer is also concerned about the decision you will make. The reason we are here in court is because we need a third party to make the decision for us. Karen Mills claims that we are at fault. We claim that Foreign Car Manufacturer is not responsible for the unfortunate disability that Karen Mills experiences today. We, therefore, have come to you as that third party and we all will rely on the decision that you will make at the end of hearing evidence that we present to you in this courtroom. Now some people just don't like to make decisions — they would much rather that someone else make their decisions for them and they certainly don't want to make decisions for other people. I can understand that. I have felt that way myself sometimes. But it is important that each and every person of this jury accept the responsibility that he or she must consider the facts and only the facts and reach a decision based on those facts. Is there anyone here who would rather not have that responsibility? Please just raise your hand and let us know that.
39. This suit is a civil suit, not a criminal suit. In a criminal case, you as jurors would be required to make only one

[1]It might be advisable to ask the judge to continue voir dire on this particular topic on a one-on-one basis so that answers would not prejudice other jurors on the panel who have not read or heard anything about this small car and its safety record.

decision: Is the defendant guilty or not guilty. In a civil case, you are asked to make a decision in two stages: (a) We will be asking you to determine whether Foreign Car Manufacturer was negligent; and (b) If you find negligence and only if you find negligence, you will then be asked to reach a decision concerning compensation to the plaintiff for the damage done to her as a result of that negligence. Do you all understand that you would consider the question of compensation only if you found negligence? Is there anyone who feels that they would not be able to separate the information dealing with these two areas without experiencing difficulty?

40. You realize that although there are twelve persons on this jury, (or six if that is all that is required) each of you will have the task of making up your own mind and voting your own convictions. Now that does not mean that you won't listen to the other members of the jury and consider what they have to say — that is essential in reaching your final verdict. But it does mean that you have to believe in that verdict and not just vote to go along with the other jurors because eight or ten or eleven of them don't see things the same way you do. Do you all feel that you would vote your own conviction and your own conviction only? Is there any person on this panel who feels that if the decision were to come down to eleven persons voting one way and one person voting the other way, that the one person who is not voting with the majority would have to be wrong? Do you all accept that one person can be just as right as eleven persons, considering the way they view the evidence?

41. Have you or any member of your family ever had any association of any nature with Foreign Car Manufacturer of America? No matter how unimportant you think that association might be, please let us know what it is. (Cover employment, purchase of services or supplies, or purchase of an automobile.)

42. Have you or has any member of your family ever had any association of any nature with any agency of federal, state, or local government that has dealt with the establishment of safety standards or safety procedures? No matter how unimportant you think that association might be, please let us know what it is.
43. Have you or has any member of your family had any association with the inspection of automobile accidents or any form of vehicle accident? No matter how unimportant you might think this association might be, please inform us of its nature.
44. I am about to read you a list of potential witnesses. If any of you are personally acquainted with anyone listed or if anyone in your family is acquainted with anyone listed or if you have any connection with anyone on the list, however remote, please raise your hand. (Read the list of witnesses.) (If such relationship is indicated by a potential juror, ask about the nature of the relationship and the extent of that relationship and whether that relationship or acquaintanceship would affect his or her consideration of the case or cause him or her to give added weight to the testimony of that witness.)
45. I am now going to read you a list of the attorneys involved in this case and the firms from which those attorneys come. If you have any acquaintanceship or relationship with any of these attorneys or with any of their firms, please raise your hand and indicate the nature of that relationship and whether that relationship would give any added weight to their presentation of their views.
46. Have you or any member of your family been involved in the establishment of rules or regulations of safety in your work environment?
47. Have you or has any member of your family ever been involved in the writing of safety manuals or safety regulations in any way or had any relationship with the establishment of safety rules or safety regulations or safety standards?

48. Have any of you or members of your family worked in quality control or environmental protection?
49. The court will instruct you that the plaintiff, Karen Mills, has the burden of proof in this case, and since this is a civil case, she must try to prove by the preponderance of the evidence that Foreign Car Manufacturer of America was negligent. Do any of you think that this is an unfair burden to place on the plaintiff?
50. Have you ever served on a jury before? If yes, was it a criminal jury or a civil jury? If it was a civil jury, could you just tell us something about the nature of the case? Especially, did they involve automobile accidents or product liability suits?
51. Is there anything about your previous experiences on a jury or even being involved with a panel and being subjected to questioning by the court and lawyers that makes you feel you would not like to sit again on a jury and in particular would you like not to sit on this one?
52. In your present job or in any previous jobs, have you ever been involved with computers of some kind, although not working for a computer company as such, but just using computers in the nature of your employment? Are any of you skilled at programming computers? If yes, please explain when and what connection you had with computers.
53. During the course of the trial you will hear words and phrases used that are and could be new words and phrases to many of you. We will have experts, including medical experts, engineering experts, and accident reconstruction experts who will be using phrasing and references to technology with which you will be unfamiliar. While we will try to be certain that all words and phrases used by our experts will be explained to you and made understandable to you, will any of you feel that you would not want to sit as a juror on a case involving technical information of a mathematical, engineering, or medical nature?
54. Obviously, there is going to be a great deal of highly

technical material presented during this trial. Can you remember well from only hearing about technical details or do any of you feel that you will need to see something to help you to remember?

55. Is there anyone who has any difficulty seeing or hearing in this courtroom?
56. It will be important that you will be able to remember what you see and hear in this courtroom for several days and even for several weeks. Is there anyone who has any trouble with their memory or who would feel they would have difficulty remembering technical material or technical details that they hear in a bits-and-pieces manner and be able to put it all together at the end of the trial when you do your jury deliberations?
57. Have you or has anyone close to you ever spent more than two weeks in a hospital?
58. Have you or has anyone close to you ever suffered an accident of any kind that has resulted in total or partial disability? If yes, would you please relate the nature of that injury and the degree of disability?
59. Have you or has anyone close to you suffered fractures of the foot or leg or multiple injuries of the body that have resulted in plastic surgery or any kind of disfigurement?
60. Have you or has any person closely related to you ever experienced a back injury of any kind?
61. Have you ever personally ever cared for a person who has been partially or totally disabled for any period of time? If so, please tell us who it was that you cared for and the amount of time that you spent in such care.
62. Will you honestly and to the best of your ability determine each question of fact submitted to you in this courtroom on the basis of the evidence brought here before you in the courtroom and on the law that His Honor (Her Honor) will give concerning this question and on that basis only?
63. Will you promise me that if you are chosen as a juror in this case, that you will decide this case solely on the

basis of the evidence that you hear in this courtroom and on the instructions of this court and that you will not consider any outside sources of information or make any independent investigation of your own outside this courtroom but that you will only use the evidence presented to you in this courtroom to decide this case?

64. When you and your fellow jurors go back to deliberate concerning the verdict, if any one of your fellow jurors states a view or opinion that indicates that he or she does have a prejudice against one of the parties to this lawsuit or is considering some matter that the court has told you not to consider or is unwilling to follow the law as given to you by the judge, will you actually carry out your oath as a juror by speaking out and stating clearly that these matters must not be considered?
65. Is there anyone who would consider jury duty at this time an intrusion on your time or on your plans, and if so, would you prefer not to be here serving on this panel? Please raise your hand if that would be the case.
66. As jurors on this case, you will be deciding whether to award damages to Karen Mills. There is no question that Karen is damaged. There is a question as to whether Foreign Car Manufacturer of America is the cause of that damage. Is there any person on this panel who will, out of sympathy for Karen, feel uncomfortable or guilty if you do not award some damages to Karen? If so, would you please raise your hand and let us know.
67. Will you promise me that if you are chosen as jurors in this case, that you will deal only with the facts of the case and not with personal sympathy for Karen and that, if the facts do not warrant the award of damages to Karen Mills, that you can come back into this courtroom and look Karen in the eye and so say, without feeling guilt or without feeling that you have not done your duty? Can you all promise me that you will deal with the facts and the facts only?

68. As my last question, I would like to ask you if you have any reason at all, however personal or private, that makes you feel that you would not like to serve on this case or that it would make you uncomfortable to serve on this case. If that is so, please raise your hand and indicate to the court such a feeling that you might have.

Sample 6: Defendant's Voir Dire for a Contract Case

PROPOSED VOIR DIRE: Civil Case
TYPE OF CASE: Contract
NAME OF CASE: City of Taron v. Consolidated Tool Co.
CASE SPECIFIC INFORMATION: The tool company had provided the city with specially tooled machines that were to assist them in their gas and electric service.
SPECIAL PROBLEMS OF CASE: A section of the contract was renegotiated after one of the specially tooled machines malfunctioned. There was some question as to whether fraud was involved in the renegotiation or whether all parties understood precisely the nature of the alterations.
FINAL VERDICT: A verdict had not reached the court.

1. Which do you believe is more binding on you, what you say or what you write?[1]
2. Do all of you accept that it is a good idea to read and understand a contract before you sign it?
3. Please raise your hand if you can think of an excuse for voiding a written contract. (If no one raises their hand ask the following.) Since no one raised a hand, does that mean that you would consider yourselves bound to honor the terms of a contract if you had signed it? Please raise your hand if that statement does not express your feelings.

[1]Since this is the defendant's voir dire there are fewer questions concerning background than there would otherwise be. However, if any of the questions that would normally be asked by the plaintiff's attorney for background information were omitted, the defendant's attorney should seek that information.

4. What is your feeling about the terms of a contract? Do you think a contract should be detailed and specific with no room for individual interpretation?
5. I would like now to find out how much experience you have had in signing a contract and in fulfilling the terms of a contract. Would you please raise your hand if you have had the following contracts:
    a. A marriage license
    b. An insurance policy
    c. An automobile loan
    d. The deed to your home
    e. An airline ticket
    f. A credit card like Visa or Master Charge
    g. A contract to build a home or an addition to your home
    h. An employment contract
        (1) Who negotiated the terms of the contract?
        (2) Did you feel that the contract protected your interests as well as your employer's?
        (3) Did you understand the terms of the agreement when you signed?
        (4) Did you seek any advice before you signed the contract?
6. What does the term in good faith mean to you?
7. Have any of you ever tried to break a contract? Have any of you had any close friends or relatives who have attempted to break contracts?
8. Do any of you own property that you rent or lease to others? If yes, do you rent or lease that property with or without a lease? Have you ever had any trouble with your leases? Do you think that a lease is binding or is it not worth the paper it is written on?
9. Are there any of you who do not feel that an agreement to buy or an agreement to purchase is not a contract?
10. If a person signs a contract because of fraud, would any of you feel that *that* contract was binding?
11. How many of you are members of a union?
12. How many of you have ever worked in construction?

13. Have any of you ever contracted or subcontracted for construction? Did you have a written or verbal contract?
14. Have any of you ever experienced any trouble of any kind by "putting it in writing"? Could you give us an idea of the nature of that trouble, as clearly as possible, without feeling that we are prying into your problems?
15. Have any of you ever experienced a bad time as a result of some kind of trouble with a utility company?
16. Have you ever heard the term fuel adjustment as it relates to utility bills? If so, please raise your hand.
17. Would you please raise your hand if you think your current utility bills are too low or reasonable?
18. Do you now work for a utility company or have you ever worked for a utility company? If yes, which company and where and for how long?
19. Do you now or have you ever worked in an energy-related business? If yes, what business, where, in what position, and how long was that employment?
20. Do any of your family members or any of your close friends work either in an energy-related business or for a utility company?
21. Do you think a contract can ever be cancelled without the agreement of all the parties involved?
22. Do any of you have any questions about contracts that you feel should be answered before we continue with jury selection?
23. If you were trying to reconstruct something that happened in the past, would you rely more on what someone remembered or said they remembered, or more on what was written by the participants at the time?
24. Do you believe that people often unconsciously tend to remember things in the light that is most favorable to themselves? Don't you believe that that is pretty much human nature?
25. Do you understand that it is one of the duties of the jury to examine each witness, each fact for the credibility of the evidence offered from the witness stand?
26. Does that idea bother any of you?

27. You understand that we probably will hear conflicting statements concerning specific elements of the case. Will any of you have any trouble at all in establishing a standard to follow in helping you to determine the truth?
28. Are there any of you who will hesitate to make a judgment about what actually is the truth? This is an important part of jury service in this case and if you would not want to be called on to make this determination, please let me know at this time.
29. Would any of you have any trouble in determining what was the difference between a true report of an occurrence and a report that just tried to save face?
30. Would you tend to place more reliance on what was written after the fact or what was written at the time of the occurrence?

Sample 7: Plaintiff's Voir Dire for an Eminent Domain Case

PROPOSED VOIR DIRE: Civil Case

TYPE OF CASE: Eminent Domain

NAME OF CASE: In the Matter of the Petition of the California State Highway Commission for Condemnation of Private Property for Highway I-275 in Warne County, California

CASE SPECIFIC INFORMATION: An apartment complex that had its entrance blocked by road construction and also lost about ninety percent of its frontage sued the state for compensation in addition to what was offered.

SPECIAL PROBLEMS OF CASE: Due to the economics of the real estate market, there were complex questions about how much damage was actually caused to the apartment complex by the loss of the frontage and by the blocking of the entrance for a six-month period. After the initial trial in which only $50,000 was awarded by the jury, the judge, finding the award to be deficient in view of the evidence that had been presented, granted a retrial. The plaintiff sought $1.5 million.

FINAL VERDICT: Very favorable to the plaintiff.

Members of the jury, this is a proceeding in eminent domain, also called a condemnation proceeding, instituted by petitioner, the Department of State Highways, to take private property for the purpose of constructing Interstate Highway I-275. At this stage of the proceeding, your function is to determine the amount of compensation to be paid to the respondents for the taking. The particular property involved in this case is about ninety percent of the frontage of the Bear Creek apartment complex (now called Maple Tree Apartments), which was taken to build the overpass carrying Joy Road over Interstate I-275.

1. Please state your name and address.
2. Please state your marital status.
3. Please state the number of children you have giving their ages and occupations.
4. How long have you lived where you now live?
5. Where have you lived before?
6. Have you ever been active in service organizations?
7. Are you acquainted with other persons on the panel — any contact at all with any of them, either as friends, neighbors, church members, co-workers, or relatives?
8. Have you ever been a witness in a lawsuit? If you have been a witness, did you testify in the court or were you just interviewed outside the courtroom with your statement being taken in the form of a deposition?
9. Now, while you have informed me that you have neither been a witness nor a party to a lawsuit in the past, have you had a member of your family or a close friend who was either a party or a witness in a lawsuit? Because of that close relationship to that person, do you have any doubts or negative feelings regarding the judicial system in this country? If you do, would you please share with us what those feelings are?
10. I asked you if any of you have ever had your statement taken in the form of a deposition. Now, a deposition is a statement taken under oath before a court reporter and then transcribed into a written form and it would be just

the same as the testimony that would be produced in the courtroom if the person could be physically present in the courtroom. However, it is sometimes impossible for a person to be physically present in the courtroom, so the deposition, that sworn written statement, is read to the jury in the courtroom. We will be having testimony of this nature in this case. Is there anyone who will find testimony that is produced in that way less credible or less impressive than if the person were actually here in the courtroom? Would you please raise your hand if you think you will have trouble listening to depositions and accepting them just the same as if the person were physically present with you here on the witness stand?

11. For your information, this case will probably take about four weeks. It will require your presence in this courtroom from 9:00 in the morning until 5:00 in the afternoon, with time out for lunch. Is there anyone here who would find that a hardship for health reasons or personal reasons or occupational reasons?
12. We are going to be working together on this trial for all of that time. For this reason, I would like to know the following:
    a. Will it cause you any hardship to stay with us that long?
    b. Will it cause any hardship on any member of your family?
    c. To any of your present plans?
    d. Do you get bored easily?
    e. Do you often take a nap during the day? If so, do you think you can function easily without having the opportunity to nap?
    f. Do you get tired easily, especially from sitting a long time in the same place?
    g. Do you suffer from headache or any physical pain from inactivity?
    h. Will your legs bother you from being required to sit so long?

13. Have you or any member of you family ever had any association of any nature with the State Highway Commission or the State Highway Department? No matter how unimportant you think that association might be, please let us know what it is (cover areas of employment, provision of services or supplies, or involvement in other land condemnation proceedings).
14. Have you or any member of you family ever had any association of any nature with any agency of federal state or local government? No matter how unimportant you think that association might be, please let us know what it is (cover areas of employment, provision of services or supplies, or involvement in other condemnation proceedings).
15. Have you or any members of your family ever worked or been associated in any way with the following: local property tax assessors, appraisals, CPAs, real estate sales, land development, or construction work?
16. Have you ever owned any income property — that is any property of any kind from which you received rent?
17. Have you ever managed income property for another person?
18. Have you ever studied real estate or land development? Or have you worked in these areas in any way so that you feel that you have some knowledge or expertise on the subjects mentioned above?
19. Is there any occasion when you would substitute your own personal knowledge of land management or planning for land use over the testimony that hear from expert witnesses from the witness stand?
20. Would you consider the other men and women who will be serving with you on a jury, who will be listening to the same witnesses and hearing the same testimony that you will hear from the witness stand, to be just as informed as you are? The reason that we are asking this is that the only information that you can consider is the information that you hear produced for you in this room from this witness stand. Is there anyone that would have any trouble with that?

21. Do you agree that no property owner should be compelled to enter into a settlement with the government?
22. Is there anyone among you who feels that the property owners should receive less than "just compensation" for his land because it is to be used for a public purpose?
23. Do you have any prejudice against a property owner who is contesting the value placed on his property by the government?
24. In this case, both the state and the property owners will present "opinion" evidence by so-called expert real estate appraisers. Do you believe that an appraiser or other expert witnesses called by the state is entitled to any special belief or credence simply because he was called to the stand by the state, or will you judge all witnesses for both sides on the basis of their qualifications and testimony on the witness stand, regardless of who called them?
25. Do you believe in "fate"? That is, do you think that something generally happens because it is time for it to happen or it is predestined to happen at that time, or do you believe that when common responsibility standards are followed, many damaging occurrences could be prevented?
26. Would you please raise your hand if you have never had a mortgage of any kind on real estate?
27. Do you contribute regularly to a savings account?
28. Have any of you invested in any stocks or bonds or land development or any buildings?
29. Have you ever experienced a major loss or a major gain through investment in real estate? Be specific.
30. Has any member of this jury heard this case discussed or has anyone on the jury read or heard anything about this case in the media? If the answer is yes, what is it you have read or heard? Is what you have read or heard going to affect your ability to sit as an impartial juror in this case, or will it be possible for you to put out of your mind anything you have read or heard since it is not testimony in this case and cannot be used in making a final decision about this case?

31. I am about to read to you a list of potential witnesses. If any of you are personally acquainted with anyone listed, or if anyone in your family is acquainted with anyone listed, or if you have any connection with anyone on the list, however remote, please raise your hand as I read the list. If you do not raise your hand, I will assume that there is no such connection. (Read list of potential witnesses.) What is the nature of your relationship and the extent of that relationship? Will that acquaintanceship or relationship affect your consideration of the case or give added weight to the testimony of that witness?
32. I am about to read to you a list of potential respondents' witnesses for this case. They are all the people who have any interest in the property involved. (Read list of respondents' witnesses.) What is the nature and extent of that relationship? Is there any reason to feel that you would be biased for or against any of the respondents? Do you feel that it would cause your embarrassment or special stress if you are required to sit on the jury in a case in which the respondents are involved? Are you personally acquainted with the respondents or any employee of the respondents or any member of the of the respondents' families? If yes, what is the nature and extent of the relationship?
33. The constitution and statutes of the State of California provide that the public has the right to take private property for public purposes, regardless of the owner's wishes in the matter. Do any of you disagree with this or have any problem accepting this constitutional concept?
34. The United States Constitution and the California Constitution both require, however, that when the government chooses to exercise that right to take private property, the government has an obligation to pay for it and that the owners of the property have the right to receive just compensation. Do any of you disagree with or have any problem accepting this constitutional idea?

35. The constitution and statutes of the State of California both require that when the government takes private property, the just compensation that is constitutionally required is determined, not by the government agency taking the property, such as the Highway Department, but by this court after a full trial. That is to say, the owner is not obliged to accept whatever the Highway Department offers, but may ask the court to determine just compensation. Do any of you disagree with that method of dealing with such issues?
36. You are all citizens of the State of California, and the petitioner in this case is the California State Highway Commission. Does it bother you or concern you in any way to know that you are going to be asked to reach a decision that you think might affect questions concerning involvement with groups pushing tax reform. If any of you have any questions or any doubt, would you raise your hand and let us know at this time?
37. The highway project with which we are concerned here is an interstate highway. That means that 90 percent of the money to pay for the project (including the award in this case) comes from the Federal Highway Trust Fund, which is financed by federal taxes on gasoline and diesel fuel. The remaining 10 percent will come from the state's Motor Vehicle Highway Fund, which is financed by state taxes on diesel fuel and gasoline, license fees for cars and trucks, and a special axle-mile tax on trucks. Does the fact that you personally have contributed in a small way when you buy fuel for your car to the overall fund from which this award will be paid prejudice you or bother you in any way?
38. Do you understand that any sum that you award in this case will not in any way affect your own taxes?
39. If the respondents prove to your satisfaction that they are entitled to a certain sum of money as just compensation, whatever that amount may be, would you return a verdict in that amount even though the federal and state governments must pay the award from highway taxes?

40. Are you or, to your knowledge, is any member of your immediate family personally acquainted with or related in any way to any of the attorneys for the respondents or any of the attorneys for the petitioner? (List all attorneys.) If the answer is affirmative, please explain the extent and nature of that relationship or acquaintanceship and explain whether you have ever been or ever contemplated being a client of that attorney.
41. Are you or, to your knowledge, has any member of your immediate family been personally acquainted with or related in any way to any of the wives, parents, or children of the witnesses previously mentioned, the petitioner, any of the respondents, any of the lawyers in the law firms mentioned above, or any of the employees of the law firms?
42. Are you aware that money is the only form of compensation that a person can seek under our system of justice? Do you accept that we cannot ask that things be restored to exactly the same condition that they were in on the date of the taking in 1970? Is there anyone who has any problem with the fact that an award of money damages is the only form of remedy that you will be able to consider in this trial?
43. Do you have any feeling against a person or corporation coming to court asking to be compensated with money for damages that may have been done to them?
44. Do you believe in awarding a fair, just, and *adequate* verdict to a person or corporation who has been damaged through the fault of others?
45. If you were damaged solely by the conduct of another, would you expect that you would be compensated by the person responsible for whatever damages had been inflicted on you?
46. Under our system of jurisprudence, people like you, the members of this jury, are required to determine what amount in a given case constitutes a fair, just, adequate, and reasonable compensation for a given injury. Do you have any quarrel with that system?

47. Naturally, you will want and need to hear all of the evidence first, but after you have heard the evidence, if, in your opinion, it would take a very substantial sum of money to make fair compensation in this case, would you hesitate to award that amount just because of the size of the award?
48. By adequate, I mean that it is sufficient to compensate for all of the elements of damage, whatever they may be, small or large. Do you understand that?
49. The purpose of these last few questions is to make sure that you do not have some predetermined financial limits that you carry around in your head beyond which you would not award any more money. I say this because some people, no matter how badly they think the taking of the land and access may have damaged the project, will, in their own mind, without telling anyone else, simply say "I will not award more than *X* amount of dollars," whatever that figure might be. Do you feel that way? Do you carry such a ceiling in your head?
50. If the evidence shows serious damage caused by the taking of this land and access and by the state's overall activities, will you award a full measure of justice in keeping with the damages?
51. The respondents claim a loss of well over $4 million in all on this project. It is not now and never has been the claim of respondents that all of this loss is directly traceable to the taking of the land for the interstate highway by the California State Highway Commission. However, we are claiming that the highway department was a substantial contributor to the damages that occurred, recognizing that there were also other contributing causes for the losses. Do you think that it will be difficult for you to sit and hear evidence and make a judgment as to the extent to which the California State Highway Department was responsible for the losses in connection with the Bear Creek apartment project?
52. Let me ask all this from another perspective. Does a million dollar verdict sound too high to you for any

damages or any loss, even if the evidence supports such a figure?

53. Can you imagine as you sit here prior to this trial a set of circumstances or facts, any set of circumstances or facts, which would be presented to you as a juror, that would demand that you award a million dollars to any party in any lawsuit?
54. In other words, does the word reasonable when it is used in relationship to the concept of damages in a civil court case imply to you a small amount of money or an amount of money that has a certain dollar ceiling on it?
55. Do any of you have a ceiling that seems to you "reasonable" in most cases, a ceiling over which you will not go? If you have a ceiling, would you raise your hand and tell me what it is?
56. For the information of those of you who have never been a juror or have never been involved as a party or a witness in any lawsuit, at the conclusion of all of the evidence and after closing arguments by counsel you will be given instructions concerning the law by the judge. Will you apply the law as given by the judge to you, even though you *might not* agree with it?
57. Will you honestly and to the best of your ability determine each question of fact submitted to you in this courtroom on the basis of the evidence brought here before you in the courtroom and on the law that His Honor (Her Honor) will give you concerning this question and on that basis only?
58. Will you promise me that if you are chosen as a juror in this case, that you will decide this case solely on the basis of the evidence that you hear in this courtroom and on the instructions of the court and that you will not consider any outside source of information or make any independent investigation of your own outside this courtroom but that you will only use the evidence presented to you in this courtroom to decide the case?
59. When you and your fellow jurors go back to deliberate concerning your verdict, if any one of your fellow jurors

states a view or opinion that indicates that that juror does have a prejudice against one of the parties to this lawsuit, or is considering some matter that the court has told you not to consider, or is unwilling to follow the law as given you by the judge, will you remember your oath as jurors to speak up and state clearly that such matters are outside the law and must not be considered?

60. If you were one of the respondents, would you be satisfied to have a juror who was in your present frame of mind sitting as a juror on your case? If you would not be satisfied to have a juror like yourself on your own case, please raise your hand.
61. As my last question, I would like to ask you if you have any reason at all, however personal or private, that makes you feel that you would not like to serve on this case, or that it would be uncomfortable for you to serve on this case. If that is so, please raise your hand and indicate to the court such a feeling that you might have.

Sample 8: Defendant's Voir Dire for a Criminal Rape Case

PROPOSED VOIR DIRE: Criminal Case
TYPE OF CASE: Rape
NAME OF THE CASE: State of North Dakota v. Dan Stevens
CASE SPECIFIC INFORMATION: Dan Stevens is a police officer in a medium-sized town. His wife is a very popular high school teacher and Dan has been on the police force for seven years. The alleged victim was a young native American woman. She is very attractive; in fact, she was a former beauty queen. The facts of the case indicated that the police officer violated three of the codes of the police department: (a) He took a police car outside the county line; (2) He called in and said that he was answering a call when, in fact, he was not; and (3) He made a confession that he had engaged in sexual acts with this young woman but claimed that she had consented. There was also evidence that the young woman had consumed extensive

amounts of alcohol and had smoked several joints of marijuana. The definition of rape would include "taking advantage" of a woman when she was in an alcoholic or drugged state.

SPECIAL PROBLEMS OF CASE: The primary problem of the case concerned the credibility of the defendant as well as the credibility of the victim. Also, extensive coverage of the incident by the media resulted in a change of venue, but that did not remove the case from the media coverage area. Two other police officers had recently been charged with crimes and as a result a member of the city council had taken on the task of "cleaning up the Police Department."

FINAL VERDICT: Not guilty.

1. Would you please state your name, address, and current occupation. Please also state the name of your spouse, if you have one, or the name of any ex-spouse and his or her occupation. If you have not been employed at your current occupation for three years, please inform us as to prior occupations or prior employment that you might have had.
2. I am going to read to you a list of the witnesses in this case and I would like you to indicate if you have any knowledge or any relationship to any of the persons on this list. When I read the list, please raise your hand if you recognize any of the names. Then we will ask you to indicate for us the nature of that relationship. (Read the list of witnesses.)
3. Have you ever been a witness yourself?
4. Have you ever been a party in a court action?
5. I am now going to read to you a list of attorneys. These attorneys include the members of my firm and the members of the firm of the local counsel and the legal staff of the county attorney's office. Please indicate after I have read the list if you know any these people or if you have done business with any of them or if you have come into any contact with their offices. (Read the list of attorneys.)

6. Do you have any children or grandchildren? If so, what are their ages and what sex are they and, if they are old enough to be employed, what employments do they have?
7. Are you related to or do you know any law enforcement personnel?
8. Have you, yourself, ever been employed in any way with law enforcement or with the court system or with the legal profession?
9. Do you have any responsibility for the hiring of people for the police department or the evaluation of them or do you know or are you related to anyone who has such a responsibility?
10. Have you ever lived in the community from which Dan Stevens works as a police officer?
11. Do you go to church on a regular basis?
12. Would you tell us what religion you are a member of?
13. Do you read the Bible on a daily or regular basis? If yes, do you interpret it literally?
14. Have you ever taught Sunday school or other religious classes?
15. Are you related to any members of the clergy or to any religious leaders or religious instructors?
16. If you have heard of this case, what have you heard or read about it?
17. Do you know Dan Stevens or any member of his family? Have you ever met his wife?
18. Do you know any of the schoolteachers of the system in which Dan Stevens' wife teaches?
19. Do you know the woman who claims to be raped, Rachel, or do you know any member of her family? She has a mother and father (list their names), and she has three sisters and one brother (list their names). Do you recognize any of those names or do you think that you might have had contact with any member of that family?
20. Are your familiar or have you ever had occasion to go to the Circle 8 Bar in ______________________ (the hometown of the police officer)?

21. Have you ever gone to the North 40 Bar in that community?
22. Are there any of you on this panel who do not drink or who believe that it is wrong to consume alcohol? If so, would you please tell us how you feel about the consumption of alcohol.
23. Do you read the daily newspaper? If yes, have you read any of the recent newspaper articles that have covered this trial? If so, please raise your hand and let us discuss the nature of the knowledge that you have of this case.
24. Do you know any male or female who claims to have been or who has been raped?
25. Have any of you ever stated an opinion concerning rape or rape victims or rapists? If you have stated such an opinion in the past, would you please share with those of us in this courtroom exactly what that opinion was.
26. Do you believe females generally fantasize about being raped?
27. When I just asked that question, how did you feel — did it make any of you angry or upset? If yes, would you please indicate what your reaction was and why you think you felt that way?
28. Have you taken any special courses dealing with sexual relationships between the sexes?
29. Do you know Dr. Smith, a psychologist? Do you know any member of his family?
30. Do you have any strong views on what kind of sex constitutes normal sexual acts? If yes, would you please explain your views.
31. You will be hearing some rather explicit language in the course of this trial, some of which you might find offensive. Will the hearing of explicit language upset you or bother you to such an extent that you will not be able to concentrate on the main question in this case, which is whether or not my client, Dan Stevens, is guilty or not?
32. Do you believe that a person can be raped without the use of weapons or without that person becoming bruised in any way, shape, or form?

33. How much or what type of actions must a person take before you believe that he has not given consent to another to have sexual intercourse?
34. Do you believe a person could actively participate in a sexual act that was rape?
35. What are your views regarding sexual activity between consenting adult partners who are not married to each other and who are of the opposite sex?
36. Are your familiar with the general area and countryside around and south of Dan's community?
37. Do rumors or gossip influence you?
38. Have you heard any rumors or gossip concerning this case?
39. Will you be able to put that gossip or those rumors out of your mind and permit us to try this case in this courtroom and will you rely only on the evidence or the lack of evidence that comes to you from this witness stand?
40. Are you aware that anyone can accuse anyone else of anything?
41. How do you judge credibility of witnesses?
42. Would you take into consideration a person's background, occupation or lack thereof before you give weight to their testimony?
43. Dan Stevens is a policeman. He will admit to you that he did not follow the regulations of his occupation. Dan Stevens will admit to you that he broke three rules and regulations on the night in question. For these reasons, he has resigned his office and will not seek further employment as a police officer. Dan will admit to you that he broke faith with his employer. For this, he has great regret. However, Dan did not do anything that was criminal. He did not commit a crime. He did make several mistakes and for these mistakes he has lost his job and his marriage has been damaged. Just because Dan was not a good employee and just because Dan was not a good husband, would you feel that he was a criminal and that he should be found guilty of a criminal act?

44. Dan is more than a man who has been charged with rape, he is a police officer who has been charged with rape. Do you feel that you would put a different level of expectation on Dan's acts because he was a police officer and because he was wearing a police officer's uniform at the time that the act of intercourse occurred? Will you treat Dan any differently than you would a man who had been in any other type of employment?
45. What standards would you expect Dan to live up to that would be different from the standards that you would expect of any other man?
46. Dan is presumed to be innocent as he sits here in this courtroom today. That is the law. Do any of you have any problem in accepting that as the right attitude to have toward Dan?
47. Do any of you think that Dan should have to be required to prove to you that he is not guilty of rape?
48. Do you think that Dan Stevens as the defendant in this case should solve the puzzle for you and explain to you exactly how it came about that these charges occurred? Do you think that is his duty or his responsibility?
49. Do you all accept that it is the state's responsibility to show guilt beyond a reasonable doubt? That is, that the burden of proof lies with the state? Do any of you have any trouble accepting that concept?
50. The court will tell you in instruction that the standard that you will follow in determining guilt beyond reasonable doubt is that you must be certain to a moral certainty before you can convict. Will you follow that instruction?
51. If the court tells you that the standard means that the judgment you will exercise in looking at the facts is the same judgment you would bring in deciding matters most serious and grave to you personally, will you follow that? Do you understand how that would help you to determine the verdict in this case?
52. If the court says that if you should pause and hesitate in your judgment that then you would have a reasonable doubt and you must acquit, would you follow that?

53. If you find yourself in a position where the evidence points toward guilt and also points toward innocence, would you accept that you *must* give Dan, the defendant, the benefit of the doubt? That that means that you must acquit Dan Stevens? Is there anyone who does not believe that that is the way that you must vote if you have evidence that points both toward guilt and toward innocence?
54. In other words, if there is a reasonable basis for you to feel that Dan is not guilty, would you vote not guilty?
55. Back in the jury room, after you have heard all of the evidence, you are looking at all of these facts that we have given you, the evidence, and you conclude that Dan could have done it the way the state says. You are suspicious that he could have done it that way. How will you vote? (Obviously, they would have to vote not guilty.)
56. You conclude, after looking at all of the facts, that it is possible that Dan did it the way the state claimed. Now, how will you vote?
57. You conclude back in the jury room, that Dan probably did it. Now how will you vote? Will you require the state to meet the standard of reasonable doubt for all elements and will you hold the state responsible for doing that?
58. Some of you indicated that you had read or heard some items about this case but that you don't really remember it very clearly. Back in the jury room, you begin to remember some of the things that you have read that did not come into evidence before the court. And you are not sure then that the state has proven its case beyond a reasonable doubt, would you let anything that you have read or heard about this case sway your judgment?
59. You realize, don't you, that only the facts, only the evidence, only the witnesses who testify in this court can be considered in reaching a verdict? Therefore, will you treat any other information or anything that you have read or anything that you have heard, like a tech-

nical foul in a basketball game — that is, you will call the memory of that evidence that has not been produced in the courtroom or that information that has not been produced in the courtroom as foul and you will take the ball out of bounds again and start the game over again without any consideration of what occurred before the foul was called? Is that okay with you? Those will be the instructions of the court. Will you accept that as the right way to conduct this ballgame?

60. If you decide that Dan Stevens is not guilty, will you be embarrassed to say so because of what you have read or because you have decided against the prosecution? Will you be swayed by the majority opinion? Will you be swayed by what you feel the community here might want you to do or by what some friend might want you to do who is not going to sit through this trial? Will you decide on your own and go back into your neighborhood and be proud of your vote regardless of which way you vote?
61. Have you ever had any special medical training or been related to someone who has had this type of training? That is, have you had any Red Cross or general first aid or hospital aid training? Any training as a L.P.N., R.N., or paramedic with the fire department?
62. Will you agree with me that someone's opinion is only as good as the facts on which that opinion is based? In other words, if the facts are wrong or not accurate, then your opinion would not be accurate. Wouldn't that be true?
63. Have you ever gone to your family doctor and had to switch to a specialist?
64. Would you go to a general practitioner or to an orthopedic surgeon if you had a broken back?
65. Would you agree that a specialist has more knowledge, training, and expertise in his particular area of study than is normally possessed by a general practitioner?[1]

[1]The general practitioner who first examined the alleged rape victim at the hospital found bruises around a shoulder and the arms that he attributed to

66. Have you had any prior jury experience? If yes, did you serve on a criminal case or a civil case? Were you the foreman on the jury?
67. You know that Dan Stevens, the defendant, is charged with rape. That is an accusation only. That information that was read to you by the judge before we began jury selection was information that was merely a method of bringing the charge. The court will tell you that it is not evidence. Will you all accept that?
68. Do you believe that since Dan Stevens is charged with a crime, that there must be something to it? That is, do you believe that where there is smoke, there is probably a fire?
69. Are we then starting uphill with you? Do we have to prove something to you in order to have you vote not guilty?
70. Do you believe that the police sometimes arrest innocent people?
71. Do you think it is possible that Dan Stevens is not guilty as charged?
72. Have any of you stated an opinion about this case or about the charges that have been brought in this case? If you have, would you just state what that opinion was?
73. Do you want to serve on this case?[2]
74. This is a serious case, especially for my client, Dan Stevens. Will you be fair in all of your considerations about

---

the rape. A specialist was to testify that these bruises came from contact with the steering column and the steering wheel and that they probably occurred during the sexual activity that occurred in the front seat of the car. He was also to testify that there were similar bruises on the defendant, Dan Stevens.

[2]Frequently lawyers will state that they do not want a juror who will say that he or she wants to serve on a case because they doubt the sincerity and the reasonableness of any person who wants to serve on a particular case. However, many jurors will state that they want to serve on a case only because they find the drama of courtroom holds high interest for them. It is important to notice the nonverbal reactions to this questions more than the verbal reactions. It is wise to distrust those persons who proclaim too strongly that they do *not* want to serve, rather than that they would serve. Also, if a prospective juror indicates that he or she would serve on the case only because "it is my duty," that person is probably more of an authoritarian type and more apt to be responsive to the arguments of the state.

this case, even though the charges of rape might be personally abhorrent to you?

75. I do not expect you to approve of Dan Stevens' actions on that warm June night. However, many people do things that we do not approve of. That makes the people who do those thing seem unwise, perhaps, or even stupid, but they should not be considered criminals. Will you look for evidence of a crime and not just for evidence of unwise or stupid acts when you deliberate in the jury room?

76. During the course of this trial, both the state's attorney and I will make objections. We make objections to information that is not necessary as evidence in this case. There are many things that occur in the investigation of a case that are interesting perhaps, but are not essential to the main items in determining whether Dan Stevens is guilty as charged. Therefore, when interesting information that is irrelevant or outside the concerns of this court is introduced into evidence, or attempted to be introduced as evidence, there will be objections. When an objection is sustained, it means that the judge agrees that the information should not come before this court and that it might confuse the issues of your decision-making. However, you might find those items to be interesting and you might object that there are so many objections offered. We might even make you angry in the way that we conduct the course of our trial. Is there anyone who will hold my actions as an attorney against my client, Dan Stevens? If we make you angry, will you hold your anger against us and not against Dan?

77. This will be a long trial, probably it will last ten days to fourteen days. Because of that, I would like to know the following:
    a. Is there any reason why you could not stay with us for that period of time?
    b. Will it cause any hardship on your family or on your present plans?
    c. Is relaxing at the end of the day difficult for you? If

we have hard days here in the courtroom, will you find it so difficult to relax that you will not be able to pay close attention to the testimony to search for inconsistencies in the testimony?

d. Will you have difficulty getting going in the morning — doing the things that you have to do?

78. Will you be able to give us your full, undivided attention for the next ten to fourteen days?

79. Now suppose at the end of the trial you find yourself in the minority. That could be either way; say the vote was ten to two or nine to three or eight to four or whatever. I would like to know, then, the following:
   a. Do you enjoy being with groups of people?
   b. Do you delay doing things you have to do?
   c. Do you see yourself as stubborn?
   d. Do others see you as stubborn?
   e. Are you good at organizing and helping others to accomplish tasks?
   f. Do you often help others solve their problems?
   g. Do you have difficulty expressing yourself?
   h. Do you usually just go along with the crowd?
   i. Is being alone upsetting to you?
   j. Even when there is disagreement among the members of a group, can you continue working with that group until you are able to reach an agreement?
   k. Will you change your mind just to please others or will you insist on knowing the reason that you should change your mind?
   l. Finally then, if you are in the minority, will you listen to others and reason with them but maintain your own view if you believe you are right?

80. Are you the kind of juror that you would want if you found a relative or a friend or even yourself in a similar situation to that which faces Dan Stevens in this courtroom?

81. Is there any reason that you can think of as to why you could not be a fair and impartial and just juror in this

case? Is there any reason at all that would make you not want to serve on this case? If you have any reservations of any kind, please indicate those to us at this time. If you do not want to discuss the nature of those reservations, feel free not to do so. Simply indicate that you would rather not serve on this jury and we can consider that indication in that light.

Sample 9: Defendant's Voir Dire for a Criminal Murder Case

PROPOSED VOIR DIRE: Criminal Case
TYPE OF CASE: Murder
NAME OF THE CASE: State of South Dakota v. Harry "Hank" Grooms
CASE SPECIFIC INFORMATION: Hank Grooms was charged with murder in the shooting death of Gary Haysacker in the holding pen on Groom's ranch at roundup time. The holding pen was just off the Indian reservation property, whereas most of the cattle pasture was on reservation land. Hank Grooms had lived all his life in the county in which he was to be tried. In spite of intense publicity and hard feelings against him in the community Grooms resisted change of venue because he "wanted to be tried by his friends, his neighbors and his peers." Mr. Haysacker, the victim, had been a cattleman of high standing in the community, but a man with a reputation for having a violent temper and for performing violent acts. He had five sons, all with similar reputations. About sixty to seventy percent of the jurors were native Americans.
SPECIAL PROBLEMS OF CASE: The defendant, Hank Grooms, was well known in the area as a cattle rustler. He had served time when he was a young man and continued to be considered by most of the people in the area to be an active rustler. Additionally, no gun had been found on the victim, yet Grooms had claimed self-defense. His claim was dependent on a remark allegedly made by the victim to the defendant: "I'm going to gut shoot you and leave you in the dust to die."

Media coverage had been excessive and there was considerable rumor connected with the case. The trial was held in a small town where almost everyone knew everyone else and where the reputation of both the victim and the defendant was widely known. The American Indian Movement (AIM) had taken the position that native Americans should not be required to serve on the "whiteman's" jury so there was some anticipation of trouble from native American leaders in the community.

The sons of the victim had "gone riding" — that is, they had contacted various members of the community, long before the actual jury list was published, to warn them that anyone who found Hank Grooms not guilty of murder would face "lots of trouble." Generally, the citizens of the community believed that the Haysacker "boys" were capable of great violence.

TRIAL VERDICT: Not guilty. (A panel of 700 jurors was called for jury duty. Of these, over 600 were excused for cause.)

At this time, ladies and gentlemen of the jury, I will ask you certain questions concerning your qualifications. I will discuss with you certain areas that may to you seem very personal. Please do not be offended or embarrassed, as it is not my intention to pry into your personal lives. I ask you these questions in good faith to make certain that we will have twelve people who will be fair, just, honest, and courageous, and who will decide this case on the evidence or the lack of evidence. I ask you these questions so that you can satisfy yourselves that you *will* be able to sit for this case and render honest, courageous, and fair judgment. You might be surprised to hear that we are seeking courageous jurors, but we are well aware of how divided the community is and has been as a result of this case and we know that it will take people not only who are honest and fair but who are courageous to sit on this panel of twelve people.

1. Where were you born?
2. What is your educational background?

3. Where did you attend elementary school and high school?
4. Did you continue your formal education past high school? If yes, where and for how long?
5. What subjects did you take in college?
6. What was your major field of study?
7. What college degrees do you hold?
8. What is your age?[1]
9. What is your marital status?[2]
10. Is your spouse employed outside the home?[3]
11. Where have you resided during the last ten years?
12. Do you own or rent your current home?
13. Do you plan to leave this community in the near future?[4]
14. Where do you now work?
15. How long have your worked there?
16. Could you share with me what kind of work you do — that is, what is the general description of your work duties?
17. Do you plan to change jobs in the near future? If yes, why? Where to you plan to go? What kind of job do you plan to seek?
18. Could you just describe for me the kinds of activities you normally would do during an average work week?
19. What kinds of decisions do you make on your job? To

[1] Avoid phrasings of this question such as "How old are you?" This implies a value judgment about ages, whereas the question "What is your age?" is neutral and eliminates any evaluation content; therefore, it is less offensive to most people. Also, if you ask men their ages, you should ask the women their ages as well. If you feel that some members of the panel will be offended by having to state their ages in years, then ask for an age range; for instance, "Are you in the age group of 20 to 40, 40 to 60, or over 60?"

[2] Avoid a question like "Are you married?" It can imply that a marrage is desirable or undesirable and as such can be offensive to either a recently divorced person or a person who has never married.

[3] It is important to use the word spouse to avoid any negative implications that some may associate with the words wife or husband.

[4] These last three questions were important in this case since community involvement and knowledge of the reputations of the people concerned was so intense.

whom are you responsible for those decisions? (Or if the person indicates that he or she does not make decisions ask: To whom do you report at your work?)

20. Do you have people working under you? If yes, how many?
21. Is there anybody with whom you work here on the jury panel?
22. Have you ever done any other kind of work than you are currently doing? If yes, what kind of work and what were your duties?
23. Do you now or have you ever belonged to any union?
24. Have you ever been an active government employee? If yes, will the fact that the government is prosecuting this case cause you to be partial toward the prosecution? That is, will you identify with the prosecution since you were at one time a government employee?
25. What is your religious preference, that is, if you have a religious preference?
26. Would you say that you attend religious services on a regular basis?
27. Do you have any children? If yes, what are their ages, sexes, residences, and occupations if applicable?
28. Are you doing any volunteer work now or have you ever done any? If yes, in what organization?
29. Are you active in any union, veteran's, or senior citizen's group? If yes, which one?
30. Is your spouse active in any of these kinds of groups?
31. Are you a member of any political party?
32. To what political organization do you belong?
33. Are any of you registered as an independent? If yes, have you always been registered as independent or was that a recent change?
34. Have you ever been in the military service? If yes, ask the following series of questions:
    a. Where and when?
    b. What branch of the service?
    c. Were you in active duty?
    d. What ranks did you hold in the military?

e. How long were you in the service?
f. Did you ever participate in a court-martial as a member of the court?
g. Did you have any experience with disciplinary activities while you were in the service?
h. While you were in the service, were you ever on military police duty?
i. Did you volunteer for the armed forces? Where and when? Or were you drafted? If so, where and when?

35. Has anyone in your immediate family or anyone close to you been injured or killed while serving in the military? If yes, ask the following questions:
    a. Was that a front line injury or death?
    b. Would you please share with me the details of that injury or death?
    c. If it was an injury, what was the extent of the injury?
    d. Is there anything about that experience that would cause you to feel that you could not judge the government and the defendant in an equally fair and impartial manner?
36. Do you believe that police officers are human just like you and me? By that I mean, do you believe they are subject to the same human weaknesses as you and I?
37. Do you feel then that a police officer may make a mistake during the course of performing the duties of his job?
38. Do you feel that under certain circumstances, that a police officer could make a mistake, maybe even a serious mistake?
39. Do you think it is the obligation of the police officer to investigate all the evidence or just to find evidence until they feel that they can prove someone is guilty?
40. Do you think a police officer should be working for the prosecution or do you think a police officer is an objective gatherer of facts?
41. If the testimony revealed that the police officer had

erred or used improper judgment or had not made a complete investigation, how would you react to such testimony?

42. Are you connected with any police department?
43. Have you ever been connected with any type of police force?
44. Do you have any immediate relatives or close friends who are connected with the police or with any type of law enforcement agency?
45. Is there anything in your lifestyle, that is, in your job or hobby or any part-time activity, that causes you to come in contact with the office of the sheriff of this county or of any surrounding county?
46. Does your lifestyle cause you to come in contact with the State Department of Criminal Investigation?
47. Have you or has any member of your family or a close friend ever worked as a volunteer or an employee for a law enforcement agency on the local, state, or federal level? If yes, when and where and what kind of activities were you (they) involved in?
48. Have you or has any member of your family or a close friend ever been a victim of a crime of violence? If yes, would you please explain the circumstances and the nature of that crime?
49. Have you or has anyone close to you ever been the victim of a crime similar to the crime charged here; for example, were you ever shot at or shot or ever threatened with a gun or weapon of any kind? If yes, please explain that experience.
50. Have you ever been injured with any kind of weapon? If yes, please tell us about that experience.
51. Have you or a relative or close friend of yours ever been the victim of any kind of crime? If yes, ask the following questions:
    a. Where and when and what type of crime?
    b. Following the crime, were you interviewed by any member of a law enforcement agency?
    c. Was he or she a state or federal official?

- d. Was there a prosecution of the offense?
- e. What was the result?
- f. Were you satisfied that the person responsible for the investigation or prosecution of the case acted competently in apprehending the alleged offender and bringing him or her to trial? Please explain your response.

52. Have you ever appeared as a witness before a grand jury? If yes, when and where?
53. Have you ever appeared as a witness in a criminal prosecution? If yes, when and where?
54. Have you ever served on a grand jury? If yes, when and where and what kind of cases were you considering?
55. Have you ever had any jury experience prior to today? If yes, please respond to the following questions.
    - a. On how many juries have you served?
    - b. Were they criminal or civil cases?
    - c. Was there a verdict rendered in any of those cases? If so, what was that verdict and were you satisfied with it?
    - d. What kind of a case was it?
    - e. Was it a state or federal case?
    - f. Did any of the criminal cases you heard in your previous jury duty affect you so that it placed a burden on your ability or desire to be able to sit on future cases?
    - g. Is there anything about your service in prior jury duty that would make you cynical about criminal trials or about trials in general?
    - h. Is there anything about your previous jury experience that would lead you to feel that you may have some leaning either toward the prosecution or against the prosecution?
    - i. In your previous jury trial, were the persons involved in those cases white or non-white?
56. Have you or has any member of your immediate family or a close friend with whom you have daily associa-

tion ever been a member of a veteran's organization? If yes, what organization and who is the person?

57. Have you ever been a member of any stockgrowers' association or organization?[5]
58. Do you belong to any organizations or groups that have as one of its primary purposes advocacy or promotion of legislation either at the state or federal level?
59. Have you ever belonged to an organization or group that has been active in working with the Bureau of Indian Affairs?
60. Have you ever belonged to an organization or group that has been active in promoting change at the local level, either in your town or in the county?
61. To what organizations or groups do you belong? For instance, please list for me your membership in such things as P.T.A., scouts, political parties, church groups, auxiliary fire department groups, country clubs, 4-H groups, conservation groups — anything or any group in which you have had an active membership during the last five or ten years? (After the person has responded with the nature of the groups they belong to, ask the following questions.)
    a. Do you attend most of the meetings of that organization or group?
    b. Are you active in the organization or group or its activities?
    c. Have you ever held an office in any of these groups? If yes, which one?
62. Are you doing any volunteer work now or have you done any in the past? If yes, in what organizations?
63. Based on any of these activities, have you formed an opinion that would affect your ability to fairly and impartially judge the evidence or the law connected with this case?
64. Have you ever heard of the John Birch Society?[6]

[5]The victim was president of the stockgrowers' association for six years.
[6]The victim was an active member of the John Birch Society.

a. Do you belong to the John Birch Society?
b. Have you ever received any of its literature?

65. Do you believe in the philosophy of the John Birch Society?
66. Have you ever belonged to any organization that had as one of its aims and purposes the impeachment of Chief Justice Earl Warren of the United States Supreme Court? If yes, would you please identify that organization?
67. Before today, have you ever heard the name Gary Haysacker? If yes, ask the following questions:
    a. How do you know him?
    b. Do you have knowledge of his reputation? If yes, in your own words, would you just tell me what you think his reputation is?
    c. Are you related in any way to the victim, Mr. Haysacker?
    d. Do you know his father, mother, brother, sister, or wife?
    e. Have you ever worked with or for the company that he owned or for him in any way, even if not directly?
68. Before today, had you ever heard the name Hank Grooms? If yes, ask the following questions:
    a. How do you know him?
    b. Do you have knowledge of his reputation? If yes, in your own words tell me what you think his reputation in this community is.
    c. Do you know his mother, brother, sister, ex-wife, wife, or any of his children?
    d. Have you ever worked with him, for him, or had any work contact with him?
    e. Have you ever had any dealings with Hank of a business nature?
    f. Have you ever entertained Hank in your home?
69. Are you acquainted with the prosecutor or any of the people on his staff? If yes, would you tell me the nature of that acquaintanceship?

70. Are you acquainted with any of the other attorneys who have been involved in the investigation of this case in any of the its stages? If yes, please identify the attorney and the nature of the acquaintanceship.
71. I am now going to list the prosecution witnesses. (List them.) Do you know any of these prosecution witnesses? If yes, which ones do you know and what is the nature of that acquaintanceship?
72. I am now going to list for you the defense witnesses. (List them.) Are you acquainted with any of the defense witnesses? If yes, identify which defense witnesses you are acquainted with and what is the nature of that acquaintanceship.
73. May I just ask what newspapers you generally read? Please include both weekly and daily papers that you frequently look at.
74. Do you tend to watch the evening news on television? If yes, on which channel?
75. Do you tend to listen to radio news? If yes, would you please indicate to me which stations you normally listen to?
76. How did you first hear or read about this case?
77. What have you read or heard about this case?[7]
78. Have you read any newspapers or any magazine article or have you seen any television programs or heard any radio coverage about this case or about Hank Grooms or about Gary Haysacker? If yes, what articles or programs did you have exposure to and what was their content?
79. Was there anything in the newspaper that you read or in the television coverage that you saw or in the radio coverage that you heard that led you to believe that

[7] This open-ended question might be undesirable when there has not been widespread media coverage of the case. At such times, the judge should be asked to permit individual voir dire to avoid the risk of contaminating the panel with this question and the questions that follow concerning predetermined opinions.

Hank Grooms was guilty or not guilty of the murder of Gary Haysacker?

80. Would you say that your knowledge of this case came from one item of exposure or many items of exposure concerning this case?
81. Most of you then are aware that there has been daily or weekly coverage of this case since it first began last November, nine months ago. Over the period of these last several months when you have read the stories in the newspaper or watched the television or heard radio coverage, have you formed any opinion about this case?
82. In other words, when you read about this case in the newspaper or saw the coverage on television, did you get the impression that Hank Grooms did commit a crime and that that crime was the crime of murder?
83. Did you read the statement in the newspaper in which the prosecutor stated that he had an open and shut case against Hank Grooms?
84. Did reading the paper leave the distinct impression in your own mind that Hank Grooms was probably guilty of the murder?
85. In other words, you formed the opinion from reading the newspaper that Hank Grooms was guilty of killing Gary Haysacker, isn't that right?
86. Would you say that those stories you read on this case were slanted on the side of the prosecution?
87. Have you ever read or heard any commentary concerning the guilt or innocence of Hank Grooms? If yes, what was the nature of that commentary and when did it occur and what was the source?
88. Have you ever discussed this case with anybody who said to you, "Well, I think Hank Grooms is innocent," or "I think that he is guilty"? Or have you ever heard such a discussion occur between other people when you yourself did not participate? If yes to either question, what was the expression concerning guilt or innocence that you overheard or that you participated in?

89. Have you yourself ever expressed an opinion about this case?
90. Within your own mind, have you ever thought, "Well, I think Hank is guilty," or "I think Hank is innocent"? Have you ever had thoughts like that?
91. From all of the information that you have gathered from the news media, from the radio, newspaper, and television, plus the information that you have gained through discussion of this case with other people, have you ever formed any opinion or any tendency to lead toward an opinion of guilt or innocence? This is especially important to us in that we need to determine if there is a burden that Hank, as the defendant in this case would have to overcome. Have you formed any opinion even as to the slightest leaning one way or the other? If yes, what is that opinion?
92. Do you have an opinion on this case at this time?
93. Would you have any difficulty overcoming that opinion that has been set in your mind?
94. When was the first time that you had an opinion about the defendant's guilt fixed in your mind?
95. Is it also a fact that you have carried that opinion until about a week ago when you became a prospective juror in this case? Would you agree that there has been a period of months in which your mind has been conditioned as to certain facts and that you have accepted those facts to be true facts? Assuming you were on trial with the chance that you would be convicted for the rest of your life, would you accept a juror who has had an opinion about your guilt for a long period of time, one who has the same frame of mind that you have in this case today?
96. Has there been anything in the many months from the time of the incident in November up until a week ago that changed your opinion that Hank Grooms had done what they said that he did in the manner that they claimed that it occurred?
97. As far as you are concerned, you have held this opin-

ion that it was an open and shut case for the last nine months and there has been nothing that you have read or seen that has changed your opinion except the fact that the judge has indicated *here today* that you should have an open mind, isn't that true?

98. In what way do you consider that you now have an open mind?
99. What has come into your own thinking that has eliminated the opinion that you had prior to your call as a potential juror that this was an open and shut case against Hank Grooms?
100. I am somewhat interested in how you can unwind. I don't mean unwinding in the sense of relaxing; I am talking about unwinding the previous, conscious mind to a point where you will undo in your present consciousness what has dwelled in there for the past nine or ten months. The fact that this is an open and shut case against Hank Grooms and that he is guilty as charged — how are you going to unwind that?
101. In the nine months since you first read about this case and heard and read about the statement made by the prosecutor that this was an open and shut case against Hank Grooms and that he was guilty as charged, you have read no evidence or seen nothing on television or heard anything that would change your mind, isn't that right?
102. Would you say that you have fixed an opinion in your mind about this case?
103. In other words, as far as you are concerned, from last November until the present time, there has been nothing to change this opinion that you have that Hank Grooms was guilty of murder. Isn't that true?
104. Well, don't you think that is a tremendous burden for you to have to overcome in a charge that is as serious as the one that Hank Grooms is facing?
105. In other words, after this long period of time that you have had this opinion, you would have to see the evidence to the contrary before you could change your opinion, isn't that right?

106. Would you expect us, as lawyers, to present evidence that Hank Grooms is innocent of the crime as charged?
107. Do you think my client has to prove that he is innocent? Mr. Blank (a member of the jury), the law presumes today that my client is innocent as he sits here in this courtroom. The judge will tell you that that is the law. Do you agree with the law or do you disagree with the law?
108. Do you think that that is the way the law should be or do you think that the law should be changed so that, as the law is in Russia, the accused must prove that he is innocent rather than the situation that we have in America that the prosecution must prove guilt? Do you approve of this law?
109. You know, don't you, that the state and the prosecutor have the burden of proof?
110. The burden of proof means that the state must prove its case against Hank Grooms to your satisfaction beyond a reasonable doubt to a moral certainty. Do you think that is placing too much of a burden upon the state?
111. Do you realize that the charge in this case is merely a formal legal pleading, nothing more than a piece of paper filed by the prosecution in order to start these proceedings and has no greater legal effect than a complaint or declaration in a civil case? You understand, do you not, that the burden of proof is always on the state and that the defendant, Hank Grooms, need not present any evidence on his own behalf at any time? Do you understand that?
112. Do you also understand that the defendant, Hank Grooms, is not required to testify on his own behalf? How do you feel about that?
113. Do you have the feeling that you want to hear *both* sides?
114. Do you realize that while in a civil case a mere preponderance of the evidence is sufficient, but in a criminal case it is necessary for the prosecution to prove that Hank is guilty beyond a reasonable doubt and to a

moral certainty to each and every one of you present on the jury? Do you have any problem with that?

115. Do you agree with our principle of law that a defendant in a criminal case should not be convicted unless the jury is convinced that he is guilty beyond a reasonable doubt and to a moral certainty? Do you disagree with the law that a man is presumed innocent until he is proven guilty beyond a reasonable doubt? Do you disagree with the law that the burden of proving the defendant's guilt beyond a reasonable doubt rests with the prosecution, with the prosecutor, and with the state? As far as you are concerned, at the present time, does Hank Grooms stand innocent of a crime or does he stand guilty of the crime as charged?

116. (To be directed toward a person who seems to have trouble with the presumption of innocence.) If the court tells you that Hank Grooms is presumed to be innocent and that you must find him to be innocent at this time, would you have any trouble with that? You wouldn't find any fault with that direction from the court? Are you willing to assume that Hank Grooms at the present time stands presumed to be innocent? If you do, please raise your hand.

117. At the present time, are you willing to accept the fact that Hank Grooms stands presumed to be innocent because you haven't heard any evidence and you know none of the real facts of the case?

118. Is there anyone who feels that they know facts concerning this case? If you do, please raise your hand.

119. Now, you would expect the prosecution to be able to give you convincing evidence beyond a reasonable doubt to prove that Hank Grooms is guilty as charged, would you not?

120. Will you promise to hold the prosecution to the fullfillment of their obligation and their duty or will you depend on previous statements that this is an open and shut case? Will you demand proof beyond a reasonable doubt and to a moral certainty?

121. Do you accept that it is not our responsibility to prove Hank Grooms is innocent? In other words, it is not Hank Grooms' duty to prove himself innocent; he doesn't have to prove anything to you, isn't that right?
122. It is up to the prosecution to prove Hank Grooms guilty beyond a reasonable doubt. Are you willing to accept that as a standard of American jurisprudence that governs this trial?
123. Would the fact that Hank Grooms has been arrested and charged with this crime create an inference in your own mind that there must be some truth or they wouldn't be holding this man all these months for trial?
124. And then the fact that the state's attorney has filed an information against him, does that create within you a state of mind that Hank Grooms must have done it or he wouldn't have been charged?
125. Would you generally take the position that where there is smoke, there must be some fire? Is that the way your mind tends to work?
126. Do you think that just because the state's attorney has charged the defendant with murder that this is evidence against Hank?
127. Does the defendant, Hank Grooms, start out with a strike or two against him in *your mind* because the state's attorney has charged him with murder?
128. Since you don't have a background in law, you probably don't know how or what is utilized to decide whether a person should be charged with murder, do you? That is, do you feel that the prosecutor knows for certain that a person is guilty when he charges the person with guilt or do you think that it is possible for the prosecutor to bring charges against an innocent person?
129. Do you feel that it is possible that persons who are charged with a crime could be innocent rather than guilty?
130. Do we have your complete assurance that your judg-

ment on Hank's cause will rest solely on what you hear in this courtroom in the form of *competent* evidence and that you will not use the fact that he has been charged with murder by the state's attorney to help you in reaching your verdict?

131. Do you think that it is possible as a matter of record or public reaction for a state's attorney to charge a person with a crime just on the basis of suspicion?
132. I want to be certain that you understand that there is no implication of guilt that can be drawn from the fact that my client is charged in an information for murder and that there is no inference brought against Hank just because he has been charged and brought to trial. Is that clear to all of you? If so, please raise your hand.
133. If you had to vote right now, before the trial has started, would you vote to acquit or convict my client? That is, would you find Hank Grooms guilty or not guilty?
134. At the end of the trial after you have heard all of the evidence you will go to the jury room and you will consider all of the evidence that you have heard. If at that time you were to have a suspicion that Hank Grooms committed the murder in the way that the prosecution states that he did, if you just suspected that Hank Grooms committed the crime in that way, how would you vote, guilty or not guilty?
135. At the end of the trial after you have heard all of the evidence, if you think that Hank possibly committed the crime in the manner that the state claims, how would you vote — guilty or not guilty?
136. That's right, we can't convict on a suspicion or on possibility. Now, at the end of the trial after you have heard all of the evidence, if you believe that Hank Grooms probably committed the crime as charged by the state and in the manner charged by the state, how would you vote — guilty or not guilty?[8]

[8]It is important to get the prospective juror to say "not guilty." Do not accept a nod of the head or a yes as an indication that he or she would

137. Does the fact that you came into this courtroom and saw all these security measures and bailiffs and guns and all of the searching procedures — does that create within you a feeling that Hank Grooms must be guilty of something or else the state wouldn't take these kinds of security measures?

138. The state will be introducing some photographs that were taken in connection with this case. It is our contention that these photographs do not have anything to do with this case. We do not deny that Mr. Haysacker was shot and that he died as a result of being shot. If you see photographs picturing Mr. Haysacker after he was shot and after he had died, we feel that these photographs may disturb you to such a point that you might feel that you would have to do something to avenge the situation as shown in those pictures. Some of those pictures are pretty gruesome. We hope that you will never have to look at them because we think they might have some effect on you emotionally. But, if the judge should let you look at those photographs and if you should become emotional after looking at them, will you try as desperately as you can to put aside that emotion and try to reach the real issue that is involved: the issue of guilt or innocence of Hank Grooms, not whether Mr. Haysacker was shot or that he died as a result of being shot?

139. When you entered the courthouse today, you passed through extensive security measures to make certain that you didn't have a weapon or that no one who had a weapon could have entered the building. Do these security measures create an aura or suspicion that there must be something here or they wouldn't be taking all of these security measures?

---

consider the not guilty vote. Since the prospective jurors have been exposed to media coverage and there is good reason to believe that they think the defendant is guilty as charged, it is important to get them to state "not guilty" so as to form the basis for so voting.

140. Do you have any feeling one way or the other about white men living, working, and owning on the Indian reservation?
141. The evidence will disclose that the deceased, as well as the defendant, owned and operated ranches on the Indian reservation. Is there anything about that fact that makes you feel one way or the other about these men?
142. Do you know what white racism is?
143. Do you believe that there is white racism in America or more specifically in this state or on this Indian reservation?
144. White racism is the feeling that white people believe they are dominant over non-white people. In some circles this is also referred to as white supremacy. Does that give you some idea about what we are talking about?
145. Do you believe that most white people are prejudiced against those people who are not white?
146. Do you belong to any clubs or organizations that are against white supremacy or against white people in general?[9]
147. Do you have any hostile feelings toward white ranchers who own and operate ranches on the Indian reservation?
148. Would the fact that Hank Grooms was convicted of a felony at one time cause you to prejudge him and to totally disregard any claim that he made or any testimony that he gave?
149. That felony was for rustling cattle. Hank was 22 years old when he was found guilty of cattle rustling. He is now over 50. Some of you are cattle ranchers; others of you sell and work with cattle all the time. Just because

[9]A substantial number of people in this area are active members of the American Indian Movement (AIM). These people have stated that they would "kill a white" with any means any chance they had. This, of course, would certainly be a negative element to inject into a murder where a white person was on trial.

Hank was a cattle rustler when he was younger, would that make you believe that he is a murderer today?

150. Are there any of you who feel that just because a person was capable of committing one act of felony, that he or she is are capable of committing any other kind of felony? What I mean is do you feel that because Hank would rustle cattle, that he would kill a man?
151. Do you understand that the defendant does not have to take the stand on his own behalf, that that is his right and that he is not required to give any testimony of any kind?
152. Would some of you feel that you had not heard "both sides of the story" if you had not heard Hank Grooms testify on his own behalf?
153. If Hank is advised by his lawyers that it is best for him not to take the stand, would you feel that there must be some negative reason for his electing not to testify?
154. On the other hand, should Hank elect to testify and should you discover that he had been in trouble with the law before, would you promise to follow the judge's instructions that you may only consider this previous trouble as a factor in your determination as to his credibility as a witness?
155. Would you have any fault to find with the law that says that a person who takes the witness stand, regardless of what his profession is, has equal dignity with any other person who takes the witness stand?
156. If the defendant in this case were to testify, would you give him the same credence that you would give to any other witness; specifically, would you feel that he were any less likely to tell the truth than, let us say, a police officer?
157. Would you take the attitude that the defendant is on trial here for his life and freedom so when he takes the witness stand would you say, "Well, he is liable to say anything because he is on trial for the rest of his life and I'm not going to believe him"?

158. Would you say that the defendant would be grasping for freedom and is liable to catch onto any straw that may come his way? In other words, do you think at this time that the defendant is likely to lie under oath?
159. Would you give the testimony of a police officer who was white more credence or more reliability than you would that of a non-white person, especially one who did not happen to belong to the law enforcement agency?
160. In this case, there will be about four times as many witnesses for the prosecution as there will be for the defendant. You wouldn't accept the combined testimony of the prosecution's witnesses just because there are more of them, would you?
161. Do you own a firearm of any kind?
162. Do you keep that firearm locked up, or do you frequently take it with you in an automobile or on a horse?
163. Do you have any objection to anybody who does own a firearm and keeps it for his or her own protection in his or her home, or car, or on his or her horse?
164. Do you believe in the citizen's right of self-defense?
165. Do you belong to any group that is training its members or its affiliates in the use of firearms?
166. Do you have any quarrel with the law that it is lawful to use any means that appear reasonably necessary under the circumstances to defend yourself?
167. Have you had any experience with weapons or firearms of any kind? What sort of experience? What sort of weapon?
168. How many of you have never owned a gun or have never shot a weapon of any kind? (If anyone answers that they have never shot a weapon or owned a gun, ask the following question.) Why is this the case for you?
169. Do you have any quarrel with the constitutional right to bear arms?
170. Do you have any view that because someone does bear arms, he or she is more prone to commit a crime?

171. Have any of you ever had to utilize the right of self-defense or has any member of your family or close friend ever had to utilize the right of self-defense?
172. Have any of you ever been jurors involving the right of self-defense?
173. Have any of you ever known anyone, either a friend or a family member, who has exercised the right of self-defense, even if it was just in a simple fist fight?
174. Do you understand that if you decide that the shooting of Gary Haysacker was justifiable, you must return a verdict of not guilty?
175. Do you understand that you can make the determination, after being so instructed by the judge, that a shooting in self-defense is justifiable?
176. If you found that the defendant acted in self-defense and used a gun or rifle to protect himself on his own land and you were instructed that that was the law and that you had to apply it, and if you believed that the defendant's testimony was credible, would you then return a verdict of not guilty?
177. Is the concept of self-defense one that you can abide by, or does it trouble you in any way? If it troubles you, please share with us at this time the nature of your feelings.
178. Would you have any problem invoking self-defense if you were assaulted or attacked or endangered?
179. If you do have a reasonable doubt about my client's guilt and, after listening to the arguments of your fellow jurors when you retire to consider the case, you still have that reasonable doubt, will you stick to your guns and refuse to change your verdict, even though it is an unpopular one or one that might result in a hung jury?
180. Would the inconvenience of having to spend the night away from your home prevent you from sticking to your guns and refusing to change your verdict, if you still had that reasonable doubt about the guilt of Hank Grooms?
181. If you are chosen as a juror, you will stand by your

opinion based on the evidence that comes before you during the trial and only that evidence, isn't that right?

182. You won't let anyone shake your opinion, will you? If you believe that the defendant is innocent or guilty and that is your true opinion, will you stick with your own opinion and not be swayed just because 10 or 11 people on the panel disagree with you?
183. If you are chosen as a juror in this case, will you stand by your own individual analysis of the evidence and not be swayed by any emotions of the other jurors? You should be swayed by the facts, but will you stand on your own individual judgment if you are chosen as a trial juror and not let emotions persuade you one way or the other?
184. Do you find it is difficult to make up your mind who is right and who is wrong in a family dispute or in a problem at work?
185. When faced with a difficult decision, would you rather leave it to someone else so you won't be blamed if the wrong decision is made?
186. If your vote in the jury room is 11 to one, would you be willing to vote your conscience even though you were sequestered and away from your family for a long period of time?
187. Would it be embarrassing to you or to your spouse if you sat on a jury in a case that had been as charged up as this one has been over a period of several months, and then the jury acquitted the defendant? Would it be embarrassing to you or to your spouse at work or at home or in discussions with your friends or neighbors or anyone else in the community?
188. Assuming that you were picked as a juror in this case and you brought in a verdict of not guilty, would you find it embarrassing in the neighborhood or area that you were living in?
189. If you were to bring in a verdict of not guilty, would you have any embarrassment at all in your church or in any of the clubs or groups that you belong to?

190. During the case, we, as the lawyers for Hank, may be making objections to testimony or evidence offered by the state. Do you understand that this is our job, so that you will not hold it against Hank?
191. If this trial lasts in excess of two or three weeks, is there anything about that length of time that would prevent your giving this case your full and undivided attention?
192. Do you realize that the state's attorney and the defense attorney are both lawyers, both equals in the eyes of the law, each doing their best to represent the client?
193. You are not going to give any more weight to the arguments of the state's attorney than to the defense attorney merely because he bears the impressive title of state's attorney, are you?
194. I have asked you many questions. At certain points you may have felt I was trying to invade your own privacy. Do the questions I have asked you infuriate you or trouble you in such a way that you couldn't be a fair and impartial juror? Do you understand why I am asking you these questions and why it is necessary for me to ask these questions? Is there anything else you want to tell us that will help the court discover whether you have any prejudgments or any questions in your own mind that will affect your decision-making process?
195. These questions that I have asked you, have they triggered off within your mind anything you want to volunteer to us?
196. Is there anything about this case that bothers you in any way?
197. Assuming that some loved one of yours was standing trial in the place of Hank Grooms for the same crime, would you feel satisfied to have 12 jurors of the same mind as yours standing in judgment of your friend or loved one?
198. If you are chosen in this case do you know of any reason why you could not sit as a fair and impartial juror?

199. You don't know of anything in your own mind's eye that we cannot penetrate or pierce into that would lead to some crevice of prejudice or prejudgment that I have not been able to reach?
200. Is there anything that I have said about Hank or the facts of this case that creates a doubt in your own mind about whether you could be fair and impartial if you served as a juror on this case?
201. Is there anything that you have felt, seen, or heard since you came here for jury duty that would lead you to believe that you might have a propensity or a tendency to accept one view, either of the prosecutor or of the defendant, more than you would accept the other view?

Table of Cases

References are to section numbers.

Index